Fire Department City of New York

Produced by the Fire Safety Education Fund, Inc., in conjunction
with the New York City Fire Department

History written by Paul Hashagen
Book edited by Janet Kimmerly

The stylized Maltese Cross depicted on the cover is from a flag presented to the New York City Fire Department on November 12, 1887. It is believed to be the first use of the initials FDNY to identify the Department. On display at the New York City Fire Museum, the back of the flag is embroidered with the inscription, "Courage and Fidelity/ Presented November 12, 1887/Department Organized May 4, 1865."

Patches for endsheets provided by Honorary Battalion Chief Fred Melahn.

Turner Publishing Company
Publishers of Historical Books
P.O. Box 3101
Paducah, Kentucky 42002-3101

Co-published by
Mark A. Thompson, Associate Publisher

For book publishing write to:
Mark A. Thompson, Associate Publisher
P.O. Box 6802
Evansville, Indiana 47719-6802

Pre-Press work by M.T. Publishing Company, Inc.
Graphic Designer: Elizabeth A. Dennis

Library of Congress
Control Number 00-131551

ISBN: 1-56311-584-0

Printed in the United States of America

Limited Edition

Fire Department Institute (FDI) is a not-for-profit foundation. For a copy of the Fire Department Institute's latest Annual Report, please send a written request to: Fire Department Institute, 300 Park Avenue, 17th Floor, New York, NY 10022.

Thank You

Numerous people – many of whom volunteered their time – contributed to this project. I want to thank the following individuals who made this book a reality:

First Deputy Fire Commissioner William Feehan
Battalion Chief George Eysser
Honorary Battalion Chief Fred Melahn
Honorary Battalion Chief Peter Micheels
Captain Walter Morris
Supervising Fire Marshal Ralph Bernard
Lieutenant Richard Smiouskas
Lieutenant Daniel Walsh
Acting Lieutenant Daniel Maye
FF Paul Hashagen
Editor Janet Kimmerly
Fire Alarm Dispatcher Micheal Boucher
Reverend James Flanagan

I especially want to thank Honorary Chief of Department Jack Lerch, whose encyclopedic knowledge of the FDNY is surpassed only by his love and affection for the Department, its Officers and Firefighters. For him, this book was a labor of love. Without him, it would not have happened.

Thomas Von Essen
Fire Commissioner

Contents

Commissioner Thomas Von Essen and Mayor Rudolph Giuliani at March 11, 1999, eight-alarm fire at Box 1323, 2823 Broadway and 108th Street, Manhattan.

Message From Mayor Rudolph Giuliani

I am especially proud to be a part of this book, which celebrates the great history and tradition of the New York City Fire Department. I remember as a child accompanying my mother to the hospital to visit with my uncle, a firefighter, who had been injured seriously in the line of duty. The thing I remember most is my uncle talking about how much he wanted to return to his duties as a firefighter. During my years as Mayor, I have seen that same spirit and desire hundreds of times as I visited firefighters injured in the line of duty. They spoke not of their injuries, but of how quickly they could return to firefighting. To me, firefighters are defined by a pure, wholesome, selfless trait. They never consider race, creed, color or religion when they are rescuing people or protecting their property. They put their lives on the line every day, on every run, for every one of us. This book tells the story of our firefighters—past, present and future. There is something here for everyone—the firefighter on the job, the retired firefighter looking to relive memories, the "buff," the historian and those with just a casual interest in the Fire Department. Above all, this book is for everyone who recognizes and stands in awe, as I do, of the Pride, Honor and Courage that define New York City Firefighters.

Message From Fire Commissioner Thomas Von Essen

When the paid firefighting force was organized in late 1865 replacing the volunteer companies, the New York City Fire Department consisted of 34 Engine Companies and 12 Ladder Companies. Today—135 years later—nine Divisions, 51 Battalions, 203 Engines, 143 Ladders, five Rescues, seven Squads, three Marine Units and one Haz-Mat Company, augmented by more than three dozen special units, provide fire protection to the seven million people who call New York City home and the millions of others who come here each day to work, visit and enjoy all this incredible city has to offer.

There is no doubt that if those first paid firefighters somehow could return today, they would be awed by how very different the FDNY is as we enter the 21st century. Even a casual observer couldn't fail to appreciate the monumental changes that have taken place during the past 135 years. What is less apparent, but no less dramatic and remarkable, are the changes that have occurred in just this past decade. The role of the firefighter today is broader, more complex and more challenging than ever. Issues that face us today were unheard of just a few short years ago. The role of the Department in responding to terrorism incidents, dealing with the consequences of weapons of mass destruction, providing assistance in the event of chemical or biological attack, are all very real issues that this Department plans and trains for every day.

With the inception of the Certified First Responder Program and the merger of EMS into the Fire Department in 1996, New York firefighters stepped into the front lines of pre-hospital emergency care, answering more than 160,000 calls for medical assistance last year. These new and different roles firefighters now play are, however, only part of the story of a vastly different Department. During those years, from the mid 1960s to the early 1980s, which New York firefighters still call "The War Years," when arson fires devastated whole communities across the city, the firefighters' slogan became "The Job is Fire." We went to an unbelievable number of fires and consequently placed less and less emphasis on Training, Fire Prevention and Fire Safety Education.

Today, those high activity years are a memory and while we still say, "The job is Fire," we mean it in a much broader sense. Fire Prevention and Fire Safety Education play an equal role with extinguishment. In the past few years, we have placed more resources into Fire Safety Education than at any time in our history. The Fire Safety "experience" at the Fire Museum and the portable Fire Safety demonstration that we bring to locations throughout the city provide dynamic and realistic Fire Safety lessons for hundreds of children each week. This fall, we will open a new and dramatic Fire Safety "experience," inside Rockefeller Center, one of the city's prime tourist attractions. This state-of-the-art facility will help us spread the message of Fire Safety to thousands of New Yorkers and visitors each year. We are extremely grateful to the Rockefeller Center Management for recognizing the importance of our Fire Safety Education Program and making this space available to us.

In calendar 1998 and 1999, fire deaths in New York were the lowest they have been in the past 50 years, clear proof that increased emphasis on Fire Prevention and Fire Safety Education pays dividends in human life. Experience tells us, however, that no matter how hard we work or how much we try, we cannot prevent every fire.

Firefighters still have to go in harm's way to face and battle our age-old enemy and that enemy today is more difficult and dangerous than ever before. New materials have made the products of combustion more toxic. Different construction practices have greatly increased the possibility of early collapses. Tighter, better-insulated buildings have increased temperatures to oven-like conditions even at minor fires. There may be fewer fires today, but they are more challenging and deadly. We have provided our firefighters with the best protective equipment available and we continue looking at ways to improve it.

We are devoting more time, money and resources to training than ever before. We have instituted programs designed to take full advantage of the variety and complexity found in a city such as New York. Newly appointed firefighters are required to spend their first three years after graduation from the Fire Academy rotating, a year at a time, to three different units with different work loads in different parts of the city before being assigned permanently. Newly promoted company officers now are assigned with career development in mind so they, too, will acquire varied and broader experiences. We have instituted a Mentor Program in which Captains slated for promotion to Battalion Chief are partnered with a senior Battalion Chief in a different area of the city for three months. During this time, the Captain's sole responsibility is to watch, question and learn as much as possible from his/her seasoned, experienced mentor. A new course was developed and given to all incumbent Chief Officers on Fireground Safety. Newly promoted Chiefs now receive the course as a separate module in the Incident Command course.

As we look ahead to this new century, there is no reason to believe that the years ahead won't produce the same profound changes in apparatus, equipment, training requirements, roles and missions that have marked our progress from horse-drawn apparatus to hazardous materials mitigation. We may not know the challenges that lie ahead, but we do know that for the past 135 years, there never has been a challenge we did not meet, an objective we did not achieve or a goal we did not accomplish.

The Firefighters and Fire Officers who have gone before us and whose deeds and stories you will read about in these pages, have left us a priceless legacy of Pride and Honor, Dedication and Duty. The Firefighters and Fire Officers who serve the people of New York today add to that legacy every day with their courage, compassion and commitment.

The story of this great Department and these firefighters—past and present—is one of the jewels in the crown of this wonderful, incomparable place called New York City. I hope the enjoyment you find in reading their story is as great as the pride I feel in being a New York City Firefighter and a part of the inspiring and humbling history of "the Bravest."

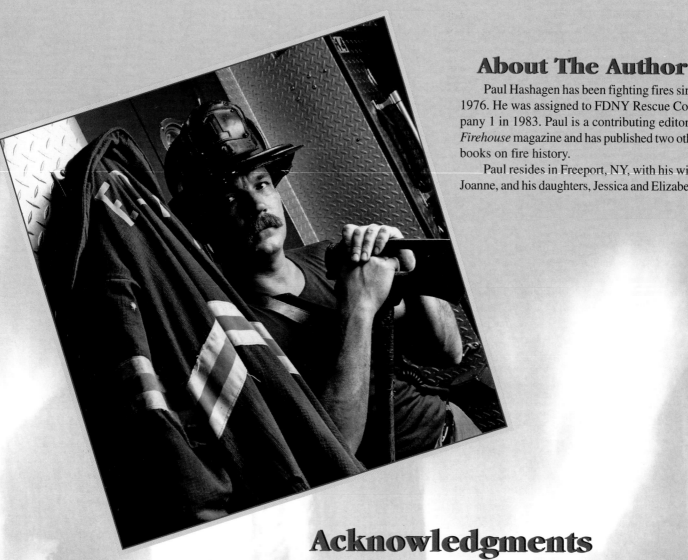

About The Author

Paul Hashagen has been fighting fires since 1976. He was assigned to FDNY Rescue Company 1 in 1983. Paul is a contributing editor to *Firehouse* magazine and has published two other books on fire history.

Paul resides in Freeport, NY, with his wife, Joanne, and his daughters, Jessica and Elizabeth.

Acknowledgments

The stories contained in this book are taken mostly from documented sources such as Department Orders, Annual Reports, Medal Day books, Reports of Meritorious Acts and other Department publications, as well as the many newspapers in print at the time. The intention of the author is not to make it appear as if the only members of the Department who made rescues or performed heroic acts are those written about in this book. On the contrary, the author had a very difficult time choosing a fair cross section of the Department throughout its history.

Although I received an enormous amount of help with this project, any errors are mine and mine alone. With this in mind, I would like to thank all those who helped to make this book a reality:

First and foremost, the late Honorary Chief Clarence Meek, who ran the Department library for many years and compiled a vast amount of historic information. I would have been lost without him.

FDNY Commissioner Thomas Von Essen, for his faith in my ability to complete the project and for his interest in keeping the history of our job alive.

Janet Kimmerly, my editor. Janet's red pen helped to make this book an accurate and correct history.

Many other people have helped along the way and I would like to single out especially the staff at the Mand library, Honorary Chief Jack Lerch and Lieutenants Danny Maye and Paul Hudak; Daniel P. Alfonso; Chief Jack Calderone; Matthew Daly; Harvey Eisner; Chief George Eysser; Herb Eysser; Warren Fuchs; John Lee Gill; Michael Goldstein; Captain Terry Hatton; Bill Noonan; Pete O'Dea; Steven Scher; Steve Spak; and Lieutenant Richard Smiouskas and the staff of the Photo Unit.

Special thanks to the Brothers of Rescue Company 1 for putting up with all the hassle.

Special thanks to my daughters, Jessica and Elizabeth, who helped with the manuscript early on. And especially to my wife, Joanne, for her love and support despite piles and piles of "important" stuff.

Line-of-Duty Deaths

(Listing Rank, Name, Unit and Date of Death)

Rank & Name	Unit	Date of Death
FF R. Wintringham	Eng. 1	8-24-1865
FF George W. Bell	Eng. 8	11-9-1865
FF Thomas Irvin	Eng. 4	12-2-1865
FF Dominick Sicot	Eng. 4	11-14-1865
FF Peter H. Walsh	Eng. 5	5-21-1866
Fore. David B. Waters	Eng. 5	5-21-1866
FF Myles L. Sowarby	H & L 10	8-27-1867
Fore. Michael Snyder	Eng. 38	4-16-1868
Fore. James Whalen	Eng. 6	10-16-1869
Asst. Fore. Thomas Roberts	Eng. 14	10-24-1869
FF Mathias Henes	H & L 4	12-4-1870
FF Jacob Edler	Eng. 16	3-27-1871
FF Edward Burke	Eng. 4	6-29-1872
FF Jacob Steigler	Eng. 25	9-8-1872
Asst. Engr. Geo. A. Erlacher	2nd Batt.	2-9-1873
FF James Plunket	Eng. 23	9-24-1873
FF John O'Neil	H & L 4	8-16-1874
BC William H. Nash	4th Batt.	9-14-1875
FF Philip H. Maus	H & L 6	9-14-1875
FF William Hughes	Eng. 9	9-14-1875
FF David Muldrew	Eng. 30	2-8-1876
FF David Clute	Eng. 30	2-8-1876
Asst. Fore. John H. Bush	Eng. 30	2-11-1876
FF Chas. J. Connolly	Eng. 6	3-14-1878
Pvt. John W. Irving	Eng. 29	1-7-1879
FF John Reilly-1	Eng. 17	1-14-1879
FF Henry C. Mount	Eng. 8	12-9-1879
FF Patrick Clark	Eng. 23	1-1-1880
Pvt. John J. O'Rourke	Eng. 6	1-25-1880
FF Thomas J. Dougherty	H & L 1	2-20-1880
FF John Cassidy	H & L 1	2-20-1880
FF Philip Holton	Eng. 24	7-31-1880
FF Thomas L. Jacobus	H & L 5	11-12-1880
Pvt. William Krattinger	Eng. 2	2-16-1882
FF Michael Connors	Eng. 14	10-31-1882
FF Edward Vincelette	H & L 4	3-14-1883
FF Joshua A. Wallace	Eng. 12	6-25-1884
FF James P. Smith	Eng. 17	2-4-1885
FF Thomas Dunleavy	Eng. 29	8-28-1885
FF John Ennis	Eng. 8	8-30-1885
FF Dennis McGee	H & L 15	1-20-1886
BC Francis Mahedy	4th Batt.	3-12-1886
FF Francis J. Quinn	Eng. 29	2-1-1887
FF J. C. O'Shaughnessy	H & L 1	5-11-1887
Engr. William Wray	Eng. 54	5-24-1887
FF James Rehill	H & L 8	6-1-1887
FF Michael J. Nolan	H & L 13	5-23-1888
FF Samuel McMahon	Eng. 56	8-13-1889
FF Chas. H. Morris	Eng. 17	1-3-1890
Engr. John Bulger	Eng. 43	10-28-1890
Asst. Fore. James H. Shute	Eng. 27	8-23-1891
FF Thomas R. Godfrey	H & L 21	5-23-1892
FF Francis Reilly	Eng. 7	8-27-1892
FF Edward Dunn	H & L 12	11-3-1894
BC John J. Bresnan	6th Batt.	12-29-1894
Asst. Fore. John L. Rooney	H & L 12	12-29-1894
Engr. Peter McKeon	Eng. 5	2-13-1895
FF Patrick Conlin	H & L 14	6-9-1895
FF Edward Walsh	H & L 5	4-1-1896
BC William Shaw	6th Batt.	5-9-1896
FF J. G. Rheinardt	Eng. 7	5-6-1897
FF M. J. Oakley, Jr.	Eng. 5	12-21-1897
FF James F. Calnan	Eng. 34	12-25-1897
FF Pierce English	H & L 22	1-7-1898
Fore. Edward Tobin	Eng. 23	1-24-1900
Fore. John J. Grady	H & L 2	1-24-1900
FF Peter F. Bowen	Eng. 21	1-24-1900
FF William J. Smith	Eng. 21	1-24-1900
FF William F. Mullin	Eng. 4	5-4-1900
FF Michael Emmett	Eng. 161	7-26-1900
FF F. Featherston	Eng. 54	1-28-1901
FF John Geary	H & L 2	2-2-1901
FF Mort. A. Roberts	Eng. 131	2-6-1901
FF Chris D. Boyne	Eng. 141	3-21-1901
FF James C. Nugent	H & L 54	4-14-1901
FF William Ryan	H & L 7	11-4-1901
FF Thomas J. Cooney	Eng. 123	3-10-1902
FF Patrick J. Quail	H & L 18	10-11-1902
BC Thomas S. Coppinger	23rd Batt.	11-26-1902
Asst. Fore. William F. Jeffrey	Eng. 126	11-26-1902
FF Michael J. O'Toole	H & L 55	11-26-1902
FF James Dawe	Eng. 19	11-29-1902
FF James G. Gorbeth	H & L 9	1-18-1903
Fore. John T. Andariese	Eng. 1	2-26-1903
FF William McNally	H & L 3	5-5-1903
BC Martin M. Coleman	5th Batt.	12-21-1903
Pro. FF Richard J. Joyce	Eng. 55	12-21-1903
Asst. Fore. George Gibson	H & L 68	1-22-1904
FF Chris Dressel	Eng. 138	1-31-1904
FF Peter J. Gaffney	Eng. 138	1-31-1904
FF Arthur J. Renk	Eng. 138	1-31-1904
Pro. FF John J. Crean	Eng. 19	4-27-1904
FF Hugh F. Arragoni	Eng. 19	4-27-1904
FF Thomas F. Madigan	Eng. 19	4-27-1904
FF James W. Gerdes	Eng. 5	6-1-1904
FF Peter S. Clark	Eng. 129	9-11-1904
FF Patrick Lennon	Eng. 160	12-1-1904
Fore. James L. Haviland	Eng. 157	1-15-1905
Asst. Fore. Geo. F. McGeary	H & L 58	3-2-1905
FF William Brown	Eng. 76	3-25-1904
FF Samuel Lilley	Eng. 38	3-30-1905
FF John Carbush	Eng. 102	6-9-1905
FF William J. Wieland	H & L 9	8-13-1905
Fore. William J. Dayton	H & L 3	8-13-1905
Asst. Fore. Daniel J. Sheehan	Eng. 67	11-6-1905
FF Geo. B. Christman	Eng. 14	3-26-1906
Fore. John F. Walsh	Eng. 14	3-26-1906
FF Denis J. Healy	Eng. 14	3-26-1906
FF Thomas F. Halpin, Jr.	H & L 24	3-26-1906
FF Jas. W. McCusker	Eng. 103	11-4-1906
E. of Str. William H. Rush	Eng. 103	11-4-1906
FF Joseph Finger	H & L 29	12-25-1906
FF Daniel J. Campbell	Eng. 32	1-6-1907
FF Thomas F. Lennon	Eng. 32	1-6-1907
FF Thomas McNamara	Eng. 166	1-23-1907
FF Henry F. Baker	Eng. 26	2-27-1907
FF Adam Damn	Eng. 26	2-27-1907
FF John Ryan-1	Eng. 80	4-8-1907
FF Gott. Messerli	Eng. 145	8-2-1907
FF James Smith	H & L 54	9-14-1907
FF Edward D. Lahey	Eng. 140	9-25-1907
FF John J. Carey-2	H & L 60	9-28-1907
FF Charles E. Parks	Eng. 43	11-8-1907
FF Geo. A. O'Connor	Eng. 72	1-10-1908
FF Thomas F. Phillips	Eng. 72	1-10-1908
FF Mathew Miller	Eng. 149	1-30-1908
FF Thomas P. Eglinton	Lad. 10	2-4-1908
FF John P. McConnell	Eng. 4	2-4-1908
DC Chris W. Kruger	2nd Div.	2-14-1908
FF Henry Hanson	H & L 62	12-14-1908
BC Mich. E. C. Graham	35th Batt.	2-15-1909
FF Francis V. A. Maher	H & L 60	5-3-1909
E. of Str. Chas. E. Meadows	Eng. 162	8-13-1909
Asst. Fore. Fred K. Schultz	Eng. 21	1-3-1910
FF Joseph H. White	Eng. 16	3-28-1910
FF John R. Fecher	Eng. 7	4-23-1910
FF James F. Barrett	H & L 22	5-13-1910
FF Timothy Cotter	Eng. 6	6-6-1910
FF William F. Healy	Eng. 10	6-6-1910
FF Daniel A. Hart	Eng. 89	10-27-1910
FF Anton Jiranek	Eng. 115	1-7-1911
FF Leo Hackbarth	H & L 32	1-13-1911
FF Stephen T. Ray, Jr.	Eng. 59	3-6-1911
BC William Devlin	Relief Off.	9-24-1911
Fore. James A. Hagen	Eng. 107	11-3-1911
Asst. Fore. John F. Timmons	H & L 55	12-23-1911
BC William J. Walsh	2nd Batt.	1-9-1912
FF George F. Farrell-2	Eng. 26	2-13-1912
FF Henry J. Kaiser	Eng. 131	4-6-1912
BC John Rush	5th Batt.	4-25-1912
E. of Str. William F. Stanton	Eng. 103	10-23-1912
FF William Maurer-2	Eng. 118	11-2-1912
BC William J. Duffy	8th Batt.	5-5-1913
FF B. E. Johnson	Eng. 77	8-13-1913
E. of Str. John B. Barget	Eng. 234	10-5-1913
FF Jeremiah Looney	H & L 106	11-28-1913
Lt. Thomas Mitchel	H & L 22	11-28-1913
FF Thomas J. McManis	Eng. 40	12-16-1913
E. of Str. John B. Doran	Eng. 156	1-25-1914
FF Jas. W. Thompson	Eng. 68	4-27-1915
FF John Duffy-3	Eng. 83	9-7-1915
FF Michael D. Curtin	Eng. 60	11-15-1915
FF Mathew J. Ward	Eng. 65	12-26-1915
FF Ignatius F. Neusch	Eng. 293	4-3-1916
FF James J. Skelly, Jr.	Eng. 280	4-16-1916
FF Raphael A. Fox	H & L 22	10-1-1916
FF Christian L. Walter	Eng. 15	3-17-1917
Capt. Thomas F. Kearns	H & L 148	4-12-1917
FF Patrick O'Connor	Eng. 289	4-12-1917
FF Harry E. Flynn	H & L 7	9-12-1915
FF John J. Frein	Eng. 65	1-4-1918
FF James Casey	Eng. 202	1-6-1918
Lt. Charles J. Murphy	Eng. 26	1-9-1918
FF John W. T. F. Kocher	Eng. 54	1-15-1918
FF Michael Wall	Eng. 151	2-3-1918
FF Francis R. J. Twomey	Eng. 55	3-16-1918
FF Henry Oltmann	H & L 28	8-8-1918
FF Henry J. Helmken, Jr.	H & L 123	10-13-1918
FF Charles J. Johnson	Eng. 58	10-14-1918
FF John J. Kelly, Jr.	H & L 1	10-18-1918
BC Matthew J. Cummings	21st Batt.	10-25-1918
FF Benjamin H. Fay	H & L 102	11-2-1918
Capt. Joseph S. Fitzgerald-2	Eng. 207	12-18-1918
FF Charles Snyder	Eng. 62	1-4-1919
Pro. FF Joseph G. Schmitt	Eng. 44	1-19-1919
FF George J. Scanlan	Eng. 44	1-19-1919
FF Fred Fempel	Eng. 257	1-25-1919
FF William E. Schalle	Eng. 16	2-4-1919
FF Alfred D. Kunde	H & L 114	2-17-1919
FF Patrick J. Lee	Eng. 221	5-16-1919
Capt. Edward F. Nealis	Eng. 226	5-17-1919
FF Charles B. Franssen	Eng. 8	5-24-1919
FF Joseph McDonough	Eng. 18	7-30-1919
FF Thomas F. Brennan	Eng. 251	2-26-1920
FF Michael M. Karkel	Eng. 251	2-26-1920
FF James Brennan	Eng. 251	2-28-1920
FF F. A. J. Callmeyer	Eng. 251	3-3-1920
FF James J. Hughes-1	Eng. 251	3-3-1920
Capt. Samuel Brown	Eng. 251	3-26-1920
FF Harry Wilson	Eng. 252	7-17-1920
FF Denis Donovan	Eng. 20	8-17-1920
FF Stephen J. Finn	Eng. 15	11-17-1920
FF John Keupp	H & L 101	12-29-1920
FF Joseph A. Flanagan	Eng. 44	7-31-1921
FF Thomas Behan	H & L 21	9-12-1921
FF William F. Sellinger	H & L 102	9-18-1921
Lt. James T. Brown	H & L 45	1-29-1922
FF Thomas D. Hassett	Eng. 58	2-13-1922
FF Fredrick G. Brandt	Eng. 208	3-25-1922
FF H. P. Reinhardt	H & L 21	3-25-1922
FF James V. O'Donnell	H & L 259	5-28-1922
FF Emmet F. Donnelly	H & L 134	6-15-1922
FF Adrian B. Curnen	Eng. 26	6-19-1922
FF James H. Malone	Eng. 219	7-18-1922
Lt. J. J. Schoppmeyer	Eng. 13	7-18-1922
FF Louis J. Farrell	H & L 33	9-24-1922
FF Michael H. Hanley	H & L 142	2-6-1923
FF John F. J. Dunne	H & L 142	2-6-1923
Lt. James Griffin	Eng. 285	2-7-1923
FF William J. Aeillo	Eng. 26	3-30-1923
FF Julius Spanier	Eng. 26	3-30-1923
FF James J. Sullivan	Eng. 230	8-21-1923
FF Raymond F. Farrell	Eng. 230	8-21-1923
Lt. A. E. Donovan-1	Eng. 303	1-21-1924
FF Thomas J. Connolly	H & L 28	4-10-1924
FF William Leichsenring	H & L 124	4-18-1924
FF James J. Murphy-3	Eng. 69	7-4-1924
FF Jas. J. McCormack	Eng. 40	7-4-1924
Capt. James R. Starkey	Lad. 112	7-16-1924
Asst. Chief Joseph Crawley	AC of Dept.	1-13-1925
FF William R. P. Fletcher	Res. 1	2-3-1925
BC Michael F. Harley	43rd Batt.	9-29-1925
FF John E. Miller	Eng. 278	11-24-1925
FF Patrick Daly	Eng. 278	11-26-1925
FF James O'Dwyer	Eng. 56	6-30-1926
FF William L. Moran	Eng. 56	6-30-1926
FF Charles R. Nagle	Eng. 306	8-11-1926
FF Christopher M. F. Quinn	Eng. 284	11-11-1926
DC John O'Hara	Bklyn. & Q	12-18-1926
FF Edward J. Fox-1	Eng. 77	1-27-1927
FF Joseph A. Heslin	Eng. 9	1-27-1927
FF John M. Grane	Eng. 77	1-27-1927
Capt. John S. Roberts	Eng. 15	1-28-1927
FF S. O. A. Williamson	Eng. 33	2-22-1927
FF Peter J. Parks	Eng. 24	2-23-1927
FF Henry Holster	Eng. 73	4-14-1927
FF M. J. Cunningham	Eng. 62	5-12-1927
FF Edward Knapp	Eng. 258-	
FF William F. Carlock	Eng. 62	8-29-1927
FF George E. Walker	H & L 40	9-26-1927
Capt. David M. Lynch	H & L 1	10-31-1927
FF Bernard O'Kane	Eng. 227	12-27-1927
FF John Dwyer	H & L 78	2-6-1928
Capt. George C. Strauss	Eng. 206	2-26-1928
FF John J. Donohue-3	H & L 2	4-3-1928

Line-of-Duty Deaths (Continued)

Name	Unit	Date
FF Jacob G. Gulde	Eng. 289	10-26-1928
FF John E. Rauch	Eng. 261	11-30-1928
FF Harry Schumann	Eng. 271	12-11-1928
FF William H. Kelly	Eng. 159	3-10-1929
Lt. John Mayer	Eng. 291	5-24-1929
FF Louis Lubcker	Eng. 50	6-5-1929
FF James H. Murphy	H & L 9	6-20-1929
Lt. Timothy E. Coughlin	Eng. 79	10-28-1929
FF William Vogel	H & L 1	11-27-1929
FF John J. Henderson	Eng. 276	12-8-1929
Pilot John J. Harvey-1	Eng. 86	2-11-1930
Capt. Charles H. Furey	Eng. 245	2-14-1930
FF Henry J. M. Hoehn	H & L 15	2-17-1930
FF Frank C. Murray	Eng. 33	3-3-1930
Lt. James A. O'Brien	H & L 116	4-19-1930
FF John J. Whelan	H & L 152	5-31-1930
FF Joseph A. Sullivan-3	Eng. 62	7-19-1930
FF F. M. Donelon	H & L 3	8-10-1930
Capt. Edward A. Dougherty	Eng. 202	10-4-1930
DC B. F. Carlock	4th Div.	11-29-1930
Lt. Thomas F. Kain	Eng. 212	1-12-1931
FF George L. Byrne	Eng. 301	2-6-1931
FF John Degnan	Eng. 35	4-7-1931
BC John J. Dooley	48th Batt.	6-6-1931
FF William Ormsby	H & L 101	9-7-1931
FF Matthew J. Dunn	H & L 14	10-14-1931
Lt. William Kostinec, Jr.	H & L 21	3-22-1932
Capt. Matthew Lynch	Eng. 251	3-30-1932
Capt. Fredrick J. Trefcer	H & L 9	5-17-1932
FF Charles G. Rappe	H & L 32	5-18-1932
FF Joseph LaGrange	H & L 108	5-20-1932
Lt. James O'Donnell	H & L 163	5-29-1932
FF Thaddius Connolly	H & L 32	7-27-1932
Lt. John H. Cosgrove	Eng. 65	8-1-1932
FF James F. Greene	Eng. 65	8-1-1932
FF Thomas S. Finn	Eng. 65	8-1-1932
FF William L. Pratt	H & L 7	8-1-1932
FF Peter A. Daly	Eng. 39	8-1-1932
Lt. James Harnett	H & L 16	8-1-1932
FF Louis Hardina	H & L 16	8-1-1932
FF Edward R. Maloney	Eng. 39	8-18-1932
FF W. M. Hackett	Eng. 13	12-15-1932
DC John J. Flood	3rd Div.	12-20-1932
FF John V. Logan	Eng. 37	1-24-1933
FF Ferd. Z. Riviello	H & L 14	2-20-1933
FF John J . Storch, Jr.	H & L 6	5-6-1933
FF John J. Feeley	Eng. 14	5-18-1933
Lt. John W. Smith-2	H & L 115	6-18-1933
FF Patrick J. Maloney	H & L 149	8-3-1933
Lt. Thomas A. Bowler	H & L 43	1-15-1934
FF Joseph P. Ahern	Eng. 48	4-10-1934
FF Frederick V. Erb	Eng. 231	7-23-1934
BC John A. Slowey	40th Batt.	8-1-1934
Lt. John H. Seeman	Eng. 227	1-2-1935
FF Cornelius Healy	Eng. 233	1-2-1935
FF George W. Sampson	Eng. 30	1-18-1935
Capt. William J. Head	Eng. 13	3-1-1935
FF Ernest Mattes	H & L 129	4-26-1935
FF John Caroll	H & L 48	4-28-1935
FF Ray M. Sands	Eng. 307	8-24-1935
FF Michael F. Logan	Eng. 321	9-5-1935
FF Charles Schoener	Eng. 13	3-7-1936
FF Joseph A. Scanlon	Eng. 293	5-13-1936
FF Joseph Dunn	Eng. 202	11-4-1936
FF William S. Neville	Eng. 217	12-10-1936
FF Joseph T. Fosse	Eng. 40	2-26-1937
FF Michael J. Mulvey	Eng. 207	3-7-1937
FF Fred Gerner	Eng. 96	8-5-1937
FF Peter J. Harmon	Eng. 61	9-24-1937
FF Joseph A. McNamara	Eng. 239	11-17-1937
Lt. John Durkin	Eng. 2	11-24-1937
FF Harry J. Kett	H & L 77	3-10-1938
Lt. Thomas Meehan	Eng. 9	4-3-1938
FF James F. Hughes-1	Eng. 48	5-3-1938
Capt. Joseph A. Tracy	Eng. 48	5-3-1938
Lt. Christopher J. Plunkett	Eng. 8	9-3-1938
Lt. Patrick McKeon	Eng. 244	10-25-1938
FF Thomas J. Hitter	Eng. 290	10-31-1938
FF John J. Jakoby	H & L 35	11-5-1938
FF Thomas Barragry	Eng. 241	12-24-1938
FF Andrew B. George	Eng. 36	1-3-1939
FF Caesar J. Macari	H & L 128	1-24-1939
FF Charles R. Will	H & L 163	3-18-1939
FF James A. Hagan	Ltd. Sq. 1	3-24-1939
FF John J. Lyons-2	Eng. 250	4-17-1939
FF William E. Lehmann	Eng. 272	8-24-1939
FF Joseph McCarty	Wnf. 50	10-21-1939
Capt. Philip W. Hublitz	Eng. 60	11-13-1939
FF John J. Finley	Eng. 201	11-17-1939
FF Gerald T. Hanley	Eng. 262	12-13-1939
FF Henry C. Foster	Eng. 321	12-23-1939
Lt. John E. Murphy	Eng. 1	12-27-1939
FF John P. Schwintek	Eng. 202	2-14-1940
FF James J. Steakem	Ladd. 30	5-15-1940
FF Patrick Devlin	Eng. 277	5-29-1940
DC James Tubridy	2nd Div.	7-30-1940
FF Charles A. Stenvall, Jr.	Eng. 69	10-16-1940
FF Harold A. Barker	Res. 2	1-5-1941
FF William J. Driscoll	Hdqtrs. Staff	1-28-1941
Lt. Benjamin Parcell	H & L 121	1-28-1941
Capt. Daniel J. Murphy-1	Eng. 315	2-20-1941
FF Thomas J. Osborn	Eng. 240	3-3-1941
FF Carl H. Bischoff	H & L 5	7-5-1941
FF Robert Mahl	Eng. 161	9-9-1941
FF Bertram Butler	H & L 137	9-17-1941
Capt. Walter Sandberg	H & L 121	10-24-1941
FF Raymond J. Cosgrove	H & L 153	1-2-1942
Lt. Thomas Blackburne	LSS 1	7-26-1942
FF John C. Huggins	Eng. 308	7-26-1942
FF Edward J. Klimas	H & L 111	10-30-1942
FF Patrick O'Keefe	Eng. 73	3-6-1943
FF Eugene F. Kelly	Eng. 240	3-22-1943
FF George Schmitt	H & L 153	3-24-1943
FF Robert W. Lane	H & L 105	4-9-1943
FF Peter J. Dannhardt	Eng. 15	7-4-1943
Capt. James H. Savage	H & L 131	7-5-1943
FF Robert G. Gates	Eng. 253	8-14-1943
FF James A. P. Dingee	Eng. 282	8-23-1943
FF C. Stephen Auditore	Eng. 243	10-18-1943
FF Robert W. Johnston	Eng. 293	12-31-1943
FF Joseph O'Flaherty	H & L 105	3-4-1944
Capt. William F. Klauck	H & L 105	3-30-1944
FF Edward J. Nelson	H & L 30	4-26-1944
FF Emile A. Steiner	Eng. 36	5-22-1944
Lt. Harold J. Curran	Eng. 161	5-30-1944
FF Bernard P. McGreevy	H & L 16	7-01-1944
Insp. Charles E. Johnson	Div. of Comb.	7-01-1944
FF Howard V. Colbert	Eng. 292	7-9-1944
FF Eugene F. Steffens	H & L 122	8-5-1944
Insp. Michael Kristal	Div. of Comb.	8-30-1944
FF George H. Cridland, Jr.	MSD	9-9-1944
Capt. Walter T. Clarke	Eng. 6	10-25-1944
FF John J. Sheehy	MSD	11-1-1944
FF Eugene J. Studer	Eng. 81	11-2-1944
FF James J. Hughes	MSD	11-19-1944
FF Robert C. Pettit, Jr.	Eng. 303	12-15-1944
Lt. Joseph A. Joyce	Eng. 40	1-1-1945
FF Vincent A. T. Schmitt	Eng. 292	1-6-1945
FF Nelson L. Tuite	Eng. 36	1-9-1945
FF Elbert Hardman	Eng. 36	1-9-1945
FF John J. Russell	MSD	1-15-1945
FF Morris Graf	Eng. 31	1-22-1945
FF Frank J. Winklarek	Eng. 36	1-24-1945
BC Anthony Jireck	32nd Batt.	1-27-1945
FF Herman Stanton	MSD	2-10-1945
FF George Nigro	Eng. 229	2-13-1945
FF James J. Ryan-4	Eng. 1	2-16-1945
FF James J. Farrell-2	Eng. 66	2-19-1945
FF George B. Weill	H & L 23	2-22-1945
FF Thomas F. Shortell	H & L 157	3-8-1945
BC Charles Kohlenberger	22nd Batt.	3-31-1945
FF James R. Hickey	MSD	4-5-1945
FF Stephen J. Butcher	H & L 5	4-19-1945
FF Stephen J. Marangas	Eng. 62	4-20-1945
FF Harold Holsten	Eng. 19	5-12-1945
FF John R. Sheridan	Eng. 89	5-14-1945
FF Henry B. Innes	H & L 33	5-15-1945
FF Thomas F. Taylor	H & L 131	6-3-1945
FF Frank Fiederliene	Eng. 257	8-31-1945
FF Charles A. Hickey	H & L 37	9-22-1945
Lt. Michael W. Tarpey	Lad. 41	10-1-1945
FF James Costello	Eng. 263	10-13-1945
FF William F. McNulty	Eng. 233	10-17-1945
FF John W. Eiserman	Eng. 299	12-14-1945
FF Walter A. Jensen	Eng. 233	1-5-1946
FF George M. Williams	H & L 49	1-11-1946
FF Frank J. Molinari	MSD	1-13-1946
FF Edwin J. Hovey	Eng. 37	1-16-1946
FF John W. Leary	H & L 122	2-9-1946
FF Michael J. Berkery	Eng. 203	6-14-1946
FF James R. Gillis	Eng. 90	7-20-1946
FF William J. Wandling	Eng. 288	11-16-1946
FF Frank Moorhead, Jr.	Eng. 93	12-12-1946
FF Daniel M. Krauss	Eng. 15	12-30-1946
FF Winfield A. Walsh	H & L 9	1-4-1947
BC William P. Hogan	5th Batt.	1-9-1974
FF Nathan Levine	Eng. 73	2-22-1947
FF Frederick Ziegler	H & L 144	6-17-1947
FF William D. Austin	H & L 144	6-17-1947
FF Howard E. Wynn	H & L 26	11-29-1947
FF Jacob Bassman	H & L 26	11-29-1947
FF James C. Farley	Eng. 92	12-16-1947
FF John T. Rynn	Eng. 89	4-10-1948
FF Joseph J. Brecht	Eng. 5	7-31-1948
Lt. Harry G. Boyle	Eng. 61	8-8-1948
Lt. Harry M. Maloney	Eng. 246	8-9-1948
Lt. George P. Oates	Eng. 283	3-3-1949
FF Lowell J. McElroy	Eng. 214	5-8-1949
FF Chris E. A. McAuley	Eng. 233	5-12-1949
FF Peter E. Farley	H & L 136	8-16-1949
BC Gunther E. Beake	3rd Batt.	8-23-1949
FF Samuel R. Doherty	Eng. 15	11-28-1949
Lt. John A. Lyden	Eng. 240	12-24-1949
FF Peter Engel	Eng. 232	1-5-1950
FF Michael R. Michelotti	H & L 116	3-12-1950
FF Walter W. Chadwick	H & L 26	3-26-1950
Lt. Robert E. Rummel	H & L 165	10-16-1950
Lt. Robert C. Davison	Eng. 75	4-22-1951
FF Arthur C. Smith	H & L 118	5-5-1951
FF James Roche	H & L 118	9-24-1951
FF Bernard Delamer	Eng. 49	10-6-1951
FF Frank E. Wolf	H & L 8	12-16-1951
Lt. William Munda	Lad. 130	1-22-1952
Capt. William J. Brady	Eng. 35	2-8-1952
FF Bernard E. Meaney	Eng. 276	2-19-1952
FF Thomas W. Cokeley	18th Batt.	2-29-1952
BC John M. J. McGowan	11th Batt.	3-8-1952
FF Denis J. Corridan	Eng. 324	4-10-1952
FF David J. O'Keeffe	Eng. 59	5-2-1952
FF Emanuel Adler	Eng. 309	11-16-1952
Lt. Packey Redican	Lad. 17	12-26-1952
FF Antonio J. Assante	Eng. 306	12-31-1952
DC Terence P. Conaty	5th Div.	2-1-1953
Lt. Louis W. Finger	Eng. 64	5-7-1953
FF Andrew L. Milyko	Rescue 3	7-1-1953
FF Julius Feldman	Lad. 43	9-8-1953
FF Daniel A. Weisse	WT 1	9-14-1953
Mar. Engr. John D. McKean	Eng. 85	9-22-1953
FF James J. Morgam-3	Eng. 203	10-13-1953
FF Thomas J. Farrell-3	Lad. 147	10-28-1953
FF Garrett W. Langdon	Eng. 298	12-6-1953
FF Harry J. Smith, Jr.	Eng. 159	12-16-1953
FF Joseph T. Mannino	Eng. 219	12-24-1953
FF William Kot	Eng. 229	4-5-1954
FF Edward J. Curtin	Eng. 63	7-17-1954
BC Edward C. Huber	20th Batt	7-27-1954
FF Joseph Delong	LSS	7-28-1954
FF Samuel A. Schiller	Eng. 324	7-31-1954
FF Joseph P. Dugan	Lad. 136	7-31-1954
FF Daniel Sullivan	Eng. 319	9-11-1954
FF John P. Hamilton	Lad. 17	10-22-1954
BC James Byrne	SS SQ	11-23-1954
FF Eric R. Anderson	Lad. 103	12-28-1954
Capt. Thomas Herlihy	Lad. 167	1-1-1955
Lt. Joseph M. Oesau	Eng. 277	1-12-1955
FF Daniel A. Dunphy	Eng. 309	1-26-1955
BC Eugene G. Dowd	44th Batt.	1-27-1955
FF Frank K. Kober	Eng. 278	1-29-1955
Capt. William L. Casey	Eng. 218	2-1-1955
FF Arnold N. Hafner	Eng. 294	3-31-1955
FF Andrew K. Wright	Eng. 17	5-4-1955
FF Fred L. Cumming	Lad. 15	5-5-1955
Lt. Thomas R. Dore	Rescue 4	6-4-1955
FF John J. Daly-2	Eng. 70	6-12-1955
FF Peter Bradley	Lad. 53	7-18-1955
BC Edward P. Scully	37th Batt.	7-24-1955
FF Vincent Laurence	LSS	8-20-1955
FF George C. Zapf	Lad. 156	9-5-1955
FF James O'Kane	Eng. 62	11-30-1955
FF William G. Brown	Eng. 156	12-6-1955
Capt. Vincent J. McGill	Eng. 96	12-25-1955
FF James W. Kojac	Lad. 128	2-2-1956
FF William Prechtel	Eng. 28	2-9-1956
Capt. James A. Walsh-1	Eng. 234	2-15-1956
Lt. William O'Sullivan	LSS	3-8-1956
Lt. John F. Molloy	Eng. 48	4-4-1956
FF Arthur G. Hanson	Lad. 44	4-4-1956
FF Fred J. Hellauer	Eng. 48	4-4-1956

Line-of-Duty Deaths (Continued)

FF William P. Hoolan	Lad. 44	4-4-1956
FF Charles J. Infosino	Hdqtrs. Staff	4-4-1956
FF Edward J. Carroll	Eng. 48	4-4-1956
Lt. Augustine Halley	LSS	5-18-1956
FF George J. Murphy-1	LSS	7-21-1956
Lt. Edward D. O'Connell	Eng. 24	8-26-1956
FF Thomas F. Maher	52nd Batt.	9-3-1956
FF Ruby Naturman	LSS	9-15-1956
Capt. Daniel T. Rice	Eng. 159	11-11-1956
FF James P. Reilly	Lad. 2	11-14-1956
FF Francis X. Casey	Eng. 18	11-18-1956
FF William McEvoy	Eng. 292	12-30-1956
FF Peter G. Peila	Res. 2	2-13-1957
FF Anthony P. Longa	LSS	3-31-1957
BC James G. Kiesling	5th Batt.	4-6-1957
FF Bernard Tully	Eng. 302	4-17-1957
FF Matthew J. Belford	Lad. 147	5-7-1957
Lt. Martin D. J. Kelly	LSS	5-26-1957
FF James E. McArdle	Eng. 75	6-14-1957
Lt. Rodman G. Chrysler	Eng. 7	6-26-1957
FF Thomas J. Walters	37th Batt.	7-26-1957
FF Michael Berenz	Eng. 258	10-22-1957
Lt. Richard MacClave	Eng. 46	11-26-1957
FF Joseph J. Tucker	Eng. 240	12-19-1957
Lt. Timothy F. O'Leary, Jr.	LSS	1-1-1958
FF Richard Gelke	LSS	1-15-1958
FF William G. Schmid	Lad. 1	2-14-1958
FF Bernard Blumenthal	Lad. 20	2-14-1958
Lt. Stephen D. Rooney	Lad. 1	3-13-1958
FF Paul C. Wrigley	Lad. 152	5-16-1958
FF Frank Zatecky	LSS	10-6-1958
FF Thomas Casey	Lad. 52	10-8-1958
FF Vincent Janczewski	LSS	11-12-1958
FF Frederick E. Glasser	LSS	1-14-1959
Capt. Thomas P. Mulvaney	Lad. 148	1-16-1959
FF Matthew F. Wieners	Eng. 256	1-28-1959
FF Charles A. Wilson-3	Lad. 166	3-19-1959
Capt. Erick W. Thomas	Lad. 34	4-3-1959
Lt. John J. Rober	Lad. 82	4-28-1959
FF Charles J. Boll	Lad. 2	5-20-1959
FF Richard W. Schultz	Lad. 129	5-31-1959
FF Ludwig A. Beckman	Eng. 31	9-26-1959
Lt. Theodore Knote	LSS	10-23-1959
Lt. James Molloy-1	LSS	11-6-1959
FF Edward J. Campbell	Lad. 78	11-16-1959
Lt. Orestes Hantjiles	Eng. 313	11-28-1959
Capt. Stephen Dyczko	13th Div.	12-11-1959
FF Ignatius V. Bell	Lad. 12	1-8-1960
FF Paul R. Cady	Sup. Eng. 1	1-13-1960
FF Michael Klein	Lad. 166	5-7-1960
FF Martin J. McCormack	LSS	6-26-1960
FF Dennis McQueenie	Lad. 126	7-29-1960
FF Robert J. Denney	Eng. 294	10-11-1960
Lt. Thomas E. Fitzgerald	Eng. 45	10-22-1960
FF John C. Cosner	Squad 8	11-18-1960
Lt. John A. McDermott	Eng. 31	11-18-1960
FF Francis J. Sammon	Eng. 31	11-18-1960
Lt. Matthew A. Sheerin	Eng. 250	11-19-1960
FF James A. Pinto	Eng. 275	1-20-1961
FF John N. Crosthwaite	Squad 2	2-4-1961
BC Anthony R. Martucci	13th Batt.	3-9-1961
Capt. Walter C. Bersig	Lad. 149	6-27-1961
FF Robert A. Meill	Lad. 120	7-1-1961
FF William J. Bryan	LSS	9-12-1961
FF John J. Garrick	Eng. 97	11-9-1961
FF Robert R. Hurst	Lad. 24	11-22-1961
FF Charles G. Lang	Lad. 24	11-22-1961
FF John J. King	Eng. 23	12-27-1961
Lt. Charles F. Hale	Eng. 14	1-12-1962
Lt. Victor Prokop	Lad. 155	1-17-1962
Lt. Michael J. Shields	LSS	1-26-1962
FF Bernard Goldmani	LSS	1-30-1962
FF Leo J. J. Ray	Eng. 55	2-15-1962
Lt. Luigi Bianca	LSS	3-28-1962
FF John Cannon	Eng. 237	5-15-1962
FF Edward M. White	Eng. 91	5-28-1962
DC Frank J. Turner	LSS	6-6-1962
FF John C. Farragher	Res. 1	7-12-1962
DC P. Joseph Connolly	Fire Emg. Div.	8-22-1962
Prob. FF Richard Andrews	Eng. 325	10-26-1962
FF Francis X. Egan-2	Lad. 115	10-26-1962
FF Richard P. Gifford	Eng. 238	10-26-1962
FF James M. Marino	Eng. 325	10-26-1962
Capt. William F. Russell	Eng. 325	10-26-1962
FF George J. Zahn-2	Eng. 238	10-26-1962
FF James J. Ruane	Eng. 69	11-17-1962

Lt. Frank W. Pickering	Eng. 156	4-3-1963
Capt. Peter J. Brennan	Lad. 36	5-15-1963
FF Raymond R. Mayr	Lad. 134	7-2-1963
FF James A. Rogers	WT 1	9-2-1963
Lt. George R. Coger	Eng. 312	10-2-1963
FF Eugene K. Byrne	LSS	12-4-1963
FF James J. Johnston-2	Eng. 310	12-22-1963
FF William J. Hanlon	Eng. 156	12-30-1963
FF Peter A. Celvini	LSS	2-16-1964
FF Martin Hanrahan	Lad. 132	5-16-1964
FF Ernest J. Marquart	Squad 3	6-26-1964
FF Edwin C. Remhild	Lad. 128	7-11-1964
FF Olin L. Blair, Jr.	Lad. 82	8-19-1964
FF Bartholomew V. Foley	DO 6	1-19-1965
FF James F. Hipple	Lad. 49	1-31-1965
Lt. Charles J. Franck	Eng. 33	4-14-1965
1st D. Comm. George F. Mand	Hdqtrs.	5-1-1965
FF Edward F. Snediker	Eng. 48	8-27-1965
Lt. Robert Niebling	41st Batt.	10-22-1965
FF Frederick M. Kubera	Lad. 82	11-23-1965
FF Robert T. Smullen	Lad. 142	3-19-1966
FF William H. O'Brien-1	20th Batt.	3-20-1966
FF Dominic Villano	LSS	5-22-1966
FF James E. Linekin	LSS	5-27-1966
FF John J. O'Keefe	Eng. 16	8-17-1966
FF William J. Farrell	Eng. 314	8-21-1966
BC Walter J. Higgins	7th Batt.	10-17-1966
DC Thomas A. Reilly	3rd Div.	10-17-1966
Lt. John J. Finley	Lad. 7	10-17-1966
Lt. Joseph Priore	4th Batt.	10-17-1966
FF John G. Berry	Lad. 7	10-17-1966
FF James V. Galanaugh	Eng. 18	10-17-1966
FF Rudolph F. Kaminsky	Lad. 7	10-17-1966
FF Joseph Kelly-2	Eng. 18	10-17-1966
FF Carl Lee	Lad. 7	10-17-1966
FF William F. McCarron	3rd Div.	10-17-1966
Prob. FF Daniel L. Rey	Eng. 18	10-17-1966
FF Bernard A. Tepper	Eng. 18	10-17-1966
FF Lorenzo Warlick	Squad 4	1-5-1967
FF James S. Hosey	Lad. 16	1-29-1967
Capt. John W. Smith-3	LSS	2-11-1967
BC Samuel H. Levine	49th Batt.	3-21-1967
Lt. Dominick Marchesi	LSS	6-21-1967
FF James C. Kearney	Lad. 114	8-28-1967
FF Carl Herer	Lad. 19	10-10-1967
Lt. Michael O. Glynn	LSS	10-22-1967
FF Lawrence Perchuck	LSS	11-27-1967
Capt. Joseph A. Fay	Eng. 61	11-30-1967
FF William P. Kelly	Eng. 278	12-27-1967
DC Perry R. Peterson	3rd Div.	1-7-1968
FF George F. Linnemann	Eng. 218	2-18-1968
Capt. Thomas F. Munroe	LSS	2-26-1968
FF Charles J. Grieco	Lad. 38	3-26-1968
Lt. Edmund A. McNulty	LSS	4-17-1968
Lt. Harry L. Miniter	LSS	9-8-1968
FF Philip C. Smith	LSS	10-5-1968
FF George L. Collins	12th Batt.	11-15-1968
Lt. Eugene R. Miller	33rd Batt.	12-24-1968
FF Lawrence Franklin	Lad. 30	2-19-1969
FF James J. Maine	LSS	4-10-1969
FF Dominick J. Rosato	Lad. 27	5-21-1969
FF Bernard P. McManus, II	LSS	7-25-1969
FF John F. M. Whelan	LSS	9-9-1969
FF Michael T. Carr	Lad. 85	9-19-1969
FF Harold R. Nelson	Lad. 156	1-3-1970
FF Carmelo J. Puccia	Eng. 53	1-6-1970
DC William G. Dusterwald	LSS	1-8-1970
Lt. John R. Eastburn	Eng. 54	2-10-1970
Lt. Edward C. Hackett	LSS	3-2-1970
FF Edward J. Ehlers	Eng. 209	4-20-1970
Lt. James W. Connelly	51st Batt.	5-17-1970
FF Edward J. Tuite	Rescue 1	10-17-1970
FF Timothy J. Gray	Lad. 34	12-7-1970
Lt. Jerome R. O'Connor	18th Batt.	1-19-1971
FF John T. Dunne	Lad. 175	3-28-1971
FF Walter J. Bozenko	Eng. 315	5-14-1971
Lt. Thomas P. Sheridan	Eng. 323	5-28-1971
FF James P. Lavin	Lad. 121	7-14-1971
FF Edward J. Heaney	LSS	7-22-1971
BC William C. Rinsdale	19th Batt.	8-1-1971
Lt. Joseph P. Connelly	Eng. 311	1-19-1972
Lt. Francis J. Martin	Eng. 70	3-9-1972
FF Henry H. Mitchell	Lad. 124	8-31-1972
Lt. Herman G. Berny	Eng. 270	10-15-1972
Lt. William C. Seelig	2nd Batt.	12-7-1972
FF Peter J. Cusumano	Squad 3	12-7-1972

Lt. Frank E. Smith	Eng. 236	1-14-1973
FF John Clarke	Eng. 268	6-2-1973
FF Joseph Johnson, Jr.	Eng. 234	9-1-1973
Lt. Frank J. Brennan	Eng. 3	9-6-1973
Lt. Allan J. Sweet	Lad. 163	11-14-1973
FF Fabian J. Echevarrieta	Lad. 109	1-7-1974
FF Anthony W. DeFalco	Eng. 298	1-9-1974
Lt. Henry J. Hinton	LSS	2-22-1974
FF Harold J. Hoey	Lad. 17	6-13-1974
FF Johnnie Williams	Lad. 17 (2)	10-29-1974
FF Russell T. Linneball	Lad. 17 (2)	10-29-1974
FF Daniel Perricone	9th Batt.	12-23-1974
FF Edward J. Winewski	Eng. 304	2-25-1975
Lt. Michael A. Maloney	49th Batt.	3-19-1975
FF Adolph A. D'Anbrosio	Lad. 151	7-4-1975
FF James W. Robertson	Eng. 235	7-8-1975
Capt. Raymond Koehler	Eng. 286	11-11-1975
FF John J. Flanagan-2	Lad. 125	12-8-1975
FF Charles K. Sanchez-1	Lad. 131	1-7-1976
FF Joseph Kenavan	Eng. 228	1-25-1976
Lt. Joseph M. Beetle	Lad. 143	2-8-1976
FF Stanley H. Skinner	Lad. 143	2-8-1976
FF Thomas J. Earl	Eng. 285	2-8-1976
FF Richard B. Marsh	Eng. 40	4-3-1976
FF Patrick J. Cleary	Eng. 219	5-30-1976
Lt. Joseph Sparacino, Jr.	45th Batt.	8-30-1976
FF William D. Prange	Lad. 8	12-9-1976
FF Donald P. Aversa	Lad. 152	1-17-1977
FF George E. Meenken	Ambu. No. 1	2-5-1977
Lt. Charles Hunt	Eng. 166	4-15-1977
Capt. John J. Stelmack	Eng. 284	6-23-1977
FF Martin R. Celic	Lad. 18	7-10-1977
Lt. Lester A. Roselle	40th Batt.	8-4-1977
FF Gerard T. Ganley	Eng. 258	7-13-1978
Lt. James E. Gutillo	33rd Batt.	8-2-1978
FF Harold F. Hastings	42nd Batt.	8-2-1978
FF James P. McManus	Lad. 153	8-2-1978
FF George S. Rice	Lad. 153	8-2-1978
FF Charles S. Bouton	Lad. 156	8-2-1978
FF William O'Connor	Lad. 156	8-2-1978
Lt. Robert G. Courtenay	Lad. 47	11-21-1978
FF John T. McKenna	Lad. 34	3-17-1979
FF Walter J. Smith, Jr.	Lad. 24	6-14-1979
FF Joseph F. Zino	Lad. 122	9-15-1979
FF Gerard D. Crowley	Lad. 134	10-14-1979
BC James M. Meyers	11th Batt.	11-15-1979
Lt. Robert R. Dolney	Eng. 332	3-5-1980
FF Donald M. Bub	Eng. 47	6-6-1980
FF Lawrence P. Fitzpatrick	Rescue 3	6-27-1980
FF Gerard J. Frisby	Lad. 28	6-27-1980
BC Frank T. Tuttlemondo	44th Batt.	8-13-1980
FF Dennis M. Peterson	Lad. 80	12-19-1981
FF Richard J. Smith	Lad. 7	1-9-1982
Lt. Robert J. Cahill	Lad. 173	2-16-1982
Capt. Alfred M. Knecht	Eng. 76	3-1-1982
Capt. Barry N. Brown	Div. 6	7-22-1982
FF William J. Ford	Lad. 50	8-21-1983
FF Tony Shands	Eng. 297	10-20-1984
FF Philip C. D'Adamo	Lad. 118	12-1-1984
Capt. James P. McDonnell	Div. 3	10-20-1985
FF Richard G. Sale	Eng. 35	6-19-1986
Lt. Peter J. Canelli	Lad. 143	2-16-1987
Lt. Joseph P. Faughnan	Lad. 162	11-17-1987
FF John J. Toomey	Lad. 123	12-6-1987
FF John P. Devaney	Lad. 131	2-3-1989
FF Alfred E. Ronaldson	Rescue 3	3-5-1991
FF Kevin C. Kane	Lad. 110	9-12-1991
Lt. Thomas A. Williams	Res. 4	2-25-1992
FF Arthur K. Tuck	Lad. 160	1-9-1993
FF James E. Young	Eng. 24	3-28-1994
FF Christopher Siedenburg	Eng. 24	3-29-1994
Capt. John J. Drennan	Lad. 5	5-7-1994
Lt. George W. Lener	Lad. 6	7-20-1994
Capt. Wayne E. Smith	Lad. 136	10-4-1994
FF Thomas A. Wylie	Lad. 18	1-3-1995
Lt. Raymond F. Schiebel	Eng. 221	3-7-1995
FF Peter F. McLaughlin	Res. 4	10-8-1995
Lt. John M. Clancy	Batt. 50	12-31-1995
FF James B. Williams	Lad. 121	1-5-1996
FF Louis Valentino	Res. 2	2-5-1996
FF Raymond H. Nakovics	Eng. 39	4-29-1998
Lt. James W. Blackmore	Eng. 332	6-5-1998
Capt. Scott J. LaPiedra	Div. 15	7-4-1998
Lt. Joseph P. Cavalieri	Batt. 39	12-18-1998
FF James E. Bohan	Eng. 262	12-18-1998
FF Christopher M. Bopp	Lad. 170	12-18-1998
Capt. Vincent G. Fowler	Div. 13	6-4-1999

Series of photos show collapse of building at a third alarm at 168th Street and Nelson Avenue, the Bronx. Summer of 1991. (Photos by Matt Daly)

Brooklyn Box 22-1055, Nostrand Avenue and Empire Boulevard, Fall of 1995. (Photo by Warren Fuchs)

Manhattan Box 55-1294, December 10, 1983. (Photo by George Tuft)

Members operate at Brooklyn Box 44-1658, 1665 Pitkin Avenue, December 12, 1995. (Photo by John Strandberg)

Ladder 114 operates at Brooklyn Box 44-1158, December 1983. (Photo by Warren Fuchs)

Members operate at 30 Allen Street, Manhattan, January 11, 1998.

Brooklyn Box 33-2585, 4312 New Utrecht Avenue, March 29, 2000. (Photo by John Leavy)

Manhattan Box 22-1686, 444 West 163rd Street, March 15, 1995.

Brooklyn Box 22-1046, New York Avenue and Lefferts Avenue, Fall of 1990. (Photo by Warren Fuchs)

15

Manhattan Box 66-725, 525 Eighth Avenue, March 1, 1996.

Brooklyn Box 10-75-780, 42 Lewis Avenue, February 2, 1997. (Photo by Peter Connolly)

Fire rages through a vacant supermarket in the Bushwick section of Brooklyn, 1979. (Photo by Harvey Eisner)

New York City Fire Department History

A five-alarm blaze was battled in the Bushwick section of Brooklyn on July 14, 1977, during a power outage. The Chief helps hard-pressed companies as he pulls hose line into position.

THESE are to certify that Thos. Franklin is pursuant to LAW nominated and appointed one of the ENGINE Firemen of the City of New York.

Decr. 30th 1799

Robt. Benson, Clk.

VOLUNTARY AID

The membership certificate of New York City Volunteer Fireman Thomas Franklin, dated December 30, 1799.

Author's Foreword

The history of the New York City Fire Department is actually the story of two departments – one volunteer and the other paid. Both of these organizations had a common bond: brave firefighters protecting the most dynamic city in the world from the ravages of fire. The volunteer department was world-famous not only for its members' abilities on the fireground, but also for their colorful apparatus, clothing, social activities and parades. Many of the initial tactics for fighting fires, tools and equipment used by firefighters across the country and around the world had their origins in the New York City's Volunteer Fire Department.

The professional department that took over from the volunteers had some large boots to fill. Using strict discipline and a highly organized approach on the fireground, the paid department soon forged its own reputation as a premier fire department.

The story of the Department is a story of men, machines and the ever-growing city around them. Ready to overcome any obstacle, the firefighters used inventiveness, raw courage and brute strength to fashion a method of operation and the tools needed to control nature itself. From leather buckets to tower ladder streams, the New York City firefighters always were willing to face a wall of flames and make a stand. Braving dense smoke and searing heat and, for the bulk of this history without the benefit of breathing apparatus, they dove into hell in search of their neighbors, trapped and helpless within the inferno. It is a story of heroics and heroes, of everyday people performing extraordinary deeds time and again. They inspire us now to continue their legacy of valor.

The Beginnings of Firefighters in New York City

The West India Company, looking for people willing to accept low-paying jobs, sought workers from any nation for their trading post of New Amsterdam. Unlike Puritan New England, this attracted a different, more rowdy type of person than the original Dutch settlers. By 1640, more than 18 languages were being spoken in a city where taverns outnumbered churches.

Peter Stuyvesant, Governor of New Amsterdam, appointed four fire wardens in 1648 and the history of organized firefighting in America began. In a stroke of political savvy, he named two Dutchmen and two Englishmen to fill the new posts. These original fire wardens were all able and honest citizens and politically correct public servants of their time.

Stuyvesant chose Dutchmen Martin Krieger and Adrian Geyser. Krieger owned and operated a popular tavern across from Bowling Green. Later, when the city was incorporated, Krieger became a member of Governor Stuyvesant's council and held a variety of other important posts until the British took control. Adrian Geyser worked for the Dutch West India Company, founders of New Amsterdam. Geyser later served as a member of the Executive Council.

The two Englishmen were Thomas Hall and George Woolsey. Hall had been taken prisoner by the Dutch and released on parole. He developed a strong relationship with the Dutch power brokers and his popularity grew. Hall owned a large and very successful farm near what is now Beekman and Spruce Streets and held a number of civic offices. George Woolsey was the second English fire warden named. He was the agent of a leading Dutch trader.

The wardens were empowered to visit every house between the Fort (the Battery) and the Fresh Water (Manhattan's largest natural, spring-fed, fresh-water pond, also called the Collect). The fire wardens were to inspect all chimneys and see that they were swept clean. They also were to ensure that no wooden chimneys were built between the Fort and the Fresh Water. If they found a chimney dirty or clogged, they could levy a fine of three gilders. The fine money was to be used to purchase and maintain fire ladders, hooks and buckets. The wardens also could fine up to 25 gilders if a house caught fire due to negligence or if the flames extended from the fireplace.

In 1657, New Amsterdam incorporated and streets were given names. The 1648 rules (chimneys swept clean and not made from wood) again were ordered to be followed and four new wardens were appointed. They had the same mission as the first group – fire prevention.

The Dutch citizens (known as Burghers) did not stop there; after a fire burned down a small log house, they designated a group of eight men to walk the newly paved streets after dark. These men watched for fires and stopped anyone who looked suspicious. They carried large wooden rattles to sound an alarm if a fire was seen. To the council, they were known as the "Rattle Watch." The citizens, however, had a slightly less flattering nickname for them. They called them "The Prowlers."

The "Rattle Watch," also known as "the Prowlers," New York, 1657.

Later that same year, the citizens realized the city needed leather fire buckets (there was none up to this point) and a tax was collected to procure them. But true to the speed of government, the buckets were not received until January 1659. Eventually, they were manufactured by the "Knights of Saint Crispin," the town's foremost cobblers who were located in Shoemaker's Pasture.

A short time later, "The Prowlers" increased in number to 50, with two men appointed in each ward or section of the city. The city fathers provided 250 buckets, hooks and small ladders to this "fire company."

In 1664, four English frigates carrying 1000 soldiers sailed into New York Harbor. Despite Peter Stuyvesant's fiery calls to resist, most of the settlers, including the Dutch, were unhappy with the West India Company's administration and gladly accepted the English terms. Without a shot being fired, New Amsterdam became New York.

The rattles gave way to bells and by 1697, four men known as the "Night Watch" were walking the streets with their bells at the ready. They rang their bells and announced the time and weather every hour. The addition of City Hall at the head of Broad Street in 1700 gave the city a new focal point.

The good ship *Beaver* arrived from England on December 3, 1731, carrying two Newsham hand fire engines. Jacobus Turck, a gunsmith, eventually was appointed to take charge of the engines and keep them in repair at his own cost after a 10-pound salary was advanced to him. Dubbed by Mayor Lurting as "Number 1" and "Number 2," the engines were stored in separate sheds in the rear of City Hall and looked upon by the citizens with a combination of excitement and awe. Jacobus Turck also was working on a pump of his own design, which was, perhaps, the first mechanical fire pumper built in America. Unfortunately, it proved to be unsuccessful.

The General Assembly of the colony established the New York Volunteer Fire Department on December 16, 1737, with the appointment of 30 men. These "Firemen of the City of New York" were to be "strong, able, discreet, honest and sober men," who would be responsible for the "care, management, working and use of the fire engines and other tools and instruments of fires" and "ready at a call by night and by day." If they failed to answer an alarm "without reasonable cause," they would be fined 12 shillings. For their efforts, they would be exempt from jury duty, serving in the militia and other mundane duties the average citizen faced.

The city's first firehouse was built in 1736, in front of City Hall on Broad Street, between Exchange Place and Wall Street. The apparatus protected a city of 1200 houses, with a population approaching 9000.

The new department's first good "job" was on March 18, 1741. At noon, a fire was discovered in the governor's house inside the fort. The alarm was sounded and the two engines were dragged to the scene. The fire rapidly extended to the King's Chapel, then next door to the barracks, as lines of buckets filled the pumps furiously being manned by the volunteers. The streams developed were exceedingly over-matched by the building flames. Despite the best efforts of the firemen, all the buildings within the fort were in ashes by sundown.

At first, the fire was believed to be caused by a careless plumber who had left a fire in the gutter between the house and the 50-year-old King's Chapel next door. Then, as a series of fires occurred during a period of a few days, an arson plot was suspected. The city was in a frenzy as rumors swept the streets. A number of people were arrested; magistrates assembled and many "conspirators" were executed. The testimony against them later began to crumble and the actual facts of the case never were resolved fully.

After battling this tough series of blazes, the exhausted firemen called for more help and 14 additional firemen were added to the department roster. This was the start of the department's expansion. It grew as the city grew.

Late in 1743, the first successful American-made apparatus was added to the department. Thomas Lote, a cooper and boat builder, covered much of the box of his hand pumper in brass and relied on hand-operated levers only. Engine Number 3 soon went into service and became known unofficially as "Old Brass Backs."

The second serious fire faced by the new volunteer department occurred on February 23, 1753, when the Free School House, which adjoined the Trinity Church on Broadway, caught fire. All of the engines – now numbering four – were brought to the scene. Flames threatened the church and embers began to cling to the wooden steeple. Firemen furiously pumped the hand engines, which were fed by buckets of water. The streams barely were able to reach the roof and firemen and citizens alike watched as it appeared doubtful the fire could be controlled. After much time and effort, amazingly, it was stopped. Weary firemen walked back to the firehouses talking about the difficulties encountered with fires that burn at a great height – a discussion that continues in New York City firehouses today.

Jacobus Stoutenburgh became the head of the department on July 24, 1761, with a salary and allowance of 30 pounds a year. The following year, the department was reorganized and Stoutenburgh's title was changed to "Engineer" (the spelling at that time was Engenier). Two Assistant Engineers were named to help direct the 72 firemen assigned to the five engine companies in the city.

The first hook and ladder company had been placed into service in 1774. Two years later, the department had grown to 170 men, assigned to eight engine companies and two truck companies. But the members of the fire department and the citizens of New York soon would have to face more than just the threat of accidental fire; the war with England was closing in on the city.

New York's first pumper made by Robert Newsham of London arrived in 1731.

Leather stovepipe hat designed by Jacobus Turck around 1731 and improved leather helmet by Henry Gratacap in 1828.

Overseer of Fire Engines Jacobus Turck created a leather stovepipe-shaped fire hat around 1731 and its use began to catch on with the volunteer firefighters. On November 19, 1762, they became an official part of the department when all New York City firemen were directed to wear the leather hats when on duty. They were the forerunner of what would develop into the American fire helmet.

General Washington had fortified the city with troops and awaited the arrival of the British, led by General Sir William Howe. The British crossed from Staten Island into Brooklyn on August 22, 1776, and began a series of battles with colonial forces. After the August 27-29 Battle of Long Island, General George Washington was forced to evacuate to New York City. Before Howe could finish off the rebel army, a miraculous retreat northward moved the colonial troops to safe ground. Virtually the entire fire department enlisted with General Washington and marched away with the army, leaving their beloved fire engines behind. Engineer Stoutenburgh – wearing the uniform of a Major – again led his firemen. They had formed into two battalions of Continental Army soldiers.

Six days after the firemen left the city, shouts of fire filled the late-night air. It was around 1:30 a.m. on September 15, 1776, when flames were seen burning through the roof of the Fighting Cocks Tavern. A brisk wind soon had spread the flames to six adjacent structures. No alarm was sounded as all the bells in the city had been carried off to be melted into munitions.

The New Yorkers who were still in town ran to the firehouses, only to find that the engines had been sabotaged and holes slashed in the bottoms of the buckets. The flames had spread to dozens of buildings before British officers could get tradesmen to repair the damaged equipment. Even after some of the pumpers were put into action, it became obvious that neither the soldiers nor the townspeople had any real idea how to effectively battle the flames. By the time the fire was over, approximately one-quarter of the city – nearly 500 buildings – had been destroyed.

On November 25, 1783, Major General Henry Knox led columns of the victorious Continental Army down Bowery Lane. Among the ranks were the tattered remains of Stoutenburgh's battalions; the commander himself had vanished. The returning firemen, at first glad to see the familiar streets of the city, soon were dismayed at the sight of block after block of charred remnants of buildings burned in the great fire. They returned to their firehouses and found only two engines working and the department in shambles.

Within a month after the British left the city, all the engines were repaired and orders were placed for hundreds of new buckets. Within a period of two years, the department was reformed by returning veterans. During this reorganization, a new custom started – the official naming of companies. Number 1 started the custom by taking the name Hudson Engine Company No. 1, in honor of the explorer.

On February 15, 1786, the Common Council passed an ordinance creating a brand-new department of 300 men in 15 engine companies and two truck companies. Five engineers were named to run the department. In 1791, one of the five engineers was placed in overall charge and the office of Chief Engineer was created. William J. Ellsworth was selected and functioned as chief.

At this time, the practice of using fire hoses attached to the smaller pumpers was being tried. The heavy leather hoses, sewed at the seams, leaked badly and those holding the line got soaked. The new, larger hand pumpers had improved and were able to create a more powerful and effective stream of water. Needless to say, belonging to a company with a larger, more powerful engine was more desirable than pushing a badly leaking "Leader," as they were called at the time, close to the fire.

After General George Washington evacuated Manhattan, the city suffered a major fire in September of 1776. Some 500 buildings were destroyed by the conflagration.

On April 30, 1789, George Washington arrived in New York City after a triumphant eight-day journey from his home in Mount Vernon. Passing crowds of well-wishers during every phase of the trip, the general finally arrived at Federal Hall and was sworn in as president. For the next year and a half, New York City was the capitol of the new nation.

On December 9, 1796, at about one o'clock in the morning, a fire broke out in the Robinson and Harshorne's Store, located on the Murray Wharf (now the east end of Wall Street). This blaze – known as the Coffee House Slip fire – was well advanced before the fire department even was notified. Arriving firemen were startled to see fire in about 20 buildings as they approached the waterfront. Flames were leaping from wooden building to wooden building, many of them large, well-stocked stores. Fire already was showing on Maiden Lane as firemen began their attack.

Union Engine No. 18 found itself cut off by the flames. The company officers attempted to rally the men and a flurry of pumping and aggressive nozzle actions could do little to ease their plight. The heat and flames had become too intense. To prevent their machine from burning, members hurled it into the river. The members then ran for their lives as the flames closed in.

Word spread along the fireground that one of the buildings contained gunpowder; the firemen held their positions. A valiant civilian, Richardson Underhill, came to the rescue. Underhill loaded the powder onboard a boat and rowed the explosives out into the middle of the river where he stayed until the flames were brought under control.

Companies worked feverishly but had little success. Chief Ellsworth decided to halt the flames by providing a firebreak. He ordered his men to virtually disassemble the Fish Market. Axes flashed and hooks yanked until the market was pulled down, board by splintered board. The fire was stopped but not until more than 50 buildings lay in smoldering ruin.

The Fire Department of the City of New York formally was incorporated by the State Legislature on March 20, 1798. The chief engineer had six assistants and commanded 22 engines. Alarms were infrequent and fires were fought about every two months.

The census of 1790 showed that 33,131 people lived in the city. (Only Philadelphia had more people with 42,000.) Sidewalks were being laid along the west side of Broadway from Murray to Vesey Streets. The streets leading from Broadway to the Hudson River were being paved with pebble stones sloped up toward the houses on either side. By 1800, the city had grown to 60,515 people.

A strong, cold breeze was blowing across the city on December 18, 1804. At about two a.m., a fire broke out in a grocery store on Front Street and began to spread. Wind-driven flames spread quickly to Wall and Water Streets. Additional engines were sent for as the conflagration mounted. A whole series of Revolutionary landmarks were burning as nearly every engine in the city went to work. When the flames were stilled, 40 houses were in ruins. The loss was estimated at $2 million and talk of arson spread as quickly as the fire had. The council appointed Dr. Browne to investigate. Browne's report called for a number of points, including a reward "for the discovery of any conspiracy to set fire to the city..."

During the first decade of the new century, the city grew at an amazing rate, with the population increasing from 60,515 to 96,373. The fire department was hard-pressed to keep up with this growth. The rolls increased from 600 to 1005 men. Seven engineers now commanded 34 engines, three hook and ladders and two fireboats (floating engines). A call went out to standardize the size of the leaders (hose) and the screws (couplings). New, bigger and more powerful apparatus were ordered to improve water delivery.

Fire plugs, the forerunner of the modern hydrant, made their appearance in lower Manhattan in 1807. The first one was placed in front of the candy store on the northwest corner of Liberty and William Streets. Hollow logs were joined together to feed water from the reservoirs. The plugs were rather like large corks that could be pulled out when needed. The first experimental working hydrant was placed at the same corner the following year. The first regular "improved" fire hydrant in the city was placed into service in 1817, in front of a dwelling on Frankfort Street. The house was owned by a volunteer fireman, George B. Smith of Engine Company 12.

An early 1800s fire hydrant. These new, improved hydrants replaced "fire plugs" that were driven into hollow-log-type water mains.

The shed that housed Engine 3 on Nassau Street, across from City Hall, in 1801.

It was common practice of the department to fine the members for using bad language, causing discord or disturbing the harmony of the company. The most important offense was missing an alarm. Excuses were far-reaching and rarely accepted, for example:

Eagle Engine Company, January 15, 1807
Harris Sage's excuse is received. He says at the time of the fire, he was "locked in someone's arms and could not hear the alarm."

His excuse was denied.

May 19, 1811, was a peaceful Sunday morning. The city's church bells had quieted as the faithful flocked to their services. A small boy named Johnny Degrauw – later to become President of the Fire Department – hurried down Chatham Street, late for Sunday School. Approaching Duane Street, he saw flames pouring from the Lawrence Coach Factory. The youngster turned and ran back toward the Old Jail behind City Hall. The panting youth shouted, **Fire! Fire!** up to men on the roof. The bells of the jail's cupola soon were sounding the alarm. This alarm spread as church bells joined in, calling the firemen for help.

The volunteers ran from their homes and dashed from churches across the city, hurrying to their firehouses. Soon the engines were rumbling across the streets, descending on the building and its column of smoke. Fanned by a strong wind, the flames were belching sparks and brands that soon were landing throughout the neighborhood.

Engineer Thomas Franklin took charge of the operation because the chief engineer was unable to respond due to illness. Flames were

racing down both sides of Chatham Street and the wind now was filled not just with sparks, but with flaming shingles and cinders. Roofs were catching fire along the path of the northeast wind. Clergy across the city, faced with some empty seats left by the volunteers, dismissed the men to go help fight the fires while the women and children remained in church.

Along the fireground, the situation was worsening by the minute. The wind was picking up, causing exposure problems to increase. The eyes of firemen and citizens alike noticed embers catching fire at the very top of the Brick Church's wooden spire. The church was emptied quickly of worshippers. But with the spire beyond the reach of hose streams and ladders, the firemen were powerless to stop the growing fire.

Suddenly, a uniformed sailor named Hague appeared on the church roof. With the wind blowing hard about him and billows of smoke hiding him at times, he grabbed a slender, metal lightning rod and slowly began the dangerous ascent. (This feat had been done once before in the city, back in 1804, under similar circumstances.) Reaching the burning spot, Hague stopped and pulled off his cap. Holding the lightning rod with one hand, he used the other to beat out the flames with his hat. To the sounds of applause, the brave sailor returned to the street and disappeared into the crowd. The fire then extended to the very cupola that sounded the original alarm as flames caught the Old Jail. Inmates of this debtor's prison were able to extinguish the fire.

The main body of the fire, however, was not being stopped. The combination of strong wind and little water made firefighting efforts extremely difficult and, for two-and-a-half hours, the firemen battled the flames. When the wall of fire reached Tryon Road (site of the Municipal Building today), some houses were ordered to be pulled down to add to the natural firebreak that the open space of the Tyron Road and Chatham Street intersection provided. With crews pumping desperately, pumpers were sending water to the fire front in relays. Replacements stepped in as tired men fell. Engineer Franklin, directing the attack, suddenly fell, due to exhaustion. With both sides of Chatham Street still raging, the chief's clothes burst into flames. Hose streams were directed on him as he was pulled to safety. A few minutes later, Foreman Peterson of Engine 15 also collapsed; unlike his chief, the foreman did not recover. He died a few hours later.

One hundred two houses were destroyed by the advancing flames, but the plan succeeded. The fire was stopped. Six months later, Chief Engineer Brown resigned due to poor health. Thomas Franklin of Engine Company 12 was named Chief Engineer after the foremen of 36 of the 38 engine companies petitioned the Council, requesting he be made chief. "Uncle Tommy," as he was known, would lead the department for the next 13 years.

The population nearly doubled between 1810 and 1824, jumping from 96,000 to almost 160,000 people. (In 1820, New York passed Philadelphia when the census counted 123,706.) Manhattan was plotted and surveyed and a comprehensive plan was in place for the expanding city. Above Houston Street, parallel streets and broad avenues were developed as the city expanded northward.

Firemen had been wearing leather stove pipe fire hats since the 1700s and during this time, the hat slowly developed into a helmet. By the early 1800s, many fire companies had determined that uniformity in design and material was necessary. The frontispiece – a leather hat badge attached to the front of the helmet – provided identification on the fireground, facilitating a somewhat smoother operation. In 1812, it was resolved that "the lettering and numbering of fire caps be as uniform as possible – no flourishes or gilt letters to be put thereon."

To improve the leather fire hat, different materials were tried and tested. Water-repellent wool, pressed felt, papier-mâché and painted oilcloth were tried, but all proved to be inadequate for firefighting uses. The leather fire hat seemed to be the answer but it, too, had some drawbacks. One of these was addressed in 1824, when New York fireman Matthew DuBois, a saddle maker by trade, added a metal wire to the brim of the leather hat for added strength and rigidity. This improvement proved very popular and DuBois soon set up a factory on Barclay Street in Manhattan.

Four years later, New York Fire Department Foreman Henry Gratacap developed the classic leather fire helmet. The early helmet had four combs, or ridges of leather, where the seam is stitched together. These combs gave added strength to the helmet and the theory was the more combs, the greater the strength. Soon, helmets featured eight, 12 and 16 combs. Special, customized helmets for presentations and the like had as many as 144, 180 or even 320 combs.

In 1836, Gratacap set up his own helmet factory and soon was selling helmets nationwide. Gratacap added two touches that remain to this day: raised, stitched lettering on the frontispiece and the eagle holder to attach the frontispiece to the helmet. The original holders were made of leather during the 1830s but by the late 1840s he had devised a brass eagle holder.

The fire department was battling fires and trying to keep up with the fast-paced city. Fires were becoming more frequent as were the deaths of firemen. On May 18, 1827, Fireman James Bradshaw of Fulton Engine 21 was crushed to death beneath a falling cornice during a fire on the Bowery. (Only a few months earlier, two firemen had been killed by a collapsing wall on Maiden Lane.) The Bowery fire involved a theater, a livery stable and a tavern. Two historic events also took place at this fire. It is believed that for the first time, a New York City fire apparatus was drawn to a fire by horses. It is also believed that this was the first time mutual aid was needed. At the height of the blaze, Brooklyn was asked for help.

In 1831, James Gulick became Chief Engineer of the New York City Fire Department. Gulick was "six-feet-two and possessed a superb physique." After a reorganization of the department by the Common Council, Gulick was now effectively the chief and commissioner of the department. In 1834, Tammany Hall came into power by winning the mayoral election. Gulick stayed out of the politics of the city and concentrated on the department. His independence annoyed many at Tammany Hall who were used to controlling everything.

At about this time, some of the bitter rivalries and brawls between companies began to hamper the effectiveness of the firefighting efforts. Gulick organized Hydrant Company #1 to take care of the water plugs and put a stop to the practice of hiding the plugs under a barrel until the preferred company arrived at the scene. At times, rival engines fought each other in the street over control of a hydrant while the structure burned merrily.

An outbreak of cholera swept the city in 1832 and more than 3000 people died during the summer. Gulick was forced to hire horses to pull the engines to the fires since so many of the volunteers were too ill to respond. By the time the epidemic had run its course, the idea of horses pulling fire apparatus was catching on. Mutual Hook and Ladder Company No. 1 purchased the first horse ever owned by the New York Fire Department on November 8, 1832. They were the only horse-drawn company for many years.

New York City was a city of a quarter of a million people in 1835. The city boasted 44 schools, more than 400 street lights, five theaters and about 35,000 houses. Only 1500 firemen protected the city and in 1835, they fought nearly 500 fires.

December of 1835 was a month that the volunteers of New York never would forget. The weather was unbelievable. The city was in the clutches of an extended cold spell and both the Hudson and East Rivers were frozen solid. During the night of the 14th, they battled a blaze at Christie and Delancey Streets. Fire tore through six houses and firemen were faced with deep snow and temperatures below zero. As they were taking up from this fire, another was reported on Water Street and they were off quickly, dragging their engines through the snow as they responded downtown.

Arriving at this scene, they were faced with a fire that eventually took seven buildings and two small carpentry shops. Weary, cold firemen, frostbitten and fatigued, battled both fires. Every company in the department was called out for one or both of the blazes. Exhausted men trudged home and climbed into bed.

The weather outside did not let up the next day; in fact, the temperature continued to drop. On the night of December 16, 1835, at about 9 p.m., William Hayes, a member of the City Watch, was on patrol and discovered a fire that would go down in the annals of firefighting. Hayes later recalled, "As I was passing the corner of Exchange Place and Pearl Streets, I smelled smoke and called several other watchmen. We found that the building on the corner was on fire and together, we were able to force open the door. We found the whole interior of the building in flames, from cellar to roof, and I can tell you we shut that door mighty quickly. Almost immediately, the flames broke through the roof and in less than 15 minutes, I believe fully 50 buildings were blazing. That was the most awful night I ever saw."

The fire building was a five-story warehouse at 25 Merchant Street. Flames that had started in the dry goods store on the first floor soon spread throughout the building. Fire was out every window and through the roof before water could be pumped through the first hose line. The entire department was summoned. Soon, 49 engines, five hose carts and six hook and ladders were pushing their way through the deep snow.

By midnight, the fire had spread over a huge area – 13 acres of buildings were in flames. Faced with the frozen rivers, firemen used ice fishing tactics by cutting holes through the ice to reach water to pump. Every trick in the book was employed to keep the men and their machines from freezing. Whiskey was poured into boots to prevent toes from icing up and fires were started under the hand pumpers to keep freezing water from building up. One company, Engine 33, brought their rig onto the bow of a ship and for more than five hours, pumped without a break.

Chief Gulick's exhausted New York firemen battled through the night. Help was sent for as the weary men began to drop where they stood. The chief then decided to try and make a stand at Wall Street. Still faced with a freezing, gale-force wind, the troops began to rally. Gulick went to the Navy for explosives to make a firebreak, a plan that, thankfully, worked.

As the new day dawned, New York firemen worked side by side with firemen who had arrived at various times during the night

from Brooklyn, Newark, Philadelphia and many other departments. The fire was halted, but the loss was high. Six hundred seventy-four buildings had burned.

The Tammany Hall politicians saw an opening to attack Chief Gulick. The ashes were not yet cool when they launched an attack, blaming him for the conflagration. In the early part of 1836, hearings were called for and an investigation was held. Even the appearance of the chief to answer the falsehoods being presented did not stop a vote to remove him from office.

Before Chief Gulick could be told of his removal, he was called out to a fire at the Union Market at Houston and Second Streets. The chief and his men began their attack and, in short order, had the fire under control. During the overhaul, a fireman came running up with news of the Council's vote to remove the chief. The chief quietly turned his hat around and walked away from the fire scene. When it

Firemen battle the flames during the early stages of the Great Fire of 1835.

The Great Fire spreads to the Wall Street area.

New York firemen worked through the night and into the next day before the fire could be contained.

nominated James Gulick for the office of City Registrar. The former chief was carried into office by the largest majority ever.

It was a number of years until the department would recover from the removal of Chief Gulick. A new mayor was elected, pushing Tammany Hall out, and when Cornelius Anderson was named as Chief Engineer, many firemen returned to service. There were still bitter feelings between those who supported Gulick and those who did not. The era of street-brawling volunteers befell the city.

On July 2, 1842, after a careful inspection of the entire 43 miles of aqueduct from the Croton Dam to Harlem, water was sent south to the city from the reservoirs to the north. Water finally filled the 42nd Street and Fifth Avenue Reservoir, on schedule, on July 4, 1842. The project was completed at a cost of about $11.4 million and ended the city's reliance on well water. The official celebration held on October 14, 1842, was a major event in the city. (One must remember the impact this would have on every citizen of the city, both rich and poor.) The entire membership of the New York City Fire Department, all 3003 men, turned out, as well as 1072 visiting firemen. Church bells rang, canons were fired and the people literally danced in the streets around the large fountain on 47th Street.

The firemen were praised by speaker after speaker for their bravery and ability in battling fires without the benefit of the newly installed water supply. A major parade followed with 4075 uniformed firemen marching up Broadway. Company rivalries and feuds were put aside for the moment and it appeared as if the volunteers could do no wrong. This public conception was about to change.

Exchange Place in ruins after the Great Fire of 1835.

was discovered by his men that he was removed as chief, they followed his example, turned their hats and returned to quarters. When the fire rekindled, the department returned, but the firemen – with hats still reversed – refused to fight the blaze without their chief. A foreman made an impassioned speech, siding with Gulick, but calling for the fire to be extinguished. Mayor Lawrence arrived and ordered the firemen to work with no effect. The re-intensifying blaze was fought only after Gulick returned to the scene and resumed temporary command.

The council then named John Riker as the new Chief Engineer. A few companies continued on duty, but the majority of the firemen called in vain for Gulick's reinstatement. Eight hundred firemen marched on City Hall and turned in their resignations from the department. The new chief refused to leave office and the council would not reinstate Gulick. The former chief's supporters became political themselves and formed the "Resigned Firemen's Association" and

The year 1845 was one of many fires and a devastating explosion. On February 4th, New York City was hit by a major snowstorm. Snow drifted and clogged the streets as temperatures dropped. It snowed through the night and at 4 a.m. (now February 5th), a fire broke out in the New York Tribune Building on the corner of Spruce and Nassau Streets in the section of the city known as Printing House Square. The small triangular area, formed by the intersection of Nassau Street, Park Row and Spruce Street, was the center of newspaper publishing in the city.

Firemen pushed, pulled and dragged their apparatus through snow-filled streets. Arriving at the scene, they were confronted with a growing fire and frozen-solid hydrants. Despite all the wonderful speeches back when the Croton water finally arrived, a water supply is only as good as the ability to tap it. Firemen from the hook and ladders went at the hydrants with axes and chopped them open.

A number of employees were trapped inside the structure on the fifth floor and were able to escape, but just barely. To the rear of the fire building was the infamous Tammany Hall. Flames belching from the rear of the Tribune Building seriously threatened the political clubhouse. Firemen battled both the weather and the flames and despite their best efforts, the fire extended into the next building. The battle continued and the firefighters began to gain the upper hand, finally getting the fire under control. The Tribune Building was destroyed as was the building next door, but Tammany was saved and no lives were lost. The firemen received high praise for their efforts in the next day's editorials.

The city was looking forward to "Robin Hood, the Outlaw," due to open on the stage of the Bowery Theater on Friday, April 25. The famous show place had a bad history where fire was concerned, having burned three times in the past. At about six o'clock, before the doors were opened to the public, flames were discovered leaping from a vault filled with wood shavings in the carpenter's shop on the theater's south side. Before the fire doors could be closed, the flames reached the scenery and the whole building soon was ablaze. At the height of the blaze, the theater collapsed, driving fire into a number of buildings nearby.

On May 31st, the department battled a fire that burned more than 100 buildings, leaving 400 people without homes. A number of thriving businesses now were smoldering ruins. Luckily again, there were no serious injuries, but the department and its men were being tested severely.

In July of 1845, the citizens of New York City ran out of luck. At three a.m., a fire broke out at 34 New Street, the sperm-oil store of J. L. Van Doren. The fire quickly spread to the chair factory next door. Firemen worked frantically, but the blaze spread across Exchange Place to Broad Street, where a large amount of saltpeter – a nitrate used in making explosives – was stored in the warehouse.

Sixty-three people were killed when the boiler at 5 Hague Street exploded on February 5, 1850.

The warehouse burned furiously for about 10 minutes and then a massive explosion occurred. The entire island of Manhattan trembled; the earth shook in Jersey City and Brooklyn and windows shattered as far north as Canal Street. When the smoke cleared, the warehouse was gone, blasted into fragments. Also gone were the lives of more than 30 civilians and four firemen. One survivor, Fireman Francis Hart, Jr., was on the roof of the warehouse when it exploded. He was carried through the air, still on the roof, across Broad Street, where he landed safely on the roof of another building.

The explosion sent flaming shards of wood throughout the entire neighborhood, causing numerous additional fires. New Street and Broadway now were blazing from Wall to Beaver Streets and Exchange Place was burning from Broadway to William Street. A call went out to Newark as it was realized that many of the New York pumpers were damaged severely by the blast.

Retired volunteers joined the ranks to render what help they could. Building after building caught fire as the flames leaped into the sky. Chief Anderson moved among the men, giving orders, encouraging and praising. For 12 hours, firemen from New Jersey, Brooklyn, Williamsburg and New York faced the raging flames until the fire finally was contained. Weary firemen faced a major job of searching and overhauling the ruins. Three hundred buildings were destroyed. The total damages were estimated at $10 million.

Following the fire, the Exempt Fireman's Company was formed by Zopher Mills, one of the most daring firemen of his day. This company, composed of veterans, outfitted themselves with a large hand-pumper and two of the new steam engines. This group stood ready to back up the regular department when needed.

The regular department included 25 engines, 32 hose carriages and six hook and ladder apparatus. There were 1998 firemen, but rivalries, poor equipment and disorganization were beginning to take a toll.

At 8:20 a.m. on February 5, 1850, the 200-hp boiler of the A.B. Taylor & Co. machine shop at 5 Hague Street exploded. The two eight-story buildings housing the company were blasted into the sky. The alarm was sounded and firemen rushed to the scene. The second of the two buildings was occupied by a hat company and was filled with workers when the explosion occurred. Under the command of Chief Engineer Alfred Carson, the firemen – faced with reports of more than 100 people trapped in the collapsed building – plunged into the flaming debris.

The flames were brought under control quickly, but the rescue work was just beginning. Twenty hours of dangerous digging, tunneling and firefighting continued as people were rescued and pockets of fire hidden in the debris was extinguished. In all, 64 people were killed and 70 were injured.

In November of 1850, the department took steps to make fire response more efficient and effective by dividing the city into eight districts. The number of bell strokes signified the district in which the fire was discovered. Only the apparatus of two districts would respond to the alarm. Then, in the summer of 1851, the bell towers of all eight districts were connected to each other and to fire headquarters by the first real fire alarm telegraph system. Bell ringers still were being employed and paid $500 per year.

Famous Department reformer, Chief Alfred Carson, who restored the good name of the volunteers, and some of his trusted men.

Chief Alfred Carson, who had taken office in 1848, continued to wage a single-handed battle against the politicians, the rowdy mobs that interfered with the firefighting force and factions of the department itself that battled each other at the scenes of fires. The rapidly expanding city was placing a major burden on the volunteer firemen and their ability to protect effectively. Carson's actions against some of the offending companies were overturned by the Common Council without an investigation. Fire companies with strong political ties were becoming difficult, if not impossible, to control. Carson's constant attention and hard work began to pay off as the firemen began to recover their good name.

A few minutes after one o'clock in the afternoon of December 10, 1853, a young office boy dropped a lamp that exploded in the large paper warehouse of Harper Brothers in Franklin Square. The huge paper-filled structure was soon a mass of flames. The heat ignited buildings across Pearl Street, as the wind carried flaming embers blocks away, starting fires along Cliff and Ferry Streets.

The Walton House, famous for its historic Revolutionary relics, soon was joining the conflagration. The large, three-story structure, built in 1754, and the Franklin Square Hotel next door quickly became just blazing memories. Fire then erupted in a second paper-filled warehouse, extending the firemen to their limits.

Large crowds formed and cheered several spectacular rescues made by Mutual Hook and Ladder 1. Soon the entire department was at work, along with four Brooklyn engines brought over by ferry. The fire had spread to 16 buildings before it was brought under control. Not since the colonial days had the firemen of New York City faced such an advanced fire condition.

That evening's *New York Herald* read: "... for three long hours, the heroic firemen worked at their engines and yielded not until they were masters of the angry element."

On Tuesday night, April 25, 1854, the members of the department would not fare as well, as this time, the fire exacted a major toll. Flames broke out at eight o'clock in the clothing store of William T. Jennings & Company at 231 Broadway, opposite City Hall. Firemen were struggling to contain the blaze and protect the American Hotel to the south and the Meade Brothers photographic shop to the north.

Eleven firemen were killed and 20 seriously injured when a wall collapsed during a fire in W.T. Jennings and Co., at 231 Broadway on April 25, 1854.

Assistant Engineer John Cregier was directing operations on the roof of the five-story Meade building, while Assistant Engineer Harry Howard led a group into the burning second floor of the Jennings building. Making little progress, Howard ordered his men out of the fire building and onto the two-story setback in the rear. Before all the men could exit the building, the rear wall of the Jennings building collapsed. The two upper floors and a large safe came plummeting down on the firemen working below.

Other firemen, unmindful of further collapse, swarmed into the blazing ruins to rescue their trapped brothers. A hose stream from above was directed down onto the flaming wreckage. Amidst cries of anguish, an order was heard from below, "Stop that water! It is scalding the men."

The decision fell to Cregier, who surveyed the situation. Even more perilous than the hot water were the flames, eating away at the already-weakened beams; the other half of the roof was ready to fall. "It can't be done. The roof will go." So under a cascade of scalding water, the rescue effort continued, a decision that proved to be correct.

For the rest of the night, the rescue work continued. Firemen, facing danger with every move they made, dug until dawn. Twenty injured firemen were pulled from the burning ruins. Sadly, 11 firemen had answered their last alarm and fallen in the discharge of their duties.

The Coroner's Jury censured the builders for flimsy construction and also concluded that the fire was caused by a gang of thieves trying to cover a robbery. Three men later were convicted and sent to prison.

The Crystal Palace was a huge exhibition hall that took up a square block on 42nd Street and Sixth Avenue next to the water reservoir. It was likened to "fairy-like palace" by local writers and drew large crowds of people to view the exhibitions of treasures on display inside. The glass-domed structure contained 1250 tons of iron and 39,000 square feet of glass. It opened in July of 1853, as part of the World's Fair.

On October 5, 1856, the fabulous collection of the American Institute was on display. The items varied from famous sculptures, suits of armor from the Tower of London, jewelry, musical instruments, carriages and machinery of American and foreign manufacture. Included in the show were two hose carriages, two engines and a hook and ladder from the New York City Fire Department.

At about five p.m., smoke was discovered issuing from a large room in the north nave and also near the front entrance. Two thousand people were inside the structure when the cry of **"Fire!"** echoed through the halls. The Sixth Avenue entrance was thrown open and the crowd safely evacuated as the fire engines pulled up.

Firemen quickly had more than 20 hose streams in operation, but they were having little or no effect on the growing fire. People were scrambling, trying to salvage some of the valuables from inside the blazing structure. The last person just had cleared the building when the dome fell with a crash.

The huge pile of melted glass and twisted metal now encased a mass of smoldering objects that included the five fire apparatus. For the next few days, thousands visited the ruins, watching the meager attempts to salvage items from the debris.

It was decided in a meeting of the department members that the quickest way to replace the lost fire apparatus was to solicit funds from the public by subscription. The rigs eventually were replaced.

By 1854, more than 4000 citizens of the city were members of the volunteer department, protecting their neighbors from fire with no reward other than the satisfaction provided on the fireground and the camaraderie of the fire service itself. The administration of such a large group was beginning to be a burden on the Common Council.

In an effort to improve overall efficiency, an ordinance was introduced, creating a "Board of Fire Department Commissioners." This board

The famous Crystal Palace blaze of October 5, 1858.

was composed of three people from each of the eight fire districts within the city and three from the section of the city known as the Twelfth Ward. Two of the three members were exempt firemen and the third was an active fireman.

At this time, the Chief Engineer was elected every three years by the members of the department. The fire department itself consisted of a "chief engineer, assistant engineers, fire-enginemen, hose men, hook and ladder and hydrant men, who all shall be citizens of the United States, of the age of 21 years and upward."

During the late 1850s, the city continued to grow although, thankfully, no major conflagrations occurred. Many serious fires were dealt with, many dangerous rescues were accomplished and several firemen died in the line of duty. A fire that had a major impact on the city

Assistant Chief William Lamb of the New York City Volunteer Fire Department.

fireproof stairs within the structure or fireproof balconies with connecting stairs attached to the outside of dwellings housing more than eight families. This went into effect June 1, 1860.

The volunteer firemen of New York City were a good cross-section of "big city Americans" by the 1860s. They were business owners, craftsmen, laborers and politicians. When the call went out for regiments to fight in the Civil War, the firemen answered President Lincoln's call with the same zeal they had answered George Washington 90 years earlier. The First Fire Zouaves left the city in April, 1861, with 1100 men and were followed by the Second Fire Zouaves two weeks later with 810 men.

By 1863, the army was in need of more recruits and in March, the Congress passed a national conscription law. The draft lottery began in New York on July 11, 1863. The practice of the rich hiring substitutes increased resentment of the system by those who could not afford the luxury of paying someone to go to war for them. On Monday, July 13th, a large crowd, including members of Engine Company 33, who thought they should be exempt from the draft, stormed the Ninth District Provost Marshal's Office at Third Avenue and 47th Street and set the building on fire. Thus started three days of rioting, arson, looting and lynching.

The remainder of the department responded to the first of what would be many fires set by the large roving mobs. Firemen were met by thugs who cut their hoses with axes taken from the responding hook and ladder trucks. The rioters' numbers were swelled by members of the city's notorious street gangs and by groups of drunks who were intoxicated liberally by generous Southern sympathizers.

and its residents occurred on February 2, 1860. A fire swept through a six-story tenement house on Elm Street. Twenty people perished in the blaze, despite several spectacular rescues. This fire highlighted a growing safety issue in the city – the need for fire escapes.

After the fire, the Common Council passed the most rigid fireproofing and building ordinance the city had yet seen. Items included

In an 1855 ordinance, members of the department were required, when on duty as firemen, to wear the leather cap as previously in use or a badge. The badge was "made of Prince's metal, bearing the words 'New York Fire Department,' each badge bearing a distinct number in raised figures thereon, of a white metal." They then were authorized for each member of the department. The same Act also directed the police to form fire lines at every fire and only allow people bearing the badge or wearing the uniform of the Insurance Patrol to pass.

Firemen's Hall on Mercer Street served as the Headquarters of the Volunteer and new Metropolitan Fire Departments.

New York City's famous "Fire Zouaves" battle a blaze in Willard's Hotel in Washington, DC, in 1861.

The firefighting difficulties came to a head on July 14th. Fire companies had been racing back and forth from one blaze to another and the drunken mobs were getting more and more dangerous. The rioters turned their attention to the "Colored Orphan Asylum" on Fifth Avenue, between 43rd and 44th Streets, and set the building on fire. The arriving firemen were under the command of Chief John Decker, who stormed into the crowd. As the burly chief fought with the mob's leaders, 200 children quickly were whisked to safety out the back door. The firemen attempted to save their chief, who was now in the hands of the drunken rioters.

Decker, with a rope around his neck, was hustled to a nearby tree. Realizing his desperate position, the chief asked the crowd, "What good will it do to hang me? You'll only stop my draft, not the government's." The crowd repeated the pun through the ranks and soon the laughing mob stepped aside and let the fire chief join his men and battle the fire.

Arriving at 14th Street and Avenue C, Assistant Chief Elisha Kingsland found several buildings burning and a wagon blocking the street. "If you touch that wagon, I'll blow your brains out!" cried a ruffian, who was backed by a large, angry crowd. The chief jumped up into the wagon to clear the street when the mob moved in. He turned and shouted to the crowd, "If this fire continues, it will cross the street and burn the houses of your friends." Some in the crowd continued to yell threats and taunt the chief, but his words began to sink in with the majority of the crowd and the wagon was moved.

Chief Decker and his assistants, Kingsland and Lamb, later battled a mob at the corner of 29th Street and Broadway. The chiefs had a hand-to-hand fight with a large crowd of rioters. Chief Lamb

was knocked down, but was rescued by firemen. Three of the ring leaders were arrested and jailed.

By July 15th, troops arrived in the city and order was restored. The losses were staggering: 1200 were killed and $2 million in damages. The *New York Herald* added: "Chief John Decker especially is entitled to the gratitude of the owners and occupants of real estate in upper sections of the city. That he absolutely saved for them their homes and contents is conceded by everybody."

A movement to replace the volunteer fire department with professionals began slowly and gathered supporters as time went on. The origins of the movement began with the insurance company executives, who felt that fire loss was too heavy. Soon, two very powerful groups joined the alliance – the New York State Republican Party members, who saw a chance to strike at Tammany Hall, and the Metropolitan Police Department, whose officers had to deal with fire-scene brawls between companies and thugs. Early in March of 1864, the Board of Fire Underwriters appointed a committee that gathered evidence that led to a bill sponsorship in the assembly.

The volunteers scrambled to set their house in order and formulated reform measures. These reforms were pushed through the Common Council in record time. Cost-cutting plans were drawn, expenses reduced and plans to trim manpower and company numbers were started. Meanwhile, Tammany regrouped to protect themselves.

On January 16, 1865, a bill was introduced in Albany, known as **"The Act to create a Metropolitan Fire District and establish a Fire Department therein."** This bill provided for a paid fire department, under the control of four commissioners appointed by the Governor, in the cities of New York and Brooklyn, which would be considered as the Metropolitan Fire District. This would give the State Republicans – and not the City Democrats – control of the department. The sides were drawn and the political battle ensued.

The bill was passed and signed by the Governor, but the battle continued delaying the appointment of the new commissioners until May 3, 1865. Injunctions were secured by New York City Mayor C. Godfrey Gunther, Chief Decker and the City Alderman, forbidding the new department to take charge of any fire department property. The entire project was back in court, delaying any action until the Court of Appeals in Albany ruled in favor of the new department on June 22, 1865.

The organization of the new department was underway when the downtown air was pierced with the loud, continuous

Chief John Decker stood up to mobs who threatened to hang him during the New York City Draft Riots in 1863.

A desperate attack was begun as hose lines were pushed in. With the flames spreading rapidly, many firemen passed the protection of the hose streams to search for trapped people and release the many harmless birds and animals that otherwise would be doomed in their locked cages.

During the early stages of the fire, a huge, snarling, Bengal tiger got loose and leaped from a second-floor window to the sidewalk below. The numerous spectators, attracted by the blaze, were crowding the street and sidewalk across from the fire. The giant animal landed before them, roaring in a frenzy from the smoke and flames. People ran in a panic, yelling and screaming. Some stood frozen with fear. Police officers used their pistols from a distance on the animal with no effect.

From the throng of working firemen stepped John Denham of Atlantic Hose Company 15. He had been stretching a hose line when the screaming attracted his attention. The "quiet, retiring" carpenter grabbed an axe and moved toward the tiger. He walked steadily, straight at the beast. The animal turned his head and with one motion leaped toward the fireman.

Denham's axe flashed through the air. With one mighty blow, the animal lay sprawled on the street. Denham checked the animal and as he walked away, the crowd began to cheer. Denham then calmly entered the burning building.

A few minutes later, the crowd cheered again as he returned to the street, carrying one of the stars of the show. "The Fat Lady," all 400 pounds of her, now was safe. Again, he entered the flame-filled structure and this time, emerged holding two children left behind by fleeing patrons. On his third trip, Denham returned with the "woolyheaded" albino woman in his arms.

The firefighting continued throughout the day, until the last of the flames were drowned. The museum was now a mass of smoldering ruins, sharing a fate common to most of P.T. Barnum's operations. The crowd dispersed, hoses were drained and rolled, life would resume its normal pace.

John Denham returned to his normal, quiet self after the fire. His actions that day became part of the legend the volunteers had added to the city's already rich history. There is no record of Denham joining the new paid department, which after a tough political battle, would take over by August of 1865.

In the *New York Times'* account of the fire, the various rescues were mentioned, as was the bravery of many firemen, but there was no mention of a snarling beast or of Denham's axe work. Was there a loose tiger? Many books relating stories of the volunteer era state it happened. In reality, it didn't matter. When Elisha Kingsland took charge of the new paid force, he and his men inherited a legacy that proclaimed that firemen's valor exceeded even fighting fire. The public believed firefighters could overcome any obstacle, even giant tigers. The new department had large boots to fill.

On July 13, 1865, the famous Barnum's American Museum caught fire and burned to the ground. The huge structure was at the corner of Ann Street and Broadway.

ringing of the fire bell at City Hall, signifying a fire in District 5. Volunteer firemen, still protecting the city during the transition, dropped what they were doing and answered the alarm. It was July 13, 1865, and the volunteer fire department was responding to a fire in one of New York City's most famous attractions, Barnum's American Museum.

This building, located at the intersection of Broadway and Park Row, was one of the most popular entertainment venues in the country. The museum was filled with curiosities and animals from around the world. Exhibits included aquariums that held whales, alligators and other exotic sea life; wax figures of famous and infamous people; sideshow-type "freaks"; and even a large, working, steam-driven model of Niagara Falls.

A fire had started in the boiler room of Groots Restaurant, located on the Ann Street side of the building under the museum offices, and was beginning to sweep through the structure as firemen arrived.

New York City Fire Department
1865 – 1946

The badge of the new Metropolitan Fire Department in 1865.

The paid Fire Department of the City of New York had its origins in "An Act to Create a Metropolitan Fire District and Establish a Fire Department Therein." This placed the fire departments of New York and the Eastern and Western Districts of Brooklyn under an organization known as the Board of Metropolitan Fire Commissioners. These first commissioners – G.C. Pinckney, F.W. Engs, James W. Booth and M.B. Brown – were appointed by and reported to the Governor of New York State.

These men met on May 2, 1865, to organize a paid department for the city. A series of court cases followed in an attempt to stop this change, until finally on June 23, the Court of Appeals ruled in favor of the new board and new department.

Volunteer Chief John Decker answered the new commissioners' request to remain as head of the department during the transition by asking to be relieved as soon as possible. Assistant Chief Elisha Kingsland was elected as chief and took control of department operations at this critical juncture.

The first of the professional units, Engine Company Number 1, went into service on July 31, 1865, at four Centre Street. The remainder of the new companies that would be the original units of the Metropolitan Fire Department were organized in September, October and November of 1865. The last of these companies, Ladder 12, went into service on December 1, 1865, and protected the city up to 87th Street. The sections of Manhattan North still were protected by volunteers.

On April 9, 1865, the Civil War ended and five days later, President Abraham Lincoln was assassinated. The country was trying to find itself after the war and cities such as New York were adjusting to the newly rejoined nation. It seemed as if all of Europe was crossing the Atlantic to jam the already over-crowded streets. "Little Old New York" was bursting at the seams. The rich began moving "up-

town" into the new brownstone buildings, while the extremely wealthy began building their mansions along Fifth Avenue.

Gaslights lined the sidewalks. Horses pulled wagons and carriages across the cobblestone streets. Pushcarts lined and further strangled the narrow streets in the poor neighborhoods. Banking and other financial interests had taken over the downtown section of Broadway; the tenements all through lower Manhattan were filled with the working poor. Telegraph wires crisscrossed the sky like a giant spider's web.

The city's skyline was made up of ships' masts and church steeples. South Street was the center of the American shipping industry and the docks and nearby warehouses bustled with activity.

The establishment of the Metropolitan Fire Department was a power play between Albany and Tammany, with the state government trying to break up the strength that the "Bosses" had developed. Many believed the base of this power was the volunteer fire department and, even if it wasn't true, the volunteers were proving hard to control.

Volunteers were, however, given preference in the hiring of the new firemen and the ranks soon were filled. By November of 1865, the paid force consisted of an Assistant Engineer (Joseph Perley), 13 Engineers (Battalion Chiefs), 34 Engine Companies and 12 Ladder Companies.

Bell Towers

When the paid department came into existence in 1865, bell towers were spread throughout the city. These bellringers watched over the city, manning each tower in three-hour shifts. Their duty was to discover fires, telegraph the location of the fire to the fire alarm Central Office in City Hall and then sound the alarm by striking the district number on the tower bell.

The central office then would telegraph the other tower bellringers south of 33rd Street, who would pick up the alarm for about 10 minutes. By November of 1865, the ringing of bells south of 14th Street was discontinued with the installation of alarm-receiving systems in the firehouses in that area. As the alarm system spread to all firehouses, the need for and use of the bell towers as a system of alarm notification was eliminated. Seven towers still were being used for lookout duty, but the duty now was covered by uniformed firemen detailed from their companies in lieu of Street Patrol duty.

Running To Fires

A fire officer leads a steamer and a ladder truck through the crowded streets.

The volunteer practice of running on foot to fires was continued after the establishment of the Metropolitan Fire Department, principally because the apparatus in use had been designed for drawing by hand and did not provide facilities for carrying more than two or three men. Running boards were added to the trucks a few years later. In the interim, the firemen ran along next to the trucks. The first fireman killed in the line of duty was run over by a steamer during a response.

During the first few years of the paid department, the District Chiefs had to make their inspections and get to fires on foot because they were not provided with horses and buggies.

The first rules of the Metropolitan Fire Department, issued on September 18, 1865, prescribed the number of men who might ride on the apparatus and specifically prohibited the Company Commanders from riding, either to or from fires.

SECTION 17 – The officer in command shall precede his apparatus in going to or returning from a fire.

SECTION 18 – The driver, engineer and stoker may ride on the Engine, and the driver and one man on the Tender, and no more.

The early records of the paid department disclose several cases of company officers being disciplined for violation of these rules. In the case of Forman McGill, Engine 13, charged with failure to fully comply with Section 17, it was shown that "having run as far as he was able, Foreman McGill was forced to get on the Engine." The Medical Officer testified for the Captain and he was let off with a reprimand.

On July 1, 1868, three years after the establishment of the paid department, General Orders No. 16 were issued on the subject of "Riding to Fires."

It is the intention of the Commissioners to furnish facilities for the men to ride to fire alarms, but until the Engines are provided with new Tenders or have the old ones altered to the style recently adopted, no general rule can be prescribed about riding.

The Foreman of Engine Companies will ride habitually upon the ash panes of Steamers with their Engineers. They will require one man to keep ahead of the horses and see that he is relieved frequently, using the Stoker for that purpose if necessary, and themselves taking the lead upon approaching a fire. No man running ahead of the horses should leave his position until relieved by someone sent ahead by the Foreman for that purpose. No more than two persons should ride upon the ash pan, except upon very smooth pavement, and where the pavement is very rough, the Foreman should require every man except the Driver to dismount.

In the lower part of the City where the runs are short and the progress of the apparatus frequently are retarded by vehicles, it will be found an advantage to have a number of men on the street ahead of the horses, clearing the way, instead of riding on the Tender or running on the sidewalk behind the apparatus.

While General Orders No. 16 permitted some of the men to ride going to fires, only the drivers were allowed to ride back to the Engine Houses. General Orders No. 11, May 18, 1868, took official notice of the increasing habit of the men to loiter on the streets while walking back from fires and expressed the disapproval of the Commissioners in this language:

The habit of loitering home after an alarm of fire must be discontinued. Hereafter, when a Company is ready to return home, either from a working fire or an alarm of fire without work, the men will be formed and marched on the street ahead of the apparatus in two ranks, with the officers ahead, or on the sidewalks abreast of the Engine or Truck horses, in one rank, with the officers ahead. The files will not be more than one pace apart, either in one or two ranks.

Most of the early rescues involved ladders. With no breathing equipment available and the normal delay in waiting for the steamer to get up enough pressure to charge the hose lines, the most effective efforts were over ladders. The standard ladder truck was pulled by two horses and carried wooden portable ladders, both extension and straight, in sizes up to 73 feet. Two officers, a Foreman and Assistant Foreman (Captain and Lieutenant), a driver and eight men were assigned to each ladder company. The company commander was required by department regulations to keep at least nine men in quarters at all times, to ensure adequate manpower to raise the ladders.

The remaining volunteers in Manhattan were abolished in 1867 with the organization of five engines and three ladder companies in the upper end of the island. The fire alarm telegraph system was extended to the new territories. In January of 1874, fire protection was provided to the newly annexed sections of the Bronx and a 900-foot submarine cable was laid under the Harlem River to establish fire alarm box coverage.

Assistant Foreman Minthorne Tompkins of Ladder Company 1, the first recipient of the James Gordon Bennett Medal.

J ust three years after the start of the paid force, the Metropolitan Fire Department began a system of recording the heroic deeds of its members. The following resolution was made by the department's Committee of appointments on November 22, 1868:

Resolved, that the secretary be instructed to open and keep under his personal supervision, a book of record, which shall be called, "The Roll of Merit M.F.D.," in which shall be entered the names of such officers and members of the department as may have, in the judgment of the board of commissioners, distinguished themselves in the discharge of their duties, with a full record of the act by which they have become entitled to the honor of being there enrolled. Opposite to each name shall be stated the action taken by this Board in making rewards in each case.

The heroic acts of Assistant Foreman Minthorne Tompkins and other members of the department the night of November 14, 1868, probably prompted this official recognition. At about 11:45 p.m., a fire was discovered in the first-floor kitchen area of the Stewart House, a hotel and restaurant located at 480 Broadway, near Broome Street in lower Manhattan. Flames raced through the rear portion of the building and to the upper floors with lightning speed.

The first-arriving firemen were informed that numerous people were trapped within the building. As many as a dozen guests were cut off, as well as nearly all of the hotel's servants who lived in the attic.

In an effort to reach the upper floors, several long ladders were placed to the upper-floor windows. Tompkins started up the first ladder as it was lowered into the building. Almost immediately, he became engulfed in hot, swirling smoke. The extended wooden ladder

was springing with each step he took. Groping in the inky blackness, feeling with his hands and feet for each rung, he continued. Step by step, Tompkins inched his way toward the sounds of a woman above him, pleading for help.

The dense smoke cleared momentarily as the fire officer approached the top of the ladder. Leaning dangerously out the window above Tompkins was a woman trapped by the flames. Nearly overcome and exhausted, she attempted to find clear air in the clouds of smoke swirling around her. Darkness closed in again as he continued up blindly.

Tompkins climbed to the very top rung. With nothing to steady himself, he slowly stood straight up, leaning in against the wall of the fire building. Choked by smoke, he told her to get ready. He extended his arms above his head slowly, until he could feel her legs. Tompkins grasped the woman firmly and carefully began to pull her toward him. She held fast to the windowsill, until he commanded her to let go. Tompkins now was holding her entire weight over his head. Only his balance held them on the ladder. Slowly, he began to lower her and placed her across his shoulder. Carefully, step by step, he descended the ladder to the street.

Assistant Foreman Tompkins paused briefly for a few breaths of fresh air after first assuring that the rescued woman was being attended. The fire officer studied the fire conditions, then returned to direct the operations of his company.

Inch by inch, the hose teams pushed in. Enduring tremendous punishment, they were able to hold the flames to the rear portion of the building. Their efforts allowed the rescue work to continue. Deep inside the blazing structure, Tompkins led his men on a difficult search.

Tompkins pressed on, despite a painful injury received during the initial phases of the interior search. Exhaustion was beginning to set in from his ladder work and operating in the heavy smoke. Even under these extreme conditions, the members of Ladder 1 were able to locate and safely remove another six people. They dragged or carried them to other firemen, waiting on ladders at the front windows.

Fireman Christopher C. Flick of Engine Company 20 made one of the most dramatic rescues as members saved another dozen people. The gutsy young fireman was able to dive into a third-floor window and locate a woman and her baby. With flames closing in, he crawled, carrying the baby under one arm, while dragging the mother to the window. Moments after he had handed the victims out to fellow firemen and scrambled out onto the ladder himself, the window filled with flames.

For his tremendous rescue efforts and his leadership on the fireground, Minthorne Tompkins became the first member of the paid force to be placed on the new Roll of Merit. Four others also were honored for their heroics at that fire: Foreman James Heaney of Ladder 9, Assistant Foreman Patrick Donohue of Ladder Co. 9 and Firemen Flick and John Kavanagh, both of Engine 20.

In 1869, James Gordon Bennett, Jr., sent a letter to the Fire Commissioner that said, in part:

My father, being desirous of adding an additional competition to the members of the Metropolitan Fire Department in the discipline, courage and honesty with which their duties are now performed and which were particularly called to his attention at the fire to his summer residence last September, has directed me to enclose the sum of $1500 and requests that you will pay $500 to Messrs. Tiffany & Co. for the die of a medal they are preparing and use the income from the balance in procuring annually a gold medal to be struck from the same, to be conferred by you and your successors in this trust, upon such members of the Fire Department as you may, in your judgment, consider best entitled to the reward.

The medal was struck and in 1870, both Tompkins and Gicquel were called to the Fire Commissioner's office. The Bennett medal then was presented by General Alexander Shaler, President of the Board of Fire Commissioners, and Joseph L. Perley, Chief of Department, to Tompkins for his rescue in 1868 and to Gicquel for his rescue in 1869. For 27 years, until 1897, the Bennett was the only medal for valor in the department.

The James Gordon Bennett Medal was endowed in 1869. For 27 years, it was the only medal of valor in the New York City Fire Department.

Foreman Benjamin A. Gicquel of Engine Company 9, the second Bennett Medal winner.

Another outstanding rescue that warranted recognition was made by Foreman Benjamin A. Gicquel of Engine Company 9. Gicquel, like Tompkins, was also an original member of the department. His actions on September 26, 1869, during fire department operations at 73 Montgomery Street, would add his name to the Roll of Merit.

The night was filled with the cries of people trapped within the building as department apparatus pulled up. As many as 20 families were imperiled by the fire as arriving firemen went to work. Battalion Chief Eli Bates, later to become Chief of Department, rescued a mother and her child using a ladder placed at a fifth-story window.

Members of Ladder 6 swarmed over the front of the blazing structure, rescuing civilians as they appeared. After many rescues had been accomplished, a rumor swept through the crowd. Two widows and their two children were believed to be trapped in one of the upper floors and probably already perished in the fire.

Acting on these rumors, Gicquel entered the top floor of the blazing structure and began searching for the missing people. The extreme conditions forced the fire officer to crawl forward on his stomach, finding air where he could. Room after room, Gicquel continued, the heat building up around him. The already heavy smoke was becoming a thick, noxious shroud around him. Nearly spent, he came upon the apparently lifeless form of a child. Scooping up the little one, he quickly retraced his path. Just inside the window, he was met by Fireman Denton Helmsworth, who also had entered the dense smoke. Gicquel handed him the child and returned for the others. Helmsworth then handed the youngster out the window to other members of Ladder 6. This process was repeated three times as Foreman Gicquel passed victim after victim to Helmsworth, who passed them to other firemen, who were perched dangerously at the top of the ladder. Amazingly, all four of the victims survived.

Across the East River in the City of Brooklyn, the growth of fire protection was moving along at almost the same pace as in New York City. The first six firemen were appointed in 1772 for the protection of the village. The first fire company, Washington Number 1, was formed on April 30, 1785, and was provided an "engine," built by Jacob Roome of New York for the sum of 150 pounds. The Legislature took action to formally organize the department in 1788. The first Hook and Ladder Company went into service in 1817 and became known as "Lafayette."

In Williamsburg, two engines were purchased and companies formed in 1834. A ladder company was started in June of 1836 and in 1837, the department was organized with David Garrett elected as Chief of the Volunteer Department of Williamsburg.

The process of establishing a paid department in Brooklyn started as early as 1858, but was unsuccessful until 1869. From 1865 until 1869, the fire companies in the Eastern and Western Districts of

The demonstration of the Scott-Uda aerial, moments before it broke and took the lives of three firemen.

The plaza at Canal Street and East Broadway was filled with spectators on September 14, 1875, waiting to see the Fire Department demonstrate a newly patented aerial ladder. At six a.m., the device was taken by department members to the corner of East Broadway and Canal Street and was run up a few sections to ensure proper operations for the 10:30 a.m. test. A rope also was tied to the top rung and the weight of nine men placed on the aerial to test its strength. Battalion Chief William H. Nash, a Civil War veteran and holder of the Bennett Medal, led the way up the fully extended ladder.

The six-foot-tall Nash wore a large, handle-bar mustache and was renowned for his fearless ladder work. As the young chief reached the top, he turned and waved to the crowd below. He was followed by Fireman Philip J. Maus of Ladder 6 and then by Fireman William Hughes of Engine 9. Four other firemen climbed up the ladder and were in the process of spacing themselves when the ladder bent forward and canted to one side.

Nash immediately called down, "Tighten those ropes!" Before anything could be done, a loud, cracking sound was heard as the ladder snapped at a point about 30 feet above the ground. The three men at the top fell to the cobblestones below. Nash and Maus were killed instantly; Hughes died a few minutes later. The four men on the bottom escaped with only bruises.

Nash, only 43 years old, left behind a wife and three children. The coroner's inquest ruled that the deaths were a result of the ladder being made of inferior wood and faulty construction. The Board of Fire Commissioners were censured emphatically for not submitting the apparatus to both scientific and practical tests before allowing the members of the department to use it. They unhesitatingly condemned the further use of those aerial ladders in the department. The four aerial ladders were placed in storage and never used. It was not until 1886 that the FDNY would purchase and finally use aerial ladders.

Battalion Chief William Nash, Civil War veteran and holder of the Bennett Medal.

Brooklyn had been part of the Metropolitan Department. By the Act of 1869, the Brooklyn Districts were removed from the Metropolitan Department and Fire Commissioners were appointed. They were directed to reorganize the department and select a Chief Engineer. On May 31, 1869, John Cunningham was appointed Chief Engineer with John W. Smith as his assistant. They were in charge of 13 engine companies and six truck companies that officially went into service on September 15, 1869. A year later, Cunningham retired and 27-year-old Thomas F. Nevins was named as Chief Engineer, a position he held for 24 years.

The New York Department became a municipally controlled organization with the creation of the Fire Department of the City of New York in 1870. The fire commissioners now would be appointed by the mayor instead of the governor. The reorganized department changed leadership, titles of rank and even its name. The large sign, Headquarters Metropolitan Fire Department, was removed from the Mercer Street building. The lettering on the apparatus was changed from M.F.D. to the now-familiar F.D.N.Y.

An 1870-style New York City fire alarm box. A key was needed to open the box and transmit the alarm.

After several title changes, the Chief of Department rank was restored with the appointment of Assistant Chief Eli Bates as the department's ranking officer in 1873.

On December 5, 1876, a fire broke out backstage at the Brooklyn Theater during a performance of "The Two Orphans." The house was packed with more than 1000 people as flames began to eat across the scenery. The actors on stage, especially the star, Miss Kate Claxton, tried their best to prevent panic, but at the sight of the flames, the 500 spectators in the balcony rushed for the exits. The stairway soon was overloaded, trapping hundreds, as the fire swept across the ceiling of the theater and roared into the balcony.

When the fire finally was brought under control, 296 people were dead. More than 100 of them could not be identified and were buried in a common grave in Greenwood Cemetery. The fire provoked immediate reaction by both Brooklyn and New York Fire Departments. Inspections were more thorough and rules were enforced more sternly. Around the world, theaters and other show houses were provided with large numbers of easily reached exits.

In 1880, the Fire Commissioner divided the title of Fireman into three grades. The grades were established according to length of service and the section of the City to which the fireman was assigned.

Third Grade – Fewer than two years of service, assigned to a company north of 43rd Street.

Second Grade – More than two years and fewer than four years of service, assigned to a company south of 43rd Street.

First Grade – More than four years of service and assigned to a company south of 43rd Street.

If First-Grade or Second-Grade Firemen were transferred north of 43rd Street, they automatically were reduced to Third-Grade status and their salaries were adjusted accordingly. Such transfers frequently were made for disciplinary reasons.

Chapter 521 of the Laws of 1880 provided that "members here-after appointed shall be known as Third-Grade Firemen with a salary of $800 a year." After two years in Third Grade, they were advanced to Second Grade and paid $900 a year. After two more years of service, they were made First Grade and given $1000 a year.

A steady snow began to fall on New York at about 8:30 a.m., on the morning of January 31, 1882. The large flakes increased steadily as the blanket of snow began to build across the city. A messenger boy was trudging through the snow when he noticed smoke coming from the Potter Building, also known as the World Building, even though the World newspaper had moved to a new location months earlier. He scampered to a fire alarm box and sent in the alarm. At 10:13 a.m., the Fire Department Dispatchers' Office received the signal and immediately sent fire companies to Park Row and Nassau Street.

The LaCours improved respiring apparatus, one of several early breathing devices tested by the New York City Fire Department (1877).

Flames quickly raced up the newly installed elevator shaft, although the elevator had not been placed in service yet. The interior stairs were filling with heavy smoke and fire was beginning to shoot up the well-hole. This central staircase was the only exit in the building and, thus, the only escape route for the approximately 150 people working inside at the time of the fire. (A defective boiler flue was believed to be the cause of the inferno.) As the alarm of **"Fire!"** was raised within the building, many escaped down the stairs. That route quickly was cut off, however, by the extending flames. Numerous people were forced back through the narrow, smoke-filled halls in an attempt to reach the windows.

It took the Chief of the Second Battalion, Francis Mahedy, approximately two minutes to reach the scene. The horse and buggy slid to a halt before the fire building. Peering through eyebrows and lashes already encased in ice, the Chief sized up the serious fire condition and transmitted a third alarm immediately.

Ladder Company 1 arrived and ladders were raised to those visible above who obviously were imperiled. This was no easy task, as the placement of the cumbersome wooden ladders was a difficult chore under ideal conditions. Overhead wires proved to be a major obstacle, as did the mounting snow, and the flames poured from the third- and fourth-floor windows.

Low water pressure began to seriously hamper department operations. Hose streams were proving ineffective and afforded poor protection to the firemen attempting to pass close to the flames and reach those trapped. Chief of Department Eli Bates arrived and assumed command. In addition to the third alarm Mahedy just had placed, Bates transmitted the "three-sixes." (This signal sent an additional 10 engines and three hook and ladders.) The Chief now had 21 engine and eight ladder companies either at the scene or responding.

A large crowd began to build despite the winter weather. People were spilling out onto Park Row and Nassau Street, pressing closer and closer to the blazing structure. Police tried their best to control the growing crowd, but with limited success.

The World Building fire, January 31, 1882.

Department Schools And
The Fire College

The first organized instruction of fire officers by the department was started in 1869, when Commissioner Shaler established an Officers School. The "Manual of Instructions for Commanding Officers of Engine and Hook & Ladder Companies" was prepared. Three classes then were formed:

- First – The Engineer Officers
- Second – Company Commanders
- Third – Company Officers not in command

In 1882, the Department purchased the first scaling ladders, called the Hoell Lifesaving Appliance. The inventor of the ladder, Saint Louis fireman Chris Hoell, was brought in to teach the methods and techniques needed to operate safely with the ladders. This directly led to the start of the School of Instruction.

General Orders No. 4 – June 7, 1883

The establishment of a School of Instruction and the rules governing it, are hearby announced to the department.

Second Assistant Chief Hugh Bonner is designated as Instructor of the School, with the power to select two assistants from the Uniformed Force, to be detailed at his request by the Chief of Department.

Until further notice the School will locate in the quarters of Engine Company 47, the third floor of which will be fitted up suitably with all necessary appliances for that purpose.

The School will be divided into two classes: The first, or Life Saving Corps, will be devoted to instruction and training in handling and using scaling and ordinary ladders, life lines, etc. and all other life saving appliances now in use or here in after introduced. The second class is to be devoted to general instruction in the practical duties of a fireman in quarters and at fires and, particularly, in the handling, care and use of all implements, tools, etc., employed in extinguishing fires.

Outdoor drills were held in the "Old Sugar House" at the foot of West 158th Street until the completion of the new Headquarters Building on East 67th Street, when the School of Instruction was located there on January 1, 1887.

Assistant Chiefs John McCabe and Francis Reilly followed Chief Bonner in charge of the school. One of the assistants selected by Chief Bonner was Captain Henry W. McAdams, who was promoted to the rank of Chief Instructor on June 1, 1897.

Company School was established by General Orders No. 8, May 5, 1888.

The Fire College was created by General Orders No. 72 of 1910. It was effective January 1, 1911. The order specified that the college consist of:
- The Officers School
- The Engineer's School
- The Probationary Fireman's School
- The Company School

The first Fire College Board included:
- Chief of Department Edward F. Croker
- Deputy Chief John Kenlon
  (CIC Officers & Engineers School)
- Deputy Chief Patrick Maher
- Battalion Chief Thomas Larkin
  (CIC Company & Probationary Fireman's School)
- Battalion Chief Edward J. Worth
- Battalion Chief Thomas F. Norton
- Captain William J. Walsh
- Captain James P. Noonan
- Captain James J. Henry
- Chief Medical Officer Herman J. Reis
- Electrical Engineer John C. Rennard
- Veterinary Surgeon William F. Doyle

Engine Company 40 vacated the quarters at 68th Street on May 1, 1918, and the College was located there until January 1934, when it moved to the Packard Building in Long Island City. Then, the College occupied the new Repair Shops and College Building in January of 1948.

Both the storm and the fire were increasing in intensity when a woman, Miss Ida Small, was seen standing at a fifth-floor window. A ladder was forced through the overhead wires and quickly was raised toward her. Fireman John L. Rooney climbed the bending ladder through clouds of smoke, hoping to reach the woman in time. Upon reaching the top, Rooney realized the woman was still beyond his reach. Looking up at Miss Small, he told her to "Keep cool, keep cool!"

Seeing the ladder's reach was short, the firemen called to the crowd for help. Their numbers now swelled with additional firemen and civilian volunteers who gripped the ladder and, on command, slowly lifted it off the sidewalk. They continued to raise it, fireman and all, until it was being held at arm's length above their heads. Rooney then carefully straightened out.

Rooney directed Miss Small to sit down on the sill and to hold onto his shoulder. He gripped her waist and told her to drop into his arms. The crowds below were cheering the heroic fireman as he carried her down to the street.

Chief Bates made several strategic moves. He placed engines on Broadway to take advantage of the larger water mains and also sent a signal to the Croton aqueduct to increase water pressure. Additionally, he concentrated his firefighting efforts at the corner of Beekman and Nassau Streets, where he made a successful stand.

For 45 minutes, the building was engulfed in flames and burned with a fury, but Bates' tactics were working and the fire was being contained to the original building.

The earliest known depiction of a medal presentation ceremony shows the hero of the World Building fire, Fireman John Rooney, receive the Bennett Medal on May 16, 1883.

More than 5000 people had filled the area near City Hall, drawn by the earlier reports of perhaps as many as 100 people being trapped by the fire. The storm changed to sleet and freezing rain and was driven by a steadily increasing wind. The flames had diminished greatly and at 11:30 a.m., the Beekman Street wall fell in with a crash. The crowds slowly left until the next morning's search of the ruins.

In all, 12 people died in the fire, but scores had been rescued, many under circumstances of extraordinary bravery. Chief Bates showed his and his department's skill by holding the fire to the original building and keeping the damage to the adjoining property to a minimum. The next summer, Rooney was presented the Bennett Medal during a ceremony at Union Square Park.

The department organized a number of double companies in 1883. Engines 12, 13, 16, 31 and 33 and Ladder Companies 6 and 9 were equipped with duplicate apparatus and increased manpower. The following year, Engines 5, 18, 26 and 27 and Ladder 5 also were made double. Engine 33 actually became a triple company, the only one in the history of the department.

At about 11 p.m. on April 7, 1884, Louis Castigan, the elevator boy in the Saint George Flats, noticed smoke in the building and descended in the elevator to the cellar to warn the building engineer and locate the fire. The apartment house, made up of two buildings, was seven stories in the front and eight in the rear and was located at 223 and 225 East 17th Street.

Castigan found the engineer attempting to extinguish a growing fire in the cellar and set off to notify the fire department. The boy raced to the street fire alarm box at Second Avenue and 17th Street, pulled the handle and ran back to the building. The boy set off in his elevator to warn the tenants above who may not have escaped.

The elevator boy went to the seventh floor to warn people in their top-floor apartment. Castigan made his way through both suites, but could find no one. He tried to return to his elevator, but was driven back by the intense heat and smoke pumping up through the shaft. The youth was forced to a window to escape the dense smoke and heat.

Chief Bresnan arrived and ordered Ladder 3 to rescue the boy with their pompier ladders. John Binns and two other firemen grabbed one ladder each and dashed to the building. Binns reached the fire building first and began his climb toward the sixth floor. Stopping one floor below the stranded boy, Binns stepped onto the top of a large extension ladder that just had been placed and raised the scaling ladder to the seventh-floor window.

The first scaling ladder rescue in New York was made by Fireman John Binns of Ladder 3 on April 7, 1884.

Castigan was forced out onto the windowsill as Binns climbed up to him. The fireman guided the youth onto the ladder; together, they slowly descended and then transferred to the extension ladder. As they stepped to the ground, the crowd of spectators began to cheer. This was the first practical test of the new ladders and it was a resounding success.

John Binns returned up the extension ladder and the scaling ladder. Then, with another fireman, they climbed through the top-floor window and continued searching. After a few minutes, they found an unconscious man and dragged him back to the window. Together, they struggled to pass the limp body out to other firemen who removed him to the street.

Battalion Chief John Binns, wearing the Bennett Medal he was awarded for his heroism at the Saint George Flats in 1884.

At six a.m., after three alarms, the last of the flames were quenched. This was the second three-alarm fire the department fought that night. The earlier fire was in Saint Peter's German Lutheran Church, at 46th Street and Lexington Avenue.

John Binns later was awarded the Bennett Medal and rapidly was promoted to Assistant Foreman, Foreman and then Chief of the Ninth Battalion.

A major blizzard swept through the city on March 12, 1888, creating conditions that made operations nearly impossible. Chief Charles O. Shay suspended all personnel leaves and numerous horses and sleighs were obtained. A special corps of linemen were assembled and put to work, restoring the fire alarm system wires that were downed by the heavy snowstorm.

During the first night of the snowstorm, there were two multiple alarms. The first was received at 6:45 p.m., March 12th, when Box 164 was transmitted. A fire started on the second floor of 9-11 Laight Street and quickly extended throughout the building. Five companies were assigned and started out through the deep snow and howling blizzard conditions. Only one engine and one ladder were able to get to the fire scene within 20 minutes and the flames soon spread to the adjoining building at seven Laight Street.

An hour after the first companies arrived, two other engines had pushed their way to the fire, while the men of two ladder companies walked, carrying their tools – but without their rigs – to the scene and went to work. The three engines stretched six lines and battled the blaze for three hours before bringing it under control.

Later that night, a patrolman discovered a fire in a five-story building at 559 West 42nd Street. The cop trudged through the deep drifts to the quarters of Engine 2 – directly behind the fire building – and turned in the verbal alarm. The company tapped out the alarm at 2:30 a.m. and started out toward the blaze. They pushed, pulled and forced their rig the 1000 feet from the firehouse to the hydrant at 42nd Street and 11th Avenue in 17 minutes. The fire had spread from the cellar to the roof and also to the adjoining five-story building.

The Engine 2 officer made his way through the deep snow and transmitted a third alarm (skipping the second alarm). Of the 12 engines and four ladders due on the third alarm, only the steamer and one-horse tender of Engine 2 and the two-horse tender of Engine 26 ever arrived at the fire. Men from Ladders 2 and 4 arrived with tools, but without apparatus, and assisted in stretching a line. Two lines controlled the blaze in about two hours.

As conditions in the city worsened, several local breweries and horse car lines (horse-drawn trolley cars) placed great numbers of horses and sleighs at the service of the fire department. They fashioned "spike hitches" that allowed four and five horses to be attached to engines and trucks, while the sleighs were packed with hose. These improvisations allowed companies to respond to alarms in a reasonable amount of time.

Before the Blizzard of 1888, only 12 pieces of apparatus were provided with three-horse hitches and a number of tenders only had one horse. The experience gained during the storm increased the number of horses available for all types of rigs. It also hastened the decision to move fire alarm wires underground.

The Department was faced with a major building collapse on August 22, 1891. The Taylor Building on Park Row suddenly crashed to the ground, taking dozens of people inside with it. Beneath the piles of debris, people were trapped, crying for help and struggling to free themselves; then the fire broke out. Arriving firemen were faced with a horrible scene, as the mounds of collapsed rubble burned with a vengeance, ending the lives of those pinned inside. The death toll was 61.

On the southeast corner of Sixth Avenue and 40th Street stood the Hotel Royal. The hotel housed about 60 regular, long-term guests and about 80 transient guests. At approximately three a.m., on February 7, 1892, a hotel employee working in the basement noticed a fire blazing up the elevator shaft. He ran to turn in the alarm, shouting **"Fire!"** and warning as many guests as he could.

Outside, an elevated train was approaching the hotel on the tracks that ran directly in front of the doomed building. The engineer, with one simple action, saved the lives of countless tenants. Stopping the

Fire companies push through deep snow during the Blizzard of 1888.

Hugh Bonner

On June 16, 1860, just two days after he came of age and was eligible to join the volunteer fire department, Hugh Bonner became a member of Lady Washington Engine Company 40. Bonner was born in Ireland and arrived in the United States when he was eight years old. He was elected assistant foreman in April 1861. In 1863, Bonner became foreman of the company and remained at this position until the department became paid in 1865.

Metropolitan Steam Fire-Engine Company No. 20 was organized on September 18, 1865, and was located at 47 Marion Street, with Hugh Bonner appointed as Foreman. Bonner was placed in charge of the first self-propelling steam fire engine and chemical engine in the department. Hugh Bonner became a Battalion Chief on May 21, 1873, and remained in charge of the second battalion for the next 10 years.

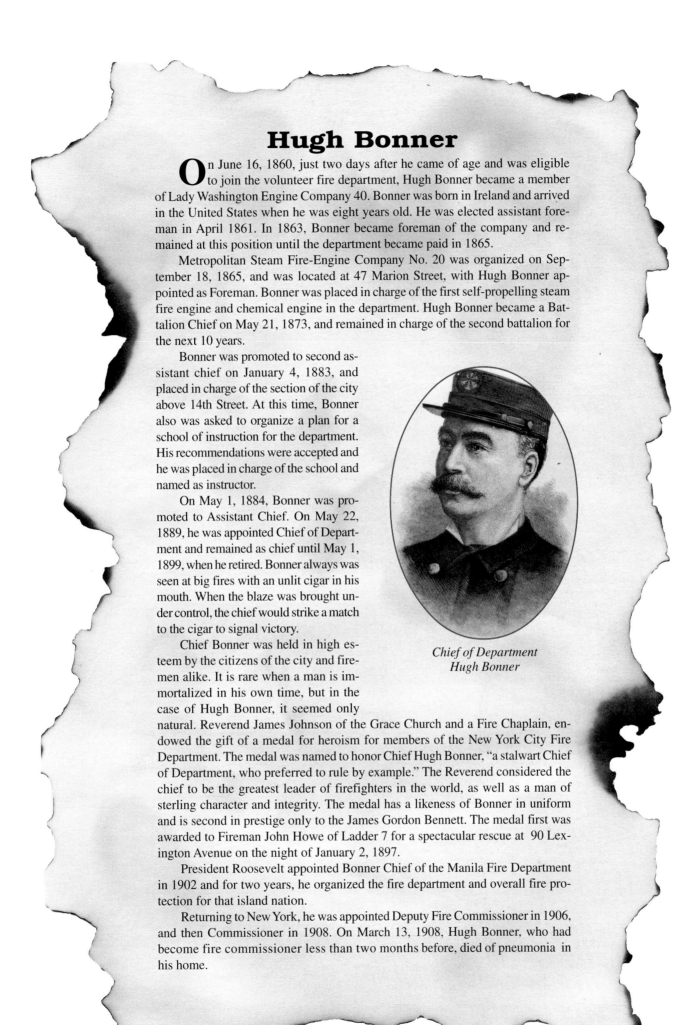

Bonner was promoted to second assistant chief on January 4, 1883, and placed in charge of the section of the city above 14th Street. At this time, Bonner also was asked to organize a plan for a school of instruction for the department. His recommendations were accepted and he was placed in charge of the school and named as instructor.

On May 1, 1884, Bonner was promoted to Assistant Chief. On May 22, 1889, he was appointed Chief of Department and remained as chief until May 1, 1899, when he retired. Bonner always was seen at big fires with an unlit cigar in his mouth. When the blaze was brought under control, the chief would strike a match to the cigar to signal victory.

Chief Bonner was held in high esteem by the citizens of the city and firemen alike. It is rare when a man is immortalized in his own time, but in the case of Hugh Bonner, it seemed only natural. Reverend James Johnson of the Grace Church and a Fire Chaplain, endowed the gift of a medal for heroism for members of the New York City Fire Department. The medal was named to honor Chief Hugh Bonner, "a stalwart Chief of Department, who preferred to rule by example." The Reverend considered the chief to be the greatest leader of firefighters in the world, as well as a man of sterling character and integrity. The medal has a likeness of Bonner in uniform and is second in prestige only to the James Gordon Bennett. The medal first was awarded to Fireman John Howe of Ladder 7 for a spectacular rescue at 90 Lexington Avenue on the night of January 2, 1897.

President Roosevelt appointed Bonner Chief of the Manila Fire Department in 1902 and for two years, he organized the fire department and overall fire protection for that island nation.

Returning to New York, he was appointed Deputy Fire Commissioner in 1906, and then Commissioner in 1908. On March 13, 1908, Hugh Bonner, who had become fire commissioner less than two months before, died of pneumonia in his home.

Chief of Department
Hugh Bonner

Ladder Company 4 at 1893 medal ceremony.

train, he began to sound the whistle of his locomotive. The loud screeching of his signal filled the night air with a warning that woke many guests from their sleep, allowing them to make a start on their escape.

Due to the advancing flames, entering the building through the front door was impossible. Ladder Company 4 arrived first and within two minutes of the alarm, members were raising ladders to those trapped above, as flames poured from the front of the hotel. Chief Benjamin Gicquel of the Ninth Battalion transmitted a second alarm on arrival, followed quickly by a third alarm.

The advanced fire conditions upon arrival did not allow rescues from the interior until the flames could be controlled. Firemen struggled valiantly to save those they could reach. Many spectacular rescues were accomplished over ladders. The fire raged on for hours and eventually the building collapsed. Many people still were unaccounted for and for the next few days, more than 100 firemen dug through the rubble until all the victims were recovered. In all, 28 people were killed in the Hotel Royal fire. This was a large loss of life, but considering the number of occupants in the building at the time (more than 150), the number rescued reflected the excellent work of the firemen.

The skyline of lower Manhattan was obscured by a major storm that was pounding the city on the night of December 4, 1898. The skyline itself was changing due to the introduction of elevators. Ship masts and church steeples now were being rivaled by taller and taller buildings and suspension bridges. The buildings were growing beyond the reach of the fire department, but few in the city were paying much attention to the fire chiefs, raising serious questions of extinguishment and rescue in buildings so tall.

At about 10 p.m., two police officers were trudging along their beat when they came upon the building of the Rogers & Peat Co. on the corner of Broadway and Warren Street, just across from City Hall. They saw a small spiral of flame spinning from a window and they dashed to turn in the alarm.

As the clock struck midnight on January 1, 1898, the Greater City of New York became a reality. Chief Hugh Bonner took command of three fire departments – New York, Brooklyn and Long Island, with 121 engines, 46 trucks, one hose wagon and one water tower, protecting 309 square miles.

A new charter accompanied the reorganization of the city and, in part, made a fundamental change in the fire department's leadership.

The Board of Fire Commissioners, in place since 1865, was replaced by a single Commissioner, appointed by the Mayor and responsible to him alone. Mayor R. A. Van Wyck appointed John J. Scannell as the first Commissioner. Scannell had been serving as head of the Board since 1894.

Another change was the new charter's provision for a Municipal Civil Service Commission. This commission would provide for "...promotions in office on the basis of ascertained merit and seniority in service and upon such examination as may be for the good of the public service."

The horse-drawn fire apparatus arrived to find every window of the five-story structure belching flames. Wind-blown bursts of fire and streams of embers poured across Warren Street and exposed the United States Insurance Company building on the northwest corner. Chief of Department Hugh Bonner positioned hose line after hose line to protect the structure.

The streets were filling with people willing to brave the weather to watch the growing blaze, which quickly was becoming one of the biggest fires in years. Chief Bonner dashed from vantage point to vantage point and rallied his men. The situation in the U.S. Life Building was stabilizing when the wind changed direction and flames appeared in the 16-story Home Life Building next door. This fire-proof structure, built in 1894, was designed by renowned architect Napoleon LaBrun (who also designed more than a dozen FDNY firehouses).

Firemen began to climb the stairs in the skyscraper and connected their hoses to the standpipe system in order to fight the blaze. Door after door was forced and the battle was joined on numerous floors simultaneously. Weary firemen were driven out of each floor by wind-blown flames as the fire took control of the building. At 11:15 p.m., after a 45-minute battle, fire was showing on the top seven floors of the pyramid-topped Home Life Building.

To add to the chief's extensive problems, the Postal Telegraph Building next to the Home Insurance Building also was being threatened on its upper floors. Again Bonner was leading the charge, as hose lines were stretched through the Postal Building. Hose streams were being directed from every vantage point. The battle raged for hours until finally the fire began to subside. The original fire building had collapsed and the Home Life Building's upper floors were burned out. The exposures sustained damage, mostly from water. Bonner's men had won, but barely.

Chief Bonner had been battling the builders of skyscrapers for some time. In 1895, he was quoted as saying, *My belief is...that a fireproof building is more dangerous in itself and to the surrounding structures than the old-fashioned structure.* The chief's prophesy about the dangers of high-rise fires would be proved again and again.

A fire of major proportions occurred on Saint Patrick's Day in 1899. The parade then, as now, proceeded up Fifth Avenue and attracted large crowds to cheer on the marchers. On Fifth Avenue, between 46th and 47th Streets, stood the Windsor Hotel, one of the city's finest hotels. The hotel was seven stories in height and occupied a plot 250 x 150 feet with a large front entrance on Fifth Avenue.

The Windsor was primarily a residential hotel, but did have some transient guests among the 275 people registered in the hotel. Many other people had taken positions at the numerous windows overlooking the Avenue to view the parade.

A discarded match apparently started a fire that quickly was out of control inside the hotel. Wisps of smoke at the second-floor windows soon became dense clouds of smoke that pumped from the building. Fire then burst through the windows on the Fifth Avenue side of

Lights

In 1877, Mr. John J. Gorman of the Board of Fire Commissioners conceived the idea of using calcium lights for Fire Department service. After much experimentation, a light was developed that could be carried on the fire apparatus. The first lights were installed on Ladder Trucks 1 and 9 and initially tested at a multiple-alarm fire on Fulton Street in March of 1878. It was reported in the newspaper the next day that "the Chief of Department considers the calcium light one of the most important additions to the service in a long time and similar lights will be provided for all of the Hook and Ladder Companies."

In 1900, a contract was given to the LaFrance Fire Engine Company to build three horse-drawn, steam-driven, electric searchlight units. The power plant was a single cylinder (five- x five-inch) engine, directly connected to a five-kw, marine-type generator, with two dismountable, 9000-candle power lights. Four hundred feet of cable to feed the lights was carried on two reels. These horse-drawn steamer searchlights were in service at Engine 20, Ladder 24 and Ladder 68 (118) until 1916, when they were replaced by calcium lights carried on the Water Towers.

During the Saint Patrick's Day Parade of 1899, the Windsor Hotel caught fire and spread rapidly. Despite numerous spectacular rescues, 45 people were killed.

William Clark, hero of the Windsor Hotel fire, of 1899. Note "Bugs" worn on sleeve.

the building. The parade halted. The music stopped. The crowd stood in muted silence as people began appearing at the hotel windows.

Fire apparatus inched their way through the throng. Poor conditions were compounding themselves. The fire and the apparatus were attracting even more people to the scene and the crush of humanity was becoming as thick as the smoke above the hotel.

First-due units were confronted with nine victims who had jumped to their deaths from the smoke-filled windows above. Firemen then raced into the lobby and attempted to gain control of the stairs with a hose line. Time after time, they pushed forward, only to be driven back.

The fire escapes were in danger of failing due to the number of people fleeing the dense smoke. Firemen used aerial ladders, portable ladders and then extended themselves above those by operating from scaling ladders.

In fewer than five minutes, Chief John Binns transmitted a second and third alarm and special-called numerous public ambulances. Deputy Chief Purroy then sent in a fourth and fifth alarm. Chief of the Department, Hugh Bonner, arrived and took command of 24 engines and six ladder trucks.

Fireman William Clark of Ladder 7 raised a 35-foot portable ladder, then built a chain of scaling ladders to a woman trapped at a fifth- floor window. Fireman Edward Ford of Ladder Co. 20 followed and together, they completed one of the most spectacular and dangerous rescues in the history of the department.

Twenty minutes after the arrival of the department, the center section of the Fifth Avenue front wall collapsed. Forty-five lives were lost in the blaze. This fire was a premonition of the dangers firemen and citizens both would face in the future.

Chief John Kenlon later recalled,

At about the time of the consolidation, a new era in building construction set in. From a five-story city in 1887, New York had begun to grow skyward to 20- and 30-story structures. Naturally, the problem of fire protection in these high buildings became acute...

It was not until several disastrous fires occurred in high buildings, such as that in the Home Insurance Building at Broadway and Warren Street, that the Fire Department officials awoke to the necessity of additional protection for such structures. I well remember the great difficulty under which the firemen attempted to stretch hose lines up through the Postal Telegraph Building next door, in an effort to arrest the flames in the eight upper stories of the Home Life Building. It was then, I believe, for the first time indelibly impressed on the minds of fire officials the need for fire standpipe equipment within structures.

The change from one century to the next is a momentous occasion. Citizens consider it a milestone in history and a major reason to celebrate. Historians use it as a benchmark, a useful way to help keep track of time passing. To the FDNY, the difference between 1899 and 1900 was not that dramatic. Two years earlier, the department had grown tremendously with the formation of The Greater City of New York. The FDNY now comprised the five boroughs of Manhattan, Bronx, Brooklyn, Queens and Staten Island. The charter called for the takeover of the many volunteer departments still operating within the new boundaries of the city.

This change would take many decades to implement completely. However, the bulk of the change took place in short order.

The day-to-day job of the FDNY had remained unchanged since the start of the paid department. Officers and firemen worked nearly a continuous tour of duty. Three hours a day were allowed for each man to leave quarters for meals. One 24-hour leave was granted each month. The entire force virtually lived their lives in the firehouse.

Firemen still wore leather helmets, the outgrowth of the original designed by volunteers years earlier. Rubber boots replaced the earlier leather version and a wide variety of coats was being utilized for battling fires. Engine men wore slicker-type raincoats that shed the hot water that rained back at them from operating hose streams, while most members of ladder companies wore cut-down wool uniform overcoats. Some truckies wore the lightweight blue denim work coats favored by railroad workers.

On March 24, 1900, companies were dispatched to 213 East 44th Street in Manhattan at 1:52 a.m. for a fire in a metal works company. Arriving units found a five-story building with fire extending from the cellar to the roof. Members of Engine Company 21 and Ladder 2 were operating on the first floor when the structure began to collapse. Captain Grady of Ladder 2 and Firemen Smith and Bowen of Engine 21 fell into the water-filled cellar and drowned. Several other members also fell into the eight-foot-deep water while attempting to rescue their brother firemen, but were pulled to safety.

One hundred forty-five passengers were killed when three North German Lloyd Liners caught fire in the North River (Hudson). A fire broke out on the piers in Hoboken, New Jersey, on June 30, 1900. As the fire swept the piers, the ships caught fire, trapping many people inside. Tugboats pulled the ships from the blazing waterfront and pushed them toward responding New York City fireboats. Twenty-eight people were saved by the fireboats' crews, either from the water or off the burning ship. Fireboats also battled fires on other ships and barges floating loose in the river.

A turn-of-the-century newspaper clipping shows firefighters caught by an explosion.

On a cold, windy and rainy afternoon, the department responded to a fire in the 71st Regiment Armory on Fourth Avenue at 34th Street. It was February 22, 1902, at about 1:30 p.m. when the first-due units were caught in a violent explosion. Luckily for these men, they were blown from the structure before a second and more violent blast rocked the structure when flames touched off black powder stores.

Flaming brands started a fire in the eight-story Park Avenue Hotel across the street. Numerous guests were at their windows watching the Armory fire, unaware of the growing fire within the hotel. Numerous rescues were made and several firemen were overcome during attempts to rescue the 21 people who were killed by the blaze.

On February 8, 1904, a major conflagration developed in the City of Baltimore. It had been burning out of control for hours and the Baltimore Fire Department was overextended and near exhaustion. Calls for help went out to several cities, including New York. Two special trains were contracted to transport nine engines and one ladder company from New York City to Baltimore to assist in fighting the blaze. Acting Chief of Department Kruger placed Battalion Chief Howe in charge of this expeditionary force of firemen. They arrived after some delays, but were eager and ready to work.

They were requested to make a stand in the southeast end of the city. With flames and smoke driven at them by a rainstorm, the companies dug in, defending a large area occupied by factories, tenement houses, icehouses and lumberyards. Their location was on West Falls Avenue, alongside Dock Street and a stream called Jones Falls. The New Yorkers held their ground all night, their water supplied by Baltimore fireboat *Cataract*. The men worked continuously and were relieved one company at a time, but only long enough for the men to be provided with sandwiches and hot coffee.

The companies faced the moving fire front with zero visibility and, finally, with reinforcements, were able to stop the advancing flames. One member of the contingent, Mark Kelly of Engine 16, contracted pneumonia and later died.

The worst disaster in the history of New York City occurred on June 15, 1904, on the East River near the Bronx. A beautiful, sunny day's excursion turned into a nightmare for both those on the water and those who watched from the shore.

The congregation of Manhattan's Saint Mark's Lutheran Church on East Sixth Street, between First and Second Avenues, chartered the excursion steamer *The General Slocum* to cruise up the river to a Sunday School picnic at Locust Point in the Bronx. Fourteen hundred happy passengers crowded the ship's rail as it started its trip from the pier at East Third Street. As they passed Randall's Island just opposite 125th Street, a fire broke out in a cabin and began to spread.

For reasons known only to him, Captain William Van Schaik did not attempt to beach his burning ship but, instead, raced upstream around the island and along the Bronx shore. The alarm was transmitted, but responding land units only could watch as the blazing ship motored by.

The pilot finally beached the ship on North Brothers Island, across from 149th Street. The poor angle of the ship still left most of the vessel over deep water. The swarm of women and children forced to jump from the flames faced drowning if they could not swim. Engineer of Steamer Lynch of Engine 60 was able to rescue 15 people by making several trips with his rowboat. Of the 1400 people on the ship, 1031 were killed.

On Sunday, January 6, 1907, at 7:48 p.m., Manhattan Box 76 was sent in for a fire in a six-story warehouse at 54 Roosevelt Street. Engine 32 was ordered to stretch a line to the third floor. As they waited for water, Fireman John Seufert removed the 1/2-inch tip from

Battalion Chief John P. Howe (shown here while Captain of Ladder Company 6), led the FDNY to help battle the conflagration in Baltimore in 1904.

Engine Company 33 takes a break during Baltimore fire, February 1904.

On June 6, 1903, the fire department held its first parade since 1867. Twenty engine and ladder companies from Manhattan and the Bronx, 10 from Brooklyn and volunteer companies from Queens and Richmond took part. More than 1000 firemen were in the line of march. The next day, the *New York Times* reported that it was, *(the) most commendable street display of the firefighting force since its organization in 1865 as a paid department.*

Chief Charles D. Purroy led the apparatus and men as they paraded from the Washington Arch, up Fifth Avenue, to the Sherman Monument at 59th Street. A flag-draped reviewing stand was set up for the mayor, fire commissioner and invited guests, including Governor Odel.

Until this ceremony, the FDNY had presented semi-annually only four medals for valor: the Bennett, Bonner, Trevor-Warren and Strong Medals. Also awarded was the Stephenson Medal to the Captain whose company was the best disciplined and most efficient.

Water Tower 1, shining brightly, passes crowd of spectators during a Department parade.

Ladder Company 8 makes its way along parade route.

The department began forming ranks before the grandstand at about three p.m. The 14 firemen to be honored were called to a place of honor before the assembled department. The awards to be presented were for acts of bravery made during the years 1901 and 1902. Additionally, the Brooklyn Citizens Medal would be presented for the first time by New York City's Mayor Seth Low. One by one, he called forward the four men to be awarded the Brooklyn Citizens Medal. The first recipient was Fireman Rudolph J. Uster of Engine Company 117, who had rescued two children, by rope, from a fire at 388 Myrtle Avenue, on March 10, 1900. The Brooklyn Citizens Medal then was pinned on the chest of Fireman James W. Trihy of Engine 107, for his daring rescue made in 1901. Then, Firemen George A. Kellock of Ladder 58 and Edward F. Nealis of Engine 103 were decorated with the Brooklyn Citizens Medal for separate rescues made in 1902.

After the presentation of awards, the mayor alluded briefly to those on the Roll of Honor, who were absent because they were too infirm to attend or had "passed to the other shore." After a moment of silence, the ceremony ended.

Uniforms

Soon after the formation of the paid department, the commissioners discussed the issue of uniforms. The first Rules and Regulations, issued in 1865, described the uniforms to be worn. The Chief Engineer and other Engineer officers (chiefs) were instructed to wear a red flannel, double-breasted shirt, dark-blue pilot cloth coat (knee length), vest and pantaloons of the same material, blue cloth cap and white fire hat. The insignia on the caps of Engineer officers read Chief, Assistant or Engineer, embroidered in gold, with the letters M.F.D. underneath. Buttons for all officers were white metal, with the letters M.F.D. inside a wreath design.

Officers and members of companies then wore a double-breasted, blue flannel shirt, with a knee-length coat, pants and cap, of the same design as prescribed for the Engineer officers. The cap device for the company officers and members was described as a white Maltese cross with emblem of the department in the center and the letters M.F.D. and number of the wearer on the points.

In 1866, the Rules were amended to include a summer uniform coat – a sack coat made from dark-blue flannel, without lining, rolling collar and of medium length.

General Orders No. 1, in 1868, promulgated a complete Bill of Dress. White shirts, instead of red ones, were prescribed for the chief officers. Red shirts then became part of the uniform for the company officers, with firemen and engineers of steamers continuing to wear blue shirts.

The trumpet was adopted as insignia of rank with issuing of the 1868 Bill of Dress, the insignia "to be embroidered in gold on caps and coat lapels, the color of the background of the design to indicate the branch of the service – blue for engineer officers, red for ladder officers, light green for chemical company officers and black for officers of engine companies."

The red shirt disappeared from the department in 1869 when General Orders No. 23 prescribed that after the first of January 1870, "Company Officers will substitute for the red shirt now worn by them, the white shirt prescribed for Engineer Officers."

In the early 1890s, metal insignia devices were substituted for the embroidered insignia previously worn by officers. The ax – instead of the trumpet – was adopted as the distinctive device for Ladder Company officers.

The drop-visor style of uniform cap was adopted in 1903.

White caps for summer wear by officers were introduced in 1907 – Special Orders 62, of May 17, 1907, prescribing that the new summer caps be worn from June 1st to September 15th, instead of the straw hats that had been worn since the summer of 1867. General Orders 15, June 2, 1868, directed that officers should wear, as part of the summer uniform, a Panama hat, with insignia, and other members a brown straw hat, with the wearer's number on patent-leather background sewn to the front of the hat.

There were no other major changes of the uniform until 1926, when the substitution of a more up-to-date overcoat was made. The Civil War cavalry-style coat, which had been worn by the uniform force since 1868, was retired. General Orders No. 68, issued August 30, 1926, promulgated the design of the new roll-collar-style of coat (still in use to this day).

the nozzle, placed it in his turnout coat pocket and then began to operate the line. Flames were eating away at the large bails of rags stored on the floor, but it was obvious that the line was doing little to control the fire. The cotton waste and paper seemed to defy the hose stream and actually were absorbing great quantities of the water.

The exposures on either side of the warehouse were occupied tenements and the companies were having little or no success in stopping the blaze. A second alarm was struck seven minutes after the initial box was transmitted, followed quickly by a third.

A short time later, Acting Chief of Department John Binns arrived. He noted the deep-seated fire in the fourth floor and sensed the potential for a collapse inside the building, due to the lack of runoff from the hose streams and the damage from the flames. The chief ordered the companies out of the building and turned to Battalion Chief Duffy and said, *Get up there, Duffy, and get every one of them out of there quick. If they don't get out, throw them out.* Suddenly, the building began to rumble and shake, then quickly started collapsing. Seufert was caught under falling bales of rags and paper. Men across the fireground scrambled for safety as the firemen on the front fire escape came tumbling to the street.

There was a sudden quiet. Firemen slowly started staggering from the building – dazed and injured – carrying other injured men. Battalion Chief Duffy was carried out unconscious; he almost had been killed. As he was being tended to in the street, he regained consciousness. Looking for the chief, he yelled to Binns, *I believe there are three men in there!*

Quick! Call a roll! commanded Binns. After a fast head count, three men were reported missing. With the fire still raging beneath the crumbled timbers, lines were repositioned in an attempt to control the flames. The thick smoke generated by the wet materials hung over the rescue workers, choking their breathing and burning their eyes and lungs. The combination of back-breaking work and inhalation of the noxious smoke knocked out a half-dozen men.

At midnight, Chief Binns and Battalion Chief Geurin made an inspection of the roof of the building next door. Due to the buckling walls and large visible crack, it was decided that all 150 people who lived there would be removed for their own safety.

As Chief Binns was conferring with Fire Commissioner Lantry, a woman came up to the Chief and asked for Jack Seufert. *Your husband has not been found,* said Binns in a low voice, *I fear he has*

Engine Company 14, around 1903.

Ladder Company 8, sporting their straw hats, in 1908.

been killed. Mrs. Seufert, despite what she was being told, kept insisting that her husband was alive and refused to leave the scene.

At two p.m. on Monday, two firemen were found dead in the ruins. Mrs. Seufert still insisted that her husband was alive in the rubble and she refused to talk with the man arranging the funerals.

Firemen worked on for the remainder of the afternoon, digging out the building debris and soaked rags by hand. At about 6:30 p.m., Deputy Chief Guerin's aide, Fireman Decker, thought he heard a noise. Calling for quiet, he listened closely. He was about to give up when he heard it again – a tapping, tapping on a pipe. First three taps, then two taps. Then again, three...two... It was unbelievable! Somewhere under all the debris, a man was alive and signaling.

The word spread at the fire scene, to the firehouses and throughout the city. Off-duty men began arriving and volunteered to help with the digging. Chief Binns, with all the help he needed at his command, could allow only a few men at a time into the collapsed structure. Working under an overhanging, free-standing wall made digging in the pile of wet material extremely dangerous. The gas pipe being tapped was located and through it, the firemen were able to talk to the trapped man. A 12-foot piece of rubber tubing was worked down along the gas pipe to him. Then, hot broth, coffee and whiskey were poured down the tube.

Firemen dug and removed tons of crumbled building materials, passing them in a chain out to the street. Father Smith, the Department Chaplain, made his way to the trapped man and first administered him the last rites. He told him his wife was at the scene, waiting to see him after he was freed. He also told him it seemed as if half of the department had arrived and volunteered to help dig him out.

Shortly after midnight, the pile of debris shifted. The scene was examined and found to be extremely dangerous. Only two men at a time were allowed to dig and the street in front of the building was cleared of apparatus. The digging continued in shifts.

At 1:42 a.m., Tuesday, the eighth of January, almost 30 hours after the time of the collapse, the crowd was asked to be quiet as two firemen gently pulled Seufert clear of his tomb. He was placed on a stretcher and carried to an ambulance.

After two days in the hospital, Seufert was allowed to return home. He had suffered only slight cuts and bruises, but his mental condition deteriorated slightly as the loss of the other men sank in. Seufert was placed on light duty and worked for many years at Headquarters. He died in retirement on December 10, 1941.

On the corner of Washington Place and Greene Street in Manhattan stood the 10-story Asch Building. This structure housed several commercial occupancies that included the Triangle Shirtwaist Company's factory on the top three floors. At about 4:50 p.m. on Saturday, March 25, 1911, a fire broke out on the southeast corner of the eighth floor and spread quickly, due to large numbers of finished garments hanging above the work tables. More than 700 people were at work in the building (600 of whom were girls between the ages of 16 and 23) as the alarm of fire was raised. Most of the girls at work on the eighth floor were able to escape aboard a large freight elevator that just had arrived at the floor; the rest fled down the stairs.

Fifty-five people on the 10th floor also were able to escape by breaking open a skylight to the roof. Many exited onto the fire escape that soon was overloaded. Two people, however, were hurled to their deaths as the fire escape pulled away from the wall.

Those on the ninth floor had little chance of escape. The fire escape was unusable after it pulled away and the doors to the interior stairs were locked to prevent theft. Their only hope was the elevator being manned by a young boy named Joseph Zito. The youngster braved flames and dense smoke as he made five trips to the doomed floor, rescuing 25 to 30 girls on each trip.

Dozens of girls were cut off from the elevator and had only one choice – the windows. They waited as long as they could but, one by one and in groups, they jumped from the raging ninth floor.

Arriving fire companies had difficulty getting into position as body after body plummeted to the ground before them. Firemen raced to help those they could. Scaling ladders were climbed and life nets were opened. It became apparent that the life nets were ineffective due to the height. Hose lines were stretched as quickly as possible. Second, third and fourth alarms were sent in to bring more help to the scene.

Before any of the frantic efforts of the firemen could make an impact, the desperate situation was over. Those who were trapped had jumped or fallen back into the growing wall of fire. High-pressure streams were directed into the building, but the damage had been done. The fire was extinguished quickly, but the grim task of searching for survivors proved fruitless.

Dozens of bodies were found piled up against a wall; dozens more lay broken on the sidewalk and in the street. In total, 146 people died at this fire. As a result of this blaze and the horrible loss of life, laws were passed nationwide, making occupancies safer. The department stepped up its fire prevention efforts and staged fire drills in factories across the city.

The Equitable Building actually consisted of five buildings erected at different times, with the tallest 10 stories high. The buildings had undergone many alterations, including openings on most floors among various structures, allowing uninhibited travel from one area to another. The building occupied the entire square block bordered by Broadway, Nassau, Cedar and Pine Streets.

On January 9, 1912, at 5:18 a.m., a fire was discovered in the basement of 12 Pine Street. Flames quickly traveled down a hallway to a large shaft containing two elevators and 11 dumbwaiters that served the exclusive Lawyer's Club and the Cafe Savarin from the eighth-floor kitchen. There were direct openings on each floor, from the cellar to the roof, with the exception of the fourth floor.

Employees tried to fight the flames with no success until finally, 16 minutes after the fire was discovered, Box 24 was transmitted. Four engines, two ladders, two battalion chiefs and the deputy chief of the First Division responded.

The first-due unit, Engine Co. 6, stretched into the cellar where they made good progress, unaware of the fire extension on the floors above. Acting Deputy Chief Devaney then received reports about fire extension on the floors above and transmitted a second alarm.

The only people in the building were cleaners, restaurant employees, watchmen, heating engineers and several bank employees. Three waiters from the Cafe Savarin took the elevator to the top floor, but flames drove them to the roof of the 10-story building.

Eight companies had entered the building and operated on the second, third, fourth and fifth floors for nearly half an hour. The structural iron and steel supports were exposed to the fierce heat and ready to buckle. At 6:35 a.m., after calling a third, fourth and fifth alarm, Chief of Department John Kenlon ordered everyone out of the building.

Now there were 22 engines, two water towers and 10 trucks working, but 65-mph winds were whipping the fire out of control. Chief Kenlon then called for Brooklyn companies to respond to the fire. This was the first borough call in FDNY history.

Using a scaling ladder, a team of firemen started toward the men trapped on the roof. Suddenly, the middle of the building started to collapse. Flames forced the victims to jump to their deaths from the Cedar Street side of the roof before they could be reached.

Caught in the collapse were Battalion Chief William Walsh and Captain Charles Bass. Walsh was killed and could not be recovered for four days. Bass was trapped on the third floor, his skull fractured.

When the building trembled, the men on the scaling ladders held fast and were not hurt. Dr. Harry Archer, the department's medical officer, accompanied a team of firemen as they worked their way through the crumbled corridors to bring out Captain Bass.

William Giblin, president of the Mercantile Savings Deposit Company, and four employees were busy in the cellar office when

The Triangle Shirtwaist fire of March 25, 1911.

A survivor of the devastating blaze is rushed to a waiting ambulance.

One of the 146 victims of the tragic Triangle Shirtwaist fire is removed from the charred building.

Companies at work during the early stages of the January 9, 1912, Equitable Building fire.

flames began eating into the inner walls. The office windows, looking out on the Broadway sidewalk, were protected with a screen of bowed-out steel bars, two inches in diameter.

When the building caved in, two men managed to escape onto Cedar Street, but the door slammed shut behind them and the warped frame locked it fast. The burning debris from above was piled about the vault like coal in a furnace. Commissioner

Engineer of Steamer Seneca Larke, awarded the Bennett Medal for his perseverance and bravery at the Equitable fire.

Joseph Johnson and the department chaplain, Reverend McGean, were nearby and heard the trapped men's cries for help.

Two firemen worked at the bars for 30 minutes with little success. Engineer of Steamer Seneca Larke had been operating the searchlight, a theatrical spotlight used to aid firefighters working at night. With daylight breaking, Larke, a former ironworker, left his searchlight and volunteered his services to Chief Kenlon. Although reluctant to put the 37-year-old father of six into such a hazardous position, Chief Kenlon agreed.

With a new hacksaw frame and a number of blades, Larke laid on his stomach by the barred window and began cutting. At this fire – where 10 million gallons of water were used – water was pouring down on Larke by the barrel-full, freezing as it fell. Broken stones, glass, flaming embers and debris fell on Larke and the Reverend McGean, who had taken a position next to Larke to give the last rights to the imprisoned if the rescue failed.

Firefighters directed hose streams into the cellar from time to time to control the fire near the trapped men. After nearly an hour, one bar was cut free, but the opening wasn't large enough. Larke continued cutting, stopping to change worn or broken saw blades 15 times.

The rescue operation was almost one and a half hours old when the second bar finally gave way and was pulled clear. Larke called for help. Giblin and one employee were pulled to safety and then hurried to a nearby hospital. The other man had succumbed to the heavy smoke. Larke also was hospitalized.

On Medal Day, 1913, for their daring work at the Equitable fire, medals were presented to four firemen and Honorary Chief Harry Archer, M.D., who received a Department Medal. Seneca Larke, Jr., was awarded the James Gordon Bennett Medal and $500 in gold from the Bankers Police-Fire Fund.

In October 1932, 17 years after the formation of Rescue Company 1, John J. McElligott, the company's first captain and now chief of department, sent a letter to the 60th Annual Convention of the International Association of Fire Chiefs in San Diego, California:

On Tuesday, January 9, 1912, firefighters worked frantically at the burning Equitable Building to release the president of the Mercantile Safe Deposit Co. and another man who were trapped behind two-inch steel bars protecting the bank windows. It required an hour and 15 minutes for the firefighters to cut through the bars with hacksaws and during the entire time, both the rescuers and the victims were in extreme danger.

On Wednesday, January 8, 1915, a car of a subway train took fire in the subway between 50th and 59th Streets. Dense smoke and fumes were produced and several hundred people, it was estimated, were either partially or completely overcome, nearly 200 being subsequently sent to hospitals. Rescue work by members of the fire department was severely delayed due to the inability of firefighters to operate for any length of time in the smoke-filled atmosphere of the subway.

At numerous fires prior to this, where persons were overcome or injured at fires, the department had been called upon to do such meager first-aid work as limited training and equipment permitted and where skilled medical attention was not available.

Such experiences, particularly those of the Equitable Building and the subway fire, emphasized the need for special equipment and specially trained men in emergencies. On January 18, 1915, on General Order 10, Fire Commissioner Adamson announced the pending formation of a squad equipped with breathing apparatus and trained to handle unusual conditions such as smoky subway fires. The result was the organization of the first Rescue Company on January 18, 1915, which after intensive training, was placed in service March 3, 1915.

Ice-covered Chief of Department John Kenlon watches his men attack the growing Equitable fire.

1914 Cadillac touring car converted by the Department Shops into the first "Heavy Rescue Rig" in the United States.

The original members of Rescue Company 1 pose for a photo in 1915 with their state-of-the-art equipment.

For the Rescue Company's first commander, Chief Kenlon picked the young captain of Ladder Company 1, John J. McElligott. The new captain led his men into some of the most hazardous situations firemen ever had operated in before. They ventured into areas that were untenable to others without the benefit of the smoke helmets. They routinely handled ammonia leaks, sub-cellar fires, ship fires and building collapses. He and his company were making quite a name for themselves, placed in the most perilous situations, and it was only a matter of time until it caught up with them. On December 27, 1916, it did.

Fireman wearing a Draeger Smoke Helmet – 1915.

The department was called to the cellar of the Park and Tilford Company, located at 72nd Street and Columbus Avenue. Members of Engines 56 and 74 and Ladder 25 entered the sub-cellar and were confronted with a raging fire. They had pushed the flames back into one corner of the room, when suddenly, several carboys of ammonia – used in an ice-making plant – exploded. The room filled with the dangerous vapors and firemen began stumbling around, choking and searching for each other and the exit.

Rescue 1 was special-called, but not before most of the first-due companies were incapacitated. Men dropped to their knees in a vain attempt to avoid the fumes and fell to the floor, uncon-

scious. Wave after wave of firemen entered the terrible atmosphere, attempting to locate their Brothers.

Rescue 1 entered the sub-cellar and searched for missing firemen and attempted to control the blaze. They located and removed the few remaining men to the street. Most of those trapped had been saved before the Rescue Company arrived. The operation had been conducted at a severe cost. The sidewalks and street were littered with a dozen men out cold, many others gasping for breath and temporarily blinded by the ammonia fumes. Some never would return to duty.

The Rescue then operated the line for nearly an hour before the fire was extinguished. McElligott collapsed into the two and a half feet of water that had accumulated on the floor and was dragged out by his men. He had used up all the oxygen in his smoke helmet, but refused to leave until a thorough search was made and the last of the flames were stilled. McElligott then was transferred to the fireboats for a rest.

Chief Kenlon watches an engine company stretch a line up a ladder. Note photographer with tripod in foreground.

The United States entered World War I in 1917 and 420 members of the FDNY entered the armed services. Every rank from Fireman Fourth Grade to Chief of Battalion was represented. Fireman Charles J. Johnson of Engine Company 38 was the first member of the department to be killed in action on October 14, 1918. In all, seven men would make the supreme sacrifice for their country.

The enemy was found mainly in the trenches of France, but the proliferation of the German U-boats made the Atlantic a very dangerous place to be. To counter this threat and be able to press the battle across the ocean, the fleet had to be expanded, outfitted and manned. In New York City, the Brooklyn Navy Yard was in full swing, its piers crowded with ships of all types, most of them laden with ammunition.

At Pier 12, one of the largest types of submarines was preparing to put out to sea; on board was its full complement of ordinance. Together, with nearby powder magazines and the other ships, there were enough munitions to wreck the Williamsburg Bridge and a portion of Brooklyn – not to mention what a chain reaction would do to the nation's war fleet. Things were about to go wrong.

Lieutenant Francis Blessing and the members on duty – Firemen Thomas Kilbride, John Donohue, John Ryan, Frank Clark, James Smith and John Mayr – responded from their quarters on Great Jones Street, Manhattan.

The chief advised Lieutenant Blessing that the fire was raging in the battery and dynamo rooms and was venting through the front hatch, exposing nearby powder magazine. There were also 20,000 gallons of diesel fuel onboard and, to compound matters, Lieutenant Sharkey and two sailors were missing below decks.

Lieutenant Blessing and two volunteers from Rescue, Firemen Kilbride and Donohue, donned Draeger smoke helmets and entered the rear hatch into the sub. As they began advancing a hand line toward the flames, other members began the dangerous task of unloading the powder magazine. Two overcome sailors were located and moved to safety. Fireman Kilbride then found Lieutenant Sharkey, dead, in the aft battery compartment. Lieutenant Commander Trever also was rescued, but later died in the hospital.

By their courage and efficiency, the members of Rescue 1 averted what probably would have been the worst naval disaster ever to take place in the New York area. Navy officials had the highest praise for the firefighters and the job they did, fully aware of the hazards they faced.

For their heroic actions, the Fire Department awarded Class 1 Certificates of Merit to Lieutenant Blessing and Firemen Kilbride and Donohue. Class 2 awards were given to Firemen Mayr, Clark and Smith. (While in the Navy during the Boxer Rebellion, Smith had been awarded the Congressional Medal of Honor for bravery under fire.)

New York Evening Sun *pictorial showing the submarine fire of October 1918.*

On the evening of November 1, 1918, the five-car Brighton Beach local-express left the Park Row terminal of the Brooklyn Rapid Transit Company, bringing people home from a long day of work. The wood and steel, five-car train crossed the Brooklyn Bridge and headed toward Fulton Street, where it switched onto south-bound tracks and continued on to Brighton Beach. Today's commute, a familiar trip for the average rider, was becoming very different. The crowded train was running 10 minutes late and the Brotherhood of Locomotive Engineers were on strike.

Submarine 0-5, hull number SS-66, was commissioned on June 8, 1918, with Lieutenant Commander George A. Trever as its skipper. 0-5 came to the Brooklyn Navy Yard to be readied for an Atlantic crossing with its division in early autumn. Somehow, the ventilator to the battery room was left closed accidentally and, while trying the port engines on battery power, Lieutenant Commander Trever became aware of the build-up of hydrogen gas. Realizing the danger, Trever and Lieutenant W.J. Sharkey quickly began actions to avert the pending disaster.

Suddenly, the after-battery exploded. Trever, seriously injured, was forced from the area by the ensuing fire. Sharkey was missing and feared dead in the battery compartment area.

The crew made valiant efforts to control the flames but extreme heat was building up. The batteries then began generating chlorine gas and the firefighting sailors were forced to withdraw.

Realizing the need for assistance, Navy Yard officials called the New York City Fire Department. First-due units were confronted with a situation beyond even their capabilities. Arriving on the scene, Deputy Chief Patrick Maher of Division 11 sized up the situation and special-called Rescue Company 1.

Twice during the trip, the motorman (an untrained man sent out by BRT management), lost control of the train. More than half of the 1000 riders left the train in fear by the time they reached the Franklin Avenue station.

At about 6:50 p.m., the train approached the dangerous, downhill S-curve at the Malbone Tunnel in Flatbush. The sign warning trains to slow to six mph was a blur as the speeding Brighton Beach local-express left the tracks. Wood, steel and flesh crashed into the concrete walls with a deafening roar. Glass and wooden splinters flew like arrows into the helpless riders. Four hundred people plunged to an abrupt halt. The dead, dying and injured lay in the dark tunnel, pinned in the twisted wreckage.

Within minutes, fire companies were on the scene. Firemen climbed into the mangled train and began the difficult rescue operations. Two hundred fifty seriously injured passengers were carried to

The Finest Firehouse in the World

Engine Company 31 always enjoyed a comfortable firehouse. They were housed in the former quarters of Fulton Engine 21 at 116 Leonard Street in lower Manhattan. This building was slated to be sold, then demolished as part of a large-scale building project being initiated by the New York Life Insurance Company. The City then made land available to the department at Elm (Lafayette) and White Streets for a new firehouse. The size of the plot, 90- x 130-feet, was large by fire department standards.

The funding for the new building would be no problem since New York Life had paid a large sum for the land they purchased from the fire department. They also offered their architects as consultants in designing the finest fire station that could be constructed. Department architect, Napoleon LeBrun & Sons, developed a design that was distinctive and imposing in character. As the American Institute of Architects Guide to New York City states: "This was a house for fire engines, disguised as a Loire Valley chateau."

Construction started in 1894 and was completed in 1896. Engine Company 31, under the command of the legendary fire officer "Smoky Joe" Martin, was composed of four officers, four engineers and 25 firemen, who manned two steamers and two hose tenders. Temporary quarters had been secured for the company on Elm Street during the construction. Thirty-one then was joined by Water Tower 1 and the Chief of the 2nd Battalion, who moved over from Chambers Street where they had been stationed with Engine 7. Later, Fuel Depot #2, with a fuel tender and two horses, moved into the rear of the building on the White Street side.

Seventeen horses lived in stalls across the rear of the apparatus floor. The firehouse was a rather busy place, especially when an alarm sounded and 14 horses charged from their stalls and firemen slid numerous poles to the floor. In a matter of moments, the rigs, men and horses were on the streets, responding at top speed.

The huge firehouse became so famous that it actually became part of the guided bus tours that wove their way through the city's streets. The "French Chateau" firehouse became another of the wonders of downtown Manhattan, just like Chinatown, City Hall, the Tombs and the Bowery.

Motorization of the department started in 1912 and ended the need for the horses, precipitating a redesign of the apparatus floor. The disbanding of the second section of Engine 31 on July 1, 1939, provided even more room, which was given over to the Fire Emergency Division.

Malbone Street where they were transferred to hospitals. Firemen worked for hours under extremely dangerous conditions as the shorted-out third rail (an act believed to be union sabotage) was re-activated by an electrician. Ambulances were in short supply and private vehicles were pressed into action.

Ninety-seven dead passengers were removed from the tunnel and lined up in the Snyder Avenue police station and the lobby of the Ebbets Field baseball stadium, three blocks away. The dead were identified and charges were brought against the motorman and the BRT officials. All parties were acquitted after six months of legal battling.

The crash prompted the introduction of safety devices designed to prevent similar accidents. Malbone Street itself was renamed Empire Boulevard to calm scared New Yorkers.

The FDNY has faced many serious fires involving oils and other flammable liquids, but probably none as difficult and costly as two blazes that occurred only five months apart. Both fires were in Brooklyn and had a major impact on the New York City fire service for some time to come.

On Saturday, September 13, 1919, at about two p.m., a fire was noticed in Tank No. 36 in the Standard Oil Co. refining yard on Newtown Creek in the Greenpoint section of Brooklyn. The sprawling complex was more than 20 acres in size, with numerous tanks – some as large as 35,000 barrels in capacity. The yard held large quantities of naphtha, gasoline, oil and alcohol and more than 1000 barrels of other explosive and flammable liquids.

Before fire companies could be notified, gas inside the tank ignited and exploded, rocking the entire area. The force of the blast ruptured an eight-inch pipe used to fill and empty the tank. The pipe was spewing flaming oil across the ground, flooding the yard with fire. Burning oil rolled down the sloped ground and traveled unimpeded (there were no dikes, fire partitions or divisions in the yard) toward the U.S. Industrial Alcohol Co. plant. The fire protection in this area also was destroyed by the initial explosion. Flames soon filled the plant.

Box 810 was transmitted, but arriving engines found the yard hydrant system destroyed by the blast. Multiple alarms quickly were sent in as arriving chiefs realized the severity of the fire situation confronting them.

Firemen pushed hose lines into the dense, noxious smoke, trying to cool exposed tanks. FDNY fireboats moved in from the creek side and were joined by nine firefighting tugs from the Standard Oil Co. in an attempt to keep the flames from jumping the creek.

At 3:23 p.m., the first of two borough calls was transmitted by Assistant Chief "Smoky Joe" Martin. Chief Kenlon arrived and assumed command of a fire that almost covered the entire yard. Tank after tank exploded, adding more and more fuel to the fire. Operations were directed to contain the fire and protect exposed homes nearby.

A number of firemen were manning hoses, cooling two large naphtha tanks, when it was noticed that the tanks were bulging at the seams. Just as they were moving back, the tanks exploded. Firemen dove into the oil-covered rivers of water at their feet and covered each other with protective streams. Amazingly, no one was injured seriously by the blast. The fire was fought under extreme conditions and could not be brought under control for four days.

The Standard Oil Company fire in Greenpoint, Brooklyn, September 13, 1919.

Heavy smoke pumps from fires raging in large fuel storage tanks in the Standard Oil yards.

Smoky Joe Martin

One of the most famous FDNY firefighters of all time, "Smoky Joe" Martin. (Smokey the Bear was named after him.)

Probably the most colorful and well-known New York City fireman of all time was Joseph B. Martin, Smoky Joe. He was born in New York City and grew up on East 13th Street, just around the block from the quarters of Engine 5. Young Joseph knew right from the start that he wanted to be a fireman, but at his father's request, he attended City College for two years before realizing his dream on January 18, 1884, when he joined the fire department. He was assigned to Engine 27 and later transferred to Engine 5.

Martin was one of the few members of the department at that time who had a college education and it was only a matter of time until he began his rise up the promotion ladder. On November 19, 1889, he was promoted to Lieutenant, then to Captain in 1893.

As Captain, he served with Engine Companies 30, 31 and 39. While commanding Engine 31, Martin earned the famous nickname that stayed with him his entire life.

On a cold night in the winter of 1899, the Captain responded with his company to Box 41, a stubborn basement fire in a warehouse at Hubert and West Streets. The initial hose line advance proved to be nearly impossible and Martin and his crew soon were being forced back by the hot, dense smoke. Reorganizing his men, he made another push.

"Take it in relays!" he shouted, leading the nozzle team as they disappeared into the smoke. Pressing forward foot by punishing foot, they slowly advanced. After battling the fire for five minutes, the first nozzle team came stumbling out, one by one. Gasping and choking, they collapsed in the street. The next wave of men crawled in and took their place next to the Captain at the nozzle. After a while, they, too, either crawled or were dragged out of the cellar.

As the entire company was laid out in the street, the second and third alarms were transmitted. Other companies attempted to relieve on the line, but conditions in the cellar were so severe that they, too, were unable to advance. After watching yet another team stumble senseless from the cellar, Chief of Department Edward Croker, fearing further injuries to his men, ordered all members to the street. When Martin failed to leave the cellar, Croker went in himself to find him.

Croker, who was no stranger to dense smoke, followed the hose toward the sound of water rushing from the nozzle. He came upon the Captain operating the hose line alone, refusing to give up the ground his men had worked so hard to gain. Croker ordered Martin to shut the line down and

follow him outside. The Captain reluctantly agreed and together, they crawled out from the blazing cellar.

Chief Croker escorted the Captain over to a group of reporters and said of the soot-stained fire officer, "Gentlemen, this is 'Smoky Joe' Martin. By the gods, he certainly does love it."

Years later, when asked about the name, Martin replied, "No man's got a corner on the smoke market. There are thousands of men who are just as much entitled to the name as I am. And they're named everything from Ike to Aloysius."

Martin was designated as Acting Chief of Battalion in June, 1895, and then was promoted to Battalion Chief on March 1, 1900. After a stint as Acting Deputy Chief, the position was made permanent on January 1, 1906.

When Chief Croker retired in 1911, Joseph Martin was made Acting Chief of Department. Later that year, after a grueling exam, John Kenlon became the Chief of Department and Martin returned to the rank of Deputy Chief. Kenlon named Martin as Assistant Chief on January 1, 1919.

Chief Martin was a veteran of many of the worst fires seen in the city. Smoky Joe was no stranger to bravery and was placed on the Roll of Merit many times.

For 46 years, Joseph Martin battled fires in New York City. Fire after fire, "Smoky Joe" beat the odds. Injured on numerous occasions and nearly killed several times, he stubbornly refused to quit. But everyone, even Smoky Joe, has his limits.

A little after two p.m., on April 15, 1930, the department was called to a fire in a five-story, converted brownstone building, surrounded by skyscrapers on East 33rd Street, near Fifth Avenue.

An afternoon crowd of nearly 20,000 people watched the firemen fight the three-alarm blaze. The flames were confined to the upper three floors being used as an antique furniture storeroom. For two hours, the firemen worked under Martin's command.

Suddenly, the chief's legs buckled as he was about to shout a warning to a man operating on a ladder. Two firemen quickly caught the chief before he fell and carried him across the street and into a hallway. Doctor Archer administered to the chief, who asked his friend to allow himself to be taken to the hospital. The 66-year-old fire chief politely refused to give up command until the fire was under control.

Flat on his back on a stretcher, Martin watched the fire, trying to wave off two priests, busy doing their duty in Latin. Not until his son, Captain Joseph Martin, Jr., came personally with the report of the flames being extinguished, did the little chief finally relax. Martin agreed he should be taken home. Behind a flying wedge of police officers, the chief, covered with a bright red blanket, was whisked through the crowd.

Martin was placed on sick leave until he returned to active duty for one day, as Acting Chief of Department. Then Chief Medical Officer Doctor Joseph E. Smith announced that "Smoky Joe" never would be allowed to perform fire duty again, due to his heart condition.

On November 1, 1930, Martin officially was retired, a retirement that seemed to agree with him. He lived at his home on East 15th Street. From there, he responded to major fires and "buffed." Chief Martin died on October 25, 1941.

In the official report to the Board of Merit, Assistant Chief Martin and his committee stated:

...that the duty performed at the fire in the Standard Oil Plant...is deserving of the highest Commendation for the energy, efficiency, courage and fidelity displayed and the effective service rendered under the most hazardous and trying conditions...

At the recommendation of this committee, the Board of Merit awarded Service Rating Class "A" to 409 officers and firefighters who operated at the Standard Oil conflagration.

Another fire that involved dangerous flammable liquids occurred on February 26, 1920. The members of the department operated with equal bravery, but the results were catastrophic. It was about 8:10 p.m. and the night was cold and windy when units were called out to a street box alarm near the Nassau Plant of the Brooklyn Union Gas Company on Kent Avenue.

As Acting Battalion Chief Issac Ludgate rolled in, he was met by an excited plant superintendent who shouted, "For God's sake, keep it away from those two coal tar tanks or we'll be blown to hell!" Ludgate began his size-up; fire was raging in a tank of highly volatile drip oil. There were two rows of these tanks with a seven-foot passage between them. The tanks, open at the top, were housed inside a sheet-metal shed used as a pump house. The piping, pumps and valves needed for the tanks made the tight area inside even more cramped. Immediately alongside the shed were tanks of coal tar.

Engine 251 was directed to stretch a line inside the shed and cool the outside of the burning tank. Engines 211 and 221 operated lines onto the outside walls of the shed to cool them and protect the coal tar tanks. The fire had been fought for some time when Ludgate noticed oil coating the water on the floor of the shed, creating a very dangerous situation. He ordered the line to be backed out and as he helped with the withdrawal, there was a sudden flash. The firefighters were engulfed in a sheet of flames that danced across the surrounding area.

Firemen staggered from the shed, their gear in flames. A line was directed on them to extinguish the fire. Deputy Chief Patrick Maher transmitted second and third alarms as a badly burned Ludgate approached him with the report of men trapped. Maher ordered men to hold the fire spreading toward the coal tar tanks as others plunged into the dense smoke surrounding the downed firemen. All were removed from the inferno but, unfortunately, all the members of Engine 251 died as a result of their injuries.

The members lost were Captain Samuel Brown and Firemen Michael Karkel, James Brennan, James Hughes, Frank Callmeyer and Thomas Brennan. (Brennan's son, Thomas Brennan, Jr., who was 16 years old when his father was killed, would follow in his dad's footsteps and join the FDNY. He was awarded the Bennett Medal while working in Ladder Company 111.)

Because of the need to expand the Brooklyn Navy Yard in 1941, Engine 251 was moved in with Engine 211 and their quarters were razed. On November 1, 1946, Engine 251 was disbanded.

The Rockaways are a popular place for New Yorkers to pass time during the summer months – ocean breezes, salt air, the ocean and summer homes for those who can afford them. On July 15, 1922, the calm summer day was interrupted by an alarm of fire in the Far Rockaway home of Lillian Russell, a popular stage star of the day. During the fire, a chimney collapsed, instantly killing Fireman Emmet F. Donnelly of Ladder 134. Fireman Adrian B. Curnen of Engine 26, who had volunteered his services while off-duty, was taken away in critical condition and later died in the hospital. Several other firemen also were injured by the collapsing brickwork.

Later in the afternoon, while still operating at the Russell fire, Battalion Chief William Lawrence was notified of a serious fire that already was at three alarms and burning out of control in the Arverne section.

This fire situation evolved slowly at first, when Box 4962 was received at 5:15 p.m. The blaze was started when a cigarette was dropped accidentally by a painter. The fire started and the painter tried for some time to extinguish the growing flames. His efforts had no effect and only delayed notification to the fire department.

Companies – including Engine 266, which was relocated into Engine 265 – responded to the scene to witness an amazing sight. Captain Harrigan, riding in the front seat of first-due Engine 266, saw two large, 20-room homes on both sides of Beach 59th and 60th Streets burst into flames simultaneously. Embers from the blazing Hotel Nautilus ignited the dried, cedar-shake shingle roofs of the homes. Harrigan immediately ordered second, third and fourth alarms.

Chief Lawrence arrived shortly and transmitted a fifth alarm. He also requested that the water pressure in the mains feeding the fire area be increased to their maximum. Even with the fifth alarm in, Chief Lawrence and the first-alarm units were on their own for quite a while. The multiple-alarm companies had to travel from the mainland via the old Rockaway Boulevard, through Far Rockaway, down to Arverne.

The first-arriving units were unable to move into the blazing hotel. As a matter of fact, Engines 266 and 267 and Ladder 121 were driven back and forced to leave behind hose and hydrant connections. Firemen scrambled with their apparatus to escape the growing waves of heat. They made their escape under the protection of a water curtain provided by Engine 265 who, luckily just had arrived at the scene.

Engine 265 then attempted to follow the escaping rigs as the growing fire storm roared in. Their Christie Tractor failed and fleeing firemen had to leave their pumper to be consumed by the flames.

The burning buildings were raising the temperature in the area to the point that nearby wooden buildings were reaching their ignition temperatures and bursting into flames. Boats at nearby slips had to be launched to prevent their ignition.

Thirty homes were burning as Deputy Chief John O'Hara, in charge of Brooklyn and Queens, arrived at the scene. Faced with a conflagration of major proportions, the chief called for gasoline pumping engines from Brooklyn. (Motorization was not completed yet and the majority of the pumpers then being used by the department had not been designed for the long run needed to get to this remote fire.)

Deputy Chiefs Joseph B. "Smoky Joe" Martin and John Davin arrived. Chief Martin assumed command and quickly devised a plan of attack. He placed Chief O'Hara in charge of the east flank and Chief Davin in charge of the west flank. Smoky Joe was going to attack the fire from both sides at the same time.

The flames raced through homes, hotels, boardinghouses and anything that got in the way. Until now, the efforts of the firefighters had little effect on the growing fire. Some companies had to dash through to the other side to get into position to flank the body of fire. Martin also called for fireboat tender 13 and requested aid from 10 boats from the auxiliary fleet. These boats had no impact on the battle as the water was too shallow for them to operate effectively.

Relaying water from a distance, a battery of streams began to close in on the body of fire and drive toward its heart. "Smoky Joe," right in the forefront, led the attack. The plucky old chief crouched behind a door, using it as a shield to protect him from the waves of heat. He directed operations as pumpers moved into position, covered by the streams of the engines they passed. The engines leap-frogged deeper and deeper into the inferno.

At about nine p.m., the western front held and the advance of the wall of flames was halted. Firemen finally had the upper hand. Watch lines were put into position as most of the victorious firemen were withdrawn. The watch lines continued to operate until seven p.m. on June 17th.

The losses were severe: 13.5 acres and 141 structures, valued at $2 million. Because of this blaze, fire-resistant roofs were mandated and an additional engine company was established in Far Rockaway.

About a month after the Arverne fire, Chief Kenlon went on vacation leave and named Chief Martin his replacement as Acting Chief of Department. Smoky Joe then faced one of the most difficult building fires in the city's history. This blaze caused the death of two firefighters, one directly and the other indirectly.

The Manufacturer's Transit Company occupied a large, seven-story, fire-resistive garage converted into a warehouse. The building extended from Jane Street through the block to West 12th Street. During the morning hours of July 18, 1922, workers were seen loading wooden cases in a large freight elevator (originally designed to carry automobiles).

Suddenly, one of the cases exploded, scattering the workers. The ensuing fire spread to other cases, prompting other explosions. Some of the workers attempted to throw sand on the burning boxes to no avail. A merchant watching from his store across the street ran to pull the fire alarm box. At 8:15 a.m., Box 593 was received by the Manhattan Fire Dispatchers Office.

The flames spread quickly up the open elevator shaft and soon reached the roof. Cases were burning briskly in the street, a fountain of white sparks shooting from the boxes, at times reaching as high as the three- and four-story buildings nearby. Black, acrid smoke pumped from the roof was settling down like a blanket across the street as the first of the fire apparatus arrived. Faced with a severe fire condition that was threatening to spread soon, efforts were made to get hose lines into position and simultaneously get all the people out of the nearby buildings.

As companies responded in, they reported to Martin at the front of the building. Lieutenant Schoppmeyer of Engine 13 and members of his company began to enter the fire building when a major explosion rocked the warehouse. The officer and his men were thrown backward and before they could regain their feet, an avalanche of debris descended upon them. The firemen frantically dug each other out. Suffering what would be fatal injuries, Lieutenant Schoppmayer quickly was uncovered and gently carried away. The fire officer lived long enough to be given the Last Rites at the scene.

Acting Chief Martin and nearly every fireman working near the warehouse also were knocked flat by the same blast. Smoky Joe was blown backward across Jane Street through a closed wooden door. A blinding flash and a shower of bricks enveloped Greenwich Village. A sheet of flames reached across Jane Street and nearly ignited a garage under construction.

Multiple-alarm units began arriving in numbers and Chief Martin, his face badly burned, ordered their placement. Hose lines were stretched from every available high-pressure hydrant. Lines even were stretched from two blocks away, through cellars and across streets to the fire.

Mayor Hyland arrived and was given a rundown by Smoky Joe. As they stood knee-deep in the run-off water, the chief said, "Mister Mayor, this is the toughest and worst fire I've ever witnessed in all my career in the fire department." Five alarms and a Borough Call

Chief Martin briefs Mayor and Mrs. Hyland and a police Captain at the scene of a multiple-alarm fire.

were placed, the largest assembly of apparatus for a building fire since the Equitable Building fire 10 years earlier.

While relocating to the quarters of Engine 207 (which was at the fire), Engine Company 210 struck a curb at the Flatbush Avenue extension and Johnson Street. Fireman James H. Malone was killed and Fireman James Carroll was injured seriously when they were thrown from the rear step of the apparatus.

Dense smoke enveloped the entire neighborhood. Martin's command post in front of the building was in the thick of it and he maintained this position as he ordered the placement of the 63 hose lines that had been stretched from 16 high-pressure hydrants and pumpers. Two water towers were put into operation and more than 28,000 gallons per minute were being directed into the building.

At 4:30 p.m., Martin finally was convinced to report to Doctor Harry M. Archer. "Smoky Joe," with his faced burned and eyelashes and eyebrows singed, had his inflamed eyes bandaged by the doctor, who himself was suffering from lacerations, contusions and had been overcome by smoke. Martin then directed operations from a cot, placed in a window of a store across the street from the fire before returning to his post at eight p.m.

Because of the building contents – photographic flash powder, whiskey, tons of rubber and rolled newsprint – the fire was defying all efforts to extinguish it. The fire acted in a strange fashion. From time to time, it would erupt. Building parts, bricks, windows, doors, glass, the building's contents and flames would shoot into the sky. Due to this unusual situation, the fire became known as the "Greenwich Village Volcano."

Finally, the fire was declared under control at 6:15 p.m. the next day (July 19). Water still was being poured on the smoldering remains. Investigations revealed that cases of magnesium powder, stored without the proper permits, was the reason for the explosions. Firefighters initially believed the sparks were from fireworks and the application of water on the magnesium caused a violent reaction.

The blaze re-ignited at midnight the next night and required four engines to knock down the flames. To complicate an already difficult situation, a deranged man ran into the fire-ravaged structure. He soon appeared at a smoke-

filled, third-floor window. Deputy Chief Helm asked for volunteers to remove the man. Firemen Steven Hanan, Thomas Ward and Lee Easop groped their way up the darkened stairs and dragged the man back to the street where he was restrained physically and taken to Bellevue Hospital.

January 27, 1927, was the coldest day in 56 years. With the thermometer reading in the teens, Brooklyn firemen operated at a second alarm in the American Molasses Company, located at the foot of Richard Street. This quick-spreading afternoon fire featured an aerial ladder rescue made by the members of Ladder 101. A man was saved from the roof of the burning building.

Box 55-433, a fifth alarm for a fire in a rag shop on East 5th Street, January 12, 1924.

Chief Martin and Chief Helm confer during fire operations.

The mercury continued to drop as the day wore on. At eight p.m. that blustery night, smoke was seen coming from the third floor of 144 Goerck Street and the alarm was transmitted. (Goerck Street was located under the Williamsburg Bridge and ran from East Houston Street to Grand Street.) Responding to Manhattan Box 416 were Engines 11, 15, 25 and 28, Ladder Companies 11 and 18, the Third and Fourth Battalions and two fireboats, the *William L. Strong* (Engine 66) from Grand Street and the *Seth Low* (Engine 232) from Noble Street in Brooklyn.

Department units arrived to an advanced fire condition in the seven-story loft building. A number of explosions accelerated the fire and hastened its spread upward. Companies set up for an exterior attack as second and third alarms were struck. Ten additional engines, two ladder companies, a Water Tower, Rescue 1 and the fireboat *The New Yorker* were dispatched. Also responding were the Chiefs of the Second Battalion, the 19th Battalion (Marine Battalion) and First Division.

After an hour, it appeared that the fire was knocked down enough to allow companies to enter the structure for the last stages of the battle and then overhauling. Assistant Chief "Smoky Joe" Martin and Deputy Chief Henry Helm were conferring on the possibility of releasing units, as members of Engine 77 and Engine 9 entered the fire area with hand lines.

Without warning, the building collapsed. A huge, debris-filled hole from the seventh floor to the basement now imprisoned the men of at least two companies. Firemen reacted immediately, but attempts to enter through the front entrance proved impossible. As fallen ladders were being raised, an injured fire officer crawled from the debris and appeared at the second-floor window, then fell from sight. Moments later, he was removed and the search for the trapped men started. The fire began to rage again; the flames had to be controlled without jeopardizing the imprisoned men.

Shortly after the digging began, a fireman was found and slowly uncovered. Still pinned and injured, he requested a priest who, a short while later, crawled on hands and knees through the charred and twisted remains of the collapsed building to the trapped man and administered the Last Rites.

At about 11 p.m., after hours of careful digging, he was freed. Shortly thereafter, two additional firemen were found and removed unconscious to Gouveners Hospital. The fire now was extinguished and the only battle remaining for the firemen was with the ice and frozen rubble. A groan was heard and new spirit removed the fatigue from the weary rescuers. They renewed their work with the strength of fresh men.

Two more firemen were found and, after a careful tunneling operation, they were rescued. Two more firemen were located among the timbers but, unfortunately, they were dead. The hopes of finding men still alive dwindled as the night dragged on.

Many of the companies were placed back in service. Rescue 1 worked on into the morning, using spotlights and block and tackle to remove timbers and other debris. At 6:20 a.m., the last fireman was found in an upright position, still holding the nozzle. All work was stopped as a priest was summoned.

Later, it was determined the cause of the collapse was a build-up of ice on the building, added to the tons of water soaked up by stock on the upper floors.

For their collective bravery and perseverance under tremendously dangerous conditions, the Board of Merit placed the names of all the men of Engines 11, 15, 17, 25, 33 and 55, Ladders 6, 9, 10, 11, 18 and 20 and Rescue 1 on the Roll of Merit. A total of 112 members were awarded a Class II.

On the corner of Broadway and 66th Street in Manhattan stood the Lincoln Square Arcade Building. This six-story structure was home to more than 250 people (mostly writers and artists in residence and their families). At 11:30 p.m., on January 29, 1931, a fire was discovered in the building. It was a freezing night, with the wind blowing in off the Hudson River. First-alarm units rolled in and went to work on the fast-spreading fire, already on its way to the roof. Chief William Bowen, of the Ninth Battalion, transmitted a third alarm on his arrival, as occupants streamed out into the frigid night air.

The speed of the fire extension and the heavy smoke spreading throughout the structure trapped those unable to exit quickly or those not hearing the initial cries of their neighbors. Ladder Company 25 quickly moved their aerial ladder into position and rescued a woman trapped at a fourth-floor window. Braving the roaring flames, several dangerous rescues were made by firemen inside the building.

The northwest wind was pushing the flames throughout the building, yet firemen continued to attack the fire aggressively. Dangerous attempts were made to control the fire in the stairways to allow the searches to continue.

Engine 26 was protecting the stairs on the fourth floor when the stairs collapsed beneath them. Battalion Chief Bowen and seven members of 26 plunged two stories with the falling debris. The trapped men were removed quickly by other firemen as an emergency treatment area was set up by Doctor Archer. Some were treated at the scene; others were hospitalized.

Chief McElligott stood in the street, ice forming on his coat and helmet, rivers of freezing water racing around his feet. He already had transmitted a fourth alarm and a fifth alarm and then decided to transmit a *simultaneous alarm*. (Basically, this was a borough call within the same borough.) Signal 9-9-982-3-3326 rang across the bell circuits. This brought nearly 60 percent of all the fire companies in Manhattan to the fire.

Thirty-five engines poured tons of water into the burning structure. Four water towers – including the 65-footer assigned to Water Tower 3 – were operating. Hose lines were placed on the roof tops of all exposed buildings.

The fire was under control at 2:15 a.m., following more than two hours of heavy firefighting. Seventeen people, including nine firemen, were injured. Miraculously, no lives were lost.

John J. McElligott assumed command of the uniformed force with his appointment as Chief of Department on March 1, 1932. Two months later, on May 5th, the department responded to a five-alarm blaze at the Cunard Docks at 14th Street and the North (Hudson) River. Almost 300 firemen were overcome or injured by the thick, creosote-laced smoke.

Five alarms and a borough call were needed to extinguish a fire that began under the boardwalk in Coney Island on July 13, 1932. Four city blocks burned as 43 engines, 12 ladders and men without apparatus converged on the scene. Approximately 5000 people were left homeless as the fire spread from concession stands to apartment houses to bathhouses and private homes.

August 1, 1932, was a beautiful day in Manhattan and across the city. The Ritz Tower Hotel at Park Avenue and 57th Street had many visitors ready for a day of sightseeing and window-shopping, in and around the hotel. In a storeroom in the second sub-cellar, a building engineer noticed smoke issuing from a paint vault. The vault itself was nine- by six-feet and nine feet high and was contained in a storeroom that was 30- by 45-feet with 12-foot ceilings. The vault, not vented to the outside air, contained paints, kerosene, gasoline, turpentine, varnish remover and other flammables.

The engineer attempted to fight the fire with a house standpipe hose unsuccessfully and was forced to exit through the single door leading in and out of the storeroom, only to return with the chief engineer. Now unable to even approach the vault area, they finally sent a man to call the fire department. At 10:36 a.m., Box 918 sent Engines 26, 8, 65 and 39 and Ladder Companies 2 and 16, along with two Battalion Chiefs and Acting Deputy Chief Roche.

Upon arrival, Engines 8 and 39 stretched a line down the stairs to the cellar area. The smoke these companies encountered proved to be impenetrable. After several attempts, Rescue Company 1 was special-called for use of their masks.

Companies still were attempting to press to the seat of the fire and a ladder was placed down through a sidewalk hoistway to the sub-cellar. Members descended to the base of the small shaft to force the door leading into the building from the hoistway shaft. At the sidewalk level, a line was fed down to the nozzle team.

Firefighters were taking quite a bit of smoke while working in the interior staircase. Engines 39 and 8 followed Ladders 16 and 12 as they continued searching for a way to reach the fire. Rescue 1 had arrived and members of that company, wearing filter masks and smoke helmets, began to enter the building.

As the door at the base of the sidewalk hoistway was forced open, a violent explosion shook the building. The tile partition of the paint locker crumbled and became airborne shrapnel. The sidewalk hoistway elevator track was twisted and deformed and the two 15-ton machines of the ammonia system ruptured. Flames roared over the heads of the firemen in the hallway just outside the storeroom, as they were hurled violently to the floor and covered with debris.

All electric power to the building was knocked out, plunging the smoke-filled structure into darkness. Clocks in the building stopped; the time was 10:56 a.m. The dense smoke condition now became total blackness. Injured men groped, searching for their Brother firemen. Stunned, they tried to lead each other out; many were injured seriously.

Three minutes after the first blast, a second – even more powerful – explosion occurred. The windows in a jewelry store splintered and, along with gems from the displays, were blown across the Avenue. All the firemen, police officers and civilians in the immediate area were thrown to the ground. One fireman was thrown up through the hoistway shaft, from the sub-cellar to the street.

A second alarm was transmitted and ropes were lowered down the shaftway. The dead and injured were hauled up.

Firemen sat in the glass-covered street, burned, cut and bleeding, blackened from the blast. They tended the wounded as best they could until arrival of the ambulances and second-alarm units. Firemen arriving on the second alarm began to attack the fire. The fire was extinguished without any further extension.

The cost to the department was extreme; eight men dead, eight injured seriously and many other firemen, policemen and civilians injured, mostly cut by flying glass. Those who were killed in the line of duty were Lieutenants Cosgrove, Engine 65, and Harnett, Ladder 16, and Firemen Daly and Maloney of Engine 39, Finn and Greene of Engine 65, Hardina, Ladder 16, and Pratt, Ladder 7.

The investigations into the explosions never reached a definite conclusion pinpointing the causes. However, steps were taken (automatic sprinkler and alarm systems to protect sub-surface areas) to ensure similar situations would not occur again in the future.

On April 13, 1933, FDNY units converged on a smoky fire in the Morris Packing Company on Brook Avenue in the Bronx. Four alarms were transmitted as firemen began the long, involved battle. During the operation, an excited citizen ran up to the chief and reported a fire with numerous people trapped in a nearby tenement at 506 Brook Avenue. Box 2209 was received at 2:02 a.m. (now April 14th) and companies scrambled from the scene of the multiple alarm and raced to the tenement.

Battalion Chief John J. McElligott, later to become Chief of Department.

The situation was so urgent that a Deputy Chief filled in as a tillerman on one of the ladder trucks. First-arriving units found the fire in complete possession of the stairway from the first floor to the roof. Several families were reported cut off on the top three floors in the rear of the building.

An aerial ladder was placed to the fifth floor and Fireman George J. Grau of Ladder 26 entered the window under severe conditions and began his search. Lieutenant John J. Metz, also of Ladder 26, followed Grau into the window. Flames were pouring out of a bedroom door, stopping the rescue team. Fireman Grau crawled up to the door and was able to close the door, thus buying some time.

Lieutenant Metz then searched for and located several members of the Brosinki family. A 60-year-old man and a 22-year-old woman were passed out to members on the aerial ladder. Fireman Grau then carried two children to safety as Lieutenant Metz brought two additional women to the aerial ladder. Their daring rescue at extreme personal risk saved a family and earned the firefighters medals for valor.

Not all fires faced by the FDNY involve multiple alarms and tremendous numbers of firefighters. Quite often, the most severe conditions encountered by firemen are at "all-hands fires." One such job was faced by Brooklyn companies in the early-morning hours of November 3, 1933. Signal Station 1664 was transmitted for a fire in a three-story, wood-frame building at 361 Bristol Street. It was just after three a.m. and flames were burning up the stairway and into apartments on each floor as Ladder 120 arrived.

Fireman Charles H. Smith ran to the rear, carrying a 25-foot portable ladder. Smith climbed up to the second floor setback and entered a window that was chugging thick smoke. Smith, driven to the floor, began a search. He came across the unconscious form of the Reverend William Carter lying on the floor. Fireman Smith grabbed the man and dragged him back toward the window.

Under extreme heat and smoke conditions, he was able to pass the Reverend out the window to firemen, who carried him to the ground. Smith was helped down, suffering from "smoke narcosis" and placed on medical leave. Smith later was awarded a medal for this rescue.

On the last three days of 1933, the city was in the grip of a major cold spell. Firemen struggled to operate as the department responded to more than 1700 alarms. New Year's Eve provided the largest fire of the year, as flames swept the nine-story Brevoort Hotel on Brevoort Place in Brooklyn. Five alarms and then a borough call were placed to provide the manpower and equipment needed to bring the blaze under control.

Election night in New York City brought bonfires and vacant building fires, year after year. Extra manpower was held as chief officers expected the worst. In 1934, the FDNY responded to 747 alarms on election night, extinguishing 1670 bonfires. The response to these fires required the use of pumpers, hose wagons, police and even the street-cleaning "flushers."

On February 23, 1940, Chief John J. McElligott retired as chief, but continued on as Commissioner. Mayor LaGuardia named Patrick Walsh as Acting Chief of Department. The 40-year veteran served much of his career as a downtown Manhattan fireman and had worked many of the most famous blazes in the city, including the Equitable Building and Triangle Shirtwaist Factory fires. McElligott retired from his role as commissioner on May eighth and the mayor appointed Walsh to take his place.

The responsibilities of chief were expanding greatly as the nation watched the growing problems in Europe and Asia. A war seemed imminent and New York, as a major port, would have to be protected. Many still remembered the lessons learned during the first war, when German saboteurs left a trail of destruction and fire in their wake.

With the threat of war looming over the city, the FDNY sent three members to observe firsthand the operations of the London Fire Brigade as they faced the "London Blitz."

Battalion Chiefs Frederic J.G. Wedemeyer and Daniel A. Deasy and Fireman George T.J. Scott flew to England in October of 1940. The New Yorkers toured the London area, met with engineers, architects, military attaches, London County Council members and Chief Officers of the Fire Brigade.

They then fell into a familiar routine of responding and working with the fire crews at night after the bombing, then examining the damage and attending meetings the next day.

The trio also visited Coventry (very hard hit by the bombers), Birmingham and Liverpool. For three months, they dodged bombs and collapsing buildings and battled flames and fatigue. They returned to New York on January 14, 1941. All three were awarded medals.

One of the most stubborn fires in Department history – The Furman Street Fire, April 20, 1935, Brooklyn.

A 20-flag FDNY color guard and the FDNY band led the sold-out crowd in the National Anthem at the Midnight Alarm.

The most stubborn fire in the history of the New York City Fire Department occurred on April 20, 1935, in a Brooklyn waterfront warehouse complex filled with crude rubber. The fire was reported at 1:15 p.m. and went to five alarms in quick succession. The "Furman Street Fire" involved a row of five-story warehouses that faced the water.

One hour and 15 minutes after the initial alarm, a Master Station was transmitted, followed by a second. For 18 hours, firemen battled the blaze, forced to operate in a dense smoke condition. Fireboats fed lines to water towers and deck pipes. In all, 66 streams were directed on the fire to finally bring it under control. This fire caused 1068 injuries, mostly to firemen, hundreds of whom were blinded temporarily by the pungent smoke.

The year 1935 saw two performances of *The Midnight Alarm,* a show presented by the Department on two nights in Madison Square Garden. The funds raised by the show were used to purchase an ambulance for the Boroughs of Brooklyn and Queens.

Two-way radios were installed on all fireboats in 1937.

Hugh A. Halligan

Halligan is much more than the name of one of the most versatile of firefighting tools. The tool's namesake was a fireman who made more than a name for himself. Hugh A. Halligan was appointed a New York City Fireman on June 16, 1916, and assigned to Engine Company 88. Halligan's career was interrupted by service in the army during World War I. Upon his return, he was assigned to Engine 35 and worked there until he was promoted to Lieutenant on April 16, 1922. The new officer worked In Engine 22 for two years before he was promoted to Captain on February 1, 1924. He commanded Engines 86, 82, 35 and 73 before being appointed a Battalion Chief on June 1, 1929.

On October 1, 1934, two weeks after his 40th birthday, Hugh Halligan, reached the rank of Deputy Chief. Commissioner Patrick Walsh appointed Halligan First Deputy Fire Commissioner on August 20, 1941. He had risen from the ranks and become one of the top men on both sides of the command structure in just 22 years.

It is the tool Chief Halligan designed, refined and manufactured that virtually gave him fire service immortality. The first forcible entry tool in the FDNY was the claw tool, a heavy and basically "off-centered" tool that was especially dangerous to the man holding it as it was driven into doors. The next generation forcible entry tool was the "Kelly Tool," named for Captain John F. Kelly of Ladder Company 163. This tool removed the curved end at the striking end, allowing a straight drive. The down side of the tool was its great weight.

Various other tools came along with improvements in design, but were welded and subject to breaking. They still were heavy. Chief Halligan worked on possible designs and methods of manufacture for quite awhile: "My primary thought was to provide the firemen with an easily handled, light, straight-drive tool that would be used with confidence."

Every curve, corner and dimension of the tool was studied and changed many times by the "trial and error" method before the dies were laid down. The result was a tool that could be held in one hand; one that would not chip or break at a critical moment; would not fatigue a man; and could be used with safety and full efficiency.

The first tools then were made. They represented 18 hours of labor. They were cross-drop forged from one piece of No. 4140 (high carbon content) steel, weighed only 8.5 pounds and were designed to protect the arms, hands and body of the user. The first tool was handed to Fire Commissioner and Chief of Department John McElligott who twirled the tool around in his hand and examined it closely. He turned it from side to side, checked each of the striking points available, then turned to Chief Halligan and said, "You can do anything with this tool."

In a short time, the tool went on the market and was a success. The Boston Fire Department bought one for every ladder truck. The FDNY struck a roadblock though, when it was decided that there was a "conflict of interests" with a member of the department selling tools to the department. The department's hands were tied and could not purchase the tools. Ladder companies across the city began to buy the tools with their own money until eventually the problem with purchasing the tools officially was straightened out.

Today, few, if any, of the original "Halligan tools" are being used. Tools with the basic design, with slight improvements (of which the chief would have been proud) even though they have their own names, still are called "Halligans" by the fire service.

On September 5, 1938, the World's Fair 55th Battalion was organized. Two new Engine Companies, 331 and 332, were organized and placed in service on the grounds of the fair. Two 1000-gallon Ahrens-Fox pumpers were assigned to Engine 331, temporarily made into a double company. They were located near the northeast end of the grounds, near the Administration Building. Engine 332 was assigned a 500-gallon Ahrens-Fox and stationed near the Horace Harding Gate.

T he new fireboat, *Fire Fighter*, was placed in service at Battery Park in lower Manhattan on November 16, 1938.

Firemen are called upon to make rescues of every type. One unusual incident occurred under Brooklyn's Foster Avenue, in the sewer line on February 15, 1939. Three men working for the W.P.A. (Works Progress Administration) were cleaning sewer lines when a sudden flood trapped them inside a trunk sewer line. Rescue Company 2 arrived and life preservers were procured from a fireboat. Fireman Frederick C. Smith volunteered to make an attempt to reach the trapped men. Smith removed his outer clothing and donned a life preserver and life belt and coiled 20 feet of rope. With a rope attached to the life belt, he climbed down into the sewer. In total darkness, he swam about 300 feet and located the men.

Fireman Smith took the loose rope and attached each of the men to himself. He then signaled the firemen on the street above to pull up the rope attached to his belt. The rescuer and the rescued were pulled into position below the manhole opening, where they were pulled up and out, one by one.

It was nearing 1:30 a.m. on June 10, 1939, and the Staten Island Ferry was running at full speed in the lower harbor. One of the passengers, Fireman Olaf W. Matson of Ladder 80, was informed that a man was drowning. Matson leaped from the boat into the water and started for the drowning man.

The fireman swam more than 200 feet to reach the man, a crewman of the British freighter, *City of Manchester*. He literally had jumped ship. Matson struggled in the water with the man for a half-hour before the ferry could be turned around. Both men then were pulled from the water.

On May 30, 1939, Engine Company 224 arrived at Storehouse No. 66, located at the foot of Joralemon Street in Brooklyn. Two men, who were removing sediment from the bottom of a buried tank, were overcome by gas. With no masks available, Fireman James Hussey volunteered to enter the tank and attempt to remove the men.

Hussey was lowered by rope and immediately rolled both men onto their backs to prevent them from drowning in the water at the bottom of the tank. Hussey then attempted to raise one of the men, but collapsed himself and immediately was removed from the tank. He was given inhalator treatment and regained consciousness. The men were removed by members wearing masks.

Another sewer rescue evolved on August 23, 1939, when an employee of the Bureau of Sewers was overcome while working in a sewer 57 feet below street level at the intersection of Hanson and Fort Greene Places, Brooklyn. Rescue Company 2 arrived and Fireman Harold A. Barker, wearing a mask, descended into the sewer. Barker searched for and found the man, dragging him to a point where they both could be pulled to the street.

During the rescue, Barker's mask was dislodged, causing the fireman also to be rendered unconscious. He was revived in the street.

For their efforts at these various emergencies, Firemen Smith, Matson and Barker were awarded medals.

On August 18, 1941, a flash fire spread to stored hemp and sisal on Pier 27 at the foot of Baltic Street in Brooklyn. Thirty-four civilians were killed as the flames raced through the pier and spread to the *S.S. Panaco,* a Cuban freighter moored nearby. The dangers of protecting the piers and waterfront again proved extremely hazardous and difficult.

Despite the strong objections of Mayor LaGuardia, members of the department pressed to enlist in the armed forces as America went to war. Between June and October of 1941, 83 members of the FDNY changed their blue fire uniforms for those of the Army, Navy and Marines. By the end of the war, 1832 firemen were serving in the military.

To supplement the strength of the firefighting force – especially in case of enemy attack on the city – an Auxiliary Corps was formed. These civilian volunteers responded on FDNY apparatus and supported department operations with exterior functions. They helped stretch hose, operated deck pipes and helped in any way they could. This program remained active for the duration of the war and provided a trained and dedicated additional force if needed.

It was a bitterly cold night on January 8, 1942, when a blaze broke out in the New York Central Railroad pier at Municipal Pier 83, located on 12th Avenue and 42nd Street in Manhattan. Box 783 was transmitted at 5:14 a.m. and reached five alarms before it was brought under control. Numerous firemen were overcome by the dense smoke and many others suffered from frostbite. The hose wagon of Engine 65 plunged through the burning pier into the Hudson River. A fire officer also fell into the river and had to be rescued by his comrades.

While this fire was being fought, another was being battled in a loft building on Sixth Avenue and 13th Street. Four alarms and two water towers were needed to quell this blaze.

The liner Normandie *burned and capsized in February of 1942.*

On February 9, 1942, five alarms were transmitted for a major fire onboard the *S.S. Lafayette*, known until recently as *The Normandie*. The ship was being converted from a luxury liner into a troop transport when a welder's torch accidentally started a fire among piles of stored life preservers. The 1000-foot-long ship held hundreds of workers who were rescued by responding firemen. Naval personnel, including sailors using semaphore flags to send messages back and forth between the ship and the chiefs on shore, helped firefighters battle the blaze. The ship capsized the following morning. It then became a training site for Navy divers. The salvage operation took many months and the Navy used it as a school for hard hat divers until the ship eventually was righted and restored to service.

O n Valentine's Day, 1942, Mayor LaGuardia made the following remarks in regard to the war clouds darkening the horizon:

All along the Atlantic Coast, we must be ready every hour of the day and night. Our industrial cities are natural objects of attack and New York is one of the most important...

The United States entered the war in December 1942.

By the beginning of 1943, the manpower levels of the FDNY were becoming acute and Chief Walsh established Squad 21 in the quarters of Ladder Company 24 at 115 West 38th Street in Manhattan. This unit provided needed extra manpower at the scene of major fires. (During the first world war, a squad company was placed in service at the quarters of Engine 40 on West 68th Street. The manpower it provided, however, was made up of civilian volunteers, rather than uniformed members of the department.)

Two additional squads were formed during the war; Squad 24 was organized on November 30, 1943, in the quarters of Engine Company 204 in Brooklyn and Squad 22 was organized on January 20, 1944, in the quarters of Engine 20 in Manhattan. These additional units prompted the temporary closing of the two engine companies. After the war, all three squads were disbanded and Engine 204 and Engine 20 were reorganized.

At 5:30 p.m. on April 24, 1943, the Jersey City Fire Department was notified of a fire onboard the steamship *El Estero,* which was docked at the Caven Point Terminal at the foot of Chappel Avenue in Jersey City, New Jersey. The ship was being loaded with ammunition bound for the war. Twenty minutes after the initial alarm was received, Jersey City requested help from New York City's fireboats. Engine 57, the fireboat *Fire Fighter* (now known as Marine 1), and Engine 86, the fireboat *John J. Harvey* (now known as Marine 2), responded with Acting Deputy Chief John J. Hurton in command. Hurton and Battalion Chief John J. Lowery responded to the fire in the tender *Smoke.*

The burning ship was being moved away from the Jersey docks by two tugboats as the FDNY boats arrived. Chief Hurton checked the tides and decided to have the *El Estero* towed toward Robbins Reef Light in New York Bay. It was hoped that if the fire caused the detonation of the munitions, damage would be limited to the surrounding waterfront. During the towing operation, the entire New York Harbor area was at peril. At any moment, the *El Estero* could detonate and ravage the buildings and ships along both sides of the river.

Using hawsers (very thick ropes), the tugboats pulled the ship toward the lower harbor, as flames roared below decks in the ammunition ship. The fire obviously was gaining in intensity and fireboat crews were well aware of the blazing ship's cargo. One hold contained blockbuster bombs, each of which weighed 4000 pounds. Nearby holds contained magnesium bombs and other explosives.

Chief Hurton had two choices: either the fire had to be extinguished or the burning ship sunk before the flames reached the stored bombs. The two fireboats moved in, monitors flowing. Twenty-five streams were directed into *El Estero.* The ship finally surrendered to the attacking fireboats and submerged to its superstructure about a half mile northeast of the Robbins Reef Light.

On Medal Day, Mayor Fiorello LaGuardia pinned 26 Department Medals (recognizing Class 1 valor) on the chests of the crew members of the two fireboats. Eleven of these men also were presented citizens medals for their valor.

With the great number of firefighters who answered the call to arms and were overseas serving in all branches of the armed services, the remaining members of the department were called upon to protect the homefront from the added dangers the war brought to the city. Sabotage, stores of munitions and increased activity on the waterfront were just a few of the potential problems.

On the positive side, firefighters were extremely active in War Bond drives. They also spearheaded blood donation programs and other morale-building activities.

After nearly four years of war and its horrors, New Yorkers and other Americans across the country were shocked at what transpired on July 28, 1945. A U.S. Army B-25 Bomber crashed into the north side of the Empire State Building shortly before 10 a.m. A thunderous crash was heard throughout midtown Manhattan and the streets and neighboring structures were covered with glass and debris. Engine 1, Ladder 24 and the Third Division, housed only blocks away on 31st Street, were on their way before the alarm box was pulled.

The twin-engined plane, lost in a dense fog, crashed into the building at a point more than 915 feet above the street. Fourteen people, including three occupants of the plane and 11 people working in the building, were killed. Twenty-six others were injured. The plane wings were sheared off by the impact, but the fuselage and engines ripped a hole 18-feet-wide and 20-feet-high in the outer wall of the 78th and 79th floors. Flames then shot as high as the 86th-floor observatory, 1050 feet above Fifth Avenue, as the bomber's gasoline tanks exploded. One engine hurtled across the 78th floor, crashed through the south wall, then plunged into a penthouse/art studio of a 13-story loft building on West 33rd Street.

Rivers of flaming gasoline poured through the 78th and 79th floors of the Empire State Building. The most severely affected areas were the offices of the National Catholic Welfare Conference and their War Relief Services. It was in these offices that the 11 people were killed. Seven employees were able to take refuge in a small office space on the floor and later were rescued by members of the fire department.

In addition to the raging fire at the point of impact, a major fire also was developing in the basement, at the base of one of the elevator shafts. A third fire was evident in the top floor of the loft building on 33rd Street.

Gerhardt Bryant, Deputy Chief of the Third Division, was the first Chief Officer on the scene and immediately assumed command. He ordered two engine companies and one hook and ladder, under the direction of Chief Massett of the Seventh Battalion, to operate on the fires within the Empire State Building itself. One engine company and one hook and ladder from the first-alarm assignment were sent across the street to 10 West 33rd Street, where a fire was burning vigorously on the roof and in the top-floor studio.

Second, third and fourth alarms quickly were transmitted at 9:55, 9:59 and 10 a.m., respectively. The 24 responding companies and special-called apparatus were deployed between either of the two buildings involved. Fifteen standpipe lines were stretched and placed into operation to bring the fires in the Empire State Building under control.

The coordination of firefighting efforts at three separate, yet related fires, was enhanced greatly by use of the department's relatively new short-wave radio backpack sets. Operated by Firemen Meyerson and Gertzen, they helped to fill the void made by the loss of telephone communications to the upper floors of the Empire State Building.

The fire was under control 19 minutes after the initial alarm was transmitted and was extinguished entirely within 40 minutes. The official report by the department stated the following about damage to the Empire State Building:

Building, 78th floor: Considerable
Contents: Slight

Building, 79th floor: Considerable
Contents: Considerable

Building, 80th Floor: Slight
Contents: Trifling

"G" and "F" elevator shafts: Considerable

Fire Commissioner and Chief of Department Patrick Walsh reported to Mayor LaGuardia:

Because of the excellent character of their work performed under circumstances most novel and most hazardous, I feel impelled, in the name of the people of the City of New York, to recommend to the Board of Merit of this Department that all Chief Officers and all Company Officers who reported to Station 4-4-681, and all Members of Companies or Units that responded on the First or Second Alarms, receive a Service Rating "A" for their work done with initiative, capability and personal bravery. For all other Members who operated at this fire, I recommend a Service Rating "B."

In 1945, a special medal was endowed by the Uniformed Firemen's Association to be awarded annually to the families of FDNY members who died in the line of duty. The Fireman's Medal of Supreme Sacrifice was designed by a special committee and bears on the front a bas relief figure of a fireman carrying a child from a burning building. This design was taken from an oil painting by C. C. Beal, a war correspondent and artist with *Collier's Weekly*. Beal also had been the official illustrator for the Treasury Department for War Bond drives of World War II.

A view from above the point of impact made by a B-25 into the 78th and 79th floors of the Empire State Building, July 28, 1945.

In the cellar, firemen battled the fire, while people trapped in fallen elevators were rescued. To reach the upper floors, men had to climb stairs from the 60th floor to the 78th and 79th to fight the blaze. Broken standpipe risers also had to be bypassed manually with hose lines to get water to the upper floors. Spectacular rescues were made under cover of hose streams as firemen pushed their way through the high-octane, gasoline-fed fire.

To control the loft fire at 10 West 33rd Street, three engines and two trucks, as well as a water tower, were needed to subdue the stubborn flames. Chief George A. Winter of the Sixth Battalion assumed command of the fire burning on the roof in the elevator bulkhead and the top-floor combination art studio and living quarters. Three lines were stretched from the standpipe and extinguished the fire.

Without a doubt, the fact that the crash occurred on a Saturday contributed to the fact that only 14 lives were lost. On a weekday, as many as a thousand people could have been affected by the devastation.

Fifth-alarm fire was fought under brutally cold conditions on February 2, 1961, at 137th Street and Third Avenue, Manhattan.

New York City Fire Department 1946 –1969

During the early-morning hours of June 25, 1946, several civilian members of the FDNY's Telegraph Bureau were working at the Staten Island Ferry Terminal at Saint George. At about two a.m., they discovered a fire and quickly transmitted Box 30.

The flames spread with amazing speed and quickly trapped and killed two civilians working in the ferry terminal. Harold Clandening, one of the FDNY Telegraph Bureau employees, was attempting to move an FDNY work truck to safety when he collapsed in the heavy smoke and later died.

The flames spread from the ferry area and extended to slips and railroad cars. A large portion of the terminal, slips and railroad cars lay in smoldering ruins before the fire could be controlled.

The month of September, 1946, was a sad one for the FDNY as two of its beloved retired chiefs passed away while in retirement. John J. McElligott and Patrick Walsh had risen through the ranks to Chief of Department and Fire Commissioner.

One of the worst disasters in the history of the city developed slowly after a series of fires apparently were started by "mischievous boys." On Wednesday, December 11, 1946, FDNY units were dispatched to a fire in an abandoned ice plant, located at 2517-19 Amsterdam Avenue, near 184th Street in Manhattan. The fire was reported at 5:45 p.m. and was extinguished using a first-alarm assignment.

Just before midnight on that same night, a tenant in the apartment house next door smelled smoke, then saw sparks coming from the roof of the ice plant. He ran to a fire alarm box a block away and transmitted the alarm. Box 1753 was transmitted again, sending units to the ice plant building that formerly was occupied by the Knickerbocker Ice Company and had been unoccupied for eight years. The plant building was the same height as the tenement next door and had massive brick walls insulated with cork, supporting a heavy concrete roof, supported on steel members.

The fire apparently was started near a pipe shaft on the east end of the structure, where a partition wall separated the storehouse and the main plant. Flames extended through the shaft to the hanging ceiling and the cork insulation in the walls. Lines were stretched and companies were operating to extinguish the intensely burning fire.

Twenty minutes after firemen went to work, Rescue Company 3 was special-called to join in a search for a suspected ammonia leak inside the old structure. At about one a.m. (now December 12th), without warning, the roof of the ice plant collapsed onto the top floor, pushing out a fire-weakened, 36-inch wall onto the adjoining occupied tenement next door. Inside the tenement were more than 60 unsuspecting, sleeping residents. On the roof were a number of people watching the firemen battle the flames.

The rear of the tenement tore away from the front section and collapsed. The icehouse wall and the shattered tenement became one large pile of twisted debris and rubble, entombing many people. Fireman Frank Moorehead of Engine Company 93 was carried down with the roof of the icehouse and was trapped somewhere within the huge pile of rubble.

The department began operations in earnest as members began the dangerous task of digging, tunneling and shoring in an attempt to reach those trapped within. A second alarm was transmitted at 1:09 a.m. and numerous ambulances were special-called. Ten minutes later, a third alarm was transmitted and two minutes later, a fourth. Five alarms and many special calls were placed, including Rescue 1, to provide the necessary manpower for the mammoth undertaking.

The firemen worked for more than 48 hours and pulled off many heroic rescues. In all, 37 people were killed and 40 were injured. A very dangerous tunneling operation, conducted by Acting Deputy Chief Joseph J. Scanlon and his aide, Fireman Adolph H. Bahruth, facilitated locating and removing Fireman Moorehead. Unfortunately, he had succumbed to his injuries.

The chief and his aide were awarded medals for their heroic rescue attempt. Six other members of the department also were awarded medals for rescuing trapped victims from the collapsed building.

The economy of the country and city shifted from the needs of the military during the war, to beefing up the homefront. The FDNY took delivery of 20 new pumpers and began the process of replacing antiquated equipment.

One of the positive results of warfare are the improvements and inventions made by industry to support the military efforts. One of these was the adaptation of the Scott Aviation Company's breathing equipment used by pilots and gun crews during high-altitude flights. This gear was redesigned with firefighting in mind and used during a nine-month test period during 1947. The Scott Air-Pak self-contained breathing apparatus (SCBA) was used by FDNY Rescue Companies during the trials. Periodic reports and suggestions for modifications and improvements were passed along to the manufacturer. This one piece of equipment arguably could be the most important invention ever to work its way into the fire service.

In an unusual twist, one of the victims pulled from the collapse by firemen was a 10-year-old boy named A. Joseph Popper. Young Popper lost both his parents, brother and sister in the collapse. A. Joseph Popper later joined the ranks of the FDNY and became a Probationary Fireman, assigned to Engine Company 7. He got to meet the man who dug him free and carried him from the rubble, Neil Kinnick, who had advanced through the ranks to become a Battalion Chief by the time young Popper joined the force.

During the last tour of duty for 1946, the Manhattan Dispatchers Office received street Box 396, Broadway and Eighth Street. Engine Companies 72, 33, 25 and 18, Ladder Companies 3 and 20, Water Tower 2, Rescue Company 1, Battalions 6 and 3, Division 2 and Fire Patrol 2 were all turned out. The first-arriving units found a well-advanced fire in a seven-story loft building at 749 Broadway, between Eighth Street and Astor Place. Two additional alarms were transmitted as the fire spread from the fourth floor to the three floors above.

At 7:10 p.m., one hour and 43 minutes after the initial alarm, the fire began darkening down in the 40- x 100-foot building, when a section of the top floor suddenly collapsed. Acting Deputy Chief William Hogan ordered everyone out of the structure and dashed inside to make sure his men knew of the dangerous conditions above.

The collapse of the floors then caused the failure of the staircase, trapping the chief and nine men. Efforts shifted to rescuing the trapped men and a fourth alarm was transmitted. Firefighters of every rank, including Honorary Chief Medical Officer Harry Archer, M.D., dove into the collapse and began the dangerous task of rescuing their Brothers.

A disaster unit from Bellevue Hospital and doctors and nurses from St. Vincent's Hospital converged on the scene. Heavy streams operating from water towers and turret pipe streams were shut down to relieve the growing weight of water in the toppled structure as the rescue effort expanded. Off-duty officers and firemen arrived at the scene to help however they could. Radio broadcasts, including replays of live coverage of rescue operations, drew a large, curious crowd of New Year's Eve revelers, who only further congested the already-packed streets and sidewalks.

A rescue effort started through the adjoining wall of a building next door and into the collapse building. Con Edison provided power compressors to help with the breaking and breaching. Fear of an explosion due to leaking illuminating gas was ended when Chief Frank Murphy ordered the gas for the entire block shut off.

The dangerous tasks of tunneling and shoring continued until the last of the trapped men were rescued and taken to the hospital, many with serious injuries. Several rescuers also received injuries that required hospitalization. In all, 12 members of the department were admitted. As a result of their injuries, Fireman Winfield Walsh of Ladder 9 and Acting Deputy Chief William Hogan both died on January 4th.

After the fire was extinguished, several companies took up hose for the last time; they previously were slated to be disbanded on January 1, 1947. The companies were: Engine 4 – 119 Maiden Lane, near Pearl Street; Engine 19 – 355 West 25th Street, between Eighth and Ninth Avenues; Engine 20 – 243 Lafayette Street, near Spring Street; Engine 25 – 342 East Fifth Street, between First and Second Avenues; and Engine 29 – 160 Chambers Street, near West Broadway.

The third fire and collapse to strike the FDNY in little more than a month occurred on January 10, 1947. At 2:12 a.m., a fire was reported on the third floor of a four-story loft building at 131 John Street in lower Manhattan. Firemen were extinguishing the fire on the third floor – a cabinet and carpentry company – when suddenly, the fourth floor of the loft collapsed on them.

The fourth floor contained a large concrete oven used by the die casting company that occupied that floor. The oven, portions of the fourth floor and the third floor collapsed onto the second floor, trapping three firemen and an officer amidst tons of water-soaked, smoldering or burning debris.

Three members quickly were rescued and removed through windows and down ladders. Rescue 1 was special-called and quickly shored up the third floor and then began tunneling and shoring toward the trapped officer, Lieutenant Thomas Rice of Engine 6, who was pinned beneath beams, machinery and rubble. For an hour, the rescue continued until the officer was pulled from the collapse and rushed to the hospital.

Luckily, even though several members were injured seriously, all of the trapped firemen were removed alive from the rubble.

In 1947, Harold Burke was promoted to Chief of Department. Burke had a very colorful career, including being awarded the Crimmins and Department Medals for a rescue he made on April 22, 1928, while Captain of Ladder Company 30. These medals were presented to him by Mayor Jimmy Walker. Burke also served as a Captain in the United States Navy and was in charge of the Naval firefighting school during the war.

Forty-two people were killed as a DC-4 passenger airliner crashed into a vacant lot adjacent to the Academy of Aeronautics Building at Grand Central Parkway and 86th Street in Queens on May 29, 1947. It was just after eight p.m. when FDNY Airport Crash Unit 31 responded to the scene to find the plane nearly completely engulfed in flames. Burning gasoline and oil covered the ground surrounding the plane as Lieutenant Edwin Rankin split his men into teams. The first team, under the direct command of Rankin, moved quickly toward the rear right side of the plane and made their way through dense smoke and high heat to a small utility door. The door was opened and Fireman Charles Ortlam entered the 18- x 24-inch door and began a search. He located an unconscious stewardess and brought her to the door where Rankin pulled her through and carried her clear, while Ortlam returned for a second woman also overcome by smoke. He carried her from the blazing plane, squeezing through the small door once again.

Meanwhile, on the right side of the plane, Fireman Edward Stegmaier moved in close to the burning aircraft and began to cut an opening through the side of the plane. Conditions were so severe that he had to work under the protection of a fog line. Stegmaier entered the plane, located an unconscious man and removed him to the outside. He then returned to the plane and assisted in the removal of other passengers.

Nearby, Fireman John McLaughlin raised a portable ladder and entered through a section of the plane that had burned away. Under cover of a fog nozzle stream, he carried a male and female passenger to the utility door where other members of the unit assisted in removing the people to safety.

Forty-two people were killed in this crash, but several lived due to the heroic actions of FDNY Airport Crash Unit 31. For their actions at extreme personal risk, Rankin, Ortlam, Stegmaier and McLaughlin each received a Department Medal.

A 5-7 signal (one engine and one truck assignment) was transmitted on June 17, 1947, for a speedboat fire near Whitestone, Queens. Engine 295 and Ladder 144 responded to the foot of 150th Street and, using a small civilian boat, approached the blazing vessel. As they moved in close, the speedboat exploded, violently knocking most of the firefighters into the flame-covered water. The fuel tank of the exploded boat struck three firefighters as it crashed through the deck of the second boat.

Several hours later, the bells of the city's firehouses sounded the signal 5-5-5-5, announcing the line-of-duty deaths of Firemen Frederick Ziegler and William D. Austin, both of Ladder 144.

The day after Christmas, 1947, New York was blanketed with 25.8 inches of snow (nearly five inches more than the "Blizzard of 1888"). Without warning, the storm moved in from the Atlantic and caught the city off-guard. With the streets impassable, the day tour was held over, doubling the available manpower. By 11:30 that night, the decision was made to place the department on continuous duty.

Apparatus picked up stranded members and transported manpower from train and subway stations to firehouses. Members then set out to clear intersections and hydrants from the grip of the drifting snow and assist stranded motorists.

By New Year's Day, conditions only got worse. For more than 40 hours, the city was pelted by a major ice storm. Nearly 4000 fire alarm boxes failed as a coating of ice was added to the deep snow.

A violent explosion tore through a four-story rubber warehouse across the street from Engine Company 23's quarters on West 58th Street. A woman showed at a third-floor window and was about to jump, when members of 23 Engine scrambled out into the street with a life net. They caught the woman, then set about battling the fire. Heavy smoke banked down in the street and obscured everything, even the deep snow. Engine chauffeurs hunted for hydrants as firemen guided arriving apparatus into position through the thick smoke.

A fifth alarm was transmitted as the flames extended into the eight- and 12-story buildings on either side of the warehouse. Apparatus was hampered by the deep snow as they responded in and operated. More than 25 firemen were overcome by the heavy smoke. Only the large complement of men available, due to the standby, allowed the fire to be extinguished without resorting to a Borough Call.

The weather finally eased up on January 3, 1948, and the department returned to normal manning levels and duty hours.

The city celebrated the 50th Anniversary of the founding of the Greater City of New York in 1948. The city had grown in leaps and bounds since the merger and the department had struggled to keep pace. A sign that the times were changing was the noticeable increase in the FDNY's work load. In 1948, a fire alarm was transmitted every nine minutes and an actual fire occurred every 12 minutes.

In the 30 years since 1918, fires increased from 13,971 to 40,522. Structural fires doubled from 10,639 in 1918, to 20,825 in 1948. Civilian fire fatalities rose from 125 to 143 during the same period. The rise in these numbers could be attributed to the increase in the city's population. There were 5.8 million New Yorkers in 1918 and 8.1 million in 1948.

Individual fire companies also were increasing their activity levels significantly. Engine Company 58 and Hook & Ladder 26, who shared a firehouse on East 114th Street in East Harlem, also shared the distinction of being the busiest companies on the job in 1948. Ladder 26 had 2224 runs and Engine 58 responded to 1890 alarms. Both companies also led in workers.

Another change in the nature of the fire duty was the shift of fires from commercial to residential. The three busiest Battalions for fires in 1948 were the 17th in the South Bronx and the 16th and 12th in Harlem.

It was 23 minutes after noon on July 12, 1948, when benzene and paint ignited on the second floor of the three-story tenement house at 5805 Third Avenue in Brooklyn, trapping a woman and her son on the top floor. Heavy smoke filled the stairs and flames poured out the windows on the second floor, making it impassable.

As Ladder 148 arrived, Fireman Thomas J. Mulgannon dashed up the stairs and began a search and located the mother and son. Moments later, he was joined by Lieutenant Frank Malthaner, covering in Ladder 114. At this point, the interior stairs filled with flames from the apartment below, cutting off their planned escape route.

The firemen brought the family to a window as a 30-foot portable ladder was lowered into place. The ladder was obscured by the dense smoke pumping out the second-floor windows. Waves of heat from the venting fire made the climb down even more dangerous as Lieutenant Malthaner started down the ladder with Mrs. Swartout in his arms. He was followed quickly by Fireman Mulgannon, who brought George Swartout to safety. Mother and son were reunited in an ambulance and taken to a nearby hospital.

Fireman Mulgannon and Lieutenant Malthaner also were reunited the next June on the steps of City Hall as they were awarded medals for their valor.

Peter Loftus assumed command of the FDNY in 1948 when he was promoted to Chief of the Department.

The FDNY's first metal aerial ladder, an 85-foot Seagrave, went into service in 1948 and was assigned to Ladder 110, then located on Jay Street in Downtown Brooklyn. Ladder 24 was assigned an 85-foot American LaFrance and Ladder 4 placed an 85-foot Pirsch ladder truck into service.

The working conditions for firefighters had improved considerably as the job adjusted into peace time operations. The work week was down to 45 hours from the war time 84 hours. A firefighter's salary had increased from $3420 in 1946, to $4150 in 1949, and vacation days increased from 21 days to 30 days.

Friday the 13th lived up to its reputation in May of 1949, at 8:48 a.m., when a 16-ton trailer truck, loaded with 80 55-gallon metal drums, filled with carbon disulphide, caught fire in the Holland Tunnel. Flames impinged on the drums and caused a series of fiery explosions. The fire and explosions stopped the New York-bound traffic 1500 feet into the tunnel and quickly spread to 10 other trucks. Drum after drum ruptured and exploded, spreading the highly inflammable contents within the confined space.

Some passenger vehicles and trucks not involved in the fire were backed out of the tunnel. The remaining drivers and passengers of the cars and trucks unable to retreat from the growing fire escaped before the fire reached extreme levels. Flames soon reached the cargo of the other trucks caught in the blaze. Turpentine, alcohol, bleach, baled paper and the gasoline stored in the vehicles soon were feeding the fire.

The New York City Fire Department was notified by the Holland Tunnel's New York Office. Rescue Company 1 was special-called to Box 327 (West and Spring Streets) at the report of chemical fumes escaping in the tunnel. Meanwhile, the fire was affecting more than just traffic, as telegraph, telephone and television cables were severed. Communication suddenly was cut off from the city to the rest of the nation.

On the New York side of the tunnel, Chief John Heaney of the Fifth Battalion and members of Rescue 1 descended into the westbound tube and moved in about 6000 feet before crossing over to the eastbound tube. They then were confronted with a major fire. The chief had Box 308 transmitted at 9:30 a.m., bringing four engines, two ladders, another Battalion and the Division. Rescue 2 was special-called two minutes later and directed to respond through the Lincoln Tunnel and operate from the Jersey side. (Eventually, Rescues 3 and 4 also were sent to the fire, marking the first time in the history of the department that four Rescue Companies operated at the same incident.)

All the members assigned to the box left their apparatus, boarded Engines 30 and 27 and entered the eastbound tube. Hoses were stretched and the battle was joined. For more than two hours, firefighters on both sides of the tunnel pushed hose lines toward the seat of the blaze. Tiles and sections of concrete dropped from the ceiling and walls as the terrible heat assaulted the tunnel itself.

The fire finally was brought under control five hours after it began. The overhauling of the charred vehicles and cargo took hours. Pockets of trapped gases exploded during operations and endangered members. Foamlite and other chemicals were used to blanket the tunnel and prevent further reactions.

Although amazingly no civilians were killed in this explosion and fire, the cost was high for the department. Despite the fact that nine Medical Officers responded to the scene, the smoke

"Cavendish," the mascot of Ladder 26, stands guard over Ladder 43's roofman, who suffered a broken leg, circa 1950. (Photo courtesy of George Eysser)

Harry M. Archer, M.D., Honorary Chief Medical Officer and Second Deputy Fire Commissioner, passed away on May 17, 1954, at the age of 85.

and gases took their toll on the firemen. The debilitating effects of the poisonous smoke mixture took the life of Battalion Chief Gunther E. Beake, who succumbed four months later on August 23, 1949.

The new decade of the 1950s continued the upward trend in responses and fires. In just two years (1948 to 1950), the total number of runs increased from 57,949 to 62,021. More dramatic, however, was the increase in fire duty, which jumped up by almost 4000 to 44,370.

Another change that affected the FDNY was the expansion of the radioactive materials as the nation moved into the "Atomic Age." One retiring Deputy Chief commented, "I've seen everything from horse manure to isotopes in this job."

A major disaster struck the city on Thanksgiving Eve with the collision of two Long Island Rail Road trains in Queens. Off-duty Fireman Benedict Barry of Ladder 8, a passenger on one of the trains, transmitted Queens Box 9680, prompting a response featuring some of the most dramatic and effective rescue operations ever performed by the department. For the second time in the department's history, four Rescue Companies operated at one emergency. Firemen separated the telescoped cars with jacks – both hydraulic and mechanical – blocks, wedges, cutting torches, hand tools and brute strength to free trapped passengers.

Firefighters crawled into the wreckage to treat the injured and recover the dead. Firemen even squeezed into the twisted debris to administer hypodermic injections under the directions of physicians. Despite more than 11 hours of dangerous rescue work, the death toll from the crash reached 79.

The department purchased seven Ward LaFrance "Quad" apparatus in 1951. These rigs received their names from their design and capabilities. They were a combination pumper, hose wagon, booster apparatus and ladder truck. They were placed in service in areas of Brooklyn and Staten Island where ladder companies were few and far between.

A major improvement in the FDNY's ability to dispatch and communicate with units in the field was made in 1952 with the completion of two-way FM radio installations on FDNY apparatus. Less effective two-way AM radio-telephones had been in service since 1937. These were used in fireboats, several high-ranking chief vehicles and a few isolated fire company rigs.

Famous Paul Thayer Harlem fire photo titled, "A chief watches over his men."

The new FM radio system was far superior to the antiquated AM system and allowed fire companies to be more mobile and redirect companies as needed or return those not needed. The FM radio system was designed "in-house" by FDNY personnel at a time when professional radio manufacturers were saying the system could not do what the department wanted.

On December 3, 1951, the department was called to a reported fire onboard the *SS American Miller*, berthed at Pier 60 on the North (Hudson) River. Arriving companies found fire burning in hold No. 5. The hold reportedly was filled with general cargo and firefighting efforts commenced. Hose lines were stretched into the hold and the fire quickly was knocked down. During overhaul, the odor of burning sulfur was detected. Despite the use of smoke ejectors, the build-up of sulfur gas was greater than the ability to remove it. It became impossible to operate in the hold without mask protection.

Rescue 1 was special-called to enter the hold and wearing masks, they began to remove the cargo. During this operation, they came upon 150 steel drums, each of which contained 250 pounds of sodium hydro-sulphide, a chemical that burns spontaneously in the presence of heat or moisture or both. A number of these drums were on fire and some of them had ruptured and gas was escaping.

During the removal process, several of the drums exploded, knocking the Rescue unit off their feet and splattering them with the hot, caustic chemical. To avert other explosions, holes were punched in the remaining drums to release the pressure. The cargo then was removed safely without further incident.

In the spring of 1954, the FDNY began the practice of "Apparatus Field Inspection Duty." AFID, as it was known to the companies, was possible because of the addition of FM radios to the apparatus. Fire communications no longer were tied to the bell system exclusively. Companies brought fire prevention to the streets of the city but still were in touch with the respective borough dispatchers. Despite the active fire prevention program, the numbers of fires the department faced increased each year.

During 1954, the arrival of 25 1000-gpm Mack pumpers and their assignment below 42nd Street allowed the department to discontinue their reliance on the high-pressure water system. The high-pressure hydrant system had served the department well for many years, but apparatus technology had advanced to the point that the new pumpers could supply the needed water pressure themselves.

Another advancement in the department's firefighting capability came when the new, 129-foot fireboat was placed in service in 1954. This new, radar-equipped craft was named for Marine Engineer John D. McKean, who died in the line of duty on September 17, 1953, after an explosion onboard the fireboat *McClellan*. McKean, burned seriously by live steam, remained at his post, vainly trying to keep the vessel under control.

Despite the accelerated fire prevention efforts, fires in residential areas of the city still were increasing in 1955. The fire death toll was also on the rise. It was decided to establish manpower units to respond and work in the high-incident neighborhoods of the city. These units were known as Squad Units.

Squad Units

On April 16, 1955, **Squad Unit No. 1** was organized in the quarters of Engine Company 59 in Harlem. Department Order No. 44 laid out the department's plan for the staffing and utilization of the squad units.

The unit consisted of four lieutenants and 25 firemen. They responded with one officer and five firemen in a converted 1940 Mack Hose Wagon, provided with a two-way radio system. They were equipped with eight air paks (with spare cylinders), two claw tools, two lock breakers, four six-foot hooks, two six-pound flat-head axes, two eight-pound flat-head axes, a $2\frac{1}{2}$-gallon soda and acid extinguisher and a standard deck pipe with a complete set of tips.

Their primary purpose was to provide added manpower at fires or emergencies. Chiefs also were reminded that the squad was not to be detained doing overhauling after the fire was under control.

Squad Unit 2 was organized on August 1, 1955, in the quarters of Engine Company 73 in the South Bronx. On November 16, 1955, two additional squads went into service in Brooklyn. **Squad Unit 3** quartered with Engine 235 in Bedford Stuyvesant and **Squad Unit 4** was stationed in the quarters of Engine 231, Ladder 120 and Battalion 44 in Brownsville.

The squad units became extremely busy firefighting units. Eventually, nine squads were formed and went into service at the following locations:

Squad 5 – organized April 1, 1959, at Engine 5 in Manhattan;

Squad 6 – organized November 1, 1959, at Engine 74 in Manhattan;

Squad 7 – organized December 19, 1959, at Engine 212 in Brooklyn;

Squad 8 – organized May 1, 1960, at 243 Lafayette Street in Manhattan;

Squad 9 – organized July 17, 1961, at Engine 22 in Manhattan.

Squad Company 3 went into service in August of 1955. Shown here with new rig in 1958.

The Fire Fighter *operates at the Luckenback Steamship Pier at the foot of 35th Street in Brooklyn on December 3, 1956. (Courtesy of the* Daily News*)*

On October 1, 1955, Peter Loftus retired as Chief of Department and Edward Conners was appointed in his place.

A torrential rainstorm virtually swamped the town of Danbury, Connecticut, on October 16, 1955. The Still River overflowed its banks, adding to the flooded conditions in the downtown section of Danbury. Buildings were under water, walls were compromised and the local resources were insufficient to cope with the problem.

A call was sent to Fire Commissioner Edward F. Cavanagh, Jr., by Mayor John A. Define of Danbury, requesting assistance. Cavanagh quickly conferred with Mayor Wagner, Governor Harriman and members of the Civil Defense Office, all of whom agreed the FDNY could send help.

A 65-2 message was sent out requesting volunteers. By late afternoon, more than 150 men had responded. The necessary manpower was chosen; the remainder were thanked and released. A convoy of 22 CD pumpers, Gas-Oil Unit 12, Searchlight 23, a department wrecker, a department mechanics truck and the Canteen Field Kitchen Unit set out at 5:50 p.m. for Danbury.

Once the rain stopped, the FDNY went to work. For two days the town throbbed with the sound of New York City pumpers. The pumping was so successful that all but eight pumpers, which stayed for an additional day, returned to the city. Ninety-one officers and firemen, 57 auxiliaries and eight civilians worked more than 1249 man-hours. The "expeditionary force" left with the thanks of the Danbury officials and citizens alike.

Hellauer of Engine Company 48, Firemen Hoolan and Hansen of Ladder Company 44 and Fireman Infosino of the Headquarters Staff.

At 3:16 p.m. on December 3, 1956, the Brooklyn Central Office received a phone alarm for a fire on the Luckenback Steamship Pier at the foot of 35th Street, Brooklyn, and transmitted Box 1499. The first-arriving unit, Engine Company 228, arrived to an advanced fire in the 175- x 1740-foot pier structure. The building was typical of most piers; it was one story, with corrugated iron, a tarred roof and a concrete deck. The flame of an acetylene torch accidentally ignited stored foam rubber and spread toward hundreds of boxes of detonators. Acting Lieutenant Al Kraemer sent in a second alarm.

Additional alarms followed in quick succession. Companies from the first three alarms were operating; fourth-alarm units were responding and the fifth alarm just had been sent in when a major explosion rocked the pier. Engine 278 was preparing to stretch a line from the fireboat *Fire Fighter*, Engines 279 and 282, Ladder 114 and Rescue 2 were operating on the pier and Ladders 109 and 148 were working on the roof when the blast occurred. Firefighters were thrown from their feet and sent flying in various directions. Several landed in the water and quickly were rescued by their comrades.

Famed FDNY photographers Ray Hellriegel and Jim Heffernan were responding and stopped their car on the top of the high bridge over the Gowanus Canal to take a "long shot" of the blaze when the explosion occurred. A huge, flame-filled mushroom cloud loomed up before them and dissipated before they could get their cameras ready.

The fireboat *Fire Fighter* was close to the center of the blast and sustained serious damage. Several of the crew were injured badly and several were thrown into the water. Those men were rescued by other firemen. Hundreds of windows in the neighborhood were broken by the blast and several other fires were started.

The explosion took the lives of 10 civilians and injured 250 more. Dozens of firemen also were injured. Miss Pauline Tornello, RN, helped the injured and worked with Rescue 2 as dozens of injured were pulled from the pier. For her outstanding medical care, given under dangerous conditions, she was presented awards by the department, the Ner Tamid Society and the members of Rescue 2.

The year 1958 was a year of change for the Department. Among the most noticeable was the discontinuance of the FDNY Band, which was organized in 1913. The official reason given was increased fire prevention efforts.

Another change was the retirement of the last man holding the rank of "Engineer of Steamer," Otto Kutzke. He had been promoted in 1921 from the last list ever promulgated for this rank. When Engineer of Steamer Kutzke retired, he had 45 years of service, having been appointed to Engine 217 in 1914.

The department also took possession of three new fireboats in 1958 – the fireboats *Archer* and *Wilks*, along with the Tender *Smoke II*.

Again, the errant use of a torch sparked a fire of major proportions for the New York City Fire Department. A demolition worker's cutting torch started a fire in the six-story, heavy-timber, mill-constructed building at 507-25 West 132nd Street, between Amsterdam Avenue and Old Broadway in Manhattan. The structure originally was occupied by a textile mill.

Tragedy struck the department on April 4, 1956, when six firemen lost their lives at a four-alarm fire in the Bronx. Box 2904 was received at 8:40 p.m. for a fire in a commercial building at Third Avenue and 173rd Street. Companies went to work, ventilating the stubborn smoky blaze. A cellar pipe was set up and operated in front of the building by members of 48 Engine.

During the height of the fire, the entire parapet wall of the fire building, which also supported a marquee, collapsed, pinning numerous firemen.

A frantic rescue operation was launched to free the trapped men. Many men were removed from the debris, several with serious injuries. Unfortunately, six could not be saved. The Brothers who made the Supreme Sacrifice were Lieutenant Molloy, Firemen Carroll and

Determined Harlem firemen make their way to a victim, June 16, 1952. (Photo by Paul Thayer)

The fire originated in the cellar where the old standpipe system was being removed. The flames quickly found the elevator shaft and spread with lightning speed. On arrival, first-due companies had heavy fire in the cellar and first and second floors. Within five minutes, the fire was roaring out every window on all six floors and extending to the exposures. Four alarms were transmitted within nine minutes and a fifth was sent in as the building's north, south and east walls all collapsed 12 minutes after the original alarm was transmitted.

Conditions were so severe at one point that Fireman Tom Sexton of Engine 36 had to be covered with a hose line as he directed his rig's deck pipe. The fire extended to six tenements to the north, one tenement to the east and six tenements to the south before it was brought under control less than two hours later.

Hell's Hundred Acres is a section of lower Manhattan that has taken a terrible toll on the members of the department. Thousands of firemen have been overcome and many firemen have been killed, battling the stubborn blazes in the loft buildings and old converted tenements in this area. These old structures are crowded into a wedge-shaped area formed by Chambers Street on the south, the Bowery on the east, West Broadway to the west and West Eighth Street to the north.

Valentine's Day, 1958, saw a fire in this area take the lives of two firemen and four members of the New York Fire Patrol. The city was blanketed by heavy snow and suffering with bitter cold and icy conditions. A fire on the fifth floor of the loft building at 137 Wooster Street was ignited by a careless smoker. The six-story building, owned and occupied by the Elkins Paper and Twine Company, was built in the 1890s and fronted 50 feet on Wooster Street with a depth of 100 feet.

The first five floors were supported by cast-iron columns, while above, the sixth floor and roof were timber supports. The building was stocked with paper in 800-pound rolls, twine and other materials. There was also twine-making machinery within the building.

At 6:20 p.m., seven employees at work on the ground floor heard breaking glass, then saw fire reflected in the windows of the building across the street. They quickly telephoned an alarm and simultaneously, Box 334, at Wooster and Prince Streets, was pulled by a passer-by. Ladder 20 and Engine 13 responded from their quarters on Mercer Street, only two blocks away. Fire Patrol 2 also had a quick response from their quarters on West Third Street. As the ladder truck approached the building, Captain Thomas McGrath saw heavy smoke on the upper floors of the building and ordered the aerial placed onto the roof. The captain sent in a second alarm as firemen began operations and members of the Patrol entered the building and began to throw covers over valuables on the third floor.

Firemen dig through the rubble at the February 14, 1958, Wooster Street collapse. Two firemen and four fire patrol members lost their lives.

Members of Ladder 20 climbed the aerial and began chopping holes in the roof to vent the thick smoke. Lines were stretched to the fire area as Patrol 1 reinforced Patrol 2 on the third floor.

Approximately 12 minutes after the arrival of the fire units, the building collapsed without warning. The men on the roof scrambled for the safety of the adjoining building. As the roof dropped away, Captain McGrath hung from a window ledge until his men could pull him up. The ladder officer looked around and realized that two of his men were missing.

At 6:36 p.m., a third alarm was transmitted. Special calls for the department ambulance, chaplain, medical officer and Fire Communications Unit 1 also were placed. Additional alarms brought more than 200 firemen to the scene. Icy conditions became so severe that the thawing apparatus was special-called.

The flames were brought under control by eight p.m. and the work of digging and clearing rubble in search of those trapped began in earnest. A heavy smoke condition enshrouded the three-story pile of smoldering debris. Firemen dug under the glare of spotlights as others kept watch on the weakened front wall. They worked at a fevered pace, hoping to somehow find their brothers alive beneath the mound. At about 11 p.m., the bodies of Firemen Blumenthal and Schmid of Ladder 20 were found. The search for the other missing men, known to be from the Fire Patrol after a roll call was conducted, continued.

The news of the collapse spread quickly and off-duty firemen began to arrive at the scene to volunteer their services. The ice continued to build, hampering operations further. Another thawing rig was called. Con Ed and FDNY compressors powered tools to help break up the heavy masonry facing the rescuers.

At 2:40 a.m. (now Saturday, February 15), the Signal 65-2 was sent over the department radio: Urgent: The Commissioner calls for off-duty firemen to report to Box 334.

The work stopped only long enough for a wrecking crane to clear the threatening front wall on Saturday morning. Three rescue companies and hundreds of on- and off-duty men pushed their way through the frozen, charred building remains. Hampered by the nine-inch-deep snow and temperatures that went as low as four degrees, the digging and clearing operation continued on through the next day. The bodies of Fire Patrolmen Devine and Tracy were recovered Monday night, February 17. Sergeant McGee and Fire Patrolman Brusati were located and removed the following day. The men were buried with firemen and fire patrolmen from many other cities in attendance.

There is no reward that can repay a man for risking his life. Certainly no one who worked to recover a lost brother would even think about recognition. But due to the nature and severity of this operation, the department took appropriate action. Department Orders No. 118 and 193, of 1958, published the findings of the Board of Merit as it related to department operations at the Wooster Street collapse. For heroic action involving unusual personal risk, 31 members received Class III awards and eight members were granted a Service Rating "A." For responding off-duty and operating at the collapse, the orders published more than 26 pages, listing the names of more than 900 fire officers and firemen, each of whom was awarded a Voluntary Duty Class "A."

At 3:55 p.m. on March 19, 1958, the gas drying oven in a five-story textile factory located at 623 Broadway exploded, filling the third floor from front to rear with flames. Sixty-six people were in the building at the time and employees on the fourth floor and above were trapped with no means of escape. The structure measured 35 feet across the front and ran nearly 200 feet through to Mercer Street. Box 341, at the corner of Broadway and Houston Street, was pulled, sending Engines 13, 30, 33 and 55, Ladders 20 and 9, Rescue 1, Battalions 2 and 5 and the chief of the 1st Division speeding to the scene.

Ladder 20 arrived first due and was faced with numerous women trapped at the windows above, obscured by the dense smoke billowing across the face of the building. Ladder 20 broke out their life net

and ran into position under the trapped people on the Mercer Street side of the building. Several women had jumped before the department's arrival. More then jumped successfully from the fourth floor; others missed the net and landed on the sidewalk. One girl landed on another who had just been caught in the life net.

The Fifth Battalion gave this preliminary report on the department radio, "Fire at 623 Broadway; five-story brick; 25 x 90...(later revised); fire third floor...using all hands...doubtful will hold...exposures (1) street; (2) eight-story brick, 50 x 100; (3) rear, street; (4) eight-story brick, 50 x 100.

Lines were pushed up the stairways in an attempt to reach the people trapped above. Lieutenant Kelly and Fireman Re of Ladder 9, second-due truck, completed several dangerous rescues and later were awarded medals.

In all, the toll on life was great. Twenty-four persons were killed and many were injured by the blaze. Forty-seven years earlier, these same companies had faced a similar fire at the Triangle Shirtwaist Factory. This time, the numbers were less, but the pain and suffering were as great. Eight fire prevention laws that required added safety precautions to these types of buildings were passed as a result of this fire.

Another significant change for the FDNY occurred on June 11, 1958, when George David was promoted to Chief of Department from the Civil Service list. David became the 14th Chief of Department. George David rose rapidly through the ranks after being appointed to Ladder 5 in Greenwich Village in 1927. At 35 years of age, he had been the youngest Battalion Chief on the job and helped to organize the Sixth Division in the South Bronx in 1956 as the department reacted to the sharp increase in fire duty.

June 25, 1958, saw land units and the Marine Division called out once again to Manhattan Box 125, a notorious false alarm location. This response, however, evolved to become the biggest threat to the Port of New York since the *El Estero* caught fire during World War II. At approximately 12:24 a.m., just opposite Pier 29 in the East River and directly under the Manhattan Bridge, the freighter *Nebraska* and the gasoline carrier *Empress Bay* collided and caught fire.

The *Empress Bay*, with its storage tanks filled with 280,000 gallons of high-test gasoline, was struck amidships on the starboard side. A large amount of gasoline poured out, covering the entire structure of the *Nebraska* from the waterline to the boat deck and coating the river with large patches of flaming gasoline. The entire East River near Piers 29 and 31 were blazing. Radiant heat from the fire ignited the railroad ties of the BMT subway that crossed the Manhattan Bridge above.

First-arriving land units gave preliminary reports, then the Second Battalion requested three extra fireboats to the scene. The Fireboat *Gaynor* left its berth after hearing four blasts of a ship's horn. The *Gaynor* moved out to the center of the river and made speed toward the blazing vessels. The fireboat drove through sections of burning gasoline and with all its turrets operating, moved in on the port side of the *Nebraska* in an attempt to rescue the ship's crew.

The Senator Robert F. Wagner *gives a water display off Pier A.*

After removing crew members from the forward amidships, others became visible on the Port fantail and the FDNY moved in to rescue these men. During this operation, the fireboat was struck by the *Nebraska's* propeller, ripping a hole through the hull beneath the waterline. Taking on water, the *Gaynor* moved toward Pier 31 with 35 rescued crewmen. Damage control was initiated in an attempt to keep the fireboat afloat.

Responding onboard the Tender *Smoke II*, Acting Battalion Chief Olsen observed an injured man in the burning water. Olsen tore off his coat and dove into the river and pulled the victim to safety. The *Smoke* then shuttled land units out to the fire. Lines were stretched and firemen, utilizing Scott masks, operated in holds of the *Nebraska*. The fire on the *Nebraska* was brought under control and the ship was towed to a pier on the Hudson River.

Companies also responded to the bridge, extinguished the burning subway ties and inspected the bridge for other damage. The hazardous conditions posed by the gasoline floating on the river remained until noon on June 27th, when regular use of the river was resumed.

Tragedy struck the New York Harbor on the New Jersey side on September 15, 1958, when a rail road train plummeted off the Bayonne Bridge. Two of the newest boats in the FDNY Marine fleet responded to the accident. The *Wilks*, Tender *Smoke II* and the *Fire Fighter* operated at the disaster that claimed the lives of 48 passengers.

The department made major strides to improve and update the firefighting arsenal with the purchase of 64 new Mack pumpers. These new rigs had enclosed front cabs and jump seats and were the start of the department's plan to unify the fleet for ease of maintenance and standardization. The following year, 20 more Macks rolled into the FDNY Shops.

The end of the 1950s foreshadowed the dramatic increase of fire duty the department would face in the near future. In 1959, for instance, despite the most vigorous fire prevention efforts in the city's history, fires increased from 48,101 in 1958, to 56,529 in 1959.

The FDNY Marine fleet placed the new 105-foot fireboat, *Robert F. Wagner,* into service. This boat was named after the father of the mayor. It was the third of four boats received between 1958 and 1961.

The year 1959 also saw a small, but significant, change in the fire helmet worn by New York City firemen. The leather frontpiece on FDNY helmets changed in style and design. It was no longer a single-piece frontpiece, colored to designate the branch of service. The colors remained the same, but all firemen wore a similar frontframe with a colored insert to designate branch and company number.

For example, members of ladder companies had a red insert with white numbers, rescue firemen had a blue insert and squad members had yellow. Enginemen wore a black leather insert and firemen assigned to fireboats wore green. This required changing only the insert if a member transferred. More than 40 years later, this basic design still is in use by the FDNY.

On March 14, 1960, the FDNY provided mutual aid to Nassau County when the Inwood Volunteer Fire Department requested help at a major fire sweeping through the seven-story (plus penthouse), one-block-square Nautilus Beach Club apartment house on the boardwalk in Atlantic Beach, Long Island. (Atlantic Beach was under the fire protection of the Inwood F.D.)

Ten engines eventually were put to work as the FDNY joined forces with Lawrence, Cedarhurst, Woodmere, Hewlett and Valley Stream Departments. FDNY units responded to the blaze at 11:51 a.m. and operated until 5:40 p.m.

April 13, 1960, saw a rather difficult and fast-spreading fire handled in a smooth and professional manner by midtown Manhattan companies. The electric motor in an old wooden escalator that served the Flushing line in the subway station at Broadway and 41st Street caught fire. The air movement through the Times Square station, caused by trains moving through the tunnels below, acted like a bellows and accelerated the fire. Flames raced up the large escalator, feeding on grease, dust and the wood of the moving stairs themselves.

Flames soon were roaring up the 60-foot-long escalator through various levels of the station. Arriving firemen were unable to enter the subway from the street level due to the extreme smoke and heat venting through the entrance stairs. Instead, they first directed their efforts to prevent the fire from entering the stores at the street level. The build-up of heat was intense (it was estimated to have reached 1500 degrees), plaster spalled from the walls and ceilings, concrete buckled and 6- x 6-inch wooden turnstiles were burned to nubs.

The initial operation employed fog lines by Engines 54 and 26 on the street level to cool and control the heat threatening the stores. Engines 34 and 1 teamed up to stretch a line into position from the entrance at 41st Street and Seventh Avenue (a block away). Engine 34 ventured through a passageway and attempted to cut the fire off from above.

Ladder Company 4 arrived first and made their way to the upper level of the subway station. Fireman Farrell of Ladder 4 donned a mask and made his way past the fire and located and removed three men cut off by the blaze. Ladders 21 and 24 searched the other levels of the station. Engine 65 managed to get a line into good position by stretching down a ramp that wound around the escalator. They pressed down to the next to last level and operated their line.

The company found an excellent spot and quickly was able to knock down the bulk of the fire on the lower levels, allowing both Engine 34 and Engine 26 to move in with their lines. The fire was brought under control within 35 minutes. Every fireman who operated at this fire was compelled to wear an air mask due to the extreme conditions.

The loft area of lower Manhattan was the site of a major FDNY fire prevention program. Field inspections and familiarization's were conducted in an attempt to reduce the terrible toll these buildings had taken on New York firemen for many years. Despite these efforts and mandating sprinklers in many occupancies, the danger of firefighting never can be removed totally. This became tragically evident on the evening of November 18, 1960.

United Airlines plane crashed into Pillar of Fire Church at Sterling Street and Seventh Avenue, Brooklyn, on December 16, 1960.

FDNY units operated for 104 continuous hours at the crash scene.

At 6:30 p.m., Box 199 was transmitted for a fire in a building on the corner of Broadway and Grand Street. Flames quickly raced through the 100- x 175-foot, five-story building and five alarms rapidly were transmitted. Suddenly, a localized collapse trapped three members operating in the cellar. Despite the heroic efforts of Brother firefighters, Lieutenant McDermott and Firemen Sammon of Engine 31 and Cosner of Squad 8 lost their lives.

During December 1960, the FDNY was called upon to operate at two of the most complicated and tragic fire operations in the history of the department. The members of the department proved themselves, once again, to be up to the task no matter what. But even the most experienced and battle-tested among them never would forget December 1960.

A mixture of rain and snow was falling on the city the morning of December 11, 1960. Visibility in the sky above New York was poor, with an estimated ceiling of only 600 feet. A United Airlines four-engine DC-8 jet was heading to Idlewild Airport (now John F. Kennedy International Airport), with 84 people aboard. Another plane, a TWA four-engine Super Constellation, was bound for LaGuardia with 44 people onboard. Supposedly, the two planes were "stacked" at different altitudes as they approached the New York area.

The two planes collided at about 10:34 a.m. over Staten Island's south shore. The flaming TWA Super Constellation crashed into Miller Field, a little-used Army Air Field on Staten Island. The three sections of the plane narrowly missed the homes of nearby New Dorp.

The second plane, struggling to stay in the air roared on for 10 more miles before it began plummeting toward one of the most densely populated sections of the city, Brooklyn's Park Slope. Just before it hit the ground, the jet's wing clipped an apartment building, leaving the wing jutting out of the roof. It then dove into a corner building, shearing its tail section, which traveled onto the intersection of Sterling Place and Seventh Avenue. Numerous other parts of the plane smashed into a nearby church, a garage and a row of brownstone buildings, causing fires within the structures.

The residents of the Brooklyn neighborhood scrambled for safety. Mothers with young children in their arms ran for cover as the wall of fire grew. Several people opened their front doors, only to be confronted by a curtain of flames. Many escaped through the rear exits of their buildings.

One elderly man standing at the corner of Flatbush and Eighth Avenues watched the growing ball of fire. He reached over and pulled the fire alarm box handle, transmitting Signal Station 1231. This began the response of Engines 269, 280 and 219 and Ladders 105 and 132. First-responding units sized up the situation as they pulled in. They were startled to see the words, "United," become clear through the smoke and flames.

As the 48th Battalion pulled up to the scene, Chief Panarella transmitted a 7-5 signal (All Hands Working). Moments later, he transmitted a second alarm with a third requested only five minutes after that at 10:44 a.m. On the fire scene, first-due Engine 269 stretched lines and immediately began operating at the south-west corner of Sterling Place and Seventh Avenue.

Ladder 105, the first-due truck, arrived and sprang into action. Lieutenant James F. Bush made a quick size-up and split his forces.

One of the FDNY's most difficult and dangerous firefighting and rescue operations ever undertaken. Thousands of workers were trapped below decks with a major fire extending from deck to deck.

More than 250 trapped workers were rescued over FDNY aerial ladders during the Constellation *aircraft carrier fire, Brooklyn Navy Yard, December 19, 1960.*

The airliner struck several buildings in its descent before slamming into the street and breaking into several pieces. The sections of the plane quickly were enveloped in flames fed by jet fuel. On the corner, the five-story brick building at 26 Seventh Avenue was damaged heavily by the crash and the resulting fire and was in imminent danger of collapse. The first and fifth floors were involved heavily in fire as were the exterior, side and rear of the structure. Lieutenant Bush sent Firemen John C. Rogan and John Dailey to attempt and rescue anyone in the plane's fuselage, while he entered the corner building with Fireman John J. Browne, Jr., and began a search of the blazing building.

Searching rapidly, Fireman Browne came upon an elderly, crippled woman on the fourth floor and, with great difficulty, he was able to remove her to the floor below, where he found himself exhausted and barely able to continue. He called out to Bush, who joined him quickly and, together, they were able to remove her to safety and medical assistance.

Firemen Rogan and Dailey approached a large section of the burning plane, surrounded by a large spill of jet fuel. It had crashed between two buildings, both of which now were involved heavily in fire, severely damaged and in imminent danger of collapse. Several persons were visible, still strapped in their seats, surrounded by flames and writhing and twisting in their seats, attempting to free themselves. Rogan and Dailey found several fire extinguishers abandoned by civilians who had been driven back by the extreme heat. Both men picked up the extinguishers and entered the blazing wreckage.

Without benefit of a protective line, they braved the intense heat and pushed back what fire they could with the hand extinguishers. Then, as Dailey tried to hold back the flames, Rogan cut two passengers free and both were pulled alive from the burning plane. Rogan suffered second-degree burns during this rescue operation.

Lieutenant Bush and Fireman Browne had just placed the injured woman in an ambulance when they were informed of a man, badly burned and lying on the sidewalk, adjacent to several burning and exploding automobiles near the corner building. Bush and Browne dashed down the street and were able to pull the injured man to an area of safety and begin first aid. Moments later, the building collapsed.

As the additional units began to arrive, lines were stretched, multiversals set up and deck pipes, large-caliber streams and numerous hand lines placed into operation. Special attention was placed on cutting off fire extension and breaking up the growing body of fire.

Search and rescue efforts began as neighboring structures were entered and searched. Firemen made their way across sidewalks and up stairs that were strewn with Christmas decorations and wrapping paper. The searches continued inside the twisted remains of the jet and in the surrounding buildings.

Just west of the plane's tail section, a major fire was growing at 123 Sterling Avenue, the Pillar of Fire Church. Adjacent to the church, a large section of the four-story 20- x 40-foot brick building at 24 Seventh Avenue was sheared off and fire was spreading throughout the structure. To the north of this building, the next three structures had fires burning in the rear apartments on all floors. Across Sterling Place from the church, three one-story brick buildings were destroyed. The corner building, 26 Seventh Avenue, had flames fully involving the top two floors. The next building to the south also had fire in an apartment on the first floor.

As the fire was brought under control, the grim task of recovering the dead began. In all, 83 passengers of the DC-8 died instantly as it crashed into the Brooklyn neighborhood. One young boy was thrown clear of the plane, but died the next day in the hospital. Six people on the ground also were killed and 15 were injured. Seventeen firemen received injuries battling the fire.

In Staten Island, the crash site was a field and the only firefighting problem was the plane itself. Two alarms were transmitted for Box 2047 at Lincoln Avenue and Baden Place. The fire was declared under control a little more than an hour later. Three of the passengers were extricated from the plane and rushed to nearby hospitals, but they died shortly after their arrival. The total on Staten Island was 44 dead, all passengers of the plane.

The last of the FDNY units operating at Sterling Place and Seventh Avenue in Brooklyn took up 104 hours after their arrival. The heroic efforts of the members who operated at this crash did not go unnoticed. For their rescue efforts at extreme personal risk, Lieutenant Bush and Firemen Browne, Rogan and Dailey all received medals. The many members who responded and operated while off-duty in both Brooklyn and Staten Island also were recognized officially by the department as more than 190 Voluntary Duty Service Rating Bs were awarded. This was one of the largest operations the department ever had faced and while companies still were operating at the site of the plane crash and fire, a dark column of smoke became visible over Brooklyn, pinpointing another historic fire department response.

The New York Naval Ship Yard was bustling with activity on December 19, 1960. The huge aircraft carrier, the *U.S. Constellation* (at the time of the fire, one of the largest ships ever built), was in the final stages of fitting-out. The ship was more than 1000 feet long and 250 feet across at its widest point. The finished ship would displace more than 60,000 tons of water. Above the hangar deck were nine levels, with seven levels below, containing more than 1200 compartments.

Because construction still was being completed, the steel ship had a tremendous amount of wood below decks. Onboard the carrier were 3200 workers, with most of them working below decks. There was no Navy fire crew assigned to the ship; it was protected by the Navy Yard's fire department of 15 men, manning two pumpers and a ladder truck.

At about 10:20 a.m., a dumpster truck working on the hangar deck pushed a heavy trash bin into a steel plate, which bent upward and sheared off the plug of a 500-gallon tank. The contents of the tank, 450 gallons of JP-5 fuel (used to power emergency generators and other equipment), began to pour out onto the hangar deck. With no coffer-dam or dike protecting the spill, the call went out to halt all cutting and burning on the deck.

An attempt to stop the flow was made and a call to the yard fire crew was placed. Some of the escaping fuel ran down a bomb elevator, where a welder was at work, touching off a fire. Hose lines were placed into operation and CO_2 was discharged with no effect. The fire then spread rapidly as the flaming fuel came into contact with wooden scaffolding and other flammables on the deck.

The FDNY received their first notice of the fire at 10:30 a.m., when a special building box at Building 213 at Kent Avenue and Clymer Street was pulled. Within the next 37 minutes, five alarms were sounded for the fire.

Arriving units were faced with a well-advanced fire situation in a structure the equivalent of five city blocks long, a block wide and 14 stories high. Shortly after the fire started, the lighting in the ship failed, plunging the entire vessel into total darkness. Deep within the maze of black compartments were hundreds of workers, cut off from any avenue of escape with acrid, dense smoke and flames closing in.

On arrival, the fire was in complete control of a large section of the hangar deck, forward of amidships. Fire also had extended to galley decks (01, 02, 03 decks), immediately above the hangar deck and the flight deck.

Firemen placed ladders to every opening they could reach in the ship and removed more than 250 trapped workers. Quick-thinking crane operators swung a large platform onto the carrier deck and lifted workers to safety. The crane platform then was converted by firemen into a makeshift ambulance, as injured and unconscious workers (and firemen alike) were lowered to medical treatment on shore.

Two outboard elevators, used to raise and lower planes, were positioned at the hangar deck level and from each of these, stairways went down pier. Hand lines were stretched. Members of the Rescue, Squad and Ladder Companies donned masks and made their way below decks and began one of the most difficult and dangerous search and rescue operations ever attempted in the history of the New York City Fire Department.

At the Welfare Island training site, Assistant Chief James T. Ward realized that a major fire was developing and instructed 100 probies and 14 instructors to board Marine Unit 6 and respond to the fire. Fifty other probies went via department vehicles to the scene. The probationary firemen stretched hose lines, operated cellar pipes and distributors, transported hose and helped in virtually every aspect of the operation.

Probies stretched 3½-inch lines directly from the fireboat to the stern of the flight deck. These lines then were gated down to supply hand lines.

The Mask Service Unit responded to the scene with 25 demand-type masks, 115 extra cylinders, 30 gas masks and 50 extra canisters, two inhalators and one resuscitator with 13 extra cylinders. The unit refilled 50 air cylinders on-scene. In all, 220 masks were on the scene and they were used by members of five ladder companies, six squads, four rescue companies and 35 engine companies. The firefighting force on hand was 580 members (plus more than 100 who would be awarded Voluntary Duty Service Rating Bs).

At the height of the fire, another working fire was reported in a factory at Morgan Avenue and Frost Streets, about a mile away from the Navy Yard. A second alarm was transmitted by the first-arriving units.

A new style of military-type insignias were being worn by firemen and officers by late 1961. The Chief of Department wore three gold stars on his shirt collar, Assistant Chiefs wore two and Deputy Assistant Chiefs had one gold star. Deputy Chiefs had a gold eagle insignia, while Chiefs of Battalions had gold oak leaves. Captains were recognized by two silver bars, Lieutenants had one silver bar and Firemen wore a traditional Maltese cross on their collars. Marine Pilots were issued anchors, while their Marine Engineers sported a propeller.

The Marine Division continued to modernize its fleet with the addition of the 105-foot fireboat *Governor Alfred E. Smith*. A native New Yorker from the Lower East Side, Governor Smith was a great admirer and supporter of the New York City Fire Department. Attention also was turned to the shallow water areas of the city where the larger boats could not navigate. The small, 20-foot fireboat *Blaze* was purchased with these areas in mind. Its two portable 160-gpm pumps fed a multiversal bow monitor.

On land, the FDNY received their first two rear-mount aerial ladders during 1961. These Magirus aerials were 146-foot seven-section ladders mounted on Mack chassis. They originally were assigned as the regular apparatus of Ladder Companies 13 and 24. They later were redesignated as "High Ladder Units 1 and 2."

In 1961, eight members of the department were killed in the line of duty. Two of these men were lost as fire swept through the Times Square Building located at the intersection of 42nd Street, Broadway and Seventh Avenue. This building is familiar to the millions of people who flood Times Square or watch the television coverage of the New Year's Eve White Ball dropping on the roof of this building.

At 8:40 p.m., Box 786 was transmitted for a fire in the subcellar of the 20-story building. Heavy smoke filled the entire structure and five alarms were transmitted. Firemen Hurst and Lang of Ladder 24 were overcome by the thick smoke as they searched the upper floors for victims. An elevator operator also lost his life at this fire.

I n February, 1962, the Staten Island Fire Alarm Dispatchers moved into their new headquarters on Slossen Avenue. They had been working from the Staten Island Borough Hall Office since 1906.

On April 23, 1962, five alarms and a borough call were transmitted for a major brush fire that extended to a number of buildings on Staten Island. The flames raced through a large area in the 23rd Battalion, in the vicinity of Arthur Kill and Richmond Valley. The fire and smoke were so bad that bridges were closed and the rapid transit system on the Island came to a halt. For the first time in FDNY history, New Jersey was asked to provide mutual aid. Six pumpers from Jersey City responded to help battle the blaze. This was the worst of a series of bad brush fires on the Island. During the eight-day period of April 21 through April 28, 1962, there were 51 greater-alarm brush fires on Staten Island.

The clear blue skies over the Mill Basin section of Brooklyn filled with ugly, black smoke as a fire broke out and spread quickly in the Sinclair Oil storage yard on May 10, 1962. Violent explosions, fed by gasoline, fuel oil and solvents, spread the fire throughout the plant.

Arriving units were faced with a series of complications that hampered their ability to battle the blaze. Limited hydrants were available in proximity to the fire, as were areas available for pumpers to draft water directly from the Mill Basin.

Burning petroleum covered the water in the vicinity of the plant. Cans and drums were exploding, throwing flames high into the air and spreading the fire to the wooden piers of the adjacent warehouse, which also was fully involved.

Three fireboats used 200,000 gallons of foam to battle the fire from the water side. On the land side, eight alarms were transmitted to provide the needed manpower to complete the three-hour operation.

Losses were more than $1 million, but the flames were stopped before they could spread to other tanks within the plant and other industrial plants in the area.

A fire was discovered in a huge air-conditioning unit located in the basement of Bonds Clothing Store at 163-36 Jamaica Avenue in Jamaica, Queens, on May 16, 1962. Employees and customers were moved quickly to the street, as the FDNY was notified at 10:42 a.m. First-due units arrived and worked their way into the store, seeking access to the cellar. Members began to descend the cellar stairs when a violent backdraft occurred in the cellar, hurling some members through the store's show windows. Although burned, all members were able to reach the street.

Within 30 minutes, three alarms had been transmitted. Yellow and black smoke poured from the two-story brick structure. Firemen quickly were overcome by the smoke. The fire attack was shifted to a defensive exterior operation and Rescues 1 and 2 were called to penetrate the brick walls to allow streams to reach the seat of the fire.

Marine 6 moves in on blazing Brooklyn oil storage yard, May 10, 1962.

The fire finally was brought under control at 2:20 p.m. Five alarms and a borough call had been transmitted to relieve companies that had been heavily engaged, rapidly exhausted and overcome by the extreme heat and dense smoke.

On October 2, 1962, the new Fire Academy was opened on Welfare Island (present-day Roosevelt Island). Consolidating the various training sites around the city greatly increased the FDNY's ability to provide a high level of training to members of all ranks.

A fire swept through the two-story building at 44-15 56th Road in Maspeth, Queens, on October 26, 1962. Box 7027 was received at 9:33 p.m. and went to four alarms as flames fed on stored fat in the Sefu Fat and Soap Company plant. Chief of Department George David declared the fire under control at 10:42 p.m. and left the scene in his sedan. David had driven about two blocks when he heard a sound he dreaded – the roar of a collapse.

Firemen were overhauling under a loading shed when the wall above them started to collapse. Shouts were stilled by the rumble of the falling masonry. Twenty firemen were caught beneath the pile as their comrades moved in to save them. Chief David transmitted a fifth alarm and returned to the scene.

Injured men crawled from the rubble as the dust settled around them. Firemen worked their way into where the men were trapped.

The chief's fears were becoming real as he realized that six firemen were trapped by the collapse. One by one, the men were located and removed. Everyone's worst fear was evident – all the men still trapped were dead – six men, six firemen lost. The body of the last man was discovered at 12:45 p.m.

For the first time, a funeral for six fallen FDNY firemen was held in one church – Saint Patrick's Cathedral in Manhattan. Thousands of firemen lined Fifth Avenue as six FDNY pumpers, carrying the flag-draped coffins of Captain William Russell, Fireman James Marino and Probationary Fireman Richard Andrews of Engine Company 325, Firemen Richard P. Gifford and George Zahn of Engine 238 and Fireman Francis X. Egan of Ladder 115 rolled to a stop before the cathedral.

On January 1, 1963, the 40-hour week went into effect for the uniformed members of the Department. An additional 470 firemen were appointed and 66 lieutenants, 22 captains, 12 battalion chiefs and three deputy chiefs were made, to complete the new chart.

Arthur J. Massett, a 37-year veteran, was appointed as the new Chief of Department on January 14, 1963, to replace the retiring Chief George David.

The temperature in Harlem on February 18, 1963, had dropped to two degrees below zero and the wind was blowing across the roof tops at about 30 mph. A young girl awoke to find her apartment house on fire and she promptly spread the alarm. The FDNY was notified of the blaze at 3:44 a.m. and the first-due units were faced with heavy fire showing on the northeast portion of the fourth floor of the seven-story, 100- x 100-foot building. Thick smoke obscured the upper floors, but an elderly woman clearly was visible on the fourth-floor window ledge, threatening to jump.

Ladder 28 pulled into position to remove the woman, but had to block the closest hydrant to do so. She was calmed as the aerial was set up and the ladder elevated to the ledge. As the woman was removed from her perch, other members of Ladder 28 and second-due Ladder 30 dashed into the building to locate and remove the remaining 300 people within the building.

Engines overcame the loss of the prime hydrant, the difficult stretch was accomplished quickly and hoses were stretched into position inside the fire building. Engine 69 and Squad 1 stretched lines up the interior stairs with reinforcement by Engine 59. The hallway was held and fire was pushed back toward the fire apartment to keep the one and only stairway open for evacuations from above.

Despite the aggressive attack on the fire, the flames were spreading through the burned-out floor into the fifth floor and horizontally across shafts. With conditions deteriorating, additional alarms were transmitted quickly until the fifth alarm was struck at 5:12 a.m., as the fire had taken hold of the entire structure. Amazingly, no lives were lost and of the 23 injuries to firemen, none was serious.

Brooklyn companies responded to the collapse of a water tank at 61 Clymer Street on February 18, 1963, at 5:10 a.m. The tank plummeted through the roof of the five-story loft and crashed through to the cellar, carrying all the floors and the equipment that was on them, into the cellar.

Arriving firemen were faced with a civilian trapped within the collapse at the first-floor level and the danger of further collapse. Fireman Bethel of Ladder 119 entered the building and worked his way to the man who was pinned under a beam. Bethel dug around the man and exposed the beam, then used a saw to cut the beam to free the man. The victim was handed out and rushed to the hospital. Fireman Bethel later was awarded a medal for his actions.

Just after noon on March 4, 1963, a Department of Hospitals bus was traveling along the east roadway on Welfare Island. The driver suddenly slumped over the wheel and before any of the 10 passengers could react, the bus veered off the road, went through a fence and catapulted over the sea wall. The bus landed on the rocks 15 feet below, then slid into the dark waters of the East River. Four people escaped the bus as it sank; the others were not so lucky.

The Mask Service Unit, located on the Island, requested a first-alarm response over the City-Wide frequency. Box 920 was transmitted with a special call to Rescue 4 at 12:24 p.m. Subsequent calls sent Rescue 2, Marine Companies 6 and 7, Tender *Smoke II* and SCUBA equipment and divers. Chief of Department Massett took command of the operation.

Ladders were placed to access the water from the roadway as the fireboats lowered small boats and began to grapple for the bus, the exact location of which was yet to be determined. Members of Marine 6, operating from a small boat, reported they had snagged something solid about 40 feet from shore. Another grapnel attached to a cable was deployed and made taut from the shore. With the air temperature at 35 degrees and the water temperature 29 degrees, Fireman George Jablonski of Rescue 2, wearing a rubber exposure suit, face mask and extension hose, entered the frigid waters.

Jablonski worked his way to the submerged bus, as divers and equipment were assembled above. Lieutenant Franklin Fritz of Rescue 4 and Fireman Martin Cunniff of Ladder 7 arrived on the scene with their personal SCUBA gear. *Smoke II* had transported additional SCUBA equipment, which then was used by Acting Lieutenant George Rathjen and Firemen Edward Surko and Patrick Burke, who alternated dives.

Fireman George Jablonski of Rescue Company 2, wearing a rubber exposure suit and a Scott air extension, prepares to enter the 35-degree water, March 4, 1963. (Photo by R. Johnstone)

Fireman Jablonski enters East River in search of sunken Welfare Island bus. (Photo by R. Johnstone)

The Welfare Island hospital bus is recovered. (Photo by R. Johnstone)

Reports from divers indicated that the bus was on its side, windows broken and filled with water. Sadly, none of the passengers was alive. Divers again submerged and attached cables from the U.S. Army Engineers' lighter *Gorham,* which hauled the bus to the surface. Members of the Department once again proved their devotion to duty and their readiness to be of service, even underwater.

Fire protection on Staten Island was enhanced with the organization of Engine 166 and Ladder 86, in new quarters at 1400 Richmond Avenue. The Island's firefighting force now consisted of 28 fire companies, doubling the 14 companies first established when the paid department was extended to Richmond in 1905.

April of 1963 was tinder-dry in the northeast United States. In the Bronx, a brush fire spread to the Wheeler Shipyard and Yacht dry dock in the Classon Point section. The fire was discovered at 1:33 p.m. on April 12th and required 16 engines, seven ladders and three special units. It was brought under control at 2:42 p.m. Less than an hour later, a fire broke out in a tenement on Southern Boulevard in the Bronx and was battled by a third-alarm assignment.

A week later, conditions became worse, especially on Staten Island. Hot, gusty winds were blowing across the already dried ground.

Operations began on April 20th at 10:08 a.m., with the report of a fire at the corner of Englewood Avenue and Arthur Kill Road on the southwest shore of the Island. Winds, gusting to 44 mph, whipped through grass and brush lots and drove brush fires into huge walls of flames that headed to occupied neighborhoods.

Conditions were becoming severe and at one p.m., an "all-hands" recall was placed, requesting all off-duty firemen in Staten Island to report for duty. Off-duty firemen from other boroughs volunteering their services also were put to work. By mid-afternoon, 67 of the city's 215 engine companies were massed on Staten Island. During these operations, the FDNY had to turn down the Bayonne, New Jersey, Fire Department's request for six engines to help battle fires on that side of the river.

In Brooklyn, an explosion and fire damaged a one-story building in East New York. The fire spread from the Hygrade Oxygen Corporation at 701 Chester Street to a junkyard and threatened a gasoline station. The five-alarm fire also caused the evacuation of a four-block area.

Then, four alarms were needed to control a fire in a six-story apartment building at 510 Ocean Parkway that extended to two adjacent stores on Church Street in Flatbush. Many of the units operating at these fires were relocated from other boroughs to cover for Brooklyn units moved to Staten Island.

This turned out to be the busiest day in the history of the Department. Nearly 2000 calls were received and 850 alarms transmitted in a 24-hour period by the five borough fire alarm offices. At least 75 families lost their homes or saw them severely damaged by the wind-driven brush fires on Staten Island. Mayor Wagner wrote to Fire Commissioner Edward Thompson: *Never before in its history has the Fire Department been faced with such a great strain upon its resources. The heroic response to this challenge has brought new glory to our city's firefighters. Please convey to them the undying gratitude and appreciation of the people of our city.*

On August 1, 1963, Edward P. McAniff was appointed Acting Chief of Department with the retirement of Chief Arthur Massett.

On Thursday, November 19, 1963, Robert O. Lowery, an Acting Lieutenant and president of the Vulcan Society, was sworn in as Third Deputy Fire Commissioner by Mayor Wagner. Mr. Lowery was the first African-American to hold this position within the Department. The 47-year-old Lowery joined the FDNY as a Probationary Fireman in 1941. In 1946, he was assigned to the Bureau of Fire Investigation in the Fire Marshal's office.

In December of 1960, he was awarded a Department Citation for effecting the arrest of an armed arsonist. He also was commended in 1946 by Chief City Magistrate Edgar Bromberger for effecting the arrest of a burglar who had committed more than 30 acts of arson in Harlem.

He then was named as Chief of Department on August 12th. The six-foot, three-inch, 195-pound McAniff joined the Fire Department in 1936, was made a lieutenant in 1941, a captain in 1948, battalion chief in 1951 and deputy chief in 1954. Before taking over as chief of department, he was deputy chief in charge of Manhattan's Fourth Division.

A classic Manhattan fire broke out on October 23, 1963, in Times Square. The alarm was placed at 10:35 a.m., as dense smoke began to pour from behind a large advertising sign on the front of a store at 1487 Seventh Avenue, near 43rd Street. The sign wrapped around the corner building, covered the third and fourth floors and rose above the roof line. Apparently, the fire started in a ground-floor discount store and swept up to the top two floors and through the roof.

The large sign featured the portrait of a young girl with tears rolling down her cheeks, to reflect her suffering from a cold. (The sign advertised aspirin.) Smoke began to pour through the sign as paint blistered on the girl's cheek. Firemen on ladders chopped through the painted child's face to expose the flames blazing behind it.

Four alarms were transmitted as the smoky fire defied ventilation. Traffic in the area slowed to a crawl as motorists watched the fire operations. The fire was brought under control by about 12:30 p.m. Two firemen suffered minor injuries battling the blaze.

The Division of Safety was established on January 13, 1964, with the objective to reduce the number and severity of accidents involving personnel and apparatus. Procedures were instituted by the division to accomplish its assigned mission through investigations of accidents, analysis of accident cause data, inspections, education of personnel and research in the field of safety.

The operating unit of the division responds to all major alarms of fire, vehicular accidents involving department apparatus and incidents causing multiple injuries to personnel. During fire operations, they assist chief officers, as directed, in the prevention of accidents and the safety of operating personnel. They also conduct on-the-spot investigations of vehicular accidents to determine their cause.

On February 3, 1964, a special unit, designated High Ladder Unit No. 1, was placed in service in the quarters of Ladder Company 24 in Manhattan. The 144-foot, rear-mount aerial ladder was an addition to the company's regularly assigned apparatus. Two firemen were on duty with the unit at all times. The rig responded only on special calls to incidents requiring its use.

A roaring blaze swept through a six-story textile building at 47-49 White Street in Manhattan on February 25, 1964. It took nearly five hours of stubborn effort by 57 fire companies to bring the blaze under control. Box 164 was received as an automatic sprinkler alarm at 6:44 p.m., with Engine 31 and Ladder 8 first due. These units did not take up until February 29th, four days later.

Even the Safety Chief is not always safe. Chief Nolan is helped from a mezzanine collapse in 1970.

Four alarms were banged in within 28 minutes, with Chief McAniff placing the fifth shortly after his arrival. The flames ate through all six floors and into the subcellars. During the battle, a backdraft knocked a fireman from a 15-foot ladder. He was transported to the hospital. Two other firemen were injured when a burst hose threw them against a wall. Three firemen suffered smoke inhalation.

A borough call brought enough help to the scene (nine alarms worth) to control the fire and stop its spread. Hell's Hundred Acres had beat up the FDNY once again.

It was 2:09 a.m. on March 6, 1964, when Manhattan Box 329 was transmitted for a fire on the third floor of a six-story tenement building at 190 Avenue of the Americas (Sixth Avenue). Flames nearly had complete control of the third floor as units rolled in. Fire was extending out into the public hall, up the light shaft and blowing out the front windows of the south apartment. Fireman Naples of Ladder

Street Medicine

The members of the FDNY have been providing emergency medical services to the people of the city since the days of the volunteers. New York firemen helped to pioneer various procedures that are now standard practice. In 1960, a study was done by the FDNY Chief Medical Officer, Gamliel Saland, M.D. In this study, the success and failure rates of people who received the new mouth-to-mouth resuscitation procedure were tracked. In January of 1962, external cardiac massage was added.

New York City firemen were among the first of the new, state-certified emergency medical technicians when the program originally was offered in the early 1970s. The FDNY began a pilot program of its own in September of 1975. More than 1200 members volunteered to be trained, but only 320 could be selected. They had 96 hours of classroom and hands-on training, then spent 10 hours in a hospital emergency room. This totaled 106 hours of training, all on off-tours.

The members who successfully completed the course were certified as New York State Emergency Medical Technician-I.

Company 20 saw three people trapped at a front window with flames cutting off their access to the fire escape. He dropped the fire escape ladder and climbed to the third floor.

Naples stepped between the victims and backed toward the blazing window. Shielding the people with his own body, the fireman began to move them to a position of safety. This calculated action, in assisting, encouraging and guiding these people, without the protection of a hose line, resulted in the ignition of his turnout coat. Naples literally became a flaming torch and received serious burns to his back, legs, arm, neck, ears and face. His rubber coat almost completely was burned off his back.

This courageous action, under conditions of great personal risk, was evidenced by the fact that the persons rescued were uninjured, while Fireman Donald Naples suffered severe burns in effecting their rescue. For his bravery and determination, he was awarded the Bonner Medal.

The downtown Brooklyn waterfront area featured numerous large warehouses that dated back to before the turn of the century. These structures were built using heavy-timber or mill construction. Columns, beams and girders are of massive wooden construction.

At 10:25 a.m., on Friday, March 6, 1964, Box 491 was received for a fire in a warehouse at 167-181 Plymouth Street in Brooklyn. The building was six stories, 100- x 150-foot, with indications of heavy fire on the fourth, fifth and sixth floors. The fire escalated quickly to four alarms. This extremely smoky and stubborn fire was battled for more than 20 hours.

A fire believed to be electrical in origin started in or near two trains parked at the terminal end of the shuttle line of Grand Central Station. It was 4:56 a.m. on April 22, 1964, when FDNY units were dispatched to Box 789 at Park Avenue and East 42nd Street. Upon arrival, it was apparent that this was not an ordinary subway fire. The fire quickly had involved both trains, the wooden section of the platforms and the ties and grease on the tracks.

Radiant and convected heat and direct flame spread the fire quickly within three mezzanines. Smoke and heat pushed into two arcades that connected the east mezzanine with Grand Central Station and the Biltmore Hotel. Flames eventually reached a restaurant and terminal lunchroom on the north side of the east mezzanine.

Five alarms were transmitted as firemen donned masks and crawled into the heat-filled subway entrances and made their way along the maze of corridors to battle the fire. Companies were sent into all buildings affected by the heat and smoke and conducted searches.

A line was advanced from a protected ramp slightly below and at a right angle to the fire. Eventually, three lines moved in from this vantage point and the fire was brought under control. The extreme heat caused the failure of metal columns adjacent to the platform which, in turn, caused the surface of 42nd Street above the fire area to sink eight to 10 inches. The street was closed to traffic as exhausted firemen began to take up their hose.

The early-morning hours of May 26, 1964, saw two four-alarm fires erupt almost simultaneously. The first, which broke out at 3:48 a.m., routed nearly 100 people from their beds, as three three-story dwellings burned in the Woodside section of Queens.

The other blaze started 18 minutes later in a block-square lumberyard in Brooklyn's Williamsburg section. No injuries were reported at either fire.

At the Woodside fire, the three multiple dwellings were damaged heavily. All of the residents were evacuated safely from the structures at 52-29 Skillman Avenue. Twenty-one companies, including 12 engines and five hook and ladders, brought the fire under control in one hour.

The other blaze, Box 283, Porter Avenue and Ingraham Street in Brooklyn, was more stubborn. Twenty-four units, including 14 engines and five hook and ladders, raced to the scene in response to the four alarms. This fire took almost two hours to subdue.

On August 9, 1964, Commissioner Edward Thompson stepped down, due to his nomination as a candidate for Justice of the Supreme Court, 17th Judicial District (Queens), New York. The FDNY Chief Fire Marshal Martin Scott was appointed as the new Fire Commissioner by Mayor Wagner.

Brooklyn fire companies raced through the streets on September 20, 1964, to a reported fire on the 12th floor of a 14-story housing project building at 224 York Street. It was just after 8:30 a.m., when Rescue 2 arrived at the box to see a woman climbing out of a fire apartment window on the 12th floor. With the elevator unavailable, the firemen hit the stairs at a run.

Members entered the fire-floor hallway and began to force the locked apartment door as Fireman James E. Bowler and Fireman George Lee of Rescue 2 continued to the 13th floor. The woman below them was dangling three-quarters of the way out of the window. Bowler grabbed the 1½-inch standpipe hose and wrapped it around himself and returned to the 13th-floor window. Below, it was obvious to the fireman that the excited woman either would fall or jump from the window if action wasn't taken.

One of the most important modern developments in firefighting arrived in New York City in 1964 when the Department took delivery of the first Mack "aerialscope." This unique apparatus, dubbed "Tower Ladder" 1, was put into service at the quarters of Ladder Company 1, at 100 Duane Street, near City Hall.

Department Order 170, on August 28, 1964, outlined the new rig's purpose, assignment, location and description. It officially went in service on August 31st.

During the period from December 19, 1964, to February 5, 1965, the Tower Ladder went to work at four fifth alarms, eight fourth alarms, five third alarms and one second alarm.

The week of January 29th to February 5th (1965), the Tower Ladder worked at three fifth alarms, three fourth alarms and one third alarm. All of these fires were fought in sub-freezing temperatures. All these operations were in addition to the normal boxes the company responded to in lower Manhattan. A new era in firefighting had arrived.

Another "innovation" introduced to the FDNY in 1964 was the rotary power saw. This new tool was 2¼-feet long, approximately 25 lbs. and developed 5½ horsepower. The portable saw ran on a gasoline and oil mixture and developed 6000 rpm. The saws came with three types of blades to cut metal, concrete and wood. Primarily, it was intended to be used to cut quick ventilation holes in roofs and floors, but firefighters always have been able to adapt to any situation and the saw began to be used for various jobs at fires and emergencies.

The Tower Ladder added a new tool to the FDNY arsenal. Tower Ladder 1 operates in the 16th Battalion in the mid-1960s.

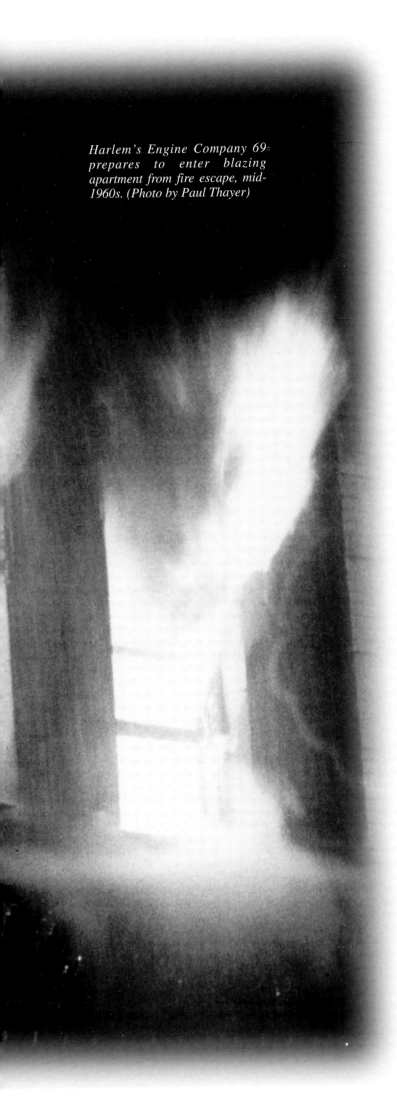

Harlem's Engine Company 69 prepares to enter blazing apartment from fire escape, mid-1960s. (Photo by Paul Thayer)

Fireman Bowler, with the hose secured about his waist, climbed out of the 13th-floor window. Fireman Lee, using a steam pipe as a source of friction, slowly lowered the hose and Bowler to the window below. When he reached the hysterical woman, he wrapped his legs around her and moved her inside away from the window ledge.

At this time, the door to the apartment was forced and firemen dashed under the flames and reached Bowler and four family members. All were removed from the apartment and rushed to Cumberland Hospital, suffering from smoke inhalation. Bowler received the James Gordon Bennett Medal for his efforts.

The new Verrazano-Narrows Bridge opened on November 21, 1964, resulting in vastly improved fire protection for Staten Island. Brooklyn fire companies now could respond to greater-alarm fires or relocate at Staten Island fire company quarters with a saving of 30 to 60 minutes over previous response times. The municipal ferry from Manhattan now is reserved as a secondary means of reaching the Island.

On December 19, 1964, Chief Edward McAniff retired and a new head of the uniformed force was named. John T. O'Hagan, a 39-year-old father of two placed number one in a competitive exam for the chief post. He was the youngest man ever to lead the uniformed force of the FDNY. O'Hagan assumed command with only 17 years on the job.

During 1965, the FDNY closed one of its most famous firehouses- "The Big House" in Jamaica, Queens, once the home of Engine 275, Engine 298, Engine 299, Ladder 127 and the Chief of the 50th Battalion. These companies were relocated to three new firehouses in eastern Queens. (The building now is used as a child care center.)

A Vacant Building Inspection program was initiated in February, 1965, because of the high incidence of fire experienced in vacant buildings in 1964. Inspections were increased and better follow-up procedures were instituted to ensure that owners complied with orders to board up or demolish buildings. Methods of reporting fires in vacant buildings were improved with the establishment of a new monthly vacant building report that helped to pinpoint areas with numerous incidents.

During the early-morning hours, an explosion and fire destroyed the Black Muslims' Harlem headquarters on February 24, 1965. It was believed that the blast and blaze were set off by a fire bomb hurled through a window of the Black Muslim Mosque No. 7, at 102 West 116th Street, from an adjacent roof top.

The fire bombing was an apparent reprisal for the murder of Malcolm X (assassinated while giving a speech on February 21st), who was being laid out in a funeral parlor 10 blocks away from the fire scene. Another fire occurred in a mosque in San Francisco at about the same time.

The mosque fire on West 116th Street was battled by 115 firemen, using 20 pieces of fire apparatus. Three alarms were needed to still the blaze, fought in freezing weather. Six firemen and a civilian were injured by falling debris. The roof of the four-story building collapsed at the height of the blaze and a brick wall crashed into the street, burying Engine 91 and Ladder 40 beneath tons of debris.

Just before 10 a.m. on May 31, 1965, Rescue Company 3 was special-called to the emergency room of Lincoln Hospital in the Bronx. The dispatcher had advised them by phone that a young man had his hand enmeshed in a commercial meat grinder.

Upon arrival, the situation was examined and various extrication methods were discussed. It was agreed that the new "Partner Saw" was the tool of choice.

The anesthetized patient was protected with asbestos blankets and moved to a lounge area to provide better ventilation. All safety precautions were in place and firemen prepared to begin the delicate operation. Two members held the boy's hand and the grinder steady while two other members worked the saw. One man brought the saw up to full rpms and the other gently guided the saw into the work while holding the saw guard.

Cuts were made until the hand became visible and the Chief Surgeon was able to make an examination. The doctor directed the work to continue and the firemen made two additional cuts. The Chief Surgeon then took over and removed the patient's hand from the grinder. The young man lost one finger and the tips of two others but the Chief Surgeon stated the boy had the FDNY to thank for saving his hand.

The Fire Department of the City of New York celebrated its Centennial on June 1, 1965, with a parade and ceremony at City Hall. About 5000 off-duty firemen marched up lower Broadway. The parade was led by a modern diesel pumper and followed by the United States 1st Army Band. Old and new fire apparatus were mixed among the firemen and dignitaries in the line of march.

The ticker-tape parade through "The Canyon of Heroes" was more than fitting, as thousands of New Yorkers turned out to cheer the firemen as they have since the days of the volunteer department. Mayor Wagner praised the firemen during his speech as "the bravest of the brave." He spoke of the growth of the department to its then 13,186 men and 282 firehouses and of the 609 men who had made the Supreme Sacrifice, giving their lives in the line of duty.

The Fordham-Kingsbridge section of the Bronx suffered two four-alarm fires on May 22, and 23, 1965. The blazes struck two Jerome Avenue taxpayers within a mile and a quarter of each other. Eleven firemen were injured battling both fires and 19 stores were damaged or destroyed.

The first fire broke out at 8:40 p.m. on May 22nd, at 3533 Jerome Avenue at Gun Hill Road. A dairy store, fur shop and auto parts store were involved and the flames then spread to six other occupancies. Firemen used the elevated subway tracks as a vantage point to direct streams into the burning stores. Several of the injured firemen were struck by exploding pressurized paint cans when the flames reached a paint shop.

Less than 27 hours later, 10 stores were damaged heavily as fire swept through 2748 to 2766 Jerome Avenue. The alarm was transmitted at 11:35 p.m. and required an hour and 15 minutes to control. Four firemen were injured at this fire.

A 10-alarm fire roared out of control for more than four hours after an explosion rocked a lumberyard at Varick Avenue and Stagg Street in Brooklyn. Box 290 was transmitted at 1:40 p.m., August 12, 1965, and quickly became a fifth alarm. Sixty pieces of fire apparatus brought 350 firemen to the scene to battle the blaze. Flames shot 100 feet into the air as firemen battled radiant heat and a fast-moving wall of fire spreading toward gasoline and kerosene storage tanks on Newtown Creek, only several blocks away. Twenty buildings were destroyed as the fire was driven by a brisk wind.

Two borough calls and the arrival of the Super-Pumper (its first fire) were needed to control the blaze. Two fireboats helped feed the fire department pumpers and it is estimated that in four hours, about 3.6 million gallons of water were poured on the fire.

During this battle, another blaze broke out about three miles away, in the Red Hook section of Brooklyn. Flames tore through two abandoned, two-story buildings at 55 and 57 Sullivan Street, then spread to two three-story frame houses. Four alarms were transmitted before this fire could be controlled.

At 5:28 p.m., November 9, 1965, most of New York City went black. Except for Staten Island and the Bay Ridge section of Brooklyn, the city and a major portion of the northeast United States and parts of Canada suffered a major power failure. FDNY emergency radio facilities quickly were up and running, as were the members of the Department.

A total of 662 alarms were sounded within the five boroughs during the period of the blackout. Fire company response was slowed by extremely heavy traffic and the lack of traffic controls and street lighting. Three 7-5s, two second alarms and a dispatcher's third alarm fires were handled without difficulty. Numerous calls for emergency lighting in hospitals and other high-priority locations were answered by the FDNY.

Hospital operating rooms, delivery rooms and recovery rooms were supplied with light and power. Blood bank refrigerators, iron lungs and incubators were powered. Corridors, stairways and emergency rooms were lit.

Hundreds of people were removed from stuck elevators. These operations became more difficult due to the lack of available lighting. This also caused panic and hysteria among those trapped. Thousands of riders were removed from stalled cars in the pitch-black subway system. By the light of the next morning, the City had returned to "normal."

By the end of 1965, it had become painfully obvious that the growing levels of runs and workers the FDNY was experiencing was only going to continue. In an effort to meet the increasing demands of fire and emergency operations, coupled with the tremendous rise in false alarms, the FDNY administrators sought to increase protection in the high fire activity areas. Ladder 54 was organized on April 22, 1966, and quartered with Engine 96 in the Bronx. Squad 4 went in service with a pumper, to respond in the East New York and Brownsville sections of Brooklyn. Engine 232 was organized in Brownsville on July 8, 1966. Starting in September, Ladder Company 15 was relocated from lower Manhattan to the quarters of Ladder 103 on Sheffield Avenue in Brooklyn from 6:15 p.m. until midnight, under the identity of "Ladder 193." Engine 331 and Ladder 173 were organized in Queens on December 2nd.

As the swelling fire load was being addressed, another ominous cloud began to form on the FDNY's horizon – a New York City fiscal crisis. In June, Mayor John Lindsay explained to the public that the 15-cent subway fare was going to be lost. He also projected a 10 percent cut across the board of all city services, including the police and fire departments.

The year 1965 was an important one for FDNY apparatus. The Department received the new Super-Pumper, ordered in 1963. Three Super-Pumper satellite tenders, 10 pumpers powered by diesel engines and 35 new chief's cars went into service.

The Super-Pumper went into service on October 1, 1965, and brought to land operations power equal to that of the mighty fireboat *Fire Fighter*. The six-stage pump, driven by a 2200-horsepower, Deltic design, 16-cylinder, opposed piston engine, was capable of pumping 8800 gallons per minute at 350 pounds per square inch (psi) or 10,000 gallons per minute. A water cannon with a five-inch tip was mounted on the tractor and could deliver 7500 gallons per minute.

The Tender was a Mack tractor and semi-trailer with numerous inlets feeding an eight-inch McIntyre Monitor nozzle. The flat hose bed also carried 2000 feet of 4½-inch hose.

As part of the Super-Pumper System, three satellites also were put into service. Each satellite was a Mack four-wheel, cab-forward-type hose truck. Besides the 2000 feet of 4½-inch hose they carried, a six-inch Stang "Intelligent" monitor nozzle was mounted on the rig.

The Super-Pumper Unit was stationed at 26 Hooper Street in Brooklyn; Satellite 1 was located on Lafayette Street in Manhattan. Satellite 2 was quartered on East 138th Street in the Bronx. Satellite 3 was on Fifth Avenue in Brooklyn.

The FDNY brings out the big guns with the introduction of the Super Pumper System in 1965. Here, a member fits a nozzle on the Tender's monitor during a multiple-alarm fire.

The Super Pumper went into service in 1965, with the capacity to pump 10,000 gallons a minute.

R obert O. Lowery became Fire Commissioner, effective January 1, 1966, at 9 a.m. The 24-year FDNY veteran had served the Department as a fireman, fire marshal and Deputy Fire Commissioner. Lowery, 49 years old, was the first African-American to be named Fire Commissioner of New York City.

On January 27, 1966, a six-story building at 462 Broadway in Manhattan collapsed, trapping several people. Box 199 was transmitted and fire companies arrived to find that the three upper floors of the 103-year-old loft building had collapsed due to extreme overloading.

Firemen tunneled and shored to reach two people trapped for more than an hour. A careful search could find no further signs of life and the operation was suspended by Chief O'Hagan, due to the extreme danger of further collapse.

The following week, 21 two-man teams of fire inspectors fanned out in Hell's Hundred Acres in an attempt to locate dangerous buildings and prevent a recurrence of the fatal collapse.

Seven firemen were injured in a stubborn fourth-alarm fire that ravaged a supermarket and nine other stores in the Bronx on January 28, 1966. Twenty-eight companies descended on the Jerome Avenue taxpayer. The blaze had broken out shortly before 7:30 p.m. and was not declared under control until 10:10 p.m.

Flames spread from the food store and also damaged a drugstore, laundry, bake shop, florist, candy store and several other businesses. Five of the injured firemen were treated at Montefiore Hospital. The Tower Ladder also was special-called and operated at the blaze.

On February 23, 1966, Tower Ladder 1 and the Super-Pumper also played an important role in the extinguishment of a five-alarm fire that spread quickly through 10 attached two-story homes. The fire affected 2086 to 2104 Tiebout Avenue, Bronx, and was battled for an hour and a half.

Firefighters were shocked by 28 deaths in 18 fires in Brooklyn and Queens in the first three months of 1966. In late March 1966, the FDNY launched an intensive campaign to educate residents in some of the city's poorest sections.

In Brooklyn, 13 of the dead were children. Seven had been left alone and were playing with matches. Four died in one fire and three in another. Hardest hit by the deadly fires were Brownsville, East New York and Bedford-Styuvesant in Brooklyn and South Jamaica in Queens. These areas were given maximum attention from the highly trained Bureau of Community Relations.

On April 17, 1966, a fire broke out in the Jewish Theological Seminary of America at Broadway and 122nd Street. The building had two wings that were separated at the corner by a tower, which housed a collection of 200,000 volumes – some very rare – and all dealing with Hebraic and Judaic culture.

The red brick tower had only one steel stairway to reach the books and periodicals that were stacked eight rows high in steel shelves on steel floors on every level of the tower. The fire started in the stacks at sometime around 10 a.m., but the alarm was not turned in until 17 minutes later.

Enginemen were unable to reach the seat of the blaze with their lines. Ventilation also proved to be as difficult as stretching lines had been. Deputy Assistant Chief Alfred Eckert called for the Department's high ladder (144-foot aerial). This ladder enabled the firemen to reach an offset of the building on the 10th floor.

Despite the tremendous heat, water was used sparingly and firemen wearing masks climbed the steel stairs and placed tarps over the books. Sixty firemen were injured battling the blaze.

The Jewish Theological Seminary fire, April 17, 1966. The 144-foot-high ladder in operation.

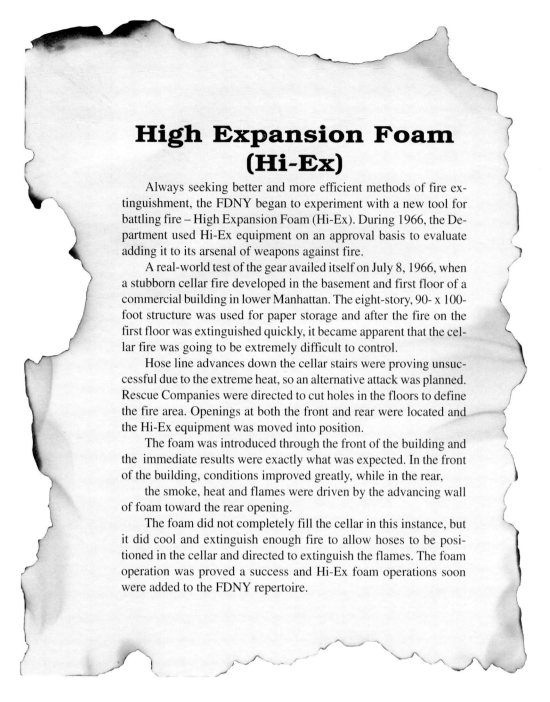

High Expansion Foam (Hi-Ex)

Always seeking better and more efficient methods of fire extinguishment, the FDNY began to experiment with a new tool for battling fire – High Expansion Foam (Hi-Ex). During 1966, the Department used Hi-Ex equipment on an approval basis to evaluate adding it to its arsenal of weapons against fire.

A real-world test of the gear availed itself on July 8, 1966, when a stubborn cellar fire developed in the basement and first floor of a commercial building in lower Manhattan. The eight-story, 90- x 100-foot structure was used for paper storage and after the fire on the first floor was extinguished quickly, it became apparent that the cellar fire was going to be extremely difficult to control.

Hose line advances down the cellar stairs were proving unsuccessful due to the extreme heat, so an alternative attack was planned. Rescue Companies were directed to cut holes in the floors to define the fire area. Openings at both the front and rear were located and the Hi-Ex equipment was moved into position.

The foam was introduced through the front of the building and the immediate results were exactly what was expected. In the front of the building, conditions improved greatly, while in the rear, the smoke, heat and flames were driven by the advancing wall of foam toward the rear opening.

The foam did not completely fill the cellar in this instance, but it did cool and extinguish enough fire to allow hoses to be positioned in the cellar and directed to extinguish the flames. The foam operation was proved a success and Hi-Ex foam operations soon were added to the FDNY repertoire.

The afternoon of June 16, 1966, was a beautiful day to be on the water. The air temperature was 85 degrees, the wind was from the southwest at about eight knots and the water temperature was approximately 62 degrees. At 2:12 p.m., in Staten Island's Kill Van Kull (a narrow estuary connecting Newark Bay and the Upper Bay of New York Harbor), the tanker *Alva Cape* collided with the tanker *Texaco Massachusetts*.

The *Alva Cape* was loaded with 132,854 barrels of naphtha in 21 tanks (42 gallons per barrel = 5,579,868 gallons). The *Massachusetts* was empty, after unloading her product earlier that day. The crews of both tankers and the tugboats that were powering them took actions to disengage and clear the two tankers.

For three minutes, everything was quiet and there were no signs of fire or smoke from either vessel. Naphtha (a flammable liquid) was escaping from the ruptured *Alva Cape*. The vessels continued to move slowly and were about 450 feet apart when a tremendous explosion was heard near the *Alva Cape*. Suddenly, the water between the tankers was a sea of flames.

A nearby tugboat captain reported the explosion by radio to his dispatcher, who relayed the information to the FDNY Marine Administration Division at Pier "A," North River. A visual check of the report was easy, as a large, black cloud was visible near Bayonne, New Jersey.

The FDNY fireboat fleet was underway moments later. Even the *Fire Fighter*, out of service due to superstructure painting, soon had her decks cleared and was steaming toward the growing fire.

As the fireboats converged, they were confronted with the waters around the *Alva Cape*, covered with flaming naphtha. From bow to stern, the paint on her hull was burning off. On the main deck, in the amidships and after superstructures and from the hole in the hull, heavy fire was visible.

Both vessels were drifting toward a tank farm on the Jersey shore, but luckily, were able to drop anchor to stop their motion. Smaller police, Coast Guard and private boats moved in and began to remove people from the water. Firemen ascertained the cargo and commenced operations. The *Smith*, Marine 8, moved in between the two tankers and, at full propulsion and pumping capacity, drove a wedge of water between the two tankers. The *Fire Fighter*, Marine 9, maneuvered in behind the *Smith*, utilizing her 20,000-gpm capacity, both to hit fire and protect the *Smith*.

Lieutenant Robert Summerbell and Fireman Gerard Hogan boarded the *Massachusetts* and conducted a quick primary search that proved negative. A tugboat captured the *Massachusetts'* anchor line and raised it, while other tugs pushed the tanker away from the blazing *Alva Cape*. The *Fire Fighter, Smith* and *McKean* (Marine 1) then were positioned and streams brought to bear on the fire. Foam was directed into the blazing tanks.

The tender *Smoke II* shuttled manpower and foam out to the fireboats. The fire was proving extremely difficult to control, as naphtha re-ignited several times, until the tanker's hull was cooled sufficiently. Final extinguishment of the blazing crew's quarters was made by firemen wearing masks.

The loss of life on the *Alva Cape* was 19 crew members. Three were lost on the *Massachusetts* and 11 men perished on the two tugboats originally pushing the tankers. The FDNY honored the actions of the Marine units for their heroics, especially Lieutenant Summerbell and Fireman Hogan, who were awarded medals.

The world of the FDNY fireman was changing drastically by mid-1966. They now faced vandalism, staggering numbers of false alarms and personal attacks on operating members.

A far-reaching program was initiated by the office of Mayor Lindsay on March 31, 1966, to combat the serious false alarm situation. It was noted that the Department responded to 32,895 false alarms in 1965, an increase of 30 percent compared to the year before. False alarms had risen 300 percent since 1955.

These false alarms were beginning to take a heavy toll on both the firemen and the citizens of New York City. Some fire units were being bombarded by false alarms so heavily that in some areas of the City, people were without immediate fire protection for as many as 15 hours out of 24.

The 12th Battalion in East Harlem – where 18 civilians were killed in 1965 – responded to nearly 1200 false alarms. On Tuesday, March 29, 1966, four children were asphyxiated in a fire on the sixth floor of an apartment house at 445 Claremont Parkway, the Bronx. According to Fire Commissioner Lowery, the firefighting units that normally would have responded to the alarm – Engine Company 46 and Ladder Company 27 – already were responding to a false alarm.

On March 19, 1966, Fireman Robert T. Smullen, 31, the father of five children and a veteran of five years on the FDNY, was killed accidentally while his ladder company was responding to a false alarm in Brooklyn.

A two-alarm fire roared out of control for nearly three quarters of an hour and injured two firemen late in the afternoon of Saturday, July 23, 1966. The minor blaze on Boerum Street in Brooklyn mushroomed in size, as hydrant after hydrant in the area was found to be out of service. Neighborhood children apparently had damaged the hydrants to control the water flow for games on the hot City streets. Objects had been lodged on the hydrant nozzles to provide a spraying effect. This diminished the flow of water so greatly that hydrants more than a block away had to be used.

Firemen also were becoming easy targets for the social unrest that was brewing across the country. Two firemen in Brooklyn had been injured by objects thrown at them from the roofs of tenement buildings. One fireman received a head injury that required 27 stitches to close a wound caused by a brick. Another received 11 stitches to a leg injured in the same fashion.

Extra fire units were being relocated into the troubled areas and helmeted policemen patrolled the neighborhoods in an effort to keep the uneasy peace in Brooklyn's East New York section. Firemen were baffled, trying to explain why only a week before, nine people had been rescued from a burning tenement and a week later, bricks were being thrown at the firemen from the very same building.

On the night of July 25, 1966, at approximately four a.m., a Molotov cocktail was used to start a fire in a parking garage on West End Avenue in Midtown Manhattan. As Engine Company 40 responded, the three youths, believed to be responsible for the first fire, also threw a fire bomb at the pumper as it rolled down West 64th Street. The fire bomb missed the apparatus and failed to ignite.

The final bomb was tossed at the building housing Engine 40. It hit the firehouse's outside brick wall and caught fire. By the time the engine returned, the fire had burned itself out. The suspects, reported as teenagers, fled and police and firemen were left with no idea what sparked the incident.

Part of the ongoing efforts by the Department to control the rising number of vacant building fires was identification. Since the new program began in February of 1965, nearly 4000 vacant buildings had been identified. By the first week of August, 1966, the FDNY already had extinguished 580 fires in vacant buildings. The Commissioner of Buildings called on the City's District Attorneys to help track down the building owners.

A fast-spreading fire swept through five decks of the ocean liner *Hanseatic* while it was berthed at Pier 84 (foot of 47th Street) in Manhattan. Five alarms were struck for Box 817 as the fire moved from the German liner's engine room to its upper decks.

The dangers faced by FDNY members increased as a new problem was added – attacks on firemen by civilians. Starting in the 1960s and continuing for the next decade, these attacks injured scores of firemen and damaged apparatus.

FDNY units arrive at the ocean liner Hanseatic on September 7, 1966. The ship fire went to five alarms.

Only three of the 425 passengers were onboard at the time of the fire, which was reported at 7:30 a.m., on September 7, 1966. The 500 crew members and the few passengers onboard had been removed quickly from the ship. The blaze, which had spread undetected, now was escaping on the various passenger levels, feeding on the fancy wood paneling and other flammable finishings.

Three fireboats, 35 engines, 10 ladder companies and 20 special units descended on the pier and went to work. Two hundred fifty firemen pushed lines into the blazing ship. The toughest assignment was moving lines down into the engine room areas. The heat encountered was so intense that the steel decks and doors warped. Firemen finally were able to penetrate into the deepest recesses of the engine room and delivered 300 gallons of foam to the seat of the fire.

With the blaze controlled, the ship was examined and damages were determined to be more than $1 million. The dogged efforts of the firemen, 12 of whom were injured during the battle, were praised by Chief O'Hagan, who proclaimed that his men did an "amazing job."

On Monday evening, October 17, 1966, at about 9:30 p.m., Herbert Brown, 42 years old, was informed by his wife, Marion, that she detected an odor of something burning. The Browns lived with their four children on the fourth floor of seven East 22nd Street in Manhattan. At first, Brown did not smell the odor, but checked through his apartment for the source. Failing to discover anything wrong in his apartment, he went to the third floor – which was occupied by the Daniels Lamp Company – to locate the source of the burning odor.

Again, he found no signs of smoke, heat or fire. Brown then went to the roof of an extension at the third-floor level. There, he saw smoke issuing from around the roof and skylight of the two-story extension that connected the seven East 22nd Street wing of the building with the five-story structure at six East 23rd Street.

Brown returned to his apartment and told his wife to telephone the Fire Department, which she did immediately. The Manhattan Fire Alarm Office received this call at 9:36 p.m. and transmitted Box 598 (Broadway and 21st Street). Mr. and Mrs. Brown decided to wake up their children, dress them and take them to the street as a precautionary measure, even though there was no smoke present in their apartment yet. As they began to awaken the children, the apartment began to fill with smoke. In a matter of seconds, the apartment was filled with thick smoke and the lights went out.

Engines 14, 3 and 16, Ladders 3 and 12, Battalion Six Chief White and Division Three Deputy Chief Thomas Reilly, were responding as Mr. and Mrs. Brown descended, groping their way down the stairs with the aid of a flashlight. As they reached the sidewalk, the first-due fire companies were rolling to a stop in front of the 20- x 100-foot building.

The companies encountered a heavy volume of smoke in the cellar and the lower floors of this building, which were occupied by lamp and lampshade manufacturers. The cellar was filled with the fabrics and plastic used in making the lampshades.

At 9:46 p.m., the Holmes Protective Company received an indication of a break in their circuit at six East 23rd Street. Two Holmes employees walked the few blocks between their offices and the 23rd Street location. They arrived and opened the drugstore and found a light smoke condition there. Due to the design of the buildings, the fire was able to burn for some time before being detected.

Ladder 3 forced entry to the first-floor art store at seven East 22nd Street, while Ladder 12 raised a ladder to the roof, vented at that location and searched the upper floors. While Ladder 3 searched the first floor, Engine 14 advanced a hose line through the store to the interior stairs on the east side of the store. They encountered intense heat as they descended the stairs to the cellar and began to push back fire rolling across the ceiling.

Engine 3 stretched a line to the second floor via the stairs and operated the line after being confronted with a tremendous heat condition.

At this time, the men in the cellar were ordered to withdraw to the head of the stairs. An additional line was stretched down a portable ladder to the cellar through the sidewalk cellar entrance, where fire was being hit.

At 9:58 p.m., Chief Reilly transmitted the "all hands," which brought Rescue Company 1 and the Seventh Battalion to the scene. Rescue Company 1 was directed to 22nd Street, where they stretched a line with Engine Company 14. Battalion Seven, Chief Walter Higgins, operated with Ladder Company 3 on the 23rd Street side.

At 10:08 p.m., a second alarm was transmitted and six minutes later, Deputy Assistant Chief Harry Goebel arrived and assumed command. Chief Reilly was sent to take charge of the 23rd Street operations. Engine Company 5 and Ladder Company 3 entered the cellar of the drugstore at six East 23rd Street, where their original examination showed no extension of fire. Engine Company 18 and Ladder Company 7 were directed into the first-floor drugstore. These four companies were operating under the supervision of Chief Higgins, while Chief Reilly examined the building and assessed the situation.

Chief Reilly, on the roof of six East 23rd Street, noticed fire extension via the shaft between seven East 22nd Street and 940 Broadway and suggested to Chief Goebel that a third alarm be transmitted.

Chief O'Hagan addresses the members assembled in Madison Square Park, across the street from the 23rd Street collapse, after the last fireman is recovered on October 18, 1966.

Companies in the drugstore were not encountering any of the difficulties being found on 22nd Street. In the cellar, the tin ceiling was removed and a minimum amount of fire was found and quickly extinguished. They operated at a position they believed was at the rear of the drugstore above them.

On the first floor of the drugstore, only a light haze was visible around lights at the ceiling level. Smoke was issuing out of a small, foot-square opening, eight feet above the floor on the rear wall. Two members of Ladder Company 7 joined members of Ladder Company 12, venting and searching the upper floors.

Fireman Nicholas Cicero of Engine Company 5, whose company was operating in the cellar, had been stationed at the head of the stairs at the front of the store. He was directed to clear stock away from the stairs and keep an eye on any developments that could affect the members in the cellar. While moving stock, he noticed a large-scale movement of air into the drugstore from the street. Immediately, Cicero went to the head of the stairs and called down to his Captain. Before the fireman could repeat his report to his officer, who had moved to the bottom of the stairs, a tremendous blast of heat drove him to the floor.

Conditions suddenly had gone bad and Fireman Cicero, now being burned, was driven from his position and shouted, "Get out! Get Out!" This warning did not penetrate to the members operating a hose line at the rear of the cellar. The men in the cellar began an orderly withdrawal, then quickened their retreat as they heard Cicero's anxious calls. Upon reaching the top of the stairs, they were blasted by a wave of heat with several of them being burned.

The men in the cellar did not know that the wall before them cut the depth of the 100-foot building to 65 feet in the cellar. Members on the first floor of the drugstore were unaware that they were actually directly above a major fire that had been burning for a prolonged period, shielded from detection by the insulating effect of the five-inch-thick cement floor beneath their feet. When the beams beneath them burned away to the point they no longer could support the weight, they collapsed without warning.

Deputy Chief Reilly and the members of Ladder Company 7 and Battalion Chief Higgins and the members of Engine Company 18 were thrown into the blazing cellar. Fireman Kaminsky of Ladder Company 7 and Fireman McCarron, Aide to Chief Reilly, were caught on the first floor by a huge mass of flames and felled by the intense heat and resultant shock.

Deputy Chief Allan Hay regrouped firemen in the street outside the collapse and began a rescue effort. A hose line was brought to the front of the building and under extreme conditions, firemen pushed into the blazing store in an attempt to reach the 12 trapped inside. Another line was positioned to protect them as fire appeared behind them.

During this operation, Fireman John Donovan of Engine 18 – who had been away from his company, issuing summonses in the area when his company had been called to the fire – reported to the scene. Learning that his company apparently was trapped in the building, Fireman Donovan geared up and began to help move the line in. In the darkness, the group unknowingly reached the area of collapse. Fireman Donovan was holding the nozzle and as he crawled forward, he fell over the edge. Fortunately, he held onto the nozzle and dangled over the blazing cellar until firemen could pull him back to safety. Donovan was burned and forced to leave the building.

The rescue and fire extinguishment efforts continued, but were hampered by three major collapses and a series of minor collapses of the first-floor flooring. Fourth and fifth alarms were transmitted and additional rescue operations were attempted.

The bodies of Firemen William McCarron and Rudolph Kaminsky were removed from the first floor before 1:30 a.m. Attempts to retrieve the bodies of the 10 men in the cellar continued while the battle against the fire was fought. The rescue operation

was aided greatly by the alertness of Fire Patrolman Edward Pospisil, who had observed some of the lost men operating on the east side of the drugstore. Pospisil drew a map of the location for Chief O'Hagan and from this sketch, the operation was re-directed.

The east wall of the building was breached in two places from the adjoining cellar. From this point, firemen were able to reach their fallen comrades. Across the street in Madison Square Park, thousands of off-duty firemen stood solemnly as throughout the morning of the 18th and into the afternoon, the tragic task continued. As each of the fallen firemen was carried out, the crowd stilled and helmets were removed and weary heads bowed. At approximately 1:45 p.m., the last man was removed.

During the course of the fire, 29 firemen were treated for injuries. Seven of them were removed to Bellevue Hospital. Twelve hundred off-duty members arrived at the scene and volunteered their services. Two officers, Captain Patrick Murphy of Engine Company 5 and Lieutenant Royal Fox of Ladder Company 3, were singled out for their heroic, superhuman efforts to save their men from the cellar. Their actions saved a dozen firemen.

The signal 5-5-5-5 was transmitted and firehouse flags were lowered to half staff in honor of:

- Deputy Chief Thomas A. Reilly – Division 3
- Battalion Chief Walter J. Higgins – Battalion 7
- Lieutenant John J. Finley – Ladder Company 7
- Lieutenant Joseph Priore – Engine Company 18 (covering)
- Fireman John G. Berry – Ladder Company 7
- Fireman James V. Galanaugh – Engine Company 18
- Fireman Rudolph Kaminsky – Ladder Company 7
- Fireman Joseph Kelly (2) – Engine Company 18
- Fireman Carl Lee – Ladder Company 7
- Fireman William McCarron – Aide to Chief Reilly
- Fireman Bernard Tepper – Engine Company 18
- Probationary Fireman Daniel L. Rey – Engine Company 18

On Friday, October 21, 1966, the FDNY and the City of New York paid their last respects to the heroic men who made the supreme sacrifice. More than 10,000 firemen lined Fifth Avenue as 10 of the 12 were given simultaneous funerals at Saint Patrick's Cathedral and Saint Thomas Episcopal Church. The services for the two other firemen were held on Long Island. The 12 firefighters left behind 12 widows and 32 children.

A raging fire was discovered in a clothing store when flames burst through a common wall into a bookstore that shared the first floor of the four-story building at 1169 Avenue of the Americas (Sixth Avenue). A customer grabbed a fire extinguisher, while the bookstore owner began to pull down shelves, trying to prevent the spread of the flames. The alarm was transmitted at 9:11 p.m. on December 22, 1966.

Members of Engine 54 arrived at Box 813, moved a line into the burning bookstore and began to operate. Without warning, the three upper floors of the building collapsed shortly after 10 p.m., trapping seven firemen below. One fireman working on the roof fell down to the third floor where he quickly was rescued. The seven under the huge debris pile would not be removed so quickly.

A tunneling operation began from the front of the collapse structure as firemen began to work their way to the trapped men. Fireman Raymond Brown of Rescue Company 1 spearheaded the rescue effort and tunneled himself into a position where he could establish voice contact with the trapped men.

At this point, a leaking gas pipe caused an accumulation of gas that ignited and exploded. Brown was forced to retreat briefly from the tunnel, then returned and continued his rescue efforts. The danger of a secondary collapse increased as the front wall of the building began to buckle. Despite the danger, Brown continued until he freed the first of the trapped men. Fireman Brown had to drag each member through the tunnel, then re-enter and

The collapse of the four-story building at 1169 Avenue of the Americas. The collapse became "The Miracle on Sixth Avenue," as the last man, Fireman Harry Foy of Engine 54, was freed from the rubble by Fireman Ray Brown and Lieutenant Erwin Alexy of Rescue Company 1 (inset photo).

dig and free another. Six separate times, Brown repeated this operation and six men were saved.

As one of the injured firemen, blackened from smoke and dirt, was being carried to an ambulance, he noticed Commissioner Lowery among the large crowd watching the rescue efforts. "Merry Christmas, Commissioner," he said weakly. The Commissioner snapped to attention and saluted the injured man. "Merry Christmas, Fireman!" he replied. This brought a loud cheer from the firemen surrounding the rescue area.

Brown had crawled back in again and located the last man, Fireman Harry Fay, who was trapped at the legs by some timbers. Brown sawed the beams until he was near exhaustion. (Brown spent three hours working in this tunnel.) Lieutenant Erwin Alexy joined Brown in the tunnel and helped with the final cuts needed to free Fay.

Anxious firemen waited at the mouth of the tunnel as Alexy, Brown and Fay appeared. All were exhausted, but happy. As Fay was placed on a stretcher and placed in an ambulance, a fireman shouted, "Atta' boy Harry!" A smile spread across the grime-covered face of the now-freed fireman as the door to the ambulance was closed.

Amazingly, the seven men who were trapped suffered no major injuries. For their efforts at the "Miracle of Christmas," Fireman Raymond Brown and Lieutenant Erwin Alexy were awarded medals of valor.

A spectacular, yet tragic, rescue effort occurred during a four-alarm fire in the 12-story Standish Arms Hotel at 169 Columbia Heights, Brooklyn. Box 479 was received at 12:45 p.m., on December 30, 1966, as fire swept the top three floors of the apartment building.

During the operation, the crowd began to yell that a woman was trapped at a window. The word spread quickly from fireman to fireman. "Woman in the window. Woman in the window." Fireman Ed Rizzo looked up and saw

Fireman Ed Rizzo at the tip of Ladder 119's 144-foot-high ladder, with Lieutenant Mike Chicko backing him up, approach woman trapped in 11th-floor window, December 30, 1966. (Photo by Francis Murphy)

The woman, with a box in her hands, jumps. Rizzo grabs her, but is unable to hold her. Inside the box: a cat and $50. (Photo by Francis Murphy)

the woman, surrounded by fire at an 11th-floor window. The window next to her belched flames and the fireman knew he had little time.

Rizzo ran to his rig, the 144-foot-high ladder assigned to Ladder 119. The fireman moved onto the ladder. As it was being positioned toward the window, a strong wind swirled around him. Lieutenant Michael Chicko moved in to back Rizzo up as he climbed the aluminum aerial. Rizzo reached the top of the ladder, 138 feet in the air, and realized they still were too short. He looked up at the woman and yelled, "Don't jump, lady!" Rizzo then opened two locks that released a thin, six-foot ladder that extended from the tip of the aerial and started to climb it.

The woman now was surrounded by fire and held a box in her hands. Rizzo pleaded with her to drop the box as he moved to the

very end of the swaying ladder. The fireman rested one hand against the face of the building and raised the other toward the woman and told her to reach for his hand. The flames now were blowing out around her as she dropped the box, curled up, then tumbled out of the window, her clothes on fire.

Rizzo lunged toward her. For one brief moment, he had his hand on her, but in a second, she was gone. The two firefighters laid against the ladder, flames belching out the window above, the wind blowing around them. They slowly climbed down and joined the companies inside battling the fire.

Both men received medals for their heroic efforts, but never would forget the woman surrounded by flames, holding a box – a cardboard box with a cat and $50 inside it.

The year 1966 found some amazing numbers being amassed by FDNY companies. Leading the list of "Runs and Workers" were Engine Company 82 with 6234 runs and 2214 workers, Ladder Company 120 with 6476 runs and 2759 workers and Squad Company 4 with 7483 runs and 1139 workers.

The Department's second Tower Ladder was placed in service during 1967 in the quarters of Ladder Company 14, East 125th Street, Manhattan, a densely populated tenement area. Tower Ladders were proving their versatility in rescue operations and placement of high-level fire streams. Members of the Department were developing new and improved techniques in operations as they gained fire experience.

A roaring five-alarm fire destroyed the century-old Tremont Methodist Church at 178th Street and Washington Avenue in the Bronx. The blaze was discovered by the church organist at about midnight on February 25, 1967.

All of the first-due companies were operating at a nearby two-alarm fire. Companies quickly were filled in and firemen went to work in the sub-freezing temperatures. The Super-Pumper and two satellites also operated at the blaze.

Three four-alarm fires were battled by the FDNY during a three-day period in 1967. On Saint Patrick's Day, eight two-story dwell-ings were damaged heavily or destroyed in Corona, Queens. The fire broke out at about eight p.m. in a Roosevelt Avenue restaurant and quickly spread to a stationery store, dry cleaners, a beauty parlor, a private house and a supermarket.

A major snowstorm hampered operations as firemen battled flames, snow and 13-degree temperatures. Residents of 25 apartments in seven two-story houses were removed as fire extended with lightning speed from one wood-frame to another in Bushwick.

The last of the weekend fourths was in a former Brooklyn high school being used as a training center. The three-story building at Nostrand Avenue and Macon Street soon was destroyed by flames. The Super-Pumper operated at all three fires.

A child playing with matches in an empty classroom closet caused the evacuation of 700 students and the transmission of four alarms on April 12, 1967. The kindergarten through fifth-grade students of P.S. 5, at 30-11 29th Street in Astoria, calmly exited the school as fire units rolled in. Children stood watching as the firemen battled the flames.

One of the first firemen to arrive on the scene, Harold Maloney of Engine Company 263, scanned the sea of children's faces with an anxious look. Were his grandchildren okay? Maloney's wife caught his eye and shouted that they were all right.

One student caused a few moments of anguish as a head count proved the class one student short. Firemen pressed the search as a police radio car sped to the child's home. The boy was located at home and returned to the scene.

Twenty-one firemen were injured battling two four-alarm blazes in Manhattan and the Bronx on May 13 and 14, 1967. The first fire was at Box 147 for a fire at the corner of Hudson and Harrison Streets in Manhattan. The fire was in a six-story olive oil and cheese warehouse.

Unique aerial shot shows Bronx companies operating at a mid-1960s multiple alarm. (Photo by Steven Scher)

Operating members were withdrawn from the building a few minutes before a major collapse occurred. The smoky blaze was battled by 225 firemen and 31 units, including the Super-Pumper and Tower Ladder 1.

The second four-alarm fire roared through a row of taxpayers on Southern Boulevard in the Bronx. Box 2373 was received at 5:33 p.m. and sent Engine Companies 94, 82 and 73, Ladder Companies 48 and 31, Squad 2 and the Third Battalion.

Members of Engine Company 94, under the command of Captain John Nova, had advanced a hose line into the Ber-Ben clothing store at 968 Southern Boulevard. A terrific explosion occurred and showered the firemen with glass, plaster, flooring and other objects as a ball of fire rolled over their heads.

Captain Nova, with a serious neck laceration, began to drag two members of his company out of danger. Other firemen dashed in to help and all those inside soon were outside, taking stock of their injuries. The captain's laceration required 50 stitches to close. Sixteen other firemen also were injured at the fire.

Two firemen were injured and a third treated for smoke inhalation at a fire in a three-story frame house on 873 Fairmount Avenue in the Bronx. Fireman Hugh Flynn of Ladder Company 27 rescued a 200-pound Saint Bernard named Neil from the dense smoke condition. Both the fireman and dog were treated for smoke inhalation.

Alarm Box 4758 came into the Queens Fire Communications Office at 5:19 a.m. on the 13th of January 1967; Friday, the 13th, to be exact. The companies normally assigned to the box were operating elsewhere, so the next closest available units were sent.

Engine Company 298 and Ladder Company 127 reached 101st Avenue, between Brisbin and Allandale Streets, and rolled into a thick concentration of natural gas. Both rigs stalled, starved for oxygen. The ground around the trucks rumbled and vibrated from the force of the gas escaping from a 24-inch, high-pressure gas main. The natural gas was not escaping from a break in the main as first thought but, rather, was caused by the tilting and dislodging of a drip pot cover. (A drip pot is used to collect moisture and condensate in the main.)

The officers ordered the rigs abandoned and the firemen were directed to knock on doors and evacuate the entire neighborhood. The noise levels caused by the leak not only hampered Fire Department communications, but caused much confusion among the civilians being removed from the area.

Chief Fay of the 51st Battalion transmitted a second alarm at 5:31 a.m. Five minutes later, Deputy Chief Weinhofer, still 500 feet from the box, called for a third alarm as the gas cloud ignited. A loud boom was heard and flames shot 85 feet into the sky. Fire also shot out from underneath parked vehicles and, within minutes, the fire apparatus burst into flames.

Within minutes, 14 homes and buildings were burning and firemen were struggling to protect houses not yet on fire. Chief O'Hagan assumed command and additional alarms were transmitted. By 6:57 a.m., the equivalent of 13 alarms were transmitted. The Super-Pumper helped to feed the 76 lines used to halt the spread of the fire. The building fires finally were controlled by 9:58 a.m. But the blazing gas leak itself continued to burn until 3:30 p.m.

Bronx firemen battle a stubborn fire in a row of stores. (Photo by Steven Scher)

Almost 1000 men and 80 pieces of apparatus were needed to control the fires. Nine homes, a garage and a paint factory building were destroyed and eight other buildings were damaged to varying degrees. Due to diligent efforts of firemen, there were no civilian injuries.

A major fire in the Bronx on May 1, 1967, brought out Tower Ladder 14, Marine 4 (Fireboat *Glenn*), Marine 5 (Fireboat *Wagner*) and the entire Super-Pumper System. The blaze occurred in an Army surplus truck yard at Lafayette and Zerega Avenues. The first alarm was received at 4:09 p.m. and escalated to four alarms as flames spread through 10 large storage sheds and dozens of trucks.

The fire was fought from the land side and the water side for one hour and 59 minutes. The flames and smoke could be seen for miles, especially by crews and passengers of planes landing and taking off from nearby LaGuardia Airport.

New York City and other major cities were beginning to suffer from the expanding ravages of incendiary fires, as social unrest was boiling in the inner-city areas across the nation. In 1965, the Los Angeles Fire Department battled numerous fires as a serious riot developed in the Watts neighborhood. The Fire Marshals of the FDNY had their hands full as the incidence of suspicious fires in vacant buildings in New York City rose dramatically.

On Monday, July 17, 1967, two Fire Marshals, John Connell and Michael Proust, were patrolling Brownsville after a rash of vacant building fires. In early June, five incendiary blazes were started in a single night. Fire Marshals stepped up their surveillance in answer to the problem.

As they drove down Amboy Street near Blake Avenue in an unmarked car, they observed a group of eight or 10 youths scatter from a burned-out, two-story, wood-frame building.

The marshals approached the structure and smelled a strong odor of gasoline fumes. On the front steps of the building, they found bottles and rags. As Proust took off in pursuit of the youths, Connell entered the structure. Inside, he could not believe his eyes – four completed Molotov cocktails, three nearly completed fire bombs, 24 empty bottles, rags and tar to seal the fire bombs. Connell also found seven gallons of gasoline neighbors said had been siphoned from parked cars.

This did not stop the rash of vacant building fires, but it did quiet things in this neighborhood, at least for a few nights.

The summer of 1967 was proving very hot for firemen across the country. Major riots caused severe fire situations in Detroit, Newark and Milwaukee. During a six-week period in the summer of 1967, New York City firemen had been shot at nine times and were the targets of bricks, stones and bottles on at least 70 occasions. Things were bubbling in New York, but had not yet reached a boil.

In an effort to protect the firemen, the Fire Department began altering apparatus in 1967. Plywood paneling was used on the side of the cabs and vinyl roofs (strong enough to withstand the impact of a brick tossed from four stories) over the cab portion of the apparatus. Tillers also were fitted with a roof cover to protect the tillerman.

Another aspect of firefighting during dangerous civil unrest situations was the Department's instruction of companies in Emergency Command and Control Procedures. This began in early 1967 at the Welfare Island training facility. These procedures, which established firefighting strategy to be adopted in the event of large-scale disturbances, activate command posts and staging areas. The plan also included the convoy system of apparatus response and fireground operations as integral fire control teams.

Destruction by fire and its growing effect on the people of this nation became a matter for Congressional attention during 1967. Fire Commissioner Robert O. Lowery and Chief of Department John T. O'Hagan appeared at hearings in the nation's Capitol in support of federal assistance and the institution of a National Fire Research Program.

In Mayor John V. Lindsay's Executive Budget Message on April 15, 1967, he reported on the tremendous workload increase the FDNY had experienced in fire alarm response during the period 1955 to 1966. Covered in the remarks was the 355 percent increase in false alarms and an 82 percent increase in fires during this period. Not included in the report was the added administrative workload that resulted from these increases. The increase in 7-5 signals (all-hands working) was 796 percent, as the numbers grew from 191 in 1955, to 1712 in 1966.

Rarely do individual firemen capture the imagination of the civilian world, but Fireman Daniel Tracy is an exception. Tracy performed three major rescues within two years.

On July 21, 1967, the FDNY was called to Box 1655, for a fire in a two-story frame dwelling at 1587 Saint Mark's Avenue in Brooklyn. When Ladder Company 120 arrived at the scene, the fire had complete possession of the basement and was extending through an open cellar door, up the stairs, into the interior hall and was extending into the rooms on the first floor. Entrance through the front door was cut off completely by fire.

Fireman Tracy went to the rear of the building to ventilate when he was informed of a child trapped inside the blazing structure. Tracy was boosted up and through a window by another fireman. The high heat condition drove Tracy to the floor. He crawled from the rear bedroom, toward the extending fire and into the middle bedroom.

Despite the introduction of saws in the FDNY, their use was limited. The tried and true method of roof ventilation was with an ax. (Photo by Steven Scher)

Nearing exhaustion, Tracy searched three beds in the room, located seven-month-old Terry Sykes and started back toward the window. At the same time, an engine company, unaware of Tracy's position, opened the nozzle, driving heat and smoke into the bedroom where Fireman Tracy was with the child. Tracy made it to the window, handed the child to another fireman and collapsed.

For this spectacular rescue, Fireman Daniel Tracy was awarded the Brooklyn Citizens Medal. Tracy, a 1959 graduate of St. John's College of Business Administration, also had rescued five children at a fire in 1965 (and received the Commissioner Edward Thompson Medal) and rescued a mother and daughter in 1966 (awarded the Brummer Medal). The Daniel Tracy Scholarship was named in his honor. This four-year scholarship is for an FDNY (present, retired or deceased) member's dependent who is chosen by a competitive exam. Full tuition and fees at any of St. John's University's four-year colleges is provided.

Fireman Gene Dowling starts up Ladder 25's aerial with scaling ladder at Morgan Post Office Annex fire, December 15, 1967.

Firemen Dowling, Williams and Pizzuto remove victims from blazing Post Office in gusty, 30-mph winds. (Photos by F. Murphy)

It was the height of the Christmas Season when a postal fore- man working in the Morgan Annex Post Office saw smoke pour- ing up out of chutes from the basement and turned in an alarm. Box 676 was received at 9:07 p.m. on December 15, 1967, for a fire in the 10-story, 200- x 800-foot structure with 20-foot-high ceilings at 341 Ninth Avenue at 30th Street in Manhattan. The Post Office, built in 1935, had large, wide-open areas that were pierced with numerous unprotected vertical openings, consisting of conveyor belt systems, spiral mail chutes, duct systems and flush floor openings.

The staff quickly began to evacuate the more than 1800 postal workers, out into the cold, windy night. First-arriving FDNY units reported heavy smoke issuing from cellar vents and mail chutes on the loading platform on the 30th Street side of the building. Know- ing that the standpipe fittings in the cellar would not make up to FDNY fittings, hand lines were stretched.

At 9:49 p.m., a second alarm was requested. Special calls and additional alarms and borough calls were placed until the equivalent of 11 alarms worth of firemen and equipment were on-scene. Heavy smoke billowed from the structure as chief officers directed compa- nies to battle the blaze and search the huge floor areas.

As Ladder Company 25 arrived at the fire, three postal employ- ees were observed trapped at a sixth-floor window (equivalent to 10 stories). Ladder Company 25 positioned its apparatus and ran up their 100-foot aerial. It was obvious the ladder still would be short, so Firemen Gene P. Dowling, Donald A. Pizzuto and Clyde W. Will- iams started up with a 14-foot scaling ladder. With the cold, gusty, 30-mph winds swirling around them, they placed the scaling ladder carefully across the ornamental masonry to the bottom of the case- ment window.

Fireman Dowling climbed the scaling ladder and helped the first victim out onto the ladder and handed him to Firemen Williams and Pizzuto at the tip of the aerial ladder. This operation then was re- peated twice more as the victims became increasingly hysterical. The victims were taken to the street and given medical attention. The firemen were greeted warmly by the chief who praised their efforts.

The fire was fought by some 350 firemen, 96 of whom were injured, and 120 pieces of equipment. For relief purposes, the last special call was placed nearly 31 hours after the initial alarm. In all, 10 million out of 14 million pieces of mail were salvaged.

The sounds of screaming in both Spanish and English hung in the two-degree midnight air as a fire swept through a multiple dwell- ing in the Williamsburg section of Brooklyn. The gray stone build- ing at 232 Johnson Avenue housed a paper box factory on the first floor and three floors of apartments above. Box 270 was received at 12:49 a.m. on January 9, 1968.

First-arriving units were faced with a major fire condition with more than 100 people trapped inside. Parents were hanging out of top-floor windows, with children in their arms, their sleepy eyes now wide with fear. Firemen hurried to raise ladders, stretch lines and connect to hydrants. With the below-freezing temperatures, the street, apparatus and ladders soon were slick with ice.

Firemen and policemen scrambled to catch children being thrown from upper-story windows by hysterical parents. Numerous children, some without clothing, were caught. Several of the children were not caught and were injured by the fall.

A hair dryer left on a bed by a woman who went to answer a telephone started a fire that required six alarms to bring under con- trol. After attempting for some time to extinguish the fire herself, the woman picked up her telephone. Unable to remember the phone num- ber to report the fire (911 was not in service yet), the frantic woman then ran to a nearby alarm box, Signal Station 2848, which was re- ceived at 2:31 p.m. on January 11, 1968.

The flames now were spreading from the fourth-floor apartment, at 1124 Stratford Avenue in the Bronx, out into the hallway and into the cockloft above the top-floor apartment. Dozens of tenants were driven out into the freezing air as the fire roared through the cockloft and spread over the apartment house.

The year 1968 was a turning point for the FDNY. The continued rise in the number of runs and workers reached amazing proportions. The Department responded to 228,020 runs, of which 127,826 were fires and, of these, 619 required multiple-alarm assignments to control. Second sections were added to five engine companies, three ladder companies and five battalions located in the high-response areas of the Bronx, Brooklyn and Harlem.

In an attempt to equalize the tremendous workload being placed on certain companies, an interchange program was developed. Approximately 60 engine companies and 50 ladder companies were paired. The extremely busy companies were paired with less-active units located in more stable neighborhoods. After responding more than 20 times or performing more than six hours of fire duty during a night tour, the busy company exchanged firehouses and response areas with the less-active unit on the next night tour.

Engine Company 10 from lower Manhattan was sent to the quarters of Engine 225 in the East New York area of Brooklyn from 6:15 p.m. until midnight.

Fire companies faced a fast-moving fire that was extending rapidly and numerous civilians flooding out of the building. Lines were dragged to the top floor and truck companies moved into position to open up the top-floor ceilings. As firemen pulled open a section of ceiling, a backdraft occurred in the cockloft overhead, blowing down the ceilings with a huge blast of flame, heat and smoke. Firemen were driven to their knees with seven of them requiring medical attention.

At the height of the blaze, more than 170 firemen battled the fire. Thirty pieces of apparatus lined the slush- and snow-filled streets around the building. Flames spread to the adjoining building before the fire could be extinguished more than two hours after it began.

This fire was right in the middle of a series of major fires that confronted the Department during the most bitter and freezing weather the city had faced in a decade. January 9th through 12th, 1968, saw eight multiple alarms in Manhattan, Brooklyn and the Bronx.

As if extreme bitter cold and social unrest were not enough, the Fire Department was challenged with yet another serious complication to fire protection: On Friday, February 2, 1968, the Sanitation Department went on strike.

In short order, thousands of tons of uncollected refuse began to pile up in alleys and streets. Rubbish was piled high near occupied dwellings and other structures and even was piled high around fire hydrants, obscuring them from view.

On Sunday afternoon, February 4, 1968, a fire apparently started in piles of rubbish against the outside of a three-story, wooden, row-frame dwelling at 23-35 38th Street in Astoria, Queens. The flames raced up the inside wall and then into the cockloft. Box 7552 was received at 12:58 p.m. and was not brought under control until 2:52 p.m.

The fire and smoke routed more than 24 families from the row of homes. Five alarms were transmitted before firemen could stop the spreading flames. Four buildings were damaged severely, with the original fire building finally collapsing. Two firemen were injured by collapses and two were overcome by smoke.

The Department then started a plan of patrolling the streets, advising landlords and superintendents to keep hallways, cellars and other outside areas clear and keep the growing mountains of garbage away from buildings. Apparatus patrolled the streets of the South Bronx, Harlem, the Lower East Side of Manhattan, the north and central parts of Brooklyn and the South Jamaica area of Queens. These areas, the most densely populated tenement districts, were the worst areas for trash build-up.

Brooklyn firemen climb wooden aerial ladder in the late 1960s. (Photo by Steven Scher)

Fire Marshals

New York City always has been a city of fire. Colonial New York suffered numerous accidental fires due to the nature of lighting, heating and cooking. Candles, fireplaces and kerosene mixed poorly within the closely spaced wood-frame and brick-and-joist buildings. Inadequate water supplies and inefficient fire apparatus could do little to overcome fires that quite often grew to major proportions. Accidental and careless fire sources were bad enough, but then arson became part of the mix. Arson for profit, arson for revenge, arson for political ends and arson as a by-product of the mentally unstable.

Just prior to the Civil War, the fire department was made up of volunteers, men who also held full-time jobs and had little time or training to find out how and why fires started. The Municipal Police Department came into existence in 1845 and was modeled after Sir Robert Peel's Metropolitan Police in London. The New York force did not wear uniforms until 1853; instead, they affixed a large copper shield to their clothes; hence, "coppers" or the shortened version "cops." The force replaced a corrupt City Watch and the new force had a relatively small membership and no true detectives. So investigations, especially of fires, received little attention.

Alfred E. Baker, a reporter for the *New York Herald*, a paper published by James Gordon Bennett, "was struck by the number of peculiar fires of doubtful origin." He brought his concerns to Chief Engineer Alfred Carson of the volunteer fire department. Carson, in turn, asked the Board of Police Justices for their backing. Baker was appointed as the board's clerk, "to investigate the cause of fires, but without pay." Chief Carson was able to convince the insurance companies to raise a fund that would pay Baker for his services.

Baker was recognized by the title of Fire Marshal after several successful investigations, including the arrest of Charles A. Peverilly for attempting to set fire to a warehouse at 147 Front Street, in lower Manhattan. About a year later, the insurance companies met again and increased Baker's salary and allowed for an assistant. To help make his investigations as official as possible, he was authorized by Chief Carson and the Board of Engineers to "wear the uniform of a fireman – red shirt, fire cap and fire coat." The Board of Police Commissioners issued Baker a police sergeant's badge that proclaimed his new title, Fire Marshal, New York.

Baker's work during the Civil War Draft Riots helped to break up the Confederate plot. He determined that the accelerant used in the scores of fires set in hotels and other targets was "Greek Fire," an ancient concoction of "phosphorous dissolved in a sulfert of carbon." This was based on chemical analysis performed on evidence he recovered from the scenes of fires. Baker also determined that the whole scheme was planned and executed by "Southern emissaries" (Confederate army secret agents) and Northern "Copperhead" traitor accomplices.

Baker eventually became a city employee, technically working for the Board of Police Commissioners. Baker, however, had the title and duties of a fire official. When the department became professional in 1865, Baker continued his fire investigations. He turned in semi-annual reports on the fires and fire alarms within the city and also used the report as a forum to extol the virtues of fire safety.

Baker was a strong opponent of "hot-air furnaces" as a source of heating. He explained why hot water was the safest method of heating; much safer than steam pipes that when "brought into contact with pine wood, they are liable, after a certain length of time, to produce combustion."

Alfred E. Baker worked hard at his new job and eventually set the benchmark for all future fire investigations. He employed scientific methods and plotted fires and alarms using statistical analysis. He was setting a new standard and did not hesitate to explain how good a job he was doing. In his report for the six months ending November 30, 1857, he includes the following:

It appears, from examination of the records in the office of the Clerk of the Court of General Sessions, that only seven convictions of arson have taken place from 1819 to 1853, a period of 35 years. Since my investigations into the origin of fires, embracing three years and a half, 12 persons have been indicted for arson and 10 convicted for that offense.

Baker went on in his report to acknowledge the Mayor, the Police Justices and the Police Department for the willing cooperation they afforded him in the discharge of his duties. He then gave special thanks to the engineers (chiefs) and members of the Fire Department, for the energy and promptness of the aid they rendered on all occasions.

Alfred Baker was succeeded in the spring of 1868 by Police Captain Charles Beckett, who served as Fire Marshal for about two years. Thomas McSpeden, a former Alderman, then became the Fire Marshal in 1870. The City of New York then legislated the "Act to create a Fire Marshal," which changed appointing the Fire Marshal from the police to the fire department. The Board of Fire Commissioners replaced McSpeden with George H. Sheldon, who took over the office on May 21, 1873.

Despite occasional bureaucratic changes, the Fire Marshals basically have been an integral part of the Fire Department since then. Sheldon had a record as exceptional as Baker before him. From May 21, 1873, to February 1, 1886, his office made 142 arrests for arson. One hundred thirty were indicted, with nine discharged by the Magistrate. Three were dismissed by the Grand Jury. Sixty-one were tried and convicted; 11 were tried and acquitted. Three were tried and used as witnesses. Two died before they could come to trial.

On February seventh, the Department extinguished 746 outside rubbish fires (the average per day was 70) and on the eighth, 888 rubbish fires were handled. Newspapers reported it was only a combination of simple luck and the adeptness of the city's professional firemen that prevented a tragedy.

The Fire Department coordinated trash burnings at 18 sites where citizens could bring trash to be burned in a controlled and safe fashion. Fire Officers Training School and Probationary Firemen's Training School were detailed to provide manpower at the protected burn sites.

Another serious fire occurred in the Astoria section of Queens on February 11, 1968. Four three-family dwellings were gutted as flames raced through 14-14, 14-16 and 14-20 31st Avenue. Box 7449 came in at 4:03 a.m. and escalated, due to the number of special calls to a "Dispatcher's" fifth alarm. Twelve families were left homeless by the blaze.

On the following day, February 12th, a four-alarm fire was battled in a two-story frame building at 3434 Third Avenue in the Bronx. This building was a salvage house used by the Saint Vincent de Paul Church to store articles contributed for donation to the poor. Box 2561 brought 34 units, including Tower Ladder 14, the Super-Pumper, Tender and two Satellites. Six firemen were injured battling the blaze. The fire was brought under control at 12:43 a.m.

A taxpayer fire at 40 Burnside Avenue in the Bronx proved difficult to control on the 15th of February 1968. The blaze burned in a supermarket and eight stores in a two-story taxpayer next door.

After battling the fire for more than an hour and a half, the Foam Unit was special-called. The new Hi-Ex foam was delivered into the cellar by members of the unit. Both of the Department's Tower Ladders also operated. The stubborn fire eventually was subdued, but not before seven firemen were injured. They were treated for a variety of injuries, including frostbite. The fire was declared under control almost five hours later.

Three off-duty firemen were riding together at eight a.m. on February 25, 1968. Fireman Daniel Dooley of Ladder Company 108 was driving with his passengers, Firemen Daniel O'Gallagher of Engine Company 219 and William Flood of Engine Company 280, when they saw a fire at 537 Vanderbilt Avenue in Brooklyn. They were faced with numerous children screaming from four-story tenement windows. Several of the excited children jumped.

The alarm was transmitted and the three off-duty firemen sprang into action. Ladder Company 105 arrived and ladders quickly were placed. Dooley made three trips up ladders and rescued a woman and three children, one of whom was found unconscious on the roof. O'Gallagher and Flood each carried a person down a ladder to safety. Fireman Walter Carroll of Ladder Company 105 searched through the dense smoke and located an unconscious woman. He dragged her to a fourth-floor window and then carried her down to the street.

All four of these firemen were injured making their rescues and 14 residents of the building also were injured. But due to the heroic actions of the firemen who operated at the two-alarm fire, both on-duty and off, only one person died at the fire.

Thirty-mph winds whipped a fire into an eight-alarm inferno on Rockaway Park's oceanfront on March 31, 1968. Three boys were seen lighting a rubbish fire in a parking lot next to Curley's Atlas Hotel and Baths, landmarks in the Rockaway Park area.

The strong sea winds swirled embers into the sky, depositing them on roof tops for a four-block area. Embers soon burst into flames on the roof of Curley's Atlas Hotel, a three-story wooden structure built before the turn of the century. It was vacant at the time. Towering tongues of fire and thick billows of smoke soon filled the sky. FDNY alarm Box 1380 at Ocean Promenade and Beach 117th Street was transmitted at 2:33 p.m. The fire spread to the three-story Green Isle Hotel, which burned and collapsed to the ground, then to homes on Beach 117th Street. The nearby Sullivan's Hotel on Beach 116th Street soon was roaring with wind-whipped flames, as was a seven-story apartment house behind the Green Isle Hotel.

Eight alarms brought 415 firemen responding to the conflagration. Sixty-one pieces of apparatus from Queens, Brooklyn and Manhattan went to work as the fire continued to spread. The Marine Parkway Bridge was closed and the Cross Bay Bridge was restricted to essential vehicles. The boardwalk, six stores on Beach 116th Street, a penny-arcade and a supermarket soon were burning. A separate fire even damaged three bungalows and a garage more than a block and a half away from the main fire area.

The civil unrest in American cities was growing by the summer of 1967. For firemen, it was becoming a major public safety problem. Riots, looting and fires had occurred in the big cities and it was expected to renew itself again in 1968. Government officials had taken proactive moves in preparation for this possibility.

With the assassination of civil rights leader Dr. Martin Luther King, Jr., on April 4, 1968, the streets in New York and other cities erupted in violence. There were numerous instances of rock- and bottle-throwing. Looting and arson also were reported in Brooklyn and Harlem, starting at about 11 p.m. Gangs of youths in both areas were reported roaming through the streets, occasionally taunting policemen and firemen on duty.

A group of adults moved along 125th Street in Harlem and attempted to convince the younger people to go home. Two blocks away, scores of young people gathered at the corner of Seventh Avenue and 125th Street. Almost immediately, a fire broke out in a John's Bargain Store. Several of the local residents fought the fire until firemen arrived. The blaze was extinguished quickly.

At 11:30 p.m., several outbreaks of rock-throwing, looting and arson occurred in several Brooklyn neighborhoods. As the sun rose over the city, several areas were cloaked in a haze. Several fires had raged in Harlem during the early-morning hours. At three a.m. on Friday morning, April 5th, firemen were busy with fires along Eighth Avenue near 130th and at 136th Streets and along Lenox Avenue between 127th and 131st Streets.

At 5:30 p.m. on Friday, April 5, 1968, Fire Commissioner Robert Lowery declared that "a fire emergency exists in the city" and ordered all fire units held over. One thousand extra firemen now were on duty.

New York City firemen were faced with numerous multiple-alarm fires, including two four-alarm fires and a fifth-alarm blaze within a four-day period. Arsonists touched off more than a dozen multiples in Harlem, Bedford-Stuyvesant and Brownsville in the wake of Doctor King's murder. The situation did not reach the same level as in several other cities, however, where troops were needed to restore order.

Tensions were high as fire apparatus moved through the streets. Jeering crowds, mostly teenagers, threw bottles and rocks at responding and working firemen. The Department also fought several major fires not related to the rioting.

On Monday night, troubles started in East New York at about 10 p.m. when a Molotov cocktail was hurled through the window of a television repair shop. This fire quickly was contained. Several blocks away, a five-alarm fire, apparently started by another fire bomb, swept through a two-story lumberyard building at Hopkinson and Dumont Avenues. Two hundred firemen battled this blaze.

On Tuesday night, April ninth, there were five multiple alarms and 20 smaller fires in Brownsville. The majority of these were in vacant factories and tenements. The most serious of the fires destroyed two warehouses and an occupied apartment building. Shortly after eight p.m., units responded to a reported fire at 1628 Saint Mark's Avenue in Brooklyn. Arriving companies were confronted by two attached factories ablaze. The first radio report was "send all available police – they're throwing rocks and bottles." For the remainder of the night, fire companies responded with an escort of two police cars leading and two police cars following the fire apparatus.

Chief Fire Marshal Vincent M. Canty stated that at least 60 of the fires in that past week were set by arsonists. He added that since it was believed the arsonists were groups of teenagers, identifying them would be difficult.

The local community began to speak out against the violence and burning. Groups organized to protect property, including schools, and called for an end to the fires and assaults. Community leaders rode with policemen in an effort both to keep open the lines of communication and show their support for law and order.

The FDNY Vulcan Society released a statement on April 8, 1968, expressing their shock at the tragic murder of Doctor King. They further stated that their sorrow was heightened by unprovoked attacks against black and white members of the Department and that they were pained by the actions of those who interfered with the firemen and their duties. *We, as Firefighters and Fire Officers, take great pride in devotion to duty and the exemplary efforts of members of this Department in the protection of property and saving of lives, regardless of color, religion or political persuasion.*

Thankfully, tensions began to cool somewhat and firemen breathed a tentative sigh of relief.

The large, spectacular, multiple-alarm fires gain notoriety and look good on the evening news. To the average fireman, the good "all hands" blazes quite often are more challenging and dish out more punishment than the larger, multiple-alarm fires. These are the "bread and butter" of the FDNY; the pay-off of aggressive interior firefighting. The hard work, danger and punishment so often taken without much notice from the outside world, keep fires from getting out of control and ultimately save lives and property.

On the night of April 21, 1968, the evening roll call was held in firehouses across New York City. In the quarters of Engine Company 217, Fireman James N. Tempro was assigned the nozzle position by Lieutenant Dresch. Fire gear was put in place, equipment was checked and the company was ready for the night tour.

At 10:23 p.m., Engine Company 217 was assigned to Box 677 and responded to 711 DeKalb Avenue, Brooklyn. The pumper pulled up to the four-story building to find flames pouring out of two second-floor windows on the left side of the building. A line was ordered stretched as civilians began to yell that there were children trapped in the apartment.

Fireman Tempro and the members of Engine Company 217 quickly had the line in place and were on the second-floor landing. They were the only unit on the scene; the first-due ladder company still was responding. While they were waiting for water, Tempro volunteered to make an attempt to reach the children.

He quickly entered the rear of the fire apartment through the hallway door and found the fire moving quickly through the railroad flat, headed toward the rear rooms. Knowing the chances were good that the children would be in the rear, Tempro began his search. Under conditions that were deteriorating by the moment, he pressed on. Groping in the dense, hot smoke, he came across a young child. Tempro picked up the child and made a sweep on top of and under a bed.

Conditions were becoming extreme and Tempro was being burned, but he refused to give in. He was guided back toward the hallway by the voices of his comrades. Fireman James Tempro collapsed into the arms of the other firemen and was rushed, along with the rescued child, to Cumberland Hospital. Tempro had received second- and third-degree burns of the face, hands and knee. He was placed in the intensive care unit and required to remain in an oxygen tent for three days. James Tempro was awarded the Bennett Medal for his heroic actions.

The dangers of fire and flammable liquids are known only too well to firemen. Sometimes, however, fires occur where they are expected least. On Sunday, May 19, 1968, a few minutes after noon, Fireman Albert Jilek was fueling his pumper, Engine Company 94, inside the firehouse they shared with Ladder Company 48 at 1226 Seneca Avenue in the Bronx. A spark from the nozzle of the gas pump caused a minor explosion, knocking the fireman off his feet and igniting the open gasoline hose. Jilek and the housewatch warned the nine men in the kitchen area of the fire.

Firemen James Carew and William Cody made a dash for the hook and ladder truck as the nearby pumper burned furiously. Flames continued to grow, fed by the flowing gasoline. Other firemen raced from the kitchen to the 40- x 80-foot apparatus floor as the hook and ladder started up. Through a wall of flames, Carew and Cody drove the rig at an angle to shield the men who had jumped on the far side running board.

Firemen ran to a nearby hydrant and stretched a line directly from it and dragged it back toward the firehouse. Fireman Walter Porr grabbed a smoke mask from the ladder truck and under the protection of the hose line, dashed back into the blazing firehouse. Porr was able to reach the gasoline pump and shut off the flow of fuel. The fire had reached the second floor of the three-story firehouse before the two-alarm assignment extinguished all the flames.

Chief Officers of the FDNY always have been concerned about the dangers of collapse and take whatever actions they can to avert injury to operating members. The collapses on 23rd Street, Wooster Street and many others gave few, if any, signs of danger until it was too late. When the Department is faced with a defensive operation, the Chief tries his best to position his lines and large-caliber streams in effective locations, while staying out of the collapse zone. This worked to good effect during fire operations at a two-alarm blaze in the Bronx.

Members scatter as wall collapses during two-alarm fire at 2060 Bronx Avenue, Bronx, May 27, 1968.

Battalion Chief William Demarest of Battalion 18 was faced with a taxpayer fire at 2070 Bronx Street on May 27, 1968, at 7:34 p.m. The deep-seated fire was in a vacant 75- x 100-foot, one-story and basement garage building. The fire was in the first floor and cockloft upon arrival of the first-due units.

Based on prior knowledge and previous experience with this kind of building, the Chief repositioned his forces clear of the anticipated collapse area. Fifteen minutes after the FDNY began to battle the blaze, the structure collapsed into the street without warning. Luckily, no members were injured as tons of brickwork and twisted steel slammed into the sidewalk and street.

One lasting effect of the rioting continued to occur in several areas of the City – the added danger of objects being thrown at responding and working firemen. On June 6, 1968, members were operating at a seven-alarm fire in a garage, warehouse and three other buildings in the Melrose section of the South Bronx.

While operating at the scene of this major fire, a fireman came under attack as broken bottles and other objects rained down from the roof of a nearby building. Arriving police also were bombarded and ended up scuffling with several youths before reinforcements arrived and took control of the rooftops. Besides the injury incurred by flying missiles, three other firemen were transported with smoke inhalation injuries from the 163rd Street fireground.

Brooklyn firemen size up third-alarm fire in 1968.

Unfortunately, it was becoming more and more common for firemen to be assaulted. A WCBS Radio editorial broadcast several times on July 11th and 12th, 1968, cited this very problem. The editorial stated that 56 firemen had been injured seriously enough to require hospitalization and medical leave as a result of attacks by residents of the City.

The Uniformed Firemen's Association took out a series of advertisements asking that these attacks be brought to an end. Newspapers took up the crusade and many civic and church groups joined in. The attacks on firemen and the growing false alarm problems were addressed.

Fires occur in all kinds of buildings— high-rise offices, tenements, factories and multiple dwellings. One of the most underrated dangers to both civilians and firefighters is the house fire. Apart from being built of wood, a major design feature that presents problems during fires is the open interior staircase found in the vast majority of private dwellings. This allows fire, smoke and super-heated gases an easy and direct path from the lower floor to the sleeping areas above.

Bronx units faced a fast-moving fire in a 2¹/₂-story private dwelling at 1767 Clay Avenue on June 17, 1968. The fire started in a second-floor front bedroom and extended to the hallway and took possession of the hall and stairs leading to the attic. Fire made its way into the attic, a large open area except for two small rooms at the front and rear.

Arriving companies were informed that a 34-year-old man, partially handicapped by polio, was trapped in the attic and threatening to jump. Fireman Gerald W. Crabtree of Ladder Company 44 went to the rear of the house to help place portable ladders. In the rear, it became apparent that the smaller extension ladder being used would prove short, due to the many obstructions.

A unique "tool" that became widespread in the fire service had its origins in the basement workshop of a firefighter in New York City. Lester T. Bourke was an eight-year veteran of the FDNY assigned to Engine Company 231 in Brooklyn. Bourke came up with an idea for eye protection and set to work designing and fabricating his invention.

Bourke's invention was a plastic, fold-down eye shield that was attached to the front brim on the fire helmet. After 13 working models, he came up with his nearly finished product. After contacting the manufacturer of the leather FDNY helmet, the eye shields were improved slightly and put into production. The Bourke eye shield was an immediate hit and is used by FDNY firemen to this day.

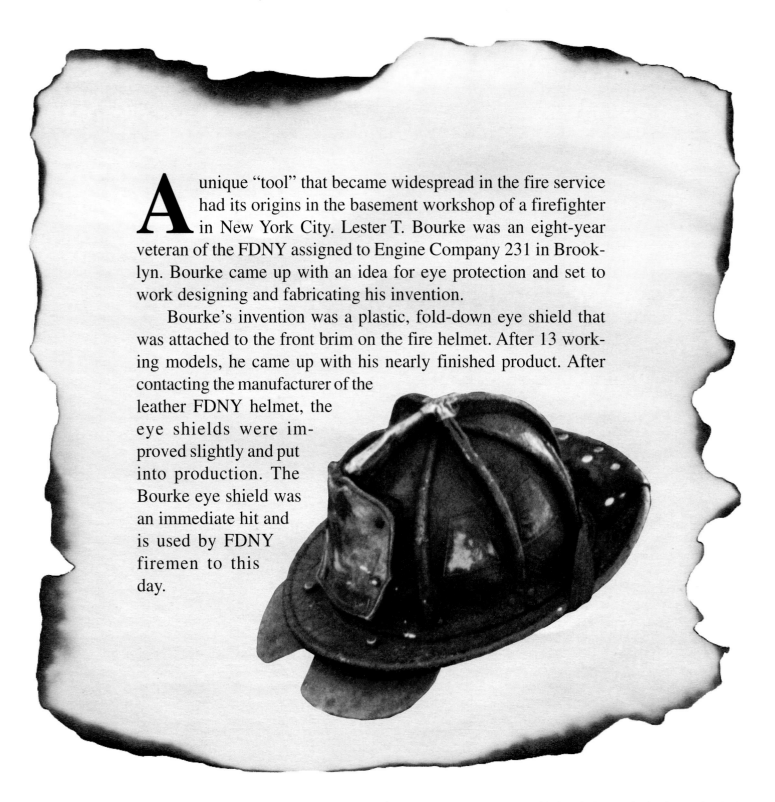

A significant event in emergency telecommunications took place on July 1, 1968, with the introduction of the "911" system in the City of New York. Until this time, citizens had to call the operator or emergency phone numbers such as "440-1234." To help make this system operational, the telephone company began to change outside public telephones to "dial tone first." This allowed anyone to pick up a pay phone and call "911" or an operator without cost.

Crabtree climbed the 20-foot ladder and raised a scaling ladder to the attic window and climbed to the waiting victim. The fireman then realized that the victim would not be able to climb out onto the ladder. Crabtree grasped the beam of the scaling ladder with both hands and directed the man to roll out the window across his arms. The fireman then began to climb down the ladder carefully with the 190-pound man on his arms.

When he reached the top of the 20-foot ladder, he carefully transferred the man and himself onto the ladder, while backed up by another fireman. Fireman Crabtree was awarded a medal for his tenacious rescue.

In 1968, the quarters of Engine Company 33, located at 44 Great Jones Street in Manhattan, was placed on the official rolls of the New York City Landmark Preservation Commission. The firehouse, designed by architects Ernest Flagg and W. B. Chambers, was completed in 1898. The committee felt that the firehouse had unique character and special historical and aesthetic interest and value. The building is a distinguished example of French Beaux Arts architecture.

A fire broke out in the Floyd Bennett Field Naval Base's enlisted men's club at around five p.m. on December 9, 1968. Bitter cold winds gusted to more than 40 mph and soon whipped the flames beyond the control of the Navy's firefighters. The call went out to the FDNY at 5:15 p.m. with the transmission of Brooklyn Box 3814.

Flames could be seen for miles as the two-story, 50- x 100-foot frame building burned with a fury. Traffic along the nearby Belt Parkway came to a standstill as motorists stopped to view the inferno. The fire eventually grew to four alarms that included the entire Super-Pumper System, Tower Ladder 1 and a fireboat.

The temperature dropped into the teens as the fire continued. The fire finally was declared under control at 7:17 p.m. The club was a total loss. Two firemen suffered frostbite injuries.

The year-end totals for 1968 included numbers that showed just how bad things were becoming for FDNY firemen. The Department fought 128,929 fires and answered 61,023 false alarms. A piece of fire apparatus rolled every two minutes, 18 seconds, as a record 229,287 fire alarms were received. Engine Company 82 led the list with 9111 runs. Ladder Company 31 responded 8597 times, Battalion 44 had 11,598 runs and Squad Company 3 did 8275.

Some apparatus changes were being made in 1969 as the "crew cab" concept was initiated. This design feature allowed all members to ride safely inside the apparatus and avoid possible injuries from thrown objects.

The FDNY also took delivery of the first two 100-foot, rear-mount aerial ladders. (Two 146-foot, rear-mounted "high ladders" had been purchased in 1961.) The remaining two Squad Companies were assigned pumpers, replacing the vans they had been using.

The WOR radio traffic helicopter was making one of its evening reports at 5:27 p.m. on Friday, January 10, 1969. The pilot-reporter Frank McDermott was 15 seconds into his report when he said on the air to newscaster John Scott, "You've got it, John. Hold on, I've..."

The helicopter crashed into the roof of 20-60 20th Street in Astoria, Queens. The pilot was killed and the crash set fire to the occupied apartment building. Three alarms were needed to contain the blaze that gutted the top floor. Only the pilot was injured.

A number of fatal fires struck the city in early 1969. In one 12-hour period on January 27th and 28th, 1969, seven people perished in the smoke and flames. Extreme cold and high winds hampered firefighting operations across the city. The first blaze spread quickly through a three-story home at 22-44 75th Street in Jackson Heights, Queens. A mother and three sons were killed as the fire burst from the cellar and cut off their escape.

Another fire struck at 592 Prospect Place in Brooklyn. Using icy ladders, firemen rescued a number of people from the five-story building. The strong winds drove the flames through the roof as frost-bitten firemen tried in vain to reach a mother and her two daughters.

On the corner of Fifth Avenue and 48th Street in Manhattan stands a white marble and granite, five-story office building. Housed in the structure are the Dixie Kitchen in the basement, a United Airlines sales office on the ground floor and an optometrist's office and vision center on the second floor. The fourth floor featured an international rare stamps dealer, with a law firm on the fifth floor.

The entire third floor of the building, 595 Fifth Avenue, housed the architectural firm of David Rosen and Associates. The office was divided into two rooms, a squarish one about 25 feet wide, facing Fifth Avenue and a rectangular room about 100 feet long, running the length of the building along 48th Street. The office held

All-Hands fire at 120 Orchard Street in Manhattan, January 1969. (Photo by A. D. Donne)

Midtown firemen stretch up exposure #2 fire escape at Holy Cross Lyceum, on 43rd Street between 8th and 9th Avenues, March 23, 1969. (Courtesy of The New York Times*)*

draftsmen and designers and contained large amounts of paper rolled into tubes. Containers of rubber cement also were stored in the drafting area.

Somehow, a fire broke out on the third floor at approximately 4:30 p.m., February 25, 1969. A few moments later, a person on the street transmitted Box 839 on the corner of Fifth Avenue and 48th Street. Fire was visible venting from the third-floor windows along 48th Street.

Ladder Company 4 arrived first-due at the box and witnessed fire pushing out of four windows on the third floor and lapping up to the roof level. Fireman William Moore and Lieutenant O'Rourke dashed up the interior stairs to the fire floor. On the second floor, they encountered two police officers carrying a badly burned woman down the stairs. They advised the firemen that a man was trapped behind the door on the third floor.

The two men from Ladder Company 4 reached the door and found it slightly ajar, with heavy smoke chugging from the small opening. With tremendous effort, Fireman Moore forced the door open about 15 inches and squeezed through. Inside, Moore found a scene of unbelievable horror – a pile of people, burned, crying and moaning. Conditions were becoming untenable at this position and his officer ordered Moore to move back to the hallway.

Just then, Fireman Martin J. Cunniff of Rescue Company 1 arrived, wearing an air mask. Cunniff worked his way through the door and found a body on the floor of the foyer. With flames rolling over his head, he tried to remove the victim from the area. Moore, seeing that Cunniff would not be able to get through the small opening with the victim and the air tank on his back, moved to the door with a claw tool and began to pry the heavy door from its hinges.

With flames closing in, Moore pulled on Cunniff's air tank to guide him out. Cunniff shouted to the other firemen that there were more people inside and dove back into the roaring foyer. Cunniff found a victim. He realized it would be more effective to pass the victims out rather than carry them. Now assisted by Fireman William Bessman of Rescue Company 1, they began to remove victim after victim.

Seven people were pulled from this blazing room without the benefit of a hose line for protection. Cunniff suffered second-degree burns to his face, neck and ears during the rescue. With the people removed from the fire area, Cunniff joined other firemen, including William Moore, in providing first aid and mouth to mouth to victims on the floor below. Cunniff and Moore later were presented medals for their valor.

The four-story building at 925 Fulton Street in Brooklyn had a store on the first floor and apartments above. At 7:40 a.m. on April 12, 1969, a fire started in the second-floor apartment. Flames soon filled the flat and burst out into the public hallway and staircase, trapping those above.

Ladder Company 105 pulled up first-due and was confronted with heavy fire conditions and numerous people, trapped and helpless. As the aerial truck pulled into position in front of the building, Fireman Joseph D. Grosso, the tillerman, moved quickly to the turntable as the chauffeur raised the ladder. Grosso, seeing a woman holding a young child and waving frantically from a third-floor window, raced up the ladder as it was being placed into position.

Grosso entered the apartment and guided the woman and child onto the aerial. The woman gasped that there were more children still inside. Grosso passed the woman and child to another fireman and climbed back into the smoke-filled apartment. Crawling on his hands and knees to avoid the heat and dense smoke pressing down on him, Grosso made his way deep into the apartment and located two semiconscious children. With a child in each arm, he returned to the window and handed them out to safety.

Once again, Fireman Grosso crawled back through the building in smoke and heat. Under extreme conditions, the young fireman found another child and returned to the window. This child, too, was

Improvements
Polyox & The Voice Alarm System

In January of 1969, the Department began to experiment with the water additive known as Polyox. When added to water, this Union Carbide product allows water to pass through hoses with reduced friction loss. In tests conducted by the Bureau of Training on Welfare Island, the "slippery water" proved an increased nozzle pressure was available while at the same time reducing engine pressures.

A prototype apparatus was outfitted to provide the solution for testing at real fire situations. These results were combined with the controlled testing to devise procedures and equipment that would be needed to introduce the operation on a wider range within the Department.

Another improvement in the FDNY in 1969 was in the area of communications. The introduction of the "Voice Alarm System" in Brooklyn, with installations in the Bronx and Queens underway, added flexibility and clearer, more concise information available to units responding to alarms from their quarters. The system had been in use in Staten Island for several years and had proved successful. This system relegated the bell system to a back-up method of notification.

handed out into the fresh air as Grosso, not sure if anyone remained, re-entered the boiling smoke condition. After a frantic search deep in the apartment, the sound of the forcible entry team working at the door was music to Grosso's ears. Near exhaustion, he made his way past members entering the apartment through the door, reported his search efforts and worked his way downstairs. He was informed that his efforts had saved all those trapped and that they were on their way to the hospital and would recover from their ordeal. For his determined actions under severe conditions, in saving the lives of five people, Fireman Joseph Grosso was decorated with the Dougherty Medal.

The quiet, early-morning hours on Harlem's West 119th Street were broken by the shouts of *Fire!* as neighbors tried to wake all those asleep in the five-story old law tenement. Box 1420 was sent out at 5:41 a.m. on July 12, 1969, with both Ladder Company 26 and 26-2 arriving at the scene.

Fire was roaring out of the first-floor front windows and had control of the hallway and stairs of the building. People were visible at the front windows and on the front fire escape. Fireman Robert F. Love, the roofman of Ladder Company 26, knew from his quick size-up that more people would be trapped in the building and that his reaching the roof to vent would be of paramount importance.

Love dashed up the interior stairs of the adjoining building and promptly was on the roof, venting the skylights and bulkhead door. He was joined in this operation by Fireman 4th Grade Patrick J. McGroary of Ladder Company 26-2. A quick check of the air shaft showed fire visible at every level of the building. When the team checked the rear, they saw two people trapped at a fourth-floor window and called for roof ropes.

The ropes arrived quickly on the roof and Fireman Love donned the first rope. The fire situation was worsening as flames now were in full possession of the top floor and cockloft beneath them. Love was lowered past a floor of fire to the two panicked victims. He quickly grabbed both of them and holding firmly, he steadied them and tried to calm them.

Meanwhile, McGroary was being lowered from the roof. The young fireman, gaining experience "on the fly," arrived and took one of the victims – an elderly crippled man – into his arms and both were lowered to the ground. Fireman Love was lowered, holding the woman whose apartment now was filled with flames.

While the rope rescues were in progress, Fireman Eugene Hoffman of Ladder Company 26-2 observed a man at a fifth-floor window and re-positioned the aerial as soon as the ropes made the roof. Fireman Siegel of Ladder Company 26-2 ascended the ladder and removed the man to the street. Hoffman then ascended the aerial and entered the raging apartment. On hands and knees, Hoffman searched the apartment until he located an unconscious man. He dragged the man back to the window and handed him out to another fireman. Hoffman then continued to search until it became so severe, he was forced from the building.

Conditions on the roof and top floor had become so dangerous that minutes after the lowering team moved to the adjoining building and Hoffman returned to the aerial ladder, a section of the fire building roof collapsed. Love, Hoffman and McGroary were awarded medals for their heroism.

I n September of 1969, the first issue of the Fire Bell Club's newsletter was published. This organization was started in 1939 and is considered the oldest buff club in the city. The now-familiar, four-page, yellow newsletter advises club members and members of the FDNY regarding the current events, noteworthy fires, recent apparatus deliveries and historic tidbits about the FDNY.

A series of pocket-sized incendiary bombs exploded on five floors of the gigantic Macy's Department Store in Manhattan's Herald Square on October 12, 1969. There were no injuries in the pre-dawn explosions. The bombs only caused minor fire damage, but the thick smoke, water from the sprinkler systems and some overhauling with hose lines caused considerable damage.

The bombs themselves were considered highly sophisticated, housed in crush-proof cigarette packs. Each had a cheap wristwatch as a timer, a small battery, a small coil, a bulb and potassium chlorate. The bombs were planted in pockets of clothing displayed on racks, in furniture drawers and under rugs. The five devices that activated were placed on the second, third, fourth, fifth and ninth floors.

The FDNY Fire Marshals worked with the police and the FBI in an attempt to find those responsible for the bombs. Macy's was one of four major department stores that were the targets of arsonists in March of 1968. Fires were set in Gimbel's, Bloomingdale's and Klein's, but the device left in Macy's failed to ignite.

The epidemic of vacant building fires was continuing to ravage the poorer sections of the city. These fires stripped the fire protection available for blazes in occupied buildings and severely taxed firemen and their equipment. The Department called for the demolition of these structures by the city as quickly as possible. The Bureau of the Budget initiated a study of the problem.

Meanwhile, firemen faced major fires in vacant buildings at an increased rate of 800 percent compared to just six years earlier. One report cited the fact that as many as 2000 to 3000 buildings were being abandoned each year in the city.

Half an hour after an anonymous telephone call was received warning that explosives had been planted in the buildings, bombs went off in three Manhattan skyscrapers on Tuesday, November 11, 1969. The almost-simultaneous explosions did extensive damage to the 70-story RCA Building at Rockefeller Center, in the new 50-story General Motors Building at 59th Street and Fifth Avenue and in the Chase Manhattan Building in the financial district.

Shortly after one a.m., the bombs exploded. An elevator operator in the GM Building suffered minor injuries when his elevator fell six stories. He was the only person injured. These blasts were the latest in a series of explosions that included Macy's Department Store and the U.S. Army Induction Center on Whitehall Street in October.

In November of 1969, in a plan worked out among the city, the FDNY and the Uniformed Firemen's Association, Tactical Control Units and newly formed regular companies went into service. TCU Engine Companies 512, 513 and 531 and TCU Ladder Companies 712 and 731 were added to the firefighting force. The TCU members reported at 2:30 p.m. and then traveled to their assigned fire company where they assumed the duties of that unit as first-due until 12:30 a.m.

As part of the agreement for each two new companies formed, three Tactical Control Units could be established. The total number of TCUs could not exceed 22. Also, between the peak hours of three p.m. and one a.m., an adaptive response policy was implemented. Only two engines and one ladder would respond to pull boxes in high incidence areas only. Three engines and two trucks still would respond on telephone alarms of structural fires.

A flash-fire – apparently touched off by defective Christmas lights – swept through an old two-story frame building at 31 Covert Street in the Bushwick section of Brooklyn on December 18, 1969. Ten members of a family, six of them children ranging in age from three months to 14 years, were burned to death as a two-alarm fire tore through the house. Nine other members of the family also were trapped on the second floor of the 80-year-old structure.

A widow and seven children managed to flee the blaze that broke out at 5:20 a.m. on December 18, 1969. Eighteen members of the Tate family were asleep in various rooms of the second floor and attic. Arriving firemen could do little to save those trapped as the wooden building burned quickly. It was estimated that at least 27 people were living in the two-and-a-half-story house at the time of the fire.

On December 23rd, a large funeral was held for the family at the Lutheran Church of the Savior, not far from the burned-out home. More than 350 people, including an honor guard of firemen, attended the services.

I n 1969, the FDNY responded to 239,318 alarms. There were 47,492 structural fires, 588 of which became multiple alarms. Non-structural fires numbered 78,712, for a total of 126,204 fires during the year. Emergency responses totaled 41,054 and there were 72,060 false alarms. FDNY studies concluded that 55 percent of all the responses occurred from four p.m. until 12 midnight.

New York City Fire Department
1970 – 1979

The decade between 1960 and 1970 saw the beginnings of an era in the FDNY that few ever could have predicted. Fires had risen from 61,644 in 1961, to 127,249 in 1970. Civilian deaths had risen from 166 in 1961, to 310 in 1970. The economic times were hard on the city and the fire load was hard on the firemen.

On the morning of January 1, 1970, Fireman Harold J. Hoey, Jr., was on his way home after a night tour in the Bronx's Engine Company 60. Hoey was approaching the Triboro Bridge toll plaza when he spotted flames coming from a top-floor apartment at 700 East 134th Street. Hoey whipped his car around and sped up to the old five-story building. He ran to a nearby alarm box and sent in the alarm before dashing into the building.

Hoey raced up the staircase, warning residents as he climbed. On the top floor, he made his way down the smoke-filled hallway to the apartment adjacent to the fire. Inside, he found six trapped people, one of them an elderly woman. Hoey proceeded to guide them out into the smoke-charged hallway because the fire escape was covered with ice and too dangerous to navigate with the elderly woman. All six people were led to safety.

A series of major fires in freezing weather taxed the efforts of the FDNY during January of 1970. The first multiple of the year went to the Bronx on January 2nd, as fire swept through a large, six-story apartment house. One woman and two children were killed and more than 200 people fled into the sub-freezing temperatures. A four-alarm fire was battled for more than four hours at Box 4268 in a row of nine stores at Coney Island Avenue and Kings Highway in Brooklyn on January 3rd. Four alarms were transmitted at Box 616 for a blaze in commercial buildings located at 167 West 23rd Street in Manhattan on January 19th. Another four-bagger was battled in Brooklyn on Bay 14th Street, as a number of private dwellings burned at Box 3498 on January 24th.

Department Order Number 19 on January 28, 1970, included a letter to Fire Commissioner Lowery from Mayor John Lindsay, who expressed the admiration of all the citizens for the heroic efforts of the firemen who battled the series of fires in the cold January. "...despite brutal weather conditions, the men of the New York City Fire Department have fought fires courageously and effectively. Please let the men and officers of the department know how much pride and gratitude all New Yorkers hold for this country's finest Fire Department..."

On the third floor of 204 West 141st Street in Manhattan, a woman was searching for a lost object under her bed in apartment C-3. To aid in her quest, she lit a match to a candle and moved back into the darkness beneath the bed. Suddenly, flames burst across the underside of the bed, driving the woman from the room. Within short order, the fire was raging and Box 1592 was pulled.

It was 11:37 p.m. on February 19, 1970, when Ladder Company 28 pulled up to the building. Nothing was showing from the front, but the seasoned firemen could tell there was a job somewhere inside. Firemen Thomas D. Ferraiuolo and Joseph T. Boylan went into a courtyard where they saw a woman threatening to jump from the window ledge on the fourth floor. Additionally, two people were climbing out onto the window ledge on the floor above.

Inside the building, flames had burst out into the hallway and raced up the stairs, trapping all the occupants in the eastern portion of the six-story building. Members of Ladder Company 28 raised a 35-foot portable ladder and placed it against the building. Fireman Ferraiuolo climbed the ladder and then raised a scaling ladder to the sill of the fourth-floor window. He climbed the ladders and entered the apartment where a woman was trapped. He helped her onto the ladder where Fireman Boylan had positioned himself. The woman was brought down to the portable ladder and the scaling ladder was raised to the fifth-floor window.

As Ferraiuolo reached the fifth floor and was climbing in the window, Fireman Leonard F. LaRotondo of Ladder Company 30 was being lowered, on a roof rope, by members of his company. As LaRotondo reached the fifth floor, he signaled the men on the roof to stop his descent. Fireman Ferraiuolo had brought a woman to the window and helped her out into the waiting arms of LaRotondo.

Conditions were becoming extremely dangerous in the courtyard; heavy smoke was obscuring the rescue efforts and fire was raging in several apartments, threatening to vent through the windows at any moment. The very action of climbing a ladder was becoming so difficult that a life net was brought into the courtyard and held in readiness.

War Valor

The bravery and daring of the members of the FDNY during fires and emergencies are well-known. Many citizens owe their lives and their livelihoods to the heroics of the men who wore the leather helmets. Some members of the department traded those for the drab-green metal helmets of the United States Armed Forces.

In the spring of 1776, the entire force of New York City firemen formed themselves into two military companies and fought with General Washington. New York firemen again went to war in 1812. Several New York firemen manned guns on the *U.S.S. Constitution*; others were with Perry at Lake Erie. Nearly 300 joined in 1846 and fought with General Winfield Scott in Vera Cruz, Mexico.

The most famous group of New York firemen were the colorful Zouaves, who first fought with Colonel Ellsworth and then with Lieutenant Colonel Farnham of Hook and Ladder 1. They fought at Alexandria, Centreville, the first battle of Bull Run, Newport News, Williamsburg, Chantilly, Fredericksburg and 2nd Bull Run. They also had important battles at Gettysburg before joining Grant in the fierce battles of the Widerness and Cold Harbor, Virginia. After the war's end, the once-proud 1100 men returned as a tired little band of 200.

The Spanish-American War saw 275 firemen join up for a war that only lasted four months.

In World War I, 600 men from the FDNY joined and saw action at the Battles of the Marne, Meuse, Argonne, Chateau Thierry and Belleau Wood. When the firefighting ranks refilled after the war, 2300 war veterans had entered the job. Eight firemen had been lost in the war. The first was Fireman Charles J. Johnson of Engine Company 38, who was killed in action in France on October 14, 1918.

During their tenures in the military, many New York firefighters were awarded medals for heroic actions during battle. Fireman James Smith, who served with Rescue Company 1 during the 1920s, was decorated for bravery during the Boxer Rebellion in 1903. Smith was awarded the Congressional Medal of Honor while serving with the Navy in China.

Fireman William L. Willis left his brothers in Engine Company 13 when he was activated as a Lieutenant in the United States Marine Reserves during World War II. His heroics were recorded in the following citation:

For extraordinary heroism in action against the enemy on PELELIU ISLAND, PALAU GROUP, on 15 September, 1944. Second Lieutenant WILLIS was serving as leader of a rifle platoon when ordered to capture and hold a 30-foot-high coral point of land, which commanded the entire landing beach and from which the enemy was delivering devastating 40-millimeter anti-boat and heavy machine gunfire on our personnel and landing craft on the beach.

Willis led his men forward in a daring and skillful assault. They penetrated the Japanese ring of infantrymen with fierce hand-to-hand fighting, then assaulted the fortified pillboxes themselves. Willis and another marine crawled ahead and flanked the enemy position. They threw white phosphorous grenades while under withering fire from pillboxes on either side of them. They moved in closer and were able to capture this strongly defended position with a hand grenade attack in close quarters. This action inspired the remaining marines to attack the other enemy strong points.

The assault resulted in the complete annihilation of approximately 80 enemy defenders. In executing this attack, more than half of the platoon was lost, but the threat to the entire beach and our landing craft was eliminated. For his heroic actions and leadership, William L. Willis was awarded the Navy Cross.

Firefighters from across the city returned from World War II, Korea and Viet Nam with many awards for bravery and Purple Hearts for wounds they received during battle – Heroes in leather or steel helmets.

Ferraiuolo then started down the scaling ladder with a male victim who had taken too much smoke and was becoming dizzy. It was decided to stop with him at the fourth-floor window. With help from Fireman Boylan, the man was taken into the apartment and held by the window until the fire in the interior stairs was controlled. All three firemen had placed themselves in extreme danger with fire threatening to vent into the shaft at any moment. For their efforts, they were awarded medals.

A new crop of revolutionaries presented an added peril for firemen, police and civilians in the late 1960s and early 1970s. One group, the Weathermen or the Weather Underground Organization – a splinter group of the Students for a Democratic Society (SDS) – set off more than 4000 bombs in 1969 and 1970. The terrorist organization set bombs that were timed to detonate precisely in the early-morning hours and then warned police so that no one would be killed or injured by the explosions.

On March 6, 1970, two members of the Weathermen (one male and one female) were constructing bombs in the basement of 18 West 11th Street in Greenwich Village. The bomb makers were surrounded by shelves filled with sticks of dynamite, alarm clocks used for timers, batteries, wires, blasting caps and other completed bombs filled with roofing nails and explosives.

Suddenly, a tremendous roar was heard. One of the bomb makers had made a wrong move and the device detonated, causing all the other explosives in the basement to explode. Most of the building collapsed immediately in a cloud of smoke and dust. Two more blasts followed as gas mains burst into flames. Windows in the neighborhood splintered and residents fled into the streets. The bomb makers and one other person in the building were killed. Two other members of the group also in the structure at the time escaped relatively unharmed; they wandered away and went underground to avoid the authorities. Firefighters, Fire Marshals and members of the police Bomb Squad worked for many days, combing the debris for victims and searching for possible survivors.

On the night of March 6, 1970, an alarm came in for Hopkins Street and Sutter Avenue. It was a false alarm. This alarm placed first-due companies out of position as a real fire alarm was received for a fire in a three-story brick building at 1342 Saint Mark's Avenue, near Ralph Avenue. Arriving firemen found a raging fire on the second floor of the structure.

Firemen entered the third-floor apartment and began their searches, only to find six dead children – two in a kitchen in the rear, huddled between a refrigerator and a stove, one on a bed in a front room, one near the apartment door and two on the floor near a window. A seventh child was found on a bed on the second floor.

Two other children were rushed to the hospital in serious condition, as was a woman who jumped from a third-floor window. It took firemen 51 minutes to bring the fire under control.

The city again was rocked by bombs on March 12, 1970. Devices exploded in the Manhattan skyscraper offices of three of the nation's corporate giants after anonymous tips warned of the blasts.

Extensive damage was done to the offices of Mobil Oil Company, International Business Machines (IBM) and General Telephone and Electronics (GTE). The first blast caused extensive damage on the 34th floor of the Mobil office on East 42nd Street. A 25-square-foot hole was blown through the floor of 425 Park Avenue, the 12th-floor offices of IBM.

The third explosion occurred in the offices of Sylvania Electric Products, part of GTE. The 21st-floor explosion demolished the entire floor of the building at 730 Third Avenue. The fears of city officials were being realized: even with the explosion of the Greenwich Village bomb factory, the radicals were still in business and "making their statements."

An already jumpy city virtually leaped when an explosion rocked the construction site of the World Trade Center's south tower on March 16, 1970 at 1:31 p.m. The exploding propane tank injured six workers and sent a flame more than 100 feet into the air. Many windows in nearby buildings were broken by the blast.

Fire Marshals determined that the blast was purely an accident. A truck apparently struck a tank of propane gas, loosening the valve and allowing gas to escape and find a source of ignition. The twin 110-story towers were expected to be completed in 1973.

The Hotel Edison is a 23-story fireproof hotel located at 228 West 47th Street in Manhattan. On March 24, 1970, Box 811 was transmitted at 7:52 a.m. for a fire on the top floor. Ladder Company 4 arrived first-due and members were confronted with flames venting out the windows and two male civilians in adjacent rooms hanging outside their windows screaming for help.

Heat, smoke and flames had entered the hallway, cutting off this means of escape for the victims. Lieutenant McKee and Fireman John Cerato proceeded directly to the roof. Below them, one man was standing on the window ledge in a very dangerous position, straddling a window air conditioner with smoke pushing out around him. Fireman Cerato was attached to the roof rope and lowered into position by Lieutenant McKee. Cerato grabbed the hysterical man and tried to calm him as he swung clear of the smoke and away from the window.

Arriving at the roof at this time was Fireman Frank DeBellis of Rescue Company 1, who offered his assistance. A plan was devised and Cerato, using great strength, began to raise the victim high enough to allow DeBellis to reach him and with the aid of the officer, pull the man onto the roof.

Meanwhile, the second victim had been reached through the interior and removed to safety by a team of firemen. Cerato then climbed back onto the roof with the help of DeBellis and McKee.

Fireman Cerato was cut and bruised around the neck and hands, but had saved this panicked man's life. He later was awarded the Scott Medal for his actions.

The six-man crew of Ladder Company 28, under the command of Captain James Gorman, were at it again on the morning of April 25, 1970. They responded to a working apartment house fire at 309 West 147th Street in Harlem. Heavy smoke and flames had forced numerous tenants to the windows. Using their aerial and two portable 35-foot ladders, they were able to rescue 25 people from the blazing building.

The two-alarm fire was believed to be incendiary in origin. Fourteen of those rescued required hospitalization for smoke inhalation, minor burns and a broken pelvis. This could have been a real catastrophe," Deputy Chief William Alford said. "Gorman and his men will be put in for a Unit Citation for the tremendous job they did in getting all those people out without serious injuries."

A stubborn four-alarm fire started at 4:30 a.m. on April 12, 1970, at 37 Union Square West in Manhattan. The blaze apparently started in a discotheque and tavern on the ground floor. Heavy smoke pushed from the five-story, 100-year-old building, as fire extended up a plumbing shaft to the four upper floors.

Firemen were able to contain the extension to the upper floors in the bathroom areas, but water and smoke damaged all of the occupancies to some degree. During the battle, the ceiling and mezzanine section collapsed on the first floor, trapping and injuring a number of firemen who were rescued by their comrades.

The blaze was fought for seven hours and injured 28 firemen. Located on the fourth floor of the building were the law offices of a firm that was representing several radical groups being tried for plotting to bomb public places. Their clients included members of the Black Panthers and Weathermen groups.

Social unrest of a different type exploded on the streets of Brownsville at about two a.m. on the night of June 12, 1970. After mounds of uncollected garbage began to pile high on the sidewalks of Sutter Avenue, two men began to "make a statement" by building a pile of garbage in the middle of the street. The arrest of the two men sparked a wild riot that saw a police car firebombed, numerous giant rubbish fires set, two two-story buildings set ablaze and several stores looted.

At first, the firemen were unable to move close to the fires because of a reported sniper. As firemen extinguished the remaining pockets of fire, sanitation crews moved in to clean up the litter-strewn streets. Mayor Lindsay toured the area after many workers and equipment had cleaned the neighborhood. One young man shouted, "Hey, Lindsay, you should have been down here at four o'clock this morning!"

A second night of trouble started as dozens of vacant tenements were set ablaze. One fireman was bombarded with bottles and bricks and required 20 stitches in his head. Numerous Brooklyn units were used, as were 10 companies from Manhattan and another 10 from Queens.

Two days later, violence and arson erupted in East Harlem after the arrest of a member of the Young Lords, a militant Puerto Rican group. Members of the group and their supporters rampaged after a 16-year-old member of the group was arrested on charges of kidnapping, assault and robbery.

The garbage burning, rock-tossing and window-breaking melee broke out after a rally for the youth's release. One hundred members and their supporters surged from 111th Street and Lexington Avenue to Third Avenue where the problems started. Rubbish and a number of mattresses were set ablaze in the middle of the street and firemen were bombarded as they responded. Two firemen were injured by thrown objects.

As firemen doused the blazing piles of garbage, they saw a group of youths surround and attack two cops a block away. Firemen dove into the pile of youths and rescued the outnumbered policemen. A number of stores were looted before order was restored a few hours later.

On Thursday night, June 16th, two clean-cut young men in their early 20s were walking along Second Avenue in Manhattan's East Village when they tossed a firebomb into a parked Cadillac. The two then walked to a construction site at West 4th Street at 11:05 p.m. and threw a firebomb at a construction site. Three minutes later, another firebomb was tossed in a large garbage bin at Greene Street, near West 4th.

A few hours later, at 2:33 a.m. on June 17th, an occupied tenement was set on fire. The six-story tenement at 8-10 Avenue B proved difficult to control and a second alarm was transmitted. During the fire, the two men apparently returned and this time, firebombed a pumper hooked up to a hydrant at Avenue B, between Second and Third Streets. One member attempted to extinguish the burning pumper with a water can and another member ran to his assistance. The second fireman collapsed, apparently from a heart attack, and was rushed to the hospital and admitted in serious condition. Fourteen other firemen also were treated for injuries.

Three Woolworth stores were set on fire by incendiary devices within 45 minutes of each other in Manhattan on June 30, 1970. No one was injured by the fires that broke out after the stores were closed. The first fire occurred at 6:38 p.m. at 120 West 34th Street where eight incendiary devices were triggered. Sprinklers held the fire, but damaged stock. At 7:02 p.m., the second fire broke out at 1527 Third Avenue where two fires were started and four other devices were found. The last fire was at 2222 Broadway at 79th Street. This fire was at 7:14 p.m. and nine of 10 devices detonated.

All hands went to work at Manhattan Box 406, on August 1, 1970, as a speeding Cadillac lost control, swerved onto the sidewalk and smashed through the side wall of 214 Forsyth Street, causing the collapse of the occupied building. The five-story, century-old tenement at the corner of Houston Street collapsed with many of the 38 residents still sleeping at eight a.m.

FDNY units responded and began to dig out the trapped residents. Ten people were pulled from the rubble and only one required hospitalization. The only fatality was the 23-year-old driver of the car.

It was nearing six p.m. on August 5, 1970, when a man working in the lobby of Four New York Plaza was told by several young women returning from dinner that "Someone ought to call the Fire Department; the building across the street is on fire." The man checked outside and sure enough, flames were shooting out of the 33rd floor of the glass and aluminum, 50-story office building known as One New York Plaza.

Box 23 was transmitted and arriving firemen were faced with an advanced fire situation with reports of people trapped. Lieutenant John C. Griffin of Ladder Company 8 and his company, Firemen Frederick Fugazzi, Thomas A. Wissman and Alvin H. Galter, took an elevator to the 31st floor and started up the stairs.

At the 33rd floor, they found conditions so bad that the officer ordered a house line stretched from the standpipe to cool the door enough so that it could be forced. A second house line was stretched to the door as Lieutenant Griffin and Fireman Fugazzi prepared to enter the extreme conditions on the fire floor. The rescue team advanced toward the elevator bank where they believed the trapped people to be. Behind them providing cover with the house line streams were Firemen Wissman and Galter, who alternated covering the advancing firemen and wetting each other to allow them to maintain their positions.

Crawling down a long corridor, Griffin and Fugazzi found the bank of elevators. One of the cars was stalled and three civilians were inside, unconscious on the floor. Griffin helped Fugazzi lift one and they started back toward the stairs. The combined efforts of the officer and remaining men, who already had run out of air in their cylinders, removed the two remaining civilians from the fire area.

On the 31st floor, Fireman Fugazzi was administering mouth-to-mouth resuscitation on his victim, as the second wave of rescuers began to work on the other two. The fire escalated to a third alarm and was brought under control just before 11 p.m. Two civilians died from the intense heat and smoke of the fire. One of them was a security guard on his first day at work. For their efforts at extreme peril, the members of Ladder Company 8 were awarded medals.

In September of 1970, the New York Road Runners and the New York City Department of Recreation sponsored the first Marathon in the city. The event was held in Central Park and the winner of the grueling 26-mile, 365-yard run was Fireman Gary Muhrcke of Engine Company 328.

It was eight minutes after seven on the night of October 16, 1970, when Brooklyn Box 613 was received for a fire at 442 Adelphi Street. First-arriving units found an extremely heavy smoke condition pushing from the commercial, garage-type structure. The one-story, non-fireproof building had been used in the past as a light factory occupancy and, at the time of this fire, it was vacant.

Entrance to the 60- x 100-foot building was through two large overhead sliding doors and two standard doors located on Adelphi Street. The front doors were forced and the rear windows were vented as hand lines were moved into the building. Heavy smoke and moderate heat were encountered as members moved into the building. Roof ventilation was commenced as a third line was stretched to an outside cellar entrance.

Reports from the third line stated a heavy body of fire in the cellar. On reports of the extensive area of fire in the cellar, a second alarm was transmitted. The lines taken through the front doors were ordered to be backed out as the members were above a serious fire area with the possibility of collapse.

Lieutenant James G. Geraghty and the members of Engine Company 219 were making their way back to the front door with the line when Geraghty and Fireman Albert Orokos fell through an open unprotected (4- x 4-foot) hatchway to the cellar floor. The officer was rendered unconscious by the fall and Fireman Orokos was left in a dazed condition in the raging cellar.

A rescue effort commenced immediately. Lieutenant Richard R. Hamilton and Fireman William F. Polera, both of Rescue Company 2, donned their facepieces as members of Ladder Company 105 placed a 25-foot extension ladder through the opening. Hamilton and Polera descended into the inferno in search of the missing men. Conditions were so severe that a hose line and roof rope were called for immediately.

On October 5, 1970, the 911 system finally was able to transfer reports of fires to the appropriate fire dispatcher's office automatically. The 911 system, on-line since July of 1968, was used only for police or ambulance emergencies. At the time, citizens called the operator and were transferred to the FDNY.

Members take a break, moments after Lieutenant Geraghty and Fireman Orokos were rescued from blazing Adelphi Street cellar, Brooklyn, October 16, 1970.

As the year 1970 drew to a close, several initiatives were being implemented or planned within the FDNY. New $1^3/_4$-inch hose was being evaluated. The FDNY was pioneering the use of this hose, with 18 engine companies in the field operating with the new hose and $^{15}/_{16}$-inch controlling nozzles. The hose, with the correct nozzles, could deliver 50 percent more water than the $1^1/_2$-inch hose it was replacing.

In autumn of 1970, the first of the ERS fire and police alarm boxes were being installed. The first 100 boxes were placed in the borough of Brooklyn. It was hoped the requirement for voice communication would lead to a reduction in false alarms. The number of false alarms had tripled from 1964 to 1969. Additional boxes were installed in Manhattan the next year.

In the area of fiscal management and department manpower levels, the end of 1970 was a mix of needs and realities. Factions that included the Brooklyn Borough President and the Uniformed Firefighters Association were calling for additional firemen, while the mayor was ordering a job-hiring freeze and talking about possible layoffs.

In the year 1970, the FDNY fought an average of 350 fires a day. This was the most in the history of the Department. Despite the fact that there were 20 percent fewer fires that reached the fourth- and fifth-alarm level, the death toll from fires mounted to 319. This number included nine members of the Department who died in the line of duty. (In 1969, 313 people died in fires, six of whom were firemen.) False alarms also had increased 24 percent from the previous year.

Due to the extreme heat and smoke condition venting from the cellar, members at the street level near the top of the ladder barely could maintain their position at the hatch opening. The line operating at the rear was ordered shut down to prevent pushing any additional heat or fire toward the rescue operation.

Fireman Orokos was located first and quickly was assisted up the ladder to the street. Lieutenant Geraghty then was located. Due to the deteriorating conditions, Fireman Polera was forced to tie a bowline on a bite on the unconscious fire officer while Hamilton operated the hose line to cool the area and hold the fire back. The ladder was removed from the hatchway and the 200-pound officer was pulled up and out of the cellar. The ladder was re-positioned and Polera and Hamilton climbed to the street level.

All four men were taken to the hospital and treated for burns and heat exhaustion. For their outstanding rescue efforts, Lieutenant Richard Hamilton was awarded the Bennett Medal and Fireman William Polera was awarded the Brooklyn Citizens Medal.

As soon as the rescue was completed, all lines were placed back in operation. A third alarm was ordered and Foam Unit 81 was special-called. The fire then was extinguished using High-Ex foam. The Department displayed both personal valor of the highest order and the latest methods of fire extinguishment at this operation.

A four-alarm fire took the lives of three people on December 4, 1970. An unlicensed sheetmetal worker's torch touched off a fire in a pile of carpet remnants. The fire roared through the new, 49-story office building at 919 Third Avenue, near 56th Street in Manhattan. Box 905 was received at 9:45 p.m. and the blaze required two hours and 32 fire companies to control. The three dead men were located on the fire floor. Fifty-two other people, including a dozen firemen, also were injured at the fire.

An uncapped gas main caused a major explosion of a tavern near City Hall on December 11, 1970. Ryan's Bar and Grill at 11 Park Row was leveled as the leaking gas ignited at about two p.m., scattering flaming debris across Broadway.

Among the first on the scene were firemen's and officers associations union officials who had offices on Broadway. U.F.A. President Michael Maye, Secretary Frank Palumbo and Lieutenant James Cersosimo and Joe Lafemina and Deputy Chief John O'Reilly of the officers union ran into the burning three-story building and rescued numerous dazed and injured victims.

The fire spread to the building next door and firemen battled the fire for an hour and a half. Five alarms were transmitted for Box 97. The death toll rose to 10, as firemen worked into the night and the next day, digging through the debris. Fifty-five people were injured by the blast.

The week before Christmas 1970 was devastating for churches in Queens. On Monday, the 21st, at 6:27 p.m., a two-alarm fire destroyed the 123-year-old Saint Saviour Episcopal Church on 57th Drive in Maspeth. Two alarms were transmitted as fire roared through the block-long structure. Quick work by firemen and some neighborhood teenagers saved many of the sacred objects from the church. Three 12-year-old boys later were arrested for setting the blaze.

Two days later, fire wrecked the 120-year-old First Congregational Church of Flushing at 38th Avenue and Bowne Street. The fire started at 12:54 p.m. and flames soon engulfed the 150-foot steeple. Within minutes of arrival, three alarms were transmitted. A freezing rain added to the already dangerous operation.

New Year's Day 1971 started the year off for New York City firemen with two tragic and difficult fires. A snowstorm was battering the city as an alarm was received for a fire at 1213 Intervale Avenue in the Bronx. Firemen raced through the snow on foot from their firehouse, a half-block away from the three-story brick building.

They entered the thick smoke on the second floor and crawled into the blazing apartment. Inside, one woman was found dead, but her unconscious roommate was revived using mouth-to-mouth resuscitation. Two firemen were injured battling the fire.

Another two-alarm fire drove seven families out into the snow at 351 Rutland Road in Brooklyn. Three firemen were injured fighting this apartment house fire.

Thick smoke drifted across lower Manhattan on January 9, 1971, as firemen battled a blaze in an abandoned structure on Pier 13, at the foot of Wall Street at the East River. The fire spread to the structure on Pier 14, just to the north. Five alarms were sounded and 250 firemen worked in the sub-freezing weather.

Dense smoke stopped traffic on the FDR Drive and drifted among the skyscrapers in the financial district. Two firemen were injured as they had to scramble down a ladder to avoid a collapsing section of roof. The fire was fought for nearly two hours before the flames could be brought under control.

A light snow was falling on the evening of January 24, 1971. The residents of Flushing, Queens, were asleep in their beds as the night slowly began to give way to the coming day. At about 5:30 a.m., a fire broke out at 150-16 33rd Avenue, a two-and-a-half-story private house.

A barking dog woke up off-duty Fireman Alfred Della Valle, who looked out the window to see his next door neighbor's home in flames. He directed his wife to telephone the alarm and ran out into the snow in his bare feet, pulling a coat on over his pajamas. His entrance through the front door was blocked by flames. Inside, he could hear his neighbor's voice. Della Valle told him to get to a window as he sought a way into the blazing home.

Della Valle soon was joined by fellow off-duty Fireman Francis Hogan, who lived around the corner. Both firemen dashed to the rear of the building and Hogan smashed in a window in the back door. With blood pouring down his badly cut hand, he reached in and opened the door. The two firemen entered the smoke-filled kitchen and began to crawl toward the stairs as the sounds of sirens grew in the distance.

Despite their best efforts, the men were forced back by the flames and had to back out of the house as fire companies arrived. The entire front of the house was now a sheet of flames. Firemen later found the six family members dead in their bedrooms. All three children were found in their parents' bed with their mother kneeling at their side.

A three-alarm fire swept through four homes in South Jamaica at 1:15 p.m. on January 27, 1971. The blaze left six families, including 19 children, homeless in the freezing weather. Companies fought the heavy fire and smoke, driven by strong winds, and gained control only after one hour and 20 minutes.

One hundred twenty firemen braved freezing temperatures as they worked to stop the spread of flames from home to home. The wooden private dwellings were two stories in height and burned quickly. The houses were 103-12 to 103-18 169th Street near Liberty Avenue.

The thundering sounds of a gas explosion tore through a restaurant filled with people at 10:31 a.m. on February 9, 1971. The Golden Goose Restaurant literally was ripped apart as the explosion opened a 20-foot crater in the sidewalk outside the one-story eatery.

Arriving firemen found severe damage to the structure with numerous civilians trapped and injured in the rubble as flames roared nearby. Broken glass covered the street as firemen moved in to rescue those trapped inside. Ladders were laid across the hole and the injured were carried out to waiting ambulances. In all, 13 people were injured, two seriously.

One of the most difficult nights in the history of the FDNY occurred on February 4, 1971. Throughout the day, the temperatures were below freezing and between six p.m. and midnight, they hovered between 13 and nine degrees. The Department spent eight hours that evening performing fire duty – above and beyond the normal punishment and dangers they faced every night.

Firemen operate at building explosion and collapse. Selected debris is removed and voids are searched for trapped civilians. (Photo by Steven Scher)

At 2:23 p.m., Bronx Box 3127 was received for a fire in a row of three-story, occupied, frame multiple dwellings. The fire, at 1190 Bathgate Avenue, near 179th Street, went to four alarms before being brought under control.

Manhattan Box 1468 was transmitted at 6:15 p.m. for a fire in the Woolworth department store at 208-10 125th Street in Harlem. The building was 48- x 201-feet and ran through to 124th Street. The structure was in the process of being altered to interconnect with a similar-sized occupancy next door to the east. Half of this structure was to be occupied as a Miles Shoe store.

Arriving units found a heavy fire condition on the 124th Street end of the Woolworth store and heavy smoke in exposure 4 (Miles). Conditions were deteriorating quickly and help was requested. Four alarms were transmitted as firemen battled the extending fire.

A defensive operation was set up, using Stangs and Tower Ladder streams. At about eight p.m., the front wall of the Miles store started to pull away. Members were directed to move to safer locations. A few minutes later, the wall collapsed into the street. Satellite monitors finished off the fire.

Meanwhile, two other major fires were being fought; one that started at 6:36 p.m. at Box 1341, a six-story, occupied multiple dwelling at 237 West 111 Street near 8th Avenue. This fire escalated to two alarms. Then at 8:21 p.m., a blaze was reported at 91 Lenox Avenue, a five-story multiple dwelling. This fire required the transmission of three alarms to control.

Brooklyn had its own multiple at 1689 Saint John's Place near Buffalo Avenue, in a row of vacant tenements. This fire went to two alarms.

A 13-year-old boy and his two younger brothers returned to the three-story old law tenement at 1090 Halsey Street in Brooklyn after fighting with a fourth child who lived on the second floor. They set fire to the building in apparent retaliation to the earlier dispute.

Box 820 was received at 12:57 p.m. on March 27, 1971, and arriving units found an advanced fire condition with flames already involving both exposures. Reports crossed the fireground of children trapped in the building. Second-due Ladder Company 175, with Captain John T. Dunne in command, went into action. The officer gave orders to his crew and donned a mask. After finding the interior stairs fully involved, he dashed to the rear fire escape, accompanied by Fireman Raymond Ross (detailed from Engine 233-2).

Despite the high heat and thick smoke, they searched the second floor, then proceeded to the third floor. Flames were pouring from the windows and onto the fire escape. Dunne ordered Ross to climb back down, as a stream was directed into the window from a line in the street. Meanwhile, unknown to Dunne, the trapped children had made their exit by jumping out windows and landing on a mattress. When the fire was knocked down, Captain Dunne climbed into the window and under extreme conditions, began searching for the children.

Soon after the determined officer entered the window, the room became engulfed in flames. Despite furious and persistent efforts by firemen to reach him, they were unable to do so. When the flames were finally beaten back, Captain Dunne had been claimed by the fire.

Dunne had been the Captain of Ladder Company 175 since it was organized in February 1970. The 15-year veteran was awarded the Brooklyn Citizens Medal posthumously. Also awarded a medal posthumously in 1970 was Lieutenant Jerome R. O'Connor of the 18th Battalion, who rescued a number of people while off-duty on January 19, 1971. O'Connor then succumbed to a heart attack at the scene of the fire at 1929 Washington Avenue in the Bronx.

Thirty taxi cabs were destroyed as a five-alarm fire raced through Katz's Taxi Garage at 127-80 Metropolitan Avenue, Kew Gardens Queens. The one-story brick building poured thick clouds of smoke that blanketed the neighborhood. High winds spread the fire along the Long Island Rail Road tracks nearby.

The fire spread from the rear of one cab at 8:30 p.m. and soon filled the entire structure. More than 200 men operated 40 pieces of fire equipment, including the Super Pumper and a tower ladder. The intense heat caused the roof to collapse. No major injuries were reported and the blaze was brought under control in about two hours.

On April 22, 1971, Manhattan fire companies were called to a reported bomb blast at 355 Lexington Avenue, the offices of the Soviet export-import agency, Amtorg. A telephone warning reported that a number of bombs were set to go off in the 22-story building near 40th Street. Fire units reported to the site of the explosion on the 19th floor and searched for victims and surveyed damages to the structure.

As the firemen expanded their search to the floor above, Fireman John Mitchell of Ladder Company 2 located a suspicious bag. The Bomb Squad was informed and moved in to check. The device turned out to be four sticks of dynamite with a timer that had activated and was only seconds away from exploding. Bomb technicians disabled the device and removed it from the building.

The fiscal crisis within both city and state governments was threatening both job security and the level of public services, both emergency and non-emergency. The papers were filled daily with projected cuts in various government agencies and programs. Firemen worried, along with the rest of the city workers, not only about their level of pay, but also their jobs.

On May 5, 1971, a rally against state and city cuts in welfare and other programs turned into widespread violence in Brooklyn's Brownsville section. After a police officer was wounded by a shotgun blast in an ambush on Sutter Avenue, gangs of youths took to the streets, overturning automobiles and setting fires.

At least 11 structure fires were reported during the day, including a four-alarm blaze that broke out about 2:30 p.m. in a three-story frame house at the corner of Christopher and Sutter Avenues. The radiant heat ignited a two-story building across the street. Another fire, believed to have been started by a Molotov cocktail, roared through a vacant building at Pitkin Avenue and Powell Street.

During the firefighting operations, bottles and bricks rained on the firemen. The disturbance covered a 14-block section of Pitkin Avenue and spread to Sutter, Blake and Rockaway Avenues. In all, 15 firemen were injured by attacks from the angry crowds.

As if the fiscal crisis and rioting were not making the operations of the Fire Department difficult enough, a gasoline strike began in early May. The FDNY was forced to limit the movement of all vehicles, except in response to fires. With deliveries to firehouses stopped, the city issued credit cards to some units and authorized the purchase of fuel at private service stations.

A three-alarm fire at Manhattan Box 872, West 52nd Street, June 6, 1971.

On Friday, May 14, 1971, a tenant in the Park House, a six-story, 92-unit apartment, smelled smoke and notified the building's superintendent. The super was unable to enter the cellar due to dense fumes and he called the Fire Department. A 17-year-old student was charged with setting fire to a cardboard box and some stored bedding, which he placed underneath a row of gas meters. The heat melted one of the gas lines, allowing a build-up of the vapors.

Box 9851 was transmitted and Queens fire companies soon were on the scene. Members of Ladder Company 125 entered the cellar, extinguished the small fire and attempted to ventilate the dense mixture of smoke and natural gas. Unaware of an order to back out of the building, several members continued their attempt to vent the area.

Suddenly, at 10:53 p.m., an explosion tore through the cellar. Fireman Walter J. Bozenko of Engine Company 315 – who had done a mutual to allow a member of the truck the night off – was killed, as a wall toppled onto him. Fireman Eugene J. McGarry, also in the cellar, suffered serious trauma injuries.

Sixteen firemen were sent into the first floor to evacuate tenants when a second explosion rocked the building. Several people were injured as sections of the front wall were blasted across the sidewalk and street in front of the structure. Sixty-two people were injured by the explosions with five civilians and three firemen admitted to the hospital.

The fire, explosion and collapse of sections of the building required the response of a four-alarm assignment. More than 200 people were left homeless by the blast.

The third three-alarm fire to strike the Sutphin Boulevard-Jamaica Avenue section of Jamaica in 1971 occurred on June 25th at 5:05 p.m. The fire broke out shortly after the Paramount Coffee Shop closed for the day at about 4:30. The fire spread quickly through the two-story brick building that contained nine stores on the street level and the Jamaica branch of the Labor Department's unemployment offices, which occupied the entire second floor of the structure.

Flames quickly made their way through the roof and began to spread to other stores within the building. By 5:24 p.m., the fire had grown to three alarms as heavy, black smoke covered the front of the building. The L-shaped building turned the corner from Jamaica Avenue and continued on Sutphin Boulevard. Also destroyed in the blaze were the offices above, a Woolworth's, a card store, a Chinese restaurant and a bar.

Night tours are 15 hours long – sometimes busy, sometimes slow. One particular night tour was rather productive for a fireman named Samuel D. Panasci. Nicknamed "Super Sam" by his brother firemen, Panasci entered quarters of Ladder Company 11 on the night of August 5, 1971, and readied himself for fire duty.

The six-foot, 205-pound former Marine responded with his company at 11:40 p.m. to a fire at 411 East 10th Street. The fire was on the 13th floor of the 25-story apartment complex known as the Village East Towers. Panasci fought the smoke and flames to rescue two unconscious men.

At 12:40 a.m., Ladder Company 11 rolled from their East Third Street firehouse to a blaze at 222 East Second Street. Inside the burning, six-story building, Panasci located and rescued a man trapped on the second floor. Not a bad night's work.

Fire Marshals investigated 11 fires that were set in supermarkets in the lower East Side and Spanish Harlem within 13 hours of each other on August 22, 1971. The fires were caused by small incendiary bombs made by filling ping-pong balls with sulfuric acid and gasoline. The bombs then were placed on the paper goods, cereal and spaghetti counters around closing time. There were no injuries, although two of the supermarkets did suffer extensive damage.

On Fifth Avenue and 81st Street stood the 16-story, 150-room, exclusive Stanhope Hotel. On October 14, 1971, a smoky fire broke out in the basement of the posh hotel at 10:25 a.m. Within minutes, the fire spread from a utility cabinet adjacent to a basement kitchen, to an elevator shaft, allowing dense smoke to fill the stairs and hallways throughout the building. Arriving firemen were faced with numerous people showing at upper-story windows, crying for help.

A second alarm was transmitted and Deputy Chief Halford, using a bullhorn, urged the trapped occupants to stay calm and remain at their windows. Fearing that some of the more excited residents might fall or jump from the windows, the chief sent a team to the roof.

Fireman John Driscoll of Rescue Company 1 was lowered by roof rope to the 15th-floor ledge along the Fifth Avenue side of the building. Hundreds of people crowded the sidewalks and stairs of the Metropolitan Museum of Art, watching the rope operation. Driscoll worked his way along the ledge and calmed numerous people. Several guests were treated for smoke inhalation, but no serious injuries were reported.

A spectacular three-alarm fire, with numerous special-called units, destroyed a financial district restaurant, injured 35 people, tied up traffic and disrupted subway service. On December 13, 1971, at around one p.m., a fire broke out in the kitchen grease duct of Schwartz's Restaurant at 29 Trinity Place. The 250-foot-long restaurant, made up of two buildings that were connected back to back and ran from Trinity Place through to Broadway, was filled with luncheon patrons.

At first, the kitchen help battled the fire with an extinguisher until they were driven from the kitchen by the growing flames. Thick smoke began to fill the 100-year-old building as the fire spread inside the structure. Box 37 was received at 1:04 p.m. Numerous people began to show at upper-floor windows and were rescued by aerial ladder.

Three unconscious men also were rescued by mask-equipped firemen. As the fire condition worsened, multiple alarms were transmitted. Thousands of people were evacuated from neighboring buildings as the fire threatened to extend and the heavy smoke worked its way inside. More than 150 firemen operated for five hours to subdue the stubborn blaze.

Water run-off caused subway traffic to halt through the Rector Street station throughout the rush hour. Thirty-six firemen were injured by the fire. The fire also destroyed about $250,000 worth of spare parts stored by the Xerox Corporation for daily repairs needed in the Wall Street area.

It was New Year's Eve and 1971 was about to become 1972. It was cold out as Brooklyn units raced to Box 671 for a reported fire in a four-story multiple dwelling at 103 Sanford Street. Units were advised by radio that children were trapped on the top floor of the building.

The inside team of Ladder Company 102 was unable to reach the front rooms because the door was sealed and the only entrance was a mass of flames. The OVM (outside ventilation man) Fireman Steven C. DeRosa climbed the aerial ladder, realizing he was the only fireman able to reach the trapped children.

Crawling through the dense smoke and building heat, DeRosa came upon an unconscious man and dragged him to the front window and passed him outside to the chauffeur on the aerial. DeRosa knew the heat was reaching critical levels because he was being burned while handing the victim out. He climbed out onto the aerial and vented another window in the apartment to release more heat and smoke. Then, he re-entered the blazing apartment.

Crawling toward the building heat, he entered another room, well involved with flame, and found an unconscious, three-year-old child. DeRosa made his way back to the window and handed this second victim off to another fireman. With fire now in the front room, DeRosa again attempted to crawl into the far room, but was driven back by the advancing fire.

Fireman Steven DeRosa suffered second-degree burns, yet saved the lives of two people. For his outstanding rescue efforts at extreme personal risk, he was awarded the Bennett Medal.

In January 1972, the FDNY – no strangers to newspaper headlines – this time made it to the *New York Times* Best Sellers List. Fireman Dennis Smith's *Report from Engine Co. 82* broke onto the national scene, relating the story of the world's busiest firehouse and the men who worked in the fire-plagued South Bronx. The book also became a Book of the Month Club alternate, a *Reader's Digest* condensation and a dual selection of the Playboy Book Club.

Smith's book gave readers a real look at the day-to-day battles of New York City firemen, including the 30 calls a day his company responded to and the heat, smoke and grime of fighting fires.

Politically fueled arson struck New York City again on January 26, 1972, when at about 9:30 a.m., an incendiary device exploded in the offices of entertainment impresario Sol Hurok. Just prior to an anonymous phone call to both the Associated Press and the National Broadcasting Company, the explosion and fire sent thick flames and dense smoke throughout the 20th floor of 1370 Avenue of the Americas, killing one young woman and injuring 13 other workers.

A separate bomb exploded almost simultaneously at another talent-booking office located at 165 West 57th Street, only a few blocks away. The continuing plague of bombing was becoming all too familiar to FDNY units. From 1965 to 1970, a total of 465 bombs of various types – 98 of which did not explode – were placed in the city. As of mid-December 1971, 40 bombs had been placed.

It was 4:17 p.m. on February 25, 1972, and the city was beginning yet another rush hour. As thousands of commuters began to descend on Grand Central Station for their train ride home, a fire broke out in the basement of a store in the Commodore Hotel. The 26-story hotel was built above the terminal in 1919 and housed more than 500 guests at this time. As smoke began to make its way from the fire area into the hotel itself, Box 789 was transmitted at Park Avenue and 42nd Street.

Members of Engine Companies 8 and 20, first-in at the alarm, moved in to attack the fire in the basement of Model's Davega Store at 111 East 42nd Street, just east of the entrance to the hotel. Thick billowing clouds of smoke chugged into the street and the adjoining building areas.

The fire and smoke situation worsened and a second alarm was transmitted at 4:27 p.m. A third was sounded at 4:40, the fourth at 5:20 and the fifth at 5:40. Firemen, wearing masks, began a room-to-room search of the giant, 2000-room hotel. More than 100 guests were removed by firemen through the heavy smoke.

Walls from adjoining cellar areas were breached to allow hose stream penetration on the deep-seated blaze. The fire was fought for nearly eight hours and as many as 30 people, including several firemen, were taken to Bellevue Hospital for smoke inhalation.

The fire was declared under control at 12:10 a.m. on the 26th. Fifteen minutes after the blaze was declared out, Chief of Department John T. O'Hagan was taken to the hospital, suffering from chest pains.

During this Manhattan blaze, two other multiples were fought in Queens at the same time. The first fire was at the Reliable Travel Bureau at 59-28 99th Street. The first alarm was received at 7:46 p.m. and went to a third by 8:19. The fire spread to five adjacent stores within the one-story brick structure.

The second Queens fire was in an optometrist's store at 45-04 46th Street in Sunnyside. The fire swept through 12 stores and burned for nearly three hours. This two-alarm fire was extinguished at 1:10 a.m.

A cigarette was the apparent cause of a fire that roared though the Sloane House YMCA at 356 West 34th Street on March 22, 1972. It was 9:54 p.m. when the call was received for a fire in the 15-story building about a block from Madison Square Garden. The "Y" was opened in 1930 and had been the temporary home for thousands of men newly arrived in New York City.

About 1000 guests were registered in the building when the fire broke out on the seventh floor and quickly spread to the eighth. Arriving units, assigned to Box 712, were confronted with numerous people pleading for help from upper-floor windows. Many spectacular rescues were made, both from the tips of fully extended aerial ladders and through the dense smoke and flames inside the building.

Reporting to the command post were Firemen James T. McCarthy and Bill Moclair of Rescue Company 1. They were directed to move an aerial ladder truck to the rear to assist people trapped there. The duo ascertained the area of most danger in the building and began their operation to assist those in the most jeopardy.

The ladder was raised toward a seventh-floor window. Because of its angle, the ladder was short of its objective, so McCarthy climbed to the top rung, reached for the face of the building and grabbed the windowsill. The victim then used McCarthy as a "human bridge" and climbed down the fireman to the top of the ladder.

A small child is cradled in the arms of a Brooklyn fireman, 1972. (Photo by Steven Scher)

The aerial was repositioned and two more people were pulled from the blaze. As the exhausted duo stood on the turntable helping the last victim down, another victim showed and McCarthy duplicated his original feat, with Moclair guiding the civilian as he climbed down the fireman's back.

Fireman McCarthy realized there were additional people trapped on the floor and hauled himself through the window. As he started down the hall, he quickly was pressed to the floor by hot smoke and gases. McCarthy was reaching his limits. He ducked into a room and grabbed a few breaths at the window before continuing his search. Working his way down a long corridor, he came across a window that he opened to help vent the hallway. Fireman McCarthy was surprised to see a civilian straddling a chimney duct on the outside of the building. The fireman stayed with the man until a ladder was positioned and McCarthy was able to help him climb from his perch.

Four people died and 36 were injured by this fast-moving fire. For his outstanding operations on the aerial and his determined search and rescues on the fire floor, Fireman James McCarthy was awarded the Trevor-Warren Medal.

April 2, 1972, was Easter Sunday and many on their way to church services saw Queens fire units with their hands full as a blaze broke out in a row of stores on Bridge Plaza North at about 9:45 a.m. Dense smoke poured from the building and covered the roadways leading to the Queensboro Bridge.

The fire wormed its way from store to store in the block-long, two-story building. A second alarm was sent in at 9:48, a third at 10:35 and a fourth at 11:17 a.m. More than 160 firemen battled the fire, which now was roaring in 18 stores. After a 3½-hour battle, the fire finally was brought under control.

Except for the fact that two auditors were coming, May 3, 1972, seemed as if it would be just another day for the workers in General Public Utilities offices in the 40-story skyscraper at 80 Pine Street in Manhattan. The holding company, associated with several New Jersey and Pennsylvania utility companies, had offices on the 36th and 37th floors of the 12-year-old structure.

At about 11:15 a.m., a small rumbling sound increased in volume in a matter of seconds, when suddenly, a 14-inch, high-pressure steam pipe exploded in the walls. Ceilings fell and partitions crumbled as a wave of super-heated steam jetted into the occupancy.

Workers who could, fled; others too close to the point of the explosion did not have a chance to get out of their seats. Seven people, including the two auditors, were killed instantly. Arriving firemen battled their way through the dense clouds of steam and dug through the rubble, searching for trapped workers.

About 800 occupants of the building were evacuated. The 500-degree steam filled a three-room section of the floor, killing everyone in the area. The steam was diverted from the riser and firemen and the Buildings Department began to investigate the explosion. Later, it was determined that a failure of an expansion joint triggered the blast.

On June 17, 1972, the Boston Fire Department suffered a major catastrophe as the Hotel Vendome collapsed, just after a raging fire inside the old structure was brought under control. Nine Boston firemen were lost in a matter of seconds as a major collapse occurred without any warning.

In the spirit of brotherhood, as practiced in the past and still done to this day, a contingent of FDNY members headed off to Boston to attend the funeral of their Brother firemen. While on the return trip to New York in a chartered Greyhound bus, one of the firemen noticed another bus leave the road and overturn. The FDNY bus was halted and the firemen sprang into action.

Crawling inside the bus, Fireman Ed Sere of Engine Company 35 found an unconscious woman who was not breathing. Sere began mouth-to-mouth resuscitation on the woman and restored her breathing. He had to duplicate his efforts a second time when she again stopped breathing.

I n June of 1972, Rescue Companies 1 and 2 each received a Hurst Tool. This hydraulic rescue tool was tested extensively and operated in real and drill situations. Various techniques and operating procedures were developed by the companies and after two years, the companies recommended that two additional tools be purchased in 1974. By 1984, there were 32 Hurst Tools in service and by 1995, there were 97 tools in service.

New York firemen swarmed all over the bus, tending to the injured until the arrival of local rescue teams and police. At least five of the victims were admitted to nearby hospitals with a variety of injuries. Connecticut State Police at the scene stated that the quick action of the New York firemen saved the life of at least one woman.

During the last week of July 1972, a fire was extinguished in a vacant tenement at 108 Belmont Avenue on the corner of Stone Street. While the firemen from Engine Company 290 were working at the blaze, several neighborhood youths broke into the Sheffield Avenue firehouse and stole helmets, boots, a transistor radio and $12 in cash.

Nearing midnight that Sunday night, Supervising Fire Marshal Michael DiMarco and Fire Marshals Rudolph Dick and Michael O'Connor were on their way to the firehouse to investigate the robbery when they smelled smoke. They noted smoke coming from 108 Belmont, the scene of the earlier fire.

The marshals radioed in the alarm, then noted what they believed to be a teen-age girl running from the burning building. They took her into custody, brought her to the local police station and began questioning her. During the course of the interview, the woman, 23-year-old Priscilla Haynes, revealed that she was one of the busiest arsonists in the history of the city. She admitted to setting more than 2500 fires, as many as three or four a day, in the vacant buildings in Brownsville. She was charged with arson and held for arraignment.

On August 31, 1972, a series of fires swept the city from the lower East Side to Harlem, Brooklyn and Queens, leaving a toll of one fireman and three civilians dead and three civilians and 12 firemen injured.

At just after midnight, a blaze broke out in a second-floor bedroom of a private house at 103-18 177th Street, Jamaica, Queens. Despite efforts of family members and firemen to save them, two children were killed in the fire.

At about the same time, the body of an unidentified man was found on the fourth floor of a seven-story tenement at 117 Avenue C, near Eighth Street. Another man was rescued from the building and suffered burns. Twenty of the 30 apartments in the building were unoccupied and it is believed that some of those in the building at the time of the fire were squatters.

Another fire broke out around the corner at 329 East Eighth Street, where a fireman rescued a number of people and then had to be rescued himself, as dense smoke rendered him disoriented. Four firemen were treated at Bellevue for smoke inhalation.

Queens Box 3534 came in at four a.m. for a blaze in a vacant, three-story frame building on West 29th Street and Mermaid Avenue in Coney Island. As firemen went to work, a group of youths launched an attack on them. Bricks and bottles flew; they even pulled extinguishers

Nozzle teams hunker down during a three-alarm fire in a Park Slope, Brooklyn, lumberyard, August 1972. (Photo by Steven Scher)

from the rigs and covered the apparatus with foam. Several youths were arrested and one fireman was hospitalized after being struck by a brick.

In Brooklyn, Box 733 was transmitted at 5:48 a.m. for a fire in a three-story multiple dwelling at 122 Wilson Avenue. When Engine Company 271 and Ladder Company 124 rolled up, the fire had possession of most of the first floor. Heavy smoke and high heat were venting from the second and third floors and because of the hour, it was believed victims might be trapped and overcome on the upper floors.

Fireman Henry H. Mitchell of Ladder 124 made his way to the roof to provide ventilation. After completing his vent, Mitchell radioed that he was entering the top floor to search. After covering the third floor, he dropped down to the second floor where conditions were becoming extreme.

At 5:58 a.m., a second alarm was transmitted as more than 15 elderly people, including a blind woman, were taken from the building. Back inside on the second floor, conditions had deteriorated to the point that Fireman Mitchell was overcome and collapsed on the floor. An intensive mission to save the downed fireman was initiated but, despite their efforts, Fireman Henry Mitchell could not be revived.

In Harlem, a three-alarm fire was being fought at the same time, as firemen were working frantically on their downed Brother in Brooklyn. A furniture warehouse fire was battering the companies on East 126th Street. Dense smoke and limited ventilation made for another difficult fire.

The following June, that terrible night in August was relived as the widow and the six small children of Fireman Henry Mitchell were presented the Brummer Medal for his heroic actions in that second-floor inferno.

On October 4, 1972, a violent explosion tore through an abandoned factory at the corner of Myrtle and Nostrand Avenues in Brooklyn. Box 671 was received at 6:05 a.m. and responding units were greeted with two demolished buildings, fully involved with flames leaping 50 feet into the air.

In the intersection, a police car had been blasted into a city bus. The radio car literally was thrown through the side of the bus. The two officers inside the car and 11 passengers in the bus were injured. Dazed and injured people began to come down from adjacent buildings. The huge volume of fire also was threatening surrounding exposures.

Five alarms were transmitted before the disaster could be brought under control. Besides the bus passengers and policemen, 15 other people were injured and almost 200 people were left homeless by the blast, believed to be the work of an arsonist.

It was 4:15 in the morning on October 16, 1972, when Ladder Company 40 pulled up in front of 2066 Seventh Avenue. Fire was blowing out of the second- and third-floor windows of the five-story old law tenement. Flames were filling the air shafts on both sides of the building as well. Engine Company 36 pushed their line into the kitchen and stopped long enough only to relieve the nozzle team, whose nozzleman had burned his neck and face.

Captain Abseck and Fireman Raymond G. McCann, after completing their initial truck work, moved in to place the line into operation. Suddenly, without warning, the ceiling collapsed, pinning both members. Within moments, a secondary collapse occurred as partition walls and cabinets came down. This added to the mound of flaming debris that now was blocking the exit.

McCann struggled to free himself from the burning pile with no success. With great effort, he was able to pull his feet from his boots, still pinned in the burning pile. Without a helmet or boots and in extreme pain, McCann looked around as well as he could, only to realize that the exit was blocked and he would have to get out through the rear.

The injured fireman then heard the anguished calls of the captain, who was buried almost completely under the smoldering mound. Despite his own injuries, McCann searched for and located the officer.

Literally pulling the semi-conscious captain from his boots, McCann half-carried, half-dragged him to the rear fire escape, where they were found by another fireman.

Fireman Ray McCann then collapsed from exhaustion and his own injuries. Both men were removed to the hospital with second- and third-degree burns, smoke inhalation and other injuries. McCann was awarded the Bennett Medal for his heroic efforts.

A five-alarm fire blazed through an abandoned Penn Central railroad warehouse, in sub-freezing weather, on the evening of January 5, 1973. Box 183 came in at 6:31 p.m. The fire erupted in a warehouse behind the 1000-foot-long Pier 29 on the North River at Vestry Street. The fire also worked its way into sections of Pier 30 and 31.

The West Side Highway was closed to traffic from the Brooklyn Battery Tunnel to Canal Street as heavy smoke banked across the road, blinding motorists. Sections of West Street also were closed as nearly 200 firemen manned 39 pieces of apparatus and three fireboats to battle the blaze.

On January 7th, Box 113, Warren and Washington Streets, was received for a fire at Pier 20. This blaze required four alarms and two and a half hours to control.

As the cold weather continued, firemen responded to a fast-spreading fire in a six-story apartment building in New Dorp, Staten Island, on January 11th. Box 2274 was transmitted at 3:01 a.m. for a phone alarm reporting fire on the fourth floor of the building at Cuba Avenue and Ebbits Street. The top three floors of the building were destroyed, leaving 300 people homeless.

A three-alarm fire was fought on January 13, 1973, in a construction area adjacent to the 110-story south tower of the World Trade Center. More than 4000 people were evacuated from the building due to a heavy smoke condition. The blaze broke out shortly before five p.m. in heavy timbers under a ramp that traveled beneath the south tower. The ramp was being used to construct an entranceway into the structure. Burning timbers extended five floors below the tower and sent billows of smoke up through elevator shafts.

Construction workers helped more than 150 firemen dismantle sections of the ramp to allow extinguishment. The timing of the fire helped to completely jam up rush-hour traffic. The fire was declared under control at 6:45 p.m.

Forty-three workers were killed in a huge liquefied natural gas tank explosion in the Bloomfield section of Staten Island on February 10, 1973. The explosion occurred at 1:40 p.m. in the 600,000-barrel, eight-story, domed structure. The tank, which was undergoing repairs, was designed with a heavy, reinforced concrete roof that was intended to collapse into the tank in the event of an explosion, thereby suppressing the explosion. The roof did exactly what it was designed to do. Unfortunately, the tank was not designed to have people inside and the workers were buried under tons of concrete.

Rescue Companies 1 and 2 were special-called quickly and, despite the heavy smoke and high heat, a rescue effort was started. When it was determined that it would be a recovery and not a rescue operation, a rotation system was devised. One rescue company and several truck companies worked together for several hours until relieved by another rescue company and several other truck companies. This system continued for several weeks until the last body was recovered. This operation was conducted under some of the most severe weather and cold temperature conditions ever encountered in the city.

On February 24, 1973, the city suffered four major apartment house fires. Four people were killed in three of the fires. A three-alarm blaze came in at 1:56 a.m. in a six-story building at 559 West 158th Street in Washington Heights. Fifty-five tenants were evacuated. Ten of them, plus two firemen, were hospitalized.

The second fire was reported at 2:03 a.m. in a six-story tenement at 309 West 113th Street. Firemen used an aerial ladder to rescue an 85-year-old woman, confined to a wheelchair, from her third-floor apartment. A 35-year-old woman was burned to death in her second-floor apartment.

At 2:27 a.m., firemen raced to 349 East 49th Street in Manhattan. The fire that started in the living room of a second-floor apartment trapped and killed the occupant when he was unable to open a locked window gate in his bedroom and then tried to return through the heavy smoke to the hallway, where he succumbed.

The fourth fire took place in a four-story brownstone building at 39 Quincy Street in Brooklyn. The fire quickly spread from the second to the third floor, driving residents to the windows and roof. A mother, with her child in her arms, jumped from a top-floor window in the rear and both were killed. Another person was injured jumping from the same window.

A thunderous explosion rocked Queens Village at 11:45 p.m. on March 15, 1973. Three buildings were leveled and bricks, steel beams and debris were scattered over a wide area on the corner of Jamaica Avenue and 218th Street.

An apparent gas leak led to the explosion and fire that required a dozen fire companies to control. Store windows were broken in 34 shops and eight apartment houses along the Avenue.

Engine Company 91 was returning to quarters on May 7, 1973, when they noticed a well-advanced fire condition in a five-story tenement at 25 East 115th Street. They transmitted Box 1377 at 8:02 a.m. Ladder Company 26 arrived and were directed to attempt the rescue of six people trapped at the windows of two interior bedrooms fronting on an enclosed light and air shaft.

Captain John S. O'Regan and Firemen Seaman and Bernard dashed to the roof of the adjoining building. Seeing that a rope rescue would take too much time, they descended to the fifth floor of the adjacent structure.

Conditions behind the trapped people were deteriorating rapidly as fire was eating through the door. Realizing speed was essential, Captain O'Regan improvised. He climbed up onto the windowsill and lunged his right leg across the shaft where a woman and her three children were huddled in fear. With the two firemen holding his left leg, O'Regan then handed the two small children and an older, heavier boy across the shaft to safety.

At this point, other members of Ladder Company 26 arrived on the roof and seeing the situation, lowered their new, 40-foot personal ropes to the captain. The end of the first rope was fastened around the pregnant woman and she was swung, pendulum fashion, across the shaft. When the woman was untied, O'Regan tied the rope around himself to allow some margin of safety as additional ropes were lowered from above and two men were swung across the five-story-deep gap.

For his heroic and quick-thinking actions, Captain John O'Regan was awarded the Brummer Medal.

On May 8, 1973, a two-alarm fire took the lives of six people in Brooklyn. Six young gang members started fires at 2:39 a.m. in the front and rear vacant apartments of the three-story building at 532 Christopher Avenue, near Lott Avenue in Brownsville. The arson was an apparent attempt to "get even" with a rival gang member.

The fire quickly spread, trapping several families above. Seven members of a family on the second floor escaped by dropping mattresses out the window and jumping on them. One of the seven, a 47-year-old woman, broke her back when she landed.

The family on the third floor was not as lucky. Five victims were found in one bedroom and the sixth was found in another bedroom. Two alarms were sounded to bring the fast-moving fire under control.

Supervising Fire Marshal John S. Barracato led the investigation into the fatal fire. His determined efforts in an intensive investigation led to the arrest of seven youths, six within 24 hours of the fire. For his skill and resourcefulness, Barracato was awarded the Commissioner Martin Scott Medal.

Shortly before one a.m. on June 2, 1973, a collision occurred between the tanker *Esso Brussels* and the container ship *Sea Witch*, resulting in an explosion and spectacular fire. Marine Company 9, the first fireboat on the scene, approached from the port side, opened up all eight of her monitors and began to move across a sea of flaming fuel. They burrowed their way through the flames to a point where they could extinguish fire along the side of the tanker. They then could see the bow of another vessel imbedded in the tanker. During a quick search of the area, 31 members of the *Sea Witch* crew were located, trapped on the ship's fantail.

The *Sea Witch's* Captain, an apparent cardiac, quickly was removed to the fireboat and given first-aid. The remaining members of the crew were removed to the fireboat as the flaming waters all around them were held at bay by the monitor streams. *The Fire Fighter* rushed the injured to pier in Brooklyn, then returned to the fire.

The ships separated and became grounded in Gravesend Bay, south of the Verrazano Bridge, resulting in two distinct operations. Firefighting operations continued for 22 days. Land units were shuttled out to the ships by fireboats. The rescue companies took turns searching the below-deck areas of each ship and recovered 16 bodies.

In 1975, Lieutenant James McKenna and several members of the crew of the fireboat, *The Fire Fighter,* were awarded the National Maritime Meritorious Service Medal, the highest civilian award given by Congress for their rescue operations. The Lieutenant and fireboat Pilot Matthew Fitzsimmons also were awarded the American Merchant Marine Association Seamanship Trophy, a silver cup, with their names engraved on it. Marine Company 9, *The Fire Fighter* was designated a "Gallant Ship" for its role in the fire rescue. This is the highest award the government can bestow upon a non-naval vessel.

The collapse of the old Broadway Central Hotel (later named University Hotel) marked the end of the city's oldest hotel. The eight-story structure was built in 1854 and had gone from youthful elegance to a shabby old age. The building had housed the likes of "Diamond Jim" Brady to welfare recipients. On August 3, 1973, the 119-year-old building collapsed onto Broadway. Box 365 was transmitted at 5:06 p.m., sending FDNY units to the scene.

Ladder Company 9 arrived and members were confronted with a huge debris pile that spilled out onto the street. Visible above were people at windows adjacent to the collapsed section. Fireman Frank P. Clark and members of Ladder Company 9 located a woman pinned under a marquee and worked quickly to free her and remove her from the collapse zone.

Clark then jumped into the Tower Ladder basket and raised himself toward the people trapped at the windows above. He gently guided the bucket into position where he first removed a woman from the third floor, then repositioned to the fourth floor, where he began to help an invalid man. Clark worked as quickly as he could because the sections of building above him looked unstable. Just as the man was pulled into the basket, a secondary collapse occurred.

On November 6, 1973, after months of negotiations, members of the Uniformed Firefighters Association staged a five-hour strike. A settlement of the strike was reached in the chambers of Supreme Court Justice Fine. The Justice announced that the union would desist from striking or threatening strikes or work stoppages and that an impasse panel would be formed immediately to begin deliberations.

Fireboat Archer *moves in on the* Sea Witch, *June 2, 1973.*

Fireman Clark pulled the victims close and shielded them as debris rained down. When the dust settled, he pulled the debris clear, calmed the victims and returned the bucket to the street. Four people were killed and scores of people were injured. Members of the Department rescued numerous victims from the rubble. Fireman Frank Clark was awarded the Scott Medal for his actions.

December 29, 1973, saw the new Sav-Tee harness and 40-foot personal ropes prove their worth again. At 6:25 a.m., a fire broke out on the third floor of 338 East 108th Street in Manhattan. Ladder Company 26 arrived to see flames spreading quickly within the six-story building. As Fireman William Murphy stepped off the rig, he saw an entire family trapped at their fifth-floor apartment window.

Murphy ascended the aerial ladder to the roof, strapped himself into the new harness and was lowered over the roof by Firemen William Barbuto and Lawrence Fitzpatrick. Murphy arrived at the window but the children were afraid to exit. The fireman spoke to the father in Spanish and English and told him to step out onto the windowsill and grab him around the waist.

The burly fireman then kicked off and swung across the alley below, to the fire escape on the adjoining building. He dropped off the father, then returned for the mother. The children were next. Calming them, he brought them one by one to the fire escape. In this Tarzan-like fashion, Fireman William Murphy saved six people.

There was a crib and four bunk beds in the bedroom of the burning apartment. Fireman Michael J. Gurry of Ladder Company 27 was crawling, hugging the floor of the burning apartment. He had heard that five children still might be inside the flat. As he entered from the fire escape, he found one of them and passed the child to a fireman outside. He knew there were four more.

As Gurry again moved deep into the apartment, the Engine Company had entered through the front and began to extinguish the fire. The more the Engine progressed, the worse conditions became around Gurry. He found two more children and hustled back to a rear window. After a few quick gulps of fresh air, he dove back into the thick, hot atmosphere.

He found the fourth child and returned to the fire escape. There was still one to go. Nearing total exhaustion, Gurry plunged back into the apartment to make one more desperate try for the last youngster. He found the fifth child – the most severely burned – in the hallway leading to the front of the building. He removed him to the fire escape.

On March 21, 1974, at 8:45 p.m., Fireman Michael Gurry singlehandedly saved the lives of five children from the most extreme of fire conditions. For his valor at 1985 Daly Avenue, Michael Gurry was awarded the Crimmins Medal.

Fires and the South Bronx were becoming synonymous. The fire duty being handled by these companies was reaching epic proportions and the level of firefighting was more than meeting that challenge.

It was 8:35 p.m. on April 4, 1974, when Bronx units descended upon Box 2550 for a fire on the top floor of 1050 Home Street, a four-story multiple dwelling. Double-parked cars did not allow ladder company apparatus to gain the position needed to reach the pregnant woman and child visibly trapped at a top-floor window. With flames pouring out the two adjacent windows of the apartment, Ladder Company 31's forcible entry team assumed first-due duties.

Upon their arrival at the door to the apartment, two police officers reported that they had been driven back by the fire. Aware that the only way to reach the mother and child was through this door, Fireman Thomas J. Neary and Lieutenant Donald H. Butler entered the super-heated hallway without hesitation. With thick flames rolling over their heads, they crawled down the 40-foot hallway toward the sounds of the woman screaming.

Both firefighters were at the point where they knew if they continued, they would be burned. They continued. Diving through a wall of flames, they advanced toward the victims. In an adjacent bedroom, the duo found the pregnant woman and her small son, wedged in the child window guard. They tore away the window guard and freed the distraught woman and protected her as best they could.

Returning the way they had come now was impossible because they were surrounded by fire. Their only hope was outside. As Butler straddled the windowsill, Ladder Company 48's aerial came into view. It had to be raised parallel to the front of the building in the cantilever position.

Ignoring his own severe pain, Fireman Neary now shielded the Lieutenant and the woman with his body as she was guided to the aerial. Next, Neary grasped the child, straddled the window and with arms fully extended, passed the child to Butler on the aerial.

His clothes smoldering and his strength about spent, Neary leaped headfirst out the window to the unsupported ladder wavering about three feet away.

Both mother and son were hospitalized for burns and smoke inhalation. They were released the next day. Neary suffered first-, second- and third-degree burns of the face, wrists and legs and was placed on medical leave. For his absolutely amazing endurance and bravery, Fireman Thomas Neary was awarded the Bennett Medal. Lieutenant Donald Butler was awarded the Brummer Medal for his exceptional heroism.

In 1913, the two-story firehouse of Engine Company 294 and Ladder Company 143 at 101-02 Jamaica Avenue in Richmond Hill, Queens, was built. The firemen who worked in this house all those years had seen their share of fire duty and suffered their share of injuries. On May 14, 1974, they got the lion's share of fire where they least expected it.

It was the change of tours and the day shift was preparing their equipment, while outside, a truck was delivering a supply of gasoline to the firehouse. The officer was writing his roll call and the Brothers started about their work. Fireman Alfred J. Bold approached the inside cellar entrance to check the fuel oil gauge as his officer had instructed at roll call. At the door, he noticed an odor of gasoline and descended to check the source. Bold noticed a widening pool of liquid and knew by the smell it was gasoline.

Bold shouted up to Lieutenant Walter C. Mischke that there was a gasoline leak in the cellar, then moved to shut off any source of ignition, knowing it could touch off an explosion. The officer jumped up from the watch desk, ordered all sources of ignition on the apparatus floor to be secured and descended the stairs to ensure sources of ignition at that level were safe.

As Bold approached the emergency shut-off switch, a powerful explosion tore through the cellar. Mischke was blown back up the stairs and onto the apparatus floor. Bold was thrown upward through an open cellar door and onto the street in a ball of flame.

Firemen, briefly stunned by the explosion, dashed to Bold and Mischke, extinguished the fire and provided first-aid. Fireman Bold was burned over 75 percent of his body and Lieutenant Mischke was burned over 30 percent of his body. They were taken to Jamaica Hospital. Bold then was flown to Jacobi Hospital Burn Center via Coast Guard helicopter.

On June 6, 1974, a three-alarm fire was fought in a six-story tenement with stores on the first floor. Bronx Box 2739 was transmitted at 6:54 p.m. and sent units to 862 Jennings Street, at the corner of Intervale Avenue. The fire was fought using hand lines on the interior and in the stores, while Stangs covered the rescue of a civilian via an aerial. After the severity and amount of fire was reported, the attack was changed to a defensive mode and lines were withdrawn.

After the fire was knocked down and conditions had stabilized, members moved back into the building to complete overhauling. Work had been going on for a while when at 8:08 p.m., without warning, a collapse occurred within the building. Seven firemen were caught in the collapse, two of whom were removed quickly from the top of the pile. Two additional Rescue Companies were called for as firemen moved in to save their Brothers.

Fireman Alfred Bold (in wheelchair) after being presented the Hugh Bonner Medal for his actions attempting to prevent the explosion in quarters. (Photo by Steven Scher)

The flag-draped coffin of Fireman Harold Hoey is carried from church by members of Ladder Company 17. At right is Fireman Neville Martin, who would lose his life on April 27, 1976, rescuing fellow passengers from a plane crash in the Virgin Islands. (Photo by Steven Scher)

two people the year before at a fire on Willis Avenue. Tonight, June 13th, only a week after Medal Day, things were as Fireman Hoey liked it – no fanfare, just fire duty.

The tower ladder was set up in front of the five-story building at 412 East 148th Street in the Bronx. Hoey and Fireman Francis Duffy were ascending in the bucket, heading for two people trapped on the roof of the blazing building. Somehow, the edge of the bucket became lodged at the cornice. Duffy jumped onto the roof to ready the victims for removal while Hoey tried to release the bucket. The bucket broke free, catapulting Hoey, who fell five stories and landed on the tower ladder.

Hoey was rushed to Lincoln Hospital, then transferred to Jacobi Hospital, where he died at 12:30 a.m. on June 14th. Even in death, Harold Hoey was not done helping people. His wife, Doris, gave permission to doctors to use skin grafts from her husband for critically injured Fireman Al Bold, who had been burned at the gasoline explosion in the Jamaica firehouse on May 14. The skin graft helped to save yet another life. Two thousand off-duty firemen lined the streets in Kings Park, Long Island, to say good-bye to Harold Hoey.

A five-alarm fire swept through a large, six-story apartment house at Riverside Drive and 250th Street. Box 1649 was received at 8:40 p.m. on September 21, 1974. High winds, whipping off the Hudson River, fanned flames and caused a severe brand problem that threatened the exposures.

Tragedy again struck Ladder Company 17 in the Bronx on October 29, 1974. While operating at a three-alarm fire in the Mott Haven Yard of the Penn Central Railroad, the 35-foot aluminum portable ladder being lowered by Firemen Johnnie Williams and Russell Linneball came in contact with 11,000-volt overhead wires. Both men were killed.

Despite extremely dangerous conditions, members worked without rest until the last man was dug free at 10:11 p.m. Several of the trapped men suffered serious injuries.

It was 10:30 p.m. when Ladder Company 17 rolled from quarters, heading to Box 2230. Riding on the side of the tower ladder was Fireman Harold J. Hoey, Jr. Life had been going well for Hoey; he enjoyed an excellent reputation as a fireman and quietly performed charity work, careful not to make a big deal out of it. He had just earned his Masters degree in mathematics.

On June 4th of 1974, Hoey stood with his family before the Mayor, Chief of Department and the assembled members of the Department and was presented the Dougherty Medal for his rescue of

In late November of 1974, a grim-faced Mayor Beame announced that 12 fire companies would be closed as part of an attempt to close a $330 million budget gap. The fire unions went to court to try and stop the closings. The case was lost.

Arson and Old Lace

Two "elderly women" were indicted on arson charges on February 6, 1975. The operation conducted by the FDNY Fire Marshal's Office was dubbed "Arson and Old Lace." The two women, sisters aged 73 and 66 years old, had headed up a ring that collected millions of dollars in insurance by setting more than 500 fires in Queens during a 10-year run.

They attempted to hire a "torch" to burn a new, unoccupied residence in Far Rockaway owned by one of the women. The "torch" happened to be Fire Marshal Thomas Russo, who had worked his way into the gang several months earlier. At a meeting to discuss the arson, Fire Marshal Russo was wired with a tape recorder. A number of the duo's accomplices, including a son of one of the women also were arrested.

In late 1974, the movie, *The Towering Inferno*, opened across the nation. The film, based on two novels, told the story of a fictitious fire that ravaged an occupied high-rise building. Since the time of its opening, firemen across the country were asked by friends, relatives and strangers: Could it really happen? The answers varied, of course, from fireman to fireman, city to city. The official answer by the chiefs in most of the major cities was, "No. It is only a movie."

On February 13, 1975, at 11:58 p.m., Box 67 was sent out for a fire in tower "A," the northern most of the two towers of the World Trade Center. The fire apparently started in electrical wiring on the 11th floor and spread to several other floors before – without the help of Steve McQueen – the blaze was extinguished.

A major fire, which raised health questions for FDNY firemen for decades to come, struck the New York Telephone Company building at Second Avenue and 13th Street at 12:25 a.m. on February 27, 1975. This fire proved to be one of the most difficult operations ever faced by the Department and one of the worst disasters to befall the Bell System.

The fire spread from the cable vault in the cellar, up through openings to the first and second floors. Dense, acrid and potentially toxic smoke, generated by the polyethylene – and polyvinyl chloride-covered cables, chugged from the fire area and poured from the few points of ventilation within the building.

Five alarms brought 500 firemen, who were rotated for a 16-hour battle to control the blaze. More than 200 firemen were injured battling the blaze. More than 170,000 phones were out of service, including the 911 service.

A seven-story apartment building at the corner of West 83rd Street and Broadway was the scene of a five-alarm fire on December 20, 1974. Box 1136 was transmitted after an accidental spill of lighter fluid started a raging fire on the top floor.

The fire swept across the top floor and burned into the cockloft. Fireman Daniel Perricone, aide to the Chief of the 9th Battalion, collapsed from exhaustion, then suffered a fatal heart attack after making numerous trips into the building and assisting residents down stairs.

The end of 1974 saw the Department's totals reaching all-time highs virtually across the board. Alarms totaled 353,458. False alarms reached 164,401; fires totaled 130,324; and structural fires numbered 52,473 with 651 multiple alarms. Despite these numbers, eight companies were deactivated in mid-December.

Terrorism reared its ugly head again in New York City at 1:30 in the afternoon on January 24, 1975. A bomb tore through the 3½-story building at 54 Pearl Street in lower Manhattan, occupied by historic Fraunces Tavern. The blast killed four people and injured about 50 others.

Two alarms were transmitted for Box 23 as firemen helped sift through the smoldering rubble. Windows were shattered within a two-block radius. The bombing was politically motivated, with the F.A.L.N., a Puerto Rican independence group, claiming responsibility.

Thick, acrid smoke pours from the New York Telephone building at Second Avenue and 13th Street in Manhattan on February 27, 1975. (Photo by Steven Scher)

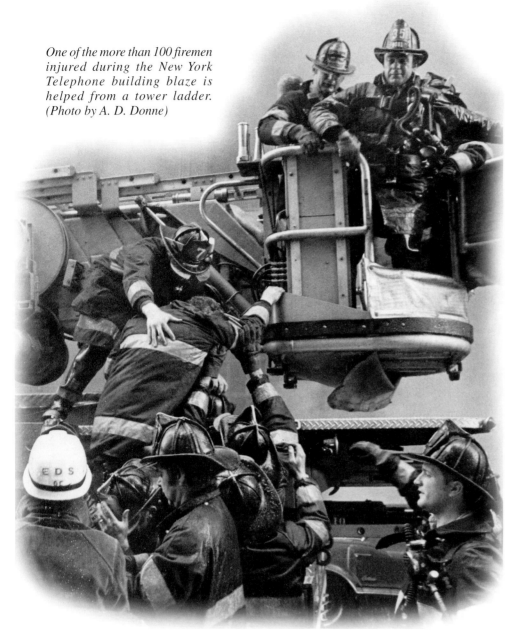

One of the more than 100 firemen injured during the New York Telephone building blaze is helped from a tower ladder. (Photo by A. D. Donne)

Heavy smoke poured from the top-floor windows of the three-story dwelling at 678 Broadway in Brooklyn. Companies had been alerted to the alarm at 12:19 a.m. on March 2, 1975. Fireman Julian R. Tavalaro of Ladder Company 102 had positioned his apparatus and was operating from the turntable when he heard that people were trapped in the rear of the building on the third floor and that there were no fire escapes.

Tavalaro placed portable ladders to a roof extension, then to the third-floor window. Faced with thick smoke pumping from the window, Tavalaro entered it without hesitation. He began his search as the super-heated gases above his head burst into flames. Locating an unconscious man, he dragged him back to the window and handed him to another fireman on the ladder. Tavalaro then re-entered the apartment and ventured even deeper into the blazing structure, where he found a badly burned girl and returned toward the ladder.

Nearing exhaustion, he arrived at the window, now venting fire from the top. Staying as low as possible, he handed the girl out and then hunkered down as a hose line pushed the flames back from over his head.

Both victims were rushed, in critical condition, to Jacobi Burn Center. For his courageous actions in saving the two victims, Fireman Julian Tavalaro was awarded the Brooklyn Citizens Medal.

Engine Company 263 pulled first-due at 30-05 44th Street in Astoria, Queens, on May 6, 1975, at 4:39 a.m. They found the entire front of the three-story building a sea of flames. Smoke and flames were coming out every front window and through the roof. Terrified tenants were jumping from the second-floor windows onto the roof of a *Daily News* delivery truck that had been pulled close to the building by its driver. Among the crowd of excited people was a mother, frantically telling anyone who would listen that her baby was still in the apartment.

Fireman Kevin G. Collins heard her pleas and sprang into action. Collins pulled a portable ladder from the pumper, raced to the rear of the building and lowered it to the child's second-floor window. He ascended the ladder, took out the glass with his helmet and dove into the room. Under severe conditions, he searched for the slender legs of a crib. Unable to stand to remove the child, he dragged the crib back across the room, handed the baby outside, then dove again – this time, out the window.

As Collins was helped to the street, the room he had just left burst into flames behind him. The child was revived by firemen and spent eight days in Jacobi Burn Center, treated for smoke inhalation and second-degree burns. For his courageous actions under extreme conditions, Fireman Kevin G. Collins was awarded a medal.

An explosion in an empty auto repair shop rocked a six-block area of downtown Flushing on June 1, 1975. Seven people were injured by the blast and the building at 133-31 36th Road was destroyed by the ensuing blaze.

The dwelling across the street from the blast took the brunt of the flying debris. Windows were shattered, curtains shredded and furniture upended. A man taking a shower at the time was injured by flying glass. Two blocks away, on Main Street, Northern Boulevard and across College Point Boulevard, windows were blown out in numerous buildings. Firemen combed the rubble for hours, looking for additional victims.

Engine Company 201 and Ladder Company 114 arrived at the scene of a rubbish fire at 51st Street and Third Avenue in the Sunset Park section of Brooklyn. The officers looked around cautiously; this was the scene of several attacks on firemen recently.

An unidentified man walked toward one of the officers and whispered a warning. "Watch out. They are out to get you. They've got 19 Molotov cocktails on the roof of that building." The man left the scene after pointing out a one-story, vacant, brick factory building. Members of the truck went to investigate and found the tip to be accurate. Fire Marshals were notified and investigated the incident.

On June 2, 1975, arsonists set 40 fires within a three-hour period in the already fire-ravaged South Bronx. Fire Marshals moved into the area in an attempt to capture the individuals responsible for the series of fires. On the 4th of June, 17 fires of incendiary origin occurred in South Bronx neighborhoods.

A father and son, seen carrying five Molotov cocktails into a three-story tenement owned by the father at 944 Washington Avenue, were arrested. The arrests were made at 12:30 a.m. on June 5, 1975. Their plan was to burn the building for the insurance money.

At 1:45 a.m., a suspicious fire was fought in a vacant structure at 1427 Ogden, 171st Street. Then, the worst fire of the day started at 2:40 a.m. in a row of seven two-story frame buildings on Washington Avenue, near East 180th Street. The two-alarm fire started in a vacant structure at 2161 Washington Avenue and spread to 2159, 2163, 2165, 2167, 2169 and 2171, all of which were occupied. Nineteen families were made homeless and firemen battled the blaze until 4:05 a.m.

At 3:22 a.m., the same morning, a fire broke out in a four-story occupied building at 199 Brook Avenue. No injuries were reported. Eleven minutes later, companies went to work at a fire in a liquor store at 726 Courtlandt Avenue, near 155th Street. Flames raced throughout the three-story building.

A Molotov cocktail smashed against the door of an apartment at 957 Aldus Street at six a.m. Damage was slight. A three-alarm fire was fought at 7:55 a.m. in a drugstore at 988 Southern Boulevard, near 163rd Street. The flames spread to a bank and an appliance store.

Yet another fire at three p.m. drove people from their apartments at 457 East 135th Street when someone ignited flammable liquids in a third-floor hallway.

The South Bronx was being compared to Dresden, Germany, after the devastating bombings of World War II. City and Fire Department officials moved all available investigative resources into the area in an attempt to stop the arson.

Breathing Apparatus

A pilot program that tested new breathing apparatus for the FDNY was completed on September 12, 1975. For about nine months, members of Squad Company 4 in Brooklyn and Ladder Company 19 in the Bronx operated at fires and other emergencies requiring mask usage. The prototype SCBA was provided by the National Aeronautics and Space Administration (NASA). Scott Aviation, NASA, the Mask Service Unit and the field companies worked together to ensure the reliability and serviceability of the new masks. The new lightweight and easier breathing Scott Air-Pak 4.5 passed with flying colors and soon became available to the FDNY and fire departments across the nation.

Firemen still were operating without masks well into the 1970s and when they did use a mask, it was the old, cumbersome Scott II, until the new, lightweight 4.5s would pass their trials. (Photo by Steven Scher)

In June of 1975, the FDNY changed the decorations signifying awards of heroism to be worn by members of the Department on their dress uniforms. Since Special Order #69, dated June 17, 1908, members had been wearing insignia specifying the awarding of Department honors for heroism.

The original designs were small badge devices (a type of Maltese cross) that came in three colors: gold (highest), silver and bronze, to coincide with the level of the award granted. They commonly were known within the job as "bugs." These small badges were worn on the sleeve with the top of the emblem pointing to the shoulder. The bottom of the cross was located $^{1}/_{4}$-inch above the seam line.

Sixty-seven years later, the FDNY adopted chest insignia (ribbons). Compared to the bugs, it was hoped the new chest insignia would greatly enhance the image of the members when appearing in uniform in public. The military-style ribbons are positioned on the left chest above the badge or where the badge would be if no badge was worn. Ribbons designate the rating class of the award and specially colored ribbons designate individual medals awarded.

New York City Firemen were dodging bricks, bottles and insults on their way to arson fires on a regular basis. To complicate an already dangerous job, political extremists were planting and exploding bombs throughout the city, including the Weather Underground blast of the Banco de Ponce at Rockefeller Center on June 16, 1975.

Six firemen from Engine Company 302, who rescued 12 passengers from an Eastern Airlines jet crash near Kennedy, received a standing ovation from the New York State Assembly on June 30, 1975. In one hand, they held commendations. In the other, they held pink slips – they were being laid off within 24 hours. In all, 896 firemen were laid off on July 1, 1975.

Added to the already extreme pressure of fires, false alarms and violence, were the pending lay-offs, company closures and other actions the city was planning to help close an ever-widening budget gap. Plans to eliminate 26 fire companies and a manpower reduction in 206 companies was going ahead on schedule in the first week of July 1975. Eight companies in Manhattan, eight in Brooklyn, five in Queens, three in the Bronx and two on Staten Island were slated to be closed.

A carelessly discarded cigarette caused a fire that drove thousands of office workers out of the 33-story Squibb Building at 40 West 57th Street on July 11, 1975. The fire on the 18th floor sent thick clouds of acrid smoke through the ventilation system from the 16th floor to the roof. Firemen led 2600 frightened evacuees out of the smoke-filled high-rise.

The first alarm was transmitted at 10:54 a.m. and the second went in at 11:27 a.m. Several people were found unconscious by masked firemen on the smoke-filled upper floors. Thirty-five people were treated for smoke inhalation and seven of them were taken to the hospital.

The Bronx is burning. This was almost an understatement in 1975. To combat the growing arson problem, the Fire Commissioner established "The New South Bronx Task Force." To form the nucleus of this elite force, only the most experienced Fire Marshals were considered. Two of these men were Supervising Fire Marshal Eleuterio R. Graniela and Fire Marshal Thomas J. Russo. On July 12, 1975, members of the Task Force were closing in on a suspect they knew to be armed and dangerous; someone they had been seeking since July 4th.

After receiving a tip, they arrived at about noon at 2357 Walton Avenue in the Bronx. Graniela surrounded the building with five Marshals as he entered the building with Russo. They reached apartment 1-C, positioned themselves and announced their presence. As the door opened, a young woman, trailed by two small children, came to the door. As the Marshals began speaking to her, the suspect suddenly appeared from inside the room.

The suspect was wearing only a pair of shorts, his trousers draped over his arm. He moved up, shielding himself behind the children, waving a pistol in each hand. The Marshals were careful not to make any sudden moves and directed the suspect to drop his weapons. Still shielding himself behind the children, the suspect opened fire on the Marshals.

Both Marshals were hit by his gunfire, but both held theirs for fear of wounding the children or the woman. Though injured, they blocked his path to the street, forcing him to flee to the roof. On the roof, other Marshals closed in and a heated gun battle commenced, leaving the suspect in serious condition.

Back in the apartment, Graniela lay critically injured with gunshot wounds of the chest, lungs and spine. Russo also was critically injured with gunshot wounds of the neck and face. Russo recovered from his wounds, but Graniela was left partially paralyzed. For their bravery and professional discipline, they were awarded medals.

An early-morning fire caught most of the tenants of a 42-unit Harlem tenement asleep on July 30, 1975. Box 1638 came in at 4:33 a.m. for a fire on the second floor that was spreading quickly to the top floor of the seven-story building.

Four alarms (and a Dispatcher's fifth alarm) brought 21 engines, seven ladders and 10 special units. One woman perished and numerous others were injured, including 29 firemen.

More than 60 families were driven by flames into the streets of the Bronx on the night of September 10, 1975. Starting at 9:45 p.m., an arson wave struck a two-block area in the Hunts Point section. Firebombs struck six different buildings, the first of which was 1027 East 167th Street and 1058 Simpson Street. These fires quickly spread to the adjoining buildings. Firemen evacuated exposed occupied buildings that soon were burning as well.

Four more vacant buildings were set ablaze on East 165th Street between Bryant and Longfellow Avenues. Thirty-fire companies, manned by 150 firemen, arrived to battle the flames. Numerous firemen were injured, including two who were hospitalized.

At 8:22 a.m., a blaze broke out in a Ridgewood lumberyard. It was the third "suspicious" fire in five days to strike within a six-block area. The November ninth blaze in the Metropolitan Avenue lumberyard was heavily involved upon the arrival of the first fire units.

Five days earlier, a fire had been set in a knitting yarn warehouse on Menahan Street. Three days later, a social club on Menahan Street burned. Both fires were set at about the same time in the morning – 6:30 a.m.

A wind-driven three-alarm fire took the lives of six people, including a mother and three of her children, in Richmond Hill, Queens, on December 9, 1975. The suspicious blaze at 118-04 Atlantic Avenue, a three-story building with two floors of apartments above stores, came in at 3:02 a.m. High winds spread flames to the adjoining structures faster than protection lines could be stretched. Firemen were able to rescue several residents from a flaming second-floor apartment. Several other residents jumped from second-floor windows to the roof of a shed in the rear and escaped uninjured.

The Blue Angel Night Club, an upscale entertainment venue, was located in the fashionable East Side of Manhattan. On December 18, 1975, a night of enjoyment turned tragic as a fire broke out in the rear stage section of the club. Using pitchers of milk, employees of the club initially attempted to fight the fire for 20 to 25 minutes, while as many as 50 patrons continued to party, unaware of any problem.

Members push line into the blazing Blue Angel night club. Seven people were killed at this fire on December 18, 1975.

Unbeknown to those attempting to fight the fire they believed to be in some insulation, flames actually were taking hold of the entire cockloft above the club. Overhead, the heat build-up began to ignite other materials at the ceiling level. A dense toxic smoke quickly dropped down from the cockloft, filling the club as flames erupted around the stage.

Patrons hurried from the club area, but many went to the coat check area to retrieve their valuable fur coats. At about this time, a call was made to 911, reporting the fire. At 2:11 a.m., companies raced to the East 54th Street address. Upon their arrival, they were faced with extremely hot smoke pushing out the front door of the club, which was located in two adjoining buildings that had been altered on the ground-floor level.

Numerous patrons were in near hysterics reporting people trapped within the club. Several people still were attempting to re-enter the club to retrieve their furs. Lines were stretched and searches started in extremely punishing conditions. With the situation worsening, second, third and fourth alarms were transmitted.

The year 1976 was record-setting in several areas for the FDNY. The Department responded to 425,014 alarms (a number that would be topped only in 1977 and 1978). A total of 153,263 fires were extinguished by the FDNY. Of those, 56,810 were structural fires, with 816 greater alarms, both records. False alarms still were very high at 207,227. As the workload reached an all-time high, the strength of the uniformed force was at a new low of 10,662, down from 14,325 in 1970. Faced with a severe fiscal crisis, the City continued to close firehouses and disband companies.

It was also quite an artistic year for the FDNY. A special contest was held within the Department to help celebrate the nation's bicentennial. Fire companies painted patriotic designs on the firehouse apparatus doors.

Another piece of art that still is seen today is the FDNY Department patch. A contest for best Department patch was opened to all members. The winning design for the patch was made by Fireman Athos "Chris" Yonick of the graphics unit. The red, white, blue and gold design officially was adopted and placed on all uniforms and vehicles starting the next year.

Searches and line advancement proved to be extremely difficult and punishing for Department members because of the maze-like layout of the club. For three and a half hours, firemen battled the stubborn blaze, which also extended into the four floors of apartments above. Sadly, seven victims perished in the inferno.

The explosion of a "high-intensity" device in LaGuardia Airport on the evening of December 29, 1975, left 13 dead and more than 60 injured. The bomb blast took place at 6:33 p.m. in the Trans World Airlines terminal, crowded with holiday travelers.

Thousands of terrified people ran from the terminal as glass and debris were blasted out into the street and parking areas. Two hours after the blast, a phone call stated that another device was set to go off in the American Airlines terminal. Members of the Palestine Liberation Organization (PLO) claimed credit for the explosion.

Firemen dug through the collapsed sections of the building, searching for those trapped under tons of rubble. The blast, believed to have originated in a public baggage locker, caused major structural damage to the terminal.

On January 4, 1976, units responded to the Patchogue Oil Terminal in Brooklyn to find an extremely heavy fire condition and a large volume of thick, black smoke. Six oil storage tanks were involved in fire and on January fifth, a seventh tank exploded, creating even greater problems for operating units.

The Department used 22,000 gallons of foam to bring the fire under control. A total of 51 engine, 16 ladder and two rescue companies worked during the 42-hour battle. More than 20 firemen were injured battling the blaze.

On January 7, 1976, Brooklyn units raced to the scene of a fire in an A&P supermarket at 173 Atlantic Avenue at Clinton Street. Box 532 was received at 5:51 a.m. for a fire in the one-story, 45- x 95-foot commercial building. During operations, the floor of the structure collapsed, trapping two officers and five firemen in the cellar. A rescue effort was initiated and multiple alarms transmitted.

A foundation wall was breached into the blazing cellar and members prepared to move in. Fireman Peter J. Bondy of Rescue Company 2, nearly exhausted from the breaching operation, entered the cellar. Bondy located three of the trapped men and attempted to pull the men to the hole in the wall, but he was unable to do so and called for assistance. The three men were moved to safety as conditions continued to deteriorate.

As the companies regrouped, Captain Frederick W. Gallagher of Rescue Company 2 arrived at the breach and took charge of the operation. He ordered the men to remain at the hole and cover his search with a hose line as he probed the collapse area. Gallagher located Fireman Charles Sanchez of Ladder Company 131, pressed against a wall of debris, apparently killed by the impact of the collapsing structure. Gallagher was unable to free him, returned to the hole and guided Lieutenant Anthony Limberg of Rescue Company 3 back to Sanchez.

As Fireman John F. Carney of Rescue Company 2 covered their operations with a hose line, Gallagher and Limberg moved toward the trapped fireman when suddenly, a secondary collapse toppled a huge refrigeration unit into the cellar. The rescuers now were trapped.

Gallagher, Limberg and Carney struggled to free themselves from the burning timbers, twisted metal and piles of debris. Fireman Carney cleared himself enough to again operate the line to hold the fire back from the others. The Captain freed himself, then helped clear the debris from Limberg and returned to the hole.

After some of the fire was knocked down with hand lines, the officers again plunged into the burning cellar. They pressed on in the direction they believed Fireman Robert Penta to be. Calling for help, they were joined by other firemen and began to dig Penta free. Gallagher then led a team to Sanchez and while they dug the trapped man out, Gallagher continued searching for any other trapped firemen. Gallagher collapsed himself and was carried out of the cellar, unconscious.

The successful rescue of Fireman Penta, who required a lengthy hospital stay, was due to the dedication and bravery of many firefighters, but especially Gallagher, Limberg, Carney and Bondy, all of whom were awarded medals.

There is a saying among firemen that no fire is a routine fire. There is danger in every facet of firefighting. On the night of January 24, 1976, this proved to be true when members of Engine Company 228 were extinguishing a fire in an abandoned, derelict vehicle. Captain Robert J. Verdonik was supervising his men and watching for their safety as traffic moved by their location on 37th Street, between Seventh and Eighth Avenues in Brooklyn.

As a car approached, the Captain realized it was not slowing down and actually was heading straight for his men. Verdonik yelled at the driver while he rushed forward into the auto's path to push his men clear. He did manage to push one man, Fireman Thomas Costello, enough so that he only suffered a glancing blow, breaking his leg.

The car continued moving, striking Fireman Angelo Volpicella, who was thrown more than 50 feet and suffered a fractured skull and leg. It also hit Fireman Joseph Kenavan, who sustained multiple injuries and died the next day. With Captain Verdonik on the hood, the auto continued its course until it crashed into the rear of the pumper, pinning the officer. Verdonik suffered a fractured pelvis and ribs while trying to move his men to safety. He was presented with the Brooklyn Citizens Medal.

The month of January 1976 ended with more than double the number of multiple-alarm fires than the year before. In 1976, there were 90 multiple alarms, including 66 second alarms, 16 third alarms, three fourth alarms and one five-alarmer.

An early-morning fire swept through a West 94th Street apartment building in Manhattan on February 4, 1976, taking the lives of 10 people. The fire apparently burned for 20 to 30 minutes in a first-floor apartment before the Fire Department was called. The six-story building housed about 30 families.

The alarm was called in at 12:21 a.m. and went to three alarms. Two of the victims, both children, were found in the first-floor fire apartment. Eight other victims were found on the top floor. Despite the heroic efforts of firemen at the scene, none of the victims could be resuscitated.

In early 1976, the residents of Richmond Hill, Queens, were extremely fearful that an arson ring was at work in their neighborhood. They feared for their property; they feared for their lives. Sixteen fires, one of which claimed six lives on December 7, 1975, had occurred within a two-month period on 118th Street.

The wave of fires turned tragic for the FDNY on the night of February 8, 1976. Queens Box 6057 was received at 1:30 a.m. for a fire in a row of taxpayers at 119-23 Liberty Avenue. Fire was working its way through three stores as firemen went to work. Companies entered the Jolly Jiant Restaurant, operating hose lines and searching in the thick smoke.

Suddenly, the fire-weakened roof gave way under the weight of several roof-mounted air-conditioning units. Nine firemen were buried beneath the blazing rubble. Fireman Ronald C. Morstadt, the aide in the 51st Battalion, was leaving the building when the collapse occurred. Morstadt moved back into the collapse area and worked his way to the sounds of the men trapped beneath the debris.

Without benefit of a mask or hose line protection, Morstadt began to dig into the rubble with his hands until he located a trapped fireman. A secondary collapse pounded Morstadt with concrete and other debris. Undaunted, he continued burrowing until he reached Fireman Richard Citowitz of Ladder Company 143.

Under an extremely heavy smoke condition, he was able to free Citowitz and pull him safely to the street. Firemen were working feverishly to free the other imprisoned men. Injured firemen were dug free and carried to the street. Unfortunately, three firemen were injured fatally by the collapse. Lieutenant Joseph M. Beetle and Fireman Stanley H. Skinner, both of Ladder Company 143, and Fireman Thomas J. Earle of Engine Company 285 had made the Supreme Sacrifice. Among the thousands of firemen attending the funeral was Al Bold of Ladder 143, still receiving therapy for his serious burn injuries. Fireman Bold, in uniform, sat in his wheelchair among the throng of blue.

For his bravery and perseverance in digging out his Brother, Fireman Ronald Morstadt was awarded a medal.

A tower ladder drives its stream into a blazing row frame in Brooklyn's Bushwick section, mid-1970s. (Photo by Steven Scher)

America's bicentennial was celebrated across the nation on July 4th, 1976. In New York City Operation Sail brought huge sailing ships from around the world to the famous harbor. At noon, Marine Company 1, the fireboat *John D. McKean*, put on the first red, white and blue water display in the history of fireboats (not counting trial runs). The tri-colored display lasted five minutes to the delight of the thousands of people who crowded the shoreline to watch the ships sail by and wait for the spectacular fireworks show that was presented after dark.

Another "hit" with the citizens were the patriotic FDNY firehouse door decorations. The generally red overhead apparatus doors took on white and blue and a host of designs created by the members themselves. Children in passing school buses, cheered the firemen's progress as they painted the doors each day. The most difficult part of the painting process was the constant raising and lowering of the doors as the companies responded to fires and false alarms by the score.

A serious fire broke out in the former Erie-Lackawana Railroad pier on the Hudson River, between West 11th Street and Bank Street, on March 7, 1976. Box 533 went out at 1:28 p.m. and went to the equivalent of eight alarms before being declared under control 25 hours later.

Thirty-five firemen were injured battling the blaze. One fireman was injured seriously, when a portion of the pier's super structure collapsed.

A four-alarm blaze raced through a turn-of-the-century, five-story commercial building at 1241 Broadway in Manhattan at 11:37 p.m. on March 30, 1976. The fire burned through the roof and flames shot into the night sky, threatening a 15-story building next door. Gusting winds spread flaming embers across the neighborhood as firemen battled the blaze.

Four alarms and five and a half hours were needed to control the fire. Pockets of fire still were being doused, more than two weeks later. Eighteen firemen were injured fighting the fire.

On April 27, 1976, two New York City firemen were onboard an American Airlines B-727 when it crashed in the Virgin Islands. The two firemen, Neville Martin, a 20-year veteran with Ladder Company 17, and Cecil Shackelton, a retired member, survived

Ladder Company 8's Bicentennial apparatus door, July 4, 1976.

the crash. Without any thought of their own safety, they risked their lives as they re-entered the burning plane, attempting to save their fellow passengers. Each man made several trips into the plane and pulled people from the flames. Shackelton received burns from the waist down during his rescue operations. Neville Martin's bravery cost him his life. Thirty-seven people perished in the crash.

Three fires broke out within a four-block area of the University Heights section of the Bronx on May 28, 1976. Twenty-three firemen were injured battling the blazes and 60 families were left homeless. The first fire was called in at 7:56 a.m. for a fire in a row of stores at Jerome and Burnside Avenues. It went to two alarms. Ten stores were destroyed and one fireman was injured.

At noon, a five-alarm fire broke out at 1950 Andrews Avenue, a six-story, H-shaped, apartment complex. The fire reached the cockloft and burned with a fury across the top floor, taking all 30 apartments on the sixth floor with it.

A fire then was fought at 1945 Loring Place South, just behind the building on Andrews Avenue. While 200 firemen worked around the corner, the fire on the fifth floor of this building was extinguished quickly.

A three-alarm fire also was fought in the Greenpoint section of Brooklyn that same day. This fire spread from 158 Greene Street, a four-story building adjacent to the four-story structure next door at 1025 Manhattan Avenue.

Three greater-alarm fires and an all-hands erupted within a four-hour period in the early-morning hours of July 12, 1976. These fires cost the life of one civilian and also caused the collapse of two fire buildings. The most serious alarm, fire-wise, was a suspicious four-alarmer that broke out shortly after 1:30 a.m. in a vacant, four-story, residential structure at 808 Flatbush Avenue in Brooklyn. A two-year-old boy was killed in an all-hands fire at 840 Castle Hill Avenue in the Bronx.

The four-alarm fire was in a four-story, 100- x 100-foot vacant building where arsonists were seen running from the structure just before the fire became visible. Within minutes, fire was throughout the entire structure, which suffered a partial collapse shortly thereafter. Several firemen suffered minor injuries.

A third alarm was sent in for a fire in an electrical supply company building at 935 Westchester Avenue in the Bronx. While venting the one-story building, a member of Ladder Company 42 was blasted across the street by an apparent backdraft. A two-alarm fire damaged a row of stores at 174th Street and Topping Avenue in the Bronx.

On the night of August 30, 1976, newly promoted Lieutenant Joseph Sparacino, Jr., was working one of his first tours in his new rank. The 40-year-old firefighter was in command of Engine Company 291 as they responded to a blaze at 66-99 Fresh Pond Road in the Ridgewood section of Queens. The new officer entered the burning factory to locate the fire, then lead his hose team to the seat of the blaze.

Without warning, knitting machines on the second floor of the building came crashing through the floor and continued on to the basement, carrying the young officer with them. Fellow firemen attempted to reach him by breaching walls from adjoining structures. However, they were unable to save him.

A fire bomb tossed into an illegal South Bronx social club erupted in flames and took the lives of 25 men and women on the night of October 24, 1976. The Club Puerto Rico, located at 1005 Morris Avenue, had no valid public assembly license and only one exit from the second floor. The fire started at about 2:40 a.m. when a fire bomb was tossed on the club's only stairs and quickly roared out of control. Hysterical people jumped out windows to avoid the growing wall of flames. Twenty-five other people were injured in the fire.

Long Island City was rocked by a powerful explosion within the American Chicle Company plant at 30-30 Thompson Avenue. The four-story, 200- x 600-foot building housed 1600 workers when the blast occurred. At 2:42 a.m. on November 21, 1976, Queens Box 7276 was received and members in a firehouse more than a mile away knew something was up – they had felt the blast.

As companies arrived, flames were showing on the top floor rear of the building. Numerous workers, some severely injured, poured from the building and onto the glass-covered street. Companies moved in to search and extinguish the fire as the injured were treated. Six people were killed and more than 50 others were injured or burned by the blast, which was caused by magnesium stearate dust, the white powder seen on chewing gum.

A Brooklyn truckie makes his way through the fireground while neighborhood children make their way to the playground in 1976. (Photo by Steven Scher)

Manhattan firemen operate at a stubborn Lower East Side cellar fire on November 11, 1976. (Photo by Steven Scher)

Fireman Murtagh of Ladder 36 guides blind man along fire escape, 521 Sherman Avenue, Bronx, November, 1976. (Photo by Harvey Eisner)

Tower ladders move in on a warehouse fire in the Williamsburg section of Brooklyn, 1976. (Photo by Steven Scher)

The cold weather continued and so did the fire duty. Both men and machines found the going rough. (Photo by Steven Scher)

Freezing conditions leave the smoldering remains of the seven-alarm fire coated with thick ice, January 8, 1977. (Photo by Steven Scher)

January 8, 1977, Manhattan Box 77-675. A Borough-Call to blazing warehouses on 30th Street, near 11th Avenue. (Photo by Steven Scher)

RALEIGH WHSE.

A major fire hammered the main shopping section of Brooklyn when Box 590 was struck on December 22, 1976. Twelve people perished in this fast-moving pre-Christmas fire. Arriving units were faced with a five-story department store at the corner of Fulton Street and Hanover Place with fire in control of the entire ground floor and heavy fire showing at many windows on the upper floors.

Multiple alarms quickly were transmitted as a rescue effort commenced. A line was stretched and operated to protect the search effort, but the fire rapidly was involving the entire structure. Firemen were withdrawn and a defensive operation began.

For 20 hours, exterior streams operated as sections of the interior floors and walls of the building collapsed. As conditions eased, a thorough search was initiated. The first victim was located on December 24th and the last (number 12) was removed on January 4, 1977. The fire operation lasted for 18 days and required the services of 120 FDNY units.

Firemen practice CPR skills during drill period in a firehouse kitchen, 1977. (Photo by Steven Scher)

I n early 1977, the last of the firemen who had been laid off since 1975 were rehired. Some firemen were separated from service for only one tour, while the vast majority came back in groups as the money for their rehire was found.

A blast of Arctic weather made firefighting extremely dangerous and difficult in early January 1977. Manhattan Box 675 came into the dispatcher's office for a fire at 30th Street and 11th Avenue. This fire became the largest fire fought in the City since the Morgan Post Office fire in 1968.

The fire swept through a complex of six warehouses on West 30th Street, between 11th and 12th Avenues. Firemen battled the flames, 30-mph winds off the river and 18-degree temperatures (which translated into a wind chill factor of 21 degrees below zero). For 10½ hours, firemen fought the blaze. Eight alarms were struck, including a borough call. Two dozen firemen were injured by smoke and from falls on the ice.

The cold spell took its toll on both men and machines. A four-alarm fire at 210 West 102nd Street in Manhattan on January 18th spread from one five-story tenement to the similar attached buildings on either side. A half-hour after arriving at the scene, first-due Engine Company 76 developed a frozen pump. Three hand lines lost water as the nine-degree temperature solidified water within the pumping system.

Firemen scrambled to overcome the problem and soon had water flowing again. Twelve firemen were treated for various injuries and about 100 people left homeless were aided by the Red Cross.

On the 23rd, Box 2172 was transmitted in the Bronx for a fire in a six-story apartment building at 600 East 141st Street. Four alarms were transmitted for the fire, which left 200 homeless.

The next day, January 24th, saw the third four-alarm fire of the week. Flames poured from a vacant, six-story tenement at 209 East 150th Street in Manhattan. About 100 people were relocated from the adjoining tenements. Eight firemen were treated for smoke and other injuries.

O n January 26th, the Fire Commissioner presented 376 firemen with New York State EMT diplomas. The total number of EMT-certified FDNY firemen was now more than 1000. All members who participated in the course had done so on their own time.

It was just after 10 in the morning on March 3, 1977, and Ladder Company 176 again was responding through the streets of Brooklyn. Their destination this time was Box 1647, 345 Saratoga Avenue. As 176 pulled up, the Brothers of Ladder Company 123 were rescuing a woman from the top-floor front room of the four-story building. The woman was distraught and screaming – her kids were still inside!

Fireman James H. Battillo of Ladder Company 176 was off the rig and on the run. He quickly climbed the side fire escape to the fourth floor. The windows were heat-stained and smoke was pushing out around the frame. Battillo instinctively knew this was a dangerous situation. The room was in danger of flashing over. He raised the window enough to squeeze through and hit the floor on his belly.

Without a mask, he pressed forward through the dense smoke toward the yellow glow of fire visible ahead. The room adjoining his was filling with fire as was the next room. Flames were beginning to roll into the room through which he was crawling. Sweeping as he moved, the fireman struggled to breathe in the gagging smoke. Suddenly, in the reflection of the light from the blazing room, he saw what appeared to be the leg of a doll hanging from the edge of a couch.

Shielding his face from the searing heat, Battillo moved closer and saw it was a small boy. As he picked up the three-year-old and started back toward the window, Battillo noticed another small form lying on the floor in the burning room. Following the voice of a fireman on the fire escape, Battillo pushed himself through the dense smoke. Reaching the window, he handed the child outside and returned for the second child.

The heat was so great that Battillo could not approach the child from the front. Using his body as a shield, he backed into the blazing room. Stretching his arms out, he grabbed the one-year-old. Suffering burns on his wrists and knees and nearing exhaustion, Battillo crawled back toward the fire escape with the baby.

For his "raw courage," Fireman James H. Battillo was awarded the 583rd *Daily News* Hero of the Month Award. The following June, he was presented with the Bennett Medal for the most outstanding rescue of the year.

A spectacular three-alarm fire erupted on March 8, 1977, on the site of the 48-day eighth alarm that broke out two months earlier. Flames destroyed the seven-story, 90-year-old Raleigh Warehouse building at 650 West 30th Street in Manhattan. Box 674 came in at 10:43 p.m. Rescue Company 1 arrived at the box first and transmitted a second alarm on arrival. An additional alarm brought the Super-Pumper, satellites and two fireboats.

At 11:13 p.m., a second-alarm fire was fought in a building that had five stores on the ground-floor level and apartments above at 77 Essex Street. Then at 3:07 a.m., Box 1191 came in for First Avenue and 90th Street for a cellar fire. Four alarms were needed as firemen were faced with a chemical company occupying the fire area (cellar) and the floor above. Two floors of apartments were above that and at one point, fire was raging out of 30 windows on the upper floors. Firemen pushed hand lines and used foam for nearly six hours to extinguish the blaze.

As firemen battled the 90th Street blaze, two suspicious fires occurred at 201 Avenue B, at 12th Street, at 4:41 a.m. They quickly extinguished that fire and had returned to quarters when at 6:15 a.m., the same building was roaring again.

The historic Trinity Lutheran Church, about 500 feet into the cemetery grounds at the corner of Metropolitan Avenue and Pleasantview Street in Middle Village, Queens, was the site of a devastating fire during the early-morning hours of April 12, 1977. The blaze was discovered at 2:30 a.m. and quickly went to three alarms.

Standing on a hill, the three-story Gothic landmark, with flames shooting from the bell tower and through the roof, could be seen for miles. The church had been the scene of several fires throughout its 120-year history. The church suffered fires in 1895, 1906 and then was struck by lightning in May of 1975.

A two-alarm fire then was discovered in a one-story taxpayer on Union Turnpike. Several stores were destroyed by the 2:51 a.m. fire. A Deputy Chief and a fireman were injured during the blaze.

A New York Airways helicopter landed on the roof of the 59-story Pan Am Building at 44th Street and Vanderbilt Avenue. It was 5:30 p.m. on May 16, 1977, and the red and white, 30-passenger copter, with rotors still spinning, waited to unload some passengers and pick up others. Most of the 21 passengers had disembarked. Fifteen to 20 other passengers were lined up, waiting to board the copter and take an eight-minute flight to Kennedy Airport.

Apparently, a tire on the helicopter blew and a supporting strut gave way. With the main and secondary rotor still whirling, the giant copter rolled over on its side. The impact with the roof tore off the main rotor, sending the blades flying. One blade cut right through four passengers waiting nearby. Three died immediately; the other died later.

One blade tore up the roof-top landing pad, broke through the parapet wall and went spinning into the

Foam is applied to the roof of the Pan Am building after New York Airways helicopter crash.

The fire was declared under control at 12:30 a.m. Only the half-collapsed shell of a building was left. The skeleton of this severely damaged structure now joined the remains of the other warehouses destroyed earlier in the year by fires.

The Raleigh building was also the scene of a serious fire on April 27, 1904, when three firemen from Engine Company 19 were killed by a collapsing wall. Engine Company 19 was housed on West 25th Street until the end of World War II when they were disbanded.

After marching up Fifth Avenue on March 17, 1977, as part of the Saint Patrick's Day parade, New York City firemen got clobbered just after the start of the night tour. At 6:43 p.m., firemen responded to a factory and warehouse fire at 630 West 51st Street in Manhattan. This fire escalated to three alarms before being controlled.

side of the building. The blade then broke in two after striking the building. Pieces of the building rained down on the streets around the Pan Am Building. The second piece of the blade traveled more than a block away, killing a woman on Madison Avenue.

FDNY units arrived and provided what first-aid they could for the eight injured people and took immediate precautions to prevent fire due to the spilled fuel. Foam lines blanketed the crash area until the area could be made safe.

A mattress fire in a Manhattan bathhouse turned deadly on May 25, 1977. Box 661 was transmitted for a fire at 28 West 28th Street, the Everard Baths, and went to a fourth alarm. The three-story structure, popular with gay men, had as many as 100 patrons within the maze-like interior. Arriving fire companies were faced with numerous men hanging from the windows.

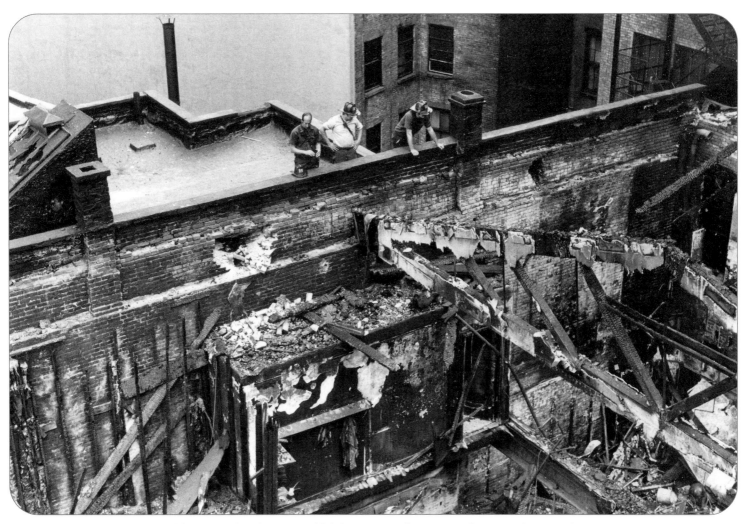

Firemen look over the remains of the Everard Baths on West 28th Street in Manhattan. Nine lives were lost, May 25, 1977. (Photo by Steven Scher)

Numerous patrons, clad only in towels, underwear or trousers, were streaming from the smoke-filled structure. Fire was roaring in the rear section of the building, weakening the structural stability. When special-called Ladder Company 3 arrived, fire already was shooting out the fourth floor and heavy smoke was chugging out of the third floor.

Fireman John P. Fogarty and the other members of Ladder Company 3 were ordered to search the third floor, where there was a complex series of corridors and cubicles. To the rear of the floor was a large dormitory area that was engulfed in fire. Heat conditions were becoming so severe that members were driven to their knees. Fogarty passed an operating nozzle team and continued searching. He came upon two firemen dragging an unconscious victim out. Fogarty continued deeper into the inferno.

Fogarty had ventured more than 70 feet into the deteriorating conditions when he came upon an unconscious man at the end of the corridor. Using all of his remaining strength, he began to drag the 200-pound man back along the route to safety. The fire had gained considerable headway during his search and conditions had become severe.

Passing a wall of fire, he finally reached the stairway door. Upon reaching the comparative safety of the second floor, Fogarty began mouth-to-mouth resuscitation on the victim, which he continued until the victim was removed to the hospital.

In all, nine lives were lost at this tragic fire, with numerous serious injuries to several men who jumped from upper-floor windows. The man rescued by Fogarty recovered. For his heroic actions, Fireman John Fogarty received the Crimmins Medal.

An explosion in a varnish and paint factory killed two civilians and critically injured six others on May 27, 1977. Workers in the Atlantic Lacquer Manufacturing Company factory at 306 Greenpoint Avenue, Brooklyn, apparently were cleaning the floors with a flammable liquid when a source of ignition touched off the explosion and ensuing fire.

The blast drove two men through a loading dock door, killing them instantly. Several others ran from the building, their clothes in flames. Fire companies arrived and pushed hand lines into the blazing structure. Several unconscious workers were pulled from the inferno by firemen from Engine Company 238 and Ladder Company 106.

Nine firemen were injured battling fires on May 31, 1977. At one a.m., a two-alarm blaze destroyed a shoe store and pizza parlor at 166-33 Jamaica Avenue, Jamaica. An extremely heavy body of fire and dense smoke confronted arriving units. The fire was placed under control after a 45-minute battle and declared suspicious.

Then at 1:47 a.m., FDNY units responded to a three-alarm fire in a row of stores in the heart of the Forest Hills shopping area. Six stores at 71-14 through 71-22 Austin Street were destroyed. The blaze, believed to have started in a florist shop, spread to several clothing stores, a shoe store and a decorator shop. This blaze was fought until four a.m. and left seven firemen injured.

A Molotov cocktail set a private house on fire at 175-25 89th Avenue, Jamaica. This fire occurred at 2:35 a.m. when the fire bomb set the porch on fire. Damages were kept to a minimum.

In yet another fire bombing, three people were arrested for throwing a Molotov cocktail through the window of a house at 147-20 106th Street, Jamaica. The bomb failed to ignite and the three suspects were picked up on charges of attempted arson. Their actions were the result of an argument over ownership of a tape deck.

Arson fires, always a burden on firefighters, became a personal attack on July 2, 1977. Arsonists touched off the fifth floor of an abandoned building at Eighth Street and Avenue C, on the Lower East side of Manhattan. When companies moved in to extinguish the fire, a separate fire, on the second floor, was ignited in the building below the operating companies.

Looking for the arsonist, Fire Marshals knocked on doors and followed lead after lead for three months. On September 23rd, Supervising Fire Marshal Ronald DeLucia and his team of Marshals – Donald Forster, Joseph DiGeorge and Ronald Caffiero – arrested a 17-year-old high school student for setting the fires that killed Celic. (DeLucia received the Commissioner Martin Scott Medal for this investigation and also for investigation of an arson fire that took the life of a member on Fourth Avenue in Brooklyn.)

It was 9:40 a.m. on July 4th, 1977, and fire companies in Elmhurst, Queens, were responding to a fire in a warehouse at 78-11 51st Avenue. A large column of dark smoke marked the location of the job. Large sheets of flame shot from the 10,000-square-foot, one-story, L-shaped building. The arson fire destroyed thousands of dollars worth of Christmas decorations. Numerous large Santa Claus mannequins and other expensive materials were consumed by the flames.

The arson problem continued on July 5th, when four suspicious fires occurred in Jackson Heights, Queens, within 90 minutes. At noon, a grocery store on 92nd Street burned. While that fire was brought under control, fires broke out in two private garages around the corner at 34-26 and 34-28 93rd Street. A car in one of the garages was destroyed.

The original fire started at about 3:10 p.m. and witnesses saw several youths leaving the structure shortly before the fire was discovered. A youth then was observed entering the structure again after the arrival of the firemen, but prior to the start of the second fire. On the fifth floor of the building were several firemen, including Fireman Martin R. Celic of Ladder Company 18.

Conditions on the floor deteriorated quickly due to the growing body of fire below. Celic and four other firemen now were trapped above. Two of the firemen found their way to the windows, hoping to escape the dense heat and smoke; three of the firemen were overcome. A tower ladder bucket was raised to the window and one of the men climbed in. As Celic moved to cross over to the bucket in the dense smoke, he tripped and fell five stories.

Firemen ran to Celic's side and the 25-year-old was rushed to Bellevue Hospital in extremely critical condition. The three firemen overcome on the fifth floor were rescued by other firemen employing masks in the dense smoke.

For a week, Celic's fiancee sat by his side, hoping for a miracle that never came. On July ninth, Martin Celic died as a result of his injuries. A reward was offered by the Uniformed Firefighters Association for information leading to the arrest of the arsonist.

Then, shortly after one p.m., a large pile of rubbish was set ablaze on the roof of the two-story building at 34-26 93rd Street. The fire burned through the roof and into the cockloft and apartment below.

Three teenagers started a fire in a vacant, five-story, brick knitting mill at Knickerbocker Avenue and Bleecker Street in the Bushwick section of Brooklyn on July 18, 1977. The fire spread quickly throughout the large structure. Prior to the arrival of the second-alarm units, radiant heat ignited a row of three-story row houses 66 feet away. As Tower Ladder 124 was attempting to operate to break the building wall of heat, conditions became untenable at their position. Under the protection of two Stang streams from Engine Companies 237 and 217, the chauffeur was able to move the smoking rig.

Multiple alarms brought additional units to the scene, but the stage already was set. The weather was not going to help; 100-degree temperatures and hot, humid conditions were extremely debilitating to firefighters. The 10-mph wind helped spread the fire.

During operations, the dreaded sounds of collapse were added to the usual cacophony of the fireground. The building, 246 Bleeker Street, adjacent to the original fire building, had collapsed. A hose line still was leading inside the structure. Lieutenant James P. Ellson dashed into the building and up the stairs, where he found some firefighters in a dazed state. Ellson directed those men to leave and continued upstairs while calling for additional help on his handie-talkie. At the top of the stairs, the line disappeared beneath the collapsed ceiling and roof. Ellson frantically began to dig through the flaming rubble in search of his Brothers. He uncovered Fireman Barrett of Engine Company 237 and pulled him from the rubble. As help arrived, Ellson collapsed from exhaustion.

Meanwhile, Fireman Parchinsky was rescued from the rubble by Lieutenant Martin Fetzer of Engine Company 229. Lieutenant James Ellson was awarded a medal for his actions.

The fire spread in every direction. Flames blew out the rear of the mill and ignited six more buildings. Then, that fire jumped the street and added four more buildings to the conflagration. A fire storm was brewing. The equivalent of 10 alarms was transmitted, bringing 37 engines, 12 ladders and 12 special units.

Three hours and 18 minutes after the receipt of the alarm, the fire was brought under control. In all, 23 buildings were leveled.

In early August of 1977, the New York City Personnel Department and Fire Department announced that a new test for fireman would begin filing on September 7, 1977, and continue until October 25th. The written and physical tests then would be given on dates to be announced later. This particular test was unique because for the first time in the history of the FDNY, women would be eligible to compete for the position. The official exam was known as Fireman, F.D. Exam No. 3040.

A third-alarm fire in a vacant candle factory at Reid and Lexington Avenue in Brooklyn, July 20, 1977. (Photo by G. Tufte)

A four-alarm fire in a vacant Greenwich Village warehouse brought firemen from other boroughs to help battle the blaze. The initial alarm was received at 12:44 p.m. for Box 509, Hudson and West 10th Streets. Firemen found fire fully involving the fourth through seventh floors with flames visible 50 feet high through the roof.

The fire prompted the evacuation of five nearby buildings as the radiant heat threatened to extend the blaze. The warehouse, built in 1892, was spewing embers across a wide area of the neighborhood. Finally, the walls began to collapse; one brick wall crushing two cars on the street and damaging a water main that added even more problems as Greenwich Street began to flood. Four firemen were injured in the two-hour battle.

Arsonists struck downtown Flushing, Queens, on October 27, 1977. Flammable liquids were poured in a former bagel shop being renovated into a vegetable store at 41-16 Main Street. Witnesses reported hearing an explosion and seeing three youths running, one with his clothes in flames, from the rear alley of the row of stores.

A second explosion spread the fire to a Jahn's ice cream parlor, an appliance store and a florist. Arriving fire companies were faced with a large body of fire in the row of stores. Two firemen received minor injuries during the two-hour operation.

Bronx Box 4794 sent Ladder Company 33 to 2055 Grand Concourse at 8:20 on the morning of December 14, 1977. Fireman Thomas J. Mannion pulled the big rig up to the address and sized up where to place his tower ladder for possible use. Mannion quickly realized he had two problems: a woman with a young child at a smoke-filled, top-floor window and the inability to get his rig into position to reach her location in the seven-story, H-type building. The 47-year-old chauffeur wasted no time. In short order, he was on the roof with a roof rope in hand.

He tied the rope off around a chimney and threw the remaining rope over the side. Shouting encouragement to the woman, the fireman took turns on his Sav-Tee harness and slid down the side of the building to the frightened mother.

At the window, he looked up to see additional members ready to follow his lead. Mannion took one child, a two-year-old girl, in his arms and slid five stories to the courtyard below. Mannion immediately began mouth-to-mouth on the youngster and continued en route to the hospital.

Fireman James Roach slid next, picking up a four-year-old and sliding with her to safety. Meanwhile, firemen were making a difficult push through the interior to reach those trapped and were able to rescue the mother. Both children were admitted to North Central Bronx Hospital where they recovered. Fireman Thomas Mannion was awarded the Walter Scott Medal for his bravery.

The year 1977 came to a close with the following statistics: Alarms – 459,567; Fires – 129,619; Structural fires – 50,941; Civilian fatalities – 290; and False alarms – 262,998. The false alarm statistic was a new FDNY record. Sadly, it stood for only a year.

A suspicious two-alarm fire took the life of a man at the landmark Chelsea Hotel in Manhattan on January 14, 1978. The fire occurred at about 11:40 p.m. in a third-floor apartment in the west wing of the 11-story building at 222 West 23rd Street. Smoke filled the hallways and many apartments as firemen evacuated tenants into the rainy streets.

The victim apparently tried to flee his apartment but was felled by the smoke and heat and collapsed at the doorway, which remained in the open position and allowed the fire to enter the hallway and reach blowtorch intensity. Teams of firemen moved down the flame-filled, 70-foot hallway of the 94-year-old hotel, which was the first cooperative apartment house in the city when built in 1885.

Several tenants were rescued from their smoke-filled rooms via aerial ladders. An hour after FDNY arrival, the fire was declared under control.

On January 17, 1978, newly elected New York City Mayor Ed Koch named Augustus A. Beekman as Fire Commissioner. The 53-year-old Assistant Chief, a rank he had held since 1970, replaced John O'Hagan. Chief Beekman, the second African-American to be named as Fire Commissioner, joined the Department in 1947 and started his career in the ever-busy Engine Company 58 in Harlem. In place of O'Hagan, Francis Cruthers was named Chief of Department by the Mayor. Cruthers also joined the FDNY in 1947.

It was 4:22 p.m. on January 28, 1978, when Ladder Company 22 responded to Box 1254 for a fire in an eight-story multiple dwelling at 315 West 99th Street in Manhattan. The building was divided inside as an S.R.O. (single room occupancy.) Upon arrival, a woman with a child in her arms was seen on a narrow, seventh-floor window ledge. In the courtyard below the fire area and the trapped pair was the body of a person who had jumped to his death from the fire apartment. Lieutenant Collister looked twice and ordered the tower ladder raised to attempt to reach the victims as he led his forcible entry team through the inside.

Fireman Clint Williams, the chauffeur, realizing the basket would be short of its objective, took a 12-foot scaling ladder with him. When the tower ladder reached its maximum height, Williams began to position the scaling ladder, obstructed at the tip by metal fencing. Williams stood on the top railing of the basket, without benefit of a life belt to securely place the ladder, all the while calming the woman who was threatening to jump.

With high winds buffeting him, Fireman Williams climbed up to the window and took control of the woman and child. He radioed to Lieutenant Collister that he could see another adult, who was throwing pails of water on the apartment's fire-exposed entrance door. The officer advised him to remain at his position while the attack on the fire commenced.

Fireman Clinton A. Williams showed initiative, nerves of steel and a high degree of personal bravery to save the life of a mother and her child. He was awarded a medal for his actions.

On March 9, 1978, at 6:14 a.m., Brooklyn Box 1838 was transmitted for a fire at 606 Pine Street with a report of people trapped. Number 606 was the fourth in a row of 15 attached frame, two-story dwellings. The rigs slid their way through snow-covered streets to find fire on both stories of 606, with fire visible above the roof level, venting through an air shaft between buildings.

The size-up after a 10-75 was given showed heavy fire in two of the attached buildings and smoke conditions in eight cocklofts. A second alarm was transmitted at 6:22, followed by a third at 6:40. In all, 14 buildings sustained light to heavy fire damage.

Thirteen firemen were injured, three of them seriously, when a 55-gallon paint drum exploded in their faces on May 19, 1978. The firemen were attempting to extinguish a fire in a walk-in oven at a metal processing plant in the South Bronx.

Companies had responded to the Associated Wire Products Corporation two-story warehouse at 860 East 136th Street when smoke was seen seeping from the 10- x 10-foot oven. The oven was being used to temper bed and furniture springs. Unaware that the drum of paint was inside the oven, firemen opened the door. An enormous ball of fire burst from the oven.

Three firemen were taken to the Jacobi Burn Center where they were admitted in stable condition, although they were placed in Intensive Care as a precaution. Ten other firemen were treated and released.

FDNY units responded to a serious motor vehicle accident on the rain-slick Major Deegan Expressway when a Liberty Coach Lines bus lost control and plowed into a concrete pillar not far from Yankee Stadium on May 24, 1978. Thirty-one of the 40 people onboard were injured, with the driver of the bus sustaining serious injuries. Firefighters worked Hurst tools and hand tools and provided first-aid to the victims who were taken to the hospital as they were disentangled from the wreckage.

A powerful explosion tore apart an ice cream truck and rocked lower Manhattan during lunch hour. At 1:49 p.m., the June 20th explosion sent glass and debris flying, injuring 158 people, 16 of them critically. The truck, a Mister Softee soft ice cream truck, was parked at Nassau and Fulton Streets serving the shoppers and workers using the pedestrian-only street on the beautiful 80-degree day.

The force of the blast threw people to the ground, shattered and scattered glass and blew in storefronts. Lieutenant James Cline and his crew from Engine Company 10 were inspecting buildings only 150 feet away. Cline transmitted the alarm and ran to help the injured. Several people were in a state of panic; running, their clothes in flames. The sounds of breaking glass and the screams of the injured soon were overwhelmed by the growing apparatus sirens and air horns. Arriving fire units tended to the injured and checked the structural stability of damaged buildings.

It was determined that a 2½-gallon can of gasoline, stored inside the truck, caught fire and exploded, causing a secondary explosion of the truck's ruptured gasoline tank.

The arson plague struck everywhere in New York City. Even the Fire Department, it seemed, was not safe. On Friday night, July 7, 1978, an arsonist struck the former FDNY fireboat house on a pier at 90th Street and the East River. The all-hands fire burned for nearly an hour, destroying almost the entire roof of the structure.

The fire was just the latest misfortune the old fireboat house had suffered. On May 3rd, a hit-and-run barge plowed into the newly renovated pier just north of Gracie Mansion. Nearly half of the 120-foot pier was demolished in the accident. The tugboat company responsible was identified and made repairs to the structure.

The fireboat house first fell on bad times in the summer of 1965, when the fireboat *Senator Robert Wagner* was radioed the message, "Go back to your quarters. Your house is on fire."

It was nearing the change of tour on August 2, 1978, when an alarm rang across the circuits in Brooklyn. Box 3300 was transmitted at 8:51 a.m., sending companies to the one-story, 100- x 150-foot structure at 2829 Ocean Avenue in Brooklyn, a supermarket undergoing some renovations. No one responding realized just how difficult and costly the next few hours would be for the FDNY.

Inside the Waldbaum's supermarket, workers were busy on a major renovation within the store. Besides the construction workers, employees and more than a dozen shoppers were busy within the market. Smoke was spotted in the mezzanine area, the Fire Department was called and the building evacuated. Engine Company 254 arrived and minutes later, transmitted a 10-75. A second alarm then was requested at 9:02 a.m.

Hole breached through side wall allowed members to penetrate the collapse area to rescue or recover trapped firemen. (Photo by Harvey Eisner)

August 2, 1978, Waldbaum's supermarket, Ocean Avenue, Brooklyn. Front of store after truss roof collapsed. (Photo by Harvey Eisner)

Twenty-four firemen climbed to the roof to ventilate the blazing cockloft of the Sheepshead Bay store. Ladder Companies 153 and 156 and Engine Company 254 were busy with saws and hose lines when suddenly, 32 minutes after arrival, the roof collapsed. Twelve firemen plunged into the raging fire below, while several men clung to the parapet wall at the roof's edge. A rescue effort was started immediately. The men at the edge were removed by aerial ladder and firemen pushed their way into the burning store in search of the fallen men.

Inside the store, a number of companies were at work when the roof collapsed, narrowly missing them. Fireman John J. Pritchard of Rescue Company 2 quickly made his way to the blazing collapse area. On the pile, he found Fireman Thomas Vallebuona, also of Rescue Company 2, who had plunged through the roof with 11 others. Vallebuona, seriously injured, directed Pritchard to where he believed several other firemen were trapped.

Pritchard located a dazed, injured fireman, helped him outside, then continued his search. He then found a pair of boots sticking out from beneath flaming debris. Without benefit of a mask or hose line, Pritchard dug out the trapped man and brought him to safety. Although injured himself, Pritchard ventured into the roaring supermarket once again and worked his way to the rear. A secondary collapse drove all members from the store. (Pritchard later was awarded the Bennett Medal for his actions.)

Regrouped outside, forays were made through a side door and a large hole was breached through the side wall, allowing firemen a direct route to where they believed the trapped men to be. One by one, the fallen men were found and carried out with a reverence known to few. Twenty-two engines, nine ladders, four rescue companies, a squad, three battalions and two divisions worked the fire and collapse. The entire fire, rescue and recovery operation lasted more than 16 hours.

The toll was staggering. Six members had answered their last alarm: Lieutenant James E. Cutillo, Battalion 33; and Firemen Charles S. Bouton and William O'Connor, Ladder Company 156; James P. McManus and George Rice, Ladder 153; and Harold F. Hastings, Battalion 42.

Thirty-one firemen were injured. This was the third worst disaster to befall the FDNY. The collapse on 23rd Street in 1966 took the lives of 12 firemen and the explosion during fire operations in the Ritz Hotel in 1932 claimed seven firemen.

A pleasant morning was interrupted with the transmission of Bronx Box 2451. It was 10 a.m. on August 18, 1978, when FDNY units responded to a fire at Oak Point Avenue and Barretto Street, an area filled with factories. On arrival, companies found the fire building totally involved, with explosions occurring inside the blazing, 50- x 100-foot, one-story structure. Each explosion sent huge blasts of fire from different openings in the building, causing severe exposure problems in virtually every direction.

The fire building, occupied by Sealed Liquid Products, was used to package and distribute paint thinners, lacquer thinners, benzene, kerosene, alcohols and other flammable solvents. The first two hose lines stretched did not even dent the wall of flames, so large-caliber streams were requested. Tower ladders were moved into position and a Stang nozzle set up.

The streams stopped the spread of the fire and High-Expansion foam was delivered into the structure. Under a huge blanket of foam, conditions calmed down and by 12 noon, it seemed as if the fire would be designated "probably will hold." About a half hour later, a series of explosions sent flames bursting through the foam. The Department fell into the pattern of calming the fire and then reacting to explosions and flames piercing the blanket of foam.

Foam leaks through various openings in the building were handled to better control the foam blanket. Operations continued for 30 hours with eruptions at various times until the fire was brought completely under control. The Department finally took up from the scene on August 22, 1978, at 11 a.m. Units delivered 415 five-gallon cans of High-Expansion foam and 235 five-gallon cans of three percent protein foam into the building during the fire.

Seventy sleeping families were driven from their beds by a roaring, four-alarm fire that destroyed the upper floors of their six-story, H-type apartment building at 2090 Walton Avenue in the Bronx. Nearly 300 residents fled into the freezing night air as firemen battled the spreading top-floor and cockloft fire.

The blaze started at 4:44 a.m. on December 12, 1978, and jumped with lightning speed. Firemen evacuated families as the fire spread from one wing to the other. Amazingly, no civilians were injured and the only fireman hurt slipped and fell on ice.

A week later, residents of 3045 Grand Concourse were not as lucky as a pre-dawn, four-alarm fire killed one person and injured 14 tenants and firemen. Forty families were forced out into the 22-degree temperatures on December 19th. Box 3527 was transmitted at 2:30 a.m. for the six-story, 100- x 100-foot apartment house.

Ladder Company 37 rolled in first-due and found a well-advanced fire condition on the first floor, with flames out three windows in the rear. Reports indicated a woman trapped in the fire apartment and Fireman Richard C. Lailer proceeded through an alley to the rear with a 25-foot ladder. Lailer was informed by neighbors that a woman was seen at a window in the fire apartment, then disappeared. He climbed the ladder to the fire apartment on the second-floor level in the rear and entered the blazing apartment.

With heavy fire adjacent to the room he was searching Lailer crawled deeper into the apartment looking for the woman. With conditions worsening around him, the fireman located the unconscious woman, dragged her back to the window, lifted her up and removed her down the ladder. Within minutes of their exit, the room filled with flames. For his valor, Fireman Lailer was awarded a medal.

The year 1978 finished with two dubious FDNY records that stand to this day. The Department responded to 472,405 alarms and 285,290 false alarms during the year. The number of fires was down slightly – 120,792 – although it was still twice as many as in 1960.

On the night tour of January 3, 1979, Engine Company 92 left their quarters in the Bronx and were sent, as part of the Department's interchange program, to Engine Company 307 in Queens for an easier tour. At six a.m. (now January 4th), Queens Box 7736 came in and Engine 92 was out the door. Arriving at 26-12 96th Street, a four-story multiple dwelling, a heavy smoke condition was pumping from the cellar.

The second-due 92 moved up to help stretch the first line when a report came of a missing civilian. Lieutenant Maxwell ordered Fireman George E. Muller to conduct a search. As the line was being stretched, Muller pulled the rubber straps of the mask across his head and started down the stairs and into the thick, swirling smoke chugging up from the cellar.

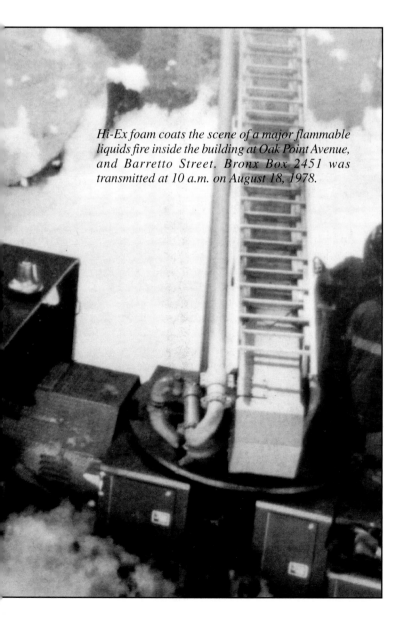

Hi-Ex foam coats the scene of a major flammable liquids fire inside the building at Oak Point Avenue, and Barretto Street. Bronx Box 2451 was transmitted at 10 a.m. on August 18, 1978.

Muller reached the floor and using his ungloved hand, checked to determine the direction from which the heat was coming. Crawling low below the building heat, he made his way toward a bedroom and found the unconscious man on the floor. Seeing the victim was having difficulty breathing, he placed his mask over the victim's face and then dragged the man back toward the stairs. Muller was joined by other firemen, who helped him remove the victim to the street. Despite Muller's efforts, the victim succumbed to his injuries. Fireman George Muller was awarded a medal for his bravery.

The year 1979 saw the adoption of the "Modified Response Plan," which eliminated responses to ERS boxes when the button was pushed and voice contact was not made. This plan was in effect during high false alarm hours. Additionally, the new, lightweight Scott 4.5 was issued to all fire companies. This provided more air with better visibility and reduced weight.

On January 3, 1979, FDNY history was made the hard way. At 7:06 p.m., Ladder Company 28 responded to Manhattan Box 1634 for a fire at 301 West 147th Street. As they rolled up, fire was blowing out two windows on the third floor of the five-story tenement with heavy smoke visible on the floors above. Lieutenant Thomas J. Neary, hearing reports of a trapped child in the fire apartment, raced to the apartment door.

Due to a police lock, it was decided to take the door on the hinge side and the door was removed. Fire was in possession of the entire apartment and the heat level was intense and increasing. Neary made a trip into the apartment and was driven back by the intense heat. Hearing the trapped child cry inside the apartment, Neary picked up the apartment door and started back into the inferno, using the door as a shield.

Neary pushed through the kitchen and into and down the interior hallway where he found the child. Neary discarded the door, scooped up the child and shielded him as best he could as he dashed back through the flames. When the Lieutenant reached the hallway, he handed the child to his forcible entry team and collapsed.

Lieutenant Thomas J. Neary suffered second- and third-degree burns of the face, ears, neck, arms and back, in addition to heat exhaustion. The severity of his injuries placed him on medical leave for 29 days. The young boy was admitted to the hospital in fair condition and survived his ordeal. For the first time in the history of the New York City Fire Department, one man – Thomas Neary – was awarded the Bennett Medal for a second time.

Ten firefighters were overcome by chemical fumes when they ventured into a smoke-filled basement at 116-11 139th Street in Ozone Park, Queens, on February 11, 1979, at 11 a.m. The members of Engine Company 302 and Ladder Company 155 made their way into the basement to find the origin of the smoke condition. They located a smoking canister, removed it from the building and then began to develop shortness of breath and chest pains.

The firemen were taken to Jamaica Hospital for tests. One officer was admitted for observation. The device apparently was a military smoke bomb used in training.

The coldest February of the century took its toll on the citizens and the Fire Department. Frigid temperatures, high winds and frozen hydrants and equipment made firefighting both more difficult and dangerous than usual. Civilians were using any method possible to ward off the cold: Ovens, stoves and portable heaters were pressed into service. Between February 10th and 14th, the Fire Department battled 23 multiple-alarm fires.

On Valentine's Day, 1979, the FDNY operated at numerous major fires around the city. A five-alarm fire raged out of control, sending flames 30 feet into the sky, in a 19th-century loft building in Greenwich Village. The fire started inside 653 Broadway just after midnight, in a third-floor pillow factory. The fire was not discovered until sprinklers were activated in the Infinity disco downstairs.

Winds and freezing temperatures compounded the difficult nature of the blaze. As dozens of patrons left the disco, flames began to spread to the adjoining structures. Efforts were adjusted to halt the spreading fire. Ultimately, the three adjoining buildings also were destroyed.

Firemen in Brooklyn were faring no better than their Brothers in the other boroughs. At 12:26 a.m., Box 1242 came in for a fire in a four-story tenement at 92 Saint Mark's Avenue. As Ladder Company 132 arrived at the location, Fireman Richard E. Hickey was informed by civilians that two children were trapped in the rear bedroom. Heavy fire was in control of the second-floor hallway. With no fire escape on the rear of the fire building, Hickey lowered the drop ladder of the fire escape on the adjacent building. Hickey could see heavy smoke in the rear bedroom. He vented the window and using a small sign protruding from the rear wall, he carefully stepped across to the window.

Without a mask, he entered the hot, smoke-filled room and began a search. He came upon a young boy and hurried back to the rear window, where he passed the youth outside to firemen on a ladder. Hickey again plunged into the building smoke and heat and crawled until he found a second child on a bed. Hickey handed the child outside, then climbed down the ladder himself into the frigid night air. For his bravery, Fireman Richard Hickey was awarded a medal.

At 4:30 a.m., a fire broke out in a row of stores at 72nd Street and 37th Avenue in Jackson Heights, Queens. The fire began in a laundry and spread to the adjoining occupancies. The blaze was fought for two hours and went to three alarms before it was extinguished.

Another fire – this one at 851 Woodward Avenue in Ridgewood – came in at 4:30 a.m. This two-alarm fire started in a bar and spread to a two-story building next door. The fire was declared suspicious due to the volume of fire on arrival.

At noon, three-alarm fires burned at 83 Bowery in Manhattan and Belmont Avenue and 176th Street in the Bronx. Shortly after three p.m., a three-alarm fire gutted four stores on Central Avenue in Far Rockaway. The owner of the building apparently died of a heart attack during the fire.

Multiples also were fought on West 122nd Street, 116th Street and Saint Nicholas Avenue, and 100 Church Street in Manhattan. In the Bronx, another third-alarm fire was extinguished at 176th Street and Tremont Avenue. Probationary firemen from Randall's Island were pressed into duty. They chopped ice to free hoses and then packed the iced hoses on waiting pumpers at several locations. The Probies wore their "sunshine yellow" rain slickers and Civil Defense helmets.

On June 12, 1979, at 4:08 p.m., Manhattan units responded to a reported fire in Macy's department store at 34th Street and Seventh Avenue. Crowds watched as the firemen entered the huge Herald Square store. Inside, a fire in a sixth-floor sporting goods area was burning from a storage room up into the plenum, virtually unseen by most shoppers.

Arriving at the location, members of Ladder Company 24 ordered the shoppers from the area and went to investigate. In a matter of seconds, conditions changed from relatively normal to extreme, as the raging fire hidden in the hung ceiling burst down with a dark, hot vengeance.

In the scramble to return to the stairway, Fireman Walter Smith was unable to reach safety. As conditions worsened, his comrades made attempt after attempt to penetrate the inferno. Four alarms were transmitted before the fire could be controlled. Thirteen people, mostly firemen, were injured. Walter Smith became the second fireman to be killed in the line of duty in 1979.

Radiant heat spread a fire to terrifying proportions in Douglaston Queens, during the early-morning hours of September 11, 1979. It was a cool, clear morning when Box 3935 sent companies to 70th Avenue at 1:24 a.m. Upon arrival, units were met with a tremendous volume of fire, completely involving eight attached, three-story, frame buildings under construction. Firemen were faced with a wall of flames 100 feet high and 150 feet wide.

On arrival, Lieutenant Ginal transmitted a second alarm from the front seat of Engine Company 313. The fire went to a third alarm and an attack was made using tower ladders and Stang nozzles. The radiant heat from the fire caused the ignition of five similar attached, three-story, occupied dwellings, 94 feet away from the original fire.

In all, eight of the attached buildings were destroyed, six were damaged and 28 motor vehicles parked in between were involved in flames. The severity of the fire on arrival was attributed to flammable liquids used by an arsonist. A good water supply and a better fire attack held the fire from spreading even further.

A three-alarm fire in a row of stores tested the Department during the early-morning hours of November 20, 1979. Units responded to 59-09 Myrtle Avenue in the Ridgewood section of Queens to find fire extending into three adjacent stores. Until they all could be forced, heavy security roll-down gates slowed the fire attack.

The fire was darkened down and appeared to be just about under control when a large, roof-mounted air-conditioning unit collapsed into a pharmacy. Luckily, firemen were aware of the unit and had been kept clear of it while operating. The fire flared up again, but was brought under control at 8:01 a.m.

The following day, while backing into a loading dock at the Mobil Oil storage yard in Greenpoint, Brooklyn, a gasoline truck sheared off a 10-inch pipe. Moments later, a thunderous explosion rocked the entire neighborhood. The blast and fire destroyed the 3000-gallon truck, two other trucks parked nearby and a loading bay. Three alarms were transmitted and firemen battled the flames for one hour and 20 minutes.

Rush-hour traffic was building on the Bronx's Bruckner Expressway on the morning of November 1, 1979. From the vantage point of the highway, a fire in a nearby two-story house could be seen. Two cars pulled of the road and headed toward the fire. Pulling up at 1407 Manor Avenue, the two drivers were confronted with fire blowing out of six windows on the second floor of the house. People were visible and trapped at second-floor windows and a woman lay injured after jumping.

Moving toward the house, the two men, off-duty firemen, made introductions on the run, "Barry. Ladder 31."..."Keenan. Ladder 55." Still running, they entered the burning home. Heavy flames blocked the top of the stairs, but both men climbed the banister and dove over the railing onto the floor. They separated and crawled toward bedrooms in the front of the house. Keenan found a dazed woman, removed her over the railing and lowered her by her hands to the landing below, then joined Barry, who was in the process of removing a heavy-set man.

Barry lifted the man onto the railing and in one motion, pushed the man and himself over. Both men fell to the first floor as the skylight over the stairs exploded, showering the area with molten, wired glass. Keenan double-checked the area and made his escape out a front bedroom window. Firemen Thomas Barry and Michael Keenan were awarded the *Daily News* Heroes of the Month.

New York City Fire Department 1980 –1989

On February 1, 1980, the temperature had plummeted to 14 degrees, with a biting, 40-mph wind coming in from the northwest. At 3:48 a.m., Box 462 was transmitted at the corner of Henry and Pineapple Streets in Brooklyn. Engine Company 205, Ladder Company 118 and the 31st Battalion arrived at the corner and saw nothing. A few minutes later, making a search of the area, Engine Company 205 found a fire at Columbia Heights and Orange Street.

Companies were confronted with heavy fire showing on the ninth and 10th floors of the 11-story Hotel Margaret. Flames were extending to the 11th floor and dropping to the lower floors via an elevator shaft. In the first few minutes of operations, a solarium, added after the building was constructed, collapsed, taking with it a large section of the original roof structure. They fell into Orange Street in a shower of flaming debris.

The five upper floors now were fully involved and the wind was driving a major brand problem across the neighborhood. A third alarm was transmitted. Fourth and fifth alarms also were sent in. Nearby buildings were evacuated and exposures monitored and protected.

Three hours and 39 minutes after the initial alarm, the fire was declared under control. FDNY units remained on the scene for more than 10 days, however, until final extinguishment was accomplished.

The year 1980 had its share of fires, emergencies and false alarms. The Department began testing and using the cross-band repeater system to improve high-rise fire communications. This system utilized the existing two-way radios and handie-talkies to allow for a reliable, local, mobile repeater.

Numerous spectacular rescues were made by the members of the Department as the 42 medals of valor attested. The year will be remembered, however, by the way that three brave men made the Supreme Sacrifice, "Tragedy, coupled with the ultimate heroism."

Brooklyn fire companies responded to a reported fire at 1041 and 1045 Sutter Avenue at about four a.m. on the morning of March 5, 1980. The fire was in two abandoned wooden structures and arriving companies went to work as usual. Engine Company 332, under the command of Lieutenant Robert R. Dolney, a 30-year veteran, operated their line to protect the building to the rear, then repositioned to attack the blazing structure. Members of Ladder Company 103 worked on the roof and vented horizontally where they could.

Engine Company 332 was waiting in the doorway in the rear of 1045 Sutter when at 4:35 a.m., conditions began to change rapidly. A blast of heat and the sound of collapse pushed from the rear of the building. Dolney's years of experience told him what was happening and he reacted in kind. He shouted a warning and pushed his nozzleman, Fireman Patrick Quinn, through the doorway in one motion. The building collapsed in a shower of sparks, flames and darkness.

Fireman Quinn, caught beneath part of the collapse, was injured seriously, but still alive. Fireman Steve Filippelli was blown into the street by the blast of hot air forced out of the building by the collapse of the roof. Five truckies on the roof jumped and fell 20 feet, but walked away with minor injuries. A rescue effort was commenced and Quinn was extricated and rushed to the hospital. Dolney, who had taken the full brunt of the collapse, was dug out and rushed to the hospital as well, but he could not be saved.

The night tour of June 27, 1980, had just begun when numerous calls alerted the Department to a fire at 512 West 151st Street in Manhattan. Members of the busy 16th Battalion were informed en route that people were reported trapped in the building. The Harlem firefighters went to work.

As Rescue Company 3 arrived, they were sent to the roof of the seven-story building to help ventilate. Below them, members of Ladder Company 28 were making a tough search for those reported trapped. Suddenly, Firefighter Gerard Frisby of Ladder Company 28 appeared at a top-floor window. The young fireman was cut off. Flames were pouring out of the two windows adjacent to his position and roaring unseen in the cockloft over his head.

Members of Rescue Company 3 responded to radio reports and prepared to remove Frisby from the top floor. Fireman William Murphy was lowered on a personal rope and steadied Frisby, while Fireman Larry Fitzpatrick was lowered on a roof rope. A protective water curtain was sprayed over the firefighters as conditions continued to deteriorate.

Fitzpatrick arrived at the top-floor window and took Frisby onto the roof rope. The rope then parted and both Frisby and Fitzpatrick plummeted seven stories to the courtyard below. Murphy was lowered one more floor and climbed in a window. The two men were rushed to Columbia-Presbyterian Hospital but could not be saved.

On August 13, 1980, Box 1672 sent Brooklyn units to 124 Osborn Street for a raging fire in a three-story frame building. Companies went to work under the watchful eye of Battalion Chief Frank T. Tuttlemondo. A civilian approached and told the chief that squatters were in the building. Tuttlemondo ordered, "All hands at work. Give me another engine and truck."

Another person advised the chief that he was certain that someone was in the fire building. (Reports were correct. Two men were found dead in the fire building.) The chief ordered a second alarm and sent Rescue Company 2 to the adjacent burning building. Engine Company 227 was moving a line into the first floor and Chief Tuttlemondo joined Lieutenant Michael Ramos to get a better idea of the conditions.

Members of the Department at line-of-duty funeral. "We will reform the line that has been broken." (Photo by Steven Scher)

A tremendous roar announced the collapse of the fire building. Wood, steel and heavy timbers fell with a shower of hot tar. In the seconds that stretched before those underneath the falling building, purposeful actions were taken. Chief Tuttlemondo threw his own body on the fallen Lieutenant Ramos to shield him from the collapse. As the injured lieutenant regained consciousness, he realized his head was being cradled by the chief's arm.

Three different men, three different fires – one common thread – humanity. All three firefighters were given the only token the Department has for bravery – medals. The small golden tokens seem so insignificant compared to the acts.

The collapse that took the life of Battalion Chief Tuttlemondo also trapped several members under tons of flaming debris. With their Brothers trapped beneath beams and other debris, firemen dove into the wreckage. For more than two hours in grave danger of further collapse, they worked to rescue the pinned men and remove their beloved chief. Many were involved in the rescue effort, but the Board of Merit singled out Lieutenant Arthur F. Connelly and Firemen Thomas D. Murphy, John P. Thomas, William Hewitson and Lee A. Ielpi of Rescue Company 2; Fireman Frank B. Tooker of Engine Company 232; Fireman Michael J. Loftus of Engine Company 283; and Fireman Edward F. Wawrzonek of Ladder Company 176. For their heroic actions, they were awarded medals.

Two hundred eight firefighters battled a five-alarm blaze that swept through the Long Island Rail Road's Holban Yards, located at 183rd Street and Liberty Avenue in Queens. The "engine only" alarm for a minor fire in the yard rapidly escalated on May 27, 1980. The fire started in a remote area in rubbish underneath skids containing cable reels and drums containing flammable liquids.

The small fire rapidly intensified and extended, helped by a brisk northwest wind. The fire soon engulfed a locker shed, a storage shed,

numerous 55-gallon drums of flammable liquids and stored acetylene, oxygen and propane tanks. The flames also extended to dozens of reels of insulated copper wire, railroad box cars, 10,000 board feet of lumber and the west end of the main storage building.

Tower ladders and Stangs battled the flames. The fire, now at five alarms, finally was brought under control. Twenty-one engines, nine ladders (including five tower ladders) and three Satellites were pressed into service.

An explosion virtually leveled a one-story, 20- x 70-foot building that housed both a dry cleaners and self-service laundromat. Bronx Box 3318 was transmitted on June 11, 1980, at 11:21 a.m. Companies responded and found the structure a pile of burning timbers and scattered bricks. The roof of the dry cleaners was pancaked with the laundromat section of roof found in an unsupported, lean-to type of collapse.

Reports indicated that several people already had gone to the hospital and that more still could be trapped under the flaming remnants. Rescue Company 3 and Ladder Companies 33 and 38 searched for trapped people, while Engine Companies 48 and 75 controlled visible fire. One person was located and removed. The search continued.

Using air bags, a victim was located and removed from under the fallen brick wall. Expecting an extensive search, Rescue Company 4 was special-called to the scene. All voids were checked and proved negative. The roof then was cut up systematically and removed and the debris cleared. Luckily, no other victims were located. The FDNY worked for 36 hours at the scene before the last unit "took up."

It was the night before Thanksgiving, November 26, 1981. Ladder Company 17 responded to a reported fire at 401 East 154th Street in the Bronx. The six-story, non-fireproof, multiple dwelling had commercial occupancies on the first floor. As the rig pulled up, heavy black smoke from burning foam-rubber seat cushions was visible pumping from the front, while flames poured from the rear. Arriving companies realized they would be alone for a while. One and one would have to do until additional help arrived.

Lieutenant John Mitchell of Ladder Company 17 made his way to the second-floor apartments and began searching. Below him, the store was completely involved and conditions above were getting worse by the second. Mitchell searched two apartments with negative results. Then, as he moved through the third apartment, he became entangled in illegal electrical wiring. Unable to free himself, he abandoned his mask and continued.

Crawling on his stomach, Lieutenant Mitchell came across an unconscious man. He dragged the victim outside, then dashed back into the swirling, hot smoke in the staircase. Mitchell heard screams from the third floor and responded. There, he found a woman and her child in a dazed panic. The woman cried that her baby was still inside. Mitchell found a safe haven for the pair and plunged into the apartment. Under extreme conditions, he was able to find the baby in a crib and carry her from the apartment. The officer rejoined the mother and carried the two infants down.

Mitchell took a brief second to gulp some clear air and ventured again into the third floor where he rescued two adults and a child. He started down the stairs with them. At the second floor, the heat, smoke and physical punishment caught up to Mitchell and he collapsed. Members of the second-due truck brought him outside.

On Medal Day 1982, Lieutenant John H. Mitchell was awarded two medals of valor, one for his efforts on November 26, 1980, and the other for rescuing several people at 637 East 140th Street on January 11, 1981. (Fireman Eugene Vitelli of Ladder Company 17 also was awarded a medal for his rescues at the same fire.)

On December 16, 1980, at 8:12 p.m., an alarm was received for 21-11 21st Street in Astoria, Queens. Units were met with a heavy fire condition in the cellar of a one-story taxpayer, occupied by a bedding supply company. Additional alarms were requested. Battalion Chief Thomas Scott of the 49th Battalion sent Rescue Company 4 to the cellar of exposure #4 to check for extension and provide an alternative approach to the fire.

Fed by box springs, mattresses and other bedding materials, the fire produced a high heat level, coupled with a heavy smoke condition. In an exposure, Rescue Company 4, under the command of Lieutenant Charles G. Moran, pulled the ceilings and began to breach the wall adjoining the fire area. As Firemen Thomas Prin and Owen McKenna enlarged the hole, it was evident that the fire had gained complete control of the cellar next door. Engine Company 260 stretched a line into position to operate through the breach and hit the seat of the fire.

Lieutenant John Mitchell of Ladder 17 removes young victim from Bronx fire in 1983. (Photo by Harvey Eisner)

Meanwhile in the street, Ladder Company 154, with Lieutenant Howard R. Kennedy in command, reported to the command post. Simultaneously, a collapse occurred and the handie-talkie blared, "Mayday! Mayday!" Two members were reported missing and Lieutenant Kennedy volunteered to attempt a rescue. Kennedy sent two members to the rear, as he entered the front of the fire building with the remaining members of the company.

In the exposure #4 cellar, Lieutenant Moran heard the radio reports, then faint cries of the members. Immediately, Moran and Prin climbed through the hole and began a search. The hose line in the cellar was opened up in an attempt to cover their advance, but the steam knocked off the officer's helmet and facepiece. Returning to the hole, Moran requested the line not be operated to allow them to hear those trapped inside. Moran then rejoined Prin.

On the first floor, Kennedy and his men came upon the nozzle of Engine Company 312's line, but could find no indication of collapse or any sign of the missing men. Suddenly, a cry for help was heard and the team moved across sections of burned-out floor and past obstacles to find a stairway opening. Kennedy sent his men back for a portable ladder while he attempted to reach down to Fireman John Masterson of Engine Company 312.

Once the ladder was in position, Kennedy descended, despite the fact that the low-air alarm was sounding on his mask. After a quick search, he located Masterson, who already had suffered burns over 30 percent of his body. Lieutenant Kennedy dragged him back to the ladder, then lifted the unconscious firefighter and climbed onto the ladder. At this point, Kennedy's mask was depleted. Holding Masterson with one hand and the ladder with the other, Kennedy could not remove the empty mask. Trying to hold his breath, the officer made one super-human effort to reach the first floor. Kennedy tumbled off the ladder with Masterson and in the dense smoke condition, tore off his mask.

In the cellar, Lieutenant Moran and Fireman Prin had located the unconscious form of Lieutenant Anthony Spalma, who also was burned severely. The two men struggled to drag the injured man across piles of mattresses and box springs that seemed to grab and hold the unconscious man. Inch by inch, they continued. Prin's mask had given out, but he continued in the choking atmosphere.

As they neared the hole, other firefighters jumped in to help pass the burned member through. Prin climbed into the adjoining cellar and collapsed. Moran made it as far as the stairs and collapsed. Both men were hospitalized with smoke inhalation, heat exhaustion and burns.

For their heroic efforts in saving the lives of two Brother firefighters, Lieutenant Howard Kennedy was awarded the Bennett Medal and Lieutenant Charles Moran (at this time, the most decorated member of the Department) and Firefighter Thomas Prin were awarded medals.

A raging four-alarm fire in the annex of the Hotel Wellington was tackled by midtown units on February 4, 1981. The smoky fire drove more than 350 residents from the hotel, as dense smoke filled the 15-story building. A 50-year-old woman living in the main section of the hotel apparently panicked and fell two stories to the roof of the annex.

Propane truck leaking product on the George Washington Bridge in August of 1980. This operation by Rescue 4 was instrumental in the training of Rescue 4 as a Haz-Mat unit and the later formation of a separate Hazardous Materials company. (Photo by Harvey Eisner)

Hazardous Material Unit

In 1981, the Department qualified Rescue Company 4 as the Hazardous Material Unit. Members of the company received specialized training at the National Fire Academy to meet the dangers of hazardous materials within the city.

In the area of identifying hazards, both to the public and the firefighting force, one substance received widespread attention – polychlorinated biphenyls. Commonly referred to as PCBs, these carcinogenic agents came to light after several fires were fought and leaks of the substances confronted the FDNY. A new Department procedure was established to help ensure the safety of members and the public.

The 9:30 a.m. blaze started in the basement boiler room of the annex at 147 West 55th Street. The fire in the ceiling caused a localized collapse that took down the sprinkler system. The blaze required 25 companies and took 150 firemen an hour and a quarter to control.

A flaming bottle of gasoline was thrown in the hallway of 143 Thames Street in the Bushwick section of Brooklyn on the evening of February 8, 1981, at about 10 p.m. Two mothers and their three young children perished in the blaze, apparently ignited by two men, members of a family evicted from the building a week before.

Firemen pushed into the burning building and found the children on the stairs leading to the roof. One child had reached safety that way. The women entered the hall and were driven into a vacant apartment where they perished. Fire Marshals hunted the two brothers believed to be responsible.

A smoky two-alarm fire in the New York Hilton, the city's largest hotel at the time, drove hundreds of guests to the street. The "suspicious" blaze in the 46-floor hotel, located at 53rd Street and Sixth Avenue, was the third suspicious fire in a city hotel in seven days. (Three people were injured at a fire in the 360-room Beaux Arts Hotel on 44th, near the United Nations, on February 15th.) The Hilton fire was confined to a second-floor conference room. The 8:04 p.m. fire brought 100 firemen and 28 pieces of apparatus to the scene. They extinguished the fire and searched all of the 2131 rooms in a little more an hour. There were 1665 guests in the hotel at the time of the fire.

John Carney and his partner, William Mulhall, sat in their Arson Task Force van on May 9, 1981, on surveillance, as part of the Department's Red Cap program. Earlier in the morning, they had arrested a 12-year-old arson suspect who had set fire to a three-story building in the Sunset Park section of Brooklyn. A 17-year-old girl had been forced to jump to escape the blaze. She broke her pelvis and eight firemen also were injured at the fire.

The youth was arrested and when his mother refused to take custody of him, he was transported to a precinct where he would be transferred to a detention center. The two Fire Marshals, who had been upgraded from provisional status only days before, returned to 42nd Street and Fourth Avenue in Brooklyn to complete some paper work and keep an eye on things.

Suddenly, at 2:35 a.m., they heard a woman scream and responded on foot toward her. A short distance away, there was an altercation underway and a shot rang out. The Marshals continued, drawing their weapons. Another gunshot sounded and the Marshals observed a lone gunman with a silver-plated handgun.

"Police officers. Don't move. Drop your gun," they yelled. The perpetrator turned toward the Marshals, then wheeled around and fired a third shot that hit a man. Fire Marshal Carney took the combat stance and squeezed off two rounds. Mulhall held fire as the crowd became larger and the growing altercation continued.

Mulhall subdued the main combatants while Carney cuffed the wounded gunman. The Marshals then backed off and awaited reinforcements. For subduing a gunman and defusing a potentially volatile situation, the FDNY proudly awarded both men medals.

Rope rescues always have been a part of the FDNY arsenal. New members train in the basics while in "Proby School." The knots are practiced and the ropes are examined and repacked weekly. A high degree of professionalism and daring was displayed when Firemen Joseph H. Dirks and Gene J. DiMarco put the evolution into play at a fire at 306 Montauk Avenue, Brooklyn, on July 15, 1981.

DiMarco lowered Dirks in a picture-perfect evolution as he picked up the trapped woman at a third-floor window. Both firefighters operated with a cool precision, even though below them in the courtyard lay three people who had jumped prior to the Department's arrival. Feeling the addition of the woman's weight and hearing Dirks' call, DiMarco continued lowering.

As the rope passed a second-floor window, another woman appeared at the third-floor window above. Without hesitation, she jumped for the rope and began to slide down, out of control. Dirks grabbed her and held on as tightly as he could. Up on the roof, DiMarco was struggling to keep control of the lowering process as he physically was dragged across the roof toward the edge.

The weight of the woman proved to be too much and Dirks lost his hold on her, just 12 feet from the ground. She fell the remaining distance to the ground but was alive. Fireman Joseph Dirks was awarded the Bennett Medal and Fireman Gene DiMarco received the Brummer Medal for saving two lives while risking their own.

A three-alarm fire ravaged an East Side hotel that would have been only a one-room fire had the sprinkler system been in operation. The blaze broke out in the Elton Hotel at 101 East 26th Street at 12:09 p.m. in a fourth-floor room. Eighty guests fled the smoke and heat. Several, including one man who was dangling from a window ledge, were rescued by firemen.

The fire raced unchecked through the fourth and fifth floors of the 65-room hotel. Ninety-five firemen operated, bringing the flames into check. Records showed that the sprinkler had been shut down for repairs that apparently never were made. The Department ordered the damaged hotel vacated.

A carbon monoxide leak in a four-story Brooklyn apartment building took the lives of three people and injured 35 others. Fire units raced to 984 Greene Avenue in the Bedford-Stuyvesant section at 6:30 a.m. on November 6, 1981. A disconnected flue from a hot water heater had filled the 20-unit building with the deadly gas while tenants slept.

Firemen raced through the building removing tenants, many suffering classic CO poisoning symptoms: cherry-red coloring, headaches, vomiting and weakness. Twenty-two people were overcome and rushed to nearby hospitals. A seven-month-old baby and his parents were found dead in their third-floor apartment.

Brooklyn units battled a three-alarm blaze at 284 Harman Street at Knickerbocker Avenue in Bushwick. The initial alarm was received at 7:39 a.m., November 15, 1981, and was declared an "all-hands" on arrival. Heavy fire was visible on the first and second floors in the rear of the fire building, a three-story, vacant, multiple dwelling. The first line went into the fire building and the second was stretched to the top floor of exposure #2, a three-story, occupied, multiple dwelling.

Conditions continued to deteriorate and second and third alarms were requested. Ladder Company 111 Firemen Richard Spatafora and Daniel Perrella were operating the tower ladder's stream at the second-floor level of the blazing exposure #4, when suddenly, without any warning, the three-story portion of the building collapsed. As the building fell, it took off the tower ladder's bucket and threw it 25 feet to the ground with the members still in it.

Firemen scrambled to free the two men. Both were extricated quickly and rushed to the hospital. Perrella suffered facial cuts and other injuries, while Spatafora received back and other injuries. The attack continued with large-caliber streams and two hours later, the fire was extinguished. A contributing factor to the collapse was the $1/16$-inch steel plating on the extension portion of the exposure #4 roof that continued across the second-level flooring of the three-story section.

On November 29, 1981, fire was reported at 345 East 52nd Street in the East Flatbush section of Brooklyn. Engine Company 283 turned out at 11:14 p.m. and arrived at the two-story building. Flames were pouring from the second-floor window and lines were being stretched hastily. A civilian reported to Lieutenant Jim McCarthy that children were trapped in the bedroom. McCarthy directed Fireman Shaun M. Reen, detailed to Engine 283 for the tour from Ladder Company 174, to attempt the rescue. Reen placed a portable ladder to the window and climbed through.

The searing heat pressed Reen to the floor as he searched for the child. At the same time, Fireman Roy Conner of Ladder Company 123 had worked his way into the room. Reen felt the forms of two unconscious infants on a bed. Conner found the third. All of the infants were burned badly and the conditions in the room were untenable.

The two firemen crawled back to the window and passed the injured infants out to a firefighter on the ladder. All the critically injured children were rushed to Kings County Hospital. Firemen Shaun M. Reen and Roy Conner, Jr., were awarded medals for their daring rescues.

A hot, smoky and toxic fire was battled on January 20, 1982 at the Hobbs Electrical Supply Company at 541 West 34th Street in Manhattan. The fire began at about 6:15 p.m. on the fifth floor of the block-long brick building. Five alarms brought 250 firefighters to the blaze.

Acrid smoke and toxic fumes filled the upper floors of the six-story structure. Plastic insulation on 150 one-ton rolls of copper electrical tubing burned, giving off polyvinyl chloride fumes. Small amounts of chemicals, including cyanide, were stored on the second, third and fourth floors. The fire was contained to the top two floors.

A pre-dawn blaze broke out in the upper floors of the unfinished Trump Tower on Fifth Avenue at 56th Street in Manhattan, on January 29, 1982. A sky crane operator was trapped 300 feet above the street by a heavy body of fire that was spreading on the 27th and 28th floors. Firefighters teamed up to effect the rescue. Engine Company 23 pushed back the fire and cooled the red-hot metalwork, allowing Lieutenants James Curran of Rescue Company 1 and Owen Byrnes of Ladder Company 16 to climb a 40-foot steel ladder inside a steel shaftway to reach the trapped man.

Engine 23 covered the operation, as the crane operator was rescued from his perch surrounded by flames. He was sitting directly above a tank filled with 300 gallons of diesel fuel. The blaze required four alarms to control. Fire Marshals declared the fire to be arson.

Lieutenants Curran and Byrnes received medals, as did the nozzle team who covered them – Firemen Joe Pierotti and Harry Wehr of Engine Company 23.

Brooklyn Box 1036 was transmitted at 1:01 a.m. on February 3, 1982, for a fire in a four-story, frame, multiple dwelling at 258 Albany Avenue. The fire was in complete control of the interior stairs, raging up through the bulkhead and entering the apartments on each floor. Numerous victims were seen and heard trapped at windows above. One person already had jumped as companies went to work.

Ladder Company 123, first-due, placed their aerial ladder to front-floor windows and rescued numerous people from the horrific atmosphere. Ladder Company 111 placed their tower ladder into operation and also removed several people from front windows. With flames roaring from windows on the second floor and blocking access, Fireman Kenneth Connelly called to Engine Company 227 to use their hose line to hold the fire in the second-floor windows. Rising above the fire, Connelly reached the third-floor window and dove into the room.

Inside the room, he found a 250-pound woman, badly burned and wedged behind a bed. Unable to move the woman and driven to the floor by the building heat, Connelly radioed for help. He then noticed an 11-year-old girl farther in the apartment. Connelly crawled from the bedroom and with flames rolling over his head, he noticed a nine-year-old boy. He started back to the front window with the girl, hoping to have time to return for the boy.

When Connelly's radio message reached Fireman Robert Johnson, who had been trying to reach the upper floors through the interior, he returned to the tower ladder. Seeing the empty bucket at a window, he knew Connelly was in a bad situation. Johnson's only alternative was to scale the tower ladder's emergency escape ladder to reach the bucket. Within seconds, he was inside, trying to free the wedged woman. Connelly appeared through the smoke. "There are more in there!" he said and handed Johnson the unconscious girl. Then, he disappeared into the smoke. Connelly returned with the nine-year-old boy, then disappeared yet again.

On June 1, 1982, the term "Fireman" was changed to "Firefighter" in the New York City Fire Department. This was in response to the decision by a Federal Court judge on March 5, 1982, throwing out the Fireman's physical exam given between November 1977 and April 1978. The judge also ruled that the city must appoint 45 female applicants if they could pass a new test. The new test was approved in August and administered at the Randall's Island training facility on September eighth, ninth and 10th. A medical exam then was given to those who passed the physical.

On September 22, 1982, 155 Probationary Firefighters were sworn in to the ranks of the Fire Department of the City of New York. Among that number were 42 women who had qualified by passing the new physical test. They completed six weeks of firefighting and physical training. On November 5, 1982, 11 female Firefighters graduated from the Training School and were assigned to firehouses across the city. Twenty-nine females and six males were re-admitted to the school for additional training.

Johnson placed the girl, then the boy, in the tower ladder bucket and returned to the blazing apartment. The middle room now was totally involved in fire and Connelly and another small victim were cut off, but just visible through the fire. Johnson lunged through the flames, grabbed both Connelly and the victim and pulled. The three tumbled back through the fire into the front room. As Johnson placed the third unconscious child in the bucket, Fireman William Ostrander of Ladder 123 joined them in the room.

Ostrander and his partner had rescued five persons over the aerial. Then, he entered the fire building, trying to reach the upper floors. He, too, responded to Connelly's radio message, repositioned the aerial next to the bucket and entered the room. The three firemen were almost out of time as the fire closed in. They struggled to free the heavy woman and get her to the window. Johnson climbed out and lifted as Connelly and Ostrander pulled. With one last effort, they moved the woman out. Ostrander looked over his shoulder at an oncoming ball of fire and shouted, "Here she comes!" They dove out the window and grabbed the bucket's railing and Johnson's outstretched arm as the fire ball burst through the window.

At the same time, two separate, dangerous rescues were being made from the rear fire escape. Fireman John Ferry of Squad Company 1 rescued an unconscious 12-year-old boy and Fireman Glen Harris of Rescue Company 2 rescued an eight-month-old girl.

All five firemen were awarded medals for their heroic rescues. Fireman Kenneth Connelly received the Bennett Medal.

A suspicious five-alarm fire destroyed a large portion of the Queens Mall in Jamaica on February 16, 1982. The blaze started in the rear of a men's clothing store shortly after two a.m. and spread through 10 other stores before it could be extinguished at 6:28 a.m.

The new 800-foot pedestrian mall was begun about four years earlier as part of a 10-year effort to revitalize the downtown Jamaica shopping and office area. The arson fire drew 150 firemen and 40 pieces of apparatus.

A wave of bombings rocked the very symbols of American financial power in the heart of wall street on February 28, 1982. The bombs were made of three to four sticks of dynamite with a timer. The explosions occurred at 11:25 p.m. in the Merrill Lynch Building at One Liberty Plaza. Both the Chase Manhattan Bank Headquarters, at One Chase Manhattan Plaza, and the New York Stock Exchange, at Broad and Wall Streets, were bombed at 11:35 p.m. The American Stock Exchange, at 86 Trinity Place, was bombed at 11:55 p.m. The FALN, a Puerto Rican terrorist group, claimed responsibility for the blasts.

A four-alarm fire broke out on the third floor of a former RKO theater, next door to the quarters of Engine Company 36 on 125th Street in Harlem. During this March 24, 1982, fire, the huge ceiling of the theater collapsed, injuring five firefighters. More than 150 firefighters battled the flames as they extended to a church and flea market, also housed inside the structure. The firehouse was used as a vantage point from which to operate hose lines during the battle.

A Lebanese restaurant in Brooklyn was destroyed by fire on April 5, 1982. A caller said that the Jewish Defense League (JDL) took responsibility for the fire. He claimed the restaurant was a meeting place for Palestine Liberation Organization members.

A 75-year-old woman lost her life in the blaze and seven people were injured. The fire started in the front dining room of the restaurant and spread to three floors above. More than two dozen people were left homeless by the fire. The five-story building at Atlantic Avenue and Clinton Street was set ablaze at 1:56 a.m. and evidence indicated that flammable liquids had been used.

A three-alarm fire damaged the landmark West End Collegiate Church on West End Avenue and 77th Street in Manhattan on December 18, 1982. The fire was confined to the roof and steeple of the 90-year-old, Flemish-style brick church. The blaze apparently was touched off accidentally by workers repairing the roof. The church, an official city landmark and on the National Historic Register, suffered water damage and lost an $80,000 stained-glass window.

The next day, Brooklyn fire companies battled a fire in the Williamsburg Christian Church during Sunday services. A fire in a ground-floor ladies lounge drove 250 parishioners outside into the freezing temperatures.

On March 24, 1983, at one a.m., there was a frantic banging on the apparatus doors of the Harlem Hilton. Inside, the men on duty knew there definitely was a fire nearby. The companies rolled just down the street from the firehouse, to 307 West 143rd Street, where flames were blowing out the windows of a five-story apartment house. Firefighter Ross Gerbino set up the aerial and raised it. The report from inside stated that fire was out into the hallway on the third floor. Gerbino spotted the aerial at the fifth-floor fire escape balcony and helped a number of people to safety.

Searching deep into the apartment, he found a heavy, unconscious woman and dragged her 50 feet back to the window. With great difficulty, he was able to get the woman outside and onto the fire escape. He radioed for help and began mouth-to-mouth. The victim was rushed to the hospital and survived. Firefighter Ross Gerbino later was awarded a medal.

Ladder Company 80 pulled up to a blazing wood-frame house at 279 Herberton Avenue, Staten Island, on the morning of May 3, 1983.

The first week of August 1982 was proclaimed New York City Firefighters Week by Mayor Koch and the five Borough Presidents. The five-day celebration started on Monday when a memorial Mass was held to commemorate the 50th anniversary of the Ritz Tower explosion and fire on August 1, 1932, that took the lives of eight firemen. The second Mass took place in Brooklyn to memorialize the six firemen who died in the Waldbaum's fire and collapse on August 2, 1978.

Tuesday featured open houses at all city firehouses. Many families of members killed in the line of duty visited the former firehouse of their loved ones. At 10 a.m. on Wednesday, the new Fire Headquarters building was dedicated at 250 Livingston Street in Brooklyn. On Thursday, the Fire Commissioner, Charles Hynes, presided at the graduation of 60 probationary firefighters. At the ceremony, the Commissioner also bestowed the title of "Honorary Deputy Chief" on two former firemen, Augustus Mille and William Gibson. Both men received permanent injuries while performing in the Department's Midnight Alarm Show in Madison Square Garden in 1947.

The Commissioner also announced that six new scholarships were being endowed for children of deceased firefighters. Then, on Friday 150 new candidates were sworn in on the steps of Brooklyn Borough Hall.

Reports indicated an elderly woman was trapped on the second floor of the home. While operating with the engine company, Firefighter Anthony Picozzi tried, but was unable to advance with just his extinguisher. The line was charged and established some control of the hall and soaked Picozzi, who dashed up the stairs into the superheated hallway.

Under severe conditions, he found the victim, radioed for help and began the removal. He was joined by an officer, Lieutenant Pecora of Engine 157. Together, they dragged the woman back the way they had come and down the stairs. Firefighter Anthony Picozzi was awarded a medal.

Firefighter George Kreuscher of Rescue Company 1 operates a hose line under a pier in the East River at 118th Street. The FDNY designated Rescues 1 and 2 as in-water firefighting teams in 1983. (Photo by John Redin)

FDNY Scuba Team

On July 20, 1983, Department Order 97 officially designated Rescue Companies 1 and 2 as in-water firefighting teams. Since the Welfare Island bus crash in March of 1963, firefighters had been talking about the lifesaving use of self-contained underwater breathing apparatus (SCUBA). This, coupled with difficult fires that burned underneath city piers, stimulated action. Rescue Company 2 had a SCUBA club for years and after a stubborn pier fire at 17th Street and the Hudson River in July of 1981, plans for in-water firefighting began.

Equipment was purchased and several successful operations quickly extinguished pier fires. On January 22, 1983, Firefighter Lee Ielpi of Rescue Company 2 made a successful rescue dive into a submerged van. The vehicle was in 12 feet of ink-black water at the foot of the India Street pier in Brooklyn. Ielpi removed a young man who later was resuscitated on shore, even though he had been under water for 30 minutes. This proved that underwater search and rescue was possible for FDNY units. Advanced dive training was completed by members of the FDNY Scuba Team in November of 1983.

A blaze erupted in a sixth-floor apartment of the luxury East Side high-rise at 240 East 27th Street in Manhattan on August 1, 1983, at about 10 p.m. Heavy smoke filled the building, causing some panicked tenants to flee to the roof of the 27-story structure. The fire was brought under control quickly with only two civilian injuries.

Less than two hours later, an arsonist set fire to a Washington Heights apartment building at 2185 Amsterdam Avenue, near 168th Street, at 11:35 p.m. The fire started in a third-floor stairwell of the six-story building and quickly spread inside. Flames engulfed the three upper floors and the roof. A man plunged five floors to his death while trying to escape by climbing down a drain pipe. Twenty-four people were injured in the three-alarm blaze.

On April 4, 1984, two buildings under renovation suddenly collapsed. Two workers were killed and a third was trapped. Firefighters searched the rubble and voids, looking for the trapped man. He was located in the basement that could be reached only through a void.

Utilities were cut and the floor was shored as a rescue operation began to free the trapped man. A 20-inch water main was broken, filling the cellar. Two Hurst Tools were brought into position and used to make the final lift to free the man. Five members of the Department were awarded medals for risking their lives to save the trapped worker.

On the 23rd of April, 1984, Ladder Company 26 responded to a fire at 50 East 104th Street in Harlem. The fire was on the 12th floor of the high-rise fireproof building. Upon arrival, heavy fire was blowing out the windows. A panic-stricken man was seen briefly at the last window of the apartment. Lieutenant John J. Fanning and his forcible entry team took the elevator to the floor below and raced the stairs to the 12th floor, where they met a frantic woman screaming that her child also was trapped.

They hurried down the smoke-filled public hall to the fire apartment. Heavy fire conditions involved the living room and hall. Fanning ducked and dashed past the fire. Despite the extreme heat, the officer crouched and ran, knowing his time would be limited. Making the rear hall to the bedrooms, the officer now was trapped. With conditions deteriorating, he found a bedroom, dove in and closed the door.

In the room, he found the man and three small children huddled by a window. With no way out except the way he came, Fanning explained his plan. He protected the children under his coat and gave his air hose to the man to hold onto and returned to the oven-like conditions. On his way back, he was met by his forcible entry team, who helped to remove the children. Lieutenant John Fanning was awarded a medal for his bravery.

On August 30, 1984, Ladder Company 2 was returning from a run when they noticed a worker dangling next to a broken scaffold, nine stories above 51st Street. With the worker's belt attached only by a small piece of rope and with the possibility the scaffold could break away at any moment, Firefighter Dennis Anderson positioned the aerial directly under the swaying scaffold and climbed up to the dangling worker.

The man was wedged between the wall and scaffold and was suffering with a broken arm. Anderson carefully pushed the scaffold away, to allow the worker release. The man could not be released from his safety belt, so Anderson moved directly under him and took the worker's weight on his shoulders until additional help arrived.

A lifesaving rope with a pre-tied bowline on a bight was lowered from the 11th-floor setback. While perched on the top of the 100-foot aerial, Anderson slipped the leg loops around the victim and tied a slippery hitch. The small safety rope was released and the worker was pulled up and in a window on the floor above. Firefighter Dennis Anderson was awarded a medal for his strong-armed, acrobatic rescue.

On November 10, 1983, the FDNY officially welcomed the newly formed organization – The Honor Legion of the New York City Fire Department. The Legion is open only to Department members who have been awarded Class I, II or III awards for deeds of valor performed at imminent risk to their lives.

In early 1984, the FDNY adopted personal distress alarm devices for firefighters. (The devices had been tested in the field since 1980.) The PASS alarms (Personal Alert Safety System) were purchased for the Department by the New York Fire Safety Foundation and Chase Manhattan Bank. The device emits a 95-decibel alarm when no motion is sensed for 20 to 30 seconds.

On October 15, 1984, Hazardous Materials Company 1 went into service. Haz-Mat was quartered with Engine Company 288 in Maspeth, Queens. The new, specially trained and equipped unit responded city-wide to handle most any kind of hazardous materials incident.

On the morning of November 23, 1984, Ladder Company 35 arrived at 166 West 72nd Street in Manhattan for a fire on the sixth floor. Reaching the floor, members were confronted with a distraught woman, mumbling that her baby was trapped. Without hesitation, Firefighter Thomas Bala entered the room and began a search. Arriving second-due, Ladder Company 25 raised their aerial to the fire floor and two members, Firefighters Kevin Yard and Stephen Johnson, started up.

Suddenly, Firefighter Bala was at the window with the entire room behind him filling with fire. He could not reach the aerial and he faced a six-story drop. A portable ladder was taken up 25's aerial by the chauffeur, Firefighter Bruce Newbery, and a bridge was made across to the trapped firefighter, who now had flames blowing out over his head.

Meanwhile, in the street, Rescue Company 1, re-directed from another run, had arrived and entered the building just prior to Bala showing at the window. Firefighter Thomas Baker, the Rescue chauffeur, saw Bala as he was getting his gear on and dashed for the idle tower ladder nearby. With no time to lose repositioning the rig, he dropped the jacks where they were, flattening a Cadillac in the process. Baker jumped into the bucket and started up directly under Bala, the precarious, improvised ladder bridge and the debris being blown from the window by the raging fire.

The fire was almost engulfing Bala. Johnson took action and began to climb out onto the unsupported ladder bridge. He reached for Bala, who calmly handed him his mask. Johnson dropped the mask and continued toward Bala. Reaching the burning firefighter, Johnson was about to pull Bala out of the window when Newbery told him to wait. He could see the tower ladder rising up below them.

Kevin Yard, standing on the tip of the aerial, held the top of the ladder while Newbery held the bottom. Johnson grasped Bala while he laid across the ladder, attempting to avoid the terrible heat pouring out the window above him. Baker arrived just below Bala, now with both legs out the window, holding the sill with one hand and leaning on the ladder with the other. The room behind him completely filled with fire and Bala's coat ignited as Baker reached across the ladder and pulled the firefighter out of the window and across the ladder into the bucket.

Baker quickly beat the flames out on Bala's coat, helped him remove it and then started back to the street. Bala was transported to the New York Hospital Burn Center with first-, second- and third-degree burns. Firefighters Yard, Johnson and Baker were awarded medals for saving the life of a Brother firefighter. The trapped baby was a bird named Baby.

"An odor of smoke" was the description of the alarm Brooklyn units responded to on January 22, 1985, at 2:56 a.m. Companies responded to 41 Hall Street, a knitting mill building, in the Navy Yard section of Brooklyn. Firefighters reached the second floor and found only light smoke. It then was determined the fire was in the basement. Faulty sprinklers, bolted doors, frozen standpipes, a bitter-cold, 11-degree temperature and the complex of buildings – a labyrinth of structures – all worked together to create a major fire situation.

The Department ended up with a building with nine floors of fire. Several other buildings in the square-block complex also were affected in what became a 10-alarm fire.

A verbal alarm from the quarters of Rescue Company 1 at 7:26 p.m. evolved into the largest single-building fire to strike New York City since 1967. This blaze also went to 10 alarms with lightning speed on the sub-freezing night of January 23, 1985. The eight-story 125- x 90-foot Wieser Piano Company warehouse, located at 524 West 43rd Street, in the heart of Hell's Kitchen, burned with a vengeance for three hours. The building's north wall collapsed and destroyed the quarters of Rescue Company 1, next door.

July 15, 1985, was the hottest day of the year and about to get hotter. Ladder Company 43 was sent to 150 West 84th Street on the West Side of Manhattan as an extra truck above the "All-hands" at 12:38 p.m. Water problems were evident as they rolled in to the top-floor fire in the five-story multiple dwelling. A report indicated firefighters were trapped.

A concerted effort was begun to reach Captain Kevin Byrnes, who was cut off at a window with a major cockloft fire burning over his head. Ladder Company 22's roofman, Firefighter Robert J. Hannon, saw the officer at a window and told him to hang on; a rope was on the way. Firefighter James G. Sears of Ladder Company 43 arrived with the lifesaving rope. Hannon tied the knots on Sears. Both firefighters were aware the spongy roof beneath them was about ready to collapse.

Sears went over the five-foot parapet and was lowered to the fifth-floor window, where he picked up the Captain as thick, hot smoke pumped out the window around them. Both were lowered to the ground by Hannon, who was taking quite a beating on the roof. Hannon quickly left the roof after the evolution was completed. Firefighters James Sears and Robert Hannon had saved the life of a Brother firefighter. For their heroic actions, they were awarded medals.

A smoldering fire in an Ozone Park, Queens, metal-processing plant on August 14, 1985, proved difficult and complicated to extinguish. August 14, 1985, was already a hot, 95-degree day when companies got called to 100-15 94th Avenue at 2:08 p.m. Fire was smoldering in the roof beams of the Liberty Heat Treating Company, a one-story commercial building.

The plant was a virtual hotbed of hazardous materials – sodium and potassium cyanide, nitrates, hydrochloric and other acids, chemicals and oils – all used in the treatment of metals for electroplating purposes.

An accidental failure of the cooling system, due to a broken fan, started the ensuing fire. The resulting situation for the FDNY seemed like a primer on what could possibly go wrong. The combined efforts of the Haz-Mat Units and the 100 firefighters operating at the two-alarm fire took a prudent and careful approach to extinguishment. With every possible hazard from poison to chemical reactions caused by water from fire hoses (a big sign on the building announced: "Use no water. Cyanide on premises"), chemical protective suits and carbon dioxide extinguishers were employed.

Firefighters possibly exposed to toxic chemicals were decontaminated. Fifteen firefighters suffered minor burns and smoke inhalation.

Grand Central Terminal was shut down for 10 hours by a 10-alarm fire on August 28, 1985. The alarm was received at 5:15 a.m. and firefighters made their way deep into the tunnel system below the majestic station. Four separate fires were started simultaneously in four unattached commuter coaches stored three levels underground. Four hundred firefighters from every borough rotated in shifts. Operating for 15 minutes at a time, the duration of their masks, firefighters battled the heat, smoke and the long trek through the maze-like tunnel system. They positioned hose lines across five city blocks, suffered through dense smoke and operated on greasy, perilous railroad ties.

Fire Marshals determined the fire to be arson. Signs indicated that homeless people had been living in a least one of the cars. By 9:02 a.m., the fire was brought under control. Fifty people were treated at the scene, with 10 civilians and 19 firefighters taken to area hospitals.

Fire companies responded to an above-ground air compressor fire at 182nd Street and the Harlem River Drive in Manhattan on September 4, 1985, at 5:26 p.m. Operations at this fire led to the discovery of 90 water tunnel workers trapped in a 550-foot-deep tunnel. The generator fire spread, knocking out electrical power to lights and work elevators in the "Third Water Tunnel," one of three being built to provide the city with water from upstate.

Firefighters rescued 12 workers stranded in a work elevator stalled 50 feet below ground. Five others stuck at the base of the shaft climbed a ladder to get out. The remaining 73 "sandhogs" navigated their way toward a tunnel exit on Roosevelt Island and exited at eight p.m.

Arriving firefighters were startled by a 60-foot geyser of high-octane gasoline erupting in Willowbrook, near the Victory Boulevard exit of the Staten Island Expressway on September 23, 1985, at 9:15 a.m. A backhoe accidentally had knocked out a pipeline valve, spilling 58,000 gallons of fuel. Three hours were needed to plug the three-inch gash in the pipeline, while 7000 gallons of foam was blanketed across the huge pool of fuel.

Absorbent booms were placed to contain the spread, while a huge vacuum was used to separate the gas from the water and to remove sand, water, gas and foam residue. Thirty homes were evacuated and more than an hour into the operation, vapors were still near the explosive range. The quick and efficient work of the FDNY paid off: there was little reported damage to the nearby wild life preserve and most of the gas was retrieved by absorbent pads and vacuuming. There were no injuries.

At 9:10 a.m., on October 11, 1985, Ladder Company 42 responded to Bronx Box 2261 for a fire at 634 Prospect Avenue. Smoke was pushing out the windows on the fourth floor of the six-story building. Tenants were pouring down the stairs as firefighters weaved their way up. On the fire floor, Captain James F. McDonnell and his forcible entry team, Firefighters Peter Bielfeld and Daniel Saitta, crawled into the fire apartment beneath the heat.

The trio worked deeper into the apartment until they found the living room, where they spread out. Leading the way, Captain McDonnell reached the entrance to the next room, the master bedroom. Some 40 feet into the apartment, the officer realized conditions had turned for the worse and a flashover was imminent.

The Captain turned and shouted his last order, "Get Out!" No sooner had he done this than the room ignited into a fireball. Fire engulfed McDonnell, but the officer's instincts overrode even self-preservation – he shoved Firefighter Peter Bielfeld clear, then fell to the wave of heat and fire. Captain James McDonnell made a sacrifice that saved the life of the men with whom he was working. For his unimaginable bravery, he was awarded the Bennett Medal posthumously.

Ten days before Christmas 1985, a five-alarm fire spread through the Briar Wyck apartment complex in Briarwood, Queens. The accidental electrical fire broke out in the seven-story building at 86-25 Van Wyck Expressway and spread inside the walls. For two and a half hours, firefighters fought both water pressure problems and the spreading fire. One hundred fifty residents were left homeless, but uninjured.

A three-story, brick, three-family house at 1740 Richmond Terrace, Staten Island, was the scene of a five-alarm fire on February 1, 1986, at 5:28 a.m. Firefighter Steven Ruggirello of Ladder Company 80 spotted the fire while driving home and turned in the alarm. Then, he raced to the building to search for trapped occupants. The building had only two exits, a front and rear stairway, fully involved. There were no fire escapes or sprinklers.

As fire companies arrived, the scene was one of pandemonium. Three adults and three children had escaped earlier before the stairs filled with flames. Two adults had jumped from third-story windows. Their three children were saved by firefighters, but later died of cardiac arrest and smoke inhalation at Saint Vincent's Hospital. A four-month-old and her grandfather also succumbed to the heavy smoke.

Off-duty firefighters forget they are not working whenever and wherever they see a fire. Firefighter John P. Sullivan, II, a 29-year veteran of the FDNY, was driving on Interstate 95, heading home after a visit to a friend in Throgs Neck. As he approached the New Rochelle toll plaza, he saw a burning van lying on its side, a crushed car beneath it. He instinctively raced to the scene, leapt onto the van with flames shooting 15 feet into the air and methodically pulled two adults and two children from the smoldering interior. Then, he proceeded over to the wrecked car, forced the door open with his bare hands, disengaged the seat belt and lifted the unconscious driver from the car. Moments later, the gas tank exploded.

By the time State Troopers and Westchester firefighters arrived, Sullivan already had saved five lives, but made no mention of it. He simply stated his name as a witness and went home; other witnesses alerted authorities to his heroism.

Acting as a private citizen in a jurisdiction outside of New York City, the 53-year-old aide to the Chief of the Fifth Division was ineligible for official Department recognition. However, he did receive a special commendation from the Mayor of New Rochelle and at a ceremony at City Hall, he was awarded the Presidential Medal of Honor.

On July 11, 1986, at 5:19 p.m., a one-alarm fire swept through the lower floors of the 17-story Brooklyn Arms welfare hotel in Fort Greene, killing a family of four brothers and sisters. The young children, aged seven years to 18 months, were left alone all day in a 12- x 12-foot, second-floor room while their parents collected bottles and cans.

When the parents returned to the 268 Ashland Place Hotel, the fire had been out for two hours. The parents were arrested for endangering the lives of the children. The cause of the fire was a mattress fire started by one of the children playing with matches. The hotel, formerly known as the Grenada Hotel and converted several years ago from a YMCA into a welfare hotel, housed 263 homeless families.

On September 21, 1986, another fire struck Grand Central Terminal. This time, it was an accidental two-alarm fire that was discovered at 6:40 p.m. in a small switching station room, two stories below the Waldorf Astoria Hotel. The estimated 90,000 commuters who ride the Metro-North experienced delays all night and for several weeks thereafter.

Forty-year-old traffic reporter Jane Dornacker was in the middle of transmitting rush-hour traffic updates on the air when she abruptly shouted, "Hit the water!" Seconds later, there was dead silence. It was October 22, 1986, at 4:45 p.m., when people in the vicinity of the Intrepid Sea, Air and Space Museum on Pier 86 at 45th Street in Manhattan, saw the WNBC Radio helicopter hover as low as 40 feet off the ground, swoop over the carrier and attempt an emergency landing alongside the West Side Highway. The engine stopped suddenly, emitted a grinding noise, tore through a fence, plunged into the water and sank in 25 feet of water.

Rescue Company 1 received a teleprinter message one minute later and was out the door while members donned SCUBA gear in the back of the rig. At the scene two minutes later, Firefighter Paul Hashagen dove into the dark waters and located the submerged craft on the river's bottom. Opening the cockpit door, he removed the pilot, William Pate, and swam him to the surface, where he was turned over to other members of the company who had entered the water. Mouth-to-mouth was begun in the water until the victim could be pulled to the street level.

Hashagen returned to the water-filled copter, located Dornacker and brought her to the surface. In the street, a major lifesaving operation was underway as members of Engine Companies 54 and 34 and Ladder Companies 4 and 21 were handed the victims and began resuscitation efforts, which were supplemented by the arrival of EMS. Both victims had been underwater for more than nine minutes and were not breathing when brought to the surface. Dornacker could not be revived and died three and a half hours later in Saint Vincent's Hospital.

Pate's breathing was restored by FDNY members and he was rushed to Bellevue in critical condition. After a long convalescence, he made a full recovery. Firefighter Paul Hashagen was awarded a medal and the members of Rescue Company 1 were given the first Burn Center Unit Citation Medal.

On the night of December 3, 1986, FDNY units responded to an explosion at a New York Telephone Company garage at 640 West 153rd Street. A truck off-loading gasoline was leaking the fuel into the cellar of the garage, which ignited with explosive force. The blast ruptured a natural gas main. In turn, the escaping natural gas and gasoline from ruptured tanks in the cellar were burning and the truck still was leaking fuel.

At 8:50 p.m., an ERS box was received. Engine Company 84 was on-scene within minutes and transmitted a 10-75. Ladder Company 34 arrived quickly with Lieutenant William F. Maloney in command. The officer ordered a nearby multiple dwelling evacuated and onlookers to be moved back. Maloney then moved in for a closer size-up.

Approaching one of the gaping holes in the concrete floor created by the blast, Maloney could hear a voice calling for help through the darkness. The fire officer moved into the blazing, rubble-strewn structure. Climbing over a buckled section of concrete, he saw a man conscious, but bleeding from a severe gash in his head. Additionally, he possibly was suffering a broken leg. Maloney radioed the chief, then extracted the man and carried him back over the buckled concrete with flames – being fed from several sources – blazing around them.

After bringing the victim to safety, Maloney returned to search for additional victims who reportedly might still be inside. Three cylinders were expended by Lieutenant Maloney during his searches, each of which could have been ended by an explosion of gasoline of accumulated natural gas vapors. For his extraordinary courage, Lieutenant William Maloney was awarded the Bennett Medal.

Gasoline again was the problem faced by FDNY units as they battled a five-alarm fire on Sunday, December 28, 1986. The blaze started at 1:18 a.m. at a Long Island City oil storage facility during a fuel transfer. The fire burned through a large part of the block-long Ditmars Oil Associates company at 53-02 11th Street and threatened six large storage tanks that were located extremely close to major traffic arteries and the Long Island Rail Road.

More than 200 firefighters from every borough battled the river of fire that rolled down the yard, across the sidewalk, around 53rd Avenue and into the sewers. Foam was used to press the attack as tower ladders doused exposed tanks to keep them cool.

On February 18, 1987, an electrical fire burned out cables on the first floor of a telephone switching station in Brooklyn, cutting service to a 200-square-block area of Bushwick and Bedford-Stuyvesant. This affected 41,000 customers, 10 hospitals and two police precincts.

One hundred mask-equipped firefighters battled the stubborn fire for eight hours. Toxic PVC fumes affected five firefighters who received medical attention. Mobile cellular telephones were installed in the hospitals and the police precincts. Banks of pay phones were installed in the area for public use. A month passed before regular service was restored completely.

A seemingly minor trash fire turned into a high-rise inferno that took the lives of seven people and caused numerous minor injuries. A sprinkler system that was shut down set the stage for catastrophe in the Schomburg Plaza apartment complex at 1295 Fifth Avenue in Manhattan on March 22, 1987. Smoldering trash was lodged between the 27th and 29th floors, unchecked by sprinklers, then burst into flames. The Department was notified at 7:57 a.m. on that otherwise quiet Sunday morning.

Fire extended through construction openings into several apartments on the 23rd, 33rd and 34th floors. Missing closet and chute hopper doors allowed fire to extend onto the 29th floor. Three people, unable to escape from their 33rd-floor apartments, jumped to their deaths. Four other victims were found during searches.

A gas explosion tore through a Bronx grocery store at 3:48 p.m. on April 8, 1987. The store, located at 2634 Third Avenue, was rocked by the explosion and then flattened as the vacant, three-story building next door fell on it. Six people were killed instantly and 29 others were injured. Two men were trapped in the cellar beneath eight feet of tangled wreckage. Lieutenant Paul J. McFadden and Firefighters Nicholas J. Giordano, John Norman, Robert W. Greene and Harry Christensen of Rescue Company 3 earned medals that day for their tunneling, shoring, cutting and lifting, while in extreme danger due to secondary collapse. After six hours of toiling, they were able to free the two trapped workers.

Aerial ladders converge on a four-alarm fire at Amsterdam Avenue and 148th Street in Manhattan, February 1987. (Photo by Harvey Eisner)

On May 26, 1987, at 12:21 a.m., Box 693 sent Brooklyn companies to 251 Hart Avenue, the site of a fire that was fed by highly volatile chemicals used to process "crack" cocaine. Heavy fire on the second floor trapped people on the third floor. Members of several units teamed up to make several spectacular rescues.

Firefighter Peter Hassler placed Ladder Company's 102's aerial to a third-floor window and ascended the ladder with Firefighter Patrick Brown of Rescue Company 2. Driven back by extreme heat several times, Brown dove in the window, while Hassler maintained his severely exposed position on the ladder's tip, backing up Brown. Fire began venting from the second floor, but Hassler refused to move from his position. Moments later, Brown crawled up to the window and handed Hassler a child. Shielding the child from the fire below them, he descended the ladder.

Meanwhile, Firefighter Joseph Borst of Ladder Company 111 rescued a semi-conscious man from a third-floor window, then entered the smoke- and heat-filled third floor, found four people and removed them to the bucket. Borst then re-entered the top floor, joined up with Brown and helped remove one of the unconscious children, then the mother. Frederick H. Lawrence of Squad Company 1 also entered the top floor over the aerial ladder and rescued a six-year-old girl from the blazing hallway.

The collective lifesaving efforts of these members earned them medals, but more importantly, saved several lives.

A thunderous explosion tore through a plumbing supply store in the Borough Park section of Brooklyn on the morning of July 21, 1987. Workers dropped a 20-pound propane tank down a stairwell into a basement, where 12 additional propane tanks and nine acetylene tanks were stored. The leaking gas found an ignition source and caused a tremendous explosion.

Passersby were hurled into the street and the plumbing store and two other stores collapsed. Box 2533 at 9:44 a.m. brought fire units racing to the scene. First-due Engine Company 250 stretched a line to protect injured victims on the surface of the rubble. Ladder Company 148 began removing people from the roof and helped remove injured from the surrounding rubble.

As the second-due Engine Company 330 arrived, reports stated that people were trapped on the second floor. Firefighters John Fassari and Brian Foley (Foley of Ladder Company 172 was working in Engine 330) made their way into the building and located a trapped man. Fassari, with Foley holding him by the ankles, stretched down into a tunnel-like vertical void and pulled out the trapped man. With fire burning nearby, smoke made the operation even more dangerous. A second venture retrieved an older gentleman.

Changing places, a third void entry saw Foley push aside an appliance to free and remove an elderly woman. All three rescues were accomplished without the benefit of protective hose line and the tight space denied them their ability to wear masks. Firefighters John Fassari and Brian Foley were awarded medals for their exceptional bravery and teamwork. Four alarms were needed to control the fires touched off by the explosion. Four people lost their lives and 35 people were injured, including a dozen firefighters.

Four teenagers ignited gasoline in a fifth-floor hallway of the Hamilton Hotel, near 138th Street in Harlem, at 3:02 a.m. on October 1, 1987. Five people, including a 10-month-old boy, were injured critically and 25 others were treated for lesser injuries.

Flames swept the floor, driving 112 families, including 400 children, into the street. Thirty people were rescued over ladders and another 30 were led down stairs.

Rescue Company 5 responded to the United States Navy home port construction site in Stapleton, Staten Island, on December 28, 1987. A hard hat diver was trapped beneath an 87-ton concrete pipe in 60 feet of water. Firefighters David H. Riechel, Jr., and Michael P. Barone dove to help the trapped man. Barone worked directly under the huge pipe, attempting to free the diver. Reinforcing rods punctured his suit, allowing cold water to enter and limit his time in the water. Riechel made the initial dive, located the trapped man, assured he was able to breathe and sized up the problem.

Riechel then helped devise a plan to lift the pipe, made a second dive to monitor the diver and controlled the lift by communications. Operating in cold, dark and dangerous water, he was able to successfully free the trapped diver. Both Riechel and Barone were awarded medals for their dangerous underwater rescue operation.

In 1988, a new tool was field-tested by FDNY units and ordered for purchase. The Rabbitt Tool, a hydraulic forcible entry tool, allowed one member to force a door in a fraction of the time needed previously. The tool was also relatively lightweight and reliable and became very popular with the members of the Department.

Borough Park plumbing supply house propane explosion, July 1987. (Photo by Harvey Eisner)

Another new tool to the FDNY – a Thermal Imaging Camera – was issued to Rescue Company 1, in Manhattan, in early 1988. This electronic device is capable of discerning less than one degree difference in temperature and has become an extremely useful tool to search for victims in building collapses and dense smoke.

Four lives were lost in the first five-alarm blaze to hit New York in more than a year and a half. Eventually, 200 firefighters and 50 pieces of equipment responded to the 10-story, 100-apartment building at 135 East 50th Street in Manhattan. The fire started in a doctor's office on the ground floor, but doors in the stairwells were chocked open, allowing the smoke and heat to be drawn up through the entire building.

Three victims were found on the 10th floor and the other victim was found between the first and second floors. Although most of the residents had fled safely, firefighters rescued several and removed them to safety. Nine civilians and 16 firefighters received minor injuries.

A quick-spreading fire destroyed seven stores at 205-07 Hillside Avenue in Hollis, Queens, on January 21, 1988. The 10:28 p.m. blaze started in a second-floor restaurant and spread to other stores, including a bank and a city councilman's office. Four alarms were required to extinguish the fire.

Another four-alarm fire was fought in the Bronx, four days later on January 25th. This fire at 603 and 605 Beech Terrace forced the evacuation of 100 residents. The fire started in the first floor in the center of the "H" shaped, six-story building. Flames extended up both wings of the building and traveled as far as the fourth floor before it could be stopped by firefighters.

Four alarms were sounded for a fire on the seventh floor of 360 East 72nd Street in Manhattan on January 29th. This afternoon fire proved difficult to extinguish because of an extremely high heat condition that developed in the 30-story fireproof building. The extra units were utilized to search the smoke-filled upper floors of the high-rise.

A fire in the six-story Liberty High School gutted the building and went to five alarms on February 13, 1988. The building at 120 West 46th Street in Manhattan was built in 1880 and designated as a landmark in 1982. This building was the former site of the High School of Performing Arts and the school on which the 1980 film *Fame* and the subsequent television show of the same name were based.

Seven hours later, a fire in a lacquer factory fed on chemicals and spread quickly in the three-story building at First Avenue and 53rd Street on the Brooklyn waterfront. The fire extended to the adjacent five-story warehouse and did major damage. The blaze was fought for five hours and required the efforts of 200 firefighters. Twenty-nine firefighters were injured.

Manhattan Box 1514 was transmitted at 10:40 a.m. on March 14, 1988. Ladder 23 was assigned and found heavy fire venting from several windows on the fifth floor. Firefighter Robert M. Marcoux of Ladder 23 made his way to the roof of the blazing structure and began to vent at that level, along with the roofman from Ladder Company 30, Firefighter Jim Ryan.

Below in the fire apartment, Lieutenant Michael Rogers led the nozzle team from 37 Engine into the burning flat. Suddenly, an explosion of flames injured the officer and separated him from his men. Disoriented and in an effort to escape the growing body of fire, Rogers crawled into a room and made his way to a window on an enclosed shaft. The exhausted and injured officer then transmitted a "Mayday" over his radio.

The two roofmen raced to the shaft and were joined by Firefighter Hugo Herold of Rescue Company 3. The conditions in the shaft were growing extreme as the fire extended from the fifth floor to the sixth. The shaftway was filled with smoke, pumping from the growing fire area. The officer was taking a terrific beating just staying at the window. He was relieved when voice contact was made with the members on the roof.

Within moments, Marcoux was lowered on a lifesaving rope by Herold and Ryan. Reaching the floor, Marcoux found himself a window away from the trapped officer and had to swing across to his location. Marcoux then removed a window gate to allow him to pull the injured officer clear. Holding Rogers firmly in his arms, Marcoux was lowered past venting fire to a lower-floor window that had to be forced.

Lieutenant Mike Rogers was taken to Cornell Burn Center and treated for burns and smoke inhalation. Firefighter Robert Marcoux (the great grandson of Battalion Chief John J. Bresnan, killed in the line of duty on December 29, 1894), was awarded the Bonner Medal for his rescue.

Two Manhattan tenements sustained heavy damage on March 20, 1988, when a fire swept through the buildings at 536 and 538 West 153rd Street in Harlem. The blaze broke out at 8:07 p.m. and drove the 100 residents from the building. During the operation, a massive natural gas explosion erupted within number 538. Forty-foot flames blasted through one of the floors. Later, the top four floors of 536 collapsed inward.

Miraculously, despite the widespread devastation and damage to the buildings, no one was killed. Eight firefighters and two civilians were treated for minor injuries. It took several hours before the fire was declared under control.

Three days later, an arson fire went to four alarms at 60 West 129th Street in Harlem. The seven-story apartment building sustained heavy damage with almost half of the apartments rendered uninhabitable. Apparently, the fire began in a vacant apartment being used as a crack den. Forty people were left homeless.

As the result of an explosion, thick clouds of black smoke pumped into the evening sky on April 21, 1988, as a carbon paper factory burned at 1075 Irving Avenue in Brooklyn. Four alarms were transmitted, bringing 35 companies and 120 firefighters from both Brooklyn and Queens.

Five tower ladders and deck pipes directed large-caliber streams into the burning factory to knock down the tremendous heat build-up. Exterior streams gave way to hand lines and firefighters entered the badly damaged structure to accomplish the final extinguishment. Two factory workers and three firefighters were injured.

An early-morning fire raced through a six-story, H-shaped building at 2185 Grand Concourse on June 10, 1988. Fire broke out at 4:51 a.m. in the recently renovated Bronx apartment building. Flames moved quickly through the top floor, cockloft and floor below. The damage to the top two floors was heavy and a partial collapse occurred on the top floor. Twenty-one firefighters were injured, including three members who required extended care at the New York Hospital-Cornell Burn Center. One firefighter was treated at the hyperbaric chamber on City Island.

On Friday, August 5, 1988, at 2:59 a.m., a man set fire to a shack that stood in a vacant plot being used as a vegetable garden. The flames soon were out of control and spreading into three adjacent apartment buildings at 161 Noll Street and 1004 and 1006 Flushing Avenue, in the Bushwick section of Brooklyn.

Four passersby braved intense heat and smoke to pound on doors and wake sleeping occupants. The last of the tenants was led clear of the building just before the interior stairs collapsed. The fire went to four alarms, bringing 120 firefighters to the scene. Eleven firefighters were injured, including one who broke a wrist and ankle in a fall.

The Rescue Liaison Unit was added to the FDNY in June of 1988. They acted as an inter-agency coordinator during rescue operations and at joint operations between the FDNY and other city agencies. The unit also helped to coordinate the Rescue Companies, Haz-Mat and the Marine Division.

Five designated ladder companies, one in each borough, were trained as Ladder/Rescue Companies in 1988. Their function was not to be special-called as rescue companies, but to augment the operations of a rescue already in progress.

At 1:02 p.m. on August 12, 1988, the steaming hot streets of midtown Manhattan began to fill with the sounds of sirens and air horns. A stubborn, smoky fire was burning in the Empire State Building at 34th Street and Fifth Avenue. The flames were brought under control rather quickly, but the fire had done enough damage to knock out one television and eight radio stations. One thousand people evacuated the building during the fire operations.

At 12:38 p.m., August 21, 1988, Bronx Box 2935 sent companies to 1748-54 Jerome Avenue, a one-story taxpayer that contained six stores. An accidental fire started in the cellar and spread quickly. Arriving units had no way of knowing that the below-grade area was being used as an illegal social club until they were met by frenzied civilians, blackened by the smoke, emerging from the club.

The club – "El Hoyo" (The Hole) – was operating in full swing as 100 people jammed the 24- x 48-foot "storage area." With only one way out, the stairs quickly became clogged. Ladder Company 27 arrived to face complete pandemonium. Captain Richard Jacquin of Ladder Company 59, working overtime, was in command. He made his way through a crowd of hysterical people. Smoke was pouring from every opening in the structure; burned and injured civilians were lying on the sidewalk, in the street and on parked cars. Other people were pounding frantically on steel roll-down gates of the store adjacent to the fire building, screaming that people were trapped inside.

Fire Department units literally had to fight their way through the crowds. Jacquin kept his cool, set up a guide rope and prepared to enter the building. The Captain managed to squeeze under the gate that could be opened only 18 inches. He was followed by

his forcible entry team, Firefighters James Forsyth and Dennis Fennell. Inside the shop, they were confronted with a high heat and dense smoke condition. Heavy fire was already in the cockloft above them as they began to search.

Weaving through a maze of disabled autos, car parts, motorcycles and other obstacles, they located an entrance to the cellar. Hot, acrid smoke pumped up the small stairway. Jacquin descended and continued searching until he located an unconscious man. The officer dragged and carried him to safety. Firefighter Fennell also found an unconscious victim in the cellar and was removing her when met by Jacquin, who helped carry her to the street where Fennell began resuscitation efforts.

Firefighter Forsyth had located an unconscious man in the cellar and was almost out of air as he reached the bottom of the stairs. Jacquin joined Forsyth and together, they removed the victim to the street, where he was revived by Forsyth. Six people died as a result of this fire and 40 were injured. As stated in the official report, there were many acts of heroism performed at this fire. The actions taken by Forsyth and Fennell, without the benefit of hose line protection,

"El Hoyo" social club fire, Jerome Avenue in the Bronx. Six people were killed in this illegal, after-hours club, August 21, 1988. (Photo by Harvey Eisner)

Members work feverishly, attempting to revive smoke inhalation victim rescued from "El Hoyo" social club. (Photo by Steve Spak)

were deemed worthy of medals. The Bennett Medal was awarded to Captain Jacquin for his bravery and leadership.

A four-alarm warehouse fire at Cypress Avenue and 132nd Street in the South Bronx lit up the night sky and forced the closing of the Triborough Bridge on September 7, 1988. Five hundred feet of the several thousand-foot-long building were involved.

Two hundred firefighters battled the blaze which, at one point, was so intense that its heat scorched the paint off the underside of the bridge span above. A poor water supply complicated matters and a low tide ruled out fireboats supplying water. Long stretches and tower ladders extinguished the fire.

A gasoline delivery truck overturned and exploded at the corner of Metropolitan and Union Avenues in the Williamsburg section of Brooklyn on October 11, 1988, at 9:20 p.m. Arriving FDNY units were confronted with a fireball that spread from the wreckage into a diner, a commercial building and two homes. The flames were fed by 3000 gallons of gasoline spilling from the overturned tanker. Amazingly, no one was killed. The truck driver, four people in the car, two people in the diner and a firefighter were injured, however. Two hundred firefighters responded and used 500 gallons of foam to quell the blaze.

Construction workers trying to fix a cracked wall excavated a trench alongside a six-story commercial building at 24 West 31st Street in Manhattan on October 24, 1988, at 3:15 p.m. Office workers in the structure felt a trembling, then the building opened outward and collapsed, spilling its contents into the parking lot next door. The luckier individuals were able to cling to sections of walls and floors and quickly were rescued by arriving firefighters.

Several surface victims and a person partially pinned were removed from the pile as Rescue Company 1 began to check voids. Special-called Rescue Company 3 and the collapse rig arrived and augmented the void search. Firefighter John P. O'Connell found a void and was able to locate a man pinned beneath tons of debris. With the assistance of Lieutenant Peter Lund and Firefighter Bryant Stiles, O'Connell worked for 30 minutes to free the trapped man.

Nine hours after the initial alarm, the last victim – a woman – was dug clear by rescuers. One man died in the collapse, but several were saved from deep within the debris, thanks to the heroic efforts of firefighters. John O'Connell was awarded a medal for his bravery and skill.

A 72-unit apartment building blaze became the first five-alarm fire the borough of Staten Island had transmitted in more than 11 years. The fire began in a fourth-floor apartment when sparks from a faulty splice in a lamp cord ignited a mattress on a bed. The family spent 10 minutes attempting to extinguish the blaze before calling the Fire Department.

Arriving units pulled into an advanced fire that was spreading rapidly within the building at 320 Vanderbilt Avenue. Fire raced through the walls, along beams directly to the roof. Twenty-two apartments were destroyed and another 22 were damaged severely. About 100 people were left homeless 10 days before Christmas.

Twenty FDNY units responded to John F. Kennedy International Airport on January 25, 1989, at 7:26 p.m. The three-alarm fire broke out in a storeroom and forced the evacuation of 600 people and delayed the flights of four different airlines.

An extremely heavy smoke condition made firefighting especially hazardous. Thirty-four people were injured: 25 firefighters, seven Port Authority police and two civilians. Half were treated at the scene and the other half were transported to nearby hospitals, all for smoke inhalation.

On Friday, February 3, 1989, units responded to a fire at 217 Van Brunt Street in Brooklyn. An overloaded electrical outlet sparked a blaze that soon was spreading rapidly, trapping many people within the four-story tenement. Trapped occupants were removed through windows to waiting Fire Department ladders. Four civilians were rescued from the roof.

Ladder Company 131 was one of the first units on the scene and Firefighter John P. Devaney, the outside vent man, put his own personal safety aside and entered a third-floor window to search for a mother and children reported to be in the room. Within seconds, the room flashed over. Devaney was found by firefighters, but had suffered fatal burns. Unknown to Devaney, the victims he was searching for had been rescued by other members. Firefighter John Devaney was awarded the Brooklyn Citizens Medal posthumously for his heroic efforts.

Deputy Chief Vincent Dunn supervises rescue efforts at building collapse on West 31st Street in Manhattan. Nine hours after the initial alarm, a woman was removed alive from the rubble, October 24, 1988. (Photo by Steve Spak)

Deputy Chief Vincent Dunn, retired Division 3, spent 27 of his 42-year Fire Department career as a Chief Officer. Chief Dunn regularly contributed to the Department's Official Training Publication, *WNYF*, as well as to numerous other fire service publications. His three books, *Collapse of Burning Buildings, Safety and Survival on the Fireground* and *Command and Control of Fires and Emergencies*, have become operational bibles for firefighters and officers throughout the Fire Service.

In recognition of Chief Dunn's extraordinary contributions to the FDNY and to the cause of Firefighter Training and Safety, the Department proudly presented him with a special award for his dedicated and exemplary service at the Annual Medal Day Ceremony on June 7, 2000.

A young boy playing with friends stepped on a piece of carpet that had been placed over an open manhole near the pier at the foot of Tiffany Street in the Bronx. The child plunged into the water-filled sewer below and disappeared. His friends alerted the Fire Department and Engine Company 73 rolled out of quarters at 5:41 p.m. on that Sunday, April 30, 1989, and were at the scene within minutes.

With several frantic stories being told at once, Firefighter Timothy L. Brown knew this was for real and time was running out. Brown grabbed a Scott mask and the lifesaving rope. Realizing the mask would not allow entry through the small manhole opening, Brown climbed into the bowline-on-a-bite, was tied across the chest and lowered into the dark, 40-degree water below.

Making a series of breath-holding dives, Brown searched the area, feeling for the form of the young boy in the blackness. After several dives, he became aware of several discharge pipes that emptied the storm drain waters into the East River. Unable to swim the distance, he probed carefully with a 10-foot hook, then a 20-foot hook.

At this time, Firefighter Brown was near exhaustion and hypothermic. He was helped from the hole. The rescue effort continued as Rescue Companies 1 and 2 arrived and entered the sewer from both directions with SCUBA gear. The body of the boy was found about an hour later by FDNY divers. For his heroic rescue attempt in the black, dirty water, Firefighter Timothy Brown was awarded a medal.

A traveling carnival set up operations at Beach 92nd Street and Holland Avenue in Rockaway, Queens, on May 8, 1989. At about 9:30 p.m., five teenagers and three adults became trapped on the "Super Loop" ride after a metal light cover broke loose and became wedged in the track mechanism.

Several of the riders managed to free themselves and climb down to the ceiling of the car, which was stuck in an inverted position at the very top of the ride's circular track. For nearly three hours the riders were stuck until they were brought down in pairs via tower ladder.

A four-alarm fire raged in a vacant apartment building at 3603 Broadway in Harlem on June 1, 1989. The building had been taken over by squatters and had a fire earlier in the week. The blaze, labeled a probable arson, spread to a neighboring building, which the city was using to shelter homeless families. The occupants of both buildings managed to escape the fire without injuries, but the firefighters were not as lucky. Thirty-eight firefighters suffered smoke inhalation and heat exhaustion and were treated at hospitals. Two members required treatment at the City Island hyperbaric chamber.

On July 8, 1989, at 5:25 p.m., a 15-year-old boy climbed a six-foot-high spiked fence to retrieve a ball. The lad slipped and a spike pierced his neck and emerged through his mouth. Rescue Company 4 arrived and carefully cut the fence with an oxyacetylene torch. The four- by six-foot section of the fence, with the youth still impaled, were rushed to Elmhurst City Hospital, where firefighters helped doctors in the final removal process. The boy suffered only a minor jaw fracture and required some stitches as a result of the accident.

At 3:27 on the afternoon of July 15, 1989, a natural gas explosion tore through a four-story Washington Heights rooming house. A huge column of fire, shrapnel-like fragments of glass and an intense shock wave erupted from the building at 430 West 145th Street. The blast also caused structural damage to the adjacent buildings and shattered automobile and apartment windows within a 50-foot radius.

Arriving units found the entire inside of the building and the front concrete stairs had collapsed. Train and vehicular traffic was halted to reduce vibrations. Firefighters were able to save a seriously burned man who had survived in an air pocket created by marble windowsills that had fallen over him but, luckily, had not crushed him.

Children playing nearby were caught in a shower of glass and flying debris; two were injured seriously. A man standing across the street also was injured seriously in the throat by flying glass.

A 24-inch section of an underground steampipe ruptured at 6:30 p.m., August 19, 1989, near 20th Street and Third Avenue in the Gramercy Park section of Manhattan. Three people were killed, 29 were injured and thousands of residents were evacuated. Chunks of concrete bombarded apartment windows and automobiles along 20th Street.

First-due units found scores of mud-caked civilians wandering about near the 10-foot-wide crater that was spewing a geyser-like, 100-foot column of steam, asphalt and debris. The force of the escaping steam was deafening and severely hampered communications.

Tower ladders plucked frightened residents from their windows and roof tops. The explosion occurred as Con Edison workers were turning the steam pipe on after completing repairs. Immediate shut down was delayed by the 400-degree heat of the escaping steam. The pipe finally was shut down at 10:15 p.m. To complicate a serious situation, a health emergency was declared when traces of asbestos were discovered five days later.

The FDNY responded to LaGuardia Airport at 11:21 p.m. on September 20, 1989. A USAir Boeing 737, with 55 passengers, slid off the end of a runway after an aborted take-off. The jetliner split into three large pieces, settled halfway in the water and slowly began to sink.

Arriving FDNY units started a major rescue operation. Victims on the surface were retrieved as other members, including FDNY divers, raced the clock to remove people trapped within the sinking fuselage. Firefighters Gerard Murtha and Christopher Blackwell of Rescue Company 3 and Michael Milner of Rescue Company 4 donned cold-water exposure suits and entered the sinking plane. Lieutenant Albert Warta and Firefighter Kevin Smith of Haz-Mat Company 1 donned life jackets and entered the chilly water wearing only their uniforms. Firefighter Carl Feilmoser arrived in the Rescue Liaison unit, donned dive gear and joined the others in the plane.

As the rescuers worked to free trapped people inside, efforts were begun by the three FDNY dive units at the scene to attempt to stabilize the sinking plane. All members were subjected to the dangers of aviation fuel and hydraulic fluids that covered the surface of the water. Additionally, the jagged edges of torn and twisted metal and aluminum seemingly were everywhere.

Warta, Smith and Feilmoser freed a trapped woman and brought her to safety, while Murtha, Blackwell and Milner worked to extricate a woman deep in the jet's tail section. As the rescue efforts continued, the water level inside rose. Undaunted, the rescuers continued their dangerous work. As the trapped woman was being removed, FDNY divers descended beneath the sinking tail section with a large, metal sling, which was attached to the "A-frame" on the rear of Rescue Company 5's rig. This action gave some measure of safety as the sinking had stopped temporarily.

Sixty FDNY units operated in the finest traditions of the Department, helping to rescue numerous passengers. Unfortunately, two women were killed in the crash. Thirty-nine others were injured, six of whom had very serious injuries and were admitted to area hospitals. About 50 rescue workers were treated for exposure to jet fuel and the cold water and assorted minor injuries.

Firefighter Gerry Murtha was presented the Bennett medal for his actions. Lieutenant Warta and Firefighters Blackwell, Milner, Smith and Feilmoser also were awarded medals.

On September 9, 1989, Ladder Company 113 responded to a fire in the five-story tenement at 1776 Bedford Avenue in Brooklyn. Flames were blowing from three fourth-floor windows as Captain Lawrence Brennan and his forcible entry team, Firefighters Thomas Sullivan and Dennis Dowdican, raced into the building.

On the fourth floor, they opened the apartment door and were greeted by a blast of fire that shot across the ceiling above them. Knowing a child was trapped inside, Captain Brennan and Firefighter Sullivan crawled in under the flames as Dowdican attempted to cover them with the extinguisher.

Harvey Eisner's shot looking west down 43rd Street at the height of the January 23, 1985, 10-alarm fire in Manhattan.

Fireman backs down aerial after holding a door against a fire escape window to hold back flames while members clear fire escape above at Eighth Avenue and West 115th Street, Harlem, December 1987. (Photo by Harvey Eisner)

John Lee Gill's outstanding photo of the 10-alarm fire next to the quarters of Rescue 1, January 23, 1985.

Traveling in separate directions to cover more ground, the two moved deeper into the blazing apartment. After searching three rooms, Sullivan found a door to an unsearched bedroom. Conditions in this room were almost untenable, but Sullivan pushed in, flat on his stomach. As his ears began to blister, he found a small child. Turning, he made his way back and tumbled into the hallway.

Sullivan immediately began CPR on the infant, even though the baby's lips and nose were disfigured by the fire. Sullivan was directed to the back seat of a patrol car that raced to the hospital as he continued resuscitation. Due to his valiant efforts, the baby, with burns over 60 percent of his body, survived. Firefighter Thomas Sullivan was presented the Prentice Medal on the steps of City Hall the following year.

On November 13, 1989, Engine Company 92 rolled in on a job at 1110 Washington Street in the Bronx. The three-story, wood-frame apartment building was hidden by smoke pumping out the front door. Lieutenant Richard McVey and his nozzle team, Firefighters John McGowan on nozzle and Robert Bergin, the back-up man, worked their way to the top of the stairs that led down into the basement.

With only booster tank water available until the hydrant could be connected, a holding action was initiated to protect members going above the fire to search. The nozzle team slowly prepared to inch down the cellar stairs. As McGowan tested the strength of the step, the stairs collapsed beneath him. Bergin grabbed hold of McGowan's mask harness and held him in position. The nozzleman's feet dangled in the abyss, with smoke and flames visible below.

The officer attempted to assist, but was unable to reach the imperiled firefighter. The only thing stopping McGowan from falling into the fire below were his arms pressing against the remnants of the stairway and the vise-like grip of Robert Bergin. As fire lapped over their heads and searing heat burned at their skin through their protective gear, Bergin summoned strength that only can be found in situations of life and death. He pulled and lifted the 235-pound McGowan – and his 100 pounds of gear – out of the hole and onto the stair landing, clear of danger.

Firefighter McGowan was treated for burns and later received skin grafts on his hands and legs. Firefighter Robert Bergin was treated for first- and second-degree burns and also was placed on medical leave. For saving the life of a Brother firefighter, Bergin was awarded a medal.

The 1980s went out with a bang for the FDNY. On December 29, 1989, a natural gas main exploded when a backhoe accidentally gouged a high-pressure gas main at 132nd Street in the South Bronx. At 1:10 p.m., an enormous fireball and a rumbling, earthquake-like blast shook everything within a 10-mile radius. The backhoe, nearby automobiles and buses were melted, as a pillar of flame gushed from the 100-foot-wide, 25-foot-deep crater.

Five alarms were transmitted as firefighters evacuated the neighborhood and set up tower ladders and stretched hose lines to keep the area surrounding the blaze cool. One worker was killed immediately and a young man was blown into the river by the powerful blast and died later. Twenty-six others were injured, most of whom were firefighters.

A contractor's backhoe ignited a huge column of flames from a high-pressure gas main on 132nd Street in the Bronx, December 29, 1989. (Photo by Steve Spak)

New York City Fire Department 1990 – 2000

The first four-alarm fire of the 1990s started at 4:55 a.m. on January 3, 1990, at 735 Knickerbocker Avenue, Brooklyn. The blazing four-story building fire injured 18 civilians and 14 firefighters. A mother and her three children were rescued from their third-floor apartment by firefighters.

In 1990, the FDNY became part of the Federal Emergency Management Agency's Urban Search and Rescue program. The FDNY members are a major part of the New York City Task Force 1 (NYTF-1). Also on the team are Emergency Medical Service personnel and police officers. The members are trained in building collapse operations and specialized rope rescue and tool operations. New York Task Force 1 is headed by Battalion Chief Ray Downey, a highly decorated fire officer, former Captain of Rescue Company 2 and Chief of the Special Operations Command, Rescue Operations. NYTF-1 is one of 26 teams across the country and can be deployed rapidly with a complete cache of tools, supplies, food and water. The team can act independently and be self-sufficient for up to seven days.

Bronx Box 4788 was received at 11:49 a.m. on January 21, 1990. Engine Company 88 responded to the working fire on the third floor of 2119 Hughes Avenue, a five-story apartment house. Lieutenant Louis J. Visconti transmitted a 10-75 signal over the Department radio, ordered a line stretched and entered the fire building.

Upon reaching the fire floor, fleeing occupants screamed that a child was trapped in the rear bedroom of the fire apartment. The door

was hot and the officer paused briefly as the charged line was bled. Visconti opened the door and scanned the apartment as flames burned up the walls and across the ceiling in the living room. Beyond the flames, he could see an open door that led to a bedroom. The Lieutenant made a quick decision. He told the nozzleman he was going to make a quick search and to control the door until he returned.

Visconti crawled under the flames and made his way to the rear bedroom where he found a four-year-old girl, unconscious and not breathing. He placed his facepiece over the child's face and shielded her from the heat and flames as he returned to the entrance door. He placed the child in the care of other firefighters and led the attack on the blazing apartment.

The young girl was rushed to Jacobi Hospital, then to the hyperbaric chamber in City Island, where she was treated for severe smoke inhalation. Lieutenant Louis Visconti was awarded a medal for his actions.

Four alarms were transmitted for a fire that involved several apartments on the upper floors of a modern, seven-story apartment house at 3255 Randall Avenue in the Throgs Neck section of the Bronx on January 30th, at 10:06 p.m.

Firefighters responded to a fire in a three-story, brick, occupied tenement at 1033 College Avenue in the Bronx on February 21, 1990, at 1:54 a.m. Units found the structure fully involved upon arrival, with fire spreading to two attached buildings. The fire quickly went to four alarms. One civilian perished in the blaze and numerous other residents and firefighters were injured before the fire could be brought under control.

In February of 1990, the Department organized the new Special Operations Command to address the administrative and training needs of nine diversified units of the Department. Now under one command were the Rescue Companies, the Marine Division, Haz-Mat, Squad Company 1, Rescue Liaison, Mask Service Unit, Field Communications Unit and the Decontamination Unit.

Firefighter Leonard L. Johnson of Ladder Company 132 wheeled his rear-mount, 110-foot aerial ladder truck onto Washington Avenue in Brooklyn on the night of February 13, 1990. Johnson saw heavy smoke pumping from the top-floor windows of the four-story, non-fireproof building at number 682. He positioned his rig and raised the aerial ladder toward two people visible at a window.

The moment the ladder was in position, Johnson raced to the tip as Firefighter William Stark of Ladder Company 105 moved his tower ladder bucket through dense smoke and placed it 10 feet below the window, alongside 132's aerial. Stark and Firefighter Edward X. Cooper, also of Ladder 105, climbed from the bucket onto the aerial ladder and entered the window. Leonard Johnson reached the end of his aerial and met Stark and Cooper, who were removing a heavy-set, semi-conscious woman from the choking atmosphere. Together, they struggled with the difficult removal, as fire belched from windows beneath them and thick, acrid smoke enveloped them.

Firefighter Peter B. Hespe of Ladder Company 105 had made his way to the roof and provided some much-needed ventilation to the smoke-filled building. He vented the top-floor rear windows, entered an apartment and began a grueling search. He came upon an unconscious man, transmitted a 10-45 and his location over his radio and started back with the victim.

Conditions around Hespe were deteriorating to the point that a flashover was becoming evident. He managed to lift the man out onto the rear fire escape as help arrived. Hespe quickly dove back into the apartment to complete his search before returning to the fire escape. He helped carry the man to the roof, their only means of escape. The victim then was removed across the roof and through the adjacent building.

In the front of the building, the large woman was placed in the tower ladder bucket and CPR was begun. Stark re-entered the room and returned with another victim. The dangerous transfer from window, to aerial, to bucket was completed again. The two victims were lowered to the street and waited for medical attention, while Stark climbed the ladder, entered the window and assisted firefighters with another victim.

For their display of daring, strength and bravery, Firefighters Johnson, Stark, Cooper and Hespe were awarded medals of valor by the FDNY.

A four-story commercial building at 1149 Broadway in Manhattan was the scene of a four-alarm fire on March 18, 1990. The fire was reported at 8:40 p.m. and burned through stored textiles before the interior of the building collapsed, narrowly missing firefighters battling the blaze. Units remained on the scene for days, performing overhauling operations.

The entire city was shocked by the events of March 25, 1990. An arson fire that burned on the first floor of a two-story building took the lives of 87 people. The structure at 1961 Southern Boulevard in the Bronx contained the illegally operated Happy Land Social Club. A lack of second-floor exits left trapped patrons nowhere to go as the smoke and super-heated gases closed in.

The actual firefighting operation only required the services of a first-alarm assignment to control. The subsequent overhaul, investigation and removal of victims led to the assignment of 50 units over a period of time.

This was the largest loss of life at a fire in New York City since the Triangle Shirtwaist disaster, exactly 79 years earlier on March 25, 1911.

A pre-dawn fire on May 16, 1990, in the Bedford-Stuyvesant section of Brooklyn tested the skills, determination and bravery of the members of the FDNY. The rig radios crackled with reports of numerous calls being received for Box 901. Companies arrived at the large, six-story apartment house within minutes of the 5:10 a.m. transmission of the alarm.

Members of first-due Ladder Company 111 hurried to their positions. Lieutenant Pat Concannon and his forcible entry team,

Firefighters Theodore Krowl and Mike Donovan, arrived at the fire apartment after being informed that children were trapped. The smoke was banked down to the floor in the public hall as they made their way 50 feet to the fire apartment.

They found the door open with dense smoke and extreme heat pouring from the apartment. Krowl, the canman, entered the furnace-like apartment first. As the team began to spread out and search, he positioned himself to hit the flames with his extinguisher.

Meanwhile, 111's roofman, Firefighter Vincent Ungaro, worked his way to the roof by the rear fire escape. As he climbed to the roof, he saw victims appear at a window in the fourth-floor fire apartment. A young woman in the window was preparing to save her one-year-old sister by tossing her out the window into a makeshift net. As he radioed for help, Ungaro shouted to her that help was coming.

Firefighter Tom Fiska of Ladder Company 123 appeared and a rope rescue was decided upon. Firefighters Dan Quinn, Engine Company 222, and Brian Fenton, Ladder Company 132, joined them on the roof as Ungaro climbed over the parapet and began to descend through the thick, hot smoke.

Inside the fire apartment, the searching continued as conditions worsened. Firefighter Krowl suddenly heard the victims and immediately crawled into the rear room. He could just make out the young woman holding the infant out the window. As he considered his next move, Krowl convinced her to pull the child back into the room.

Through the smoke, the legs of the descending Ungaro became visible outside the window. Krowl placed the two small children in Ungaro's arms, who then was lowered to the ground. Krowl waited with the young woman for a second rope rescue, but conditions had become so severe they could wait no longer. Shielding the woman from the heat and flames, they raced from the apartment into the smoke-filled hall, where they were met by other firefighters who helped remove the woman.

Courageous actions both inside and outside the fire apartment saved the lives of three sisters. For their bravery, Firefighters Krowl and Ungaro were added to the list of Department Medal winners.

On July 8, 1990, at 7:04 p.m., Brooklyn companies were faced with a fire in a one-story, brick, carpet warehouse that quickly extended to a similar attached building, then to a five-story warehouse. The large stock of carpeting created an extremely heavy smoke condition, which severely complicated the attack on the fire. Five alarms were needed to extinguish the blaze.

More than 2000 marchers, representing 76 fire departments from seven states and Canada, participated in a grand parade and muster, celebrating the 125th anniversary of the founding of the professional Fire Department of the City of New York on May 5, 1990.

An estimated 10,000 spectators watched the parade as uniformed firefighters marched and 60 antique apparatus rolled by. A street fair on Spring Street, at the Fire Museum, was the focal point of the festivities. Demonstrations, fire prevention literature and apparatus displays drew excited children of all ages.

Tactical Support Units 1 and 2

On August 24, 1990, the FDNY placed in service Tactical Support Units 1 and 2. These two new rigs, purchased to replace the antiquated floodlight trucks, are multi-purpose vehicles, designed to provide fireground lighting, as well as carry special equipment for use at collapses, water rescues and other emergencies. TAC 1 is quartered on Roosevelt Island and TAC 2 is on Clove Road in Staten Island.

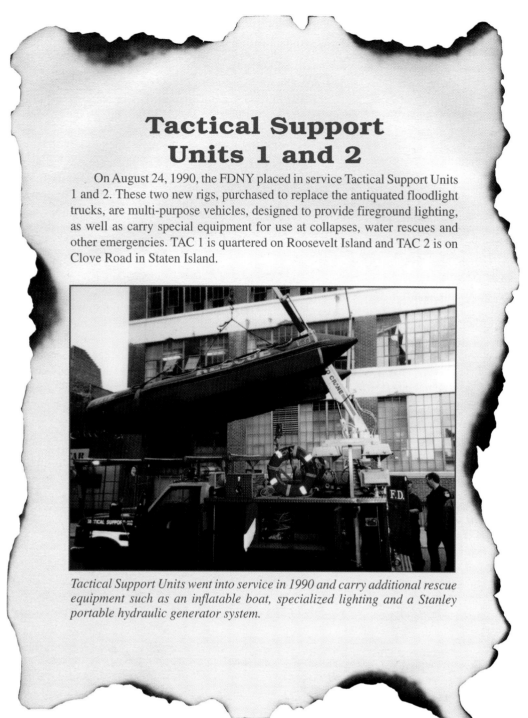

Tactical Support Units went into service in 1990 and carry additional rescue equipment such as an inflatable boat, specialized lighting and a Stanley portable hydraulic generator system.

As companies were operating inside the vacant structure, a collapse occurred. The floors gave way and Firefighter James Trainor of Engine Company 41 found himself sliding, tumbling and falling down through the third, past the second, then the first floors and into the basement, leaving him dazed and buried up to his chest by tons of debris.

Firefighter William Welsh of Ladder Company 17 was near Trainor when the collapse occurred and radioed a "Mayday" as he saw him disappear into the debris-filled void. Welsh then hurried down the stairs to a first-floor bathroom, where he knew from experience that a hole in the bathroom floor would allow access to the basement.

Captain John Keenan of Engine Company 41 worked his way down among the sections of collapse, searching for his missing man. Realizing the bulk of the rubble was in the basement, Keenan headed there. Meanwhile, the roofman of Ladder Company 17, Firefighter William Larsen, had completed his roof operations and carefully made his way to street level after the collapse occurred. Larsen located an exterior basement entrance, crawled in and began to pick his way through the debris as flaming embers and rubble continued to rain from above.

Upon reaching the trapped firefighter, Larsen, a trained EMT, cleared an airway by pulling away debris from around his head. As he did so, he confirmed that Trainor was breathing. Larsen radioed the information, requested the area be monitored for possible secondary collapse and asked for a cervical collar and backboard, anticipating the injured firefighter's removal.

Larsen was joined by Welsh and they carefully began to dig the trapped firefighter out of the tons of rubble. Captain Keenan had begun shoring the immediate area around the trapped firefighter because collapse was imminent. Larsen helped the Captain place shoring before they returned to tunnel around the trapped man. Beams and debris were moved or removed and finally the straps of Trainor's mask were cut free. The injured firefighter was placed carefully on a backboard and removed from the basement. He was treated for major trauma at Jacobi Hospital.

Captain Keenan and Firefighters Larsen and Welsh were awarded medals of valor for their efforts at exceptional personal risk in saving the trapped firefighter.

On Saturday, October 6, 1990, Brooklyn units responded to a fire in a block-long, four-story, vacant hat factory at 583-601 Grand Avenue. The fire quickly went to four alarms as flying brands caused seven other building fires. The conditions inside the vacant structure were so hazardous that the fire was fought with exterior streams for almost the entire operation. The original fire building eventually collapsed.

The seven-story commercial building at 99-80 Walker Street in Manhattan was the site of a five-alarm fire at 4:05 a.m. on November 25, 1990. The building had been the site of a two-alarm fire five months earlier. The fire spread rapidly and damaged the buildings on both sides. Eleven firefighters were injured battling the blaze.

A five-alarm fire broke out on the 51st floor of the Empire State Building on July 16, 1990, at 6:30 p.m. First-due units were confronted with an extremely heavy fire condition that vented into the hallway, injuring several members. Nozzle teams pressed in against the stubborn flames as searches commenced on the smoke-filled upper floors. Four civilians and 34 firefighters sustained injuries.

A four-alarm fire broke out in a three-story Con Edison substation at 237 Front Street in Manhattan on August 13, 1990. The fire caused a power outage that lasted for hours and affected the entire downtown business district. The flames were battled for more than five hours before it could be brought under control. The United States Coast Guard provided mutual aid in the form of a unit carrying 150 pounds of dry chemical extinguishing agent. The dry chemical was not used, however. Thirty firefighters were injured during the course of the fire.

Bronx fire companies found themselves extinguishing fire in the same vacant five-story tenement twice in the same tour – not all that unusual in the busier areas of the city. This second fire at 495 Courtland Avenue nearly cost the life of a member of the FDNY. The alarm was transmitted for the second fire in the structure at 10:10 p.m. on September 24, 1990.

December 28, 1990, was a blustery day, with snow blowing into drifts. At 5:48 p.m., an explosion rocked the Albany Housing Project at 405 Albany Avenue in Brooklyn. Rescue Company 2, quartered just a short distance away, could feel the force of the blast inside the firehouse and were on the way as the teleprinter came to life.

Arriving units saw heavy smoke pouring from the top-floor windows of the 14-story building. Members of Rescue Company 2 and Ladder Company 123 ran up the stairs against a tide of hysterical tenants fleeing the inferno. On the 14th floor, they found a severe smoke and fire condition – the result of a gas stove explosion.

Firefighters Lee Ielpi, Terrance Coyle and Anthony Errico of Rescue Company 2 reached the fire floor and split up, with Ielpi and Errico heading toward apartment 14-K to search for children reportedly trapped. Coyle made his way to apartment 14-A on the report of a child in that apartment. Lieutenant Edward Geraghty of Ladder Company 123 split his company and headed toward apartment 14-A.

Flames were pouring from what had been the doorway of apartment 14-J, the site of the explosion. Fire was spreading rapidly to other areas since the partition walls between apartments had been blown down by the explosion.

In apartment 14-A, Geraghty located a seven-year-old boy, trapped between a collapsed wall and frame of a couch. He attempted to lift the wall, but was unable to do so because of its weight. Conditions on the floor were deteriorating quickly; no hose line was in place yet and the fire was growing in size. Geraghty began to dig by hand around the victim until the arrival of Firefighter Coyle. Together, they were able to lift the wall enough to allow the boy to be pulled free. Geraghty lifted the boy into his arms and shielded him with his body as he carried him to safety.

In apartment 14-K, Firefighters Ielpi and Errico were digging out three victims buried beneath a mound of rubble. They were joined by Coyle, who had crossed from the other apartment. One by one, the three trapped victims were uncovered and rushed from the decimated fire floor. Lieutenant Geraghty and Firefighters Ielpi, Errico and Coyle were honored with medals for their heroic efforts.

During the year 1991, the Starfire II Computerized Assisted Dispatch System vendor began to install Mobile Display Terminals (MDTs) in fire apparatus in Manhattan and the Bronx. Dispatchers and field units were trained in the use and operation of this innovative new system. This ongoing project continued the following year with expansion into the other boroughs.

On Tuesday, January 15, 1991, a five-alarm fire raged out of control at 319 McKibbin Street in Brooklyn. The fire, in a four-story mattress factory located in the Williamsburg section, eventually spread to four other, similar, adjacent structures. Nine tower ladders and numerous other large-caliber streams were employed to knock down the fire. Additional units above the fifth alarm were special-called as brands from the blaze started fires on the roofs of nearby buildings.

A three-alarm fire destroyed the three-story apartment building at 198 Irving Avenue in Brooklyn on January 18, 1991. The initial alarm of fire was received at 2:35 a.m. while most tenants were sleeping. Flames extended to two adjacent structures, leaving 11 families homeless. Five firefighters were injured battling the three-hour blaze.

Ladder 17 has its hands full with a large vacant building fire at Intervale and Dawson in the Bronx, December 1990. (Photo by Harvey Eisner)

While at home in the Stapleton section of Staten Island on January 24, 1991, off-duty Firefighter Donald Clark of Engine Company 65 was on his way to bed when he heard the cry of "Fire!" from his next-door neighbor. From his window, Clark could see heavy smoke venting from the first floor of the two-story building next door. Clark called the Staten Island Command and ran outside.

Knowing an elderly invalid was in the fire apartment, Clark entered the burning apartment and crawled 30 feet down the smoke-filled public hallway and forced the wooden door. The smoke and heat condition became even worse as Clark crawled into the flat on his belly. He followed the sounds of moaning and reached the man, lying on the floor, covered with burning materials. Using his bare hands, Clark brushed away the flaming blanket and clothing and dragged the injured man back through the apartment and down the long hallway.

This entire rescue was performed without benefit of protective clothing, mask or a charged line and before the arrival of FDNY units. For his bravery in saving the life of his neighbor, Firefighter Donald Clark was awarded a medal.

Tuesday, March 5, 1991, at 12:40 a.m., Bronx fire companies were operating at a third-alarm fire in a two-story commercial building at 126 East Fordham Road. While searching for hidden fire, Firefighter Alfred Ronaldson of Rescue Company 3, a 13-year veteran, cited six times for heroism, was killed by a concrete floor collapse. Ronaldson was the first line-of-duty death since February 3, 1989, when Firefighter John Devaney was burned.

Six people were killed in an arson fire that swept through a three-story Bronx tenement on March 13, 1991. The fire building at 1074 Fox Street was filled with old furniture, large appliances and mattresses, which slowed the advance of firefighters. Marshals arrested a suspect in connection with the two-alarm blaze.

A quick-spreading fire, apparently originating in a grease duct of a ground-floor coffee shop, eventually consumed and gutted the interior of the six-story commercial building at 431 Fifth Avenue, at 38th Street, in Manhattan. The March 24th blaze started at 7:52 a.m. and took more than 175 firefighters more than five hours to control.

Firefighter Kevin Shea swings in to complete the second rope rescue at 737 Seventh Avenue in Times Square. This dramatic rescue was seen by television viewers across the nation on the evening news on May 14, 1991. (Courtesy of The New York Post*)*

The heart of the shopping district of Flushing, Queens, was ravaged by a three-alarm fire that destroyed stores and offices in the two-story taxpayer at 38-11 Main Street. Three weeks later, the commercial building next door at 38-07 Main Street was the scene of a second-alarm fire that further devastated the business area.

Rush-hour commuters found traffic in Queens and the Bronx at a standstill on Monday morning, April 22, 1991. A gasoline tank truck rolled over and its tank separated from the chassis and burst into flames on the Bronx side of the Whitestone Bridge toll plaza. More than 3500 gallons of burning fuel poured into storm drains, sending geysers of fire 20 feet into the air.

On May 13, 1991, Harlem fire companies responded to a fire in a six-story apartment building at 230 West 113th Street. Box 1358 went to a third alarm as firefighters rescued 18 people trapped by the roaring flames. Rescued victims, including children, the elderly and a paraplegic, were taken out windows, down fire escapes and through the interior.

Reacting to a "Mayday!" given by the first-due truck company's OVM (outside vent man) trapped on the floor above, Captain Robert R. Morris and Firefighter Bruce Collister of Ladder Company 40 braved extreme conditions to breach a wall, locate the firefighter and then lead him to a window and down an aerial ladder under protection of a water curtain. For saving the life of a Brother firefighter, Captain Morris and Firefighter Collister were awarded medals.

One of the most spectacular fire rescues ever captured on film occurred high above the streets of Times Square on May 14, 1991. Box 837 was transmitted for a fire on the top floor of 737 Seventh Avenue at 48th Street in Manhattan. Rescue Company 1, under the command of Lieutenant Patrick Brown, arrived and found heavy smoke venting from the 12th floor of the commercial building. Excited civilians in the street were pointing to two men, trapped at windows on separate sides of the corner building. Battalion Chief John McDermott ordered Rescue 1 to effect the rescue.

On the roof level, the lifesaving rope was readied as Lieutenant Brown climbed onto the parapet to communicate with one of the trapped men. Firefighter Patrick Barr of Ladder Company 45, detailed to Rescue 1 for the tour, climbed over the parapet and waited while Firefighter Kevin Shea got into position to lower him. With nowhere to tie off and little time to improvise, Shea took his turns of rope and sat on the roof with his feet against the parapet.

As Barr was lowered, the weight on the rope lifted Shea, who then was held down by Firefighters Bruce Newbery and Patrick O'Keefe of Rescue Company 1. Barr arrived at the window and took the man in his arms. They were lowered carefully to the 11th floor, where members of Ladder Companies 35 and 21 cleared glass and pulled the men in the window to the cheers of the growing crowd below. A quick wave of Barr's hand was seen in acknowledgment to the accolades as the rescue effort shifted to the other side of the building.

This time, Kevin Shea was lowered with Firefighter Raymond McCormack of Ladder Company 24 controlling the rope. Newbery and O'Keefe assisted again. Moments later, Shea was dangling over the streets as video cameras recorded the event. The second man was pulled through the window. The firefighters took a quick breath as the crowd below cheered the acrobatic rescues. The firefighters then fitted facepieces and plunged into the smoke and heat to battle the blaze, which had reached a third alarm.

This double rope rescue, utilizing the same rope twice, saved the lives of two men trapped in the thick, hot smoke of a growing fire. The video of the rescue was seen by millions on the national evening news. The FDNY was proud to award both Kevin Shea and Patty Barr medals for their heroic actions.

A gasoline tank truck and car collided at the intersection of Bruckner Boulevard and East Tremont Avenue in the Bronx on May 20, 1991, at 12:11 a.m., igniting a spectacular, 10-story fireball that engulfed and destroyed a row of 11 stores, economically devastating the area. More than 4000 gallons of gasoline fed the three-alarm fire,

including a river of flames that burned 10 parked cars. The truck driver and four passengers of the car were killed.

One construction worker was killed and another was rescued by firefighters when three floors of a six-story brick building under renovation collapsed on August 20, 1991. Brooklyn units responded to 1273 Pacific Street in the Crown Heights section at 10:52 a.m. The live victim was removed after an hour; the dead worker was uncovered only after six hours of work.

On August 28, 1991, at 12:22 a.m., a speeding southbound IRT subway train derailed just north of the Union Square, 14th Street station. Five people were killed and 171 were injured in the crash. Two alarms were transmitted as FDNY firefighters worked for hours in the 100-degree temperatures. Exhaust fumes from power tools added to the danger and discomfort levels as the extrication work continued. The first subway car was sheared in half and more than 20 vertical steel support beams were displaced by the momentum of the train.

Probationary Firefighter Kevin Kane of Ladder Company 110 sustained critical injuries when a ceiling collapsed on him as he searched for squatters in an abandoned, four-story, brick building in East New York. The fire was reported at 5:07 a.m. at 1004 Hegeman Avenue in Brooklyn on September 12, 1991. Kane, appointed to the FDNY the previous October, suffered severe burns and died less than 24 hours later. Kane was awarded the Brooklyn Citizens Medal for his deliberate search of three blazing apartments for people reportedly trapped. A homeless woman with a history of arrests – including arson – was charged with setting the two-alarm blaze.

A five-alarm fire raged in Maspeth, Queens, for almost 14 hours on September 24, 1991. The fire started at 7:18 p.m. at 57-27 49th Street in a huge, 600- x 1500-foot brick warehouse under renovation. High-expansion foam and large-caliber streams were utilized to bring the fire under control.

More than 100 firefighters battled a three-alarm fire in a century-old Harlem church on November 8, 1991. The blaze broke out at 9:34 p.m. at 1872 Amsterdam Avenue at 153rd Street in the basement of Saint Luke's African Methodist Episcopal Church in Washington Heights. An aggressive interior attack saved the upper sanctuary of the church.

An extremely smoky four-alarm fire that started in the basement of a book and video store did extreme damage to a six-story commercial building near Times Square on December 5, 1991, at 8:48 a.m. An interior fire attack was waged at 251-257 West 42nd Street for hours until conditions grew so extreme the Incident Commander was forced to switch to a defensive attack.

Fourteen exterior streams then went into operation. Fifty-nine FDNY units operated, with 12 more rotating for four days until all the hidden pockets of fire in the basement were extinguished.

A fire started in a wood-frame auto repair shop that caught fire when gasoline from a car leaked onto a mechanic's droplight. The car's gas tank soon exploded, spreading fire to three adjacent structures – a two-story commercial building and two three-story apartment houses.

It was 7:43 a.m. when Ladder Company 80 rolled in on Box 723, 2065 Richmond Terrace, on December 31, 1991. Dense smoke obscured the building, but trapped people could be heard screaming from within the building. Captain James Supino transmitted a second alarm upon arrival.

Firefighters from 80 went to work. Chauffeur Anthony Picozzi set up the aerial as OVM Phil Dressler and roofman Barry Lee threw a portable in the front. Captain Supino ordered Lee to hold off on his roof assignment and assist with the rescues at the front as he and his forcible entry team, Firefighters Albert Borges and Paul Cavagnaro, entered the building to begin a search.

Outside, Lee climbed the extension ladder and inched across a narrow ledge three separate times to rescue an infant and two small children. Lee returned up the ladder and went across the ledge in the other direction.

Nearby, Picozzi had the aerial in position and was helping three civilians when an hysterical woman jumped for the aerial. Picozzi managed to hold onto her, even though his knee was twisted violently by her impact. Picozzi now had four adults at the tip of the aerial. Phil Dressler had removed an infant and teamed with Lee to remove four more children.

Suddenly, an explosion tore through the fireground and the upper floors in the rear of 2065 Richmond Terrace collapsed downward. The front of the building split horizontally down the middle, clear to the second floor. The shock wave blew Dressler from his perch, three floors to the ground. Lee was blown off the ledge, but grasped the portable and hung in mid-air for a second until the ladder fell back into position.

Inside, the Captain was blown across an apartment floor and burned by the blast. Borges and Cavagnaro were hurled down the rear stairs. All three escaped while the rear of the building collapsed.

Three of the victims on the aerial were dislodged by the blast. Picozzi held one as she swayed suspended beneath the ladder. Another woman was grabbed around the waist by the legs of a man and they both dangled underneath the ladder. Lee was able to position the portable alongside and remove the couple, as Picozzi pulled the woman up onto the ladder and brought her down.

All the victims and firefighters were on the ground as the building became a sheet of flames and radiant heat drove them back. Picozzi tried to climb onto the turntable to lower the aerial, but was driven back by the heat. So he jumped into the front seat and saved his truck by driving it clear with the ladder still in the air.

Ladder Company 80 operated at this fire for only eight minutes. Despite arduous conditions – dense smoke, heavy fire and a tremendous explosion causing a collapse – they rescued 10 people. The company was awarded the New York Firefighters Burn Center Foundation Medal for the most outstanding unit operation of the year. The company also received the Father Julian Deeken Memorial Medal (for the best Burn Center Medal unit operation within a three-year period). Firefighters Picozzi and Lee also received individual medals for valor.

Ladder Company 126 was met by hysterical civilians screaming that a child was trapped in the basement of the 1½-story, wood-frame private dwelling at 133-13 103rd Avenue in Jamaica, Queens. It was January 14, 1992, at 3:42 in the morning. Firefighter Richard V. Trampas saw the fire was in possession of two rooms in the basement of the house. Flames were extending up the interior stairs and into the first floor. Trampas went to the side of the house to find a way in. He stopped at a small window that was pumping hot smoke. Leaning down, he heard the faint cries of the child.

Firefighter Trampas started through the window, only to get his mask and cylinder caught in the narrow window frame. Without hesitation, he took off the mask and dove into the room. Pressed flat to the floor by the building heat, he searched one room, then pushed on, choking and gagging in the suffocating smoke. Deep in the basement, he found the unconscious three-year-old and crawled back to his entry point, where he handed the child outside. Trampas then climbed up and squeezed through the window. Both the child and Trampas were taken to Jamaica Hospital with smoke inhalation. Firefighter Richard Trampas received a medal of valor for his actions at this fire.

On January 16, 1992, Ladder Company 18 responded to Manhattan Box 432 at 12:32 a.m. They arrived to find a fire venting from a fifth-floor window of 200 East Seventh Street, a six-story multiple dwelling. Ladder 18 went to their second-due positions with Lieutenant Dan Butler and Firefighters Albert Gonzalez and Patrick McKenna (detailed from Ladder 45 for the tour). The trio made their way through the extremely narrow hallway to the apartment directly above the fire and found the door nailed shut.

Conditions in the hallway were unbearable and the tight quarters made forcible entry next to impossible. Suddenly, the entire ceiling erupted into flames. The water in the extinguisher was useless against the building body of fire. The three men were forced to the floor. The heat mushroomed downward and flames moved down the walls around them.

Realizing it was only going to get worse, Al Gonzalez jumped to his feet and drilled his Halligan into a door. Straining and twisting, he worked the Halligan until he was able to force the door open. The team dove into the apartment, unaware of the extent of their injuries and began a search.

As fire began to show through the door, they worked their way to a fire escape. As the fire went to three alarms, Gonzalez' two comrades were taken to the Cornell Burn Unit and treated for first- and second-degree burns. The officer sustained burns to 20 percent of his body. Gonzalez received second- and third-degree burns to his knees, neck, ears and face. The other two told everyone who would listen that Gonzalez saved their lives.

For his actions in the face of excruciating pain and extreme heat, Albert Gonzalez, Jr., was awarded the Bennett Medal.

The first four-alarm fire of 1992 came in at 8:08 p.m. on February 12th. Box 1645 sent Harlem fire units to 283 West 150th Street, where fire rapidly spread through the five-story brick building. The fire made its way though several floors before extending to adjoining buildings.

The next four-alarmer was also in Harlem and came on March 13, 1992, when Box 1446 was received at 5:57 a.m. for a fire at 174 East 122nd Street. This five-story tenement blaze injured 16 firefighters.

The scene shifted to Queens on March 26th, when four alarms were struck for Box 3158 at 110-44 Queens Boulevard. This incendiary fire consumed a large restaurant and several stores. The original alarm was received at 7:11 a.m. A man later was arrested for throwing a fire bomb into one of the stores.

Five alarms were needed at Mansfield Hall, a midtown hotel, when Manhattan Box 865 was struck at 6:40 a.m. on March 29, 1992. More than 30 residents were rescued during the early-morning fire, as flames spread through the seven-story building via a shaftway.

Sunday, April 5, 1992, was a day Staten Island firefighters remembered for quite a while. Box 8480, Gateway National Park, was transmitted at 4:32 p.m. for a brush fire inside the park. Four alarms were transmitted as high winds whipped up flames that tore through 200 acres of the park. Firefighters struggled to stay ahead of the spreading fire front that was pushed by the wind in the direction of several structures. Through hard work and determination, the firefighters made a stand and the fire was stopped before it reached the buildings.

Four alarms were sent in for Manhattan Box 46, at 61 Broadway, on April 22, 1992. The initial alarm was received at 9:12 p.m. and arriving firefighters found a fire in computer rooms on the 28th floor of the 30-story high-rise. Heavy smoke filled the upper floors as firefighters made a room-by-room search. The blaze was contained to the floor of origin.

A basement fire broke out in an electronics store at 208 Fifth Avenue, on April 27, 1992, at 12:14 p.m. Manhattan Box 625 went to five alarms. High-expansion foam was used to extinguish the stubborn blaze.

On Tuesday, May 26, 1992, Brooklyn fire companies responded to a reported fire at Box 715. A fire in a store on the ground floor of the four-story building soon spread to the apartments above. The building at 899 Broadway soon had fire throughout. The blaze started at 12:52 p.m.

A "verbal alarm" to the quarters of Rescue Company 3 on July 6, 1992, at 12:41 p.m., went to five alarms. The company arrived to find the two-story taxpayer fully involved. By the time firefighters gained control, the fire had spread from the hardware store to three other commercial buildings and an apartment building.

High-expansion foam was used to control a four-alarm blaze at 164-11 Jamaica Avenue in Queens on September 12, 1992. Box 4783 was sent out at 9:50 a.m. for a fire in a three-story commercial building and took five hours to extinguish.

On September 29, 1992, Manhattan Box 1678 was transmitted for a fire at 481 West 159th Street. A strong wind was creating blowtorch conditions within the six-story building. Lieutenant Michael J. Puzziferri of Ladder 23 hustled to the top floor and found conditions horrible and getting worse. The wind-whipped flames already had burned several members of Ladder 34, the first-due truck, and fire controlled two apartments and was spreading unchecked in the cockloft.

Ordering his canman to remain at the stairs, Puzziferri proceeded down the hall with Firefighter Don Atlas to apartment 53. They forced the door and encountered even more severe conditions. Crawling toward sounds, Puzziferri located a 25-year-old, semi-conscious woman at a window that was across from windows venting heavy fire in the narrow shaft.

The fire officer pulled her away from the window and discovered she was holding the limp body of a small child. Puzziferri took the child in one arm and the mother with the other and retraced his path out into the public hall. He was forced to pass fire venting from two apartments. Dragging, pulling and carrying the mother and son, he made it to the stairs and stopped at the third floor to administer rescue breathing to the infant.

The mother and child, who now was breathing, were rushed to the hospital. Lieutenant Michael Puzziferri had saved three lives – the woman was pregnant. For his courage and tenacity, he was awarded a medal of valor.

That same night, flammable liquids contributed to a fast-moving fire at 1090 Rogers Avenue in Brooklyn. Box 3727 was transmitted at 7:46 p.m. and went to four alarms. An explosion blew out a wall of the original fire building, seriously injuring several members.

October 28, 1992, saw four alarms struck for Manhattan Box 1626. Firefighters removed numerous squatters as fire raced from the second to sixth floors in the six-story, "H-type" apartment house. This 12:30 p.m., multiple-alarm fire was the same location where the FDNY battled a four-alarmer on Christmas 1990.

Fire in a four-story building in the Brooklyn Navy Yard on October 30, 1992, required four alarms and the special call of two 95-foot tower ladders. Box 8050 was sent out at 6:34 p.m. for fire in Building 294. Two fireboats in the East River helped to augment the water supply.

In 1993, the Marine Division placed in service the first new boat since 1962. The *Kevin C. Kane*, a 52-foot, aluminum-hulled boat, with a top speed of nearly 30 knots and capacity to pump 5000 gallons per minute, was added to the firefighting fleet as Marine Company 6.

On November 10, 1992, Rescue Company 4 responded from Queens and joined Manhattan units at Box 754, a Con Edison steam plant. The company knew they were responding to a steam leak, but no one ever could imagine the magnitude of this emergency. At Waterside 2, Captain Martin McTigue and his men were told that 15 employees were missing and were directed to make a search.

During the search, the Captain and Firefighter Billy Boltja suddenly were enveloped in a cloud of super-heated steam. Members of the company, Firefighters Joseph Tufano, William Quick and Stephen Healy, witnessed the steam diversion and after being knocked back by it themselves, they regrouped and moved in to aid their Brothers.

As the trio moved into the steam cloud, Firefighter Boltja was able to dive over a railing to avoid the boiling vapors. He landed at Healy's feet and was dragged to a safe location by Healy, who then returned to help with the Captain.

Quick and Tufano had their hands on the Captain and his mask harness, trying to free him from where he was tangled, but were driven back by the scalding cloud. Again, they dove in and now, joined by Healy, each member grabbed a part of the officer and pulled for all they were worth. Suddenly, the Captain was free and toppled over on top of them.

Captain McTigue and Firefighter Boltja, along with their rescuers, were rushed to the Burn Center at New York Hospital-Cornell University. Captain McTigue required months of therapy and operations, but was alive and came to wear the gold badges of an FDNY Battalion Chief, thanks to his men. Firefighters Tufano, Quick and Healy were awarded medals for their lifesaving efforts.

Brooklyn Box 820, 1094 Hancock Street, was a five-alarm fire in a former soap factory. The Sunday evening fire came in at 6:58 p.m. on November 15, 1992. Several engines and ladders above the fifth alarm were called to patrol for flying brands. More than 30 firefighters were injured battling the stubborn blaze.

On Thursday afternoon, December 10, 1992, Manhattan fire companies raced to a reported fire at Box 793, 145 East 43rd Street, Saint Agnes Church. Built in 1877, the church was damaged heavily in the four-alarm blaze. It took more than three hours to bring the fire under control.

One of the worst storms to strike the city in 50 years hit New York on Friday, December 11, 1992, causing downed power and telephone lines, fallen trees and flooding throughout the five boroughs.

On Staten Island, ocean water rolled a mile inland, damaging more than 1000 homes and forcing an equal number of residents to evacuate. All 33 FDNY units on the Island were pressed into service assisted by 35 units from other boroughs. Companies assisted with every kind of emergency, from flooding to electrical problems. In Great Kills, firefighters stretched hose lines through neck-high water to battle a building fire.

In Brooklyn's Coney Island, FDNY units also responded to flood-related emergencies from a command post located at IS 303. Brighton Beach and Sea Gate were affected by floods, too.

January 31, 1993, was Super Bowl Sunday. Television sets across the nation were tuned to the championship football game. At about 11 p.m., the housewatch computer alarms came to life in midtown

firehouses and companies soon were on their way to 280 Park Avenue. En route, a 10-76 was transmitted by the first-arriving unit. Everyone else heard it on the air; then as they turned the corner, they saw it in the sky.

Fire was out eight windows on the sixth floor. The Battalion transmitted a second alarm and directed Rescue Company 1 to check the fire floor, then search the floor above. They searched the sixth floor, then went above. Entry on the seventh floor mandated a search rope due to the severity of the fire and the maze-like layout. Structural damage was discovered and reported. The concrete floor had buckled due to the intense heat and fire was burning directly through the floor.

Captain Martin McTigue addresses assembled members and the media after undergoing extensive burn care and therapy. He was injured while searching for trapped workers at the Waterside 2 Con Ed steam plant in Manhattan on November 10, 1992. (Photo by Steve Spak)

Lieutenant Steve Casani was going to the next floor and left Firefighters Henry Molle and Bruce Newbery to monitor conditions on this floor as he took the remainder of the company above. Moments after the company left, a broken "Mayday!" transmission was heard on their handie-talkies and Newbery made a probe out onto the floor.

With conditions deteriorating rapidly, they took turns venturing out into the fire area. Newbery called back to Molle and said he had heard voices. Molle lifted his facepiece and shouted, "Where are you?"

There was a low, but definite answer, "We're trapped!"

Using the wall as a guide, they crawled deeper into the inferno as fire raged through the holes in the floor. Reaching the elevator lobby they found two firefighters in a stalled car, sharing a mask. An empty mask lay nearby.

Newbery took off his mask and gave air to the gasping firefighter as Molle helped the other strap his facepiece back on. Each of the rescue firefighters took a Brother by the arm and retraced their way back to the stairway. They radioed that they had the "Maydays" safe and requested a resuscitator as Newbery took them to the fifth floor. Molle remained on the seventh floor.

This rescue was made without a charged hose line, directly above a free-burning fire that involved more than 6000 square feet. Firefighters Hank Molle and Bruce Newbery were awarded medals for saving two firefighters.

With the rescue of the two trapped men, the battle at the 43-story Banker's Trust Building was by no means over. The blaze was fought for hours and after all the numerous special calls for additional engines and trucks over the fifth alarm, it was decided to classify the fire as eight alarms. More than 35 firefighters were injured during the fire.

On February 26, 1993, a violent explosion shattered the cold winter afternoon air of the World Trade Center (WTC) complex in lower Manhattan. The quiet lunch hour was thrown into total chaos. The detonation of a suspected car bomb on parking level B-2, under the Vista Hotel, blew a gaping hole through the concrete and steel substructure of the complex. The blast caused extensive damage to the lower level of the WTC, setting fires, killing or injuring scores of people and causing the collapse of part of the PATH train station. The bomb not only twisted steel, broke concrete and shattered glass, but also tore the fabric of peace across the nation. Major international terrorism apparently had struck a bloody blow on the shores of America.

The World Trade Center complex consists of five buildings on a 16-acre site. Developed by the Port Authority of New York and New Jersey, the WTC houses more than 1200 businesses and trade organizations, including importers, freight handlers, steamship lines, the U.S. Customs House and international banks. Fifty thousand workers and 80,000 visitors populate the complex daily. Actually a city within a city, the WTC has its own police station and medical facility, public parking and more than 60 stores, restaurants and banks within the lower-level concourse. Mass transit stations for the PATH trains and the NYC subway also are found on the lower levels.

North Tower #1 and South Tower #2, the famous twin towers, rise 110 stories (1350 feet) above and the complex also continues seven levels below the street. Each floor level of the towers has an acre of rentable space and these areas are served by 104 elevators. An observation deck, popular to tourists and schoolchildren, is found on the 107th floor of the South Tower.

Across the street from Tower 2, on Liberty Street, is the home of 10 Engine and 10 Truck of the New York City Fire Department. That afternoon, as the pumper was backing into quarters, the officer on duty, Lieutenant Matt Donachie, was facing the WTC, watching as the snow was blowing past the tower. Suddenly, the lights in the tower flickered. Then a rumbling explosion was heard. The officer ordered his men back onto the apparatus and they responded to investigate the cause of the explosion. At this time, the men believed it was a transformer problem, a fairly common occurrence in Manhattan.

At 12:18 p.m., just seconds after the explosion, the Manhattan Fire Communications Office received the first call. Dispatcher Herb Eysser, manning the ARD position (alarm receipt dispatcher), answered a phone call from an excited woman, reporting "...an explosion in the garage of the Vista Hotel." Moments later, Box 69 was transmitted. Suddenly, all the lights signifying incoming calls blazed in the dispatcher's office. As Engine 10 responded, the officer requested that the box be transmitted and as the calls came in, the dispatchers filled out the alarm and included Rescue Company 1. Most of the calls received were reporting an explosion of some kind in the garage of the Vista Hotel.

As Engine 10 turned the corner onto West Street and pulled up in front of the 22-story luxury hotel, people were seen running from the structure. Two large overhead doors, feeding ramps that led to the lower levels, appeared damaged and light gray smoke was visible. Lieutenant Donachie transmitted a 10-75 signal.

As first-arriving companies began to probe into the fire area, slowly the damage was revealed. Voices could be heard crying through the dense smoke and the firefighters pressed on. While the initial searches were going on, members realized that the three main electrical feeders to the complex were in proximity to the explosion and fire area. They were shut off, plunging the entire complex into darkness.

World Trade Center bombing, February 26, 1993.

Rescue after dangerous rescue was made by FDNY members. People were removed from stalled elevators on the upper floors, they were rescued from beneath debris in the sub-basement and evacuated from every floor in the building. Many suffered smoke inhalation. In all, five people were killed by the blast. Fifteen individuals were injured directly by the bomb blast. There were at least 1042 reported injuries (mainly smoke inhalation), with more than 450 of those treated at hospitals. Thirty-five police officers, 44 firefighters and one EMS worker also were reported injured.

This operation was the largest movement of apparatus in the history of the FDNY. During the initial 24 hours of operations, there were 135 responding FDNY companies and approximately 775 uniformed members at the scene. The equivalent of 23 alarms were called for this emergency. The FDNY fought two other major fires, a second alarm on Rockaway Boulevard in Queens at 12:54 p.m. and a second alarm on Hancock Street in Brooklyn at 3:18 p.m. while operating at the World Trade Center.

Ten members of the Department were awarded medals of valor for operations at the World Trade Center bombing. Lieutenant John Fox was given the Bennett Medal. Twenty-five companies were awarded Unit Citations for their rescue efforts. Ladder Company 5 was presented the Burn Center Medal for their rescue of 17 trapped people and the recovery of two deceased victims during their grueling four and a half hours of dangerous work.

On May 18, 1993, Queens Box 7250 went to five alarms as fire destroyed a one-story taxpayer building at 47-53 43rd Street. The building contained seven stores, which were a total loss as the roof and ceilings collapsed into the structure.

On June 6, 1993, the units of the FDNY Marine Division were credited with the rescue of 30 Chinese immigrants from the waters of the Atlantic Ocean when the ill-fated *Golden Venture* ran aground. Marine Companies 6 and 9 launched their small boats and made numerous trips, ferrying the rescued immigrants to Coast Guard vessels offshore.

An arson fire at Manhattan Avenue and Stagg Street in Brooklyn went to five alarms on July 16, 1993. The fire began in a huge pile of rubbish in the rear of similar three-story frame stores and dwellings. Before the flames could be brought under control, a total of eight similarly attached buildings were involved.

Two days later, on July 18th, Brooklyn Box 3733 at Linden Boulevard and Utica Avenue went to five alarms. The original fire was in an open yard area of a plumbing supply firm at 769 Utica Avenue and soon involved several frame sheds, piles of lumber, a delivery truck and cylinders of flammable gas used to solder pipes. Numerous large-caliber streams were brought to bear on the fire.

A fifth alarm was requested at Bronx Box 2226 on October 7, 1993, as units battled a tough fire in a vacant, six-story apartment house at 432 East 149th Street. Bricked-up windows made firefighting a slow go as mauls were used to pound them open for entry and ventilation.

In August 1993, Manhattan fire units responded to the crash of a commercial blimp. The lighter-than-air ship apparently lost altitude, struck an apartment house and deflated.

Thick smoke began to rise up through the elevator shafts and fill the tower The number of calls for help was staggering and additional alarms were transmitted.

Firefighter Kevin Shea of Rescue Company 1 was searching determinedly for trapped people among the piles of rubble leading to the lower levels of the building, when a section of concrete collapsed beneath him. The floor and the firefighter fell more than 30 feet into the super-heated blackness below.

Lieutenant John Fox of Squad Company 1 and his men made their way toward the crater, stretching a line as they went. Fox went forward and found Lieutenant John McAllister of Rescue Company 1, hanging over the edge to pick up Shea's radio messages.

When some of the fire below was knocked down, Battalion Chief Rewkowski, who had assumed command of the rescue effort, allowed Lieutenant John Fox to be lowered on the rope. Passing the various levels of destruction, Fox reached the bottom and was able to locate Shea. From out of the smoke emerged Firefighter Jack Tigue from Rescue 5, who had found another route to reach Shea. A stokes basket was lowered to Fox and Tigue and they began to package Shea for his trip out of the hole. From out of the darkness, firemen converged from various angles to the area near Shea. With debris still falling from above, they hastened their exit and the stokes was slid up a portable ladder's rails. Finally, he was carried clear of the blast area and taken to New York Downtown Hospital.

While the firefighter rescue was being accomplished, the emergency workers of New York City went to work in earnest and began the largest search and rescue effort ever undertaken in the city.

A phone alarm came in at 3:31 a.m. on August 27, 1995, for smoke in the Saint George Hotel in Brooklyn Heights. The fire soon took on monumental proportions as flames spread throughout the structure. (Photo by Harvey Eisner)

November 23, 1993, was just another day to the tunnel workers (called "Sandhogs") at the site known as "19-B." The shaft on Grand Avenue in the Maspeth section of Queens, one of 14 under construction, had reached a depth of about 450 feet, leaving 200 more to reach what would be the junction with the uncompleted tunnel. Working in stages, the sandhogs dug out 100 feet of the shaft at a time, then lined it with concrete to create a giant pipe. When the shaft reached the 650-foot mark, it was extended laterally and tied in with the tunnel system.

Inside the shaft, a 106,000-pound steel form was used to mold the concrete into a 35-foot ring. At the mouth of the shaft, three giant winches, approximately 20 tons each, were used to raise and lower the metal form. They fed cables that dropped into the shaft and are attached to the form. The entire system was placed under tension before the actual move took place.

 Below, eight men were working on three temporary catwalks near the 350-foot mark, testing the cables that disappeared over the edge of the shaft, more than 400 feet above their heads. Work on the form itself also was underway and other necessary tasks were being completed. Operating engineers and sandhogs were working side by side, in light softened by the fog that forms in the shaft as the heat of the curing cement meets the naturally cool, damp air.

Sandhogs chipped away cement from the mold, as the engineers examined the mechanical equipment. Tension slowly was placed on the cables during this check. Suddenly, a loud Boom! reverberated across the work site and chilled the blood of the men in the shaft below. In a fraction of a second, one of the winches tore loose from its moorings and tumbled into the shaft. It plunged, ricocheting off the smooth, damp shaft walls toward the helpless men. The upper tiers of catwalks and piping were sheared through and electrical wiring was ripped apart, showering sparks into the blackness beneath the remains of the shaft's work platforms.

The massive piece of machinery splashed into the 20 feet of water that had seeped into the base of the shaft, taking most of the scaffolding and one of the workers with it. On the damaged catwalks, dazed men began to take stock of their condition.

On the surface, immediate actions were taken by the workers to save their friends as notifications were made to the FDNY, EMS and the police. Only a short distance away, Rescue Company 4 responded quickly to the scene. Initial reports were of "10 men down on a crane." Due to company drills, Lieutenant Ken Memmen was familiar with the site and had a rough idea of what he would encounter.

Lieutenant Memmen, Firefighter Mike Milner, a police officer, two EMTs and an engineer entered a basket and were lowered by a crane into the shaft. Other firefighters brought tools and equipment to the site as needed.

Moving down into the shaft, they weaved their way past debris, dangling live electric wires (220 volts) and other obstacles. They continued down slowly until the rescuers came upon three men, one clearly injured with a broken arm, stranded on what was left of one of the catwalks. They said they were fairly safe where they were and directed them further down to where a man was hanging on by his finger tips.

They threaded their way further down through jutting-out sections of damaged wreckage and moved as close to the imperiled man as they could. He had been hanging on, upside-down, literally by his finger tips for more than 30 minutes. Then, he managed to turn himself upright and wrapped his arms and legs around remnants of the catwalk. A rope was placed around the badly shaken sandhog; then he was helped across into the cage.

Meanwhile above, another device used by the workers to remove sludge and debris from the bottom of the shaft was lowered. Manned by members of Rescue Company 2 and police, they stopped and removed an injured worker (broken arm) and transported him to the surface.

At the surface, another quick conference was held. Then the cage again was lowered into the shaft to pick up the two other workers and search for additional victims. Milner tied off, climbed from the cage and carefully helped two workers inside.

They searched the wreckage and debris that littered the surface of the water as best they could. Styrofoam, used in the form collar, covered everything. Thousands of pieces, from the size of pebbles to the size of boulders, coated the scene like a blanket of ice and snow. With no signs of the injured worker, they started back up, stopping briefly to pick up a severed limb.

It was decided that even though both fire and police divers were ready to operate, it was fairly certain the remaining worker was dead and the safest way to recover him would be to pump the water from the base of the shaft.

The next day, sandhogs stood quietly by as Rescue 4 freed their fellow worker's remains from the wreckage and gently placed them in a body bag. Quietly, everyone returned to the surface.

Except for the one fatality, it was surprising to anyone who was at the scene that the situation had not been worse. Previous projects had averaged about one death per mile of tunnel. Number 3 had been dug a winding 16 miles, down into Manhattan and under the East River to Queens. And the death toll stands at 20.

A four-story factory fire on November 25, 1993, escalated to five alarms as the structure at 26th Avenue and Fourth Street became completely involved. Two walls collapsed and then the fire spread to nearby sheds and industrial buildings. The fire area eventually measured 400- by 100-feet. Two fireboats helped land units battle this waterfront blaze.

The first four-alarm fire of 1994 came in at 1:32 a.m. on January 10th. Brooklyn Box 592, DeKalb Avenue and Albee Square, involved all floors of a five-story vacant tenement. A partial collapse required the operation be conducted using exterior streams. During this job, Brooklyn firefighters also battled another fire that went to two alarms at Saratoga Avenue and Bergen Street.

A fire in a partially vacant five-story tenement at Lenox Avenue and 127th Street went to four alarms on January 22, 1994. The initial alarm for Box 1497 was received at 11:08 p.m. Flames broke out on the first floor rear, occupied by a retail food store, and extended to all the vacant upper floors before spreading to adjacent exposures.

Later that day, Box 1571 came in for Broadway and 137th Street. The alarm was received at 5:11 p.m. for a fire in an occupied, six-story brick apartment house at 600 West 138th Street. This difficult blaze was fought for nearly two hours before it could be extinguished.

On January 26, 1994, units responded to a reported explosion in a one-story diner at 38-34 22nd Street in Queens. First-due units confirmed an explosion and indicated that people were trapped within the collapsed structure. Rescue Company 4 arrived and assisted in the removal of people partially covered with debris on top of the pile. Lieutenant Terence Hatton and Firefighter Kevin Dowdell (detailed for the tour from Rescue 2) then made their way into a void of unsupported, reinforced concrete slabs, weighing about two tons each. A woman was trapped beneath this daunting, unstable mountain.

After a short while, they had shored the area as best they could, cut, dug and cleared the woman to her waist. But her legs still were pinned beneath the rubble. The rescue effort was re-doubled with the addition of Firefighters Michael Loftus of Rescue Company 4 and William Lake of Rescue Company 2, who had approached the victim from different directions to better operate with the delicately stacked tons of debris.

Through the coordinated efforts of the four rescuers, using hydraulic rams, sawzalls, air bags and their own hands, the trapped woman was freed from her tomb and carefully, but quickly, removed to a hospital. For their heroic and professional operations, Lieutenant Hatton and Firefighters Dowdell, Loftus and Lake were presented medals.

An arson fire that started in an auto parked in the basement garage of the six-story apartment house at 1487 Shore Parkway North in Brooklyn went to four alarms on January 29, 1994. The fire spread through pipe recesses and erupted above on various floors. The alarm for Box 3492 was received at 3:28 a.m. and was declared under control at 4:53 a.m.

A large, seven-story brick apartment house at 610 West 142nd Street in Harlem was the scene of a fire on February 7, 1994, that became the equivalent of eight alarms. Box 1609 came in at 1:36 p.m. and responding units found themselves faced with a wind-driven fire that was sweeping the top floor of the 200- x 100-foot building.

Flames burst through the roof and showered the neighborhood with flaming embers. The roof of the tenement to the rear of the fire building was soon in flames and an entire first-alarm assignment fought the fire in that building and then went to work in the original fire building. Twenty firefighters and 10 civilians were injured in the blaze.

A four-alarm fire involved the fifth and sixth floors and cockloft of one wing of 1631 Grand Avenue in the Bronx on February 27, 1994. The afternoon fire then was halted as it tried to spread to the other wing through the cockloft. At the height of the blaze, a firefighter became trapped at a top-floor window and was rescued via aerial ladder.

On March 14, 1994, Manhattan Box 1628 came in at 5:22 a.m. for a fire that started in a ground-floor apartment of a six-story brick building at 250 West 146th Street. The suspicious fire spread up the rear of the west wing of the building and heavily involved the first through sixth floors. An unidentified person, who had been shot, was in the fire apartment, burned beyond recognition. A woman who also had been shot, escaped the fire by jumping out the rear window.

A fire in the three-story, occupied multiple dwelling at 62 Watts Street in Manhattan took the lives of three of New York City's Bravest on March 28, 1994. While operating on the second-floor landing, the forcible entry team of the second-due truck – Ladder Company 5 – Captain John Drennan and Firefighters James Young and Christopher Siedenburg, detailed from Engine Company 24, were trapped in a sudden flashover.

The metal apartment door could not be opened in time and the team was trapped where they stood in a fireball of more than 2000 degrees. They were found by firefighters and Drennan and Siedenburg were rushed to the Burn Center at New York Hospital – Cornell Medical Center. Firefighter James Young was killed in the flames. Firefighter Chris Siedenburg died from his burns 24 hours later. Captain John Drennan fought the good fight and hung on for 40 days in the Burn Center before succumbing to his burns.

On May ninth, President Bill Clinton made an unscheduled visit to the quarters of Ladder Company 5 and Engine Company 24 to convey his sympathies. The firehouse became an impromptu shrine as neighbors and FDNY supporters filled the sidewalk in front of the Sixth Avenue firehouse with flowers.

Another piece of FDNY history was made on May 7, 1994, when Firefighter Rochelle T. Jones of Engine Company 159 was promoted to Lieutenant. A member of the Department since 1982, she is the first woman promoted to officer rank in the uniformed force. (She was promoted to Captain in 1999, another first.)

Mayor Rudolph Giuliani and Fire Commissioner Howard Safir were on hand as the first delivery of FDNY bunker gear was made at the quarters of Engine Company 227 on May 16, 1994. This was the start of the Department's plan to replace thigh-length turnout coats and high boots with bunker gear and short boots. The Department eventually delivered 11,300 sets of bunkers to the firefighting force.

The city had been suffering through another typical hot, hazy and humid summer day on July 23, 1994. Late-afternoon showers rumbled across the metropolitan area, bringing a brief cooling and some relief. In Coney Island, a section of the city in the Borough of Brooklyn, long noted for its beaches and amusement parks, a serious water emergency began to develop.

A late model, silver-colored Lincoln Continental was heading west on Neptune Avenue. For reasons unknown, the driver, a man in his 50s and apparently out celebrating his birthday, veered into a private parking lot about 50 feet past West 12th Street. The auto, filled with four middle-aged people and the driver, then barreled off the edge of the parking area, down an embankment and flipped over, crashing into the water. The vehicle, now upside down, sank into the Coney Island Creek, a body of water notorious for its polluted conditions. One fire official described the water as "straight haz mat."

The fire department received phone calls within seconds of the crash and as per Department policy, immediately dispatched units and notified both the police and EMS. Fire units normally assigned to a first alarm were dispatched, along with the closest FDNY SCUBA unit.

Engine Company 245, stationed only blocks away with Ladder Company 161 and the 45th Battalion, quickly responded to the scene. Familiar with the location, engine chauffeur Ken Grof pulled the pumper directly into the lot and rolled toward the end.

The rear wheels of the submerged vehicle were just visible above the water. Lieutenant Michael J. Lee jumped down from the cab and began to remove his shoes as civilians excitedly told him that five people were still in the car.

Lee scrambled down the muddy embankment and half swam, half waded out to the submerged car. The water at the front of the vehicle was shoulder high and got deeper as the bottom dropped off toward the rear. Realizing that immediate action would give these people their only chance to survive, the officer and his men went to work.

Reaching down, Lee ran his hand along the side of the car, searching for the door handle. The officer located the handle and found the door unlocked, but was unable to move it. As he continued to struggle with the mud-blocked door, he was joined in the water by Firefighters Tommy Ingram of Engine 245 and Jimmy Kennelly of Ladder 161. Together, they managed to pull the door open. Lee took a few deep breaths and ducked beneath the black surface and entered the front seat of the vehicle.

Moments later, he returned to the surface with the driver in tow. He handed the unconscious man off to members of both companies, who had formed a human chain down the slippery embankment. This group was augmented by the addition of members of the second-due units, who added to the chain and also set up a first-aid area for those being removed.

Back in the water, Lee made a breath-holding dive into the front seat, but came up empty before diving again. Groping in the darkness, he found a woman in the front seat area. Seconds later, he burst to the surface with his second unconscious victim in hand.

The exhausted officer then nodded to Firefighter James P. Kennelly, who disappeared beneath the surface and searched the front seat. Lee made his way to the rear and found this door stuck, too. Kennelly surfaced, satisfied that no one was in the front. Then, he joined Lee and Ingram and together, they again forced a door frozen in the mud.

O n June 1, 1994, the FDNY held its annual Medal Day ceremony on the fabled steps of City Hall. On that day, a special award was presented to a man who had shown a devotion to the members of the FDNY that few have in the history of the Department.

Honored was Michael R. Madden, M.D., of the New York Hospital-Cornell Medical Center, Burn Unit. Doctor Madden is the Clinical Director of Burns/ Clinical Associate Professor of Surgery. Madden had received a beep on his pager on March 28, 1994. This started his care for Captain John Drennan, who had suffered severe burns. Madden, who had cared for Captain McTigue after his steam burns, did not leave the city for the next six weeks so he could supervise the treatment of Captain Drennan. He performed seven operations, three of which required 10 to 11 hours of surgery.

His treatment ended when Captain Drennan passed away on May seventh. Doctor Madden had shown his deep love and respect for all firefighters with the care, concern and professionalism demonstrated in his expert treatment of Captain Drennan. In appreciation for his valiant efforts, a grateful Fire Department presented a Department Medal to Michael R. Madden, M.D. The only other civilian ever to be presented a Department Medal was Doctor Harry Archer who, like Madden, was also an Honorary Fire Medical Officer.

Directly in front of the open door, the near exhausted Lee dove again, this time into deeper water and entered the back seat of the vehicle. Moments later, he returned with the third victim. Kennelly took Lee's place at the rear and took a dive into the car. In a matter of seconds, he surfaced with the fourth victim.

Firefighters handed victim after victim from the vehicle across the water and up the muddy, 12-foot embankment. Looking back from his vantage point in the water, Lieutenant Lee watched proudly as members of the Fire Department "Put on a clinic in CPR." Behind him, Kennelly surfaced again, with the fifth victim. Ingram then dove into the sunken automobile and completed the searches.

All five victims were without pulses when they were placed on the ground and CPR was begun. By the time EMS had begun to transport them, each had regained a heartbeat.

All the members of the first-arriving units who entered the water were taken to the emergency room and treated for ingestion of polluted water. They received gamaglobulin shots, TB tracers and Hepatitis screening.

From the arrival of Fire Department units until the removal of the last victim from the submerged car, time elapsed was approximately five minutes. The 80-year-old victim died during emergency surgery, but all the other victims survived their ordeal.

On July 28, 1994, New York City Mayor Rudolph Giuliani presented 13 members of the Fire Department with Certificates of Appreciation for their work at the bottom of Coney Island Creek. Members who participated in the water rescue were cited for their heroic actions and Lieutenant Michael Lee received the Brooklyn Citizens Medal.

Manhattan units responded to Box 913, 12th Avenue and 57th Street, Pier 90, the passenger ship terminal for a reported smoke condition aboard the 612-foot cruise ship *Regal Empress*. The ship was returning after a five-night ocean cruise. Ninth Battalion companies waited as the ship was docked, then boarded and found fire in a dining area. Lines were stretched and visible fire was extinguished. Further investigation revealed a fire burning in a large shaft area. Companies cut into the shaft with great difficulty.

The fire went to four alarms to provide adequate manpower. All passengers were removed safely as the fire was fought with lines stretched from both land units and fireboats. Twelve civilians suffered minor injuries.

On the night of October 28, 1994, at 3:29 a.m., Ladder Company 30 responded to Box 1468, for a fire at 148 West 124th Street in Manhattan. Heavy fire was venting from four windows on the third floor of the five-story old law tenement. Firefighter James R. Curran positioned his rig and placed the aerial to the roof to facilitate the roofman's operations. A man showed at a fourth-floor window and as Curran positioned the ladder and began to climb, the man jumped onto the ladder. Curran helped him down the ladder to the street.

Hysterical people were screaming that there was a person still trapped inside on the fifth floor. Curran repositioned the aerial, donned his mask and climbed to the fifth floor as fire vented below him. Curran entered the window and found a handicapped man without legs, who could do little to help himself. Curran muscled him up with one arm and pulled him through the window, then out and onto the aerial.

Surrounded by hot, swirling smoke pumping from the fire below, the man then advised Curran that his wife was still inside. Curran passed the man to Firefighter Craig Buccieri, who had climbed the ladder behind him. Curran radioed the information and tried to squeeze through the window and enter the apartment once more. The inside team advised Curran that they had the victim, who later died from her exposure to the heat and smoke inhalation.

There were 10 companies working at this second alarm. Eleven firefighters, including James Curran, were injured while operating. For his strength, determination and bravery, Firefighter James R. Curran received a medal of valor for his actions at this blaze and a second medal for his heroism on May 13th at 28 West 125th Street.

Members open roof at September 29, 1995, two-alarm fire at 1575 Bergen Street in Brooklyn. (Photo by Jim Romeika)

Four alarms were transmitted as high winds whipped the flames and brands poured across the neighborhood at Manhattan Box 44-537, West and Jane Streets, November 7, 1994. (Photo by Paul Hashagen)

Brooklyn Box 44-2513, 392 East 4th Street, July 4, 1998. (Photo by Pete Connolly)

Ladder 167 removes victims from four-alarm fire at the Flushing YMCA, January 23, 1996. (Photo by Steve Spak)

On December 1, 1994, Doctor Kerry Kelly was appointed Chief Medical Officer of the New York City Fire Department. She is the first woman to hold this position.

Monday morning, November 7, 1994, was quite a busy day for the FDNY. High winds were buffeting the five boroughs and brought problems to the firefighting forces of Manhattan and the Bronx. Rescue Company 1, returning from an all-hands downtown and responding to a box in midtown, came upon a building fire at the corner of West and Jane Streets. The four-story vacant filled with fire at an amazing rate. Rescue Company 1 requested a 10-75, followed by an "All-hands with an extra truck, a tower ladder." Then, a second alarm was transmitted as fire spread to two occupied exposures.

With the first-due companies operating at the downtown box, the fire continued to spread. Third and fourth alarms were transmitted by the company just as help arrived. Box 537 went to four alarms in nine minutes. Several separate all-hands were extinguished in the neighborhood as a result of flying brands.

Three and a half hours later, Bronx units descended upon 3135 Park Avenue, a 20-story housing project. Flames broke out in an 18th-floor apartment in the building, filled with mainly elderly residents. An open apartment door allowed the 50-mph wind to drive the fire into the hallway with blowtorch intensity. Wave after wave of engine companies rotated personnel and pushed two $2\frac{1}{2}$-inch hose lines an inch at a time into the howling flames.

On the roof, a 12-foot-high bulkhead cut off the roof section where a woman was trapped at a window. Firefighter Doug Hantusch, with a lifesaving rope, literally was lifted over the wall by Firefighter James Hawkins of Ladder Company 55. This maneuver enabled Hantusch to reach Firefighter Michael Conboy of Rescue Company 3, who was lowered by Hantusch to the 18th-floor window below.

The woman refused to go out the window, so Hantusch lowered a mask to Conboy, who stayed with the woman and prayed the engine companies could make it down the hall to them. On the roof, Hantusch was preparing for another rope evolution when a person was seen trapped at another 18th-floor window. This person was reached through the inside.

Hawkins vented, then descended to the floor above the fire and under extreme conditions, searched and vented until his mask was depleted. Reporting his progress, he was ordered to the 16th floor, where he collapsed from exhaustion. After a few minutes of rest, he joined his company and helped Conboy remove the woman through the interior.

In the end, the whole operation could be summarized: some 250 cylinders were used before the fire was knocked down; one person was killed; five civilians and 44 firefighters were injured, including 17 members who were granted medical leave. Six companies were cited for their excellent unit operations at this fire. Firefighters Conboy, Hantusch and Hawkins were awarded medals.

On December 23, 1994, engine companies in Division 11 went on-line as Certified First Responders-Defibrillator. This was the start of the city-wide CFR-D program that took two and a half years to implement fully.

Brooklyn Box 224 was received at 1:02 p.m. for a fire at 252 South Fourth Street on November 20, 1994. As Ladder Company 108 pulled up, chauffeur Firefighter Jim Newman positioned the rig to cover the front and exposure #4 side of the six-story structure. Excited people in the crowd pointed out a man trapped at an exposure #4 rear window. The aerial was extended to the window, Firefighter Gregory J. Smith climbed up and the frantic man handed him two small children.

Smith advised the father and mother to wait at the window and started down the cantilevered ladder with the frightened children. Not willing to listen or wait, the mother climbed out onto the fully extended ladder. Smith felt the ladder shift to the right and slide across the window ledge. The twisting ladder was at its maximum limits when the man, despite pleas from Smith, climbed onto the ladder.

The weight of five at the tip of a twisting ladder was too much. The aerial began to buckle. Firefighter Smith knew the worst was happening: the ladder was failing and they all were going to drop. Focusing on the children, he held them tight, laid into the ladder's rungs and held on.

The ladder fell six stories to the lot below. Smith was injured seriously by the fall, but held fast to the children, protecting them as best he could. Suffering a fractured arm, scapula and spine, bleeding in the lung and numerous bruises and contusions, Smith was rushed to the hospital. For his amazing presence of mind and bravery, Firefighter Gregory Smith was awarded the Bennett Medal.

In early 1995, it was announced that three suspects linked to the 1992 arson fire that took the life of Lieutenant Thomas Williams of Rescue Company 4 had been arrested. The insurance fraud blaze was investigated from the outset by New York City Fire Marshal Robert Thompson with the help of Fire Marshal Jim DeSocio. The marshals developed the case. Then a mini task force was put together with Detective Ed Dowd of the 104th Precinct and FBI Special Agent Cindy Peele. The case was coordinated by the Bureau of Fire Investigation through the City-wide Special Investigation Unit.

Due to the sensitive nature of the investigation, it was kept secret. The Williams family, however, was kept advised as the case developed.

In May 1995, FDNY members were activated as part of the FEMA USAR Team response to the Oklahoma City bombing. The team immediately went to work on the night of their arrival and continued on the night shift, relieving the team from Los Angeles until they returned home. Each shift was 12 hours long with two hours for preparation and two hours for cleanup. The team upheld the finest traditions of the rescue service and was a major component of the operation.

On March 17, 1995, the New York City Fire Department marched up Fifth Avenue as part of the annual Saint Patrick's Day Parade. Sadly, just after the parade ended, Drum Major James P. Corcoran passed away after leading the Department in the parade he loved so much. Firefighter Corcoran was a charter member of the band and its only drum major. Corcoran was appointed to the FDNY on September 21, 1957, and started his career in Ladder Company 19.

On March 29, 1995, a fire that broke out in the Fulton Fish Market received major media attention. Box 76 came in at 12:34 p.m. and went to four alarms, as flames tore through the 100- x 100-foot, three-story, metal frame structure. At the height of the blaze, seven tower ladders were in operation, along with two fireboats.

The Bureau of Fire Investigation determined that the fire was arson and joined in a task force with the NYPD and FBI to locate the arsonist.

On Friday, April 7, 1995, units responded to a fast-moving fire at 629 East Fifth Street in Manhattan. Box 432 was transmitted at 7:50 a.m. and companies found fire on the fourth, fifth and sixth floors and in the cockloft. During the firefighting operations, a "Mayday" was declared by an officer who was cut off by fire and trapped in a sixth-floor window. Members of Ladder Company 6 and Rescue Company 1 converged on the roof above the trapped officer. A quick plan was drawn up and put into effect.

Firefighter Joseph Hodges of Ladder Company 6 quickly was tied into the lifesaving rope and lowered over the side by Firefighter Paul Baldwin of Rescue Company 1. Hodges picked up the officer and as they weighted the rope, it caused the rope to skid at the roof level, pinning Baldwin's hand. Another quick plan was devised and the rope operation was taken over by another member as Baldwin and his belt were freed.

Apart from the six-foot free-fall as the rope was freed at the roof, the operation went smoothly, considering that heavy smoke and fire were pouring up the side of the building and burning directly below the feet of the lowering members. Several members were cited for bravery at this fire and Firefighter Hodges was awarded a medal.

On June 1, 1995, Bronx Box 2747 came in as a three-story, wood-frame, vacant dwelling at 1367 Franklin Avenue. The fire spread to three similar structures at 1365, 1369 and 1371 Franklin. Only 1365 was occupied, although all were about the same 20 – x 40-feet in size. Flames leaped from one detached building to the next. The original building was destroyed and the others sustained heavy damage.

Numerous phone calls alerted responding Brooklyn units that not only was Box 954 a working fire, but people were trapped. Ladder Company 132 arrived first-due at 727 Prospect Place, a four-story multiple dwelling. It was 6:07 a.m. on June 17, 1995, and flames were roaring up the interior stairs and through the bulkhead of the building. Flames also were extending into the front apartments via two enclosed shafts.

Firefighter Gerard Triglia raised the aerial ladder and Firefighter Karcher climbed to the roof. The outside ventman, Firefighter Guardabasso, reported heavy fire venting out three of the five rear windows on each floor. He also stated that a woman was visible at a top-floor rear window and ready to jump.

Triglia climbed to the roof with the rope and found heavy fire venting up the two enclosed shafts and raging out of the bulkhead door. It was also evident that heavy fire was spreading beneath his feet in the cockloft. The only place the rope could be tied off was to a possibly unstable chimney. It was time to go, so Triglia went.

At the window, Triglia had to lean in and lift the woman off the floor, then lift and pull her out the window. With heavy fire blowing out adjacent windows and thick smoke swirling about him, Triglia called to be lowered.

The woman was rushed to the hospital with burns and smoke inhalation. For his bravery, Firefighter Gerard Triglia was awarded the Bennett Medal. (Triglia also was awarded the Archer Medal for this rescue in 1999.)

On September 7, 1995, Brooklyn Box 60 was sent out for a fire at 135 Newel Street. The building was a two-story, wood-frame, 25-x 30-foot building. Before it was over, this fire also involved exposure #3 – a rehabilitated, 150- x 40-foot frame building at 122-140 McGuiness Boulevard; exposure #2 – a four-story, 20- x 50-foot frame building at 133 Newel Street; and exposures #4 and #4A – both three-story, 20- x 50-foot frame buildings at 137 and 139 Newel Street.

There was an extremely heavy fire condition upon arrival and the flames soon were moving in the common cockloft of exposure #3. A

tower ladder was able to control that extension. The original alarm was at 1:18 p.m. and the blaze was declared under control at 2:38 p.m.

A 40-story, 200- x 200-foot office building at 605 Third Avenue (at East 40th Street) was the site of a fifth alarm in Manhattan on September 8, 1995. The fire originated in the sub-grade transformer room. A burned worker made his way to the lobby and the alarm was transmitted at 9:15 a.m. for Box 772. The fire then began to fill the building with heat and heavy smoke. A major evacuation removed the workers from the smoke-filled building. It was under control by 11:27 a.m.

On November 3, 1995, Commissioner Howard Safir broke ground for the new FDNY Headquarters in Brooklyn. The formal address is known as 9 MetroTech Center.

The George F. Mand Library and Learning Center, located in the newly constructed building at the Fire Academy on Randall's Island, officially was opened by Mayor Giuliani and Fire Commissioner Howard Safir on December 27, 1995. The 3000-square-foot building has an extensive collection of fire service-related volumes.

The library is named for the late First Deputy Fire Commissioner Mand, who left funds in his estate for the project. The reference-only library contains books, magazines, videos, photographs and other fire service items. The library is open to all members of the FDNY, as well as the general public.

On Christmas Day, 1995, at 9:22 in the morning, Brooklyn companies had been operating at 1092 Pacific Street, a vacant brownstone. The chief had pulled everyone out of the almost fully involved building to concentrate on cutting off fire spread to the exposures.

A neighbor informed Firefighter Louis Valentino of Rescue Company 2 that a woman had been living on the second floor of the building. The chief allowed Valentino and Lieutenant Joseph Downey to attempt a rescue. Making their way through the heavy smoke, a large section of the third floor already had collapsed onto the second floor in the rear and that area was involved heavily in fire.

Valentino placed a door across the exposed beams and continued his search to a room in the front of the second floor, where he located the woman on a bed. Retracing his same perilous path – now dragging a victim – Valentino reached the outside. The woman succumbed to the terrible punishment of the fire, but that did not diminish the heroic rescue efforts of Valentino.

Tragically, Firefighter Louis Valentino never received the medal the Department had planned to give him. He lost his life six weeks later on February 5, 1996, due to injuries sustained at a fire and collapse. Valentino's family was presented with the Mayor Fiorello LaGuardia Medal.

Manhattan eight-alarm fire at 525 Eighth Avenue and West 36th Street, March 1, 1996. (Photo by Steve Spak)

Five-alarm fires were battled on January 7, 1996, in a five-story brick building at 887 Hunts Point Avenue in the Bronx. Fire on all floors eventually led to the collapse of the fire building. Then, on January 23, 1996, Queens companies faced a blaze at Box 4456, the Flushing Y.M.C.A. The building, located at 138-46 Northern Boulevard, contained approximately 100 people when the fire broke out. The fire was located on the third and fourth floors. Twenty-five people were removed from the building by firefighters.

High winds drove flames into blowtorch intensity during a fire operation at 1020 Grand Concourse in the Bronx. The February sixth blaze in the 22-story multiple dwelling known as the "Executive Towers," required a four-alarm assignment to extinguish. The unfortunate tenant of the fire apartment succumbed to the intense heat and smoke conditions.

On March 17, 1996, the Bureau of Emergency Medical Service was established in the FDNY. Under the command of Deputy Assistant Chief Daniel A. Nigro, the new Bureau assumed the resources of the Emergency Medical Service previously operated by the New York Health and Hospitals Corporation.

EMS originally was formed in the early 1970s as a result of merging the ambulance service that each New York City-owned hospital then operated. The nation's largest EMS system merged into the FDNY at a time when their call volume had doubled in the past 22 years. The FDNY immediately began to implement a long-range plan to add new ambulance stations and a five-year replacement cycle for ambulances.

Assistant Chief Frank P. Cruthers was sworn in as the 27th Chief of Department on February 14, 1996. Frank is the son of Francis Cruthers, who was Chief of Department in 1979 to 1980. This was the first time in the history of the FDNY that a son followed a father as Chief of Department.

Manhattan Box 725 was sent out at 3:24 a.m. for a fire that apparently began in a street-level Chinese restaurant at 525 Eighth Avenue near 35th Street, on March 1, 1996. Fire extended to all floors of the six-story, brick, commercial, 80- x 60-foot non-fireproof structure. Five tower ladders were used to fight the fire, which went to five alarms or six, once all the special-called companies were counted.

On March 23, 1996, the wind was howling across the Bronx when a fire was reported at 3971 White Plains Road at 8:39 p.m. The fire building was a 100- x 50-foot taxpayer with seven stores. Fire was reported in a fried chicken store. The fire spread from the restaurant to the other occupancies as Bronx firefighters made a stand.

During venting operations on the roof, a member fell through the fire-weakened roof and into the blazing store below. "Mayday!" crackled across the handie-talkies and members, including Rescue Company 3, quickly assembled at the front, ready to help their missing Brother. Among those who entered the front of the store was Firefighter Bryant Stiles, the Rescue Company 3 chauffeur. Despite the extreme heat and thick smoke, Stiles followed calls for help deep within the store.

Styles found the injured firefighter and carried him back through the maze-like store. Upon reaching the street, the injured firefighter was doused with an extinguisher to cool him down. The injured man was transported to New York Hospital Cornell Burn Center with first- and second-degree burns. Firefighter Bryant Stiles was awarded a medal for saving the life of a Brother firefighter. The fire went to four alarms before being extinguished.

Thomas Von Essen was sworn in as the 30th Fire Commissioner of New York City on April 22, 1996. Von Essen was assigned to Ladder 42 in the South Bronx after completing Proby School in the summer of 1970. After 13 years in the firehouse, he was elected Bronx trustee in the Uniformed Firefighters Association. In 1990, he returned to Ladder 42 and in 1993, returned to the UFA as its President. In 1996, when Fire Commissioner Howard Safir became Police Commissioner, in an unprecedented move, Mayor Giuliani asked Von Essen to become Fire Commissioner. He is the first firefighter in the history of FDNY to be appointed Commissioner. He has made improved firefighter safety and training the Department's primary goal.

Queens Box 9382 came in as a phone alarm at 8:47 p.m. on May 5, 1996. First-arriving units transmitted a 10-75 two minutes later for a fire at 37-80 103rd Street in Corona. The 2 1/2-story building had a store on the first floor with apartments above. Exposures on both sides were similarly attached with slight differences in design. The fire started on the second floor of 37-80 and spread rapidly to the exposures on both sides.

The fire was held as it began to burn into exposures #2A and #4A. Narrow, one-way streets, with parking on both sides, slowed the attack on the fire. The fourth alarm was placed at 8:31 and was under control 35 minutes later.

On June 27, 1996, the FDNY changed the designation of the Rehab Units to "Recuperation and Care Units" (RAC Units). These units respond to "All hands" and provide members with cool drinks and cool towels during hot weather and warm drinks during cold weather. Designated areas also can be set up to facilitate cooling or warming of exposed members, depending upon weather conditions.

On July 17, 1996, the shocking news of a major airliner crash just off the coast of Long Island filled the local New York news media. TWA Flight 800 went down approximately 12 miles south of the Moriches Inlet in Suffolk County. Marine Company 6, the *Kevin Kane*, responded to assist in the recovery efforts and help support the operations of the FDNY SCUBA team. Subsequently, the Red Cross Disaster Assistance Response Team (DART) within the FDNY was activated and assisted in Red Cross operations.

Brooklyn faced a four-alarm fire in a six-story, 200- x 200-foot building under renovation on July 21, 1996. The former Pratt Institute facility also had been a public school. The building was fully involved and spread to the exposures. The blaze took nearly three hours to control.

On August 23, 1996, a fire broke out in the former B. Altman Department Store, located at Fifth Avenue and 36th Street. Box 733 was sent out at 3:05 a.m. for a reported fire in the 13-story, brick, 420- x 200-foot vacant building. The top-floor fire proved to be extremely hot and difficult to control. The fire went to five alarms before it was controlled at 1:14 p.m.

An apparent gas explosion in the Hyo Shin Bible Presbyterian Church in Queens caused major damage and a severe radiant heat problem for arriving units. The explosion occurred within the three-story, 75- x 200-foot brick church, blew the roof off the structure and sent a huge fire ball roaring into the night. First-due units transmitted a second alarm upon arrival for Box 6912. The severely damaged church was involved heavily in flames and two 2½-story Queen Annes burned as well. A separate box was transmitted for the burning homes and also went to two alarms.

At 3:59 a.m. on October 10, 1996, Box 847 was transmitted for an electrical fire on the 10th floor of 30 Rockefeller Center in Manhattan. The fire started in an electrical panel on the 10th floor of the General Electric Building, which houses both WNBC-TV (New York City Channel 4) and the national NBC Television Network.

The fire dropped down to the ninth- and eighth-floor electrical closets. Thick, acrid smoke filled the 69-story building, forcing its complete evacuation. This affected both the local and national television feeds. A 10-76 was transmitted, followed by second, third, fourth and fifth alarms.

Number 30 Hamilton Place is a six-story homeless hotel that takes up the entire block from 138th to 139th Streets in Manhattan. Approximately 300 residents live in the 147 apartments. A fire broke out in a fourth-floor apartment and quickly raced across the ceilings and out into the public hallway. Flames then shot up the south stairway and mushroomed on the top floor, rapidly extending down the sixth-floor hallway.

Box 1584 was transmitted at 3:48 a.m. and units were at the scene within minutes. Arriving second-due, Ladder Company 28 sized up the huge structure. Heavy smoke was pumping from the sixth-floor windows with two people threatening to jump. Firefighters Thomas Grimshaw, the chauffeur, and John K. Duddy, the OVM (outside vent man), placed the aerial ladder into operation. The 100-foot ladder was extended and Duddy quickly ascended to the victims.

Upon reaching the top of the ladder, Duddy noticed an ornamental fence blocking the lower half of the window. Without regard for his own safety, Duddy stepped onto the top rung of the aerial, stepped across to the windowsill and began to lift the victims, a man and a woman, over the fence and onto the ladder, where Grimshaw assisted them to the ground.

The victims informed the firefighters that two people still were inside the apartment. But before they could return to the room, two other people appeared at a window of the adjoining apartment. The aerial was placed to that window and Duddy duplicated his previous acrobatic rescue effort. Then, not wanting to wait until the ladder could be moved back to the original window, Duddy entered the apartment and began to crawl to the public hall.

Meanwhile, on the fifth floor, the floor above the original fire floor, the forcible entry team of Ladder Company 28, Lieutenant James P. Ginty and Firefighters Edwin Anzalone and John Kean, crawled into the public hall and began searching. Conditions on the floor were deteriorating rapidly as fire had complete control of two apartments. No hose lines were in position yet and the fire was raging out of control, making the public hall almost untenable.

Crawling toward the sound of moaning, Lieutenant Ginty pressed deeper into the heat and smoke and came upon a woman, uncon-

scious and badly burned. He radioed the chief and began to drag her back toward the stairs. Ginty was joined by his forcible entry team, who carried the woman to the third floor.

With numerous apartments to search and conditions getting worse by the minute, Ginty requested he be allowed to re-enter the blazing fourth floor. Under grueling conditions, two more victims were found and prevented from jumping out a window. The victims were held in place as an engine company moved in and gained control of the raging hall.

On the sixth-floor, the forcible entry team of Rescue Company 3, Lieutenant Gerard Murtha and Firefighters John Conroy and Clifford Stabner, crawled down the hall under blistering heat. In the oven-like conditions of the 100-foot-long hallway, Lieutenant Murtha located an unconscious woman and ordered Conroy and Stabner to remove her to the relative safety of the fifth floor (where the hallway door was closed and the heavy fire in the stairway held in check).

Returning to the sixth floor, Conroy located and removed an unconscious female, then entered the floor again and rescued an unconscious male. Stabner also located and removed two victims from the sixth floor.

Entering a room, Murtha found another victim and began to drag her out. Conroy arrived and took charge of the victim, while Murtha returned again to the raging hallway. Crawling down the hall for a third time, Murtha met Firefighter Duddy from Ladder Company 28, who had found an unconscious victim and needed help. They began to drag the victim out and were met by Conroy and Stabner, who assisted in the removal.

The fire required a third-alarm assignment and proved to be one of the most punishing fires in recent history. The valiant work of the nozzle teams of several companies and the persistent searches by members of the ladder and rescue companies were in the highest traditions of the FDNY. Seven companies were cited for their operations. For his heroic and acrobatic rescue work, Firefighter John Duddy received the Bennett Medal. For their bravery and determination, Lieutenants Ginty and Murtha and Firefighters Stabner and Conroy were awarded medals.

The year 1997 got off to a wild start as the FDNY was called to a wind-driven inferno on the 28th floor of the 42-story, high-rise multiple dwelling known as One Lincoln Plaza in Manhattan. The fire started in the apartment of famed musician Lionel Hampton and was seen live on televisions across the city.

The blaze broke out when a high-intensity lamp fell over onto a bed and set it on fire. The occupants of the apartment, Mr. Hampton included, evacuated, but inadvertently left the apartment door open. The window to the fire room failed and a strong wind soon drove flames down the hallway with blowtorch intensity.

Box 969 was transmitted at 2:32 p.m. and companies could see sheets of flames shooting from the 28th floor as they pulled up to the 64th Street and Columbus Avenue building. Conditions on the fire floor were as severe as they possibly could be. Lines were hooked up to the standpipe, flaps were pulled down and collars pulled up as the first of the nozzle teams attempted to inch their way into the wall of flames.

The Ninth Battalion received reports of two women seen trapped at a window on the fire floor. The chief sent Rescue Company 1 to attempt to reach them. Locating the apartment directly above the trapped women, they forced the door and quickly began a lifesaving rope evolution. Firefighter Stan Sussina was lowered out of the 29th-floor window to the trapped women below.

Firefighter Sussina twisted through the window and took charge of the situation. He requested and received two masks for the women, then checked conditions at the hallway door and took steps to stop further smoke from pushing into the apartment. Sussina calmed the women and held them at a window as the fire fight continued.

Outside the apartment door, on the 28th-floor hallway, team after team of firefighters pushed two 2½-inch hose lines down the hall. Advances were measured in inches, as the entire apartment fire was driven at the nozzle teams. It took the combined efforts of 10 engine companies to reach the fire apartment and extinguish the fire. Five alarms were sent in to provide crews on the fire floor and search the smoke-filled floors above. For his daring rope work and placing himself in an extremely dangerous and potentially untenable position, Firefighter Stan Sussina was awarded the Bennett Medal.

Twenty-five minutes after the "Lionel Hampton fire" was placed under control, Brooklyn Box 2138 sent companies to 1011 Foster Avenue, a 1000- x 750-foot, one-story, cinder-block structure with a rubberized roof covering. The food warehouse roof fire produced thick, black smoke and as different products below were ignited, flying brands became a problem.

Five alarms were requested as fire also had extended to exposure #2, a one-story, 150- x 150-foot rag warehouse. During this operation, an "All-hands" was fought in Truman High School in the Bronx.

A fire was reported in Saint Philip Neri Roman Catholic Church at 3025 Grand Concourse in the Bronx at 8:17 p.m. on Father's Day, June 15, 1997. The church, built in 1898, was the equivalent of three stories high and had a heavy fire condition on the upper levels and through the roof. Several large, stained-glass windows were removed to allow tower ladder operations. The blaze went to five alarms and ended with the collapse of the structure. In an area where potential collapse was feared, Commissioner Von Essen, who often is found on the fire floor, was "caught" with members of Rescue 3 removing statues out of the collapse zone.

On July 15, 1997, the city was suffering a heat wave, accompanied by extremely humid conditions. At one minute after noon, Queens Box 9372 came in for a fire in a 2½-story private dwelling at 35-30 101st Street. Upon arrival, the second floor of the structure was fully involved with fire in both exposures. A second alarm was transmitted upon arrival.

A five-inch supply-line from Engine Company 324 was stretched to the front of the fire building and a manifold was set up to feed four hand lines. With

the debilitating effects of the heat, four alarms were transmitted and numerous trucks were special-called. Two RAC Units supplied much-needed fluids and a city bus was utilized to cool off overheated members.

In the early-morning hours of August 6, 1997, Brooklyn units were called out for the collapse of an occupied building at 3851 Flatlands Avenue. Box 3084 came in at 3:36 a.m. and Ladder Company 159 was on the scene minutes later. The five-story, 100- x 200-foot, H-type building had suffered a major collapse. Three quarters of the B-wing bearing wall had collapsed, leaving the floors from the fifth down to the second, hanging in an unsupported, lean-to fashion. The second floor also had collapsed onto the first floor in a pancake fashion.

Lieutenant Edmund S. Lucia split the members of Ladder Company 159 into two teams. Firefighters Patrick Geraghty, Justin Van Wert and Michael Haddican were sent to the fifth floor to find and remove as many people as they could. Inside one of the collapsed apartments, Geraghty found and removed a dazed woman. The team continued searching the fifth floor, then dropped down to the third floor.

Lieutenant Lucia teamed up with Firefighter James McHugh to search the fourth floor, where they found an 88-year-old man approximately 10 feet inside the lean-to collapse that had been his apartment. Lucia and McHugh completed the search of the fourth floor and joined the men on the third floor. There, Haddican found an elderly male pinned under fallen rubble and furniture that had to be cut. Lieutenant Lucia gave the information to the officer of Rescue Company 2, Lieutenant Dennis Mojica (Mojica is assigned to Rescue 1, but was working in Rescue 2 for the tour). Mojica moved into the area with Firefighter Robert Galione.

The building was making noise – the collapse area was shifting. Realizing the treacherous position the pinned man was in, it was decided that Galione would work alone and cut the man free, with Mojica and the members of Lad-

Five alarms were transmitted for Queens Box 9656 on February 17, 1997. Flames roared through seven frame buildings along Jamaica Avenue. (Photo by Steve Spak)

The ribbon is cut on October 9, 1997, at the new FDNY Headquarters, located at 9 MetroTech Center, Brooklyn.

On October 9, 1997, the ribbon was cut at the nw FDNY Headquarters, located at 9 MetroTech Center in Brooklyn. Thanks to the efforts of Mayor rudolph Guiliani, this was the first time since 1887 that the FDNY moved into a new building designed strictly for Headquarters. It features a state-of-the-art audio-visual center, 200-seat auditorium, an Operations Command Post, where critical incidents can be monitored by senior staff, training rooms, a fitness center and indoor, below-grade parking faiclities.

The New York Post newspaper building is on South Street, near the Brooklyn Bridge. Across the street from the building and next to the river is a parking lot used by employees of the paper. On Friday afternoon, October 24, 1997, at about 2:40 p.m., 67-year-old Isaac Yorkowitz left work at the *Post* and entered his car, a black Mercedes-Benz, and apparently suffered a heart attack. The auto suddenly lurched forward and was catapulted from the parking lot out into the East River, the driver struggling with both a heart attack and a sinking car.

der Company 159 nearby to provide back-up if needed. For nearly five minutes, Galione carefully cut away the pieces pinning the victim. With further collapse imminent and a strong build-up of leaking natural gas in the area, Galione prepared to make the last cuts.

The building began to vibrate and Mojica moved in next to Galione and the victim. Galione was having difficulty with the victim because he was sliding off the angled sofa and toward the debris pile. Mojica grabbed the victim around the chest and Galione grabbed the victim around the waist. Mojica pulled the victim up and over Galione, who passed the victim hand over hand. Together, they dragged him up the steep slope of the collapsed floor to the hallway where Ladder 159 began medical treatment.

For their teamwork under extremely fragile conditions with the potential for further collapse or explosion, the members of Ladder Company 159 -- Lieutenant Lucia and Firefighters McHugh, Geraghty and Maddican, and Rescue Company 2 -- Lieutenant Mojica and Firefighter Galione, were awarded medals for their actions.

A fire in a Queens three-story frame turned the night of September 18, 1997, into a tough one. Box 7474 was transmitted at 11:21 p.m. for a fire at 30-91 Steinway Street in Astoria. The 30- x 50-foot building also had a one-story 30- x 40-foot extension in the rear. Originally a residence, the building had been converted to commercial -- a toy store.

The volume of fire upon arrival dictated a second alarm and flames soon spread to exposures 2, 2A, 2B, 4, 4A and 4B, for a total of seven similar attached structures. Seven alarms were transmitted as the glow of the flames lit up the night.

On the elevated FDR Drive above, David Weiss of Ladder Company 46 was off-duty and driving with his fiancee. Weiss saw the car sinking in the water, stopped his vehicle and sprang into action. Climbing over the roadway wall, he crossed a steel beam that supported the elevated road and made his way to the connection point where another beam met. Weiss looked for signs of life as the car slipped beneath the water. Suddenly, amidst escaping bubbles, appeared Mr.

First Deputy Commissioner William Feehan confers with Chief Officers. A water main break led to a gas main rupture and a three-alarm response on January 2, 1998. The catastrophe occurred at Broadway and 20th Street in Manhattan. (Photo by John Strandberg)

Manhattan's lower east side was the site of a three-alarm fire at 101 Christie Street on January 24, 1998. (Photo by Jim Romeika)

February 3, 1998, train derailment at White Plains Road and East 241st Street, Bronx.

Yorkowitz. Weiss slid down the girder to the concrete pillars that encased the beams at the water line and sunk into the river's bottom.

Weiss dove into the water and swam toward Yorkowitz, who could not keep himself above water. The Bronx firefighter rolled the now-unconscious driver over and tried to give him a few quick breaths. Back on land, *Post* employees were taking actions to help as best they could. A newspaper delivery driver dove into the water, but could not overcome the fast-moving water. He had to abandon his rescue attempt before becoming a victim himself. Workers called 911 as another team of drivers made their way to the water's edge. Weiss towed the victim and fought the currents and the cold water (water temperatures were about 40 to 50 degrees) as he struggled toward shore.

One *Post* driver found a sledge hammer and with other *Post* employees holding him, hung over the edge and extended the tool toward the exhausted firefighter. Weiss grabbed the tool in one hand and held the victim in the other.

Firefighters from Engine 9 and Ladder 6 arrived within moments and a ladder was lowered to Weiss, who placed Yorkowitz on it. Both men then were pulled from the river. Sadly, Yorkowitz was pronounced dead in New York Downtown Hospital. For heroism, Firefighter David Weiss was awarded a medal.

On the morning of December 17, 1997, Firefighter Joseph M. Dougherty of Ladder Company 41 arrived at his firehouse to find he had the detail. Dougherty gathered his gear and set out for Ladder Company 53 on City Island. Crossing the bridge to the Island, Dougherty saw smoke and went to investigate.

Dougherty found a house on fire at 577 Minnieford Avenue. He could see flames blowing out two side windows as he donned his bunker gear. He told a civilian to call the Fire Department and as he approached the house, he noticed a man and woman outside the building on a third-floor ledge. Dougherty made his way to the door where he met off-duty Firefighter Walter Henning of Engine Company 63, who had searched the first floor without benefit of gear or a mask

and removed a disoriented woman. Then, he had returned and attempted to reach an elderly couple on the upper floor via the interior stairs and by the exterior fire escape.

Henning advised Dougherty the interior stairs were impassable and that the fire escape stairs were cut off by fire. The two firefighters located a contractor's ladder and hurried toward the victims. Henning butted the ladder and Dougherty climbed the almost vertical ladder to the top. He guided the victims down to Henning, waiting halfway down the ladder. As they exited the ledge, they told Dougherty that a woman was still inside. He climbed the ladder and entered the window.

Searching in the dense smoke without a mask, Dougherty had to return to the window for gulps of air. Henning remained at the top of the ladder to act as an audible guide. He made repeated searches and finally as the apparatus arrived, he climbed down the ladder only to grab a mask off the rig and continue his search. Dougherty, still in his street clothes, helped stretch the first two lines.

For their heroic actions in saving the lives of three people without benefit of mask or hose line protection, Firefighters Walter Henning and Joseph Dougherty were awarded medals.

On January 19, 1998, the FDNY provided mutual aid to Jersey City, New Jersey, when a landmark building, the State Theater, collapsed onto the three-story building next door. The collapse injured at least 17 people and required two alarms of Jersey City companies. A request to the FDNY sent Rescue Company 3 with the Collapse Rig, Battalion 9 and Battalion Chief Raymond Downey of Special Operations. Rescue Company 1 later was special-called to relieve Rescue Company 3. Both companies were honored by the Jersey City Fire Department for their actions at the collapse operation.

Bronx units responding to a reported train collision at White Plains Road and 241st Street could not believe their eyes when they arrived at Box 3884 on February 3, 1998, at 9:24 p.m. Two passenger-less trains being moved to the yard collided, causing a derailment. Several cars were thrown from the elevated tracks.

One car had toppled over and landed on a parked trailer below, starting a fire that rapidly was extending. Two of the cars came to rest with one end of the car on the tracks and the other end off the tracks, with one of the cars slamming onto the roof of a two-story building. The car sat balanced between the elevated tracks and the roof of the badly damaged commercial building.

Ladder Company 39 arrived and placed their aerial ladder to the elevated tracks. Firefighters William Jutt and Robert Schiavone climbed under high-voltage wires and onto the elevated track area, carefully avoiding the still live third rail. Checking under the cars, they located the lead car and entered the dangling car. The duo found the engineer, unconscious and bleeding from a head wound.

They radioed their find and the patient's condition as they began first aid. They established an airway, stabilized his neck and spine and tended to his head wound. Radio reports were voicing real concern regarding the stability of the damaged building, which supported one end of the car. Jutt and Schiavone worked as fast as they could to place the man safely in a Stokes basket. The injured man in the Stokes was lowered with a lifesaving rope down the rails of the aerial.

For their bravery and expertise, Firefighters William Jutt (a previous Bennett Medal winner) and Robert Schiavone were awarded medals.

February 25, 1998, was a busy day for the Department. At 2:45 p.m., Manhattan Box 1076 became a 10-76. The fire was on the 26th floor of the 35-story building at 500 East 77th Street. The fire was fought for about a half hour before being brought under control.

Immediately following that job, a two-alarm blaze was fought at Manhattan Box 1558. A fire in a laundromat in the landmarked Colonial Park Houses at 3359 Broadway raced up the pipe recesses of the six-story, 25- x 75-foot brick building. Firefighters were able to head off the spread at the fourth floor.

At 9:22 the same evening (February 25th), special calls were placed for Battalion 9 and Rescue Company 3 to respond on a mutual aid to Hoboken, New Jersey, to the scene of a multiple building collapse at First and Garden Streets. The FDNY operated for nearly two hours, using thermal imaging cameras, sound detectors and performing visual searches in voids.

Friday, the 13th of March, 1998, was a cold, gray and blustery day that, among other things, featured a full moon. As expected, it became one of those days:
• Manhattan All Hands at Box 427 – fire on the eighth floor of a 14-story multiple dwelling. • Second alarm on arrival at Queens Box 8658, a 2 1/2-story dwelling on Marsden Street. • All Hands Bronx Box 2759 on Waldo Avenue – an emotionally disturbed person set himself on fire. • All Hands at Bronx Box 3280 for a fire in a five-story multiple dwelling on Reservoir Oval, where Firefighter Gary Voigt of Ladder Company 32 made the medal-worthy rescue of an elderly man from a raging fourth-floor apartment. The fires continued: • All Hands at Brooklyn Boxes 58 – a one-story commercial building on Calyer and Jewel Streets and 75-1762 for a three-story building on Fulton Street. • All Hands at Queens Box 7885, a six-story multiple dwelling on 36th Avenue. • A 10-80 code 2 at 1827 Pacific Street in Brooklyn for crystallized picric acid in a factory. • All Hands Brooklyn Box 3735 for a four-story, brick, multiple dwelling on Bedford Avenue. • Bronx Box 2578 for a fire on the 21st floor of a multiple dwelling on Ogden and East 167th Streets. • All Hands at Queens Box 5708 for a house fire on 200th Street in Saint Albans. • All Hands at Brooklyn Box 3541 for a compactor fire in an 18-story multiple dwelling at West 23rd Street and Surf Avenue in Coney Island. • All Hands Brooklyn Box 3669, for a house fire on Lois Avenue, Gerritsen Beach. • Bronx All Hands Box 3160 for a suspicious fire (second fire in building on the same day) on the third floor of a six-story multiple dwelling. • All Hands Bronx Box 2441 for fire in a two-story brick on Clarendon Road. The clock struck midnight, but three more All Hands were fought before the sun rose.

On February 26, 1998, High-Rise Unit 2 was placed in service in the quarters of Engine Company 39. The unit responds to all 10-76 signals and special calls within Battalions 2, 4, 6, 7, 13, 16, the Bronx and Queens. High-Rise Unit 1, located in the quarters of Engine Company 3, responds within Battalions 1, 8, 9, 10, 11, 12, Brooklyn and Staten Island. The original High-Rise Unit 1, went into service in 1976.

On June 5, 1998, tragedy struck the FDNY again. Brooklyn Box 2044 was transmitted at 8:22 p.m. for a fire in a three-story, wood-frame dwelling at 2530 Atlantic Avenue. Fire was blowing out several windows and people were reported trapped as units rolled in. Captain Scott LaPiedra of Ladder Company 176 and Lieutenant James Blackmore of Engine Company 332 led their men into the blazing structure.

Members were moving into position when suddenly, the floor collapsed, throwing members into the blazing inferno below. Battalion Chief Edward S. Kilduff was asked by Chief Galvin to tell the operating members of the heavy fire below them and determine the status of the searches for missing tenants. Kilduff reached the collapsed area and saw Engine Company 332's line dangling over the edge of a hole filled with fire.

Chief Kilduff raced to the first floor to inform Galvin. Members of Engine Company 321 had arrived at the front and were moving a line into the fire area. Kilduff grabbed Firefighter Eric Weiner of Ladder Company 111 and plunged into the fire area. The Chief quickly found Captain LaPiedra and shortly thereafter Firefighter Quinn. Kilduff directed the removal of the men and coordinated the attack on the fire. Lieutenants Stackpole and Blackmore and Firefighter Baiker were located and members moved in and removed the trapped men.

The operation reached five alarms as the rescue efforts and firefighting were pressed beyond the average physical limits. Two valiant members of the Department died in the line of duty as a result of the collapse. Lieutenant James Blackmore of Engine Company 332 was rushed to Brookdale Hospital, but succumbed to his severe injuries. Captain LaPiedra was airlifted to Jacobi Hospital Burn Center. The Captain clung valiantly to life until July 4, 1998. Four other firefighters were transported to the Burn Center at New York Hospital.

For his outstanding leadership during operations in an extremely hazardous and frenzied atmosphere, Battalion Chief Edward Kilduff was recognized by the Department with the Brooklyn Citizens Medal.

A verbal alarm for Manhattan Box 795 was transmitted at 8:25 a.m. on July 21, 1998, for a scaffolding collapse at the Conde Nast construction site at Four Times Square. A scaffold that contained a tracked elevator used to transport workers and equipment to the upper floors of the 48-story building under construction tore loose at the 21st floor and fell across 43rd Street. The largest section of track penetrated the concrete roof of the Woodstock Hotel and killed an elderly woman in her top-floor apartment.

The FDNY evacuated people in the immediate area and the collapse zone. Units initiated a search (and found the fatality) and reported their size-up back to the Incident Commander. The FDNY maintained units on-scene for 26 days. During that time frame, 93 engine, ladder and rescue companies and 52 battalions and other units were called.

As the dismantling work continued, the FDNY downsized their number of units on-scene. Teams stood by at the ready; rescue teams covered the work crews and Squads acted as FAST units. Paramedics stood by at the ready and chief officers supervised the operations 24 hours a day.

On July 24, 1998, Brooklyn Box 2456 came in at 11:01 p.m. with Engine Company 255 arriving first-due. Captain John Pritchard transmitted the 10-75 and was off the rig in a flash. Tenants were reporting a baby was trapped on the burning fourth floor of the six-story apartment house. Pritchard proceeded to the fire area.

At the door, he encountered an extreme heat condition with thick smoke banked to the floor. Pritchard crawled into the apartment. Pritchard searched as far as he could. The building heat was burning his skin and he was about to back out when he heard a baby's cries. Pritchard plunged ahead until he found a play pen with a baby girl inside. Flames were venting violently over the child and out the windows. There was no way to stand and lift the child, so Pritchard grabbed the play pen and dragged it back across to the apartment door.

The room was filling with flames, the play pen was melting in his hands and Pritchard was exhausted, but he continued through the apartment door and into the hallway. Firefighter George Shea and Captain Michael McGrath found Pritchard as he dragged the play pen the last few feet. They helped him and the baby to safety. McGrath and Shea returned to the apartment and continued the search.

The modern-day Squad Companies can trace their origins to December 3, 1977, when Squad Company 1 was reorganized in Brooklyn. The company was assigned a fully equipped pumper, stocked with ladder company hand and power tools and a high-expansion foam generator. They responded to local boxes as an engine and to designated battalions as a squad.

The reorganization of Engine Company 41 in the Bronx in 1990 was a similar situation, except that 41 was designated as an "enhanced engine company." They were, however, equipped, operated and responded like Squad Company 1.

With the Mayoral Directive charging the Department with the mitigation of chemical and biological agents and the decontamination of those affected by terrorist attack, the FDNY took action. Recognizing the need for additional Squads, Commissioner Thomas Von Essen selected and designated Engine Companies 18, 61, 252, 270 and 288 as Squads on July 1, 1998. Engine Company 41 was designated as a Squad Company the following day, July second.

These units received extensive training in ladder company operations, collapse, confined space, high angle and other rescue operations. Additionally, they received extensive haz-mat mitigation and decontamination training. All of the Squads have been equipped and designated as Hazardous Materials Technician Units. Each has a second piece to carry haz-mat equipment.

Shea followed the whimper of a child deep into the apartment and found a young girl. Shea crawled back past the main body of fire – shielding the child from the flames – out into the hall and brought her down to her family.

Captain Pritchard and the 10-month-old infant he rescued were admitted to the Burn Center. The child rescued by Shea also required hospitalization. For their daring, lifesaving efforts, Firefighter George Shea was awarded a medal and "Captain Jack" Pritchard became only the second member of the FDNY to be awarded the Bennett Medal twice.

In September of 1998, FDNY members were activated as part of New York Task Force 1, the FEMA team. The team was flown to the Dominican Republic and operated where possible on the island that was devastated by Hurricane Georges. Team members were dropped by helicopter in remote areas to provide medical attention to villages cut off from the outside world. Drugs were administered, first-aid provided and surgery was performed.

Other team members were transported to San Pedro de Macoris where they worked on restoring a hospital hard hit by the storm. After a grueling day's work under broiling sun, the team had refabricated the roof and restored electricity and water to the hospital. Team members were thanked in person by the President of the Republic.

To address the fatal fire problem in Jamaica, Queens, an area filled with wood-frame and Queen Ann construction, Commissioner Von Essen went to the Mayor and secured approval for a new truck company. A call went out for volunteers. A combination of seasoned veterans, sprinkled with a few probies, was chosen to fill the roster of the new company. On November 9, 1998, Ladder Company 133 went into service in the quarters of Engine Company 275. No one could have imagined just how quickly the new unit would have an impact on fire protection in Queens.

Four days after 133 went into service, Box 5018 came in, sending the new company first-due to a reported fire in an eight-story senior citizens residence. Heavy smoke and fire were venting out a fourth-floor window as firefighters hustled into the building.

Lieutenant Greg Picconi led his forcible entry team of Firefighter Greg Batkay and Probationary Firefighter Bill Schaeffer up a staircase toward the fourth floor. As the hose line was stretched from the standpipe, the trio moved down the hall and forced the door to the fire apartment. Before the water could be started, Picconi crawled into the raging fire apartment as Firefighter Schaeffer covered him with the water can.

Crawling deep into the apartment nearing the seat of the fire, Picconi found a severely burned woman, unconscious on the floor. Picconi dragged the woman from her burning apartment and back down the public hallway into a clear apartment. Engine Company 275 then pushed the line down the hall and into the blazing apartment. For his heroic rescue and setting the bar high for members of the new company, Lieutenant Greg Picconi was awarded a medal, his second.

November 25, 1998, was a clear morning and off-duty Firefighter Heinz Kothe was on the upper east side of Manhattan with his friend and colleague, Lieutenant Lawrence Blieka, also off-duty. Both men worked together in Ladder Company 12. While walking on First Avenue, they detected an odor of smoke and went to investigate. They found a hot cloud of smoke rising above the six-story apartment house at 1480 York Avenue.

Dashing into a courtyard, they entered different staircases, searching for the seat of the fire. Kothe quickly made it to the roof, crossed to the rear and saw flames blowing out a fifth-floor window. Kothe, with no tools, was able to physically force the bulkhead to vent the mushrooming heat and smoke below. Kothe then heard noise in a shaft and found two men in a state of panic, threatening to jump. He calmed them and assured them help was on the way.

Meanwhile, downstairs, Blieka had found smoke but no fire on the fourth floor. He continued to the fifth floor, pounding on doors and shouting warnings to the residents. Heat and smoke were pouring out the open fire apartment door and venting into the hall. Without gear, the tremendous heat did not allow the officer to get close enough to close the door. He dashed to the sixth floor and continued warning residents, before returning to the fourth floor and making his way to the rear fire escape.

Commissioner Thomas Von Essen introduced the new Squads in front of FDNY Headquarters at July 1, 1998, ceremony.

Aerial view of roof-top fire at 136 William Street in Manhattan. This five-alarm fire was fought on April 12, 1998. (Photo by John Strandberg)

Fire burns throughout the roof of the 128-year-old Central Synagogue in Manhattan, August 28, 1998. (Photo by Steve Spak)

By this point, Ladder Company 13 arrived and Firefighter Thomas Sabella made it to the roof with the lifesaving rope and joined Kothe. Below them, the sixth-floor public hall filled with flames. It was rope time. Kothe tied off the rope, put on the life belt and took turns, as Sabella readied himself to be lowered. Firefighter Dale McLaughlin of Ladder Company 16 arrived. After a quick introduction to Kothe, McLaughlin acted as guide and safety man as Sabella was lowered and picked up a victim.

After they were safely off the rope, it was pulled up and then McLaughlin was lowered. With conditions deteriorating rapidly, McLaughlin snatched the victim from the window and together, they were lowered to safety.

Lieutenant Blieka used the fire escape to cover the rear of the building, searching the sixth and fifth floors under extreme conditions. For their combined on-duty and off-duty rescue efforts, Lieutenant Blieka and Firefighters McLaughlin, Sabella and Kothe were awarded medals.

The year 1998 came to a sad close as Lieutenant Joseph Cavalieri and Firefighters James Bohan and Christopher Bopp were killed while operating at Brooklyn Box 4080 on December 18th. The trio were working together in Ladder Company 170 at this fire in a senior citizens residence when a window failed. The wind drove a fire ball down the hall at the unsuspecting men.

On March 11, 1999, a kitchen fire broke out at 2823 Broadway, Manhattan, in the 11-story multiple dwelling on the corner of West 109th Street. The building was undergoing renovation with a huge scaffolding erected within an open air shaft and extended to the roof. Flames in a grease duct soon auto-exposed to the wooden plank-lined and plastic mesh-covered scaffold. The kitchen fire was developing into a major blaze.

As the fire began to spread beneath them, workers were rescued from the scaffold by aerial ladder. As the scaffold operation commenced, Deputy Chief Pat McKnight was informed that an extremely distraught woman was seen at a 10th-floor window with children. An aerial ladder was positioned and Firefighter Matt Barnes of Ladder Company 25 climbed toward the frantic woman.

Reaching the very top, Barnes stood on the top rungs to see over the ledge when the woman virtually forced the infants into the firefighter's hands. With little choice and in an extremely precarious position, Barnes, with the assistance of Firefighter Steve Johnson, managed to remove them safely to the street. The mother was removed through the interior by other firefighters.

The fire continued to spread and the 11-story scaffold became a tower of flames, burning into apartments on each floor. Numerous hand lines were stretched and operated. In all, eight alarms were transmitted for this fire. Firefighter Matt Barnes' act of heroism was submitted to the Board of Merit and he received the Honor Legion Medal on Medal Day.

The day after Saint Patrick's Day, March 18, 1999, posed a serious problem to the FDNY and citizens in the midtown area. At 1:17 p.m., Box 786 was transmitted for One Times Square for a reported fallen sign with injuries to people. The building, a 22-story commercial and famous as the site of the New Year's Eve ball drop, featured a large sign – measuring approximately 80- x 50-feet and weighing 500 pounds – that became dislodged by high winds. Several people were injured by the falling debris that still was raining down as fire apparatus pulled up.

Three sides of the sign had pulled free and the wind, gusting above 40 mph, was whipping the sign about dangerously. Secured with high-angle rope equipment, Firefighter Gerry Nevins of Rescue Company 1 worked his way out onto a 14-inch-wide parapet and began attaching shackles and utility ropes. The sign, moved by the strong wind, then wrapped around a light system and began to shred the lighting systems.

Nevins was lowered down the inside of the sign on a high-angle rope system to various levels and again went about the dangerous and laborious task of stabilizing the huge sign. Using utility ropes and shackles, he tied down section after section of the sign. Working for more than one hour, on a rope, 200 feet above Times Square, Firefighter Nevins secured the sign and cleared numerous broken pieces of aluminum, plastic and metal that had been raining down on the streets below, injuring citizens.

Firefighter Gerry Nevins worked in a very dangerous position, with an unrelenting wind and made the sidewalks safe below him. For his courage and determination, he received the Thomas A. Kenny Memorial Medal.

April 1999 was a tough month for Staten Island units. On the 14th, three alarms were transmitted for Box 982, a lumberyard fire at 130 Union Avenue. The fully involved lumberyard fire began at 5:01 p.m. and extended to four nearby homes.

On April 16th, Box 2666, at Guyon Avenue and Old Mill Road was transmitted at 2:45 a.m. for a wind-driven brush fire. Three alarms were transmitted as firefighters protected homes threatened by the advancing fire.

At 11:16 a.m. on April 27th, Box 3433 was transmitted for a fast-moving brush fire in Great Kills Park. The Box number later was changed to Box 8480 and went to four alarms. As this fire was being fought, Box 1960 was received for a fire in a two-story, wood-frame building at 38 Leo Street. This fire required a two-alarm assignment to extinguish.

On April 29th, Richmond Box 8800 was transmitted at 11:04 a.m. for a fire at 4435 Victory Boulevard. The fire was in a two-story-high, 300- x 200-foot pile of compressed cardboard boxes. The fire threatened several structures and four alarms were transmitted before the fire was brought under control.

Once again, the FDNY lost one of the Bravest in the line of duty. On June 4, 1999, Captain Vincent Fowler succumbed to smoke inhalation while operating in a cellar fire at 150-28 Old South Road in Howard Beach, Queens. Despite the valiant efforts of several firefighters and fire officers, the Captain could not be saved.

On July 3, 1999, the Queens Dispatcher alerted Engine Company 275 and Ladder Company 133 to respond to a working fire in a private dwelling at 188-01 Dormans Road. It was 5:15 a.m. While en route to Box 8621, a Dispatcher's update stated numerous calls – people trapped on the second floor.

Engine Company 275 arrived first and transmitted a 10-75. Heavy fire was visible on the first floor of the 2½-story house. Ladder Company 133, under the command of Lieutenant Carlos Gonzalez, arrived as first-due truck and went into action. The officer ordered Firefighter Daniel Barry, the chauffeur, to place the aerial to the second floor and ordered a portable to the opposite side. Gonzalez entered the first floor with his forcible entry team.

Heavy fire was extending from the fully involved enclosed porch. Gonzalez ordered his men to search the first floor while he searched for the stairs to the second floor. Crawling, he found the stairs and, despite the extreme heat, made it to the hallway of the second floor. He searched a bedroom, returned to the hall and crawled toward the second bedroom when he found a 79-year-old woman, seriously burned and unconscious on the floor.

Gonzalez transmitted a 10-45 code 2 and dragged the woman down the hall, down stairs and across the living room toward the front door. Engine Company 275 was just beginning to start their attack on the fire at this time. Members helped the officer with the final portion of the removal.

The woman was taken to the hospital in cardiac arrest and revived. She later was transferred to the Cornell Burn Center. The heroic actions of Lieutenant Carlos Gonzalez were recognized with the John H. Prentice Medal.

A phone alarm for Richmond Box 229 was received at 3:06 a.m. on August 2, 1999. While responding, units were informed that numerous phone calls were being received for 190 Bay Street and that police on-scene were reporting a working fire. A wide array of police and EMS vehicles in front of the fire building slowed the placement of apparatus as firefighters went to work on the blazing three-story. A can of gasoline had been used to ignite the interior stairs of the house.

As the officer and forcible entry team moved in, a charged line was advanced and the aerial was placing the roofman from Ladder Company 78, Firefighter Stephen Fenley, in position to vent above the raging stairs. The inside team reported the stairs between the second and third floor had burned away. At the same time, a person, his clothes catching fire, became visible at a third-floor window. Fenley radioed his officer as the aerial was repositioned.

The ladder stopped at the window where the man had been seen. Fenley raced up. The man had moved from the window and fallen unconscious. Fenley dove headfirst into the extreme heat of the top floor, located the badly burned man and dragged him to the aerial. Conditions were deteriorating quickly. Fenley, struggling alone with the victim, lost his helmet. Within seconds of removing the victim and himself onto the aerial, the room behind him flashed over.

The victim was rushed to the hospital with critical burn injuries and succumbed to his injuries the following day. Fenley received first- and second-degree burns to his face, head and ears. For his daring rescue, Firefighter Stephen Fenley was awarded the Gordon Bennett Medal.

Brooklyn units responded to Box 1048 on August 26, 1999, at 7:42 a.m., for a reported fire in a row of attached private dwellings at 12 Miami Court. A heavy smoke condition obscured the fire building as members of Ladder Company 113 moved in. They came upon a man who had just jumped from the blistering heat of the second floor. He informed firefighters that a man was still inside.

Rescue company firefighter uses thermal imaging device at 48 Wallabout Street in Brooklyn. (Photo by Pete Connolly)

O n July 19, 1999, the FDNY introduced a new signal – 10-77 – for a working fire in a high-rise multiple dwelling. This signal gives the Incident Commander sufficient units, including four Engine companies, four Ladder companies, one Rescue company, one Squad company, a FAST unit (a ladder company), three Battalion Chiefs, Special Operations Battalion, Safety Battalion and a Deputy Chief, to manage a medium fire and smoke condition.

Firefighter John Hand of Ladder Company 113 dashed up the stairs to the second floor. Searching toward the front of the building and with fire drawing across the ceiling to the window left open by the jumper, Hand moved in. Reaching the bedroom, Hand located an unconscious, 76-year-old man and began to drag him out.

Forces operating below now realized the fire was actually in the cellar and controlled the first floor as Hand made his way down the stairs with the victim. The victim was turned over to EMS for treatment and transport. Firefighter John Hand's actions were honored with the Hugh Bonner Medal.

A few hours later, Manhattan Box 1639 was transmitted for a fire in a four-story brownstone at 535 West 149th Street. Fire extended into exposure #2, a seven-story multiple dwelling. Flames ate their way through both structures and blazed through the roofs. Eight alarms were required to extinguish the fires in both buildings.

On October 2, 1999, Bronx Box 2686 came in at 11:55 p.m. for a fire in a taxpayer at Soundview and Lafayette Avenues. Thirteen separate retail businesses were contained within the 75- x 100-foot structure. After a grueling attack, members were removed from the building and an exterior operation was begun. Four tower ladders operated and a fourth alarm was requested for relief purposes.

Ladder Company 33 was assigned to a water leak at 12:20 a.m. on October 25, 1999. During the response, Lieutenant John J. Halpin noticed police cars and a heavy smoke condition at Andrews Avenue, off Fordham Road. He notified the dispatcher that he had heavy smoke pushing from the fourth- and fifth-floor windows of 2315 Andrews Avenue. He transmitted a 10-75 and went to work. Ladder Company 59 was providing first-due truck work so Ladder Company 33 assumed the second-due position and went to the floor above.

Lieutenant Halpin and his forcible entry team of Firefighters Manning and Gilhooly encountered a heavy smoke and high heat condition on the fifth floor. They crawled down the long hall to search apartments 5-A and 5-B. After entering 5-A, the officer heard the frantic screams of an adult male. Crawling deeper into the apartment, he came upon a father and his two young children, who were face down on the kitchen floor.

Halpin ordered the window vented to try and improve the worsening smoke condition. He then radioed the Battalion that he had three civilians trapped above the fire. Halpin was told that water would be delayed because of a bad hydrant. Roof ventilation was delayed, too.

Lieutenant Halpin told the father to remain by the window as he crawled back to the hall to check on conditions. Extremely heavy smoke and heat were filling the hallway. He could not take them out that way, so he crawled to the fire escape window and was met by

Peter J. Ganci, Jr.
28th Chief of Department

Peter J. Ganci, Jr., became the 28th Chief of Department in October 1999. Chief Ganci began his career 31 years ago when he was appointed to Engine Company 92 in the Bronx. He transferred to Ladder Company 111 in Brooklyn and worked there for five years before starting his way up the promotion ladder in August of 1977. He was a Lieutenant in Ladder Company 124, the Captain of Ladder Company 18, a Battalion Chief in the 57th Battalion and then a Deputy Chief in the 1st Division. He also has been in command of the Bureau of Fire Investigation, Assistant Chief of Operations, Chief of Operations and Acting Chief of Department.

Chief Peter J. Ganci, Jr., at Brooklyn Box 44-2513, 392 East 4th Street, July 4, 1998.

Twenty-five teams, known as NEST Teams, consisting of one officer and two firefighters, equipped with Chemical Protective Clothing (CPC) suits and equipment for elevator emergencies, were placed in service. The number of members on duty in the Squad Companies were increased to seven and the companies were relocated to respond as haz-mat technician units. Squad Company 1 operated from the quarters of Rescue Company 1, as did a second Special Operations Battalion and the temporary unit, Haz-Mat 2. Squad Company 41 located at Engine 39; Squad 288 located at Engine 33; and Squad 18 located at Engine 3.

Squads 61, 252 and 270 and Rescue Company 5 manpower were increased by two members. Haz-Mat Company 1 operated from Engine 8 on the east side. The Special Operations Battalion and the Containment vessel were located at Engine 8. A haz-mat command post was set up in Central Park, at Sixth Avenue and 60th Street, under the command of Battalion Chief John Fanning. Special Operations Command coordinated all the special units and was under the command of Battalion Chief Ray Downey.

The last runs of the millennium were as follows:
- **Manhattan** – Box 1401 transmitted at 11:57 p.m. Engine Company 91, Ladder Company 14 and the 12th Battalion responded.
- **Brooklyn** – Box 1059 transmitted at 11:58 p.m. for 281 Crown Street.
- **Bronx** – EMS Box 3176 transmitted at 11:57 p.m. for a cardiac at 2259 Bathgate Avenue. Engine Company 88 was assigned.
- **Queens** – Box 2356 transmitted at 11:56 p.m. for 80-62 264th Street. Engine Company 251 was assigned. (10-35)
- **Staten Island** – EMS Box 3995 transmitted at 11:47 p.m. for unconscious person at 567 Winant Avenue.

At 12 midnight, a second alarm was transmitted for Brooklyn Box 2350. The fire was at 1121 Lafayette Avenue.

The first runs for the FDNY in the year 2000 were:
- **Manhattan** – Box 712 transmitted at 12:01 a.m. for 460 West 34th Street. Engine 34, Ladder 21 and Battalion 7 responded.
- **Brooklyn** – EMS Box 3923 transmitted at 12:03 a.m. for 1098 Eastern Parkway. Engine 234 responded.
- **Bronx** – Box 3589 transmitted at 12:01 a.m. in front of 3505 Wayne Avenue. Engine 62 responded.
- **Queens** – EMS Box 4964 transmitted at 12:00 a.m. for 155-15 71st Avenue. Engine 315 responded.
- **Staten Island** – Box 645 transmitted at 12:14 a.m. for an automatic alarm at 1320 Bay Street. Engine 152 responded.

heavy smoke and fire venting from below. Halpin returned to the kitchen. He shared his mask with the family. One child now was unconscious and conditions were worsening.

The Ladder Company 33 OVM, Firefighter Robert McGrath, heard the reports being given by Halpin and moved his tower ladder basket to the fifth-floor window adjoining the fire escape. He entered the room and crawled to the kitchen where he was given the 18-month-old child. Halpin took the three-year-old and the father out through the hall, a more direct route.

All three occupants made it safely outside the dense smoke condition. Lieutenant John Halpin was instrumental in saving their lives. For his leadership and courage under extreme conditions, he was awarded the M. J. Delehanty Medal.

The final days of 1999 took on added significance as the City and the world prepared for Millennium celebrations. Despite the possible threat of terrorism and the possible effects of Y2K computer problems, New York City would host "The New Year's Celebration" in Times Square, as usual.

What was unusual, however, was the preparation taken by the Office of Emergency Management under the leadership of Director Jerry Hauer and the plans implemented by the Fire Department under the leadership of Commissioner Von Essen and Chief of Department Ganci.

Presidents Board Of Commissioners 1865 - 1897

1865-1867	Charles C. Pinckney
1867-1870	Alexander Shaler
1870-1873	William Hitchman
1873-1877	Joseph L. Perley
1877-1881	Vincent C. King
1881	Cornelius Van Cott
1881-1884	John J. Gorman
1884-1893	Henry D. Purroy
1893-1897	John J. Scannell
1897	James R. Sheffield

Commissioners

1898-1901	John J. Scannell
1902-1903	Thomas Sturgis
1904-1905	Nicholas J. Hayes
1906	John H. O'Brien
1906-1908	Francis J. Lantry
1908	Hugh Bonner
1908-1909	Nicholas J. Hayes
1910-1911	Rhinelander Waldo
1911-1913	Joseph Johnson
1914-1917	Robert Adamson
1918-1926	Thomas J. Drennan
1926-1933	John J. Dorman
1934-1941	John J. McElligott
1941-1945	Patrick Walsh
1946-1950	Frank J. Quayle
1951	George P. Monaghan
1951-1954	Jacob Grumet
1954-1961	Edward F. Cavanagh, Jr.
1962-1964	Edward Thompson
1964-1965	Martin Scott
1966-1973	Robert O. Lowery
1973-1978	John T. O'Hagan
1978-1980	Augustus A. Beekman
1980-1982	Charles J. Hynes
1982-1987	Joseph E. Spinnato
1987-1990	Joseph Bruno
1990-1993	Carlos Rivera
1993-1994	William Feehan
1994-1996	Howard Safir
1996-	Thomas Von Essen

Chief Engineers and Chiefs of Department

1865-1869	Elisha Kingsland
1870-1873	Joseph L. Perley
1873-1884	Eli Bates
1884-1889	Charles O. Shay
1889-1899	Hugh Bonner
1899-1911	Edward F. Croker
1903	Charles D. Purroy
1911-1931	John Kenlon
1932-1940	John J. McElligott
1941-1945	Patrick Walsh
1947	Harold J. Burke
1948-1955	Peter Loftus
1955-1958	Edward Connors
1958-1962	George David
1963	Arthur J. Massett
1963-1964	Edward P. McAniff
1964-1978	John T. O'Hagan
1978-1980	Francis Cruthers
1980-1984	John J. Hart
1984-1986	John J. O'Rourke
1986-1988	Robert J. Butler
1988-1990	Homer G. Bishop
1990-1991	Joseph M. DeMeo
1991-1992	William M. Feehan
1992-1994	Anthony L. Fusco
1994-1995	Donald T. Ruland
1996-1997	Frank P. Cruthers
1997-1999	Joseph A. Casaburi
1999-	Peter J. Ganci, Jr.

Bringing FDNY into the New Millennium

To tell the story of this Department without noting the great strides the FDNY has made during the administration of Mayor Giuliani and Commissioner Von Essen not only would be unfair to them, but would ignore one of the most progressive, productive times in the history of this Department. Following are some of the major initiatives they have instituted during these past several years; initiatives that benefit both the men and women of this Department, as well as the citizens of and visitors to this city. Together, the Mayor and Commissioner have written a memorable chapter in the history of the FDNY.

- The roster staffing arbitration was settled with restoration of the fifth firefighter to 60 Engines.

- NYC Firefighters and Officers now have a Cancer Bill.

- The Nederman Exhaust Systems now are installed in all firehouses. Firefighters no longer breathe in diesel exhaust.

- Excellent medical training and extra compensation for responding to medical emergencies was given to firefighters and officers in all Engines, Squads and Rescue Units, with Ladder Company training in progress.

- Bunker gear was provided for everyone – firefighter burns have decreased dramatically. The dire predictions about heat stress have proved untrue.

- A new headquarters building was designed and built with modern, comfortable, high-tech amenities.

- Lighter masks, shorts, hoods, personal face pieces, leather boots – all were purchased and issued to improve firefighter safety. Additionally, all newly purchased apparatus is air-conditioned.

- Comprehensive medicals, now given every 15 months, provide personal attention to real medical problems.

- Additional units were placed in service: a new Ladder Company in Queens; three auxiliary craft units for the Marine Division; a new unit in Staten Island is planned for next year.

- Five Engines were converted into highly trained, superbly equipped, motivated Squads, with firefighter safety as their top priority.

- The Battalion Chief quota was increased by 21.

The Battalion Chief Mentor Program was established to provide more training for Chiefs.

- Fort Totten was acquired from the Federal government. Plans for FDNY Fire and Life Safety, campus renovations and construction are underway.

- $50 million was budgeted with construction to start in winter 2001 for additional training buildings at Randall's Island.

- A new communications system finally is close to realization.

- Two new 80-foot fireboats have been designed and will be ordered this year.

- Thermal imaging cameras were funded for all Rescue, Squad and Ladder Companies.

- Increased resources and attention were given to fire safety education, resulting in the fewest civilian fire fatalities in 50 years.

- The Fire Zone, a multimedia Fire Safety Education exhibit, will provide children of all ages with a high-tech, interactive learning experience. It will open at Rockefeller Center in the fall of 2000.

- Fire Cadet Program, aimed at increasing diversity in the Department, was established. First graduates to be appointed firefighters this year.

During Mayor Giuliani's and Commissioner Von Essen's tenure, millions and millions of dollars have been allocated to FDNY for these critical projects. The past few years have been phenomenal ones for FDNY. Projects that prior administrations were unwilling to fund have become realities. The FDNY forever will be indebted to Mayor Giuliani and Commissioner Von Essen for their leadership and continued support of the men and women of this Department.

The photos on the following pages show Commissioner Von Essen
with many supporters of the FDNY.

Mayor Giuliani and Sister Marguerite (sister of Joe Torre, the Yankees Manager).

At the Police/Fire run in Central Park

Ground-breaking ceremonies for new firehouse for Engine 75, Ladder 33. Proud Bronx units who have lived in the worst NYC firehouse for too long!

Our Mayor proudly leading us on St. Patrick's Day with Chief of Department, Peter Ganci.

Deputy Mayor Joseph Lhota and Director of Mayor's Office of Emergency Management, Jerry Hauer.

Lou Anemone, NYPD Chief of Department

With Rusty Staub, Mayor Giuliani and a smiling Commissioner Safir.

At the Commissioner's Humanitarian Awards Dinner with Cadet class 1 of 2000.

Bob Blair, "Old Buffalo," at Ladder 42.

Commissioner Von Essen and wife, Rita, pay tribute to Zachary Fisher at the Intrepid. *Mr. Fisher, Intrepid Museum founder and a great patriot, has supported uniformed services and the armed forces for decades.*

Miss America, Heather French, and Alan Hevesi, NYC Controller, feeding the homeless.

UFA President Kevin Gallagher checking on his members at a fire.

Bill Cosby producing a fire safety PSA

Father Mychal Judge at Cardinal O'Connor's last St. Patrick's Day Parade (1999).

At the dedication of the New York State Fallen Firefighters Memorial with Vinny Bollon, IAFF, Jim McGowan, NYS Department of Labor and Lieutenant Doug Sloan, Squad 270. (Photo by Dee Richard)

Annual Medal Day Celebration

Rescue 3 satellite unit (just kidding), owned and operated by retired Firefighter Tom McTigue (R-3).

A great team, a proud team, Chief of Operations Daniel Nigro, Chief of Department Peter J. Ganci, Jr., First Deputy Commissioner William Feehan.

Bureaus of
The New York City Fire Department

Bureau of Communications

In a city as large as New York, with nearly a million buildings and a full-time population of more than seven million, the Fire Department must be equipped and ready to provide a variety of emergency services to the public. Nearly 150 years ago, it was realized that a means to success would be related directly to an efficient, dependable communications system. As times changed from the volunteer fire companies of the 1800s, our Fire Department always has taken advantage of technological innovations to enhance its service. Nowhere have changes been made as successfully or rapidly as in communications.

The volunteers of the 1800s were notified of fires through the use of bell towers located throughout the city, linked by telegraph and staffed by watchmen. When a fire occurred, the bells would strike out predetermined signals to indicate the location of the fire and get the "vollies" on the way. In 1865, the paid Fire Department was organized to replace volunteers and communications took another step forward.

By 1870, another link in fire communications was complete: a central fire alarm office was in operation and nearly 400 alarm boxes were installed on street corners throughout New York—"technology" of its own time that provided the public with a means of reporting fires.

In 1911, the Bureau of Fire Alarm Telegraph—now known as the Bureau of Communications—was established within the Department. Realizing that the efficient dispatch of fire apparatus is the first step in providing the public with quality fire service, the Department decided to build independent, stand-alone, state-of-the-art communications facilities. During the 1920s, four of the five existing Communications Offices, then known as Telegraph Offices, were constructed and occupied. In 1922, the Central Manhattan Telegraph Office moved to Central Park; in 1923, the Brooklyn Central Office moved to Empire Boulevard from its location on Jay Street in downtown Brooklyn; in 1924, the Bronx Central Office moved to East 180th Street from its previous location at the quarters of Engine 46 on East 176th Street; in 1928, the Queens Central Office moved to its new location on Woodhaven Boulevard from Jamaica Town Hall; and in 1962, the Staten Island Central Office moved from its location in Borough Hall to Clove Lakes Park.

As the 20th century progressed, so did the advancements in FDNY's communications. A study conducted during the 1930s concluded that the inability to maintain communication with units (once they left the firehouse) was the most critical weakness in the communications operation. In 1936, a two-way, low-band AM radio network was implemented for use by fireboats. In 1937, a two-way radio was installed in Chiefs' vehicles and Rescue Companies.

In the early part of 1940, FDNY introduced the first fireground radios known as "walkie-talkies." They operated in the ultra-high frequency, two-meter band, weighed approximately 15 pounds, measured 9- x 5- x 13-inches and were carried in a backpack. The two-way pack transmitter-receiver had its first test under actual fire conditions at the Algonquin fire in July, 1940.

In 1952, a two-way VHF radio system was implemented, placing Manhattan and the Bronx on one radio frequency, and Brooklyn, Queens and Staten Island on another. By the 1960s, all Fire Department apparatus was radio-equipped.

In 1970, a new and innovative method of dispatch that eventually replaced the existing telegraph system was implemented in the borough of Manhattan and, in the following years, throughout the city. The Voice Alarm permitted the dispatcher to give notification of

Dispatchers are a vital communications link to the responding apparatus.

the location of alarms, as well as critical details of the call. The Bells then became a secondary means of notification and remained as such until 1983 when they were discontinued. The Telegraph Bell System faithfully served the Department for more than 130 years.

In 1971, a newly developed alarm box, known as an ERS (Emergency Recording System) box, was introduced to the streets of New York. It provided the public with the ability to speak to both Fire and Police personnel from the box on the street and provided the Fire Alarm Dispatcher with more information than previously was available, enabling them to better provide the appropriate response of apparatus.

In 1959, roughly 85,000 initial alarms were transmitted citywide. By 1970, that figure had increased to more than 400,000. The intensifying fire activity throughout the city was taxing the ability to transmit alarms rapidly. Once again, the Department recognized the significance of the Dispatch Operation and Communications was given the task of delving into the evolving world of computer technology.

One of the country's first successful Computer-Aided Dispatch (CAD) Systems was designed for the New York City Fire Department. Among its many advantages, CAD provided the ability to send notification of alarms to fire companies via teleprinter and responding firefighters were availed of more specific and critical information prior to arrival. The FDNY CAD system and Dispatch Operation perform efficiently and effectively and continue to serve as a model for other cities. The CAD function in the fire Dispatch Operation has been recognized as one of the most significant improvements in Communications and is considered to be one of the Department's unprecedented achievements of this century.

During the mid-1960s, the Department introduced the use of fireground radio frequencies, otherwise known as the handie-talkie. This radio originally was piloted with Ladder Companies and later issued to the entire Department. It provided members with a means of communicating on the fireground and was a critical step in ensuring firefighter safety during operations.

By the 1980s, it was recognized that an efficient operation of an Emergency Communications Center is dependent upon the operation of many different components working in seamless synchronization with each other. By then, radio had become a critical component of the fire operation. However, increased activity and regular use of radio equipment presented Communications with the need to free up radio traffic.

The introduction of MDTs permitted the transmission of information that previously was sent over the borough voice frequency and gave the Battalions, Divisions and Staff additional frequencies in the 800MHz range for point-to-point radio communications without burdening the dispatch operation. Additionally, it created a higher level radio network for Battalions, Divisions and Staff. The additional frequencies in the 800MHz range operate on a unit-to-unit basis, thereby eliminating any burden to the dispatch operation.

During the 1980s and 1990s, a high-rise repeater system and sound-powered telephones vastly improved fireground communications. Pagers and cellular telephones were introduced to the Department as additional means of communications and notification. The Mobile Command Center was instituted, which provides an environment and communication capability for Staff-level personnel at the scene of major incidents.

Answering the need for FDNY's ever-increasing demand on radio operations, in the early part of the year 2000, we will begin converting the Department's radio network from VHF to UHF. All radio equipment, from handie-talkies to vehicle radios, will be "changed out." Using UHF will provide FDNY access to more radio frequencies.

The consolidation of Fire and Emergency Medical Service has paved a path for Communications to advance again into the technology of the future. The Department is engaged in the design of a new computer-aided dispatch system that will serve both Fire and Emergency Medical Service dispatch. In conjunction with the new CAD, the five FDNY Central Offices will be refurbished to accommodate a combined Dispatch Operation.

The teleprinter that replaced the bells of yesterday has been replaced by touch-screen alarm teleprinters in each firehouse. Telephone technology related to the receipt of calls will continue to provide the ability to identify the name and location of a caller. Automatic Vehicle Locators, or AVL, is a system that may dramatically change the way units are dispatched. Vehicle identifiers installed in units will identify a unit that is physically closer to an assignment.

FDNY, first and foremost, always has placed public safety and the safety of our members as the priority. As we move forward into this new century, the possibilities for technological advancement that will allow us to maintain that goal seem endless. What was once a whim or imagination is now within arm's reach. The Bureau of Communications will continue to explore future technologies and maintain our standards of providing the highest levels of service in our field.

Some FDNY Communications Highlights:

•**1903** — Bronx telegraph system moved from Manhattan to a Central Office established at Engine 46 on East 176th Street •**1905** — Alarm box post lantern fixtures replaced by globes, still lit by gas •**1905** — Queens Central Office established at Jamaica Town Hall •**1906** — Borough preliminary signals were established and for the first time, Department-wide notifications of multiple alarms are made by fire alarm telegraph in all five boroughs •**1922** — Central Manhattan telegraph office moved to Central Park •**1923** — Brooklyn Central Office moved to Empire Boulevard •**1924** — Bronx Central Office moved to East 180th Street •**1928** — Queens Central Office opens on Woodhaven Boulevard. Rockaway and Long Island City alarm systems are tied into Queens •**1936** — Two-way, low-band AM radio (WNYF, 1630 KC) for fireboats •**1937** — Two-way radio for Commissioners' and Chiefs' cars and Rescue Companies •**1948** — Zone system instituted as regular operating procedure for transmitting alarms to the firehouse bells •**1952** — Two-way VHF FM radio for all units; separate channels for Manhattan/Bronx, Brooklyn/Queens, Staten Island •**1962** — Staten Island Central Office opens in Clove Lakes Park •**1970** — Voice alarm to firehouses introduced as primary means of dispatching alarms in Manhattan •**1971** — Voice alarm system for Bronx and Brooklyn. First ERS voice street alarm boxes •**1972** — Last of the 1870 locked alarm boxes removed from public schools after being in service more than 100 years •**1977** — Computer-aided dispatching introduced in Brooklyn •**1983** — Bell system in firehouses discontinued as back-up to voice alarm •**1985-Present** — Development and implementation of various wireless systems; i.e., MDTs, cellular telephones, enhancements to Department-wide notification systems, improved sound-powered phones, introduction of high-rise Repeater System and 800MHz radio system

Bureau of Fire Investigation

Whenever a fire is fatal or thought to be maliciously set, Fire Marshals are called in to determine its cause and origin and apprehend and arrest anyone who may be criminally responsible for it.

The first Fire Marshal in New York City was Alfred E. Baker, who was appointed in 1854. There was no pay, but the insurance companies raised a fund to remunerate him. One year later, Baker obtained permission from Chief Carson and the Board of Engineers to wear the uniform of a firemen—red shirt, fire cap and fire coat. The Board of Police Commissioners conferred upon him a sergeant's shield, which was engraved with Fire Marshal, New York. He also was given a regular salary. In 1873, the Bureau of Fire Marshal was created in the Metropolitan Fire Department. In 1915, the name was changed to the Bureau of Fire Investigation (BFI).

In 1940, the legislature granted Fire Marshals broad powers to detect the crime of arson and bring its perpetrators to justice. These powers included arrest, the right to subpoena people, books and documents, authority to enter any building and authority to take testimony under oath.

Fire Marshal interviewing Chief John S. Ievolo at suspicious fire.

in New York County; 48 individuals were indicted.

In February of 1997, a "Joint Arson Task Force" was established with the NYPD and the Bureau of Alcohol, Tobacco and Firearms (ATF). It is ironic that when the ATF first was delving into arson investigation, they rode with the BFI to hone their skills. This joint Task Force has been successful in many organized crime cases, including one that led to the arrest of 35 members of the Giannini Crew and the largest federal indictment of the Russian mob – seven members for a third-alarm fire in a grocery store on 63rd Road in Queens.

As the BFI enters the new millennium, it is adding the power of better computer databases to its arsenal. The Marshals themselves, with their enhanced training, will continue to develop new and innovative ways to fight "the never-ending war" on fire.

In 1970, the Marshals were upgraded from peace officer to police officer status. They needed all the powers that came with their new status as they and the Department battled the growing firestorm that was raging over the city at that time.

In 1977, several teenagers set fire to an abandoned factory in Bushwick, Brooklyn. It quickly spread to more than 30 adjacent buildings. After this conflagration, Mayor Beame ordered the Fire Department to appoint another 100 Fire Marshals and an additional 100 the following year. Many of these new appointees were placed in expanded "Red Cap" units, operating from trailers positioned wherever there was an abundance of fire. At its height, the Bureau had 405 men operating in three task forces. Whenever the "Red Caps" saturated an area, not only did arson fires and false alarms go down, but so did other crimes.

On March 25, 1990, a jealous lover set fire with a dollar's worth of gasoline in the entrance foyer of the Happy Land Social Club in the Bronx. The fire killed 87 of the club's patrons, giving this incident the dubious distinction of replacing the Puerto Rican Social Club fire as the largest case of mass murder in the city's history. As a result of this fire, the "Social Club Task Force" was formed with the Marshals playing a key role. The Task Force was charged with repeatedly inspecting the hundreds of social clubs in the city to ensure they comply with the fire safety code.

For many years, the Fourth of July has been the FDNY's busiest day for individual fires. The major cause of these fires was the result of illegal fireworks. To combat this problem, the "Fireworks Task Force" was formed between the BFI and NYPD in 1995. In 1997, the Task Force confiscated 28,293 cases of fireworks. In contrast, in 1999, they took in only 2278 cases because they virtually had put "organized crime out of the fireworks business." As a result, fires on the Fourth of July have decreased 72 percent and injuries are down 87 percent.

In 1997, the BFI successfully concluded its investigation of a group of individuals who allegedly were in the women's handbag business but, in reality, were in the insurance fraud business. They would ignite a fire in another manufacturer's space on the floor above. After the Fire Department put tons of water on the fire, they put in a false claim for water damage. They would repeat this scenario at another location (after first moving the handbags out). The investigation resulted in the largest single indictment of the Russian Mafia

Bureau of Fire Prevention

The Bureau of Fire Prevention (BFP), staffed by 430 professionals, includes civilian fire protection inspectors, chemical and electrical engineers, supervisory and clerical workers and approximately 10 uniformed personnel working out of Fire Department Headquarters. The BFP generates approximately $33 million annually in inspection fees, permits and certificates.

The Bureau is commanded by the Chief of Fire Prevention, who reports directly to the Chief of Department, as mandated by the Administrative Code. That section of the code empowers the Bureau to perform the duties and exercises the powers of the Commissioner in relation to dangerous articles such as combustibles, chemicals, explosives, flammables, compounds, substances or mixtures. The Bureau also is responsible for the prevention of fires and the protection from panic, obstruction of aisles, passageways and means of egress, standees, fire protection and fire extinguishing appliances in theatres and places of public assembly.

The history of the Bureau dates back to 1865, when the Metropolitan Fire Department was formed from the Volunteer Department. Within the Metropolitan Department, there was a municipal department for the "Survey and Inspection of Buildings." The stated goal was the effective prevention of fires and the protection of life and property in the City of New York.

A "Bureau of Combustibles" was organized in 1867 and the city was divided into 52 inspection districts, co-terminus with the company administrative districts. Each district had a Company Commander in charge. This bureau, staffed by uniformed members, inspected buildings and issued permits for the storage and use of oil, dynamite and other dangerous materials.

Chapter 521 of the laws of 1880 transferred the duties of building inspection to the Fire Department from the recently abolished Department of Buildings. The authority and power to inspect buildings for violation of fire regulation and code compliance now was placed on the "Inspector of Buildings of the Fire Department."

The "modern" Bureau of Fire Prevention was formed on May 1, 1913, as a direct result of the Triangle Shirtwaist fire of 1911 and the Wagner Factory Investigation Commission. This marked the first recognition of the equal importance of fire prevention with fire suppression in the work of the Fire Department.

In 1933, the Bureau was transferred to the newly formed Department of Buildings and was returned to the Fire Department in 1940, where it remains as the premier group to carry out the fire prevention duties designated to the Fire Commissioner.

Re-organization is an on-going project at the BFP. As the fire protection needs of the city change, the Bureau is evolving to meet new challenges. In an effort to provide the public with "one-stop shopping," the Bureau now is in the process of consolidating the inspection functions of various BFP units into the District Office system. The 14 District Offices are being reconfigured into nine Fire Prevention Field offices. The BFP Field Offices will be co-terminus with the nine firefighting Divisions. The goal is to make fire prevention more efficient and user-friendly for the public, as well as for the firefighting field units.

The mission of the Bureau of Fire Prevention—"the protection of life and property from the perils of fire"—will continue to be fulfilled in the best traditions of the Department.

Fire Safety Education

Increasing the significance and impact of fire safety education has been one of the main goals of Commissioner Von Essen since his appointment. Drawing on many members from the field who have previous teaching or counseling experience, the staff has been tripled. An influx of civilian professionals also has broadened the capabilities of the unit. It clearly is evident that if we stop fires before they start, we not only save civilian lives and property, we protect our own.

With the increase in fire safety presentations in the past several years and the simultaneous decline in civilian fire fatalities—to the lowest they have been in 50 years—the direct correlation between education and safety is evident.

Based on analysis performed by the Bureau of Fire Investigations, the Fire Safety Education Unit strategically has been targeting neighborhoods that exhibit high incidence of fire fatalities. Every fire death is analyzed and any lessons gleaned from the actions or reactions of those involved may point to a lesson we can share with others, thus bringing home the messages of personal responsibility and home fire safety planning.

Firefighters and civilian community coordinators are out everyday in schools, day-care centers, senior citizens facilities, neighborhood and community meetings, delivering basic fire safety information. In the year 2000 alone, they will complete 5000 presentations. Some of the presentations are specialized in response to specific needs, such as recent high-rise fire safety education. Following a series of high-rise fires, it became clear that people did not know if they should leave the building or were safer staying in their apartments. These tailored presentations addressed those concerns and questions.

With the help of corporate partners, such as Channel 7 and Radio Shack, we have been distributing 50,000 smoke detectors annually to seniors and families in high fire districts. Additionally, we run "Change Your Battery When You Change Your Clock" campaigns, distributing 25,000 smoke detector batteries each Fall and Spring.

Hot Dog, FDNY's fire safety mascot, was brought to life in the Fall of 1997. He tours the city in his donated Hot Dog Dalmatian van, spreading the message of fire safety. Two mobile fire safety houses visit schools, playgrounds and other venues to let children practice escaping from a fire building within a realistic setting.

Each year, approximately 25,000 children visit a fire safety apartment that was built into the Fire Museum in SoHo. During Fire Prevention Week 2000, the "Fire Zone" will open in Rockefeller Center. This state-of-the-art, immersive experience will provide schoolchildren and visitors with the how-to tips of prevention and planning.

Bureau of Health Services

The Bureau of Health Services (BHS)—aka the Medical Office—and its Medical Officers predate the consolidation of the boroughs into the City of New York. Doctor Charles McMillan, an Army surgeon during the Civil War, joined the Fire Department in 1867. He recognized the need for physical standards and physical examinations were given to both incumbents and new hires. Standard physical requirements for appointment and promotion were adopted in 1879 and announced in General Orders No. 2. This established the principle that no member could be promoted who could not meet all of the requirements for original appointment.

At the time of the consolidation in 1898, there were three Medical Officers in the FDNY and three in the Brooklyn Fire Department. Appointed in 1886, Dr. Joseph E. Smith was the first surgeon of the Brooklyn Fire Department. Members were examined in both Headquarters in Manhattan and in the Medical Office in Brooklyn for evaluation for duty.

The Medical Officers were inducted into the Uniformed Force, with the rank of Battalion Chief, by Special Orders 58, dated May 21, 1904. Medical Officers' duties included determining members' fitness for duty, responding to multiple-alarm fires to evaluate injured members and evaluating candidates and incumbents.

As the Department has grown and undergone change, so has the Medical Office. The location of the Bureau has changed several times. Many members still remember when the Medical Office was located at Spring Street where the Fire Museum now is housed. Legend has it that a faulty connection here between a soda machine and an EKG machine created abnormal EKG patterns that resulted in undue worry for many a member.

The next location was 251 Lafayette Street in lower Manhattan. Under the direction of Dr. Cyril Jones, Chief Medical Officer from 1981 to 1995, many changes were instituted. Additional changes have occurred up to the end of this century with Drs. Kelly and Prezant at the helm. Let's look at some of those major changes.

Hot Dog, the official FDNY mascot, is always a big hit with schoolchildren.

#1 Staffing the Medical Office with medical officers who have a variety of backgrounds—with special areas of expertise in emergency medicine, orthopedics, physical medicine, pulmonary, cardiology and other areas—has helped provide the members with a cadre of medical specialists to care for their many needs.

#2 A psychiatrist and psychologist were added to the staff to better serve the needs of the Department. This unit also performs evaluations of incoming candidates.

#3 A full complement of nurses was added to help members make appointments for outside testing, provide follow-up during long convalescence and handle immunizations.

#4 The addition of orthopedic consultants to evaluate our members' many orthopedic problems has helped our members get needed attention in a timely and professional manner. Our goal is to continue to provide an orthopedist at BHS on a daily basis.

#5 Merging EMS with the FDNY in 1996 has increased the number of members seen at BHS on a daily basis. We have developed a system of referrals that allow the Medical Officers to order tests, authorize surgery and physical therapy and provide needed follow-up to help EMS members get treatment faster and more efficiently.

#6 The move to MetroTech has provided the BHS with a beautiful new facility that combines new technology with a warm atmosphere. The Medical Officer enters the patient notes on a computerized form. The immunization table is readily available, indicating when and which immunizations have been given.

#7 The periodic medical examination (which sometimes occurred every 16 years, whether it was needed or not), was replaced by the scheduled, 15-month medical evaluation. Recognizing how important the annual evaluation is in maintaining a fit work force, Commissioner Von Essen has given BHS many resources to accomplish this task. Scheduling medicals on a 15-month rotation has been made a top priority.

At the annual, members are given a complete evaluation, including pulmonary function testing and fitness evaluation. The necessary OSHA training for blood-borne pathogens, right to know and mask fit testing is done at the time of the annual. Blood screening for prostate cancer is performed. Needed immunizations are given and PPD (TB) testing is done at the same time.

The 10-city initiative with the IAFF will allow us to gather information about our Department that will continue to guide us in developing a fit work force. Concerns about the demands of bunker gear on the members prompted evaluation of the physiology of fitness through studies by Dr. Prezant and Lieutenant Kevin Malley. Important clinical research regarding the reduction of significant burns to our members was done through the efforts of the Medical Office.

#8 The increased exposure of our members to victims who may carry potentially life-threatening illnesses has prompted several initiatives. An MDX form for exposure to blood-borne and respiratory agents has been developed. This form has been updated as necessary to best capture the needed information. In its current form, the computerized version should allow us to better advise members after an exposure. Blood-borne pathogen follow-ups have been initiated to treat prophylactically, when indicated, to follow up on victim tracking and perform subsequent blood testing after the exposure.

#9 The counseling unit, under the direction of Malachy Corrigan, not only provides assistance to members seeking help with alcohol and substance abuse problems, but also provides a range of services to members and their families as they struggle with emotional, social and medical issues.

The all too frequent tragedies of the past few years have highlighted the role of the Medical Office as we respond to these events to help both the affected members and their families.

The Bureau of Health Services continues to play an important role in monitoring our members' health and providing needed services to help them recover from their injuries. As always, we remain committed to our mission to provide members with medical assistance and keep our members healthy.

Fleet & Technical Services Divisions
Fleet Services Division

The Fleet Services Division (FSD) operates a unique and one of the largest enterprises of its kind in the nation's fire service. The charge is to provide safe and reliable fire apparatus, ambulances and support vehicles to the field.

Two main repair facilities are used. The Long Island City location is dedicated to fire apparatus and support vehicles, while the one in Maspeth is dedicated to the ambulances. There are also five preventive maintenance shops located throughout the five boroughs. Twenty-two emergency crew mechanics work shifts that provide repairs 24 hours a day, seven days a week. They service all of the fleet at firehouses, ambulance stations or in the field.

Long Island City Location

The "Shops" are located between 34th and 35th Streets on Hunters Point Avenue. The outer area of the shop floor contains a variety of support shops opening onto the main floor. The main shop area, which provides a clear space, can service up to 70 fire apparatus in various stages of repair and overhaul.

The pumper, ladder and chiefs' car sections are the primary areas where most repairs to fire apparatus and other support vehicles are performed. The following support shops keep the fleet in prime condition: the welding and blacksmith shop repairs, fabricates and forges various metal parts of the fire apparatus; the electric shop rebuilds alternators, starters, air dryers and emergency lights and performs diagnostics of electric problems on vehicles. The machine shop, with its lathes, milling machines, grinders, planers, dull pieces, etc. provides and repairs various parts on the vehicles. It also houses the engine and transmission rebuilding shops; the tire and battery shop offers in-house and road services for replacing flats and worn/torn tires. The carpenter shop repairs portable ladders, hooks and axes and is involved in various working projects.

Maspeth Location

Located at 58th Street in Maspeth, the main area of the shop is the ambulance repair section, which has 12 in-ground, two-post lifts and is responsible for the preventive maintenance and repair of more than 425 FDNY ambulances. Within the main shop is a support shop that has four above-ground lifts and one drive-on lift. This section performs all preventive maintenance and repairs on support vehicles, such as sedans, Jimmys, Suburbans, etc.

Within the main shop is a centralized parts room. In addition, the following support shops are located at the 58th Street location: tire repair shop, battery shop and welding fabricating shop. Also available to the field units are satellite shops, with one in each borough to perform repairs on vehicles located in that area.

Technical Services Division

The Technical Services Division (TSD) includes four individual units: New Apparatus and Design, Fire Tools and Equipment, Medical Equipment and Medical Supply Units. The TSD provides new fire apparatus, ambulances, and support vehicles with fire tools and equipment, medical equipment, medical supplies and related services for the field.

New Apparatus & Design Unit

The New Apparatus & Design Unit of the TSD is responsible for designing, amending and updating specifications for new fire apparatus, ambulances and support vehicles. This unit also is charged with the purchase of fire apparatus and vehicles, as well as their replacement, assignment and reassignment.

Fire Tools & Equipment Unit

The Fire Tools & Equipment Unit, also known to the field as the "Tool Room," is located between 34th and 35th Streets on Hunters Point Avenue in Long Island City. The Tool Room is responsible for the procurement, specifications, distribution, tracking, maintenance, repair and relinquishment of all fire tools, equipment and Certified First Responder-Defibrillator (CFR-D) equipment and supplies city-wide. It also provides answers to technical questions about operating and maintaining the equipment used by the field units. A computerized inventory system that employs bar codes, tracks the equipment issued to the field units, identifies each piece of equipment and the units to which it is issued, provides a reporting system that has improved the budget planning of the unit, all of which have increased the overall equipment available to the field units.

An overhead view of the Shops in Long Island City.

Currently, there are more than 1000 individual firefighting-related items handled by the Tool Room, as well as another 115 CFR-D items available to the engine companies.

Medical Equipment Unit

The Medical Equipment Unit (MEU) is located at 58-65 52nd Road in Woodside, Queens, and is responsible for the procurement, specifications, distribution, tracking, maintenance, repair, decontamination and relinquishment of all medical equipment city-wide. MEU employees are the FDNY specialists, answering the technical questions from the field and EMSC on operating and maintaining the equipment, as well as the latest technology available.

Medical Supply Unit

The Medical Supply Unit (MSU) is located at 58th Street in Maspeth, Queens, and is responsible for the procurement, specifications, distribution and tracking of all medical supplies issued to the ambulances, as well as distribution of CFR-D supplies to the Tool Room for distribution to the fire field units. More than 420 items are stocked. The staff has the expertise in warehousing, as well as complying with the New York State Department of Health, Part 800 Regulations, New York City Medical Advisory Committee guidelines and the FDNY Office of Medical Affairs policies.

Storehouse Operations Unit

Recently, the Storehouse Operations Unit (SOU) was brought under the administrative control of the Technical Services Division and was relocated to the 58th Street location, housed with the Medical Supply Unit. The SOU is responsible for the administration of the central storehouse orders from fire companies, EMS stations and administrative units, all furniture requests and relinquishment for the FDNY from assisting in preparing the paperwork, to physically removing relinquished items to the DCAS Centre Street location for processing. An effort is underway to increase the inventory of supplies in the central storehouse to meet the needs of the FDNY for more timely service to the field units. Absorbent compound will be the first product to be added to the inventory.

Emergency Medical Service

The service traces its history to Bellevue Hospital's five horse-drawn ambulances, which handled 1812 calls in 1870. Dispatching was by telegraph and each ambulance had a physician or surgeon aboard. However, in later years, less-skilled personnel were used. In 1909, ambulance operation was placed under the management of the Board of Ambulance Service, chaired by the police commissioner. By 1929, 12 city and 33 private hospitals provided ambulances in a joint municipal-private effort. Drivers did not assist with patient care and transport to the closest hospital was not required. Ambulance management was centralized in the 1960s under the city's Department of Hospitals, when annual responses passed 400,000.

The New York City Emergency Medical Service was founded in 1970 as part of the city's Health and Hospitals Corporation. Ambulance drivers were phased out beginning in 1973 and all Ambulance Corps personnel were trained as emergency medical technicians. Paramedic training at the Albert Einstein College of Medicine began in 1974 and continued for 10 years. The first paramedic units were fielded in the Bronx in July, 1975. In March, 1996, EMS was transferred from the Health and Hospitals Corporation to the FDNY.

The emergency medical service program currently includes units operating from 27 municipal hospitals and stations and 25 voluntary hospitals.

The private hospitals that participate in the EMS program provide their own EMTs, paramedics and ambulances and operate in accordance with EMS guidance. All ambulances –city- or volunteer hospital-owned –are considered to be part of the same program and dispatched without regard to ownership.

The EMS program is augmented further by 46 volunteer ambulance corps active throughout the city. The volunteer Basic Life Support (BLS) units may be called upon when no EMS ambulances are immediately available in a given area or to assist at a mass casualty incident or special event.

The Emergency Medical Service is a command within the Fire Department Bureau of Operations. The senior EMS officer, the Chief in Charge of the EMS Command, is a three-star assistant chief. Two-star assistant chiefs manage EMS (borough) divisions and are assisted by deputy chiefs. Captains and lieutenants are the field supervisors and designated "condition cars" on the radio. One supervisor normally covers the ambulances assigned to one or two stations.

EMS communications receives the bulk of its calls through the 911 system. Operators at the 911 answering point in Brooklyn forward medical calls to the EMS Communications Center at 1 MetroTech. Incoming calls are handled by "call receiving operators" (CRO), who are either EMTs or paramedics, trained as emergency telecommunications operators. There are 19 CRO consoles; 12 to 15 normally are in use. Each call is screened (none can be refused outright), prioritized and then entered into the EMS computer-aided dispatch system. It then is forwarded to radio dispatchers handling each borough dispatch zone, while the CRO gives the caller crucial first-aid instructions when applicable. Dispatch consoles are grouped by borough, with one dispatcher for each dispatch zone, plus one additional dispatcher at each borough group. Their screens show the location and priority of the incident, cross streets and recommended ambulance assignment. The dispatcher handling the incident does not modify the recommendation, except to add a supervisor when appropriate.

The incident then is transmitted to one or more ambulances in the field, depending on the level of service required and the number of prospective patients. Dispatch is first by voice radio, followed by a message on the mobile data terminal. Each ambulance has an assigned "center of rove" area and responds from that area when the message is received. Policy calls for the patient to be transported to the nearest hospital.

The Telemetry Control Section provides voice and EKG data links between the field units and the duty physician. The Section also has voice tie lines to emergency rooms at participating hospitals, providing a link from the ambulances.

Training

BLS training is conducted at the EMS Training Division at Fort Totten, Queens. Cadets receive 288 hours of instruction before taking the New York State EMT certification exam. Then, they get 160 additional hours of local orientation, including the 40-hour Emergency Vehicle Operation Course and physical fitness training.

ALS paramedic training is not provided by the Department. Aspirants take State-certified courses and exams at their own expense and time. The curent minimum State requirement is 790 hours (300 didactic, 240 clinical and 250 internship). The program is competency-based and may be extended as required. Most institutions provide a total of 1000 to 1200 training hours. State-certified individuals selected by FDNY then receive a 128-hour ALS local orientation.

Annual refresher training by the Department is 80 hours for BLS and 120 hours for ALS.

Special Operations Command

In 1982, the Rescue Services Unit was organized. Staffed by an Acting Battalion Chief and firefighter, they were located in the quarters of Engine Co. 226 in Brooklyn. Their mission was to provide assistance with equipment and tool purchasing and training, administrative support and other issues that involved the four Rescue Companies. As their duties and unit responsibilities grew, they moved to larger quarters on Bradford Street with Engine Co. 332 and Ladder Co. 175.

In May of 1988, a Rescue Liaison Unit (Car 13D) was organized and operated from quarters located on Roosevelt Island. They shared quarters with the Manhattan Fire Marshals. The unit was manned by three Rescue Captains who responded to all third alarms, SCUBA incidents, major emergencies, special operations and performed as the FDNY Liaison at these incidents. After three months of operating with 16-hour tours, their staffing was increased and tours were changed to 24-hour coverage.

On April 13, 1990, the Special Operations Command (SOC) was established and located at the Roosevelt Island firehouse. The Fire Marshals had relocated and SOC took possession of the firehouse. The Rescue Liaison Unit was disbanded in 1994. In September 1998, the Special Operations Battalion was established.

The SOC Battalion responds to all second alarms, SCUBA incidents and all emergencies involving special operations. The Special Operations Command has four sub-commands, including the Marine Division, the Mask Service Unit, Hazardous Materials Operations and SOC Administration. SOC Administration includes Rescue Operations, the Special Operations Battalion, five Rescue Companies, seven Squad Companies, two Tactical Support Units, a DeCon unit, a De-watering unit, five Recuperation and Care Units, the Reclamation facility, the Loaner Gear Program and the daily administrative duties for the Command.

EMTs move patient to a waiting ambulance.

George F. Mand Library

The Fire Department of the City of New York has included a library among its resources since the early days of the Metropolitan Fire Department. The first library was established by resolution of the Board of Metropolitan Fire Commissioners on the 27th day of December 1867, exactly 130 years before the opening of the George F. Mand Library. The original Department library was located in a large hall above the Headquarters offices of the Metropolitan Fire Department. Charles De F. Burns was the first Department librarian.

On December 17th, 1878, the Board of Fire Commissioners decided to break the Fire Department Library up into 10 Battalion libraries. These Battalion libraries were placed under the direction of the Assistant Foreman (Lieutenant) of the company where the library was located. Charles De F. Burns, Assistant Secretary of the Department, was named General Librarian and given the task of supervision over all Battalion Libraries. Unfortunately, the Battalion libraries eventually fell into disuse and their collections were scattered throughout the Department.

Reverend Edward M.H. Knapp, Chaplain of the Fire Department, was the driving force behind establishing the next FDNY Library. Reverend Knapp succeeded in interesting Mrs. Russell Sage in his plan to install technical libraries in every firehouse in the city. Mrs. Sage donated $10,000 for the construction of these libraries. The responsibility for selecting the books for what became the Sage Memorial Library was placed with Dr. John S. Billings, the Director of the New York Public Library. In recognition of his dedication to the FDNY Library cause, Fire Commissioner Waldo designated Chaplain Knapp as Chief Librarian of the Department.

In 1938, FDNY Honorary Chief Clarence Meek began work on an FDNY Library at the Fire College located in the old Packard Building. Eventually, this library was moved to FDNY Headquarters at 250 Livingston Street where Honorary Chief Meek ran the library until his death on September 16, 1973. In honor of his dedication, the library was renamed the Chief Clarence E. Meek Library. Acting Lieutenant Paul Stolz took over the operation of the library after the death of Honorary Chief Meek. Paul Stolz had worked closely with him for many years. Acting Lieutenant Stolz eventually was designated Chief Librarian of the Department. The Chief Clarence E. Meek Library was disbanded shortly after the death of Paul Stolz in 1987.

Fortunately, the collections of the Meek Library were placed in storage at Fire Department Headquarters. The Meek Library, which incorporated much of the former Department library collections, now forms the foundation of the George F. Mand Library. Deputy Fire Commissioner George F. Mand, the benefactor of the current Department Library, collapsed and died at the scene of a third-alarm fire in the Bronx on May 1, 1965. A portion of the estate of George F. Mand was left to establish a resource center on the grounds of the FDNY Fire Academy. The result of George F. Mand's endowment is the George F. Mand Resource Center.

George Mand's vision of a modern library/resource center, located at the Bureau of Training, was fulfilled through the commitment of the Safir and later Von Essen administrations. The George F. Mand Resource Center encompasses a 5000-volume special library, conference room, audio-visual resource room and the George F. Mand memorabilia collection. The library maintains a close affiliation with the New York State Fire Academy Library and other fire research libraries around the world. Through resource sharing and collaboration, the Library is able to provide cost-effective and high-quality service to the FDNY.

The current administration's commitment to education and technology has allowed the Library to expand collections, upgrade software and modernize the computers. Soon, the Library's catalogs, indexes, full text materials and photographs will be available off-site through the Department's Web site. The Library is grateful to the Von Essen administration for its continuing support. The Library also acknowledges the previous librarians, whose dedication to the accumulation of fire service knowledge and tradition has made the George F. Mand Library the finest fire department library in the nation.

Bureau of Training

The evolution of the current Bureau of Training began in 1869, just four years after the New York City Fire Department was founded as a paid force. The Board of Metropolitan Fire Commissioners, headed by General Alexander Shaler, established an "Officers School" and wrote a "Manual of Instruction" for the commanding officers of engine and hook and ladder companies.

Up to that point, the "Foreman" (Captain) of a given company was responsible for the training of his unit. This practice continues to this day in the form of the company drill, still an important part of a well-rounded training program.

General Order #4 of June 7, 1883, created a formal "School of Instruction." Chris Hoell of the St. Louis Fire Department was hired to train members of this Department in the recently invented Hoell Lifesaving Appliance. This appliance is known today as the scaling ladder. Second Assistant Chief Hugh Bonner was designated "Instructor of the School."

The School of Instruction was made up of two classes. The first was called the "Life Saving Corps." It instructed and trained firemen in the use of scaling ladders, ordinary ladders and life lines. A second class covered the practical duties of a fireman in quarters and at fires. It particularly stressed the handling, care and use of all implements, tools, etc., employed in extinguishing fires. The School of Instruction was quartered with Engine Company 47 at 766 Amsterdam Avenue. An old sugar warehouse at West 158th Street and the Hudson River was used as the first drill tower.

In 1887, the new headquarters building was dedicated on East 67th Street. The School of Instruction moved to the fifth floor of this building. A rear yard was used as a drill ground and the rear windows were used for scaling ladder practice. General Order #8 of 1888 added a "Company School" to the School of Instruction.

General Order #72 of 1911 created the next plateau, the "Fire College." That General Order specified that the college should consist of an Officers School, a School for Engineers, a Company School and a Pro-

Probationary Firemen's School at the 68th Street site looked like this in 1936.

bationary Firemen's School. The Fire College Board was headed by Chief of Department Edward Croker and Deputy Chief John Kenlon.

When Engine Company 40 vacated their quarters on West 68th Street in 1918, the Fire College moved in, remaining there until 1932, when it moved to the "Packard Building" at Queens Boulevard and Van Dam Street. The Probationary Firemen's School, however, continued to train at 68th Street until 1963. The College, meantime, was moved again in 1948 to Hunters Point Avenue and 35th Street in Long Island City, to a site called the "Shops and College Building." This is the same building that Fleet Maintenance uses today.

Department Order No. 113 of 1960 created the Division of Training and in 1963, a new training center was completed on Welfare Island. All training activities moved to this location. Also, it was the first time "live fire" was used in training. Until that point, simulations were with dry hoses and no fire.

The current Fire Academy on Randall's Island was dedicated in 1975. The Division of Training was renamed the Bureau of Training in Department Order No. 115 of 1993. This site remains the hub of Fire Department training to this day.

Housewatch at the New York City Fire Museum.

New York City Fire Museum

The New York City Fire Museum is dedicated to the collection and preservation of the history and cultural heritage of the fire service in this city, from the time it was a colony up until yesterday. The museum's collection is an amalgamation of the FDNY and the Home Insurance Company collections.

In the early 1930s, Deputy Chief George L. McKenna, Director of the Fire College, had Firefighter Walter Beatty transferred from Ladder 116 to the College. At one time, Beatty had worked for Henry Ford, helping to preserve his historical collection in Dearborn, Michigan. Beatty, often using his own time and money, had been assembling and restoring antique fire apparatus belonging to the Department. Under Beatty's direction, the Fire College Museum was born on the seventh floor of the Packard Building in Long Island City in 1934. In 1948, the Department opened a brand-new Shops building in Long Island City with space for the Museum.

By 1959, the collection displayed at the "Shops" had grown in size and popularity. Fire Commissioner Edward Cavanaugh moved the Museum into the firehouse occupied by Ladder 1 on Duane Street. Light-duty firefighters were assigned to operate the Museum so it could be more accessible to school groups and the public at large.

Harold V. Smith had been collecting fire memorabilia since he was a teenager. After he became president of the Home Insurance Company, he moved his world-class collection of rigs, fire marks, buckets, toys, helmets, badges, prints and hundreds of other objects related to firefighting into the company's headquarters on Maiden Lane, in 1937.

In 1980, the Home Insurance Company decided to part with Smith's collection and gave much of it to the City of New York.

It was readily apparent that the fire museum on Duane Street was inadequate to house this new addition. In 1981, the Friends of the New York City Fire Museum was formed by some of the ardent supporters of the Department, including Dorothy Marks, Dick Fay and Ken Strauss. With the support of Mayor Koch, they managed to raise more than $1.1 million to renovate the 1904 beaux-arts firehouse that had been the quarters of Engine 30 on Spring Street. The "Friends" eventually evolved into the museum's current board of directors.

Fittingly, the collection from the Department's museum on Duane Street was moved into the new Spring Street building by a group of volunteers under the direction of then-Captain George Eysser.

On July 6, 1987, the first members of the public wandered into the firehouse on Spring Street to find it filled with fabulous exhibits designed by Louis Scrima, under the direction of Jim Selby. The official opening-day reception was held on October 9, 1987, fulfilling the dream Chief McKenna had almost 60 years earlier.

As the museum enters the new millennium—under the direction of Geoff Giglierano, with the support of the board of directors, staff and volunteers, along with the help of the firefighters assigned to Fire Prevention—it continues to expand its collection and mission to include teaching fire safety education to people of all ages. It is also the museum's mission to further inform the public of the sacrifice, loss and heroic nature of being a firefighter in the FDNY.

The Art of John Goss: A Retrospective of the Work of a Firefighter/Artist

This past winter, the New York City Fire Museum and the members of FDNY Engine Company 35 and Ladder Company 14 proudly presented a special exhibit of paintings by the late John Goss, firefighter and artist.

Over the years, a number of the New York City firefighters have had second careers in the arts and John Goss was one of the best known. In 1964, when Goss joined the Fire Department and was assigned to Engine Co. 35 in Harlem, he already was painting. He studied art at Hunter College and the Art Students League and entered works in a number of outdoor exhibitions. The subjects of his early paintings were mostly landscapes and scenes that he and his wife, Virginia, had seen during trips overseas. But once he became a member of Engine Co. 35, Goss' artwork increasingly focused on firefighters and firefighting.

John Goss' firefighting paintings are unique because they were drawn from his experiences and memories. He did not base them on photographs and, in fact, much of what he portrayed was seldom, if ever, seen by anyone other than firefighters. He takes the viewer down the street on the back step of the apparatus and inside burning buildings.

The images he created often represented the point where the firefighters came face to face with the smoke and flame. This intersection of light and darkness was a recurring theme of Goss' work. John Goss' art was also about the emotions of firefighters. He commented about his firefighting paintings, "I try to show that part of the fire service that is rarely or never seen. I show actual fire scenes inside a building and what things look like after the fire is out. It's the wear and tear on the men that I paint. It's the things we feel each day on the job that the media do not show."

For 12 years, his work was exhibited in an annual show at the Lynn Kottler Gallery. It also was shown at the World Trade Center and the Home Insurance Co. offices. But, it was on the walls of New York City's firehouses, at the FDNY Training Academy on Randall's Island and in the homes of firefighters around the area that Goss' work was appreciated most.

John Goss served with Engine 35 throughout his entire career. He retired in 1990 and died seven years later. This past winter, Bart Mitchell, a retired FDNY Battalion Chief and member of the Board of Trustees of the New York City Fire Museum, author Peter Micheels, also a member of the NYCFM board, and officers and firefighters at the firehouse where John Goss once worked, decided to present a retrospective of his art. With the support of Virginia Goss, John's widow, they borrowed paintings from firehouse hallways and kitchen areas, offices and the Training Academy and the living rooms of firefighters' homes. These collected works–usually unavailable for viewing by the public–were exhibited from February 25 through March 9, 2000, on the third floor of the New York City Fire Museum in SoHo.

The art of John Goss

WNYF – With New York Firefighters
An official training publication of the New York City Fire Department

WNYF's history began when the November 1940 issue was published. Written solely for the Firemen of New York City (With New York Firemen), the publication was created to provide descriptive articles on any new and efficient development introduced into the Department and explain new rules or anticipated Departmental events. In short, *WNYF* would provide information on subjects of general interest to the readership. Through this medium, a valuable, but unofficial suggestion might be offered that could be relayed to all the men of the Department. Its aim was to be devoted sincerely to the interests of everyone from the newest Proby to the highest Officer.

And, it succeeded in its mission. Through its many years of publication, *WNYF* developed into a valuable communication, training and educational tool for our firefighters. It was sought after by other fire departments around the country and, indeed, around the world. It kept retired members in touch with each other, as well as friends still on the job. It served as a written and photographic record of our Department. It was a source of pride, camaraderie and nostalgia for all of our personnel. It also was an important historical record of the triumphs and tragedies of the FDNY.

WNYF went through a name change when women joined the ranks of the uniformed personnel. While *WNYF* remained the same in content, its new name became **W**ith **N**ew **Y**ork **F**irefighters.

After continuous publication for more than 50 years (four issues per year), the magazine went through some tough times and distribution was suspended. Prior administrations did not recognize the value of the magazine as a training tool and did not think it was important enough to save. Commissioner Thomas Von Essen thought otherwise and acted accordingly. *WNYF* was rejuvenated and now it is back all the way. Once again, *WNYF* provides our firefighters with the information and knowledge needed to perform their jobs. It has re-established itself as the enjoyable morale booster it always had been. Once again, it is the pre-eminent fire service publication.

Most important of all, members and subscribers have returned to support the publication. Our writers have been willing and able to share their firefighting knowledge and experiences by submitting articles and supplying photographs or illustrations. Members are sharing their expertise and supplying articles about recent fires or operations of an extensive or unusual nature; proper use of tools and equipment; safety; tips on training and conducting drills; management; back to basics-type information; and history. Of course, for a lighter touch, the ever-popular All Hands submissions have returned, too.

Truly, *WNYF* has come full circle. The following was listed in Department Order No. 13, dated February 1, 2000: Effective with the first issue of 2000, *WNYF*, an official training publication of the New York City Fire Department, once again will be considered for inclusion in the bibliography for the Technical Knowledge portion of future promotional exams. The comeback of *WNYF* is complete.

Brooklyn firefighters take a well-deserved break after battling three-alarm fire on August 3, 1999. (Photo by Pete Connolly)

City-wide Tour Commander Steven DeRosa directs operations at Manhattan Box 44-175, 81 Mott Street, March 6, 2000.

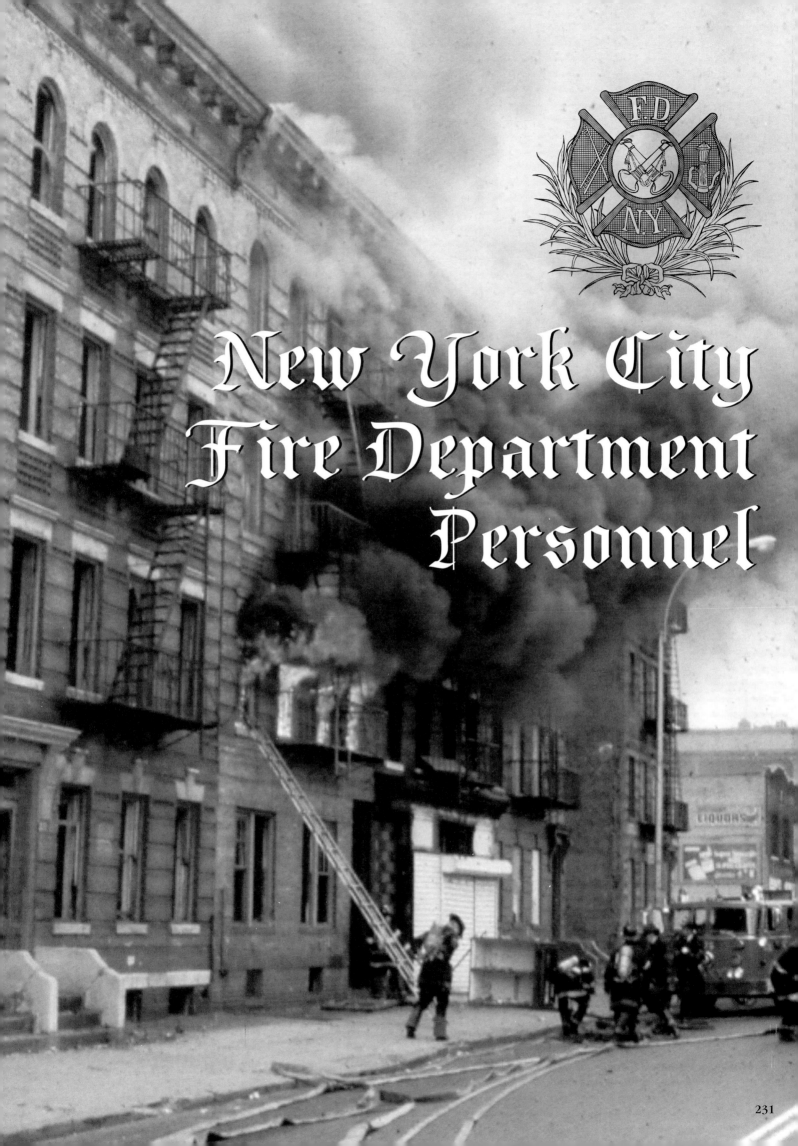

New York City
Fire Department
Personnel

DEPARTMENT ADMINISTRATION

EXECUTIVE STAFF

Deputy Comm. Mary Lynn Tierney, First Deputy Fire Comm. William M. Feehan, Fire Comm. Thomas Von Essen, Deputy Comm. Thomas Fitzpatrick, Deputy Comm. Michael Regan, Deputy Comm. David Clinton

OFFICE OF THE FIRE COMMISSIONER

1st: Debra Doyle, Sandra Trimarche, Gloribel Ojeda, Evelyn Tesoriero, Lourdes Sinisterra, Eileen Maloney, Sabrina Askew 2nd: Kevin McAllister, Deputy Comm. David Clinton, Fire Comm. Thomas Von Essen, First Deputy Fire Comm. William M. Feehan, Deputy Comm. Thomas Fitzpatrick, BC Henry McDonald 3rd: Peter Guidetti, Dave Harney, Capt. Raymond Goldbach

CHIEF OF DEPARTMENT STAFF

Lisa DeFazio, Chief of Department Peter J. Ganci, Jr., Executive Assistant Steven C. Mosiello

STAFF CHIEFS

1st: Gerard Barbara, Steven DeRosa, Donald Burns, Harold Meyers, Joseph Callan 2nd: Salvatore Cassano, Daniel Nigro, Peter J. Ganci, Jr., Frank Cruthers, Gustave Reinhold

BUREAU OF OPERATIONS

FIRE OPERATIONS

1st: Capt. Bill Bokowski, Edna Powell, Erica Decastro, AnnMarie Zaccaro, Vermell Hendriex, Islin Brown, Abigail Helm 2nd: Chief John LaFemina, DC Albert Turi, Jr., Chief Joseph Ramos, AC Daniel Nigro, AC Steven DeRosa, Chief John Peruggia, Lt. Rosario Terranova, Lt. Bradley Mann, Lt. Abdo Nahmod Third: Capt. Walter Werner, Capt. Tim Tubridy, Chief John Cashin, Lt. Rich Tarkenton, Mike Fox, Capt. George Vallebuona, Lt. Anthony Vanaria, Tom Gaby 3rd: Lt. Gary Gates, Lt. William Hayes, BC John Norman, Rich Zarrillo

EMS COMMAND, OPERATIONS

SAFETY

1st: Donna Hannon, Yvette Pabon, Cathy McCrorie, Mery Bento, Melba Alvarez, Michelle Robbins 2nd: Joseph Cahill, Lt. Roger Moore, Chief Jerry Gombo, Chief Robert McCracken, Capt. Toni Lanotte, Lt. Sophia Kwok, Lt. Bradley Mann, Phillip Ashby

1st: Crystal Devine, Brenda Sheppard-Lahens, Bruce Zamelsky, Erica DeCastro, Vito Ribaudo 2nd: Lt. Patricia Parra, Capt. Richard Tobin, DAC Gustave A. Reinhold, BC Arthur Lakiotes, Lt. Thomas Herrlich

OFFICE OF MEDICAL AFFAIRS

1st: John Cellante, Theresa Astramowicz, Jacqueline Baird, Elise Watson, Roselyn Servande, Lizette Perez 2nd: Glen Asaeda, Allen W. Cherson, Lewis W. Marshall, Neal J. Richmond, Lorraine M. Giordano, Capt. Mark Steffens, Lt. Luis Matallana, Lt. Grant Simmons 3rd: Dominick Loccisano, Jerard Allas, Monique Kusick, Louise Villanueva, Manuel Delgado, Richard Fox, Nicholas Cagliuso, Tracey Mulqueen, Maurica Zuniga, Joan Hillgardner

BUREAU OF COMMUNICATIONS

ADMINISTRATION

1st: Sam Kaiman, Doreen Yip, Roxie Pringle, Robert Carolan, Jacqueline Hughes, Ruby Purvis, Yvonne Salveggi 2nd: Cleanthis Meimaroglou, Ivan Goldberg, John Porcelli, Assistant Commissioner Stephen Gregory, Joseph Higgins, Lt. Anthony Napoli, Lt. Frank D'Amato 3rd: Francis Molinari, Mike Vitucci, Michael Weber, Martin Lewis, Eugene Edkins

BROOKLYN COMMUNICATIONS OFFICE

1st: Ronald Poe, Janice Gregory, Lawrence Feilich, Gerald Faulk, Edna Marie Ceglia, Myra Holmes, Faye Smyth, Warren Fuchs 2nd: Barbara Van Buren, Estelle Skeete Brown, Thelma Irving, Rosemary Smith, Sandra Evans, William Kelly 3rd: Allen Callahan, Eric Van Zan Ten, Kenneth Nielsen, Donette Marion, George Munch, Elizabeth Reinhold 4th: Joseph Pascalone, Richard Levoi, Peter Dodge, Brian Kuntz

BROOKLYN COMMUNICATIONS 2

Richard Lang, Eugene Naylor, Leroy McKeever, David Rosenzweig

BUREAU OF COMMUNICATIONS

BRONX COMMUNICATIONS OFFICE

1st: Robert Derskewicz, James Lee, Glen Loew, John Burke, John Willis 2nd: John Cashin, Thomas Glavin, Robert Engel, Kevin Kelley, Dennis O'Connell, Gary Greenbaum, Ronald Gonzalez, William Treanor

MANHATTAN COMMUNICATIONS OFFICE

1st: Judy Salgado, Mercedes Segui, Scott Coyne, Steven Scher, Jim Raftery 2nd: James Matheos, Paul Hedderson, Henry Dingman, James Walsh, Joseph Cittadino

QUEENS COMMUNICATIONS OFFICE

1st: John Scacalossi, Joseph Epstein, Douglas Martin, Patricia Hanna 2nd: Barbara Baumgarten, Lawrence Franks, Thomas Byers, Constance Brown, William Hartman 3rd: Edward Condon, Michael Esposito, Tina Werts, Ronald Christian, Stephen Chrobet, Phillip Drakes, Robert Langenbach

BUREAU OF COMMUNICATIONS

STATEN ISLAND COMMUNICATIONS OFFICE

1st: Stephen Wasserman, Edward Overton, John Curry, Kenneth Fisher, Patsy Alessi, Charles McLean 2nd: Michael Boucher, John La Corte, Nicholas Bruno, Cynthia Washington, Raymond Lopez, Raymond Piellucci, Steven White 3rd: Robert Stephens, Arthur Levine, Owen McAnuff, Emanuel Silverman, Frederick Katz, Raymond Stender, James Katchusky

FIELD COMMUNICATIONS

1st: Capt. John Timulty, Lt. Carlo Soranno, Asst. Comm. Stephen Gregory, Gerard Neville 2nd: Daniel Nastro, William Ladell, Jeffrey Cohen, Brian O'Hara, Richard Chiarello, Carmelo Mercado

BUREAU OF FIRE INVESTIGATION

ADMINISTRATION

1st: SFM Ralph Bernard, Jr., Patrice Roper, Barbara Fenton, Angela Betts, SFM Warren R. Haring, Jr. 2nd: Robert W. Greene, Nazareth T. Harris, SFM Christopher A. Tempro, Chief Fire Marshal Louis F. Garcia, Assistant Chief Fire Marshal Richard F. McCahey, SFM Wayne A. Corbett, JoAnn Jacobs, Melford J. Hazel

BFI SPECIAL INVESTIGATIVE UNIT

1st: SFM Fred Taylor, Richard Grassia, Dana Holland, Paula Lubin, Ken Moody, Frank Valenti 2nd: Carl Sederholt, Michael Cain, SFM Randall Wilson, SFM Robert Byrnes, Asst. Chief FM Richard McCahey, SFM Donald Vastola, Steve Steponaitis, Michael Starace, William Pepitone

BFI BROOKLYN

1st: SFM Ralph Brock, SFM Salvatore Rignola, Gerald Trimboli, Salvatore Rignola 2nd: John Foppiano, Thomas Callaghan, William Whelan, Danny Nolan, Ronald Fletcher, SFM Robert Byrnes, Lawrence Pliska

237

BUREAU OF FIRE INVESTIGATION

BFI BRONX

Paul Capan, SFM Kevin Wallace, Vinny Faggella, Brian Grogan, Phil Gibbs, SFM Wayne Sforza, Roy Haynes, Rick Barry, Joseph Kisonas, SFM Hector Hernandez, Jonathan Mercurio

BFI MANHATTAN

1st: SFM James Kelty, SFM Randall Wilson, Frederick Solomon, SFM Hector Hernandez, William Kregler, Robert Puchal, SFM Wendall Williams 2nd: Radcliff Johnston, SFM Arthur Banks, Nazareth Harris, Kevin Larkin, SFM James Kay, Seamus Ward, Charles Stychek, SFM Barry Goffred, Fred Surber

BFI QUEENS

1st: Edward Hennessy, Stanley Jaremko, Donna Graham, Roger Eckert, Peter Hoeft, Thomas Doyle 2nd: Thomas Famoso, SFM Charles Martoni, SFM Cecil Maloney, Daniel Godstrey

BUREAU OF FIRE INVESTIGATION

BFI
TRAINING UNIT

1st: Richard McCurry, SFM Thomas Williams, SFM Hector Hernandez 2nd: Daniel Matteo, Henry Raven, Michael Owney, Ronald Bucca, Vincent Faggella, Richard LeMonda

BFI RANGE
OFFICERS

1st: Vincent Fagella, Ronald Bucca 2nd: Frank Valenti, Michael Cain, Arthur Crawford, SFM John McCauley, Henry Raven, Donald Mormino, Hector Hernandez, Richard Garcia

BFI NEW MARSHALS & INSTRUCTORS
FIRE MARSHAL CLASS NOVEMBER 1999

Robert Ammann, James Brierley, James Brosi, Joseph Brosi, Gregory Buday, Patrick Campbell, John Carbone, Robert Cashman, Peter Connolly, James Costanza, Kevin Cunnane, Leonard Curcio, Thomas Currao, Joseph Depperman, John Deprizio, Andrew DiFusco, Thomas Fennelly, Charles Ferris, James Fleming, Jack Galante, Robert Giddings, Vincent Guzzone, James Halaby, William Ingram, Richard Kuzniewski, Gerard Ledwith, Robert Lee, Kevin Lenahan, James MacKay, James Mahaney, Thomas Mazza, Joseph Mazzarella, John McCarthy, Martin McHale, Thomas McHugh, Joseph McMahon, Kevin Melody, Daniel Mulhall, Keith O'Mara, Joseph Pasquarello, Peter Patterson, Robert Reeg, Kenneth Ruddick, Robert Schmidt, Thomas Silvestri, Joseph Sykes, Todd Velten, Owen Williams, David Winter, Paul Yodice, Edward Zebrowski

BUREAU OF FIRE PREVENTION

1st: Peter Carfagua, Ruby Patterson, Elsa Araya, Brenda McKiver 2nd: Sam Pepper, AC Gerard Barbara, AC Harold Meyers

1st: Lisa Horsley, Dorothy Ruiz, Sylvia Lawson, Sonia Lora Velez, Phyllis Reed, Enid Santiago, Joan Hart, Purlene Ashley, Iris Silver, Jeanette S. Withers, Margaret Gaines, Brenda L. McKiver 2nd: Carrol Bell, Robert Rampino, Joseph Barrazato, Samuel Pepper, Chief Lawrence Bazzi, Gary Sher, AC Gerard Barbara, AC Harold Meyers, Chief Anthony Ardisson, Chief Richard Powner, Judy M. Vitti, Ines Jamison, Barbara Brathwaite 3rd: Susan Hunt, Neil Criscuolo, Gerald Pearce, Daniel Flynn, James Lauer, Charles Holzinger, Nyoma Sorkin, Robert Chavis, Emiliya Ozeryanskaya 4th: Anton Ferrone, Robert Brenta, Mary Murdock, David Kahn, James Hansen, Linda Bradley, Dorothy Thompson, Hooshang Negathaim, William Vernon, Albert Robateau 5th: John M. Altre, Ivan Deleon, Anthony Scacluto, James Carroll, Linda Pasantes, Mark Cahill, Steven Addeo, John Mazek, Kam Zhan, Abu Alam, Dominic Deangelis, James Williams

BUREAU OF FIRE PREVENTION

1st: Robert Kaufman, Lisa Horsley, Dorothy Ruiz, Mary Murdock, Dorothy Cross, Agatha Actie, Delory Brown, Faried Omar, Sr., Herman Nelson, Arthur Koenemund, Christopher Afuwah, Elliott Valentin **2nd:** David Warren, John Henderson, Samuel Pepper, Chief Lawrence Bazzi, Gary Sher, AC Gerard Barbara, AC Harold Meyers, Chief Anthony Ardisson, Chief Richard Powner, Julius Squillar, Abu Alam, Frank Cifuentes **3rd:** Shaji Mathea, Benjamin Leonen, Jr., Robert Pampino, Joseph Barracato, Hiram Borrero, Ali H. Ali, Suresh Deshmukh, Cecil Cannady, Alan Hirschkorn, Sandy Camacho, Lionel Hudson, Darryl Chalmers, Edward Nolan, Sr., Ashwin Patel **4th:** Mark Smith, Lian Liu, Frederick Nicolas, Ronald Alexander, Steven Addeo, Wesley Barney, Joseph Polcha, Grady Caviness, Michael Kavolius, William Romer, Anthony Pretigiacomo, Bart Aclin, Anthony Scacluto, Leslie Dunning

1st: Novlette Barrett, Iris M. Rivera, Jacqueline Dixon, Tonita Ratcliff Palmer, Donna Ryan, Ruby Patterson, Emma Hicks, Awilda Ramos, Annette Whitley **2nd:** Heath B. Telford, Alex Skor, Alex Emokpae, Samuel Pepper, Chief Lawarence Bazzi, Gary Sher, AC Gerard Barbara, AC Harold Meyers, Chief Anthony Ardisson, Chief Richard Powner, Joseph Meegan, Mohammed Bhuiyan **3rd:** Samuel Asa Moah, Shifrin Yevgeny, Kats Oleg, Esdel Abrams, Alex Gutmakher, Alex Spektor, Peter Abraham, Arkady Mavashve, Leo Subbarao, Lyden Joseph **4th:** Ian Jonas, Carlos Lopez, Paul Samuel, Boris Shapner, Lt. Dennis Scanlon, Fitz Roy Benjamin, Juan A. Leon, Antonio Greguere, Eugene Kaplan **5th:** Steven Brocato, Phanatama Darsanlal, Pirrie Charles, Richard Shaw, Martin Vitti, Sr., Steven Smalls, George Borshchevsky, Semen Khinich, William Peters, Yeugeniy Levintov

BUREAU OF FISCAL SERVICES

REVENUE MANAGEMENT STAFF

1st: Edil Oriol, Pacencia Servande, Lillian Perry, Janet Rodriguez, Roseann Loures, Diann Mathews, Elaine Correa, Beatrice Croswell, Lucile Walker, Anna Bakradze
2nd: Delores Grice, Dirington Crooks, Maria Rodriguez, Arturo Soriano, Vermett Bulter, Jackie Ruiz, Gil Salnave, Lewis Weissman, Emma Rivera, Shaughn White, Debbie Angone, Hoang Nguyen, Tanya Carr, Mary Martin, Josefina Torres *3rd:* Ernestine Jones, William Casiere, Manny Torres, Ashton Spann, Deborah Rosa, Lizbelle Marrero, Michelle Cintron, Latisha Davis, Yahaira Borgos, Grace Taguba, Myron Hyman, Darshanie Prasad *4th:* Ammit Pandya, Alex Javellang, Mildred Santana, Elsa Bracero, Laura Toala, Nelsida Rodriguez, Kathy Ann Lewis, Jazelle Pierre, Joyce Affoon *5th:* Gregg Bajamunde, Anthony Napolitano, Gregory Jenkins

FISCAL SERVICES

1st: Dorothy Jelks, Alice Yap, Theresa Larsen, Kathryn Ford, Patricia Ruffin, Lillian Bilotti, Christina Gamban, Barbara Boatswain, Bruce Solomon, Carmen Rodriguez
2nd: Kirk Eng, Stacey Pfeffer, Alba Surace, Susan DiMarco, Milly Burgos, Adelle Goodwine, Helen Petes-Philip, Barbara Canning, Marilyn Smith, Donald Casiere, Vincent Barrett, Maria Rodriguez, Tanya Mejia *3rd:* Linda VanKerckhove, Mamerto Gamboa, Theresa Joseph, Patricia Romeo, Robert L. Scott, Barry Greenspan, Aurea Otero, Vilma Lane, Philip Muniz, Wendy Castillo, Damon Chan *4th:* Omkar Prasad, Jack Wolfman, Haydee Tineo, Marlene Carter-Ruffin, Marilyn Brettschneider, Kristina LeGrande, Sandra Chait, Gay Cabeza, Enilce Gucman, Nancy McNamara, Leonard Brochis

BUREAU OF FISCAL SERVICES

BUDGET SERVICES

1st: Alba Surace, Caroline I. McDaniels, Clarinda Matela, Lynn Lee 2nd: Terry Fiorentino, Joseph Zavaglia, Rosemary Feeney, Fred T. Novello, Richard Ross, Rudy Altre, Letitia Maxwell

CIVILIAN PAYROLL

1st: Lilieth Ferguson, Barbara Duncan, Corinne Saffarano, Ellen Gales, Mary Milauskas, Linda Allen 2nd: Caroline Matela, Jennifer Potts, Rebecca Kercado, Gerard Montesano, Resy Lorenzo, Howard Knobler, Jeanette McClarity, Jo-ann Phillips 3rd: Ernie Almazan, Russell Kinard, Nina Hepbert, Robert Johnson

UNIFORMED PAYROLL AND PENSIONS

1st: Sandra Huang, Agnes Chan, Ghalia Elashmawy, Khadiga Aboelezz, Kerri Muli, Pauline Martini, Karen David, Olga Sosa, Fatima Sandoval-Ubes 2nd: Yevgeny Radomyslsky, Maureen Dale, Irina Sklyarevsky, Ivelisse Ramos, Samford Smolowitz, Edward Healy, Mary E. Blendermann, Angel Garcia, Albert Connolly, Ernesto Escalera, Debra Person 3rd: Angelina Arlia, Patricia Sentkewitz, Debra Kelly, Andrew Valentino, Calvin Smith, Dorothy Ashley, Darlene Slater, Murray Rosen, Rodney Henry, Darlene Slater 4th: Beverly Thom, Jaime Villaruz, Merlene Ernandez, Stephen Brown

BUREAU OF HEALTH SERVICES

FIRE DEPARTMENT MEDICAL OFFICERS

1st: Pierce Ferriter, Edoardo Giuliani, Stanley Soren, Kerry Kelly, David Prezant, Viola Ortiz, Ludwig Klein *2nd:* Ronald Gasalberti, Lewis Miller, Brian Maloney, Ira Feirstein, Cristobal Alvarado, Vincent Degennaro, Michael Garvey, Neil Coplan, Cornelius Cooper

BUREAU OF HEALTH SERVICES

1st: Jocelyn Stewart, Sheree Robateau, Randall Shaw, Audrey Brown, Maryann Murray, Anabel Echevarria, Susan L. Phillips, Tadaecher Campbell, Martin Merrick *2nd:* Robin Hirschhorn, Silvia Morris, Lee Loshak, Sharon Hampton, Justine Lashkow, Mary T. McLaughlin, Capt. Richard Klein, Eileen Flynn, Christine Lee, Charmaine Olivari, Mark Fasano *3rd:* Lt. Jay Swithers, Corey Romanowski, Patsy Mason, Joseph Tripptree, Anne-Marie Bachmann, Patricia Brown, Shila Jackson, Mary Murphy, Alpheaus Vaughn, Anthony Garcia, Denise Shuler *4th:* Bonnie Regan, Guy Nichols, Carlos Nunez, Michael Palleshi, Mary Kriner, Clyde Sealey, Lt. John Mendez

HEALTH & FITNESS

1st: Michael Cacciola, Lt. Kevin Malley, Lt. Michael Giammarino *2nd:* Gerard Scarnato, Thomas Kelly, Richard Conte, Kevin Miller

BUREAU OF HEALTH SERVICES

COUNSELING UNIT

1st: Shara Pena, Patricia Cusumano, Marcy Cole, Claire Cammarata, Dianne Kane *2nd:* John D'Alberto, Michael Bradley, Bill Crawford, Ted Frett, Malachy Corrigan, Bobby West, Jim Carey, Lisa Zerndorfer

HELP TEAM

1st: Charles Sullivan, Joseph Murphy, James Herold, Michael Reap, John Flamio, James Spillane *2nd:* Thomas Bala, Ralph Perricelli, Donald Loud, James Rutter, Joseph Ditta

BUREAU OF INTER-GOVERNMENTAL AFFAIRS

1st: Anita Hinds, Gladys Bennette, Marilyn Estrada, Mary Tobin, Gladys Rivera, Mary Simpkins, Lt. Valerie Miller *2nd:* Mary Mays, Carlos Del Valle, Lt. Joseph Torillo, Capt. Thomas Tropea, Deputy Comm. Lynn Tierney, Lt. Sheldon Wright, Gabriel De La Pena, Ruby Jenkins, Cheryl Keyes *3rd:* Betty Jackson, Lt. James Scabsi, Capt. Dan Daly, Errol Anderson, Greg Evans, Lt. Angel Carrer, John Jermyn *4th:* Edgar Pitre, Lt. Rosco Brown, Gerald Claxton, John Ruiz, Alvin Kevelier *5th:* Edward Shann, Thomas Ahern, Frank Spaldo, Ronald Milletti, Paul Iannizzotlo

BUREAU OF LEGAL AFFAIRS

1st: Barbara Johnson, Iris Cruz, Sandra McLeod, Tonnie Rivera, Marva Smith-Haber, Sonia Rodriguez, Catherine Byrne 2nd: Parvesh Datta, Debra Doyle, John Fuller, Elena Ferrera, Julian Bazel, Lorna Tibby, Mary O'Sullivan, Abbey Handelsman 3rd: Pat Cain, Renaldo Hylton, Richard Velez, Jesse Querijero, Lt. Charles Rauch, Gabriel Cabassa, Harsh Sehgal

BUREAU OF MANAGEMENT ANALYSIS AND PLANNING

1st: Christopher McDaniels, Suzy Sosa-White, Minerva Santiago, Safaa Sanders, Ted Cox 2rd: Manuel Lozada, Jr., Andrea Allocca, Frank Buccellato, Vito Pulito, Kevin Heckman

BUREAU OF PUBLIC INFORMATION

1st: SFM Ralph Bernard, Marc Scott Cohen, Brian Blair, Maria Lamberti, David Billig, Adriana Bacarella, Cecelia Cox 2nd: Lt. Richard Smiouskas, James Spollen, Capt. Steve Chimento, Capt. Walter Morris, Janet Kimmerly, BC Brian W. Dixon, Deputy Commissioner Michael Regan, Lenore Koehler, Francis McCarton, Joseph Leoncavallo, Lt. Daniel Walsh, Bruce Lyall

BUREAU OF PERSONNEL

1st: Domingo Williams, Fredda Wigder, Iris Ramos, Annet Villanueva, June Coco, Altrice Tatum, Debbie Croskey-Smith, Jacqueline Bradnock-Merveil, Regina Washington, Parrese Wade, Stephanie McGaney *2nd:* Andrew Alongi, Lt. Gregg Hansson, Jannine Jordan, Margaret Quinn, Capt. Lawrence Andriola, DC John J. Francese, Sherry Ann Kavaler, BC Vincent Cordasco, Margaret Prather, James Denn, Rita Ricks, Marilyn Woodward, John Costello *3rd:* Christopher Gaidis, Elsie Sanchez, Antonia Yarnell, Shonnette Nash, Lt. Robert O'Donnell, Euis Thompson, Emma Rebovich, Camille Isaacs, Margaret Basso, Marie Socha, Novell Hopkins *4th:* Jack Gridley, Charles Dalton, Joseph Siminski, Linda Pederson, Frances Haile, Ana Johnson, Gloria Aiken, James Mims, Joann Blackwell, Lance Dubner *5th:* Deborah Francis, Neil Mendelsohn, Kenneth Stubbs, Wadell English, Richard Brown, Paul Kenny, John Leppla

CHAPLAINS

Rev. John Delendick, Rabbi Joseph Potasnik, Rev. Wilfred Callender, Rev. Mychal Judge, Msgr. Marc Filacchione

BUREAU OF SUPPORT SERVICES

BUREAU OF SUPPORT SERVICES

1st: Edward Leonard, Thomas Dematas, Maria Alexis, Gerrit Geurs 2nd: William Tsoutsouras, Ellen O'Byrne Mauser, David Mitchell, Assistant Commissioner Roy F. Katz, Cynthia Crier, Carol M. Bell

BUILDING MAINTENANCE DIVISION

1st: Pedro Matos, Kelman Caton, Gerrit Geurs, Norman Becker, Anthony Bianchino, Donna Savage, William Loheide, Christopher Galioto 2nd: Leatrice Caesar, Benedetto Digeronimo, Mikhail Altshiler, Joseph Mastropietro, McLaughlin Harris, Carlo Garguilo, Paul Soehren 3rd: Cynthia Crier, Steven Gillard, Jelphine Calder, William Hickey, James Nikol, Duane Thorne, Wilberto Gracia, Daniel Wallen, James Campbell

EMS FLEET MAINTENANCE

Tim Ramos, Ken Krejci, Kevin Schmeider, Anthony DeMaio, Mike Felico, Jesse Jackson, Carl Genna, David Leone

BUREAU OF SUPPORT SERVICES

EMS SUPPORT SHOP

1st: Bill Buchack, Larry Sehuester, Mike Nin, Manny Missud, John Cinerella *2nd:* John Shaw, Mike Germaine, Winnie Minesquero, John Peez, Richard Glass, Dave Leone, Mike Carroll, Pat Sarcone, Tim Ramos

EMS FLEET MAINTENANCE

1st: Bob Cosenza, Alan Hannula, Anthony Lintner, Rick Vella, Nguy Huu, Dave Casey *2nd:* Gary Christianson, Eddie Boharsik, Tom Ward, Kevin Bunyan, Guisspe Tirone, Eddie Ishanyan, John Podhajeri

MANAGING & PURCHASING STAFF EMS

1st: Nancy Marreso, Tom Smith, Fanny Menexas, Karen Boyd *2nd:* Mark Aronberg, Jim Nelson, Sayda Carrasco, Mike Felice, Jesse Jackson, Tony DeMaio, Alan Greenberg

BUREAU OF SUPPORT SERVICES

RANDALL'S ISLAND P.M.

Tony Grey, John Barbone, Kerry Dillon, Giochino Trinceri, Richie Booth

1st: George Murphy, Carlos Lopez, Sean Lahey, Rich Kemp 2nd: Nick Flores, John Genna, Tom Rom, Tom Dowling, Greg Burzine, Dave Teague, Mel Pineda, Suzanne Vaccaro

TECH SERVICE MEDICAL EQUIPMENT

PARTS DEPARTMENT 58TH STREET

1st: Kevin Schmieder, Sergio Vargas, Brian Kacher, Peter Paolella 2nd: Russell Bentulan, Dennis Hoey

BUREAU OF SUPPORT SERVICES

**SHOPS
EMERGENCY CREW**

1st: Louis Salazar, Jerry Fischer, Austin Gentle, Gasper Galia, Roy Culken, Kenny Appollonio, Mike Arriaga
2nd: Fred Robinson, Phil Mackie, Pat Murphy, Pete Schoepe, Artie Sampson

**FLEET MAINTENANCE
PAIDGE AVENUE**

William Mitchell, Arthur Sampson, Lt. William Cardone, Mike Arriaga

**TECH SERVICE
MEDICAL SUPPLY**

1st: Peter Cruz, Rafael Rivera, Ronald Lightfoot 2nd: James Geraci, Alice Gramlich, Carlos Ramos, Bladimir Rodriguez, Carlos Acosta, Agnes Rafferty, Samsundar Sookram

BUREAU OF SUPPORT SERVICES

PMP CREW (PM)

1st: Dave Harson, Tom Mulcany, Lucius Williamson, Ralph Caserta 2nd: Dave Brownstein, Spencer Nimmo, Andrzej Bator, Kenny Clark

STORE HOUSE OPERATIONS

Clyde Jackson, Rayvone Jackson, Nick Caropreso, Robert Feliciano, Dwayne Sumpter, Danny Ferran

TECH SERVICE TOOLS & EQUIPMENT

1st: Kurt Schwinn, Ed Hronec, Carlos Nogue, David Perez, Ken Wagner 2nd: Robin Mundy-Sutton, Phyllis Thompson, Lt. Angel Vasquez, William Hoops, Frank Sclafani, Jonas Fils-Aime, Patricia Smithwick, Ralph Esposito, Danny Kemmet, Mary Scullion, Lt. Brian Bolls

BUREAU OF SUPPORT SERVICES

FLEET MAINTENANCE LADDER SECTION

1st: Sebastien Matre, John Evangelisto, Joseph Sargent, Hugh McAllister, Esteban Rodriguez, Robert Lucey, Nick Allegretti 2nd: Rocco Tinebra, Frederic Goetz, Michael Petito, Wayne Mazzella, Thomas Hind, Stefan Mark, William Sheehan, Raymond Tuborg, Edwin Moore

SHOPS ADMINISTRATIVE STAFF

Andy Diamond, Thomas Curti, Tom McDonald, Anne Morelli, Mary Ann D'Ulisse, Frederick Rilling, Mark Tria, James Munro

FLEET MAINTENANCE SUPPORT SHOPS

1st: Joseph Leanza, Daniel Rodgers, Napolean Wallace, Richard Spoto, D.J. Strongilis, Bernard Cutrone, Carl Slocombe 2nd: Andrew Nukutos, Rudolph Veneck, Edward Topak, James Sottile, Joseph Zerbo, Salvatore Arcabascio, Jeffrey Kaplan, Pasquale Rocchio, Mathew James, John Griswold, Otto Petersen, Peter Ricciardi, Tom Prete, Frank Leanza

BUREAU OF SUPPORT SERVICES

FLEET MAINTENANCE 2 EMS

1st: Pete Morales, Delores Richardson, Fernando Dotel, Pablo Llanot, Delores Hardy, Frank Dizazzo *2nd:* Frank Montetna, Jesse Jackson, John Latimore, John Perez, Juan Marquez, Carl Crawford, Johnnie Harrell, John DiDonato, John Kolb, Alfred Broadnax, Artie Olsen

FLEET MAINTENANCE PARTS ROOM

1st: George Hicks, Mo Sherjang, Bob McDermott, Richie Vasquez, Nate Reice *2nd:* Joe DeFranco, Joe Dorce, Ramon Ross, Doug Fais, Dino Spencer, Marty Markowitz, Mike Merseberg

TIRE SHOP

Donald Myrie, Richard Mazze, David Taylor, Frank Godizzaro, Mike Dickie, Ronald Bower

FLEET MAINTENANCE PUMPER SECTION

1st: Patrick Murphy, Michael Green, Frank Blanchfield, Anthony Nardone, Guiseppe Costanzo *2nd:* Patrick Bartlett, Fred Haeseher, Joseph Mongiello, Steve Cody, John Kay, Leo Walsh, Joseph Dellavecchia, Hector Alvarez, Frank Donato, Lennox Wilhes, Mark Yeramian

BUREAU OF STRATEGIC PLANNING & REVIEW AND INTERNAL AUDIT UNIT

1st: Gerardo Afable, Carlos Ramos, William Killips 2nd: Elidia Tennenhauser, Raymond Saylor

BUREAU OF TECHNOLOGY DEVELOPMENT & SYSTEMS (BTDS)

1st: Yakov Shindel, Elena Shor, Ching Tsang, Nicol Sakur-Khan, Lalit Bhalla, Phyllis Vickers, Balaji Jayaram, Pavel Syrovatchenko, FF Edward O'Neil, FF Carl Waite 2nd: John Adams, Thomas Brucato, Ben Forman, Robert Neistein, David Litvin, Richard Glatzel, Alex Achille, Margie Iglesia, Donald E. Stanton, Paul Kaufman, Maria Vidal, Ronald Maffei, Paula Souleotis, Tom Lin, Stephen Chio 3rd: Imtiaz Khan, Michael Lee, Diptesh Patel, Levent Kocaoglu, Rhunetha Daniel, Zemfira Shapiro, Stephanie Thomas, Julia Rabinovich, Carol Chodes, Linda Shang, Robert Zito, Leroy Smith, William Minus, Adisak Ratana 4th: Gerald Joseph, Theresa Clarner, Walter Rimkunas, Hing Mak, Hollis Duke, Patricia Hickey, John Lubera, FF Glen Midbo, Dino Riojas, Jack Schulstein 5th: Capt. Thomas Ryan, Lt. Robert Salmon, Capt. Edward Linehan, Lt. Stephen Pecylak, Daniel Casucci, Joseph Friedman, Capt. George Edgeworth, FF Anthony Gonzalez, FF Christopher Staten, Philip Binik, Jordan Iotzov, David Ye

BUREAU OF TRAINING

DEPARTMENT OF FIRE AND LIFE SAFETY

EMS DC Gustave Pappas, Stephan Hittmann, PhD, Executive Director, Fire & Life Safety, DC Albert Turi, Jr., Chief of Training

BUREAU OF TRAINING AT RANDALL'S ISLAND (THE "ROCK")

1st: Lt. Joseph Jove, Lt. Daniel Bellew, Frank Pfaff, Lt. Michael Agovino, Lt. Eric Dailey, Lt. Patrick McFadden 2nd: Capt. Steven Sheil, Capt. James Johnson, Lt. Robert Stein, BC Nicholas Santangelo, AC Joseph Callan, Capt. Daniel Keenan, Lt. Walter Dreyer, Lt. John Delmaestro, Lt. Thomas Whyte, Lt. John Harten, Lt. Kevin Brennan, Lt. Edward Geiger, Lt. William McJunkin, Capt. Stephen Krupa, Kevin Mathis 3rd: Alfred Benjamin, Douglas Dien, David Luciano, Lt. Joseph Brosi, Capt. Jeremiah Meehan, Lt. Richard McCarty, Lt. Francis Farrington, William Kristoff, Lt. Paul Hudak, Lt. Lawrence Flaim, Lt. Joseph Imperato, Lt. John Barnickle, Jimmy Liebman, Lt. Robert Cadieux, Ralph Manganiello, Lt. Kevin McCarrol, Joseph Manuella 4th: Lt. Glenn Perry, Lt. James Smithwick, John Regan, William Bell, Brian Regano, Lt. John Flynn, Richard Othmer, Stephen Jantz, Lt. Kevin Dillon, Jonathan Benson, Smith, Richard Dore, Patrick McFadden, Salvatore Camilleri

BUREAU OF TRAINING

FIRST LINE SUPERVISORS TRAINING PROGRAM

Capt. Steven Krupa, Joan Birmingham, Capt. Eugene Carty, Capt. Eugene DeLuca, Capt. Francis Coughlin

CFR-D ADMINISTRATIVE AND INSTRUCTIONAL STAFF

1st: Lt. Michael Camarco, Lt. Katherine Fuchs, Capt. Marylou Aurrichio, Capt. Anthony Campos 2nd: Frank Pizzo, Dorothy Bryman, Mercedes Medina, Beatrice Quiles 3rd: Janet Decker, Julie Guevara, Joe Paz, Liz Casio 4th: John D'Andrea, Lillian Bonsignore 5th: Anthony Bonfiglio, Joseph Terry, Kim Weaver, Terri Napolitano

MAND LIBRARY

Honorary Chief of Department Jack Lerch, Lt. Dan Maye

BUREAU OF TRAINING

LAST FIREFIGHTER CLASS OF 1999

PLATOON 1 SQUAD 1

1st: Michael Schroeder, John Braunagel, Michael Doyle, Michael Burke, James Heinrich, Dana Hannon, Brian Langner, James Brennan *2nd:* Chris Jorgensen, William Sessler, Peter Fallucca, Michael Engel, Joseph Vitiello, Matthew Desjardin, Kevin Wrafter, John McGee *3rd:* Kevin Callahan, Andrew Gargiulo, Gary VanPelt, James McDonald, Mark McGinty, Leo Tineo, Michael Burke, Thomas O'Neill

PLATOON 1 SQUAD 2

1st: Douglas Barry, James O'Boyle, Sean Kearney, Jeffrey DiBenedetto, William Mulhall, Michael Curyn, Kevin Meiners, David Martin *2nd:* Vincent Casione, Douglas Caffarone, Anthony Kimball, Thomas O'Leary, John Lyons, Steven Devaney, William Farrell, Brian Healy *3rd:* Thomas Gentile, Matthew Sheehan, Kevin Farrell, Gregory Brund, Kevin Heaney, John Rodriquez, Richard Poole, Bruce Valero

PLATOON 1 SQUAD 3

1st: Vincent D'Amato, Peter Harvey, Brain McDonnell, Paul Fazio, Steve Tonrey, Michael Doda, Kenneth Kresse, Richard Kane *2nd:* Ed Quinn, Michael Liambalvo, John McNamara, James Sicilian, Michael Dennis, Brian Keag, Michael Zalzyk, John Leverock *3rd:* Ralph Cardino, Michael Peacolk, John Thompson, Brian Coyle, Steve Jiminez, Frank Romano, Michael Kane, Joseph Pagliuca

PLATOON 2 SQUAD 2

1st: Michael Harsch, Paul Liotta, Joseph Zieris, Mike Lynch, John Mayo, Paul Jamin, Kevin Lawe, Arnie Galvez *2nd:* Victor Vene, Ronnie Littlejohn, Charles LoSacco, James Sullivan, Lenny Burmester, Brian Ford, John Dunn, Michael Leahy *3rd:* Anthony Abbruzzese, Michael Canner, Chris Betta, Brian Flood, Dan Casey, Robert Dawson, Frank Somma, John Cialino, Kevin Whalen

PLATOON 2 SQUAD 1

1st: Marice Richardson, Robert McPadden, Kevin Maye, Robert Derrig, Greg Tracy, Joe Spitalieri, Rob Dorrmann, Michael Daly *2nd:* Gary Mattingly, John O'Sullivan, William Esposito, John Latham, George Porter, Thomas Bambury, Richard Lehr, Daniel McGowan *3rd:* Vincent Scialpi, Paul Barbara, Byran Campbell, William Hickey, Brian Kenny, Joseph Wakie, Chris Basil, Giancarlo Gomez, James White

PLATOON 2 SQUAD 3

1st: Robert Ravert, Jon Buchsbaum, Joe Farrell, Ibn Gaskins, Kristoffer McArdle, Kenneth McNiff, Mark Ward, Anthony Cuozzo *2nd:* Nicholas Manfredo, James Touhey, Michael Mugan, Daniel Salsedo, Vincent DeGori, Eric Mora, Frank Perrone, Peter Van Middelem *3rd:* Tom Newbert, Richard Maldonado, Sebastian Fodera, Daniel Lyon, Peter Perri, Matthew Moore, Douglas Delschlager, Christopher Mouhlas

BUREAU OF TRAINING

FIRST FIREFIGHTER CLASS OF 2000

1ST PLATOON 1ST SQUAD "A" COMPANY

1st: Kevin Seaman, William Hayes, George Corrado, Robert Hagen, Carmine Jichetti, James Moody, Vincent Barone, Greg Bourquin *2nd:* Joseph Lamaze, Jemal Braithwaite, Neil Hall, William Johnston, Robert Hourican, Samuel Cirincione, Gregory Frusci, Michael Cosgriff, James Wilson *3rd:* Patrick Nash, James Breslin, Anthony Cittadini, Peter Blaich, Daniel McKay, Jangiz Demirkan, Ronnie Stibritz, Thomas Roche

1ST PLATOON 2ND SQUAD "A" COMPANY

1st: Paul McManaman, James Cleissner, James Kirby, Paul Primavera, Daniel Stanton, Hugh Connolly, Michael Niccoll, Michael Torres *2nd:* Kevin Cassidy, Terrance McShane, Eugene Nickola, Dennis Kerrigan, Kyle Dolder, Edgar Hayes, Thomas DiLorenzo, Michael Cunningham *3rd:* Thomas Costa, Matthew Kerecka, Michael Castellano, Christopher Suhr, Anthony Rubano, Richard DeNave, John O'Conner, Jim DeMartinis

1ST PLATOON 3RD SQUAD "A" COMPANY

1st: Kenny Jackowski, Thomas Michel, Patrick Coyle, Thomas King, John Keating, Jason Groth, Glenn Knatz, Brian Carlstrom *2nd:* Brian Phillips, Sean Kelly, John Dolan, John Miller, Kurt Wesch, Thomas McDermott, James Miller, Jonathan Smith *3rd:* Joel Attis, Philip Spina, Dom Vincenti, Michael Sanseverino, Michele Lomardi, Joseph DelGiudice, Leonard Decker, Patrick Delmage

1ST PLATOON 1ST SQUAD "B" COMPANY

1st: Dave Henrich, Kevin Reilly, Paul Tegtmeier, Patrick Murphy, Steve Vele, James Rooney, Michael Rugusa, Brian Gallagher *2nd:* James Hennessey, Steven Bello, Michael Washington, Russell Dietz, Michael Coen, Richard Carroll, David Wirta, William Tracy *3rd:* Charles Lobianco, Brian Shovlin, Michael Giacoppo, Gerard O'Hara, David Rodriguez, John Lavecchia, Glen Merkitch, Jose Prosper

1ST PLATOON 2ND SQUAD "B" COMPANY

1st: Peter Qagusa, John Masera, Sal Sinatro, William Agosto, Gerard Warnock, Christopher Pickford, Jason Rigioli, Neil Rochford *2nd:* Mark Klingner, Peter Conlan, Stephan Riccio, Thomas Hogan, Michael Sabatello, Kenneth Butler, Robert Greer, Michael Ward *3rd:* Pasquale Amato, John Barry, Michael Dorgan, Vincent Morello, Brian Conlon, Peter O'Conner, Ian Tauss, Joseph Draney

1ST PLATOON 3RD SQUAD "B" COMPANY

1st: Steven Pascale, Robert Linnane, Robert Tomasulo, Michael Tenteromano, Donald Madlik, Javier Marmol, Peter Quitalino, Tom Scharfenberger *2nd:* Earl Martin, John LaBarbera, Ed Rice, Brian Larney, Alain DiNicola, Daniel Jackson, Greg Manning, Martin Curran *3rd:* Michael Murphy, Sal D'Agostino, John Taber, Ryan Egan, Eric Plesniarski, Ernian Gil, Frederick Brown, Brian Guilfoyle

BUREAU OF TRAINING

FIRST FIREFIGHTER CLASS OF 2000

2ND PLATOON 1ST SQUAD "B" COMPANY

1st: Scott Ditzel, Owen McHenry, Mark Smith, John Horan, Robby Rachoi, David Young, Andrew Mastroberti, Charles Gallogly *2nd:* Tim Sullivan, Steve Mirabell, Steve Doyle, Brian Gibbons, Robert Florio, Gary Lambdin, David Revello, Joseph Mason *3rd:* Anthony Tampa, Thomas Curran, Curtis Crowe, Kenneth Roberts, Joseph Esposito, Kevin Butler, Edward Olson, Edward Tucker, Brian Watson

2ND PLATOON 2ND SQUAD "B" COMPANY

1st: Joseph LoRusso, Michael Hammer, John McCabe, Abimael Acosta, Frank Schuffenhauer, Charles Erdey, John Tepedino, Steven Pjura *2nd:* William Sherwin, James Vangorder, Kevin Maloney, Gordan Ambeles, William Shannon, Stephen Donnelly, Louis Lopez, John Montronx. *3rd:* Kevin Delehanty, Frank Fridrich, John Johnson, Angelo Novelli, Douglas Egan, Daniel Dooley, Peter Peltonen, Sergio Villanueva, Joseph Hardy

2ND PLATOON 3RD SQUAD "B" COMPANY

1st: Frank Caccavale, Denis McCarthy, Joe Liselli, Kevin McMahon, Patrick Moloney, John Mucciola, Vincent Verrino, Kevin Kelly *2nd:* John Cadell, Robert Spear, Brian Lavan, Pete Herting, Steve Skroski, Garry Maurice, Michael McGovern, Ronald Soltysik *3rd:* Grant LaRose, Jerrold Dietz, Jamie Privitar, Michael Budischewsky, Michael Jankowski, Barry McWilliams, John Barrone, Cliff Carty, Dominick Montalto

2ND PLATOON 1ST SQUAD "A" COMPANY

1st: William Kinsley, Scott Pandolf, Charles Fragapane, Michael Hinchy, Ronald Casser, Joseph Santos, Daniel Feltham, Joseph Florio *2nd:* Kevin Burns, Thomas Goncalves, Joseph Maresca, Dale Scott, Kevin Lennon, Lester Eser, Brian Kevan, Gabriel Masaracchia, Thomas Mongiello *3rd:* Marc Von Essen, Hugh Boyle, Gerard Kane, James Keegan, Thomas Carbone, John Bellina, Mark Mullady, Robert Stuart, Steven DeCarlo

2ND PLATOON 2ND SQUAD "A" COMPANY

1st: William O'Brien, Jeffrey Smith, Douglas Lotton, Darrin Milo, Carlos Guzman, Michael Gager, Chris Girello, Tim Gorman *2nd:* Anthony Maneri, Kenneth Mcternan, Gregory Star, John Griffin, Drew D'Emic, James Brennan, Dan Campion, Andrew Owens *3rd:* Stephen Sauced, Kevin Dyer, Joel Gurrieri, Scott Sheehan, Stephen Wynne, James Dell'Alba, Sead Pekusic, Alex Streichennein, Glen Baillargeon

2ND PLATOON 3RD SQUAD "A" COMPANY

1st: James Alfano, Tim Langner, Armin Betting, James Buhre, Julian Eyre, Frank Marousek, Ricardo Sosa, Rafael Badillo, Kevin Kromer *2nd:* Mark Beekman, Peter Stissi, Michael Ansbroll, Anthony Ferraro, Stephen Duffy, Marc Jensen, Robert Witt, Henry Ryan *3rd:* James Manitta, Donald Barbour, Neil Filipowicz, Jeffery Ruffler, George Aguirre, Jeffrey Huey, Anthony LaGreca, John LaPointe, James Lodispoto

DIVISION 1

1st: DC Stephen Hession, DC Peter Hayden, DC Sal Cassano, DC John Casey, DC John Coloe. Back: Teresa French, Lt. Anthony Venezia, Christian Waugh, Daniel Newman

BATTALION 1

Kirk Pritchard, Rudolph Pillarella, BC Andrew Richter, BC Joseph Pfeifer, BC William Blaich, BC William Oehm, Jeffrey Jones, James Miller

BATTALION 2

BC Edward McSheehy, BC Joseph D. Ebert, BC Richard E. Fuerch, Leonard Roe

BATTALION 6

BC Brian McCullagh, BC Eugene Flynn, BC Peter Rice, BC Richard Burban, George Ross

BATTALION 7

BC Allen S. Hay, BC Kevin R. Byrnes, BC Orio J. Palmer, Kevin Deery

Note: Battalion 4 in photo with Ladder 18 (See page 267)

*1st: Michael Reeves, Capt. John Kitchenman, Lt. Alan Panettiere, Robert Humphrey **2nd:** Carmine DiSilvestro, Joel Quintalino, Matthew Daly, Chris Bruno, Michael Pritchett, Daniel Parker, Michael Alberico*

ENGINE CO. 4

42 South Street, Manhattan

This company, located in a large and unusual modern fire station on the ground floor of a large commercial office building, was organized on September 8, 1865, in the former quarters of volunteer City Hose 8 at 39 Liberty Street. They were disbanded on January 1, 1947, from their quarters then at 119 Maiden Lane. Reorganized on August 20, 1984, in the quarters of Ladder 15 at 73 Water Street, both units moved into their current home on May 4, 1987. Engine 4 rolls with a 1993 Seagrave 1000-gpm pumper. Also located in these quarters is the Decontamination Unit—a 1987 Mack tractor, pulling a 1995 Super-Vac trailer equipped with showers, etc. Engine 4's first-alarm district consists of numerous high-rise office buildings, including the World Trade Center, as well as the many old East River piers, South Street Seaport, Fulton Fish Market and Staten Island Ferry Terminals. They have had two medal winners and received three unit citations. Five members have died in the line of duty.

LADDER CO. 15

42 South Street, Manhattan

The original Ladder 15 was a suburban ladder company organized on October 30, 1865, in upper Manhattan at 10th Avenue and 159th Street. They became a regular hook and ladder company on January 1, 1868, and were disbanded on July 11, 1881. On November 27, 1882, they were re-organized—this time in lower Manhattan—with Engine Co. 10. They finally moved to their current quarters with Engine Company 4 on May 4, 1987, in an unusual fire station located on the ground floor of a large office building. The Decontamination Unit also is quartered here and manned by members of the company. In addition to the South Street Seaport, their first-alarm territory includes many high-rise office buildings, piers, etc. They have had eight medal winners and received five unit citations. Three members have died in the line of duty. They have a 1999 Seagrave/Aerialscope 75-foot tower ladder.

*1st: Michael Micara, Lt. John Viola, Lt. Joe Leavey, Capt. Tim McKinney, Lt. Joe Hartigan, John Paolella, Frank Vaskis **2nd:** Ed Rzempoluch, Steve Krakower, Jack Becht, Josue Recio, Scott Kopytko, Howard Blythe, Eric Olsen, Dennis Blake, Sal D'Iorio*

*1st: Lt. Henry Porcaro, Lt. Steven Sorger, Capt. Edwin Travers, Lt. James Gunning **2nd:** Paul Beyer, Thomas Rooney, Kenneth King, John Butler, Anthony Barone, Michael Rispulo, Vincent Palmieri, William Green **3rd:** Paul Schmalzried, Peter Rodriguez, William King, Alphonse Sicignano, Marco Silva, Eugene McKeon, Christopher Broughton, Robert Emans*

ENGINE CO. 6

49 Beekman Street, Manhattan

Originally organized on September 8, 1865, in the former house of volunteer Washington Engine 20 at 100 Cedar Street, they later moved to 113 Liberty Street in 1905 and eventually to their current address, which is the former quarters of the now disbanded Engine 32, on March 6, 1970. Like Engine 4, their first-alarm area consists of numerous high-rise office buildings, as well as some very old factories, the World Trade Center, City Hall and other government buildings, the Fulton Fish Market, hospitals, etc. Due to the many high-rise buildings, they are equipped with a special 1994 Seagrave 1000-gpm, high-pressure pumper, one of only seven in the city. They have had five line-of-duty deaths, nine unit citations and seven medal winners, including a James Gordon Bennett in 1877. Their former captains received Stephenson Medals in 1897 and 1945 for maintaining the most disciplined and efficient company in the FDNY.

ENGINE CO. 7

100 Duane Street, Manhattan

This company originally was established as part of the paid department on September 8, 1865, in the former quarters of volunteer Protector Engine 22 at 22 Chambers Street. Eventually, they moved to their current house on December 31, 1905, where they are quartered with Ladder 1 and the 1st Battalion. At various times in the past, various special units, including Searchlight 1, Relay Hose Wagon 1, Water Tower 1 and Smoke Ejector & Foamite Truck 1, as well as Ladder 10, Division 1 and Battalion 2 also were located here. Their first-alarm territory includes mainly commercial buildings of various occupancies, as well as City Hall and other government buildings, the World Trade Center, etc. They have had 11 medal winners and received four unit citations. Four members have died in the line of duty. The Stephenson Medal was awarded to the captain in 1889 for maintaining the best-disciplined and most efficient company. The NYC Fire Museum was located in these quarters prior to moving to Spring Street in 1987. Their new apparatus is a 2000 Seagrave 1000-gpm pumper.

1st: James Barry, Lt. James Fody, Capt. Dennis Tardio, Lt. Patrick Lynons, Stanley Jessamine 2nd: Patrick Zoda, Michael Babino, William Meade, Damian Van Cleaf, Neil Ottrando, Thomas Spinard, John Gilhooly, Richard Nappi 3rd: Daniel Caruso, Joseph Sweeney, Robert Carbone, James D'Addesa, Gary Kavakos, John Casanovas, Joseph Casaliggi

1st: Steven Olsen, Lt. Randy Wiebicke, Capt. Ron Schmutzler, Lt. Gary Lajiness, Lt. William Walsh, Lt. Gregory Gargiso 2nd: Kirk Pritchard, Christopher Connor, Daniel McCarren, Frank Esposito, Michael Kozak, Nick Borrillo, John McConnachie, Christopher Mullin, Daniel Keane, Kevin Lynch, Jan Greibesland, Robert Keller 3rd: Edward Fahey, Glenn Radermacher, James Hanlon, Donald Meinecke, Denis Noonan, James Burke 4th: William Hammel, Glen O'Connor, Christopher Ward, Steven Rogers

LADDER CO. 1

100 Duane Street, Manhattan

Ladder 1 was organized on September 8, 1865, in the former quarters of volunteer Mutual Hook and Ladder 1 at 26 Chambers Street, next door to Engine 7, which took over from volunteer Protector Engine 22 on that same date. Both companies moved to their current quarters on December 31, 1905. Ladder 10, Searchlight 1, Water Tower 1, Relay Hose Wagon 1, Smoke Ejector & Foamite Truck 1 and the First Division have been in these quarters in the past, as has the Fire Museum. The 1st Battalion now is stationed here. Ladder 1, in 1964, was the first FDNY company to be equipped with a tower-ladder. Their first-alarm area consists of large commercial and government buildings, including City Hall and the World Trade Center. They have had 23 medal winners, including James Gordon Bennett Medals in 1873, 1879, 1886, 1917, 1930 and 1938 and a Dr. Harry M. Archer Medal in 1921. Additionally, in 1891, their captain received the Stephenson Medal. They have received 11 unit citations. Eight members have died in the line of duty. Their apparatus is a 1999 Seagrave/Aerialscope 75-foot tower-ladder.

ENGINE CO. 10

124 Liberty Street, Manhattan

This unit was first established on September 8, 1865, in the former quarters of volunteer Franklin Hose 18 at 28 Beaver Street, in lower Manhattan It then had several locations until brought together with Ladder 10 in their current house on June 11, 1980. This is one of two houses in the FDNY where both the engine and ladder have the same number (the other houses Engine and Ladder 52 in Riverdale). Engine 10 is directly across the street from the World Trade Center and was first-due at the catastrophic bomb blast there in 1993. Other buildings in their first-alarm area include high-rise office structures, historic churches, piers, etc. They have had three medal winners, including a James Gordon Bennett in 1875 and the New York Firefighters Burn Center Foundation Medal, a unit award given in 1993 for heroism at a fire on a tugboat in 1992. This unit also has received 10 unit citations. One of their former members died in the line of duty. They operate a 1994 high-pressure Seagrave 1000-gpm pumper, one of only seven in the FDNY.

1st: Dan Peritore, Lt. Sean O'Malley, Capt. Gene Kelty, Lt. August DeLorenzo, Anthony Konczynski 2nd: Jeff Olsen, Mitch Castiglione, Mark Dulski, Paul Pansini, Sal Argano, Walter Dunlop, Joe Ruggirello, Vincent Geloso 3rd: Gary Kolsch, Mike Molly, Richard Zerilli, Nick Simeone, Gerard Fitzgerald, Steven Leon, Scott Gaboff

1st: Ed Thompson, Serge Pilipczuk, John Morabito, John Walstrom, Bill Tasker 2nd: Kerry Horgan, Mike Egan, Tom Basmagy, Ray Arcos, Capt. Paul Mallery, Lt. Matt Donachie, John Rohr, Patrick Higgins, John Castronova 3rd: Pete Patterson, Kevin Ekberg, Tom Maragaria, John Cassidy, Frank Henglein, Kevin Connolly, Colin Phillips

LADDER CO. 10
124 Liberty Street, Manhattan

A company that has changed location many times, Ladder 10 originally was organized in a former volunteer house, Southawk Engine 38 at 28 Ann Street, on October 20, 1865. From 1866 to 1968, they were located at 191 Fulton Street. They moved to their current quarters with Engine Company 10 on July 1, 1984. They are only one of two FDNY stations where the engine and ladder have the same number. (The other houses Engine and Ladder 52 in Riverdale.) Located directly across the street from the World Trade Center, they were first-due at the bomb blast there in 1993. Other hazards in their first-alarm area include old high-rise office buildings, historic churches, piers, etc. They have had 16 individual medal winners, including James Gordon Bennett Medals in 1874, 1883, 1889 and 1952. In 1917, 1920 and 1922, the entire company was awarded the Fire College Medal for the best time at evolutions and drills. They have received eight unit citations. Two members have died in the line of duty. Their apparatus is a 1994 Seagrave 100-foot rear-mount.

ENGINE CO. 24
227 Avenue of the Americas, Manhattan

Organized on October 11, 1865, the unit took over the quarters of volunteer Howard Engine 24 at 78 Morton Street and remained in this house until moving into their current quarters with Ladder 5 on November 25, 1975. The 2nd Battalion now is quartered here, as was the 1st Division in the past. Their first-alarm territory, in the Greenwich Village and SoHo areas, has a mix of old tenements, modern apartment houses, small townhouses, large commercial factories and the west side piers. Four of their former members were awarded medals. A Stephenson Medal for the most efficient and best-disciplined company in the department went to their captain in 1889. They have received two unit citations. Five members have died in the line of duty, including two, plus the captain of Ladder 5, at the tragic Watts Street fire in 1994. They have a 2000 Seagrave 1000-gpm pumper.

1st: Robert Beddia, John Ottrando, Lt. Joseph Mauro, Capt. Anthony Varriale, Lt. George Finnin, James Esposito, Anthony Salerno 2nd: Thomas Sheeran, Richard Billy, Joseph Graffagnino, Dennis Taaffe, James Miller, Marcel Claes 3rd: Adam Lake, Gary Jacobson, Charles Gaffney, Robert Gelling, William McCarthy, Michael Paolone, Francis McCutchen

LADDER CO. 5
227 Avenue of the Americas, Manhattan

Ladder 5 was organized on September 25, 1865, in the former quarters of volunteer Columbian Hook and Ladder 14, at 102 Charles Street. On March 1, 1884, they were re-organized as a double company with separate officers and firefighters in each section. This second section was disbanded on July 1, 1939. Ladder 5 moved to their current quarters with Engine 24 on November 25, 1975. The 2nd Battalion is in these quarters, too, as was the 1st Division at one time. Located in the historic Greenwich Village and SoHo area, their first-alarm territory has old tenements, modern apartment houses, townhouses, factories and the west side piers. They have had 10 individual medal winners, plus the New York Firefighters Burn Center Foundation Medal for team heroic actions at the World Trade Center disaster on February 26, 1993. They have received 11 unit citations. Five members have died in the line of duty. They respond on a 1991 Seagrave 100-foot tillered aerial.

1st: John Santore, Chris Waugh, Capt. Steve Cirulnick, Ed Foy, Stephen Napolitano, Paul Keating, Jeffrey Anstead 2nd: Joe Andreano, William Greco, Paul Finochiaro, Greg Saucedo, Keith Frey, John Stringle, Marty Moriarty 3rd: Nick Primiano, Mike Simon, Gregg Wasserman, Mike Brennan, John Kelly, Thomas Hannifin

ENGINE CO. 55

363 Broome Street, Manhattan

Engine 55 was organized on June 4, 1887, in the former volunteer quarters at 173 Elm Street (later known as 185 Lafayette Street), and moved to their current house on June 6, 1899, which, until recently, was also home to the 2nd Battalion. For approximately one year prior to August 1999, while their quarters were being modernized, Engine 55 temporarily was relocated to the quarters of Ladder 20. Located in an ethnically mixed area, their first-alarm territory consists of many old tenements, as well as factories, converted loft buildings and numerous restaurants and retail stores. In 1906, their captain was awarded the Stephenson Medal for having the most efficient and best-disciplined company in the entire department. They have had two other individual medal winners and have been awarded five unit citations. They have had two line-of-duty deaths, one while in the military service during World War I. Their current apparatus is a 1993 Seagrave 1000-gpm pumper.

1st: Lt. Richard Sautner, BC Dominick DeRubbio, Lt. Peter Freund, Lt. Rocco Battista 2nd: Christopher Geraghty, Paul Quinn, Kevin Erdman, Robert Siragusa, Richard Cippoletti, Anthony Castano, Scott Koennecke, Charles Ferris, Peter Metzger, Stephen Russell 3rd: Patrick Schuppel, Bryon Bodine, Eugene Cairns, Charles McElhone, John Powers, Paul Acciarito, John Olivero, Steven Bennett, Kevin Aglietti, Robert Lane

1st: Craig Carlsen, Lt. John Dopwell, Capt. John Gialella, Lt. James Donahue, Michael Macko 2nd: Robert Leanza, John Callaghan, Ronald Lipari, Kevin Dinkins, Gerard Poulin, Kurt Bugge, John Buchheit, Tony Caracciolo 3rd: Thomas Flynn, Timothy Hallahan, James Hayes, John Channell, Brian Sullivan, Oscar Garcia, Brian Mulry, Dennis Grady

LADDER CO. 8

14 North Moore Street, Manhattan

Ladder 8 was organized on October 16, 1865, in the quarters of former volunteer quarters at 153 Franklin Street. They moved to their current address on June 18, 1905. Originally, this firehouse was a two-bay, two-door house that was cut in half to widen Varick Street. Ladder 8 was made a double company for a few months in 1905, then again from 1906 to 1914, when the section was disbanded. The second section was re-organized again in April 1917, but at the quarters of Engine Company 30 at 278 Spring Street, while the first section was at the North Moore Street house. The second section was disbanded on May 1, 1918. Ladder 8 became famous when the movie Ghostbusters was filmed in their quarters. The company was disbanded on July 2, 1975, due to a budget crisis, but re-organized two days later. Their first-alarm area includes converted loft buildings, factories, apartment houses and government buildings. They have had 10 medal winners, including a James Gordon Bennett Medal in 1917 and the Stephenson Medal in 1914 and have been awarded six unit citations. In 1918, the company received the Fire College Medal. They have had four line-of-duty deaths.

LADDER CO. 20

251 Lafayette Street, Manhattan

Ladder 20 was organized on March 30, 1889. They originally were located at 155 Mercer Street, in an historical building known as Firemen's Hall. In 1900, they were made into a double company and operated as such until 1939, when the second section was disbanded. They moved to their current quarters, along with the now-disbanded Engine 13, on April 24, 1974, to a building that also had been used as the FDNY Bureau of Health Services Medical Office, prior to that unit moving to MetroTech Center. The 1st Division now is located in these quarters, as is the Manhattan Base of the Bureau of Fire Investigation. Ladder 20's first-alarm territory consists of many large factories, converted residential lofts, numerous restaurants and retail stores. They have had 14 medal winners and 11 unit citations. In 1912, a former captain received the Stephenson Medal for maintaining the most efficient and best-disciplined company in the department. They have had one line-of-duty death. They have a 1999 Seagrave 100-foot tillered aerial.

1st: Lt. John Fischer, Capt. Gregory Rodgers, Lt. Harold Banker, Lt. James Brennan 2nd: Anthony Fontana, Kenneth Escoffrey, William Cunneen, Michael Hopkins, Gregory Edwards, Randolph Regan, Robert McMahon, Thomas Papaccio, George Kozlowski, Bruce Beschner, Robert Barrett, Michael Toal 3rd: Victor Diz, Jose Maldonado, David LaForge, John Burnside, Adrienne Walsh, Richard Stewart, Thomas Boyne, James Gray, Richard Snyder, Kevin Morrow

ENGINE CO. 9

75 Canal Street, Manhattan

Located in the heart of Chinatown, this company originally was organized on September 29, 1865, in the former quarters of volunteer Excelsior Engine 2 at 55 East Broadway and moved to the current quarters with Ladder 6 on May 6, 1969. While still in their former quarters, a special unit, Bridge Chemical Engine 63, was quartered with them. Part of the Satellite Water System, they are equipped with a 1994 Seagrave 2000-gpm pumper, the only such rig in the FDNY. Satellite 1, a 1993 Mack/Saulsbury hose wagon, rolls with them on multiple alarms and special calls when needed. Their first-alarm area is made up primarily of many very old tenement buildings, as well as small factories and retail stores. They also respond to three major bridges, the Brooklyn, Manhattan and Williamsburgh. They have had four medal winners, including the James Gordon Bennett Medal in 1870 and 1873 and have received 11 unit citations. Three of their members were killed in the line of duty.

1st: Lt. Jacob Chin, Capt. Ralph Fago, Lt. Robert Blanco, Lt. Thomas Sialiano 2nd: Walter Cisek, Sherwin Chow, Nicholas Lucenti, John Starace 3rd: Daniel Hettrick, David Wong, Bruce Ross, Sean O'Sullivan

1st: Lt. Ernest W. Petretti, Capt. John A. Jonas, Lt. Frederick J. Reich 2nd: Robert L. McGuinness, Patrick J. O'Grady, Michael R. Meldrum, Dwayne M. Dewitt 3rd: Peter S. Mueller, William J. Leahy, William S. Butler

LADDER CO. 6

75 Canal Street, Manhattan

Ladder 6 was organized on September 27, 1865, in the quarters of former volunteer Harry Howard Hook and Ladder 11, at 180 Clinton Street. A second section was organized in May 1883, but disbanded six months later. They moved to the quarters of Chemical 6 at 77 Canal Street in 1877, when Chemical 6 was disbanded. They have been in their current house, with Engine 9 and Satellite 1, since May 6, 1969. Their first-alarm territory consists of old tenements, many small factories and numerous retail stores. They have had 24 individual medal winners, including two James Gordon Bennett Medals in 1873 and 1894. A former captain received the Stephenson Medal in 1898 for having the best-disciplined and most efficient company in the department. In 1990, members were awarded the New York Firefighters Burn Center Foundation Medal for an heroic team effort in 1989. They were awarded 22 unit citations. They have had three line-of-duty deaths. They have a 1989 Seagrave 100-foot tillered aerial.

ENGINE CO. 15

269 Henry Street, Manhattan

First organized on September 18, 1865, in the former ornate quarters of the famous volunteer Americus Engine 6, Engine 15 temporarily was quartered for a few months with Ladder 6, while their new house—at the same site as the original house at 269 Henry Street—was being built. They took occupancy on July 1, 1884, and have been here since. Their first-alarm area is made up mainly of old tenements, with a sprinkling of modern housing projects and some small factories. Seven of their former members were killed in the line of duty. They have had seven medal winners, including a James Gordon Bennett in 1873 and again in 1920 and have been awarded seven unit citations. Their 1989 Mack 1000-gpm pumper will be replaced in 2000.

1st: William Miller, Lt. Victor Harris, Capt. Kevin Blaine, Lt. August DeLorenzo, Lawrence Mathe 2nd: Francis Valerio, Robert Stanton, Michael Flanagan, Kevin Coursey, Modesto Gonzalez, Frank Lopresti, Ivan Albert, Christopher Barrett, Douglas DiGeorgio, Adam Schwinn, Thomas Morgan 3rd: Keith Nelson, Teresa French, Rocky Raimondi, Michael Crowley, Peter Syrett, Robert Allar, Sami Asfar, Thomas Mitchell, Joseph Brennan

1st: Lt. Kirk Kowalchuk, Lt. Thomas Murphy, Capt. Dennis Asher, Lt. William Schillinger 2nd: Daniel Walsh, Daniel Maurer, James Ippolito, Robert Salvador, Michael Kehoe, James Lopez, Joseph Esposito, Thomas Sullivan, Steven Mattera 3rd: Robert Alverson, Mark Washington, Roy Chelsen, Kenneth Hansen, Robert VanSteen, Paul Brezinski

ENGINE CO. 28
222 East 2nd Street, Manhattan

Engine 28 was organized in the former quarters of volunteer Forrest Engine 3, at 604 East 11th Street, on October 20, 1865, later occupying a new house at the same location from 1880 until moving into their current quarters with Ladder 11 on April 22, 1959. This company is located in an area of the lower east side, made up mainly of old tenement-style buildings, with many retail stores of various occupancies. Four members of this company have been awarded individual medals. This company has been awarded 24 unit citations. Additionally, in 1988, one of their lieutenants and five firefighters were awarded the New York Firefighters Burn Center Foundation Medal as a unit citation for their heroic work at a tenement fire in 1986. One former member of this company died in the line of duty. They have a 1989 Mack 1000-gpm pumper, which will be replaced in 2000.

LADDER CO. 11
222 East 2nd Street, Manhattan

Ladder 11 was organized on October 27, 1865, in the former quarters of Mechanic's Hose 47. They moved to their current house with Engine 28 on April 22, 1959. Located on the lower east side of Manhattan, their first-alarm area consists mainly of old tenements and many retail stores. They have 21 individual medal winners and 27 unit citations. These included John Gordon Bennett Medals in 1905 and 1958. In 1998, Firefighter James Kelly received the DeFranco Medal for a water rescue in the East River on November 11, 1997. In 1999, Lieutenant John Cronley was awarded the Delehanty Medal for an heroic rescue at a 7-5 at 30 Avenue D on March 13, 1998. Their apparatus is a 1994 Seagrave 100-foot rear-mount.

1st: Lt. John J. Cronley, Capt. George Carlin 2nd: Keith R. O'Mara, Richard P. Olsen, Richard J. Kelly, Jr., Richard A. Barto, Michael A. Pignataro, James T. Corcoran, Robert Annunziato, Jr., Daniel Cassidy, Robert Castelli, Stephen Eagers, Stephen G. Schwarz 3rd: Frank Licata, Kevin Murray, Philip Tesoriero, Gary Elder, Matthew S. Rogan, Robert Cherry

1st: Fred Schaaf, Rich Kelly, BC Jim Murray, John Scarcella, John Kelly, Mark Rosenbaum 2nd: Bob Newman, Chuck Wilt, John Smyth, Lt. Eric Sacknoff, Lt. Bob Dillon, Capt. Carl Grunewald, Lt. Gary Borega, Dan McGuinness, Lance Ogren, Rob Greenfield 3rd: Bob Moore, Steve Merenda, Ed Cutting, Harry Coyle, Charlie Maloney, Dan Keating, Sean Kissane, Kevin Murray, Ron Lattari

LADDER CO. 18
25 Pitt Street, Manhattan

The original Ladder 18 was a Bronx company organized on January 1, 1874, at 491 East 166th Street, with Chemical Engine 2. They were disbanded on July 1, 1882, following the organization of Combination Engine Company 50. They were re-organized in Manhattan, at 84 Attorney Street, on February 1, 1887, and later moved to 185 Broome Street. On December 12, 1973, they moved to their current quarters with Engine 17, which since has been disbanded, and the 4th Battalion. This busy company covers a lower east side area consisting mainly of old tenements, with some high-rise housing projects and many retail stores. They have had 18 medal winners and 22 unit citations. In 1993, Firefighter Albert Gonzalez was awarded the James Gordon Bennett Medal and three years later, the Dr. Harry M. Archer Medal. Ladder 18 had a previous Bennett Medal recipient in 1905. They have had three line-of-duty deaths. Their apparatus is a 1999 Seagrave 75-foot tower-ladder. The company received the Elsasser Medal in 2000 for an heroic group act in 1999. *(Both Ladder 18 & Battalion 4 are pictured in photograph)*

ENGINE CO. 5

340 East 14th Street, Manhattan

One of the earlier paid companies, Engine 5 was organized at their current address on September 25, 1865, in
the former quarters of volunteer United States Engine 23.
That house was torn down to make room for their "new"
house at the same location, which they have occupied since
March 1, 1881. This is one of the oldest, still active quarters in the Department. Engine 5 covers an area of the
lower east side, made up mainly of old tenement buildings. Fourteenth Street, itself, has hundreds of retail stores
of various kinds. The huge Stuyvesant Town and Peter
Cooper Village developments are also in their territory.
With the exception of a few months in 1899-1900, Engine
5 operated as a double engine company from 1884 until
1939. They have had five line-of-duty deaths and five
medal winners, including a James Gordon Bennett Medal
in 1891 and 14 unit citations. They operate a 1994 Seagrave
1000-gpm pumper.

*1st: Lt. Girard Owens, Capt. Michael Mullins, Lt. Charles Hubbard 2nd: Manny DelValle, Michael Connolly,
Douglas Dicks, Anthony Farrington, Gerard Gorman, Robert Mahoney, Marc Sommer, John Napolittano,
Christopher O'Keefe, Thomas Lynn, Edward Merner, John McAndrews, Patrick Keegan 3rd: Derek Brogan,
James Andnizzi, Michael Hardy, Mathew Black*

ENGINE CO. 14

14 East 18th Street, Manhattan

Originally organized on October 6, 1865, in the former
quarters of Metamora Hose 29, this company actually has
been at the same address since inception. However, the
current house dates back only to 1895, after replacing the
volunteer station at the same location. An unusual aspect
of an original endowment of a Department award, the
John T. Agnew Medal only can be awarded for an act of
heroism to a member of Engine 14. This is the only such
award dedicated to one company. This medal has been
awarded only six times, most recently in 1973. Additionally, a former captain was awarded the James Gordon
Bennett Medal in 1923 and the Dr. Harry M. Archer Medal
in 1924. In 1946, their captain was awarded the Stephenson
Medal for the most efficient and best-disciplined company. The company has received eight unit citations. Their
varied first-alarm territory includes factories, office buildings and apartment houses. Their apparatus is a 1998
Seagrave 1000-gpm pumper. They have had seven line-
of-duty deaths, two on the same day at a fire in 1906.

*1st: Salvatore J. Parisi, John A. Schunke, Capt. Charles J. Vella, BC Carl Jost, Jr., Lt. Michael D. Bordes, Robert G.
Henry 2nd: Kevin D. Cahill, Peter A. Zuk, Angelo Zecca, Robert E. Peters, Jeffrey A. Henkel, Kevin McQuilly,
Donald G. Hayes, Steven C. D'Alessio 3rd: Christopher Bilotti, Michael McClelland, John A. Crimi, Gabriel
Esposito, Daniel P. Geysen, Joshua M. Reder, Carle Jost, Jr.*

*1st: Robert Schmuck, Louis Trazino, Capt. Robert McLoughlin, Carl Orregia, Michael Ottrando 2nd: David
Arce, Brian Stapleton, Joseph Last, Steven Nuzzi, Andrew Robb, Vincent Canale, Matthew Hornung, Brian Bilcher,
Joseph Bert, Gerard Dolan*

ENGINE CO. 33

42 Great Jones Street, Manhattan

Originally organized in the former quarters of volunteer
Niagara Engine 4, at 220 Mercer Street, on November 1,
1865. Engine 33 moved to 15 Great Jones Street in 1882
and to their current house on January 1, 1899. This large
station now is the home of Ladder 9, too. Engine 33 operated as a double engine company from 1883 to 1939. This
house once was used for the quarters of the Chief of Department and for the offices of WNYF, an official training publication of the FDNY. The company was awarded
seven unit citations and six of their members have been
awarded medals. Three members were killed in the line
of duty. This company has many large factories and warehouses, as well as numerous old tenements, retail stores,
etc., in their first-alarm area. Their current apparatus is a
1998 Seagrave 1000-gpm pumper.

1st: Daniel Rowan, Lt. Paul Schmidt, Capt. Joseph Sapienza, Lt. Terence Cashin, Frederick Walker 2nd: Gary Nybro, Chris Corsi, Bertram Springstead, Craig Reimertz, Donald Casey, Anna Schermerhorn, Gregory Gessner, Thomas Baroz, Leonard Yourth, John Kazan, Kurt Bro, Kevin Duffy, Stephen Spellman

LADDER CO. 9

42 Great Jones Street, Manhattan

Ladder 9 was organized on October 20, 1865, in the former quarters of Hibernian Hook and Ladder 18 at 209 Elizabeth Street. A second section was organized on July 20, 1883, in these quarters, but was moved to 199 Chrystie Street on November 30th of that year. This was unusual—two sections in two different houses—but the second was disbanded March 30, 1889. Ladder 9 moved into Engine 33's quarters, their current location, on November 22, 1948. Their first-alarm area includes old tenements, large factories, warehouses and retail stores. They have had 15 individual medal winners and 20 unit citations. Their captains received the Stephenson Medal in 1895 and 1913. In 1913, the company was awarded the Fire College Medal for the quickest time in various drills and evolutions. In 1998, Lieutenant Paul Schmidt and five firefighters were awarded the Elsasser Medal for a team heroic action at a 3-3 at 3 Hanover Square on April 15, 1997. They have had six line-of-duty deaths. Their apparatus is a 1999 Seagrave/Aerialscope 95-foot tower-ladder.

LADDER CO. 3

108 East 13th Street, Manhattan

Ladder 3 was organized on September 11, 1865, in the former volunteer house of Friendship Hook & Ladder 12 on the site of their current house. They occupied this house on October 28, 1929, along with the 6th Battalion, which is still here. Water Tower 2 also was located here until being disbanded in 1957, as was Chemical 7 from 1876 to 1877. Ladder 3 is one of very few FDNY ladder companies to be in a house without an engine. Their first-alarm area includes many large factories, commercial loft buildings, old tenements and numerous retail stores. They have had 29 medal winners and 21 unit citations, including six James Gordon Bennett Medals in 1885, 1897, 1903, 1904, 1939 and 1945. Three of their former members were killed in the line of duty. Their apparatus is a 1994 Seagrave 100-foot rear-mount.

1st: James Wind, Lt. Dan Browne, Capt. Michael Murphy, Lt. Ray Trinkle, Lt. Kevin Donnelly, Lt. Reid Jantz, Kevin Horan 2nd: Jay Ogren, John Gates, Frank Calabro, Bob Burmeister, Steve Olson, Tim Brady, Dennis Durnin, George Symon 3rd: Pat Murphy, James Canty, Tim McSweeney, Michael Carroll, Jeff Giordano, Tim McNamara, Richard DiPadova

ENGINE CO. 1

142 W. 31st Street, Manhattan

Originally organized as one of the first engines in the paid department, Engine 1 entered service in the former quarters of volunteer Northern Liberty Engine 42 at One Centre Street, in lower Manhattan, on July 31, 1865. Disbanded in 1868, they were reorganized in midtown Manhattan at 165 West 29th Street on February 17, 1873, and moved on November 3, 1946, to their current quarters, shared with Ladder 24. Several special units, including Water Tower 3, Searchlight 21, Department Ambulance 1 and High Ladder 1, and the Third Division, were housed in these quarters. Their first-alarm area includes various factories and high-rise commercial office buildings, plus Madison Square Garden, Penn Station, the Empire State Building, Macy's Department Store and several hotels. Four members were killed in the line of duty. There have been six medal winners and nine unit citations. Three of their former captains were awarded the Stephenson Medal in 1896, 1922 and 1951, given for maintaining the most efficient and disciplined company in the Department. They have a 1998 Seagrave 1000-gpm pumper.

1st: Lt. Claude Knowles, Capt. Kenneth Erb, Lt. Blake McLoughlin 2nd: Kirk Long, Paul Castle, Anthony Salato, Kevin Duggan, Nelson Ross, Joseph Falco, Paul Bessler, Michael Cruz 3rd: Simon Porteus, Rudy Geiger, Gerard Suden, John Foertsch, Russell Bakunas, Michael Weinberg, Michael Yarembinsky, Liam Coleman

LADDER CO. 24

142 West 31st Street, Manhattan

Ladder 24 was organized on June 1, 1901, at 115 West 31st Street in midtown Manhattan. On November 3, 1946, they moved to their current quarters with Engine Company 1. Other units occupying this house in the past included Water Tower 3, Searchlight 21, Department Ambulance 1, High Ladder 1 and the 3rd Division. The first-alarm district includes factories, high-rise commercial office buildings, hotels, Penn Station, Madison Square Garden, the Empire State Building and Macy's. They have had 18 individual medal winners and 19 unit citations, including a James Gordon Bennett in 1946. Their former captain in 1908 received the Stephenson Medal for having the best-disciplined and most efficient company in the department. In 1993, Lieutenant Robert Keys and five firefighters were awarded the Elsasser Medal. They have had four line-of-duty deaths, including Firefighters Robert Hurst and Charles Lang, killed at the Times Tower 5-5 on November 22, 1961. Their apparatus is a 1999 Seagrave 100-foot rear-mount.

1st: James T. Grillo, Lt. Joseph Dilorenzo, Capt. Daniel Brethel, Lt. Donald Atlas, Lt. Edward Brown, James M. Hosford 2nd: James Halaby, Michael Pinto, Eric Sutton, Thomas Langan, John Montani, John Regan, Thomas Ahern, Steve Wojciechowski, Joseph Papillo, Sean Norton 3rd: Gregory Herth, Joseph Boneillo, Steve Belson, Robert Kirschberg, James Cody, John Suarez, Brian Thomas, Salvatore Scarentino, Stephen Halliday, James Duffy, Donald Zink

ENGINE CO. 3

146 W. 19th Street, Manhattan

This midtown company was organized in the former quarters of volunteer Jackson Engine 24 at 417 West 17th Street on September 14, 1865, moved to 216 West 20th Street on October 26, 1960, and eventually to their current quarters with Ladder 12 and the 7th Battalion on February 6, 1967. High-Rise Unit 1, a special unit with a custom-built 1997 Mack/Saulsbury, also is located here. Their first-alarm area includes many old tenements and commercial buildings, as well as the west side piers. Over the years, they have had one medal winner, 11 unit citations and two line-of-duty deaths. In 1999, one of their lieutenants and five firefighters were awarded the New York Firefighters Burn Center Foundation Medal for a teamwork act of valor at Manhattan Box 2-2-616, 206 West 23rd Street, on February 24, 1998. Engine 3 operates a 1997 Seagrave 1000-gpm pumper.

1st: John Chance, Rob Albino, Lt. Tom Colucci, Capt. Kevin Loughran, Lt. Jim Walsh, Mike Prodromides, Lloyd Stuart 2nd: Damien Martin, Tom O'Donoghue, Dave Aslan, Rick Bonadies, Pat Nelson, Glen Kittle, Scott Holowach, Rob Chyriwski, Lt. Tom McNamara 3rd: Paul Asaro, Jim Matishek, Adam Mazy, Matt Tansey, Gulmar Parga

LADDER CO. 12

146 West 19th Street, Manhattan

Ladder 12 was organized in the former quarters of volunteer Liberty Engine 50, 243 West 20th Street, on December 1, 1865. They moved to their current quarters with Engine Company 3 and the 7th Battalion on February 6, 1967. A special unit, High-Rise Unit 1, also is quartered here. Their first-alarm area includes old tenements and commercial buildings, as well as the west side piers. They have had 25 medals awarded and eight unit citations, including the James Gordon Bennett Medal in 1921. Two other former members received the Bennett Medal, plus the Harry M. Archer Medal. They were Michael McInerney, who was awarded the Bennett in 1927 and the Archer in 1930 and Rudolph Musil with the Bennett in 1934 and the Archer in 1936. In 1916, their captain received the Stephenson Medal for the most efficient and best-disciplined company in the department. They have had three line-of-duty deaths. Their apparatus is a 1999 Seagrave/Aerialscope 95-foot tower-ladder.

1st: Angel Juarbe, Charles Biondo, Lt. Brenda Berkman, Capt. Thomas McCarthy, Michael Mullan, James Sanders 2nd: Hugh Duffy, Leon Stephenson, Heinz Kothe, Charles Ehni, Lt. Thomas Ballard, Michael Murphy, Raymond Going, Michael Swift, Richard Roccabruna

ENGINE CO. 26

220 West 37th Street, Manhattan

This company has been in the same quarters since its inception on October 16, 1865. Engine 26 was organized here in the former station of volunteer Valley Forge Engine 46. Currently, it is the oldest active fire station in the FDNY, but has had many phases of interior modernization. With the exception of a few months in 1893-1894, Engine 26 operated as a double engine company with two separate sections from 1884 to 1939. They are located in the heart of the NYC garment center and most of their first-alarm area consists of large commercial buildings housing manufacturers, showrooms, offices, etc. They also respond to a few hotels and several large retail shopping areas and face the many hazards of Times Square and surrounding areas. They were awarded six unit citations and two of their members were awarded medals. Seven of their members were killed in the line of duty, including two each at fires in 1907 and 1923. Their current apparatus is a 1994 high-pressure Seagrave 1000-gpm pumper, one of only seven in the FDNY.

1st: Louis Malizia, Joseph Petrich, Capt. Robert Rainey, Lt. Donald Franz, Keith Gough, Kenneth Rossiello 2nd: Kurt Wehner, Kevin Cody, John Heffernan, Michael Egan, Robert Sorgini, Michael Incantalupo, Rory Maguire 3rd: Sean Keenan, Kevin Russell, Vincent Caposio, Robert Bruno, Brian Clarke, Joseph Murphy

1st: Nathaniel Wheeler, Paul Fusaro, Lt. Russell Touhey, Brian Kappen, Charles Stewart 2nd: Claudio Capobianco, Rune Bekkelund, Denis Reen, Kevin Meehan, Gerard Nicoletti, Michael Oates, James Stasio, Luis Rivera, Robert Garofalo, Brian Armstrong, Eric Berntsen

ENGINE CO. 34

440 West 38th Street, Manhattan

Organized on October 30, 1865, in the former quarters of volunteer Mazeppa Hose 42, at 440 West 33rd Street, they operated as a double engine company for a few months in 1893. Boat Tender 2, re-designated as Boat Tender 1, was quartered here from 1912 until 1933, with Boat Tender 5, here from 1922 until 1924. High-pressure hose wagons carrying large-diameter hose, the Tenders operated in conjunction with fireboats, but could be special-called to inland fires. Engine 34 moved into their current quarters with Ladder 21 on September 1, 1937. Rescue 1 located here from 1985 until 1989 while their new quarters were being built. Engine 34 protects warehouses, factories, tenements, the west side piers and the Javits Convention Center. They have had seven unit citations and three individual medal winners—including James Gordon Bennett Medals in 1874 and 1887—plus the New York Firefighters Burn Center Foundation Medal in 1995, awarded for a team effort at a 1994 fire. They have had one line-of-duty death. Their apparatus is a 1994 high-pressure Seagrave l000-gpm pumper.

LADDER CO. 21

440 West 38th Street, Manhattan

Ladder 21 originally was organized at 432 West 36th Street on June 1, 1890. They moved to their current quarters with Engine Co. 34, on September 1, 1937. They became a double company on June 1, 1901, and remained as such, with separate apparatus and personnel, until the second section was disbanded on July 1, 1939. Rescue Company 1 temporarily was quartered here from 1985 to 1989, following the fire that destroyed their quarters. Ladder 21's first-alarm area consists of factories, warehouses and older tenements, as well as the west side piers. They have had seven unit citations and 18 individual medal winners. A former captain received the Stephenson Medal in 1939 for maintaining the best-disciplined and most efficient company in the department. The entire company was awarded the Fire College Medal in 1919 for proficiency in drills and evolutions. They have had four line-of-duty deaths. Their apparatus is a 1997 Seagrave/Aerialscope 75-foot tower-ladder.

1st: Lt. Gerard Finnegan, Lt. Matthew Moog, Capt. Michael Farrell, Lt. Michael Fodor 2nd: Vincent Kabus, Clinton Schmitterer, Gerald Atwood, John Marr, Gerard Gavin 3rd: Thomas Merenyi, Edward Luciani, Adam Torres, Leo Skorupski, Robert Keating, Thomas Hammerton, Brian Eagers, Bryan Weckmann

DIVISION 3

1st: DC Edward Dennehy, DC Nicholas Visconti, DC Michael Weinlein 2nd: Louis Piazza, Joseph Syzmanski, Robert Leaver, Lt. Kevin McGeary, Ronald Barber, James Cunningham

BATTALION 8

1st: BC Jay Fischler, BC Tom DeAngelis, BC Jim Wendling, BC Tom Jensen, BC Robert Cantillo
2nd: Lenny Thomas, Charles Carrington, Robert Dennington

BATTALION 9

Alan Feinberg, BC Edward Geraghty, BC Stanley Dawe, BC Joseph Nardone, BC Brian O'Flaherty, James Cooney, Carl Asaro

BATTALION 10

Paul Dalessio, BC Robert Schildhorn, BC Michael Boyle, BC William Moore

BATTALION 11

1st: BC J.K. Corcoran, BC John Hughes 2nd: James Shaughnessy, Gary Sheridan, Douglas Robinson

BATTALION 12

BC Joseph Marchbanks, BC Kevin O'Keefe, BC Fred Scheffold, BC Mark Ferran

ENGINE CO. 8
165 East 51st Street, Manhattan

Organized on September 11, 1865, in the then rural quarters of volunteer Relief Hose 51 at 128 East 50th Street, Engine 8 now covers the midtown east side area from their unusual quarters shared with Ladder 2 and the 8th Battalion, where they moved on September 6, 1961. This firehouse is located on the ground floor of a large high-rise office building and is the actual site of the old quarters of Engine 8, into which they had moved back in 1869. Their first-alarm area covers high-rise office buildings and luxury apartment houses, plus the United Nations, Rockefeller Center, Grand Central Station, etc. In recent years, in number of runs, they have become one of the busiest engine companies in the City. Over the years, they have had five line-of-duty deaths, eight unit citations and three medal winners. One of these, a Stephenson Medal, went to their captain in 1903 for the most efficient and best-disciplined company. Their current apparatus is a 1997 Seagrave 1000-gpm pumper.

1st: Lt. Gerard Moreau, Lt. Mark Monnelly, Lt. Rory Houton, Capt. William Dudley 2nd: Donald Buckley, Dave Offitto, Vincent Timmons, Rob Parro, Neal King 3rd: Peter Morrissey, Edgar Atiles, James Moore, John Curatola

LADDER CO. 2
165 East 51st Street, Manhattan

Ladder 2 was organized in the former quarters of volunteer Liberty Hook and Ladder 16 at 126 East 50th Street, on September 11, 1865. They moved to their current quarters, with Engine Company 8 and the 8th Battalion, on September 6, 1961. This station is unusual because it is located on two lower floors of a high-rise office building, with a police precinct located next door in the same building. While still in their former quarters on 50th Street, Ladder 2 operated as a double company, with two aerials and separate officers and firefighters, from 1913 until 1939. Relay Hose Wagon 2 was here from 1942 to 1944. The first-alarm area of this very busy company consists of high-rise office buildings and apartment houses, as well as Grand Central Station, the United Nations and Rockefeller Center. They have had 20 unit citations and 33 medal winners, including James Gordon Bennett Medals in 1881 and 1943. They have had five line-of-duty deaths. They operate a 1996 Seagrave 100-foot rear-mount.

1st: Capt. Frederick Ill, Lt. Neil Skow, Lt. Tom Woods, Lt. Kevin Sullivan, Lt. Kevin Dillon 2nd: Bill Sankey, Gene Maguire, Dan Harlin, Joseph Harnischfeger, Greg Dennehy, Bill Scheu, Mike Murphy, Rich Manetta, John Carbone 3rd: George DiPasquale, Denis Germain, Thomas Byrnes, Chris Flatley, Dennis Mulligan, Joe Poma

8th Battalion

8th Battalion

1st: Lt. Mike Cuttino, Lt. Dennis Fischer, Capt. Nick Gaudiosi, Capt. John McKeon, Lt. Mickey Cross, Lt. Tony Lapari, Lt. Vernon Richard, Lt. Rob Kirwan *2nd:* Jerry Marrome, John Passaretti, Joe Deserto, Ron Cifu, Chuck Mendez, Matt Kelly, Joe Finley, Pat Cotton, Lou Ruggirello, Gary Cline, James Hurley, James Slevin, George Cain *3rd:* Paul Lee, Steve Marsar, Al Squire, Lt. Bob Johann, Lt. John Hemsley, Tom Gernon, Bob Foti, John Gleason, Mike Dee, Russ Jordan, Vinny Princiotta, Joe Vizzini, Gerry Bonner, Thor Johannsson, Bobby Rae *4th:* Dave Rodriquez, Nelson Haerr, Capt. John Tobin, Lt. Ed McCaffrey, BC Jim Kearns, Dan Lynch, Bob Mansberger, Anthony Castillano, Paul Miller, Jimmy Hillary, Tom Byrne, Mike Boccia, Mike Gilvary, Jack Tevlin, Capt. Paul Kozlowski, Don Carcone, Capt. George Vallibuono, Lt. Frank Gribbon, Kevin Melody, BC John Moran, Larry Thompkins, Richie Muldowney *Banner holders:* William Fanos, Brian Finley

ENGINE CO. 16

234 East 29th Street, Manhattan

This company was organized in the former quarters of volunteer Lexington Engine 7 at 223 East 25th Street on September 18, 1865, and remained at that location until moving in with Ladder 7 in their current house on August 6, 1968. Engine 16 actually was a double engine company, with two separate sections, from 1883 to 1939. Their east side territory consists of old tenements and modern high-rise apartment houses, as well as several major hospitals. Quartered here and manned by them is FDR Drive Response Vehicle 1, a 1995 Ford/Saulsbury used for response to car fires on the FDR Drive. Their regular apparatus is a 1998 Seagrave 1000-gpm pumper. Searchlight 1 also was quartered here from 1955 to 1959. They have had three medal winners, nine unit citations and five line-of-duty deaths since their inception almost 135 years ago.

LADDER CO. 7

234 East 29th Street, Manhattan

Originally organized on October 11, 1865, in the former quarters of volunteer Washington Hook and Ladder 9, at 217 East 29th Street, Ladder 7 moved to their current quarters, with Engine Company 16, on August 6, 1968. FDR Drive Response Unit 1 also is quartered here. There are several major hospitals, as well as old tenements and many large apartment houses in their first-alarm area. They have had 10 unit citations and 15 medal winners, including a James Gordon Bennett Medal in 1898. They have had eight line-of-duty deaths. Four of these—Lieutenant John Finley and Firefighters John Berry, Joseph Kaminski and Carl Lee—were killed in the tragic 23rd Street fire on October 17, 1966. Their apparatus is a 1995 FWD/Aerialscope 75-foot tower-ladder.

1st: Lt. Steve Chase, Capt. John Fray, Lt. Robert Martirano 2nd: Rob Schulz, William Woodlon, Mike Byrne, Bob Selesky, Jay Snow, Fred Sanicola, John Shotter, Sidney Parris 3rd: Tom Tommaso, Jack Sweeney, Alex Timlin, Aron Buch, Richard Brancroft, Zackery Vause, William Casey, Mike Kennedy, Dan O'Connor

ENGINE CO. 21
238 East 40th Street, Manhattan

Organized on October 2, 1865, in the former quarters of volunteer Naiad Hose 53, at 216 East 40th Street, in what was, at that time, a somewhat rural area. Their first-alarm territory now consists mainly of high-rise office buildings, luxury apartment houses, several hotels and hospitals, plus the United Nations and Grand Central Station. Engine 21 moved to their current quarters on November 1, 1940. A special unit, High Ladder 1, with a 1961 Mack Magirus 146-foot aerial, was quartered here from 1964 to 1966. Ladder 2 also was located here temporarily for two years until 1960, while their new quarters were under construction. Engine 21 lost two of its members in an interior building collapse at a three-alarm fire at 213-215 East 44th Street on March 24, 1900. They, along with the foreman (captain) of Hook & Ladder 2, were drowned in the cellar before they could be rescued. They have had seven unit citations and five medal winners. Their apparatus is a 1997 Seagrave 1000-gpm pumper.

ENGINE CO. 65
33 West 43rd Street, Manhattan

Engine Co. 65 was organized in their current quarters on June 4, 1898, and has been there ever since. Rescue Company 1 shared these quarters with them from 1960 to 1973. A former special unit, Canteen Field Kitchen 94, was located here from 1946 to 1958, and manned by a member of Engine 65. It also has been Manhattan Boro Command headquarters in the past. Engine 65 is located in the heart of midtown Manhattan. Their first-alarm area consists of numerous high-rise office buildings, apartment houses and hotels, as well as many retail stores, the Broadway theatre district, Grand Central Station, etc. They have had 17 unit citations, three medal winners and five line-of-duty deaths. Three of these deaths occurred at the Ritz Towers disaster on August 1, 1932, at 113 East 57th Street. They have a 1994 Seagrave high-pressure 1000-gpm pumper, one of only seven in the department.

1st: Frank Costa, Tom Orlando, Capt. Rich Rotanz, Kevin Kouril 2nd: DC Nick Visconti, Sal Dellolio, Joe Mazzarella, Lt. Tom Piambino, Lt. Jerry Kearns, Lt. Billy Hoag, Chris LaRocca, Bob Begley, Joe Felle, Armando Reno, Willie Franklin 3rd: Rev. Mychal F. Judge, Capt. George McQueen, BC Jim Wendling, Robert Reckerdas, Larry Montrose, Tom Courtenary, Harry Cardio, Gene Judd, Joe Petrassi

1st: Lt. Jim DiCostanzo, Lt. Ed Weinberger, Capt. John Bendick, Lt. Joe Pierotti 2nd: Brian Reehil, Robert Ingenice, Vincent Molinini, Kevin Johnston, Vincent Yorks, Paul Johnsen, Jerry Lennon, Chuck Sullivan 3rd: Mark Whitford, Paul Brantmeyer, Dominick Curci, Thomas Kelly, Edward Usher, Anthony Cotroneo

ENGINE CO. 23
215 West 58th Street, Manhattan

This company was organized in the former quarters of volunteer Equitable Engine 36 at 153 West 68th Street on October 6, 1865, but was moved in 1866 to a former volunteer house at 235 West 58th Street. They remained at that location until moving into their current quarters on July 3, 1906. Located in the midtown Manhattan area, their first-alarm territory is varied and includes many major hotels, commercial office buildings, apartment houses, theaters and large retail stores. At one time, this house also was used as the night quarters of the on-duty Assistant Chief of Department. They have had 10 unit citations and five medal winners in years past, including Stephenson Medals for their captains in 1885 and 1932, for maintaining the best disciplined and most efficient company in the FDNY. Five of their former members were killed in the line of duty. They currently have a 1997 Seagrave 1000-gpm pumper.

ENGINE CO. 40

133 Amsterdam Avenue, Manhattan

Suburban Engine 40 first was organized at 10th Avenue, between 154th and 155th Street (later known as 1907 Amsterdam Avenue), on October 30, 1865. That company was disbanded on January 1, 1868, with Engine 38 organized in those quarters on that date. In 1874, they were re-organized as a regular engine and spent many years at 153 West 68th Street. They later moved in with Ladder 35 at 142 West 63rd Street on May 1, 1918, and finally again with Ladder 35, to their current quarters, which is at the rear of the huge Lincoln Center entertainment complex. Besides Lincoln Center, their first-alarm area has many large apartment buildings, several schools and many retail businesses. They have had three unit citations, two medal winners and five line-of-duty deaths. Their current apparatus is a 1997 Seagrave 1000-gpm pumper.

1st: Kevin Kelly, Lt. John Ginley, Lt. Paul Samodulski, Capt. James Gormley, Lt. Thomas Donnelly, Bruce Gary 2nd: Edward Santore, Christopher Lynch, Nicholas Pezza, Steve Mercado, Raymond Pfeifer 3rd: Mark Kenny, Joseph Tisbe, Anthony Ruocco, Kevin Bracken

LADDER CO. 35

133 Amsterdam Avenue, Manhattan

Ladder 35 originally was organized as a double ladder company on November 1, 1907, at 142 West 63rd Street. The section was disbanded on January 1, 1915, but reorganized on April 17, 1917. They were disbanded again, this time for good, on May 1, 1918. Engine 40 moved into those quarters on that same day. On January 31, 1960, the two companies moved to their new quarters, located at the rear of the huge Lincoln Center entertainment complex. The remainder of their first-alarm district consists of many large apartment houses, schools and retail stores. They have had eight unit citations and 11 medal winners. In 1962, Firefighter Joseph Almon received the James Gordon Bennett Medal for heroism performed on December 27, 1961. He received the Dr. Harry M. Archer Medal for the same incident in 1963. They have had one line-of-duty death. Their apparatus is a 1998 Seagrave 75-foot tower-ladder.

1st: Edward McVey, James Giberson, Lt. Kevin Burke, Lt. Kevin O'Neill, Capt. Francis Callahan, Lt. Timothy Callahan, Terence Holden, Michael O'Donnell 2nd: Michael Kotula, Michael Sawula, Robert Menig, Christopher Schroeder, Chris Combs, Marion Mackey, Stephen Kelly, Gregory Petrik 3rd: Matthew Dennehy, Michael Otten, Christopher Maloney, John Schroeder, Eugene Szatkowski, Ronald Barber, Daniel Powers, Robert Hickey, Daniel O'Donovan

1st: Jeffrey Manno, Edward Jordan, Lt. Vito Emanuele, Capt. Dag J. Dorph, Lt. Thomas Venditto, Thomas Clinton, Michael Cioffi 2nd: Albert Quinones, Andrew Sforza, David Turner, Stephen Rogan, Michael Brennan, Joseph Poliseno, Paul Gill, Nicholas Lorenzo 3rd: Kevin Williams, Leonard Ragaglia, Louis Esposito, Thomas Hogan, Joseph Angelini, Ralph Talarico, Christopher Reynolds, Jose Guadalupe

ENGINE CO. 54

782 Eighth Avenue, Manhattan

Engine 54 was organized on May 26, 1884, at 304 West 47th Street. After that, Engine 54 changed locations temporarily a few times and finally moved to their current house, with Ladder 4 and the 9th Battalion, on March 15, 1974. This company covers the midtown theatre district with its numerous theatres, movie houses, restaurants and related businesses. They also have many old tenements and high-rise commercial buildings in their territory. In recent years, they have become one of the busiest engines in the department. They have had 14 unit citations and five individual medal winners. In 1996, a lieutenant and four of their firefighters received the New York Firefighters Burn Center Foundation Medal for a team effort at a fire on June 20, 1995. In 1999, the same group was awarded the Father Julian F. Deeken Memorial Medal for the same incident. They have had four line-of-duty deaths. Their apparatus is a 1993 Seagrave high-pressure 1000-gpm pumper.

1st: William Dunigan, Leonard Sieli, Lt. Robert Strafer, Lt. Thomas Meara, Capt. James Costello, William Herbst
2nd: Leslie Alvarez, William Wilson, Arthur Thies, Edward Coyle, Louis Robinson, Robert Schuff, Joseph Foti, Carl Asaro **3rd:** Keith Kern, Samuel Oitice, Russell Regan, John Tipping, Daniel Squire, Eric Kozak, Patrick Parrot

LADDER CO. 4
782 Eighth Avenue, Manhattan

Known as "The Pride of Midtown," Ladder 4 originally was organized in the former house of volunteer Empire Hook and Ladder 8 at 788 Eighth Avenue, on September 18, 1865. They moved into their current quarters with Engine 54 and the 9th Battalion on March 15, 1974. In recent years, they have become one of the busiest FDNY ladder companies, with a first-alarm territory that includes old tenements, high-rise commercial buildings, theatres, restaurants and retail stores. They have had 18 unit citations and 37 medal winners, including James Gordon Bennett Medals in 1879, 1893, 1904, 1905, 1907, 1914, 1957 and 1966. In 1926, their captain received the Stephenson Medal for having the most efficient and best-disciplined company in the department. They have had three line-of-duty deaths. Their current apparatus is a 1989 Seagrave 110-foot, heavy-duty, rear-mount aerial, one of only four in the department.

1st: Capt. Donald Striffler, Lt. Robert Wolfe, Lt. Thomas Conaty, Lt. Dennis Stanford **2nd:** Alexander Pollina, Michael Eleris, Anthony Connolly, Fred DelGrosso, Michael Ruddick, Michael Cascella **3rd:** Robert Leone, Thomas Casoria, John Grogan, Michael Sitler, Jeffery Powers, Patrick Stranzl

ENGINE CO. 22
159 East 85th Street, Manhattan

Established in the upper east side Yorkville area on October 2, 1865, this company at first occupied the former quarters of volunteer Aurora Engine 45 at 1511 Third Avenue. They later moved to their current address on May 7, 1878, and to a new house on the same site, together with Ladder 13 and the 10th Battalion, on May 11, 1961. Located in their first-alarm territory are many high-rise, luxury apartment houses, as well as many old tenements. Several major hospital complexes are also in their area. They have had two unit citations and eight medal winners, including a James Gordon Bennett Medal in 1889. A former captain received the Stephenson Medal in 1909 for having the most efficient and best-disciplined company for the prior year. Their current apparatus is a 1997 Seagrave 1000-gpm pumper.

LADDER CO. 13
159 East 85th Street, Manhattan

Ladder 13 originally was organized as Suburban Hook and Ladder 13 on October 11, 1865, at 159 East 87th Street. They were made a regular hook and ladder company on January 1, 1868. The major difference between the two were the pay differential, with the firemen in the suburban companies getting $300 per year, opposed to those in the regular companies receiving $700. A second section was organized on March 1, 1907, and remained in service until disbanded on December 31, 1915. They moved to their current quarters, with Engine 22 and the 10th Battalion, on May 11, 1961. Squad Company 9 also was located here from 1961, until disbanding in 1967. High-rise luxury apartment houses, old tenements and several hospital complexes are located in their first-alarm area. They have had nine unit citations and eight medal winners. In 1886, their captain received the Stephenson Medal for having the best-disciplined and most efficient company. They have had one line-of-duty death.

1st: Edward Duignan, Lt. Michael Donlon, Lt. Thomas Robinson, Capt. Walter Hynes, Lt. John Hemsley, James Dorman **2nd:** Vincent Tancredi, Ronald Daly, James Grishmer, Douglas Mitchell, Patrick Sherry, Frank Portelle, Joseph Graziano, Thomas Gutzler **3rd:** Thomas Hetzel, Greg Mattingly, Gerard Clement, Michael Piliere, Wayne Wright, Reggie Nickpree, Thomas Sabella

ENGINE CO. 39
157-159 East 67th Street, Manhattan

Established as Suburban Engine 39 at 58 Lawrence Street (West 126th Street) on March 20, 1875, they became a regular engine and moved to the east side. Since January 13, 1887, they've shared their six-story firehouse with Ladder 16. It was used as Fire Headquarters, the School of Instruction and the Manhattan Telegraph Bureau. In 1911, Engine 39 was assigned the first gasoline-powered and -propelled pumper in FDNY, a Waterous with a 750-gpm piston pump. It proved unsuccessful and was gone by 1914. A special apparatus, High-Rise Unit 2, is quartered here and manned by Engine 39. Their first-alarm area includes apartment houses, tenements, foreign missions, retail stores and several hospitals and schools. During major house renovations from 1985 to 1992, Engine 39 and Ladder 16 were quartered at Hunter College. They have received 10 unit citations and five medals, including Stephenson Medals in 1891 and 1907 and Fire College Medals to the entire company in 1914, 1924 and 1926, for efficiency in drills and evolutions. They have had four line-of-duty deaths. They have a 1997 Seagrave 1000-gpm pumper.

1st: Leonard Baione, Terry Shields, Lt. James McGlynn, Lt. Raymond Wick, Capt. John Donnelly, Lt. Frank Keane, Arthur Myers, Christopher Reinhard 2nd: Joseph Sherry, Louis Mancuso, Joseph Buchanan, Craig Santandrea, Dean Favarulo, Robert Curatolo 3rd: John Troutman, Keith McLaughlin, Martin Morgan, Walter Bieber, Russell Ridky

LADDER CO. 16
157-159 East 67th Street, Manhattan

Ladder 16 was organized on the upper west side of Manhattan on November 1, 1873, at 97th Street and Bloomingdale Road. That company was disbanded on August 17, 1882, and the current Ladder 16 re-organized on January 13, 1887, at their current location with Engine Company 39. This landmark building has undergone several renovations and served in the past as Fire Headquarters, as well as the School of Instruction and Telegraph Bureau. High-Rise Unit 2 also is located here. Their first-alarm area includes large apartment houses, older tenements, foreign missions, hospitals, schools and retail stores. They have 14 unit citations and 12 individual medal winners. This company was awarded the Fire College Medal three times—in 1922, 1924 and 1930—for having the best time in the various drills and evolutions. They have had four line-of-duty deaths, including two at the Ritz Tower explosion on August 1, 1932. Their apparatus is a 1994 Seagrave 100-foot rear-mount.

1st: Edward Opfer, Oscar Davila, Kenneth Ruane, Lt. Miguel Ramos, Lt. Daniel Williams, Capt. Steven Redican, Lt. Robert Sadowski, Kenneth Rogers, Edmund Sullivan 2nd: James Carroll, Robert Dana, James Long, Derek Bennett, Brian Kane, Joseph Noonan, Ronald Cammarata, Daniel Ross 3rd: Joseph Detrich, Christopher Reginella, Dale McLaughlin, Eddy Nietzschmann, Steven Wright, John Drumm, James Lanze, William Hennessy, Tim Carroll

ENGINE CO. 44
221 East 75th Street, Manhattan

Engine 44 was organized in their current quarters on April 1, 1881, and remained here continually, except for being disbanded for two days in 1975, due to the fiscal crisis of that year. Now located in their quarters is FDR Drive Response Vehicle 2, a 1995 Ford/Saulsbury, used for car fires on the FDR Drive and manned by members of Engine 44. Located in their first-alarm territory are many high-rise luxury apartment houses, older tenements, townhouses and foreign missions, plus several schools and hospital complexes. They have had eight unit citations and four medal winners and three line-of-duty deaths. Two of these deaths were the result of the men being crushed by a falling wall at a 3-3 at 423 East 104th Street on January 19, 1919. Their apparatus is a 1997 Seagrave 1000-gpm pumper.

1st: George J. Parkans, Jack Paccione, Lt. John Francis Dougherty, Edward Kennedy 2nd: Daniel D. Halvey, Michael J. Lyons, Phillip L. Piarulli 3rd: Ronald Kemly, Stephen J. Heavey, Robert E. Coppola

ENGINE CO. 53

1886 Third Avenue, Manhattan

Engine 53 was organized on January 14, 1885, at 175 East 104th Street, East Harlem. They remained in that single house until moving on February 1, 1974, into their current quarters with Ladder 43. At one time, RAC 1, as well as the now-disbanded 4th Division, also were located here. Their area consists of many high-rise project developments, old tenements and several hospitals, as well as retail stores, etc. In the past, they have had 16 unit citations and five medal winners and two line-of-duty deaths. Their current apparatus is a 1998 Seagrave 1000-gpm pumper.

1st: John Regazzi, Lt. Robert Dorritie, Capt. Kerry Hollywood, Thomas O'Conner 2nd: Dean Pappas, Frank Carino, Joe Torregrossa, Ed Cachia, Kevin Torrey, Ralph Corsini, Steve Modica, Louis Giaconelli 3rd: John Condon, Al Vega, Mike Regan, Kevin McGovern, Kevin Joos, Mark Carpinello, Matt Higham

1st: George Hear, Capt. Alexander Hagan, Lt. Douglas Gehrt, Kirk Lester 2nd: David Connolly, Daniel Manning, James Sears, Todd Frederickson, John Neumann, James McEntee, John Duffy 3rd: Lawrence Reilly, Dino Pappas, James Lanza, Frank Macchia, Robert Markardt

LADDER CO. 43

1836 Third Avenue, Manhattan

Ladder 43 was organized on November 27, 1913, at 240 East 111th Street with Engine Company 9l. They moved to their current quarters, with Engine Company 53, on February 1, 1974. Their first-alarm territory in this busy east Harlem area consists of old tenements, high-rise housing projects, retail stores and several hospitals. They have had 17 unit citations and 19 medal winners. In 1992, Firefighter Michael Dugan received the James Gordon Bennett Medal for an act of heroism performed on December 23, 1991. In 1994, he was awarded the prestigious Dr. Harry M. Archer Medal for the same act. Firefighter John Colon of this company has received three medals in recent years for acts of valor. These were the Fire Bell Club Medal in 1989, the Wesley Williams Medal in 1995 and the Henry Brookman Medal in 1997. They have had two line-of-duty deaths. Their apparatus is a 1991 Seagrave 100-foot rear-mount.

ENGINE CO. 37

415 West 125th Street, Manhattan

Engine 37 first was organized as Suburban Engine 37 at 209 East 122nd Street on October 11, 1865. Suburban Engine 37—and the other Suburban companies—were disbanded and reorganized on January 1, 1868, with Engine 37 taking over the quarters of Suburban Engine 39 on West 126th Street. They moved to their new house with Ladder 40 on September 6, 1974. No longer a suburban area, their first-alarm territory consists of old tenements, large commercial buildings, several major colleges and many retail stores. Two of their members were killed in the line of duty. They have had 12 unit citations and three medal winners. Their apparatus is a 1993 Seagrave 1000-gpm pumper.

1st: Daniel Maher, Lawrence Lanza, James Saccente, Raymond DeSimone, John Patten, Joseph Canale 2nd: William Burke, Anthony Squillante, Gary Grillo, Thomas Morrissey, James McNamara 3rd: Frank DeSanna, Frank Giaquinto, Drew Kane, Terence Nolan, George Hopkins

LADDER CO. 40
415 West 125th Street, Manhattan

Ladder 40 originally was organized in its quarters at 6 Hancock Place on January 1, 1910. They moved to their current quarters, along with Engine 37, on September 6, 1974. Their first-alarm area in west Harlem consists of many old tenements, large commercial buildings, several major colleges and numerous retail stores. Their members have received 16 unit citations and 30 medals for valor. Firefighter Raymond McCann, now retired, received the James Gordon Bennett Medal in 1973 for an act of extreme heroism on October 16, 1972. He also received the Dr. Harry M. Archer Medal in 1975 for the same brave deed. Ladder 40 has had one line-of-duty death. Their current apparatus is a 1991 Seagrave 100-foot, tractor-drawn aerial.

1st: David Segot, Michael Gallagher, Lt. Rudolf Weindler, Capt. John Rynne, Timothy McCauley, Eugene Box 2nd: Lt. James O'Connell, Lionel Horry, Colin O'Neill, Joseph Connolly, Craig Brierley, Peter Cooney 3rd: William Hroch, Peter Critsimilios, Thomas Lapp, Kendall Washington, Lawrence Marley, Bruce Collister

ENGINE CO. 47
502 West 113th Street, Manhattan

Engine 47 was originally a Bronx unit, starting as Chemical 1 at 909 East 149th Street on January 12, 1874. On October 14, 1881, that company was disbanded to form the original Engine 47 at that same location. They were disbanded on July 1, 1882, but reorganized as Combination Engine Co. 47, in Manhattan at 766 Amsterdam Avenue, on August 7, 1882. On April 1, 1891, they became regular Engine Co. 47 and moved on that date to their current quarters. Ladder 22 was organized and moved into their former Amsterdam Avenue quarters three weeks later. Their first-alarm territory consists mainly of high-rise apartment houses, tenements and retail stores, plus several hospitals and universities. They have had 11 unit citations and three medal winners, including Captain Joseph Guglielmo, who received the Albert J. Johnston Medal in 1994 for his heroics at a fire on June 4, 1993. They have had one line-of-duty death. They have a 1994 Seagrave 1000-gpm pumper.

1st: Salvatore Lia, Edward F. Callahan, Lt. Frank J. Perry, Lt. Michael Burke, Lt. William Wall, Gregory M. Voce, Gerard Keller 2nd: Michael Sarro, Allan R. Dinger, Gregory Corona, Timothy Fitzgibbons, Thomas Turilli, Richard J. Gleason, Anthony J. Apuzzo, Keith Murphy, Brian Duffy, Stephen Viola, John Russell 3rd: John T. Murray, Dennis Donoghue, Charles Truncale, Louis D. Cacchioli, Frank Beirne, Peter J. Buser, Robert Gallagher, Lance J. Lizzul

ENGINE CO. 74
120 West 83rd Street, Manhattan

Engine 74 was organized, with Ladder 25, at 207 West 77th Street, on June 1, 1901. On November 24, 1972, they were moved to their current quarters, replacing Squad Company 6 in this house. This is also the former quarters of the long-disbanded Engine 56. Their first-alarm responsibility, in the upper west side area, consists of many large apartment houses, older tenements, several museums and other public buildings, as well as an ever-growing number of restaurants and retail stores. They have been awarded four unit citations. Their current apparatus is a 1998 Seagrave 1000-gpm pumper.

1st: M. Shagi, F. Brunner, Lt. R. Weldon, Capt. D. Loeb, Lt. P. Holahan, Steven Mancino, J. Johnson 2nd: K. Diercksen, M. Hettwer, R. Hatton, C. Healy, J. Dale, J. O'Riordan, P. Carey, D. Murphy, J. Breen 3rd: D. Finnegan, J. Brown, E. Doyle, J. Abbott, S. Moss, I. Hernandez, M. Williams, R. Correa

ENGINE CO. 76

145 West 100th Street, Manhattan

Engine 76 is unusual because originally, it was organized as a double engine company, with separate officers and firefighters in each section, at 105 West 102nd Street, on April 15, 1904. The second section was disbanded on November 1, 1946. Engine 76 moved into the quarters of Ladder 22 at 766 Amsterdam Avenue on March 18, 1957, with both companies, as well as the 11th Battalion, moving into their current quarters on December 3, 1960. In addition to the many large apartment houses, projects and old tenements in their first-alarm area, they have several colleges, hospitals, etc. They have had nine unit citations and one medal winner. Two of their members died in the line of duty. They have a 1998 Seagrave 1000-gpm pumper.

1st: Douglas Robinson, Lawrence Fursich, Lt. Thomas Byrne, Lt. Edward Meehan, Lt. Kevin Guy, William Martinez, James Shaughnessy 2nd: Jerrold Scaringe, Donald Russell, Kevin Gorman, Jason Hickey, Thomas Quigley, Richard Banaciski, Efrain Pizarro, Charles Larocchia, Gary Sheridan 3rd: Arthur D'Agata, Michael Greenfield, Glen Smith, George Rodriguez, Thomas Olson, Hugo Muriel, Gerald Rice

1st: James Larkin, John O'Donnell, Lt. Gerard Reilly, Lt. Robert Savarese, Lt. Daniel Twomey, Capt. John Pellegrinelli, Fredrick Hollins, Eric Kosak 2nd: John Bynes, Charles Lipinski, Richard Quinn, Steven Klee, Patrick Hennessey, John Coyle, John Spiech, Robert Pyne, Joseph Fallen, Edward Bolger, Gregory Scott 3rd: Bryan Wilber, Albert Loyola, Fernando Camacho, John Malley, Christopher Donovan, James Schatz, James Rahill, Charles McNeely, Robert Russell

LADDER CO. 22

145 West 100th Street, Manhattan

Originally organized on April 21, 1891, in the former quarters of Combination Engine Company 47, at 766 Amsterdam Avenue, Ladder 22 moved to their current location, with Engine Company 76 and the 11th Battalion, on December 3, 1960. While still in their former quarters, they operated as a double company from February 17, 1900, to March 11, 1957, when the second section was disbanded. Their first-alarm territory consists of old tenements, large apartment houses, high-rise projects, colleges and hospitals. They have had 12 unit citations and 31 individual medal winners, including the James Gordon Bennett Medal awarded in 1991 to Firefighter William Jutt for an heroic rescue at a 2-2 at 2731 Broadway on December 8, 1990. They have had four line-of-duty deaths.

LADDER CO. 25

205-207 West 77th Street, Manhattan

Originally sharing these quarters with Engine Company 74, Ladder 25 was organized on June 1, 1901. Engine 74 since has moved; however, the 3rd Division now is located here. Ladder 25's first-alarm territory consists of large apartment houses, many old tenements and brownstones, plus numerous retail stores and restaurants. Their members, past and present, have been awarded 27 medals and the unit nine citations. Firefighter William Russo was awarded the James Gordon Bennett Medal and the Dr. Harry M. Archer Medal in 1960, for an act of heroism that took place on November 11, 1959. Firefighter James Dowling received the Bennett Medal in 1968 and the Archer Medal in 1969, for an heroic action performed on December 15, 1967. Their apparatus is a 1996 Seagrave 100-foot rear-mount.

1st: Sean O'Brien, Bob Sullivan, Lt. Anthony Montaruli, Capt. Gary Senger, Lt. John Byrnes, Robert Minara, Thomas Healy 2nd: Ray Herbst, Richard Jones, James Gormley, Michael Schnugg, Matthew O'Hanlon, Brian Englander, Brian McShane 3rd: James Elmendorf, Joseph Rivelli, Joseph McHugh, Paul Ruback, Matthew Barnes, Mario Tarquinio, William Murphy, Michael Bonner

ENGINE CO. 35

2282 Third Avenue, Manhattan

Engine 35 was organized in the former station of volunteer Columbus Engine 35 on January 1, 1868, in what was then a rural location of 223 East 119th Street in East Harlem. They moved to their current quarters with Ladder 14 and the 12th Battalion on August 29, 1974. At one time, a special unit, Thawing Unit 61, also was located here. This very busy company covers a first-alarm territory made up mainly of old tenements, intermixed with some high-rise projects. Third Avenue, itself, has many commercial buildings and retail stores. They have had 25 unit citations and seven medal winners, including James Gordon Bennett Medals in 1896 and 1903. Three of their former members were killed in the line of duty. Their new apparatus is a 2000 Seagrave 1000-gpm pumper.

1st: Frank Perez, James Stines, Lt. Brendan Whelan, Lt. Michael Hadden, Capt. Denis Ryan, Lt. Douglas Rosenthal, Lt. Thomas Fitzgerald, William Knoth, Keith Atlas 2nd: Dennis Prosick, John Jacovina, Daniel Seller, Frank Morrisey, Brendan Lowery, Thomas McGlade, Thomas Peiser, Michael Fitzmaurice, Dennis Fisher, Michael Fahy

1st: Robert M. Marcoux, Robert Faiella, Lt. Dominic Caleri, Lt. Ewald Pollich, Capt. Stephen T. Damato, Lt. Peter L. Doran, Lt. Kevin P. Wallace, Daniel F. Peters, Dennis P. Albrechtsen 2nd: John M. Hartel, Brian A. Neville, James G. Corley, John F. McGurren, William E. Bruse, Eugene R. Heghmann, James A. Bittles, Rodney Decort, Michael J. Dowling 3rd: John P. McQuade, Thomas J. Quinn, George Baade, Michael R. Hipsman, George M. Konop, Brian T. Hanrahan, John F. Hunt, Brendan Deehan

LADDER CO. 14

2282 Third Avenue, Manhattan

Ladder 14 was organized at 120 East 125th Street, on October 20, 1865, as Suburban Hook and Ladder 14. On January 1, 1868, they were re-designated as a regular company. They moved to their current quarters with Engine Company 35 and the 12th Battalion on April 15, 1975. In 1966, they were the second FDNY ladder company to be assigned a tower-ladder. No longer a suburban area, their first-alarm district consists of old tenements, high-rise projects, commercial buildings and retail stores. They have had 31 unit citations and 34 individual medal winners, with James Gordon Bennett Medals awarded to their members in 1899, 1900, 1918, 1961 and 1964. Firefighter David Crowley, who received the Bennett Medal in 1964, also was awarded the Dr. Harry M. Archer Medal in 1966. In 1995, Lieutenant Kenneth Schermerhorn and five firefighters received the Elsasser Medal for a team heroic action at a 7-5 at 15 East 131st Street on June 30, 1994. They have had five line-of-duty deaths. Their apparatus is a 1991 Mack/Baker 95-foot tower-ladder.

ENGINE CO. 36

120 East 125th Street, Manhattan

Engine 36 was organized as Suburban Engine 36 on October 11, 1865, in the former quarters of volunteer Pocahontas Engine 49 at 2333 Fourth Avenue. The address on this house and its replacement was changed to 1849 Park Avenue. The men assigned to these Suburban Engines performed the same work as those in the regular companies, but were paid only $300 per year compared to the $700 in the regular units. They were allowed to work at their former vocations during the day, but had to attend all alarms and sleep in quarters at night. Engine 36 moved into their current house—the former quarters of Ladder 14—on April 17, 1975. They have had 13 unit citations and three medal winners, including a James Gordon Bennett in 1895. Four members have been killed in the line of duty. Once a suburban area, their first-alarm district now includes old tenements, some high-rise projects and many retail stores. They have a 1993 Seagrave 1000-gpm pumper.

1st: Lt. Thomas M. Higgins, Capt. Samuel Vazquez, Lt. Thomas J. Rappe 2nd: Frederick J. Schaming, Robert W. Brunone, John Daly, Richard J. Bittles, Harold J. Johnston, John J. Hear, Joseph T. McCarney, Elliot Colon 3rd: Michael O'Donnell, Brian McGuire, Daniel McCarvill, Jeffrey Abrams, William Kline, Richard M. Leonard, David R. Preyor, Drew W. Kinash, Daniel Shortell

1st: Lt. Dan Sheridan, Lt. Sal Canale, Lt. Jeff Simms, Lt. Bob Nagel, Capt. John Newell, Capt. Charles Roberto, Lt. Ed Geraghty, Lt. John Calamari, BC James Campbell, BC Dennis Collopy 2nd: Ed Roberts, Chris Callan, Bob Canale, Rick Campbell, John Wilson, Susan Blake, John Regan, Glenn Ellingsen, Steve Bascelli, Gerard Ledwith, Joe Killeen, Lt. Mike Vecchione, Tom Nuccio 3rd: Lt. Eddie O'Donnell, Capt. Bart Codd, Bill Donohue, Greg Parr, Frank Mollica, Jim Brady, Bill Delehanty, Tom Akerberg, Dave McGovern, John Weber, Jim McBurney, John Donahue, Chris McLaughlin, Walter Porr, Jack McLaughlin, Bill Moran, Paul McMenamy, John McAllister, Dan Grogul, Will Abruzzese, Capt. Bill McCrane, Kevin Tully, Bill Rodgers, Larry Pusack

ENGINE CO. 58

1367 5th Avenue, Manhattan

Known as the "Fire Factory," Engine 58 originally was organized at 81 West 115th Street, in East Harlem, on June 1, 1893. On November 8, 1948, Engine 58 moved in with Ladder 26 at 52 East 114th Street. They moved to their current quarters with Ladder 26 on March 10, 1960. Always one of the busiest engine companies in FDNY, they led the city in runs and workers for many years in the past. In 1911, 58 was assigned an experimental Nott gasoline-propelled steam pumper. This one-of-a-kind unit was driven with a differential and shaft, with chain drive to the rear wheels. This was a one-piece unit and differed from the tractorized steamers of that era. It proved unsatisfactory and was removed from service after a short time. 58's first-alarm territory consists of many old tenements, as well as high-rise housing projects and several large hospitals. They have had 33 unit citations and six medal winners and two line-of-duty deaths. Their apparatus is a 1993 Seagrave 1000-gpm pumper.

LADDER CO. 26

1365-1367 5th Avenue, Manhattan

Ladder Company 26 was organized as a double company at 52 East 114th Street on July 1, 1904. The second section was disbanded on November 1, 1946, reorganized on March 11, 1957, disbanded on April 20, 1959, reorganized yet again on August 10, 1968, and finally disbanded on December 16, 1974. Ladder 26 moved into their current quarters with Engine 58, on March 10, 1960. For many years, they were the busiest ladder company in FDNY and gained the nickname of "The Fire Factory." Their first-alarm area includes old tenements, high-rise housing projects, hospitals and retail stores. They have had 46 unit citations and 43 medal winners. Firefighter Anthony Riccardi received the James Gordon Bennett Medal in 1947 and the Dr. Harry M. Archer Medal in 1948 for an act of valor on September 14, 1946. Additionally, they had another Bennett Medal winner in 1916. They have had three line-of-duty deaths. Their apparatus is a 1993 Seagrave 100-foot rear-mount.

1st: Capt. James Brand, Lt. Stephen Lonergan, Lt. Kevin J. Fitzpatrick, Capt. Marco A. Vitolo, Lt. John Rice, BC Robert F. Sweeney 2nd: BC William Koehler, Kevin B. Murphy, Richard N. Driscoll, Walter R. Hutter, Steven J. Connor, Patrick F. O'Connor, John Kelton, Stephen Haggerty, Christopher George, Thomas P. Keery 3rd: Timothy Hoppeg, Thomas Burke, Francis K. Trapani, Andrew S. Kolesar, Dennis Czeczotka, Joseph Bennetti, Thomas McKenna, Robert O'Dowd, Joseph T. O'Brien

ENGINE CO. 91

244 East 111th Street, Manhattan

Engine 91 was organized originally in their current quarters on March 20, 1913. Always a very busy unit, they were joined by a second section in the same house on January 1, 1916, with the manpower coming from the disbanded Engine 89. The second section was disbanded on November 1, 1946, re-organized again on October 15, 1957, disbanded again on November 15, 1958, re-organized again as Engine 91-2 on August 10, 1968, and finally disbanded for good on December 16, 1974. Ladder Company 43 also was in this very large house before moving to Engine 53 in 1974. Fire Salvage 2 was quartered here from 1979 until disbanding in 1991. RAC (Recuperation and Care) Unit 1 currently is housed here. Their first-alarm area consists of old tenements, several high-rise housing projects, a hospital complex and many retail stores. Engine 91 has had 20 unit citations and seven medal winners and two line-of-duty deaths since their inception. They have a new 2000 Seagrave 1000-gpm pumper.

DIVISION 6

1st: DC William Demarest, DC Thomas Kennedy, DC Joseph DiBernardo, DC Malachy McCann 2nd: Patrick Vogt, Larry Welch, John Scales, Bill Brennock, Sal Gigante

BATTALION 3

BC Thomas Martin, BC Charles Ditta, BC Anthony DiPaola

BATTALION 14

BC Tom Stephens, BC Bernard Mullin, BC John Quevedo

BATTALION 16

1st: BC Thomas Roby, BC Michael Rappe, BC Francis Donnelly 2nd: Robert Laird, Dominic Cassase, Mark Blanda

BATTALION 17

1st: Thomas Connolly, Kevin Adams, Patrick Murtagh 2nd: BC Jeffrey Lever, BC Thomas Fahy, BC Kevin Corrigan, BC Robert Steiniger

Note: Battalion 26 in photo with Engine 50 and Ladder 19. (See page 293)

1st: *Peter Ficke, Luis Cruz, Lt. Michael Lizzo, Capt. Doug Tripken, Lt. Alfred Gaddi, Lt. Michael Mulderrig, Elio Moschetta, Dennis Daly* 2nd: *Vincent Massa, Kenneth Hettwer, Michael Schnarr, Damon Alston, Luke Jurain, Michael Mirando, Manuel Diaz, Keith Faccilonga* 3rd: *Robert Peterson, Chris Polidoro*

ENGINE CO. 64
1214 Castle Hill Avenue, Bronx

Engine 64 was organized in a former volunteer house at 2152 Gleason Avenue on May 1, 1896, and moved to their current quarters on December 9, 1908. Ladder 47 actually is located in a slightly newer house (1913) at 1220 Castle Hill Avenue, separated from 64's house by a narrow yard. Their first-alarm territory consists of many private homes, large apartment houses and the huge Parkchester housing project, plus numerous retail stores. The unit was awarded two unit citations and in 1995, Firefighter Patsy Coppola was awarded the Pulaski Association Medal for an heroic act at Bronx Box 2660 at 580 Castle Hill Avenue, on May 20, 1994. Their one line-of-duty death was a lieutenant, who was killed in 1953 while detailed to Engine 53. Engine 64 currently has a 1993 Seagrave 1000-gpm pumper.

1st: *Cliff Mueller, Gene Mahlstadt, George Holzmann, Lt. Joe Lowney, Capt. Steve O'Donnell, Lt. Mullarkey, Tom Bruckner, Fred Burnett* 2nd: *Aux. Capt. Bob Hutton, Mike Sudol, Skip Theiss, Joe Inserra, Pat Whelan, Chris Delisio, George Diaz, Pete Klammer* 3rd: *Ken Winkler, Bob Niebler, Brian McMahon, Doug Ferretti, Tim Wren, Tom Heghmann, Greg Hopkins, Pete Grossmann, Sean Murphy*

LADDER CO. 47
1220 Castle Hill Avenue, Bronx

Separated by a narrow yard from the five-years-older quarters of Engine Company 64, Ladder 47 was organized here on November 27, 1913. Besides the huge Parkchester housing project, other buildings in their first-alarm area include private homes, large apartment houses and many retail stores. One of their officers has received two medals of valor for this company. In 1996, Lieutenant Dennis Munnelly received the Fire Marshal's Benevolent Association Medal for the rescue of a woman and five children at 2275 Randall Avenue on May 27, 1995. In 1992, he received the Third Alarm Association Medal for an act of heroism performed on January 21, 1991. They have had eight unit citations and one line-of-duty death. Their current apparatus is a 1996 Seagrave 100-foot rear-mount.

ENGINE CO. 94
1226 Seneca Avenue, Bronx

Located in an area known as Hunts Point, Engine 94 was organized in their current quarters on November 27, 1913. Ladder Company 48 and the 3rd Battalion also are quartered here. Tactical Control Unit Engine 513 responded from here from 1969 to 1971 before being disbanded. 94's first-alarm area consists of many small commercial businesses, a few factories, junkyards and an extensive wholesale produce market, as well as many tenements and retail stores. They have had 14 unit citations and two medal winners. Their apparatus is a 1993 Seagrave 1000-gpm pumper.

1st: *Terry Long, Capt. Joe Cleary, Lt. Tom Delehanty, Richard Straub* 2nd: *Dave Sinclair, Patty O'Keefe, Kenny Quinn, John Sullivan, Matthew Egan, John Farrell, Timothy Keys*

LADDER CO. 48
1226 Seneca Avenue, Bronx

Ladder 48, along with Engine Company 94, with whom they share quarters, were organized on November 27, 1913, at their current location. The 3rd Battalion is quartered here, too. A special unit, Tactical Control Unit Engine 513, also responded from here during their period of service from 1969 until 1971. Their first-alarm territory, in this area known as Hunts Point, consists of old tenements, retail stores, factories, junkyards and the Hunts Point produce market. They have had 18 unit citations and seven individual medal winners. The most recent winner was Firefighter Alan Maurer, who received the Honor Legion Medal in 1994 for an heroic rescue at 883 Longfellow Avenue on May 17, 1993. Ladder 48 has had one line-of-duty death. Their apparatus is a 1991 Seagrave 100-foot rear-mount.

1st: Ed Tietjen, Lt. Ed Boscarino, Capt. Tom Armstrong, Ed Loehmann 2nd: Rod Downey, Mike Polchinski, Kenny Quinn, Kevin Meehan 3rd: Pat Butler, Declan Grant, Pat Lindquist

ENGINE CO. 96
1689 Story Avenue, Bronx

Engine 96 was organized on October 29, 1929, at 1684 Bruckner Boulevard, with Ladder 19. On June 1, 1935, they were re-organized as a combination engine company, when Ladder 19 was relocated to the quarters of Engine 50. A Mack city service ladder truck was assigned and responded together with their pumper and hose wagon. In 1941, they moved to temporary quarters for a few months while the firehouse itself was moved, to facilitate the widening of Bruckner Boulevard. They became a regular engine company in 1951, when a new Ward LaFrance "Quad" was assigned to replace the pumper, hose wagon and city service ladder truck. On April 13, 1966, they moved to their current quarters with Ladder Company 54. Foam Unit 96 also is located here and manned by Engine 96 when special-called. Their first-alarm area includes many private homes, high-rise project complexes, retail stores and many small business buildings. They have had 10 unit citations and six medal winners. They have had two line-of-duty deaths. Their apparatus is a 1993 Seagrave 1000-gpm pumper.

1st: Robert Englehart, Daniel Ward, Lt. Thomas Yuneman, Capt. John Gleeson, Lt. George Stonebridge, Lt. Patrick Rogan, Robert Kruczowy 2nd: Robert Reynolds, Michael O'Rourke, Bernard Leech, Richard Ward, Andrew Piscitelli, Richard Bowmann, Ronnie Schlitt, Thomas Marry, Glenn Messapesa, Andrew Link, Michael DeStefano, William Tripp, Brian Corrigan, James Jackson, Craig Brannon, Michael Currid 3rd: Edward Mullamany, Edward Nietzschmann, Richard Burke, Thomas Conroy, John Murphy, Patrick Corr, Christopher Smith, James Roell, Christopher Gogerty

LADDER CO. 54
1689 Story Avenue, Bronx

Ladder 54 was organized in the quarters of Engine Company 96 on April 13, 1966. A special unit, Foam 96, also is located here. Another special unit, Searchlight 23, was here prior to being disbanded. In the short time that it has been in existence, Ladder 54 has become one of the busiest ladder companies in the department. Their first-alarm area consists of many private homes, high-rise housing projects and many retail stores. The company has had seven unit citations and six medal winners. Lieutenant Brendan Sheehy received the Uniformed Fire Officers Association Medal in 1999 for the rescue of two children at a 2-2 at 1760 Story Avenue on February 5, 1998. Also in 1999, Firefighter William McGee received the Battalion Chief Frank T. Tuttlemondo Medal for his heroism at a 7-5 at 1245 Virginia Avenue on July 20, 1998. In 1997, Firefighter McGee was awarded the Dr. Albert A. Cinelli Medal for a rescue at a 7-5 at 1029 Manor Avenue on May 5, 1996. Their apparatus is a 1995 Seagrave/Aerialscope 75-foot tower-ladder.

1st: Kevin Cunningham, Lt. Jeff Magnatta, Lt. Richard Volpe, Lt. Frank Santiago, Lt. Brendan Sheehy, Lt. Mike Kenney, Phil Smith 2nd: Robert Piser, Billy McGee, Brian Sullivan, Tom Kelly, Jose Molina, Richard Kirschner, John Foiles, David Bell, Neil Wallace, Nick Ortiz, Steven Byrne, Vincent Egbert, Lt. Patrick Woods, Desi Breslin, James Mattutat, Lt. John Corcoran 3rd: Kevin Albert, Angelo Cocciolillo, James Kadnar, John Dorn, Gerald Conlon, Joseph Martorell, Al Tarquinio, Bill Degnan, Al Johnson, Edward Cruz, Richard Bailey

ENGINE CO. 60

341 East 143rd Street, Bronx

Engine 60, known as "The Green Berets," originally was organized in their former quarters at 352 East 137th Street on January 1, 1895. They moved to their current quarters with Ladder 17 and the 14th Battalion on November 1, 1948. This very busy company has a first-alarm territory that includes many old tenements, as well as high-rise projects, a very large hospital complex, numerous retail stores, etc. They have had 15 unit citations and six individual medal winners, including the James Gordon Bennett Medal to Captain George Wolken in 1935. In 1991, two of their members, Lieutenant Michael Finer and Firefighter Thomas Keeling, were awarded the Bella Stiefel Medal and Captain Denis Lane Memorial Medal, respectively, for their heroic actions at Box 3-3-2182, 358 Willis Avenue, on December 24, 1990. Firefighter Dennis Hodges received the Frank W. Kridel Medal in 1990 for his bravery at a fire in a project building at 227 Willis Avenue on February 26, 1989. They have lost two members to line-of-duty deaths. Their apparatus is a 1993 Seagrave 1000-gpm pumper.

1st: Lt. Michael Waters, Lt. Tom Lapolla, Capt. Austin Horan, Lt. John Leonard 2nd: Jerry Rooney, John Rohr, Bill Dunn, Bob Charboneau, Steve Bowles, Jim Breen, Steve Schwartz, Paul Trunali, Sean McAuley 3rd: Tom Martin, Brad Daly, Mike Steel, Chris Murphy, Jose Maldonado, Jim Curry, Pat Maloney, Tim Parker

1st: Lt. Frank O'Grady, Capt. Chris Rearer, Lt. Ray Callinan, Lt. John DiSalvo 2nd: Tom Cunneen, Pete Lusenskas, Frank Simpson, Gerry Archambault, Kenny Francis, Kevin Kouril, Bill Larsen, Jason Goldsmith, Tom Freshour, Brian McKiernan 3rd: Joe Brosi, Joe Kennedy, Brian Connolly, Brian O'Connor, Frank Quigley, Bob Nosman, Steve Pitiz, Paul Murphy, Jack Allen

LADDER CO. 17

341 East 143rd Street, Bronx

Ladder 17, the "Green Berets," were organized on January 1, 1874, in a former volunteer house at 2608 Third Avenue, making them the oldest Bronx ladder company. They moved to their current address in 1877 and to their current house on March 1, 1907. They share space with Engine Company 60 and the 14th Battalion. They operated as a double company on two separate occasions, first from March 1, 1907, until January 1, 1915, and again from October 3, 1970, to December 16, 1974. Their first-alarm territory consists of old tenements, high-rise housing projects, hospitals and retail stores. They have had 19 unit citations and 24 individual medal winners. In 1903, their captain received the Stephenson Medal for maintaining the most efficient and best-disciplined company in the department. They have had five line-of-duty deaths, two of which occurred at a 3-3 at Willis Avenue and 132nd Street on October 29, 1974. Their apparatus is a 1997 Seagrave/Aerialscope 75-foot tower-ladder.

ENGINE CO. 71

728 Melrose Avenue, Bronx

Celebrating their 100th anniversary last year, Engine 71 was organized at 3168 Railroad (later known as Park) Avenue on August 1, 1899. In 1901, they moved to their big, new house at 3134 Park Avenue, where they remained until moving to their current station, with Ladder 55 and the 6th Division, on March 16, 1989. Rescue 3 shared their former quarters from May 14, 1951, until July 23, 1968. Other units in their former quarters included Searchlight 3 and the 4th, 5th, 6th and 7th Divisions and 26th Battalion. The current first-alarm territory for this busy unit features many old tenements, high-rise projects and numerous retail stores, as well as several government buildings and Yankee Stadium. They have had 12 unit citations and one medal winner. Engine 71 formerly was assigned one of only two 1970 Mack pumpers equipped with a 54-foot articulated Squrt boom. Their current apparatus is a 1993 Seagrave 1000-gpm pumper.

1st: Paul Passaretti, Robert Pappas, Lt. Gerard Smith, Capt. Roger Olin, Lt. Peter Vratimos, Lt. Patrick Dvignan, Dominic Nolan, Russell Moody 2nd: Steven Reisman, Joseph Prunty, Michael Rahilly, William Magrino, Shan Cody, Ben Connolly, John Gardner, Gerard Maher, Gerald Rocco 3rd: Daniel Sambrato, Gregory Penny, Anthony Stefania, Angel Vasquez, Guy Jordan, David Bruno, Patrick Sheridan, Keith Frey, Joe Curl, Michael Zofchak, Timothy McCarvil

LADDER CO. 55
728 Melrose Avenue, Bronx

Ladder 55 was organized in the old quarters of Engine Company 71 at 3134 Park Avenue, on July 23, 1968. On March 16, 1989, they moved with Engine 71 to the new quarters where the 6th Division also is located. Their first-alarm territory is a mix of old tenements, high-rise housing projects, retail stores, government buildings and Yankee Stadium. They have had 17 unit citations and eight medal winners. In 1970, Firefighter Charles Varner received the James Gordon Bennett Medal for an act of heroism performed on August 15, 1969. The most recent medal winner was Firefighter Edward Wohl, who received the Fire Chiefs Association Medal in 1997 for the rescue of a mother and five children at a 3-3 at 682 Eagle Avenue on January 24, 1996. Their current apparatus is a 1991 Seagrave 100-foot rear-mount.

1st: Gerard Amitrano, Frank Stefanak, Edward Wohl, Lt. Michael Derudder, Capt. Frank Mannion, Lt. Edward Aretakis, James Hawkins, Greg Tilearcio *2nd:* Bruce Fritz, Christopher Young, Mark Fredrickson, Paul Rickel, Donald Feldman, John McGuinness, Christopher DiBiase, Richard Blazeski, James McCarthy, Patrick Latimer, James Darcey, James Vella, Michael Karen, John Brett *3rd:* John Propura, Michael Federowski, John Zollner, Joseph Daley, Michael Nigro, James Murphy, Joseph Wills, Francis Hughavin

ENGINE CO. 83
618 East 138th Street, Bronx

Engine 83 was organized in their current quarters on February 1, 1906. They share this station with Ladder Company 29. In the past, several special units were located here, including Bridge Chemical Engine 63, Gasoline & Oil Unit 2 and Satellite 2. Their first-alarm area is varied and made up of old tenements, several high-rise projects, many kinds of factories, retail stores, a large railroad yard, etc. They also respond to both Randall's and Ward's Islands via the Triborough Bridge. They have had 17 unit citations and four medal winners, including a former captain, who received the Stephenson Medal in 1950 for having the most efficient and best-disciplined company in the department. One of their former members was killed in the line of duty. Their apparatus is a 1993 Seagrave 1000-gpm pumper.

1st: Lt. Garrett Langdon, Lt. James Neville, Lt. James Renne, Capt. Josef Winkler *2nd:* Michael Scanlan, John Conroy, Thomas Frey, Jay Fink, Michael Killarney, James Carney, Charles White *3rd:* Michael McGarvey, Mark Ward, Thomas Lennon, Thomas Schoales, David Carpenter, Thomas Eichner, William McLoughlin *4th:* Paul Falla, Robert Leanza, John Tannian, Patrick McElvaney, William Martin

LADDER CO. 29
618 East 138th Street, Bronx

Ladder 29 was organized on February 1, 1906, and share their current quarters with Engine 83. Several special units, including Bridge Chemical Engine 63, Gasoline and Oil Unit 2 and Satellite 2, were located here in the past. Ladder 29's first-alarm territory consists of old tenements, high-rise projects, factories, retail stores and a large railroad yard complex. They have had 14 unit citations and nine individual medal winners in the past. A former member died in the line of duty in 1906. Their apparatus is a 1989 Seagrave 100-foot rear-mount aerial.

1st: Lt. Wayne McPartland, Capt. George Walsh, Lt. James Byrnes *2nd:* Christopher Popp, Francis Curnyn, Scott Farrington, Dennis Molloy, Scott Watson, Alfred Zahra, Noel Heffenan, Richard Weinhart, Darryl Williams, Jeffrey Sapienza, Joseph Milianta, Anthony Raimone *3rd:* Jacob Vormittag, Kevin Cassidy, Richard Kennedy, John Henrikson, Daniel Messina, William Pfeifer, Onofrio Russo, Kevin Murphy, Patrick Corr

ENGINE CO. 59

111 West 133rd Street, Manhattan

Engine 59 was organized on April 1, 1894, in their former quarters at 180 West 137th Street in Harlem. They moved to their current quarters, sharing this house with Ladder 30, on November 1, 1962. In the past, special units, including Squad 1 and Department Ambulance 1, also were located with them. Their first-alarm territory is made up of many old tenements, as well as some high-rise projects and numerous retail stores. Engine 59 has been one of the busiest FDNY engines for many years. They have had 16 unit citations and five medal winners, including the James Gordon Bennett Medal to Firefighter Lawrence Duenas in 1963. They have had two line-of-duty deaths in the past. Their current apparatus is a 1993 Seagrave 1000-gpm pumper.

1st: Tom Moore, Jerry Simpson, Lt. John Corcoran, Capt. Jim Montgomery, Lt. Pat Tracy, Capt. Jim Day, Chris McCormack *2nd:* John McGann, Dino Kapetanakis, Rob Fenty, Tom Healy, Lt. Artie Farley, John Higgins, Bob Kaudelka, Rob Spiers, Lucien Segot, Chris Craven *3rd:* Mike Quigley, Danny O'Connor, Mike Deehan, Tom Gardner, Paul Robinson, Terry O'Connor, Brian Gavan, Rob Singer, Bill Martinson, Ken Gustavson, Rob McKeon

1st: John Barry, Douglas Huebler, Lt. James McCluskey, Capt. Abe Haiman, Lt. Edward Tierney, Anthony Scialo, Keith Nicoliello *2nd:* Timothy Sommerlad, Kenneth Haring, Stephen Elliott, Robert Ryan, Joseph Pecorella, Ali Pasha, Patrick Corkin, Kevin Shanahan, Michael O'Byren, Aloysius Grogan, Kirk Coy *3rd:* William Slattery, Thomas Gregory, Christopher Love, Thomas Glasser, Edward Snyder, James Curran, Alan Jacobs, Richard Collister, Craig Thweatt, Charles Schule

LADDER CO. 30

113 West 133rd Street, Manhattan

Ladder 30 first was organized in their own quarters at 104 West 135th Street on February 1, 1907. They moved to their current location, along with Engine Company 59, on November 1, 1962. Mobile Medical Unit 1 also was located here prior to disbanding. Their first-alarm territory, located in Harlem, consists of many old tenements, plus some high-rise housing projects, brownstone-type residences and many retail stores. They have had 24 unit citations and 30 medal winners. In 1998, Firefighter Stephen Elliott was awarded the Hugh Bonner Medal for a rescue at a 7-5 at 630 Lenox Avenue on January 14, 1997. In the same year, Firefighter Ali Pasha was awarded the M.J. Delehanty Medal for a rescue at a 5-5 at 31 Tiemann Place on August 2, 1997. They have had two line-of-duty deaths. Their apparatus is a 1993 Seagrave 100-foot rear-mount.

1st: Thomas Caldwell, John Kudlak, George Brennan, Lt. Raymond McCormack, Lt. Joseph Neubauer, Lt. Christopher Lennon, Jules Segot, Lt. Jack Corr *2nd:* Timothy Klett, Kevin Harrison, Francis Moriarty, Paul Conrad, Timothy Carter, Jack Keane, Michael Finamore, Hisham Tawfig, David Olsen *3rd:* Michael Grillo, Daniel Sullivan, Daniel O'Neil, George Clark, Greg Antonison, Vic Leeber, Thomas Barbagallo, Vincent Tessoriero

ENGINE CO. 69

248 West 143rd Street, Manhattan

Engine 69 originally was organized on July 1, 1899, as Combination Engine Company 69 at 243 East 233rd Street in the Bronx. On January 1, 1916, they were disbanded, with Hook and Ladder 39, formerly a Manhattan unit, reorganized here. 39 is still in this building. Engine 69 was re-organized on April 17, 1917, in their current quarters, where they share space with Ladder 28 and the 16th Battalion. This very busy Harlem company has a first-alarm area made up of many old tenements, some high-rise project buildings and numerous retail stores. Members have been awarded 18 unit citations and six medals for valor in prior years. Three of their former members were killed in the line of duty. Their apparatus is a 1992 Seagrave 1000-gpm pumper.

LADDER CO. 28

248 West 143rd Street, Manhattan

Ladder 28 was organized in their current quarters on January 15, 1905, as a double company. The second section was disbanded on January 1, 1915. Ladder 28, known as "The Harlem Hilton," has shared these quarters with Engine 69 and the 16th Battalion for many years. The first-alarm territory of this busy unit includes old tenements, high-rise projects and retail stores. They have had 43 individual medal winners. Firefighter Michael O'Driscoll received the James Gordon Bennett Medal in 1956 and the Dr. Harry M. Archer Medal in 1957, for an act of heroism on December 17, 1955. In 1997, Firefighter John Duddy received the Bennett Medal for heroism at a 3-3 at 30 Hamilton Place on November 25, 1996. They have had three other Bennett Medal winners in 1967, 1980 and 1988. They have had 18 unit citations and three line-of-duty deaths, including a firefighter in military service during World War I. Their apparatus is a 1993 Seagrave 100-foot rear-mount.

1st: John Duddy, Thomas Grimshaw, John Faracco, Capt. Robert Morris, Lt. Robert Carberry, Lt. Kevin Flanagan, Thomas Landau, James Cody *2nd:* Patrick O'Sullivan, John Tobin, Brian Autz, Michael LaPorta, Joseph Jablonski, Kevin Hayes, Raymond Sessa, Robert Allen, Peter Thweat, John Saropa *3rd:* Archie Booker, Paul Nigro, James Kerley, Edwin Burwell, Edwin Anzalone, David Guzick, Thomas Stringer, James Carney, Robert Rodeska, James Dunscomb

1st: Gene Hipsman, Jim Kobetitsch, Lt. Bill Dunlevy, Capt. George Gabriel, Lt. Tom Riley, Jim Bevers, Fred Vargas *2nd:* Andy Horan, Al Gotay, Mike Koesterer, George Reese, Bob Kennedy, Tom McCoy, Jerry Sillcocks, Jim McGuiness, Tom Marsich, James McNamara, John Martinson *3rd:* Bill Mackin, Tom Huber, Kevin Kean, Steve O'Hagen, John Zollner, Brian Germain, Bob Carlo, Mike Leanza, Ralph Espito, Jim Lovett, Bob Greene

ENGINE CO. 80

503 West 139th Street, Manhattan

Engine Co. 80 actually was organized as a double engine company on May 15, 1905, in their current quarters. Each section had its own steamer and hose wagon, as well as its own officers and firefighters. The second section was disbanded on January 1, 1915, with Engine 80 operating as a single engine since that time. Ladder 23 has shared these quarters since 1918. Their West Harlem first-alarm territory consists of many old tenements, large apartment houses and a university complex, plus many retail stores and other small businesses. They had 16 unit citations and one line-of-duty death many years ago. Their current apparatus is a 1998 Seagrave 1000-gpm pumper.

LADDER CO. 23

503 West 139th Street, Manhattan

Ladder 23 was organized at 504 West 140th Street, in quarters directly behind their current location, on September 17, 1898, and moved in with Engine Company 80 on May 1, 1918. The 5th Division also was located here for many years prior to being disbanded. Their first-alarm area consists of many old tenements, large apartment houses, a university complex and many retail stores. They have had 15 medal winners over the years. In 1996, Firefighter Thomas McKiernan received the Hugh Bonner Medal for a rescue at a 7-5 at 61 West 87th Street on December 28, 1995, while the company was relocated to Ladder 22. They have had 13 unit citations and one line-of-duty death – a firefighter who was killed in action during World War II. Their current apparatus is a 1998 Seagrave/Aerialscope 75-foot tower-ladder.

1st: Thomas Borsare, J.J. Moran, Robert Moran, Lt. Mike Alexander, Lt. Mike Galgano, Capt. James Duffy, Rich Lengefeld, Hienze Hilmer, Jack Kenny *2nd:* Mark Egan, Nick Ladisa, Andy Horan, John Doherty, Andy Duffy, Mark Jarmek, Rich Appenzeller, John Gormley, John Rigolini *3rd:* John Murray, Mike Anson, Mark Kurtz, Paul Martinowicz, Steve Katz, Charles Barhold, John White, Bill Butler, Chris Walsh

ENGINE CO. 46

460 Cross Bronx Expressway, Bronx

Chemical 4, the predecessor of Engine 46, was organized on January 15, 1874, and disbanded on July 11, 1881. On that latter date, Engine 46 was organized as a combination engine company at 753 East Tremont Avenue. After moving to new quarters at 451-453 East 176th Street in 1895, they became a regular engine company on June 1, 1904, and moved to their current house, along with Ladder 27, on March 14, 1972. While still in their former quarters, a second section, known as Engine 46-2, was organized on August 10, 1968, until disbanding on October 15, 1969, to become Engine 88-2. Their first-alarm territory consists of old tenements, several high-rise projects and numerous retail stores. They have had 14 unit citations and three medal winners and one line-of-duty death. They have a 1993 Seagrave 1000-gpm pumper.

1st: Thomas Cinotti, Lt. John Meara, Capt. Bryan Violetto, Lt. James Burns, Lt. Cesar Rivera, Edward Kohler 2nd: Timothy Ryan, Francis Reyes, Gerard Pirraglia, George King, Dennis Freyre, John Roche 3rd: Michael Smith, Thomas Mahoney, William Woytkiw, Gregory Sikorsky, Craig Weber, Rick Vidal, Daniel Coleman, David Gold

LADDER CO. 27

460 Cross Bronx Expressway, Bronx

Originally organized next door to Engine 46, at 453 East 176th Street, on June 1, 1904, they moved into their current quarters with Engine 46, on November 6, 1972. A second section, known as Ladder 27-2, was organized in their former quarters on February 7, 1970, but disbanded on the date (November 6, 1972) of the move to the current quarters, to organize Ladder Company 58. Ladder 27's first-alarm area consists of old tenements, high-rise housing projects and retail stores. They have had 24 unit citations and 15 individual medal winners and four line-of-duty deaths. Their current apparatus is a 1991 Seagrave 100-foot rear-mount.

1st: Robert Kselman, Stephen Dempsey, John Morris, Lt. Gary Demry, Capt. Rick Arazosa, Lt. John Tyson, John Merrigan 2nd: Salvatore Bologna, Paul Quirke, Dennis Martin, Alan Bloecker, Brian Bagot, Robert Schmitt, Terence Gallagher, James McNelis 3rd: Eugene Stolowski, Daniel McCluskey, Richard O'Mack, Charles Reilly, John Clavin, John Bellew, Wayne Warren, Joseph Lombardo

ENGINE CO. 68

1160 Ogden Avenue, Bronx

Originally organized as a combination engine company on August 23, 1898, at 1080 Ogden Avenue, Engine 68 became a regular engine on February 15, 1908. On March 1, 1947, Ladder 49, which had been located in a newer building (1913) at 1079 Nelson Avenue—directly behind Engine 68—moved in with 68 in their older house. 49's quarters then were taken over by Fire Patrol 6. Both Engine 68 and Ladder 49 moved to their new and current quarters on September 19, 1979. Their first-alarm area consists of a few high-rise projects, numerous old tenements and private homes, plus Yankee Stadium and a wholesale produce complex. They have had 11 unit citations and one line-of-duty death. Their current apparatus is a 1997 Seagrave 1000-gpm pumper.

1st: Tom Luniewski, Lt. Bruce Stewart, Capt. James Nichols, Lt. Michael Glander, Lt. Kerry Stephen, Bill Greco 2nd: Tom Gabay, Tony DeMasi, Tim Tarpey, Bob Jones, Frank Caputo, Mike Ryan, Chuck Shannon 3rd: John Johnson, Dan Foley, Hugh Duffy, Dan O'Sullivan, Mike O'Hanlon, John Amato

LADDER CO. 49
1160 Ogden Avenue, Bronx

Ladder 49 was organized at 1079 Nelson Avenue on December 23, 1913, in a single-bay fire station directly behind the much older quarters of Engine Company 68 at 1180 Ogden Avenue. On March 1, 1947, Ladder 49 moved in with Engine 68, with the Nelson Avenue quarters occupied by Fire Patrol 6 of the New York Fire Patrol. Ladder 49 and Engine 68 moved to their quarters on September 19, 1979. Their first-alarm territory, in an area known as Highbridge, is made up of many old tenements, highrise housing projects and private homes, plus a wholesale market complex and Yankee Stadium. They have had nine unit citations and eight medal winners. In 1998, Firefighter William Callahan received the Zahn/Troiano Memorial Medal and Firefighter Thomas O'Meara received the William Friedberg Medal, both for multiple rescues at a 7-5 at 1400 Jesup Avenue on October 19, 1997. They have had two line-of-duty deaths. Their apparatus is a 1990 Seagrave 110-foot, rear-mount aerial, one of only four in the department.

1st: Harry Oster, John Moran, William Bartholomew, Joe Spinelli, Bob Travis, Bill Privitar, Jack Featherstone, Bill Cavanaugh, Jeff McCarthy, Rich McCoy 2nd: Lt. Ed McCaffrey, Capt. Jim Gill, Chuck Todd, Bob Peters, Larry Hyland, Vinny Hogan, John Shurina, Lt. Rick Saracelli, Mike Gallagher, Tom O'Meara, Bill Cimillo, Bill Golden, Bill Callahan

ENGINE CO. 92
1259-1261 Morris Avenue, Bronx

Engine 92, which, for several years, has been one of the busiest engine companies in the department, was organized in their current quarters on March 20, 1913. They share these quarters with Ladder Company 44 and the 17th Battalion. From mid-1997 to mid-1998, they were quartered temporarily with Engine 50, while their house was being modernized. Their first-alarm territory consists of many old tenements, large "H-type" apartment houses, a large hospital and many retail stores. They have had three individual medal winners, including a James Gordon Bennett Medal in 1955. In 1990, Lieutenant William Mulcahey and Firefighters Heriberto Galaza, John Matthews, Lawrence Scally, Michael Schraeder and John South were awarded the Firefighter Thomas Elsasser Memorial Medal for their heroic team effort at Bronx Box 2-2-2359, 902 Morris Avenue, on March 4, 1989. They have had 18 unit citations and one line-of-duty death. Their apparatus is a 1998 Seagrave 1000-gpm pumper.

1st: Joe Martin, Larry Scally, Capt. Brian Johnson, Lt. Mike Gibbons, John Matthews, Jeff Pezone 2nd: Angelo Cozza, Kenny Knapp, Carmine Dedonato, Pat McCarvill, Joe Piegare, Brian Fox, Kevin Hogan, Bill Heaney, Joe Hoffman 3rd: Steve Lee, Paul Bailey, James Costanza, Kenny Kirby

1st: Kevin O'Hagan, Tom McGarry, Lt. Mike Finer, Capt. John L. Sullivan, Lt. Mike Everett, Lt. James Zodkowic, Todd Velten 2nd: Mike Mercurio, John McGowan, Paul Gabriellini, Charles Malara, Dan Perrella, Sal Loscuito, James Watterson, John South, Dave Preyor, Tony Mikolich, Mike Treanor, Mike Schunk, Augie Tufano, Louis Mancuso, Willie Servedio, Mike Ciampo

LADDER CO. 44
1259-1261 Morris Avenue, Bronx

Ladder 44 was organized in their current quarters, where they share space with Engine Company 92 and the 17th Battalion, on November 27, 1913. In 1969, they were the first Bronx ladder company to be equipped with a tower-ladder. Their first-alarm district is made up of large apartment houses, older tenements, a large hospital and many retail stores, some of which are in one-story, "taxpayer"-type buildings. They have had 28 unit citations and 21 individual medals for valor. Additionally, members of the company received the Elsasser Medal in 1991, for a team act of heroism on July 4, 1990. On April 4, 1956, Firefighters Arthur Hanson and William Hoolan of Ladder 44 were killed at a 4-4 at 4063 Third Avenue. Four other members of the department were killed at this fire. Ladder 44 operates a 1991 Mack/Baker 95-foot tower-ladder.

1st: Lt. Lawrence Sorensen, Lt. Lawrence Mack, Lt. Robert Spencer, BC Joseph Herir, Sparky, BC Michael McPartland, BC Robert Kilkenny, Lt. Paul Smith 2nd: Lt. Robert McDonough, Arthur McLoughlin, Michael Roberto, Peter Scally, Thomas Lynch, James Hartnett, Robert Lennon 3rd: Kevin Naughton, Gerard Baptiste, Robert Gleissner, Edward Bergamini, Joseph Ginley, Thomas O'Hagen, Stuart Keane 4th: Gerald O'Shea, Robert Meaney, Daniel Schug, Robert Brown, Thomas LoFaso, Thomas Currao, Timothy Geraghty, James Kiernan, Thomas Oswald, John Lopez, Jeffery Cool, William Katsch, Rolf Hettinger, Daniel Crowe, Steven Gladding, Steven DiMaggio, Eric Broden, Thomas Nealon, David Planken, Thomas Kelly, Lt. Robert Ginley, James McShane, Frank Ward, Lt. Daniel Finegan, Brian Healion, Patrick Manning, Charles DiMartini, Lt. Joel Gerardi, James Deering, Lt. Michael Buckheit, Capt. Robert McNicholas, Michael Tierney, Sean Parker 5th: Robert Narducci, Carmine Evola, Jeffrey Dershem, Joseph Reid, Lt. James McCaffery

ENGINE CO. 50

1155 Washington Avenue, Bronx

This company was organized as Combination Engine Co. 50 at 491 East 166th Street on June 15, 1882. They became a regular engine in 1898, but reverted back to combination status in 1899 and back again to being a regular engine on May 17, 1909. They moved to their current quarters, with Ladder 19, on July 28, 1976. This has been one of the busiest FDNY engines for many years. On May 30, 1970, a second section, Engine 50-2, was formed with separate officers and firefighters. They were disbanded on March 23, 1974. Their first-alarm area is made up of many old tenements, intermixed with some high-rise project developments. They have had 15 unit citations and six medal winners and two line-of-duty deaths.

LADDER CO. 19

1155 Washington Avenue, Bronx

Originally organized in the Highbridge area on March 17, 1880, Ladder 19 was disbanded on August 23, 1898, but reorganized at 886 Forest Avenue on November 12, 1898. They later moved in with Engine 96 and later again with Engine 50, with whom they now share quarters, along with the 26th Battalion. They have been at their current location since July 28, 1976. This very busy company has many old tenements, intermixed with high-rise projects, in their first-alarm territory. They have had 17 medal winners, including a James Gordon Bennett Medal in 1929. In 1998, Captain Michael McPartland received the Susan Wagner Medal for heroism at a 7-5 at 450 East 169th Street on April 30, 1997. Firefighter Richard Mlecz received the Thomas Kenny Medal for a rescue at a 2-2 at 1048 Sheridan Avenue on December 29, 1997. They have had 25 unit citations and one line-of-duty death. Their apparatus is a 1999 Seagrave 100-foot rear-mount.

*Battalion 26 in with Engine Company 50 and Ladder Company 19.

ENGINE CO. 73

655-659 Prospect Avenue, Bronx

Originally organized almost 100 years ago on November 1, 1900, the quarters of Engine 73 are 13 years older than the next-door attached quarters of Ladder 42. Squad Company 2 also was located here from 1955 until being disbanded in 1976. Their first-alarm area is made up of old tenements, some project buildings and many retail stores and light commercial buildings. They have had 16 unit citations and four medal winners, including the following: In 1953, their captain received the Stephenson Medal for having the best-disciplined and most efficient company. Firefighter Tim Brown received the Wagner Medal in 1990. Lieutenant Robert Henesy was awarded the Crimmins Medal in 1984. They have had four line-of-duty deaths. Their apparatus is a 1993 Seagrave 1000-gpm pumper.

1st: Lt. Kevin McCutchan, Lt. Ralph Caramanica, Capt. Robert Kilcarr, BC Richard Bienenstein 2nd: Richard Bonacorsa, Matthew Tringali, John Covitt, Kevin Halliday, Thomas Biryla, William Schauffler, Nicholas Liso, Derek Harkin, Charlie Flood, James Devane, Peter Dopfel, Robert Pennacchia 3rd: Edward Doyle, David Russell, Peter Carey, Dell Truay, Richard Cutney, Dana Bolte

1st: Raymond Murphy, Richard Glover, Lt. Michael Dugan, Capt. Thomas Pierno, Lt. James Walsh, Robert Merkel, Fredrick Gleissner, Sean McNamee 2nd: John O'Shaughnessy, John McGee, Stephen Hopkins, Brian Ahearn, Gregory Buday, Michael Vissichelli, Joseph Pietrofere 3rd: Donald Finnegan, Thomas O'Malley, Peter Bielfeld, Jerome Farrell, Daniel Tompkins, John McDonald 4th: Thomas O'Neill, Robert Blair, Brian Nicholson

LADDER CO. 42

653-659 Prospect Avenue, Bronx

This very busy south Bronx company was organized in their current quarters on November 27, 1913, in a building that is 13 years newer than the adjacent and currently interconnected quarters of Engine 73. Squad Company 2 also was quartered here from 1955 until disbanded in 1976. Their first-alarm territory consists of old tenements, high-rise housing projects, some commercial buildings and many retail stores. They have had 29 unit citations and 21 medal winners over the years. In 1984, Firefighter Robert Merkel was awarded the James Gordon Bennett Medal for an heroic rescue at a fire at 761 East 158th Street on March 29, 1983. In 1998, Lieutenant James Walsh received the Thomas Dougherty Medal for an act of heroism at a 7-5 at 745 East 152nd Street on February 26, 1997. They have had one line-of-duty death. Their apparatus is a 1999 Seagrave 100-foot rear-mount.

ENGINE CO. 82

1215 Intervale Avenue, Bronx

Engine 82, made famous by the book authored by former Engine 82 firefighter Dennis Smith, was organized on September 5, 1905, in their current quarters. Soon after, on December 27, 1905, they became Combination Engine 82 and were assigned a city service ladder truck that rolled with their steamer and hose wagon. They reverted back to being a regular engine on May 1, 1907. Most of their first-alarm territory consisted of large tenements and "H-type" apartment houses. Many of those were demolished or burned and replaced by new one- and two-family homes. Many of the old tenements still exist, as do numerous retail stores. They share quarters with Ladder 31. In the past, several other units were located here, including Engine 85, Tactical Control Unit Ladder 712, Searchlight 23 and the 3rd and 26th Battalions. They have had 16 unit citations and four medal winners and one line-of-duty death. Their apparatus is a 1993 Seagrave 1000-gpm pumper.

1st: Lt. James Leight, Capt. Thomas P. Kavanagh, Lt. Pete Wolf, Lt. Jack Apair 2nd: John DeStepano, Dave Giambalvo, Paul Kreischer, Adam Lutfi, Robert Roff, Peter Mabanta, Ken Begbie, Mark Zawgara, Kevin Miller, Mark Buckley, Mike Murray, Dan O'Brien 3rd: Vincent Sepe, Mark Doran, Richard Ramaizel, Anthony Pirro, Stanley Balskey, Brad Tellefsen, Brian Quinn, Sean Burgoyne, Patrick Dunn, James Caddigan

1st: Lt. Howard Carpluk, Lt. Jim McCaffrey, Lt. Phil Liubicich, Capt. Thomas Hoy, Capt. Ronnie Gilyard, Lt. Gerry Murnane, Dan Willett 2nd: Greg Magi, John McGongle, Bill Donlon, Kevin McGeary, Paul McKie, Vincent Pinto, Tom Dutton, Vinny Holfester, Ted Carsttensen, Pete Wasserman, Mike DeRosa, James Hudson, Troy Roberts, Bill Kology, Nich Schwartz 3rd: Craig Nesteruck, Frank Stonitsch, Ken Jurgensen, Ed Carroll, Steve Hagan, Ed O'Connor, Dan Reeber, Charles McCormack, Steve Blancato, Mike Walsh

LADDER CO. 31

1213 Intervale Avenue, Bronx

This company was made famous—with Engine Company 82, with whom they are quartered—by the book written by Dennis Smith, a former member of 82. They were organized in their current quarters on May 1, 1907. During the "war years" of the 1960s and 1970s, they were one of the busiest companies in the department. Other units located here in the past include Engine 85, Tactical Control Unit Ladder 712, Searchlight 23 and both the 3rd and 26th Battalions. The response area still includes tenements (many were demolished), but there are also one- and two-family homes and retail stores. They have had 20 unit citations and 28 medal winners. In 1975, Firefighter Thomas Neary received the James Gordon Bennett Medal for an act of heroism on April 4, 1974. Former UFA President Firefighter Michael Maye received two medals while a member of Ladder 31—the F.D. Roosevelt Medal in 1966 and the Wesley Williams Medal in 1968. Their apparatus is a 1999 Seagrave/Aerialscope 75-foot tower-ladder.

DIVISION 7

1st: DC William DeDonato, DC Thomas Neville, DC Al Santora, DC Richard DeSimone, DC James Murtagh, Lt. Douglas Rosenthal *2nd:* Michael O'Rourke, Kevin Skeahan, Pat Flaherty, Michael Stevenson, Peter Graham, John Yarusso, Denis O'Connor, Robert Shenefield

BATTALION 13

James McHale, BC Edward Lintz, BC Donald Borthwick, Joseph Morstatt

BATTALION 15

BC Thomas Fox, BC Mike Dunne, BC John Keenan, Catherine Riordan

BATTALION 18

BC Gary Ruiz, BC Tom McKavanagh, BC John Salka, BC Dennis Moynihan

BATTALION 19

1st: BC Robert W. Colley, BC James M. Keene, BC Herbert Perciavalle, BC Richard Comiskey
2nd: Steve O'Brien, Stanley Andrusczyn, Michael Dougherty

BATTALION 20

Joshua Ramos, BC Robert Stec, Alex J. Kolanik

BATTALION 27

BC George Gierer, BC Kevin Connolly, BC Frank Miale, James Saverese, William Sanagata, BC Gene Dowling, BC John Bruckner

ENGINE CO. 67

518 West 170th Street, Manhattan

Engine 67 was organized in their current quarters on August 21, 1898. During the budget crisis of 1975, they were disbanded on July 2nd, but reorganized two days later on July 4th. They are located in the densely populated Washington Heights area and cover a first-alarm territory made up of many old-style tenements, retail stores, a huge armory building and the Columbia-Presbyterian Hospital complex. They have 10 unit citations. Medal winners include Lieutenant James Shugrue and Firefighters Joseph DiGilio and Thomas Donnelly, receiving the Hispanic Society Memorial Medal, the Steuben Association Medal and the Holy Name Society-Brooklyn Queens Branch Medal, respectively, for their heroic actions at a building collapse at Manhattan Box 1715, on January 29, 1982. In 1998, Lieutenant William Welsh and Firefighters Lee Fuchs, Jason Goldsmith, Gilbert Gomez and William Staudt were awarded the NY Firefighters Burn Center Foundation Medal for their heroic actions at a 2-2 at 501 West 164th Street on December 25, 1997. They have had two line-of-duty deaths. Their apparatus is a 1993 Seagrave 1000-gpm pumper.

1st: Lt. William Welsh, Lt. Dennis Gilhooly, Capt. Paul McDermott, Lt. Francis Occhiogrosso 2nd: Robert Dugan, Robert Coffey, William Staudt, James Messmer, Scott Batterberry, Lee Fuchs, James Mara, Norberto Pratts, Matthew Madtes, Gilberto Gomez, George Brady, Jason Goldsmith, William Hanley, Michael Minnock 3rd: Joseph Vogelsang, James Brown, James Sullivan, Abdu Salim, Richard Fellegara, Paul Patsos, David Carpenter

13th Battalion

ENGINE CO. 84

513-515 West 161st Street, Manhattan

Engine 84 was organized in this house on August 1, 1907. They share these quarters with Ladder Co. 34. Their upper west Harlem and Washington Heights first-alarm area includes many old tenements and apartment houses. Additionally, a large hospital complex is in their territory, as are many schools and retail stores. They have been awarded 12 unit citations. Their current apparatus is a 1998 Seagrave 1000-gpm pumper.

13th Battalion

1st: Kenneth Mundy, Gregory Leverock, Lt. Matthew Murtagh, Capt. John Luongo, Lt. William Schall, Albin Wagner, Steven Amen, Glen Seymour 2nd: Steven Bailey, Thomas Jasinski, Thomas Lent, Chris Mandeville, Kevin Moran, Gerald Smyth, Timothy Rice, Michael Cacciola, Charles Markey 3rd: Daniel Conway, Angelo Blanda, Patrick Carley, Paul Geoghegan, Mike Coppola, Edward Egan, Kevin Quinn, Ernest Medaglia, Richard DeSimone

LADDER CO. 34
513-515 West 161st Street, Manhattan

Ladder 34 was organized on August 1, 1907, at their current quarters, next door to Engine Company 84. Their first-alarm territory—in an area of upper west Harlem and lower Washington Heights—consists of many old tenements and large apartment houses, as well as a large hospital complex, schools and retail stores. They have had 16 unit citations and 14 medal winners. Lieutenant William Maloney received the James Gordon Bennett Medal in 1987 for an heroic act on December 3, 1986. In 1990, he was awarded the Dr. Harry M. Archer Medal for the same deed. The Archer Medal is given once every three years for the most heroic of the three prior Bennett Medal actions. They have had three line-of-duty deaths. They have a 2000 Seagrave 100-foot tillered aerial.

1st: Bryan McPherson, Shawn Ashe, Lt. Albert Gonzalez, Lt. Bobby Winkler, Capt. Arthur Depew, Lt. Brian Gillen, Peter Farrenkopf, Victor Armaniaco 2nd: James Walsh, Edward Boles, Rudy Goop, Joe Feldman, John Miles, Tony Jovic, James McHale, Thomas Mullen 3rd: Thomas Leduc, Glen Perry, Steven Kearney, Richard Muratore, Joe Horgan, Mike Boeri, John Sullivan, Eric Torres

ENGINE CO. 93
513-515 West 181st Street, Manhattan

Engine 93, one of very few companies, originally was organized as a double engine company. They had separate apparatus and each section had its own officers and firefighters. They have been at their current location since inception, on March 20, 1913. Ladder Company 45 and the 13th Battalion also are located here. The second section of Engine 93 was disbanded on July 2, 1918. Rescue Company 3 was quartered here from 1968, before moving back to The Bronx in 1992. They have had six unit citations and two line-of-duty deaths. One of these was Firefighter Frank Moorhead, who was the company's only medal winner for his actions at a collapse in December 1946. Their first-alarm area consists of large apartment houses, many rows of retail stores, a hospital complex, schools, etc. Their apparatus is a 1998 Seagrave 1000-gpm pumper.

1st: Al Noney, Capt. Steve McDonald, Lt. Thomas Whyte, Vincent Diaz 2nd: Michael Heaphy, Seamus O'Callaghan, John Lenihan, Michael Lennon, Richard Walston, James Cizike, Kevin Anderson, Cliff Woods, Wayne Blatz 3rd: Robert Clarke, Michael Brockbank, Tim O'Connor, Sean McBrien, Thomas Meehan, Thomas Sullivan, Pat Shannon, Thomas Cunniffe, James O'Connor

LADDER CO. 45
513-515 West 181st Street, Manhattan

Ladder 45 was organized in their current quarters, with Engine Company 93 and the 13th Battalion, on November 27, 1913. Several other companies also were organized on this same date. Rescue Company 3 was here from 1968 to 1992. Their first-alarm territory, in this area known as Washington Heights, is made up of old tenements, many retail stores, a hospital complex and several large schools. They have had 13 unit citations and eight medal winners, most recently Firefighter Joseph Tustin, who received the Goldenkranz Medal in 1996, for an act of heroism performed on June 30, 1995. He had received the Lane Medal in 1995 for a prior heroic action on February 1, 1994. This company has had one line-of-duty death. Their apparatus is a 1994 Seagrave/Aerialscope 75-foot tower-ladder.

1st: Dan McCauley, Lt. John Frawley, Lt. John Sullivan, Dave Cunningham 2nd: Pat Heffernan, Michael Maye, Sean McNally, Gary Iorio, Al Gryner 3rd: Rich Giampaolo, Joe Byrne, Ray Griffin, Pat McKenna, Dave Kelly, William Hayes, Joe Tustin

ENGINE CO. 95

26-31 Vermilyea Avenue, Manhattan

This company has the distinction of being located furthest north of all Manhattan engines. They were organized on October 1, 1915, in a house they share with Ladder Co. 36. A special unit, known as Foam 95, is assigned here and manned by Engine 95. Their first-alarm territory, known as the Inwood section, has many old tenements, as well as several high-rise housing projects, many schools, a hospital, a few small marinas, several lumberyards and numerous retail stores. The company has received five unit citations. Their apparatus is a 1993 Seagrave 1000-gpm pumper.

1st: Lt. Paul Conlon, Capt. Thomas Van Doran, Lt. Richard Jacaruso, Lt. Ronald Rolle 2nd: Paul McGuire, Andrew Wyckoff, Eugene Meehan, Stephen Erickson, James McClusky 3rd: David Alexander, Ilya Zerakhto, Guillermo Sterling, Peter Hannon, Brian Carey

LADDER CO. 36

31 Vermilyea Avenue, Manhattan

Ladder 36 was originally a Bronx unit, organized on February 15, 1908, in the quarters of Engine Company 43 on Sedgwick Avenue. They were disbanded as such on April 1, 1913. They were reorganized on October 1, 1915, in their current quarters, with Engine Company 95. Located in the Inwood area, their first-alarm district is made up of old tenements, high-rise housing projects, schools, a large hospital, lumberyards, small marinas and numerous retail stores. They have had six unit citations and one medal winner, Firefighter Patrick Monahan, who received the Columbia Association Medal in 1978, for a rescue on January 11, 1977. They have had three line-of-duty deaths. Their current apparatus is a 1995 Seagrave 100-foot rearmount.

1st: Lt. Douglas J. Scherma, Capt. Jack Taddeo, Lt. Jose Garcia 2nd: Sean Janes, Michael King, James Marley, Christopher Williamson, Scott Atlas, Sean Hegarty, Alfred Hildreth 3rd: Steve Brunner, Douglas Feffer, Dennis Murphy, William Murphy, Jr., Richard Bendix, Patrick Ryan

ENGINE CO. 38

3446 Eastchester Road, Bronx

This unit originally was organized in Manhattan as Suburban Engine 38 at 159 East 85th Street on October 11, 1865. This is the current address of Engine 22 and Ladder 13. On January 1, 1868, they were reorganized as Engine 38, taking over the quarters of Suburban Engine 40 at 1907 Amsterdam Avenue. In 1881, they were re-designated as Combination Engine 38 and rolled with a steamer, hose wagon and city-service ladder truck. They reverted back to a regular engine in 1898 and were disbanded in 1918. They were reorganized in their current quarters, with Ladder 51, in the northeast section of The Bronx, on December 20, 1928. Their first-alarm area consists of many private homes, apartment houses, retail stores, etc. They have one unit citation and in 1996, Firefighter Craig McLoughlin was awarded the Wylie Medal for his heroic act at a 2-2 on September 29, 1995. Two members of the original Manhattan Company were killed in the line of duty. They operate a 1993 Seagrave 1000-gpm pumper.

1st: Patrick McNamee, Joseph Boyle, Lt. Thomas Swanwick, Lt. Patrick Fitzmaurice, Eugene Lynch, John Sepa 2nd: Mark Schweighardt, Steve Kwintner, Jr., Gary Theriault, Peter Collazo, Brian Watson, John Pushkal 3rd: Carl Gelardi, Eamonn McLoughlin, Gary Sharkey, Bernard O'Hara, Craig McLoughlin, Christopher Ritchie, Frank Harnisher, Leonard Curcio

LADDER CO. 51

3446 Eastchester Road, Bronx

Ladder 51 was organized in their current location on December 20, 1928, along with the current Engine Company 38. The original 38 was a suburban engine company located at 159 East 85th Street in Manhattan. They later moved and became a regular engine company at 1907 Amsterdam Avenue in Manhattan, later converting to a combination engine company at that location. They were disbanded in 1918 and reorganized, along with Ladder 51, on December 20, 1928. Their first-alarm territory, in the northeast Bronx, consists of private homes, some large apartment houses and many retail stores. They have had four unit citations and two medal winners. Lieutenant Lawrence Romano received the Columbia Association Medal in 1967 and Firefighter Anthony Mazza the Hispanic Society Medal in 1974. Their apparatus is a 1998 Seagrave/Aerialscope 75-foot tower-ladder.

1st: Don Kleint, Raymond Farrell, Lt. Frank Vignali, Capt. James J. Lucas, Keith Pettus, Frank George 2nd: Kaseem Ryan, Christopher McGuire, Charles Hauben, Ernest Ehlberg, Richard Donovan, Frank Trosa, Manuel Giron, Thomas Haughney 3rd: Michael Jackson, Matthew Daly, Patrick Neville, Thomas Lorello, John Marano, Richard Oakley, Edward Curry

1st: John Ryan, Lt. James McLaughlin, Capt. William Galligan, Lt. Patrick Welch, James Salemo 2nd: Daniel Kinzel, William Pesature, Michael Kirwin, Jack Allen, Kevin Kustka, Michael Kelly 3rd: Joseph Montanaro, William Ferrara, Paul Castle, Nicholas Schwartz, Kevin Woods, Anthony Rodriguez, Michael Bogert, Jonas Adams

ENGINE CO. 63

755 East 233rd Street, Bronx

Also located in the northeast Bronx, Engine 63 was organized on February 1, 1896, in a former volunteer house on White Plains Road and moved after a few months to 687 East 240th Street. They moved again in 1909 to 4109 White Plains Road and finally settled in their current house on 755 East 233rd Street on September 17, 1971. The 15th Battalion also is located here. Their first-alarm territory, in the area known as Wakefield, consists of many private homes, plus some apartment houses, high-rise projects, hospitals, retail stores, etc. They have had two unit citations and three medal winners. Lieutenant John Manning was awarded the William F. Conran Medal in 1997 for an act of heroism at Bronx Box 3805, 755 East 229th Street, on January 28, 1996. Firefighter Walter Henning received the Bella Stiefel Medal in 1998 for an heroic act while off-duty at Bronx Box 2-2-4526, 577 Minnieford Avenue in City Island, on December 17, 1997. They have had one line-of-duty death. Their current apparatus is a 1998 Seagrave 1000-gpm pumper.

ENGINE CO. 66

21 Asch Loop, Bronx

The original Engine 66 was a fireboat stationed at the foot of Grand Street and the East River, Manhattan. This company was organized on June 4, 1898, with the then-new fireboat, William L. Strong. Soon after, the name of this boat was changed to Robert A. Van Wyck, but later changed back to its original name. Two other fireboats, George B. McClellan and Cornelius W. Lawrence, also were stationed here for part of their careers. Engine 66 was disbanded on May 1, 1955. The current Engine 66 was organized on January 19, 1974, in the house they share with Ladder 61. This station is in the Co-Op City area, which consists of many high-rise apartment houses. Other structures in their first-alarm area include private homes and retail stores. They have been awarded one unit citation. Their apparatus is a 1994 Seagrave 1000-gpm pumper.

1st: Anthony LoMeli, Daniel Baron, Anthony Siciliano, John D'Attore 2nd: Jeffrey Nichols, Patrick Crorkin, Brian O'Connor, Lawrence McGee, Michael Killeen, Lt. Robert Russo, Stephen McGee 3rd: Timothy Bertsch, Mark Munley, Leland Maggio, Joseph Leahy

LADDER CO. 61

21 Asch Loop, Bronx

Ladder Company 61, located in Co-Op City with Engine Company 66, was organized in these quarters on March 23, 1974, two months after Engine 66 was organized here. Besides the many high-rise apartment houses in the private Co-Op City development, Ladder 61 also has a first-alarm area made up of other large apartment houses, many private homes and numerous retail stores. They have had two unit citations and one medal winner, Captain James Lynch, who received the Dr. John F. Connell Medal in 1986, for an heroic rescue at a fire in a 26-story Co-Op City building, at 2420 Hunter Avenue, on June 2, 1985. Their apparatus is a 1989 Seagrave 100-foot rear-mount.

1st: William Powers, Brian Shea, Ed Vreeland, William Schauffler 2nd: Daniel O'Sullivan, Thomas Maloney, John Murray, John Curtin, John McDowell, Greg Straub 3rd: Robert Lorenz, Paul R. Newman, Fred Davis, Dana Bolte

ENGINE CO. 97

1454 Astor Avenue, Bronx

Engine 97 was organized in their current quarters on April 1, 1931. Ladder Company 32 also was located here from April 1931, before moving back to the quarters of Engine 62 in April 1933. Currently, two special units—Brush Fire Unit 8 and Thawing Unit 2—are located here and manned when needed. Engine 97's first-alarm area features mostly private homes, intermixed with some large apartment houses, several nursing homes and many retail stores. They have had two unit citations and one medal winner. Firefighter Angelo Michelini was given the James Gordon Bennett Medal in 1952 for effecting the arrest of an armed criminal on December 21, 1951. They have had one line-of-duty death. Their apparatus is a 1993 Seagrave 1000-gpm pumper.

1st: Lt. Richard Burke, Lt. William Morris, Capt. Vincent DiPippo, BC John LaPerche, Capt. Robert Blume, Lt. William Thomas 2nd: Arthur Davila, John Matthews, George Baade, Kevin Tully, Steven Radich, Thomas Mirante, Kenneth Larm, Jose Ruiz, Wilfred Santos, Richard Nielson, Michael Verzi 3rd: Dennis Hargett, Kevin Mignogna, Orlando Ortiz, Robert Fitzgibbon, John Mongiello, John Aragona, Edwin Erosa, Charles Tapia, John Fila

LADDER CO. 39

243 East 233rd Street, Bronx

Originally a Manhattan unit, Ladder 39 first was organized with the original Engine 89 at 1799 First Avenue, on February 1, 1909. They moved to their current quarters on January 1, 1916, taking over this house from Combination Engine 69, which was disbanded on that date. At one time, the truck used to carry dynamite for the long-defunct Sappers and Miners Unit was stored in the quarters with Ladder 39. The dynamite was stored underground in a vault in Woodlawn Cemetery, across the street from quarters. If special-called, the members assigned to this unit responded to Ladder 39, drove the delivery truck into the cemetery, retrieved the explosives and then responded to the incident. Ladder 39's first-alarm area includes private homes, small apartment houses, hospitals and nursing homes, plus small businesses. They have three unit citations and two medal winners, both in 1999. Their apparatus is a 1991 Seagrave 100-foot, tractor-drawn aerial, the only tillered ladder in The Bronx.

1st: Cornelius McGovern, Lt. Craig Buccieri, Lt. James Krieger, Capt. Robert Vonderheide, Lt. Michael McMenemon, Lt. Kevin O'Kane, William Jutt 2nd: Joseph O'Brien, Robert Schiavone, Dennis McKeever, Paul Haarmann, Richard Ahern, Michael Shanley, Paul Falla, Michael Moore, Dennis McCarroll, Wayne Pokstis, Steven Roccabruna, Michael Flannagan, Martin Morgan 3rd: Vincent Slizewski, Christopher McGovern, James O'Neil, Thomas Ubertini, Thomas Scambone, Joseph Imparato, Robert Sacchi, Robert Moore, Andrew Casucci, Marques Martins

ENGINE CO. 45

925-927 East Tremont Avenue, Bronx

Engine 45 began on January 15, 1874, when Chemical 3 was organized in former volunteer quarters at 1922 Division Street (Longfellow Avenue). They were converted to Engine Co. 45 on April 23, 1879, and to Combination Engine Company 45 on December 6, 1894, with a ladder truck added. They became a regular engine again in 1896 and a combination engine again in 1898, remaining as such, with a steamer, hose wagon and ladder truck, until 1913, when they reverted to a regular engine. While at their current address since 1885, the present quarters—on the site of the original structure—was opened in 1932, with an adjoining building built for Ladder 58 and the 18th Battalion in 1974. Squad Co. 1 also was located here from October 31, 1975, until disbanded on May 1, 1976. 45's first-alarm area features tenements, project buildings, retail stores, small commercial buildings, schools, hospitals and the Bronx Zoo. They remain one of the busiest engines. They have had 22 unit citations and four individual medal winners and one company medal. They have had one line-of-duty death. Their apparatus is a 1993 Seagrave 1000-gpm pumper.

1st: Florentino Agosto, Lt. William Carroll, Lt. Joseph Saccente, Capt. Michael Keenan, Capt. Kevin Burke, Robert Straub 2nd: Steven Calcutti, Keith Scharfenburger, John Sullivan, John Wamsley, George Valente, Gerald Hart, Ciro Izzo, Dale Manners, Thomas Ward, Peter Busching, Richard DeCola, William Connelly 3rd: Robert Jobb, Daniel McGuinn, James Berry, Edward Ryan, John Marsich, Matthew Beatty, Thomas Healy 4th: Walter Powers, Michael Swiander, William Riccarduli, Chris O'Connell, Daniel Purcell, Michael Smith

1st: Edward Alfarano, Lt. Edmund Calo, Capt. Joseph Principio, Lt. James Rogers, Jacinto Urbino, William Smith 2nd: Jeffrey Ehret, James McKeon, Vincent Hubner, Robert Murray, Glenn Rohan, Mark Wesseldine, Frank Giacoio, Joseph Patriciello, Douglas Batterberry 3rd: Jonathan Henderson, Joseph Drexler, James Wallace, Todd Holgan, Brendan McKiernan, Robert Santandrea, Kevin Jensen

LADDER CO. 58

927 East Tremont Avenue, Bronx

Ladder 58 originally was organized in the former quarters of Ladder 27-2, the second section of Ladder 27, at 453 East 176th Street. This was on November 6, 1972, the day that Ladder 27 moved to their current quarters with Engine 46. The second section of 27 was disbanded to form Ladder 58. On May 15, 1974, Ladder 58 moved to their current quarters, built next door to the existing quarters of Engine Company 45. The 18th Battalion also is located here. This busy company has a first-alarm district made up of old tenements, high-rise housing projects and many retail stores, plus several schools and hospitals. They have had 19 unit citations and nine medal winners. The most recent medal winner was Firefighter Thomas Dunn, awarded the Chief Joseph B. Martin Medal in 1995 for the rescue of three victims at a 3-3 at 1123 East Tremont Avenue, on November 14, 1994. Their apparatus is a 1991 Mack/Baker 95-foot tower-ladder.

ENGINE CO. 48

2417 Webster Avenue, Bronx

Engine 48 originally was organized as Combination Engine 48 at 2504 Webster Avenue on October 14, 1881. At that time, they were the most northern company in all of The Bronx and responded first-due as far as Riverdale and Wakefield. They became a regular engine company on February 1, 1895, back to a combination engine on September 17, 1898, and finally a regular engine again on November 15, 1908. They moved to their current quarters, with Ladder 56 and the 7th Division, on June 29, 1977. For several years, they have been one of the busiest engine companies in all of New York City. Their first-alarm area consists of many old tenements, retail stores, Fordham University and a few hospitals. They have had 16 unit citations and six medal winners. Additionally, the Stephenson Medal for the best disciplined and most efficient company in the department went to their captain in 1933. They have had seven line-of-duty deaths. Their apparatus is a 1993 Seagrave 1000-gpm pumper.

1st: Dominic Lidonati, Daniel Vito, Capt. Thomas Damore, DC Richard DeSimone, Lt. Kevin White, William Martens 2nd: Jeff Johnston, Earl Hayes, Angel Torres, Lawrence Vowinkel, Joseph McKiernan, John McCann, George Netz, Frank Ferdinandi, Philip Pillet, Steven Alleva, Michael Lindy, Brian Voos, Chris O'Brien

18th Battalion

LADDER CO. 56

2417 Webster Avenue, Bronx

Originally organized in the quarters of Engine Company 42, at 1781 Monroe Avenue, on August 10, 1968, Ladder 56 moved to their current location with Engine Company 48 and the 7th Division on August 12, 1981. This very busy company has a first-alarm area made up of old tenements, retail stores, Fordham University and several hospitals. They have had 14 unit citations and 10 medal winners since their inception. In 1999, Firefighter Brian Browne was awarded the Emerald Society Medal for an act of heroism at a 7-5 at 2544 Valentine Avenue on November 17, 1998. Their current apparatus is a 1991 Seagrave 100-foot rear-mount.

1st: Anthony Pastorelli, Franz Edwards, Lt. Stephen Baker, DC Richard DeSimone, Michael Moschitta, Richard Peitler 2nd: Lester Lightbourne, Anthony Mastrelli, Matthew Casey, Brian Singer, Christopher Macri 3rd: Brian Brown, William Weinert, Rocco Lumbrazo

1st: Lt. Thomas Diehl, Lt. Patrick Murphy, Capt. Louis Kikis, Lt. Richard Johnson 2nd: Michael Saccomanno, Thomas Kanganis, James McGowan, Martin Tighe, Brian Riggs, James Beltrami, William Schumacher 3rd: Mike Hovsepian, Dennis Sullivan, James Fopeano, Anthony Perciavalle, Christopher Phillips, Joseph Harris, Daniel Powers, James Impalaria, Aidan Kelly

ENGINE CO. 88

2223-2225 Belmont Avenue, Bronx

This busy Bronx company was organized in their current quarters, with Ladder 38, on November 15, 1908. Their first-alarm territory consists of many old tenements, retail stores, numerous restaurants, Fordham University and the Bronx Zoo; hence their nickname, "First Due at the Zoo." On October 15, 1969, due to the heavy runs of Engine 88, a second section, known as Engine 88-2, was organized in these quarters. It remained here until disbanded on November 22, 1972, with its manpower used to organize Engine Company 72 on that same day. They have had 12 unit citations and three medal winners, including: Lieutenant Louis Visconti, who received the McElligott Medal in 1991 for a rescue at a 7-5 at Bronx Box 4788, 2119 Hughes Avenue, on January 21, 1990, and Captain Timothy Gallagher, who secured the Hugh Bonner Medal in 1983 for a rescue at Bronx Box 3304, 711 East 183rd Street, on May 28, 1982. Their apparatus is a 1997 Seagrave 1000-gpm pumper.

LADDER CO. 38

2223-2225 Belmont Avenue, Bronx

Ladder Company 38 was organized in their current quarters, next door to Engine Company 88, on November 15, 1908. Their first-alarm territory is made up of many old tenements, restaurants, retail stores, Fordham University and the Bronx Zoo. They have had 22 unit citations and 15 individual medal winners. In 1938, their captain received the Stephenson Medal for maintaining the best-disciplined and most efficient company in the department. In 1999, Captain Kenneth Schermerhorn received the Fire Bell Club Medal for a rescue at a 7-5 at 795 Garden Street on January 17, 1998. Also in 1999, Firefighter Kevin Kelly received the Albert S. Johnston Medal for a rescue at a 2-2 at 2041 Washington Avenue, on July 26, 1998. They have had one line-of-duty death. Their unusual apparatus is a 1990 Seagrave 110-foot rear-mount aerial, one of only four in the FDNY.

1st: Tony Scerra, Capt. Ken Schermerhorn, Lt. Mike Tarpey, Vinnie Albanese 2nd: Jack Mulvihill, Vinnie Fiumara, Rocco Dimieri, Bill Schneider, Kevin Kelly, Joe Spor, Pete Krebs 3rd: Tom Cosgrove, Kevin Bohan, Paul Malkan, Rick Kobbe, Carl Punzone, Mike Sullivan, Tom Pushkal

1st: David Dwyer, Robert Meadows, Capt. Herbert Penner, Lt. John O'Connor, Lt. Roy Levesque, Lt. Stephen Wall, George Palladino, Joseph Morgan 2nd: Richard Leonard, James Conroy, Michael Reutter, Donal Ginter, Mark Verdi, Michael Sheridan, Stephen Schadt, Walter Hyde, Michael Hettwer, James Morgan, Dominick Domino 3rd: Kenneth Vidal, Richard O'Brien, Terrance McGann, George LoMedico, Robert Dolney, Pearse Kearns, Bryan Lillis, James Higgins, William Weber, Joseph DeSalvo, Robert Labatto, Peter Brennan, Douglas Yano

ENGINE CO. 42
1781 Monroe Avenue, Bronx

One of the earliest Bronx companies, Engine 42 was organized on January 1, 1874, at 1192 Fulton Avenue and moved to their current quarters on January 1, 1915. Ladder Co. 56 and Rescue Co. 3 also were located in these quarters for many years, but at different times. This very busy company has an area made up mainly of old tenement buildings, some larger apartment houses, a major hospital complex and many retail stores. They have had 20 unit citations and one individual medal winner, as well as the Firefighter Thomas R. Elsasser Memorial Medal to a lieutenant and five of their firefighters for a team effort at a 2-2 on April 5, 1991, at Bronx Box 2985, 1881 Walton Avenue. Their apparatus is a 1993 Seagrave 1000-gpm pumper.

ENGINE CO. 43
1901 Sedgwick Avenue, Bronx

Engine 43 originally was the 106-foot fireboat *William F. Havemeyer*, which entered service on May 12, 1875, at the foot of Pike Street and the East River. It was disposed of and the company disbanded in 1903. The current Engine 43 was organized as a land company on May 1, 1904. Later that year, they were converted into a combination engine company and assigned a ladder truck to respond along with their steamer and hose wagon until February 15, 1908, when they became a regular engine. Ladder 36 was organized here on February 15, 1908, but moved to their quarters with Engine 95, in Manhattan, in 1915. Ladder 59 moved to these quarters in 1978. Also stored here from 1969 until 1972, during out-of-service hours, was Tactical Control Unit Ladder 712, which operated from the quarters of Engine 82 and later from Engine 85. 43's first-alarm area includes old tenements, private dwellings and several project-type apartment houses. They have had 13 unit citations and two medal winners and one line-of-duty death. Their current apparatus is a 1998 Seagrave 1000-gpm pumper.

1st: James Kirby, Michael Sangiuolo, Lt. Mike Fagan, Lt. James Kitson, Capt. Gary Walter, Lt. Bill Hoag, Frank Salmon, Kevin McLoughlin 2nd: John Dwyer, Gregory Jentzen, James Spencer, Walter Bieber, Gary Valentino, Joseph McGovern, James Gallager, John Fracassi, Mark Kwalwasser, Paul Torns, Michael Roberts, Richard Peterson, John O'Hagan 3rd: Luis Ostolozoga, Michael Swift, Robert Watson, Daniel McMaster, William Carroll, Anthony Lalli, Jeffery Pearson, Robert Begley, Charles Wendland, Lawrence Bell

1st: Karl Loehmann, James Dahl, Lt. Robert Hagan, Capt. John Murphy, Lt. Kevin Lavelle, Lt. James McKay, Bill Muller 2nd: Robert King, Joe LeClair, Ronald Kemly, Richard DiDonato, William Kuhens, Glen Lawson, James Leach, John Barrett, Kenneth Smith, John Sherry, Martin Murphy, Thomas McEnroe 3rd: Kevin McEntyre, Lt. Brian Healy, William Peck, Thomas O'Shea, Hugh Lennon, Patrick Mulligan, Christopher Miller, Michael Boland, John Steinhardt, Thomas Lennon, Dennis Farrell

LADDER CO. 59
1901 Sedgwick Avenue, Bronx

Ladder 59 was organized in the temporary "tin house" at 1264 Boston Road, along with the now-disbanded Engine 85, on November 24, 1972. They were relocated to their current quarters, which they share with Engine Company 43, on April 17, 1978. Their first-alarm territory consists of old tenements and older-style private dwellings, as well as high-rise housing projects. Fifteen medals for valor have been awarded to members and 13 unit citations. In 1989, Captain Richard Jacquin was awarded the James Gordon Bennett Medal while covering in Ladder Company 27. In 1998, Lieutenant Robert Hagan received the Steuben Association Medal for heroism at a 7-5 at 2222 Andrews Avenue on April 2, 1997. Also in 1998, Firefighter John Barrett received the Dr. J.W. Goldenkranz Medal for his rescues at a 7-5 at 40 Richmond Plaza on February 5, 1997. In 1999, Firefighter Barrett received the Fire Marshals Benevolent Association Medal for another rescue at a 7-5 at 1889 Billingsley Terrace on March 19, 1998. They have had 13 unit citations. Their apparatus is a 1994 Seagrave 100-foot rear-mount.

ENGINE CO. 75

2283 Jerome Avenue, Bronx

Originally organized as Combination Engine Company 75 at their current quarters on December 25, 1901, this unit became a regular engine company on May 15, 1907, when Ladder 33 was organized here. The 19th Battalion also has been quartered here for many years. All of these units are slated to move to their new house, located a few blocks away, in the near future. Engine 75 has a first-alarm territory made up of many old tenements and larger "H-type" apartment houses, intermixed with many retail stores, schools, an elevated subway line and a huge, partially vacant armory. They have had 25 unit citations and three medal winners, including Captain Frank Somsky—the Wagner Medal in 1983 and Lieutenant Peter LoCastro—the Stiefel Medal in 1986. They have one recorded line-of-duty death. Their apparatus is a 1993 Seagrave 1000-gpm pumper.

1st: Lt. Matthew Hanson, BC Dennis Devlin, Capt. John Stark, Lt. Matthew Jankowski 2nd: Timothy Grant, Richard Dore, George Jones, Thomas Zambrano, Arthur Bennett, Sean Shanahan, Kenneth Durante 3rd: Kieran Brosnan, David Winthrop, Edward Reilly, Glenn Coleman, Timothy Gimpel, William Honneger, Jay Walsh 4th: Scott Samuelson, Kevin Diercksen, James Kassel, Michael Mulvihill, Thomas Asher, Reginald Manley

LADDER CO. 33

2285 Jerome Avenue, Bronx

Ladder 33 was organized in their current quarters with Engine Company 75 on May 15th, 1907. A new fire station for the three units currently is under construction a few blocks away. This very busy company has many large apartment houses in their first-alarm area. Other buildings in their response district include old tenements, many retail stores, schools and a huge, partially vacant armory, as well as the Jerome Avenue elevated rail line. They have had 25 individual medal winners. Additionally, in 1996, Lieutenant Thomas Kelly and five firefighters received the Elsasser Medal for team action at a fire at 1 North Street on December 12, 1995. They have had 26 unit citations and two line-of-duty deaths, one of whom was a member in military service killed in action during World War II. Their apparatus is a 1991 Mack/Baker 95-foot tower-ladder.

1st: Louis Sarapochillo, Lt. John Halpin, Lt. Richard Alfano, Capt. Tom Kelly, Lt. Brian Curran, Capt. Michael Finamore, Clifford Thomson 2nd: Kevin Callan, Joseph Mullady, Brendan Manning, Jonathan Shields, John King 3rd: Kenneth Martin, Robert McGrath, Stuart Carver, Dean Gilhooley, Steve Naso, Michael Kentner

1st: Charles Harmon, Lt. Scott McLaughlin, Lt. Matthew Lonegan, Capt. Robert Boeri, Lt. Craig Groth, Robert Johnson 2nd: Peter Caoili, James Rooney, Stephen Carey, John Kavanagh, Joseph Ditizio, James Basile 3rd: Joseph Stein, Joseph Ford, Mario Marsich, John Lazina, Stephen Archambault

ENGINE CO. 81

3025 Bailey Avenue, Bronx

Engine 81 was organized in a former school building on June 17, 1905, at 3045 Albany Crescent and moved to their current quarters, located in the Marble Hill area, on June 9, 1913. They share this house with Ladder Company 46. Their first-alarm area, which includes Riverdale, is made up of many large apartment houses, high-rise project buildings, numerous private homes, retail stores, two large hospitals, schools and Van Cortlandt Park. They have four unit citations and their one medal winner was then-Lieutenant John Stark, who was awarded the Hispanic Society Memorial Medal in 1999 for an heroic rescue at a 7-5 at Bronx Box 3701, 5480 Broadway, on January 9, 1998. Their one line-of-duty death was a firefighter killed in action while in military service during World War II. Their apparatus is a 1998 Seagrave 1000-gpm pumper.

LADDER CO. 46
3025-3027 Bailey Avenue, Bronx

Ladder 46 was organized in their current quarters, which they share with Engine Company 81, on November 27, 1913. Their first-alarm territory, in this area known as Marble Hill, consists of many large apartment houses, private homes, high-rise housing projects and retail stores, plus schools, hospitals and Van Cortland Park with its brush fire hazard. They have had six unit citations and five medal winners. In 1999, Firefighter William O'Shea received the Captain Denis W. Lane Memorial Medal for rescues made at a 7-5 at 5480 Broadway on January 9, 1998. In 1998, off-duty Firefighter David Weiss received the Emily Trevor/Mary B. Warren Medal for an heroic water rescue in the East River in lower Manhattan. Their apparatus is a 1997 Seagrave/Aerialscope 75-foot tower-ladder.

1st: Richard Watts, Lt. Christopher Boyle, Capt. Richard Lee, Lt. John Woods, Dennis Gallagher, James Scheer
2nd: John Schmitt, Kenneth Wiltse, David Fullam, Daniel Bright, Brian Madden, William O'Shea, Thomas Brusca
3rd: Anthony D'Amico, Raymond O'Hanlon, Robert Solesky, Gerald Murphy, Salvatore Mancuso

ENGINE CO. 70
169 Schofield Street, Bronx

Engine 70, on City Island, was organized as a combination engine company, on August 1, 1899. They became a regular engine company on November 1, 1928, when Ladder 53 was organized in the same quarters. They have been here since May 1, 1940. During the summers from 1939 until 1971, Engine 70, which normally had two pumpers assigned, operated as a double company on weekends, etc. Detailed personnel from other units manned the second pumper, normally used as a hose wagon. On August 24, 1974, Engine 70 and Ladder 53 were disbanded to form Combination Fire Company 121. With a captain on each tour, they responded with a pumper and a 75-foot tower-ladder. CFC 121 was disbanded and Engine 70 reorganized on November 22, 1975. In 1976, they were assigned a retrofitted 1970 Mack pumper, with a 50-foot telesqurt aerial device, the only one in the department. Their first-alarm area includes private homes, restaurants, boat yards, etc. They have had two line-of-duty deaths. Their apparatus is a 1993 Seagrave 1000-gpm pumper.

1st: Lt. Raymond Alexander, Capt. Christopher O'Sullivan, Lt. Gregory Washington 2nd: John Rodenas, Mario Torres, Leroy Magee, Douglas Harkins, Jesus Cruz, Heriberto Galarza, Norbert Thompson

LADDER CO. 53
169 Schofield Street, Bronx

Ladder 53 was organized in the quarters of Engine 70 on November 1, 1928, and moved to the current quarters, at the same location, on May 1, 1940. Ladder 53, along with Engine 70, were disbanded to form Combination Fire Company 121 on August 24, 1974. The combination fire company concept did not prove successful; hence, that unit was disbanded and Engine 70 reorganized on November 22, 1975. Engine 70 operated alone for several years, but were equipped with a pumper that was retrofitted with a 50-foot telesqurt aerial. Ladder Company 53 was reorganized on May 20, 1986. The company is located in a remote area on City Island with a response area that includes many private homes, restaurants and boat yards. They have had one line-of-duty death.

1st: Lt. William Henderson, Lt. James Finn 2nd: Luis Fragoso, Orlando Davila, Bryant Barnes, Samuel Edwards, Jr., Paul Driver, Joseph Antolino, Wilson Matos, Freddie Guerra

1st: Lt. Robert Feeley, Lt. James Fenton, Capt. Thomas Cozzi, Lt. Martin Auer, Stan Freedner 2nd: Thomas Cunniffe, Liam Guilfoyle, Vincent Beckles, Michael Brown, Anthony Vecchiollo, Phillip Martini, Vaughn Peer 3rd: John Northshield, Thomas Delgrosso, Gregory Wurz・urger, Thomas Harris, Russell Post, Nicholas Telincho 4th: Kevin Griffin, Darryl Shephard, Bryan Chamberlain, James Knips

ENGINE CO. 72

3929 East Tremont Avenue, Bronx

The original Engine 72 was organized at 22 East 12th Street, in Manhattan, on July 1, 1900, and was long the home of the 2nd Division. From 1908 until 1916 and again from 1917 to 1918, they operated as a double engine company. The first actual piece of motorized fire apparatus in the department, other than chief's cars, was a 1909 Knox high-pressure hose wagon assigned to Engine 72. On October 15, 1957, Engine 72 was disbanded to form Engine 41-2 on October 15, 1957. The new Engine 72 was organized in their current quarters on November 22, 1972. Another new unit, Ladder 57, was slated to be organized here, but this never occurred. Satellite 2, a 1993 Mack/Saulsbury hose wagon, is manned by Engine 72 and rolls, along with 72's 2000-gpm pumper, to multiple alarms and special calls. Their first-alarm area includes mainly small private homes, retail stores and some large apartment houses. The original Engine 72 had three unit citations and five medal winners. Two line-of-duty deaths occurred at a building collapse in 1908.

ENGINE CO. 89

2924 Bruckner Boulevard, Bronx

Engine 89 was originally a Manhattan company, organized on February 1, 1909, with the original Ladder 39, in a leased "temporary" firehouse at 1799 First Avenue, Manhattan. They were disbanded on January 1, 1916, with their manpower used to organize the second section of Engine 91 on that same day. They were re-organized as a Bronx company on May 15, 1926, in quarters shared with Ladder Company 50. Due to the budget crisis of that time, they were disbanded on July 2, 1975, but were re-organized two days later. Their first-alarm area is mainly private homes, some large apartment houses, numerous retail stores and both the Throgs Neck and Whitestone Bridges. They have had one unit citation and three line-of-duty deaths, one from the original Engine 89. Their apparatus is a 1993 Seagrave 1000-gpm pumper.

1st: Lt. Edward Hefele, Lt. Patrick Soldano, Capt. James F. Noonan, Lt. James Favara, Lt. Michael J. O'Donnell, David Cohen 2nd: Patrick Colgan, James Schneider, Peter Shatesky, Christian Engeldrum, Anthony DelGiudice, Charles Lewis, Peter DeLorme 3rd: William Clarke, Dion Esposito, Joseph Valerio, Luigi Nuzzi, Paul Castellucci, Smajl Rugova, James DeCuffa

1st: Patrick Branley, Lt. William Padilla, Capt. Edward J. Davis, Lt. James M. Quigley, Brian J. Quinn, Thomas Duffy 2nd: Sean M. Giery, Patrick Stranzl, Daniel O'Sullivan, Darryl D. Powell, James Barrett 3rd: Justin M. McCarthy, George S. Orosz, Matthew Heffernan, Anthony Delavega, Richard J. Jahoda, Brian A. Williams, James Balles

LADDER CO. 50

2924 Bruckner Boulevard, Bronx

Ladder 50 was organized on May 15, 1926, in their current quarters, along with the second Engine Company 89. The original engine company of that number was a Manhattan unit, located at 1799 First Avenue, and was disbanded in 1916. Their first-alarm area consists of numerous private homes, some large apartment houses, numerous retail stores and the Throgs Neck and Whitestone Bridges. The New York State Maritime Academy is also in their territory. They have had three unit citations and one line-of-duty death, Firefighter William Ford, who died in 1983. Their current apparatus is a 1991 Mack/Baker 95-foot tower-ladder.

ENGINE CO. 90

1841-1843 White Plains Road, Bronx

Engine 90 was organized on May 1, 1910, in their current quarters, which they share with Ladder 41. The former 9th Division also was located here. Their first-alarm territory is made up of many large apartment houses, some older tenements and numerous private homes, as well as many retail stores. Most of these stores are located in the very dangerous "taxpayer"-type buildings. They have had two unit citations and one line-of-duty death. Their current apparatus is a 1993 Seagrave 1000-gpm pumper.

1st: Kenneth Kerr, Thomas O'Rourke, Lt. Mark Serokosz, Capt. John Gudat, Lt. James Kless, Lt. Robert Hoyt, Joseph Battista, Michael Burrillo 2nd: Gregory Brann, Gerald Lennon, Denis Hanrahan, Kenneth Meadows, Gerald Holmes, William Burke, Brian Cantwell, Al DeSimone, Christopher Tutone, Michael Callahan, Michael Hennigan, Edward Schmidt, William McCormack, Martin Sheehy

1st: Louis Torres, Arthur Watson, Lt. James Hurley, Lt. Frank Ninivaggi, Capt. Kenneth Zavekas, Lt. John McGurk, Lt. James Walsh, Patsy Adovasio, Richard Othmer 2nd: Daniel Pfiefer, Joseph OToole, Michael Cook, Edwin Santiago, Robert Aull, Ernesto Nieves, Brian Johnston, Jeffrey Fleischmann, Fred Schwarzrock, James Solesky, Patrick Smith, Mike Dougherty, Paul Deleo, Thomas Burke, Steven Robbins, Michael Simon, John Hessler 3rd: Alexander Lopez, Sean Faherty, Thomas Batis, Steven Reilly, David Valentine

LADDER CO. 41

1841-1843 White Plains Road, Bronx

Ladder 41 was organized in their current quarters, next door to Engine Company 90, on May 1, 1910. Their first-alarm territory in this, the West Farms area, consists of many large apartment houses, some older tenements and numerous private homes, as well as many taxpayer buildings containing retail stores. They have been awarded seven unit citations and six members have been awarded medals for valor. In 1998, Lieutenant John McGurk received the Company Officers Association Medal for a rescue at a 2-2 at 2186 Cruger Avenue on March 8, 1997. In 1998, Firefighter Joseph Dougherty, who assisted at the above-mentioned rescue, was awarded the Honor Legion Medal for a rescue made at a 2-2 at 577 Minnieford Avenue, City Island, on December 17, 1997, while detailed to Ladder 53. Their apparatus is a 1999 Seagrave 75-foot tower-ladder. Ladder 41 has lost one member in the line of duty.

ENGINE CO. 52

4550 Riverdale Avenue, Bronx

Engine 52, located in the remote Riverdale area, actually was organized as a combination engine at the above address on August 30, 1884. They became a regular engine on November 1, 1928, when Ladder 52 was organized. Both units moved into their current house on May 1, 1939. Their first-alarm territory consists of many large apartment houses, expensive private homes, several colleges and both private and public schools, as well as Van Cortland Park with its brush fire hazards. They have had one unit citation and one medal winner. Their apparatus is a 1993 Seagrave 1000-gpm pumper.

1st: Lt. Edward Marcoux, Lt. Patrick McKernan 2nd: James Greenfield, John Wildrick, Vincent Gergenti, David Izzo, Jack Herlihy 3rd: Kevin Melody, William Thompson, Charles Marino, James Hudson

LADDER CO. 52

4550 Riverdale Avenue, Bronx

Originally organized with Engine Company 52 at the current address on November 1, 1928, both units moved into the new firehouse at the same address on May 1, 1939. This is one of only two fire stations in New York City with the engine and ladder companies carrying the same number. The other house is Engine 10 and Ladder 10 in lower Manhattan. Their first-alarm area, in this section known as Riverdale, consists of many expensive private homes and estates, large apartment houses, several colleges and private schools, as well as the sprawling Van Cortland Park with its brush fire hazards. On May 8, 1988, Firefighter James Shanley of Ladder 52, detailed to Marine Company 6, performed a water rescue for which he received the Firefighter David J. DeFranco Medal in 1989. They have had one unit citation and one line-of-duty death. Their apparatus is a 1995 Seagrave 100-foot rear-mount.

1st: Lt. Robert Joy, Capt. Roger Gagnon, Lt. Joseph Pupino 2nd: Mike Kaner, Daniel O'Brien, Franky Simmons, Thomas Walsh, Rudy Dent 3rd: Kenneth Kumpel, Clark Mooney, James Williams, John Mark

ENGINE CO. 62

3431 White Plains Road, Bronx

This company, in the northeast area of The Bronx, originally was organized as Combination Engine Company 62 at 61 White Plains Road, on February 1, 1896. It became a regular engine in 1900, reverted back to a combination engine in 1903 and finally became a regular engine again on December 20, 1928. They have been in their current quarters since December 12, 1903. Ladder 32 also is located here. In the past, the 15th Battalion was also at this location. Their first-alarm area consists of large apartment houses, high-rise housing projects, numerous private homes, several hospitals and nursing homes, as well as retail stores, schools, etc. They have seven unit citations and one medal winner, Firefighter (now Captain) James Sollami, who received both the James Gordon Bennett Medal and the New York State Honorary Fire Chiefs Association Medal for an heroic act at a fire on January 10, 1984. They have had five line-of-duty deaths. Their apparatus is a 1994 Seagrave 1000-gpm pumper.

1st: John Black, Lt. Edward McKallen, Capt. William Chilson, Lt. Michael Finelli, Robert Conte 2nd: Kevin McNichol, John Mauer, Carlo Casoria, John O'Halloran, John Corrao, Anthony Torquato, Michael Marinaccio, Garret Barbosa, David Sedacca 3rd: Joseph Boyle, Michael Gaffney, John White, Dennis McCarrol, Phil Zeiss, Joseph Kirshman, Thomas Yagunich, Robert Biscardi

LADDER CO. 32

3433 White Plains Road, Bronx

Originally located in the south Bronx, Ladder 32 was organized on May 15, 1907, in the quarters of Engine 50 at 491 East 166th Street. They moved to their current location with Engine Company 62, on December 20, 1928. For two years, between April 1931 and April 1933, they were quartered with Engine 97 and then returned to Engine 62's quarters. Their first-alarm territory consists of large apartment houses, high-rise housing projects, private homes, retail stores and several hospitals and nursing homes. They have had four unit citations and three medal winners. In 1999, Firefighter Gary Voigt received the Holy Name Society (Brooklyn-Queens) Medal for a rescue at a 7-5 at 3280 Reservoir Oval East on March 13, 1998. They have had three line-of-duty deaths, two of which occurred in 1932 during an accident while responding to an alarm. Their new apparatus is a 1999 Seagrave 100-foot rear-mount.

1st: Tom Warkenthien, Lt. George Wicks, Capt. Richard Blatus, Lt. Brian Strenge, Dan DeMinno 2nd: Matt Blaskovich, John Wrobel, Gary Voigt, Sean O'Donnell 3rd: George Hazim, Tom Cawley, Tom McCarthy, John Kavanagh, John Kershis, Phil Zeiss

ENGINE CO. 79

2928 Briggs Avenue, Bronx

Engine 79 was organized in their current quarters, which they share with Ladder 37 and the 27th Battalion, on August 31, 1904. This area of The Bronx is known as Norwood and consists mainly of large apartment houses, with a few private homes, retail stores and a major hospital complex, as well as several large schools. In 1968, two of their members, Firefighters Anthony Palazzo and Lawrence Brigati, were awarded the Franklin D. Roosevelt Medal and Bella Stiefel Medal, respectively, for a rescue made in 1967. One of their former members died in the line of duty. The unit has eight unit citations. Their current apparatus is a 1998 Seagrave 1000-gpm pumper.

1st: Charles Velez, John Rice, Peter Acton, Darren DeBonet, Michael Reilly, Shaun Burns 2nd: Capt. Wesley Shelling, Lt. James Ferry, Kevin Nolan, Robert O'Brien, Capt. Richard McVey, Bernard Langkafel, Gregory Lehr, Brian Schumacher, Christopher Spencer, Lt. Martin Cass, Peter Quinn, Lt. Anthony Catalanotto, William Frano, William Santagata, Gene Sausto, Matthew O'Brien, Roger Hagan, Joseph Brady, Michael Courtney, Steven Guerci, Lt. Neil Halpin

LADDER CO. 37

2930 Briggs Avenue, Bronx

Ladder Company 37 was organized in their current quarters, where they share space with Engine Company 79 and the 27th Battalion, on February 15, 1908. Their first-alarm territory in this north Bronx area is made up of many large apartment houses, private homes, schools, retail stores and a large hospital complex. They have had nine unit citations and five individual medal winners over the years. The most recent winner was Firefighter Steven O'Donnell, who was awarded the Susan Wagner Medal in 1991 for a rescue at a 2-2 at 2628 Bedford Park Boulevard on June 21, 1990. They have had one line-of-duty death. Their current apparatus is a 1994 Seagrave 100-foot rear-mount aerial.

1st: Frank Bazzicalupo, Patrick Murphy, James Lennox, William O'Keefe, Michael Ricciardello, Robert Tobias, Dennis Keating, Laurie Galiato 2nd: Michael Carlisi, Kevin King, Chris Haywood, William Clark, Thomas Quinn, James Reilly, Alan Gieck, Francis Rush, Lt. Joseph Cody, Capt. Joseph Governale, Lt. Kenneth Witteck, Anthony Austin, James Manning, Kevin Finneran, Patrick McAliney, William Hatcher 3rd: Thomas Peterman, James Kane, Paul Zenir, Robert Wienert, James MacKay

DIVISION 8

Thomas Tobin, Carol Vicenti, Judith Murphy Beyar, Lt. Joseph Astarita, DC Thomas Haring,
DC Robert Mosier, DC Theodore Goldfarb, DC Ralph Racioppo, John Kaltenmeier, Ted McVey

BATTALION 21

John Farrell, BC Mark Fernen, BC Richard Posavetz, BC Robert McGrath

BATTALION 22

*1st: Paul Wittek, Kenneth Pogan, Vincent Tummino, Walter Vines **2nd:** BC Robert Wing, BC John Calderone, BC Robert Ryan, BC James Leonard*

BATTALION 23

1st: BC Richard Olivieri, BC Robert Gibson, BC Thomas Vallebuona 2nd: Daniel Ricciardi, Milan Fekete, John Conroy

BATTALION 40

*1st: BC James Esposito, BC Edward Henry, BC Vincent Mandala **2nd:** Daniel Black, Michael Triglianos, John Picarello*

1st: BC Robert Glynn, BC Steven Bernius, BC Richard Howe, BC Gordon Symon *2nd*: John Knutsen, Richard Danetti, William Tropea, Anthony Amoroso

Battalion 42 in photo with Engine Company 243 & Ladder Company 168 (See Page 323)

ENGINE CO. 152

256 Hylan Boulevard, Staten Island

Engine 152 was organized as Engine 202 on November 1, 1905, in the former quarters of Columbia Hook and Ladder 5. The house, which still is standing in Rosebank at 142 Bay Street, was opened in 1900. On January 1, 1913, Engine 202 was re-numbered to Engine 152. The first apparatus was an 1893 American fourth-size steamer. On October 18, 1921, Engine 152 received a new American LaFrance 700-gpm pumper. Part of the rebuilding program of the 1930s, Engine 152 moved into new quarters at 256 Hylan Boulevard. Assigned to Engine 152, Foam 152 was placed in service on October 1, 1986, as Foam 83 and re-numbered on December 29, 1998. Battalion 21 moved here from Engine 153's quarters on April 5, 1976. On July 2, 1997, Engine 152 received a new Seagrave 1000-gpm pumper. Two members of Engine 152 have earned medals for bravery and one Unit Citation has been awarded to the company.

1st: Joseph Mottola, Lt. Edward Morrissey, Capt. Peter Defeo, Lt. Neal Thomason, Stephen Zasa, Steven Perez
2nd: Mark Bonsanti, Lewis Pizzulli, Jeffrey LaRosa, William Fox

ENGINE CO. 153

74 Broad Street, Staten Island

Placed in service in the former quarters of Protection Engine 7, Engine 203 was organized on November 1, 1905. Located in the Stapleton section, Engine 203's quarters at 68 Broad Street were built in 1900. On August 27, 1912, Engine 203 moved to temporary quarters at 78 Broad Street. These leased quarters were replaced on January 1, 1915, with a new building at 74 Broad Street. This firehouse is the only example on Staten Island of two houses in one, with a wall separating the two companies. Ladder 77 shares the house with Engine 153. Engine 203 had its number changed to Engine 153 on January 1, 1913. Engine 153's first rig was an 1884 Clapp and Jones fourth-size steamer. The first motorized apparatus was an impressive new Ahrens Fox, with the big silver ball on the front end above the pump. The Fox could pump 750 gallons of water per minute and was received on July 1, 1916. Engine 153 has earned five Unit Citations and two members have earned medals.

1st: Kenneth Mulligan, Capt. Robert Schafer, Lt. Donald Leo *2nd*: Frank Rapacciuolo, Gerard Pace, Michael Faherty, Anthony Varvaro, Anthony Gallo, Vito Ruvolo, Robert Dillon

LADDER CO. 77

76 Broad Street, Staten Island

Ladder 102 was organized on November 1, 1905, in the former quarters of Enterprise Ladder 1. This firehouse had a unique location at Canal Street and Wright Street in Stapleton: in the middle of Canal Street with the trolley-car tracks on either side of the building made the turn onto Wright Street. Ladder 102 was renamed Ladder 77 in 1913. Their first apparatus was a 1900 Gleason and Bailey ladder truck and the first motorized apparatus was a 1915 Mack City Service ladder truck. Today, they respond with a 1998 Seagrave 75-foot tower-ladder. The area protected by Ladder 77 has a mixture of homes, projects, commercial buildings, the waterfront and the railroad yard of the Staten Island Rapid Transit. On January 1, 1915, Ladder 77 moved into new quarters at 76 Broad Street with Engine 153. One member has received a medal for heroic work and the company has been awarded nine Unit Citations. One member was killed in the line of duty in 1938.

1st: Lt. Willard Wright, Capt. Patrick Mahaney, Lt. Vincent Sobal 2nd: Raymond Ferragano, Joseph Jankunis, Gregory Stranchan, Robert Fithan, Joseph O'Hara, Sal D'Agostino, William Leith 3rd: John Yorks, Salvatore Anzalone, Peter Acquafredda, William Gorman, Dennis Farley, Peter Traut, Tom Gerrish, John McDonald, Randy Perroth

ENGINE CO. 155

14 Brighton Avenue, Staten Island

Engine 205 was placed in the former quarters of New Brighton Engine 4 at 80 Jersey Street. Established on October 1, 1905, the company moved to another volunteer firehouse at 223 Jersey Street during 1907. This house once was home for Richmond Ladder 4 and opened in 1895. Engine 205 was renamed to Engine 155 on January 1, 1913. Engine 155's first apparatus was an 1895 American Fire Engine Company, fourth-size steamer. On November 6, 1922, Engine 155 moved into the motorized era, receiving a new American LaFrance 700-gpm pumper. New quarters were built at 14 Brighton Avenue and on June 26, 1931, Engine 155 and Ladder 78 moved in. The company now responds with a 1997 Seagrave 1000-gpm pumper. Covering one of the older sections of Staten Island, Engine 155 has been an active company for many years. Seven Unit Citations have been awarded to the company and one medal winner can be counted in the complement of men.

1st: John Giobbie, Lt. Mike Farrell, Capt. Jimmy Thomson, Lt. Jimmy Manning, Lt. Pete Brady, Frank Fontaino 2nd: Dave Sgromo, Dan Nemeth, Joe Socci, Steve Reilly, Kevin Coyne, Sean Kenny, Bob Orazem, Artie Lindemann 3rd: Ron Lipari, Bob Mahala, Jay Finegold, West Ballou, Bob Ricciardi, Jeff Szczecinski, Mike Wallace, Tom Hayes

1st: Ed Latourette, Lt. Billy Hayden, Lt. Matty Cichminski, Lt. Bill Cox, Jerry Huntzinger 2nd: Mark Qualben, Ken Christiansen, Mark Volpe, Jim Marshall, Al Trentalange, Bob Grimes, Dave Caputo, Neal Fredericksen, Danny Newman, John Farley 3rd: Bob Kozlowski, Mickey Dolinger, Bob Zaleski, Richie Obermayer, Billy Lilley, Steve Monahan, Tom Tillotson, Brian Schnell, Steve Fenley, Paul Salisbury

LADDER CO. 78

14 Brighton Avenue, Staten Island

Organized on October 1, 1905, Ladder 103 went into service in the former quarters of Tompkins Hose 6 at 3 Brook Street. Their first apparatus was a new 1905 Gleason & Bailey ladder truck. Ladder 103 was renamed Ladder 78 in 1913. Ladder 78 moved into new quarters at 14 Brighton Avenue on June 26, 1931, with Engine 155. From May 16, 1948, until June 1, 1962, Rescue 5 was assigned to Ladder 78. The cross-trained crew could take either apparatus, depending on the call. This part of Staten Island is very old with many wood-frame buildings, making Ladder 78 a very active company. Besides the wood-frame buildings, the area has a housing project, city offices and many commercial buildings. Ladder 78 has earned eight Unit Citations and five members have received medals for heroism. Two members have been killed in the line of duty. FF Stephen Fenley received the James Gordon Bennett Medal, a first for Staten Island, for making a rescue on August 2, 1999. Ladder 78 operates a 1991 Seagrave 100-foot rear-mount aerial.

1st: Chris Criaris, Lt. Vincent Tavella, Lt. John Vigliotti, Capt. Tom Besignano, Lt. Tom Bailey, Ronnie Salvo 2nd: Tom Baez, Drew Feretti, Hank Decker, Frank Ciaravino, Chris D'Ambrosio, John Castagna, Frank Baker 3rd: John Deliso, Alan Bjorklund, Mark Damitz, Tom Smith, Dave Shaw, Dan Sini, Mike Barron, Rick Fernandez

ENGINE CO. 159 & SATELLITE 5
1592 Richmond Road, Staten Island

Hose 7 was placed in service on June 1, 1912, with the first expansion of the Department since 1905. Hose 7 was replaced by Engine 159 on January 1, 1913, although their first piece of apparatus was a 1912 Mack/Boyd chemical and hose wagon. On November 21, 1913, Engine 159 received a new Nott 500-gpm pumper. For many years, Engine 159 covered more area than any other company on Staten Island. The firehouse, located at 1592 Richmond Road, was built for Cromwell Engine and Hose 8. The firehouse was torn down and replaced on September 18, 1930. During the rebuilding, Engine 159 moved in with Engine 160 at 1850 Clove Road. From October 1, 1915, to June 25, 1960, Ladder 81 was quartered with Engine 159. Today, Engine 159 shares its quarters with Satellite 5, which went into service on January 1, 1983. Four members of Engine 159 have been killed during fireground operations. One Unit Citation has been awarded for Engine 159's actions.

1st: Louis Treglia, Jan Pistak, Lt. Dan O'Byrne, Capt. Dennis Moore, Arthur Carletti, Frank Sorito, Ralph Moscato 2nd: John Hourican, Frank Baldini, Richard DiCostanzo, Peter Campione, Christopher Bartley 3rd: Andrew Walters, Michael Clarke, John Zwilinske, Jonathan Backof, Dave Dionisio

ENGINE CO. 160
1850 Clove Road, Staten Island

Engine 160 was placed in service on October 1, 1915, in the largest firehouse on Staten Island. This three-story house is located at 1850 Clove Road and is home for Division 8, Rescue 5 and Tactical Support Unit 2. Engine 160's first rig, the 1913 Nott 500-gpm pumper, was obtained from Engine 159. The building was lettered for Ladder 81 when built, but they never responded from this location, except for the tearing down and rebuilding of their quarters in 1929-1930. Because of the size of the building, it was used as the Borough supply house. Spare rigs were brought over on the ferry and dropped off here. Division 8 has been located here off and on since 1930. Rescue 5 was re-established here on August 20, 1984. Engine 160 has a 1998 Seagrave 1000-gpm pumper that they received on July 13, 1998. Two Unit Citations have been awarded to the company and one member has earned a medal for his heroic actions.

ENGINE CO. 161
278 McClean Avenue, Staten Island

Hose Company 1 was organized in the former volunteer house of South Beach Hose 12 at 181 Seaside Boulevard on November 1, 1905. South Beach Hose 12 dates back to April 2, 1874. Besides Hose 1, the only other company on the south shore of Staten Island was Engine 151 in Tottenville. Hose 1's first rig was a Rumsey hose wagon from the volunteers. In 1914, a Mack/Boyd hose wagon brought Hose 1 into the motorized era. Hose 1 was renamed Engine 161 on June 11, 1923. It was several years before Engine 161 obtained a pumping engine. On December 3, 1925, Engine 161 received a new 1925 American LaFrance 700-gpm pumper. The volunteer house located on the beach was showing its age and was replaced with a new brick house at 278 McClean Avenue on June 26, 1931. Two members have died in the line of duty. One of them, Lieutenant Harold Curran, was detailed to Engine 154 and was overcome by smoke on May 30, 1944.

1st: Lt. Galletta, Capt. Jim Edwards, Lt. Roy Barbarino 2nd: Larry Ventrudo, George Gulliksen, Ron Wilton, Bill Cormican, Sal Squatrito, Jack DeNora, Pat McGarty, Bob Collaro, Joe Ricca, Jim Murphy, Chris Smith, Mark Pedersen

1st: Lt. John Delfino, Capt. Steve Pose, Lt. Pat Hayden 2nd: Steve Laureno, Ed Morri, Carl Coscia, John Franzone, Ben Scarsella, Joe Pisicolo, Bob Kafel, Oscar Orengo, Tony Castellano, Mark Matthes 3rd: John Chipura, Dave Iadisernia, Joe Pica, John Williams, Andy Morawek, Lt. Kevin Richardson, Bob Bianco, Mike Bellantomi, Mike Connoly, Rich Bostic, Steve Passburg, Pat O'Connor

(left margin: 21st Battalion)

LADDER CO. 81
278 McClean Avenue, Staten Island

Organized on October 1, 1915, Ladder 81 went in service in the quarters of Engine 159 at 1592 Richmond Road. Originally, Ladder 81 was to be placed into the quarters of Engine 160, which was lettered for the ladder truck but, instead, went to Engine 159. Ladder 81's first piece of apparatus was a new Mack City Service ladder truck. On December 29, 1929, both Engine 159 and Ladder 81 relocated into Engine 160's quarters, while the wood-frame firehouse was torn down and a brick replacement house built. The new house was completed on September 18, 1930, and both companies moved back. When Ladder 85 was placed in service, Ladder 81 was relocated to the quarters of Engine 161 at 278 McClean Avenue on June 25, 1960. Ladder 81 has received one Unit Citation. They are responding with a 1999 Seagrave 100-foot, rear-mount aerial.

ENGINE CO. 154
3730 Victory Boulevard, Staten Island

Engine 154 is the only company to move from one side of the Island to the other. Organized as Engine 204 on November 1, 1905, its first house was in the former quarters of Niagara Engine 5. This house was unique because it had two levels—44 Sarah Ann Street was the entrance for the hose wagon, while the second floor faced St. Paul's Avenue, on the hill, and was the exit for the steamer. The first rig for Engine 154 was an 1873 Clapp & Jones fourth-size steamer. On May 12, 1919, a new American LaFrance 700-gpm pumper replaced the horses. On January 1, 1913, Engine 204 became Engine 154 and on June 23, 1913, moved into new quarters at 60 Hannah Street. On November 22, 1972, Engine 154 moved to new quarters at 3730 Victory Boulevard in the Travis section. Also assigned to Engine 154's quarters are Brush Fire Unit 4 and Foam Unit 154. The company has earned a Unit Citation and one member has earned a medal.

1st: Winfield Kluth, Lt. Gary Lustig, Lt. Frank Pellegrino, Ciro Formisano 2nd: Robert Fitting, Edward Selling, Adam Polanish, John Mastropietro, Robert Caruso, Edward Zdancwicz, Anthony Muia 3rd: Richard Diorio, Joseph Enia, George Cuevas, John Lucciola, Daniel Ursomanno, Derrick Milone, George Braadt, Matthew Jasko

(right margin: 22nd Battalion)

ENGINE CO. 156
412 Broadway, Staten Island

Engine 206 was organized and located in the former quarters of Wyandotte Ladder 5 on October 1, 1905. The firehouse located at 412 Broadway was Wyandotte's second home, built in 1892. Engine 206 was returning from the St. George Hotel fire on November 13, 1907, to find their quarters on fire. The building burned to the ground and Engine 206 moved into Ladder 79's quarters. On December 6, 1907, Engine 206 moved to temporary quarters at 543 Carey Avenue. New quarters were built on the same site and opened on June 1, 1908. Engine 206 was renamed to Engine 156 on January 1, 1913. Their first apparatus was an 1881 Clapp & Jones fourth-size steamer. Motorization came to Engine 156 on November 21, 1913, with a new Nott 500-gpm pumper. Engine 156 responds with a new 1993 Seagrave 1000-gpm pumper with a 750-gallon water tank. Five members of Engine 156 have been killed in the line of duty. The company has been awarded three Unit Citations.

1st: Francis Wicinski, Lt. Gerald Obremski, Lt. Robert Burns, Lt. John Tyler, Capt. Timothy O'Neill, Stephen Stafford 2nd: Arthur Evans, Perry Pizzolo, August Simoncini, Manuel Bracero, Anthony Parello, Scott Krute, John Willadsen, Roy Smith, Lawrence Garda, Leonard Renia 3rd: Dennis Reilly, Anthony Arpaia, Edward Sweeney, Charles VanPelt, Theodore Florenza 4th: Patrick Smith, Michael Gurnick, Kenneth Kearns, Patrick Mohin, Charles Arnone, Ronald Malanga

(left margin: 22nd Battalion)

ENGINE CO. 157

1573 Castleton Avenue, Staten Island

Engine 207 was placed in service on October 1, 1905, in the former quarters of Washington Engine 1. Also placed in service with Engine 157 was Battalion 2, re-numbered to Battalion 22 on April 15, 1906. Engine 157 went into service with an 1884 Clapp & Jones fourth-size steamer at 51 Cottage Place. Engine 207 became Engine 157 on January 1, 1913. One of Engine 157's larger fires occurred on March 11, 1929, when 17 buildings were destroyed in a fast-moving lumberyard fire. Engine 157 received the only 1917 Robinson 700-gpm pumper assigned to Staten Island on April 9, 1918. On January 23, 1931, Engine 157 moved into new quarters at 1573 Castleton Avenue with Ladder 80. Currently, Engine 157 is responding with a 1993 Seagrave 1000-gpm pumper with a 750-gallon water tank. One Unit Citation has been awarded and one member has received a medal.

1st: Lt. Robert Pesce, Lt. Edward Porto, Lt. Denis Driscoll 2nd: David Sozio, James Conlon, Paul Stallone, Steven Ruggirello, John Dimino, Michael Francese, Frank Sigona 3rd: Michael Singer, Neil Fitzpatrick, Robert Caputo, Thomas Gagliardi, Roger Pfleging, Thomas Newman, Eugene Gavin

1st: Daniel Kenny, Paul Cavagnaro, Capt. John Dunne, Lt. John Zazulka, Edward Thompson, Joseph McGovern, Peter Librizzi 2nd: Jeffery Mulligan, Michael Luisi, Andrew Olsen, Cosmo Diorio, Brian Malloy, Thomas Bradley, Peter Wright, Thomas Downing

LADDER CO. 80

1573 Castleton Avenue, Staten Island

Although it was placed in service on October 1, 1905, Ladder 105 was the last ladder company to be organized with the extension of the paid department to Staten Island. Ladder 105, later re-numbered Ladder 80, was placed in service in the former quarters of Port Richmond Engine 3 at 232 Port Richmond Avenue. The original piece of apparatus was an 1887 Gleason & Bailey ladder truck. Today, they have a 1989 Seagrave 100-foot rear-mount aerial. On January 28, 1931, Ladder 80 and Engine 157 moved into new quarters at 1573 Castleton Avenue. Located in one of the oldest parts of Staten Island, Ladder 80 has been very active through the years with many multiple-alarm fires along Richmond Terrace. When placed in service, the waterfront was bustling with activity, boatbuilding yards, ferry slips and a large shopping district along Port Richmond Avenue. Seven Unit Citations have been awarded to Ladder 80 and 11 members have earned medals for their heroic actions. One member was killed in the line of duty.

ENGINE CO. 158

65 Harbor Road, Staten Island

Engine 208 was placed in service on October 1, 1905. They were located in the former quarters of Aquehonga Ladder 1 at 22 De Hart Avenue in the Mariner's Harbor section of the Island. Their first apparatus was a Silsby steamer that they kept until December 20, 1921. On that day, they received Engine 157's used 1917 Robinson 700-gpm pumper. Engine 208 became Engine 158 on January 1, 1913. New quarters were built for the company at 65 Harbor Road on June 26, 1931. Engine 158's response area is a mix of residential, housing projects, commercial, some industrial, many marine facilities and a major port in Holland Hook. Due to Engine 158's remoteness, they have to operate for long periods of time before the second-due engine or first-due truck arrives. A 1993 Seagrave 1000-gpm pumper with a 750-gallon water tank has been assigned to the company since June 23, 1993. The company has earned one Unit Citation.

1st: John Juliano, Lt. Steven Rice, Lt. Peter Danti, Lt. Anthony Barone, Capt. Gerard Tait, Edward Turner, Russel Porter, Frederick Cipoletti 2nd: Joseph Borg, George Donaldson, Thomas O'Brien, Gary Persch, Steven Wiesner, Kevin McNamara 3rd: Vincent Sobal, Edward McCamphill, Anthony Rivicci, Carmelo Brancato, Joseph Rotunno, Brian Spisto

22nd Battalion

ENGINE CO. 163

875 Jewett Avenue, Staten Island

On March 12, 1932, Engine 163 and Ladder 83 were placed in service in new quarters at 875 Jewett Avenue. Division 8 moved in from Engine 160's quarters on the same day. This style firehouse was used from 1922 until 1940; Engine 163 is the largest of the 55 houses built. Engine 163's first apparatus was a 1931 Seagrave 700-gpm pumper. Today, they respond with a 1993 Seagrave 1000-gpm pumper. The Castleton Corners area of Staten Island, their first-due area, features mostly private homes and some commercial buildings, plus the Staten Island Expressway. With Engine 163 located in the center of the Island, they respond to 99 percent of all the boxes on either the first or second alarm. The only boxes they do not respond to are around the Verrazano Bridge. On May 27, 1993, Engine 163 received a new Seagrave pumper with a 1000-gpm pump and a 750-gallon water tank. Engine 163 has been awarded two Unit Citations and two members have earned medals for bravery.

1st: James Sterner, Lt. Peter Tronolone, Capt. James Koeth, Lt. Joseph Siracuse, Lt. Jan Fulmer, James Keir 2nd: Christopher Rizzo, Douglas Palamara, Joseph Sherry, Frank Corcillo, Steven Keller, Jeffrey Rainiero 3rd: John Defazio, Michael Kelleher, William Barr, Thomas Meyers, Steven Scarfone, Mark Knipstein

LADDER CO. 83

875 Jewett Avenue, Staten Island

On March 12, 1932, Ladder 83 was placed in service with a used 1920 Robinson City Service ladder truck, the only one purchased by the fire department. The firehouse at 875 Jewett Avenue is shared with Engine 163, which also was placed into service on the same day. Like Engine 163, Ladder 83 responds on 99 percent of Staten Island, on either the first or second alarm. Located in Castleton Corners, Ladder 83's first-due area is mostly single-family homes and commercial buildings. Additionally, the Staten Island Expressway – a heavily traveled highway, with trucks carrying every kind of material from computer parts to chemicals and gasoline – is within its response area. Ladder 83 was the last ladder company to use a tillered ladder truck on Staten Island. Today, Ladder 83 operates a 1995 Seagrave 100-foot, rear-mount aerial. The company has been awarded two Unit Citations.

22nd Battalion

1st: Guy Mangogna, Edward Matusaik, Lt. Patrick Whalen, Capt. Philip Morretta, Lt. Edward Bogan, Lt. Peter Tartaglione, Richard Flower 2nd: Joseph Masullo, Steven Aiello, Daniel Surat, Lt. Greg Hansson, Michael Kemper, Steven Sosa, Vincent Milone, Bryant Phillips 3rd: Michael Kroczynski, Martin McKeon, Peter White, Walter Selliti, Richard Fugazzi, Paul Castaldo, Christopher Quinn

ENGINE CO. 166

1400 Richmond Avenue, Staten Island

The proposal for Engine 166 was included with the planning of Engine 165 in the 1957 Capital Budget. Between these two companies, there were 12 square miles with no fire companies located within the area. Engine 166 was placed in service with Ladder 86 on April 15, 1963, in new quarters at 1400 Richmond Avenue. The area was mostly marshland and had a population of only 3000 in 550 buildings. The Willowbrook State Hospital had a population of almost 5000 children and was located among Engine 166, 163 and 165. Today, Engine 166 has a unique response area. It includes a large residential area, a large commercial section along Richmond Avenue and the Staten Island Expressway. Engine 166's first rig was a used 1953 Ward LaFrance 750-gpm pumper. Today, they respond with a new 1996, 1000-gpm Seagrave pumper. One member of Engine 166, Lieutenant Charles Hunt, was killed when he fell through a pier into the water and drowned in 1977.

22nd Battalion

1st: Robert Fuentes, Lt. Gary Washington, Capt. James Heal, Lt. Mike Frusci, Dennis Clarke, Tom Boemi 2nd: Richard O'Brien, Robert Cooper, Kevin Ryan, Sal Ventimiglia, Kevin McDowell, James Hyland, Lance LaMazza 3rd: Albert Russell, Gary Weber, Alfonso Giaquinto, Bryan Platt, John Coughlin, Frank Gunther, Joseph Spagnola

LADDER CO. 86

1400 Richmond Avenue, Staten Island

Ladder 86 was placed in service with Engine 166 on April 15, 1963. The firehouse is located at 1400 Richmond Avenue. Like Ladder 85, Ladder 86 was part of the 1957 Capital Budget and tied in with building of the Verrazano Bridge, which was started earlier. The area around Ladder 86 was mostly marshland and would be built up once the bridge was completed. The Willowbrook State Hospital was located between Ladders 85 and 86 and had almost 8000 patients in three different complexes. Today, the area has a unique mixture of buildings and hazards. It includes a large residential area and a large commercial section along Richmond Avenue and the Staten Island Expressway. Ladder 86 went in service with a 1955 FWD 75-foot wood aerial, which they kept until 1971. Since then, they have had three Mack tower-ladders, a 1971, 1980 and 1988 model. A new 2000 Seagrave 75-foot tower-ladder is slated for delivery. Ladder 86 has been awarded two Unit Citations. Three members have earned medals for their heroic actions.

1st: Gregory Helfer, Joseph McKay, Lt. Robert Reres, Capt. James Melvin, Lt. Edward Costello, Lt. James Fleschner, Lt. Albert Gonzalez, Thomas Spitzbarth 2nd: James Smith, Joseph Saladis, John Troianiello, Joseph Quinn, Timothy Quin, James McHale, Paul Germann, Carmelo Composto, Joseph Fedele, Mark Blanchard, Mark Quigley, John Levendosky 3rd: Charles Salerno, Michael Donohue, Lawrence Jensen, Kevin Mullane, John Dunn, Michael Bergen, Glen Pillarella, John Brukalo

1st: Robert Widener, Leonard Smit, Lt. Michael Murphy, Capt. Frank Hudec, Lt. Steven Shapiro, Dennis Stagliano 2nd: John Czapalski, William Suroweic, Robert Cobb, Michael Duggan, Angelo Covais, Denis McCafferty, Edward Lee, Sal Dellacroce 3rd: Richard Meeks, Christopher Geissler, John Najmy, Arthur Sabatino, John Picciano, Peter Simoncini, William Ketelsen, James Tosach, John Guiffrida

LADDER CO. 79

1189 Castleton Avenue, Staten Island

Ladder 79 was placed into service on October 1, 1905, as Ladder 104. They occupy the former quarters of Mendora Ladder 3 at 1189 Castleton Avenue. Built in 1904, this is the last volunteer house still in use by the paid department on Staten Island. New quarters, combining both Ladder 79 and Engine 156, were on the drawing boards as early as 1946. Today, Ladder 79 shares its quarters with Battalion 22. Ladder 79's first apparatus was an 1890 Gleason & Bailey ladder truck. Currently, they respond on a 1994 FWD Saulsbury 75-foot tower ladder. Like the rest of the north shore, Ladder 79's area has many hazards along the waterfront with shipyards and many older buildings, as well as housing projects, private homes and a hospital. Four members have been awarded medals for their heroic actions and the company has been awarded four Unit Citations.

1st: Philip Sabella, Charles Sineri, Lt. C.B. Stivala, Capt. William Gill, Lt. Ronald Biller, Kevin Corbett 2nd: Brian McAvoy, Glen Midbo, Dennis Komar, Edward Newell, Arne Mattson, Timothy Post

ENGINE CO. 151

7219 Amboy Road, Staten Island

Engine 151 was organized on November 1, 1905, as Engine 201. Located in the former quarters of Eureka Engine 1, the house at 190 Butler Avenue was part of the Tottenville Fire Department and was built in 1888. The first rig was an 1898 Amoskeag third-size steamer. Their first motorized apparatus was a 1920 American LaFrance 700-gpm pumper, received on September 25, 1920. On January 1, 1913, Engine 201 was re-numbered to Engine 151. On February 1, 1930, Engine 151 and Ladder 76 moved into new quarters at 7219 Amboy Road. Engine 151 and Ladder 76 were combined into Combination Fire Company 131, on an experimental basis, from July 13, 1974, to November 12, 1977. Engine 151 responds with a 1997 Seagrave 1000-gpm pumper, which they received on July 1, 1997. One member of Engine 151 was killed in the performance of his duty. Two Unit Citations have been awarded to the Company.

LADDER CO. 76

7219 Amboy Road, Staten Island

Ladder 76 was placed in service as Ladder 101 on November 1, 1905, in the former quarters of Protection Ladder 1. The firehouse was located at 5445 Arthur Kill Road in the Tottenville section of Staten Island and was part of the 1st Battalion. Their first ladder truck was an 1895 Gleason & Bailey truck. On January 1, 1913, Ladder 101 was re-numbered to Ladder 76. Engine 151 and Ladder 76 moved into new quarters at 7219 Amboy Road on February 1, 1930. From July 13, 1974, to November 12, 1977, Engine 151 and Ladder 76 were combined in Combination Fire Company 131. This sleepy bedroom community was once a thriving town with a ferry crossing for the passengers and railroads. For years, after leaving Tottenville, the closest fire company was Hose 1 (Engine 161) in South Beach. For this reason, several volunteer companies were kept active around Tottenville until 1937. Ladder 76 has earned two Unit Citations. Today, Ladder 76 responds with a 1999 Seagrave Saulsbury 75-foot tower-ladder.

1st: William Leverock, Lt. Gregory Fodor, Lt. Richard Ratchford, Michael Borik, Walter Wall, Dennis Heedles 2nd: Joseph Fontana, John Kohm, Robert Walsh, Robert Vanhouton, Paul Drennan, Brian Hopkins 3rd: Susan Byrne, Peter Castellano, Christopher Catalano, John Walsh, Gregory Broms

1st: Salvatore Velez, Lt. Neil MacIntyre, Lt. Charles Maniscalco, Capt. Philip Laudati, Lt. Anthony Orlandi, Louis Rotondo 2nd: Robert Corino, John Porretto, Dennis Zimmerman, Patrick Eason, Jack Galante, Jack McHugh, Edward McHugh, Robert Tozzi 3rd: Salvatore Costello, John Gilhooly, Nicholas Mirto, Christopher Mullin

ENGINE CO. 162

256 Nelson Avenue, Staten Island

Engine 162 and Ladder 82 were placed in service in a new building at 256 Nelson Avenue on December 20, 1928. Their first apparatus was a new American LaFrance 700-gpm pumper. Today, they respond with a 1993 Seagrave 1000-gpm pumper. Engine 162 filled a big gap between Engines 151 and 159 in the Great Kills section of Staten Island. Although Engine 162's response area is predominantly residential, it has a massive brush area. During 1963 and 1964, Engine 162 responded to many large brush fires. One brush fire burned more than 200 buildings and devoured most of the south shore of Staten Island. Because of the large brush area, Engine 162 was assigned a 1993 Seagrave 1000-gpm pumper with a 750-gallon water tank. Besides sharing quarters with Ladder 82, the 23rd Battalion also is located with Engine 162. The unit has been awarded two Unit Citations.

LADDER CO. 82

256 Nelson Avenue, Staten Island

Ladder 82 was placed in service with Engine 162 on December 20, 1928, in new quarters at 256 Nelson Avenue. The first apparatus assigned to Ladder 82 was a used 1921 White Pirsch City Service ladder truck. Their current apparatus is a 1995 Seagrave 100-foot, rear-mount aerial. Ladder 82's response area is mostly private homes with a large brush area. During brush season in the spring, Ladder 82 and the other south shore companies have responded to many third and fourth alarms for brush fires. Three members have been killed in the line of duty.

1st: William Lee, Joseph Evangelista, Robert Brancato, Lt. Joseph Rimassa, Tim Calkins, Pat Devaney 2nd: Joseph Healy, Richard Grigoli, Francis Barton, Jack Baum, John Nichols, Jim Mcloughlin, Richard Fritz, Vincent Dodd, Thomas Kasprowitz, Dave Ferrero, John Heigl, Steve Fish, Ken Colacino, Harold McClutchy, Salvatore Velez

1st: Lt. Dennis Lindsey, Lt. John Bassi, Capt. John Vanden-Heuvel, Lt. Peter Ferrulli 2nd: Edward Degaetano, John Rubino, John Marks, Frank Esposito, John Staiano, Patrick Merwin, Leonard Munda, Albert Hohmann, Michael Byrnes 3rd: Robert Morisie, Robert Teryek, Richard Lukasiewicz, Stephen Dziubela, Kevin Cahill, Robert Defillipo, Victor Sciarappa

ENGINE CO. 164

1560 Drumgoole Road West, Staten Island

Engine 164 and Ladder 84 were placed in service on November 1, 1937, in new quarters at 1560 Drumgoole Road West. With the placing of these two companies, the last five volunteer companies to be disbanded were taken out of service, leaving just two volunteer companies, which still are active today. This also ended the expansion of the Fire Department on Staten Island in the 1930s. With Engine 164 now in service, the responses of Engines 151, 158, 159 and 162 were reduced. Even today, they have a large area to protect, which consists of mostly homes, with some light industry, two major highways and an oil tank farm. Engine 164's first apparatus was a used 1931 American LaFrance 700-gpm pumper from Engine 154. Today, they respond with a 1989 Mack Ward 79 1000-gpm pumper. Engine 164 has earned one Unit Citation.

LADDER CO. 84

1560 Drumgoole Road West, Staten Island

Ladder 84 was placed in service on November 1, 1937, with Engine 164 in new quarters at 1560 Drumgoole Road West in the Huguenot section. With the placement of these two companies, five volunteer fire companies were disbanded. For many years, this area was nothing but woods, but has been growing with new housing developments since the 1970s. Ladder 84's first apparatus was a used 1921 White Pirsch City Service ladder truck. On September 19, 1973, Ladder 84 received its first tower-ladder, a new Mack tower. Today, they respond with a 1994 FWD Saulsbury 75-foot tower-ladder. The company has earned two Unit Citations.

1st: Lt. James Podlucky, Lt. Robert Bolker, Capt. Richard Persichetty, Lt. Edward Vallebuona 2nd: John Wegenaar, William O'Conner, George Wilton, Patrick Mulligan, James Iosue, Francis Signorelli, Thomas Daluise, Dennis McConville, Glen Barile 3rd: Michael Banovich, Joseph Pasquarello, Joseph Fortunato, Edward Quinn, Keith Dillon, James Ahrens, Thomas Flynn

1st: Mike Canavan, Lt. George Criscitiello, Lt. John Murray, Capt. Jim Bossert, Lt. Brian Grisanti, Dom Pace, Pepe Saenz 2nd: Jeff Tkachuk, Sal Massa, Matt Mills, Paul Luffman, Pete Smit, John Lecce, Alex Capobianco, Matt Buono

ENGINE CO. 165

3067 Richmond Road, Staten Island

Engine 165 and Ladder 85 were organized and placed in service in new quarters at 3067 Richmond Road on June 18, 1960. The request for this house goes back to the 1957 Capital Budget. The closest fire companies were more than two miles away. The response area included three different kinds of hospitals with a population of 7800 patients. The regular, full-time population was 4600 and included 750 buildings in six square miles. The area was mostly wooded at the time, but has grown to a large residential area with some commercial buildings. Engine 165's first rig was a used 1946 Ward LaFrance that could pump 750 gallons of water a minute. Today, they respond with a 1993 Seagrave 1000-gpm pumper. They also respond with one of Staten Island's active volunteer fire companies, Richmond Engine 1, protecting the area since 1903. Engine 165 has earned two Unit Citations.

LADDER CO. 85

3067 Richmond Road, Staten Island

Ladder 85 and Engine 165 were organized and placed in service in new quarters at 3067 Richmond Road on June 18, 1960. The 1957 Capital Budget requested money to place these two companies in service. Although the area was heavily wooded, it had a population of more than 12,000 with 750 buildings, which included 7800 patients in three different kinds of hospitals. The closest fire companies were more than two miles away. Today, Ladder 85's first-due area includes many single-family homes and some retail stores. Ladder 85 went in service with a 1938 FWD wood aerial. Today, they operate a 95-foot, 1991 Mack tower-ladder, the tallest on Staten Island. Ladder 85 has the largest area to protect on Staten Island. They also respond with one of Staten Island's active volunteer fire companies, Richmond Engine 1, which has been protecting the area since 1903. Four members have earned medals for heroic deeds and five Unit Citations have been awarded to the company.

1st: Gregory Scalfani, Lt. Steven San Fillippo, Lt. Sal Gugino, Capt. Robert Sohmer, Lt. Joseph Palo, Lt. Mike McClatchey, Anthony Papagni 2nd: Anthony Salterelli, Wayne Spingman, Brian McDowell, Frank Ortado, Todd DeMayo, Michael Stapleton, Joseph Collica, Thomas Donato, Charles Wahren 3rd: John Thompson, Raymond Eger, Thomas Del Pino, Robert Colacino, Peter Greibesland, Gregory Orlando, Thomas Tobin, Thomas Black

1st: Carl Racanello, John Whyte, Lt. William McEvoy, Capt. Gregory Hansen, Capt. Victor Valva, Kevin McCusker, William Battcock 2nd: Gerard Fraser, Michael Catalano, Joseph Cicero, George Froehlich, Robert Christy, John Catapano, Daniel Beyar, Joseph Biserta, Gary Gibbs 3rd: Daniel Fennell, Mark Ryan, Joseph Rehak, Michael O'Shea, Robert Bornhoeft, Robert Brennan, Joseph Albanese, Mark Heintz, John O'Dowd

ENGINE CO. 167 & FOAM 167

345 Annadale Road, Staten Island

The last engine company placed in service on Staten Island was Engine 167 on November 22, 1972. Engine 167 was placed in service by disbanding Engine 208 in downtown Brooklyn. Located in new quarters built for them at 345 Annadale Road, they were located in an area that was growing at a very fast pace. Private developers were putting new homes up as fast they could be sold. Most of their first-due response area is private homes, with some commercial businesses along Richmond Avenue and an oil refinery. They also respond to the largest landfill in the world, the Fresh Kill Landfill. Because of the area, a foam unit was added to the quarters on May 10, 1985. Foam 85 was renamed Foam 167 on December 29, 1998. When placed in service, Engine 167 had Engine 208's 1970 Mack 1000-gpm pumper. Today, they have a 1993 Seagrave 1000-gpm pumper.

LADDER CO. 87

345 Annadale Road, Staten Island

Ladder 87 was placed in service in the quarters of Engine 167 at 345 Annadale Road on August 15, 1987. Their first apparatus was a 1980 Mack tower-ladder and the current one is a 1988 model Mack. The Annadale section grew at a very fast pace, with private developers building new homes as quickly as they could be sold. Ladder 87 filled a very large need because the closest ladder companies were miles away. Most of their first-due response area involves private homes. However, there are some commercial businesses along Richmond Avenue, as well as an oil refinery. They also respond to the largest landfill in the world–the Fresh Kill Landfill.

ENGINE CO. 201

5113 4th Avenue, Brooklyn

Engine 201 was placed in service on September 15, 1869, as Engine 1 of the Brooklyn Fire Department in the former quarters of Putnam Engine 21 at 633 4th Avenue. As Brooklyn grew to the south, the number of alarms started to increase in that area. The vicinity started to develop as a mix of residential, commercial and industrial occupancies. On August 20, 1891, Engine 1 moved to new quarters at 5113 4th Avenue in what was considered the very southern end of Brooklyn. Moving into Engine 201's former house on the same day was Ladder 9, now 109. Engine 1 became Engine 101 on October 1, 1899, and Engine 201 on January 1, 1913. Firefighter James P. Nevin garnered the James Gordon Bennett Medal and the Dr. Harry Archer Medal for a rescue he made in 1936. Two other members also have earned medals for bravery. The company claims seven Unit Citations. In its 131-year history, one member of the Company was killed in the line of duty in 1939.

1st: Lt. Dennis Monohan, Lt. Francis Conwell, Capt. Robert Spellman, Lt. Buffalo Orloff, Lt. John Lamiquiz 2nd: Richard Flynn, Adam Mazy, Joseph McKay, Guy Sconzo, Bryan McElwain, Thomas Imello, Peter Velloza, Frank Francchiolla, Douglas Spano, Michael Conroy, Frederick Corona, John Schardt 3rd: Greg Buck, John Travers, Michael Thomas, James Blow, John Kelly, Theodore Ropiak, Roger Montalvo, John Kadri, Thomas Guarnieri

ENGINE CO. 228

436 39th Avenue, Brooklyn

Placed in service in temporary quarters at 945 4th Avenue, Engine 228 was organized on April 17, 1890, and moved to new quarters on December 30, 1891. Beginning with Engine 228's new quarters at 436 39th Street, Brooklyn made a change in the outside appearances of the firehouses. Before 1891, all the Brooklyn houses were one of two designs—a flat roofline or a peaked roofline with a square apparatus door. Engine 228 has a rounded apparatus door and windows. The growing area of South Brooklyn required placing this company in service. Because of the number of fires along the waterfront, Engine 228 received a 1934 Ahrens Fox 1000-gpm pumper. One of the biggest fires along the waterfront was the Luckenback Pier fire of 1956. Workers using torches started the fire in the 1700-foot pier that contained detonators and rubber products. The explosion killed 10 and injured 250 people. One member was killed in the line of duty. Five medals have been bestowed on members and the company has earned two Unit Citations.

1st: Donald Meeg, Robert Gillen, Lt. Paul Fischer, Lt. Richard Smith, Capt. Michael Quinn, Lt. Rick Kotula, Vincent Minieri, Richard Henry 2nd: James Martin, John Treglia, Anthony Saccavino, Michael Lyons, Josh Reder, Steve Cipaldo, Robert Froner, Joseph Castellano, Nick Rossomando, Anthony Montella, Fred DiCrescento, Franco Riggio 3rd: Christopher Glynn, Peter Arce, John Nietzschman, Michael Morabito, Edward Wagner, John Lyons, Fred Portello, James Niebler, Michael Potter

ENGINE CO. 241

6630 3rd Avenue, Brooklyn

On February 1, 1896, the volunteer fire department of New Utrecht was replaced with Brooklyn Engine 41 and Ladder 13 of the paid department. They were located in a new house at 240 Bay Ridge Avenue. Ladder 13 was disbanded and became part of Engine 41 on April 15, 1898. The ladder truck was removed from service when Ladder 149 was placed in service at Engine 284 on May 15, 1914. The need for a ladder truck in Bay Ridge had been felt since 1914. Instead of organizing a new company, Ladder 109 was moved from 4th Avenue at 19th Street to Engine 241 on February 1, 1939. Both companies moved into new quarters at 6630 3rd Avenue on March 22, 1971. Engine 241's response area has some commercial businesses, but is mostly residential, with apartment buildings and two-family homes. Two members have died in the line of duty. One member has received a medal for bravery and four Unit Citations have been awarded to Engine 241.

1st: Michael Tobin, Stan Giammalvo, Joseph Del Grasso, Capt. Jerry Maloney, Lt. Robert Brandt, Peter Tracy, Patrick Barry 2nd: Dennis Grace, Eric Knudsen, James McCann, Eric Knutsen, James Schmidt, Jason Conelli, Christopher Conley, James Buff, Daniel Iadisernia 3rd: William O'Leary, Thomas Giardino, Thomas Love, Robert Desantis, Mark Solari, William Jennerich, Robert Maddalone

LADDER CO. 109

6630 3rd Avenue, Brooklyn

Ladder 9 was placed in service in the former quarters of Engine 1 at 633 4th Avenue on August 20, 1891. Ladder 1 had served this area before moving to Red Hook in 1872. This fast-growing area included residences and commercial buildings. Ladder 9's first apparatus was an 1891 LaFrance Hayes 75-foot aerial. In 1921, a new American LaFrance 75-foot aerial replaced the horses, the last ladder company to be motorized in Brooklyn. On February 1, 1939, Ladder 109 moved in with Engine 241 at 240 Bay Ridge Avenue in Bay Ridge. Both companies moved into new quarters on March 22, 1971, at 6630 3rd Avenue. Ladder 109's first-due area features apartment houses, private homes, a hospital and commercial and retail buildings. The current ladder truck is a 1994 Seagrave 100-foot rear-mount aerial. Ladder 109 has been awarded eight Unit Citations and 10 members have earned medals for heroism. One member has been killed while protecting the citizens of New York City.

1st: Michael Burns, Lt. James Shea, Lt. Frank Thurlow, Capt. John Molloy, Lt. James Young, Lt. Thomas Campanelli, Gerard Callahan 2nd: Timothy Butler, Joseph Pizzo, Robert Rivera, Andrew Hornbuckle, Jeffrey Palazzo, Joseph Flynn, James Matheos 3rd: Edward Prince, Joseph Arcuri, Dominick LaForgia, Joseph Kennedy, Joseph LaPointe, James Mullins, Gary DeBiase

ENGINE CO. 278

5011 7th Avenue, Brooklyn

Placed in service on March 20, 1913, Engine 278 is located at 5011 7th Avenue in the Sunset Park section of Brooklyn. As part of the Brooklyn expansion, it was located on top of the hill from Engine 201. The horses had problems pulling a heavy steamer up the hill, thus delaying the response. Engine 278 also serves the people on the south side of Greenwood Cemetery, a distance from Engine 228. This part of Brooklyn was being built up with many new brownstones. Battalion 40 has shared quarters with Engine 278 since December 11, 1917. Engine 278's first new rig was a 1912 American LaFrance second-size steamer with a Christie tractor. Today, Engine 278 responds with a 1998 Seagrave 1000-gpm pumper that they received on July 29, 1998. Two members have received medals for their bravery at fires. Engine 278 has earned four Unit Citations for their actions. Four members have lost their lives while protecting the citizens of New York.

1st: James Tozzo, Lt. Robert Lacey, Capt. John Henricksen, Lt. James Winters 2nd: Vincent Buonocore, George Pepe, Richard Paulan, Richard Vetland, John Scafidi, Robert Lodato, Peter Kohm 3rd: Gerald Coughlin, Michael Witkowski, Joseph Dunn, Scott Muldoon, Kevin McNamara, Michael Ricciardi

1st: Daniel Klein, Gregory Warnock, Lt. Dennis O'Berg, Lt. Brian Gorman, James McGuire, Robert Abiuso 2nd: Robert Adams, James Riches, Scott Armstrong, William Fitzgibbons, William Rohl, Larry Lee, Thomas Behan 3rd: Kevin Hogan, Michael Molloy, Kerry Walsh, Tim McConnell, Lt. Dave Johnson, Andrew Gilmore 4th: Robert Cameron, Kevin Anderson, Paul McManus, Victor Fiorella, Robert Gibson, Michael Falcone

LADDER CO. 114

5209 5th Avenue, Brooklyn

On September 15, 1897, Brooklyn placed Ladder 18 in service in new quarters at 5209 5th Avenue. Ladder 18 was re-numbered Ladder 14 on April 15, 1898. Ladder 14's first apparatus was a used 1889 LaFrance Hayes 75-foot aerial. A Christie front-wheel-drive tractor replaced the horses in 1916. Ladder 114's response area has a variety of occupancies, private homes, apartment houses, commercial buildings and retail stores, a hospital and the waterfront. During the 1970s, the Sunset Park area was taken over by drug dealers and Ladder 114 became one of the busiest ladder companies in the city. The citizens of the community started to fight back and by the 1980s, the drug dealers were gone and fire activity decreased. Today, Ladder 114 responds with a 1995 Seagrave 75-foot tower-ladder they received on January 24, 1997. The company has earned 12 Unit Citations and 16 members have received medals for their heroic actions, including one James Gordon Bennett Medal recipient. Three members have been killed in the line of duty.

ENGINE CO. 242 & RECUPERATION & CARE UNIT 5

9219 5th Avenue, Brooklyn

Brooklyn Engine 42 was organized in a new house built for them at 9219 5th Avenue. Brooklyn Ladder 14 was placed in service with them in the same house. Both companies replaced the volunteer department of New Utrecht on February 1, 1896. Engine 242 protected Fort Hamilton, which dated back to the War of 1812. Ladder 14 was disbanded as an individual company and became part of Engine 242 on April 15, 1898. This lasted until May 15, 1915, when Ladder 149 was organized at Engine 284. Engine 242 received its first motorized pumper, a new American LaFrance with a 700-gpm pump, on December 20, 1922. Satellite 3, part of the Super Pumper system, was placed in service with Engine 242 on October 1, 1965. It was relocated to Engine 330's quarters on December 30, 1975. Now quartered with Engine 242 is Recuperation and Care Unit 5, organized on July 1, 1996. This unit carries fans, blankets, ice water and other items for exhausted firefighters.

1st: Daniel Magrino, Michael Brancato, Michael Gargiso, Lt. Robert Picard, Lt. Michael McCormack, Donald Francomano, Mark Unrein *2nd:* James Harkins, John Imbesi, John Marsh, Michael Maiz, Michael Harty *3rd:* Paul Bednarczyk, Joseph McCormack, Joseph Miller, Mike Billotto, Anthony Regina *4th:* Thomas Buttaro, Thomas Zelios, Raymond Bartlett

1st: Anthony Rao, Peter Coyne, Kevin McCole, Andrew Graf, Joseph Dudley, Kevin Charley, Vincent Fiorentino, James Boylan, Charles Thompson, Stephen Jezycki, William Roesch, Michael Ellia, John Carlson, John Bongiorno *2nd:* Lt. Charles Cama, Lt. James Newman, Lt. Thomas Wilhelmsen, Lt. Kevin Lymn, Lt. Raymond Saxton, Joseph Larstana, Doug Mercereau, Mark Levine, Michael Abbruzzese, Walter Burtchell, Derek O'Brien, Jeffrey Sterner, Capt. Matthew MacKittrick, Lt. Gerard Campbell, BC Robert Brennan *3rd:* John Kroon, Salvatore Sciascia, Brian McBride, Gregg Stamler, Daniel Quirke, John Nastazio, Steven Conti, James Vitucci, John Mahoney, Paul Adamski, Daniel Lazzaro, James Tracey, William Curatolo, Joseph Vasta, Brian Mooney, Anthony D'Addessa, BC Martin Coyne, BC Wayne Lang, John Kirk

ENGINE CO. 243

8653 18th Avenue, Brooklyn

Engine 43, Ladder 15 and District Chief 12 were organized in a new firehouse at 8653 18th Avenue on February 1, 1896. These two companies replaced Liberty Ladder 1 of the New Utrecht Fire Department. The firehouse had two doors for the apparatus to exit and a lookout tower. It was the first Brooklyn house to have a hot water heater. The house was remodeled in 1930 with the removal of the lookout tower and smaller apparatus doors. On April 15, 1898, Ladder 15 was combined with Engine 43 to form one company. With the removal of the ladder truck on October 28, 1929, from Engine 243, it became Ladder 168. Engine 243's response area includes commercial and residential buildings. On April 20, 1922, Engine 243 received its first motorized apparatus, an American LaFrance 700-gpm pumper. Two members have received medals for bravery. Two Unit Citations have been awarded to the company. One member was killed when the apparatus collided with an asphalt truck in 1943.

LADDER CO. 168

8653 18th Avenue, Brooklyn

Ladder 168 was placed in service as Ladder 15 with Engine 43 of the Brooklyn Fire Department on February 1, 1896. They were part of the largest expansion of the BFD. During an eight-month period, they placed 24 engines, 13 ladder companies, one chemical engine and four district chiefs in service. Ladder 15 was disbanded and the apparatus assigned to Engine 43 on April 15, 1898. On October 18, 1929, Ladder 168 was placed in service with a 1929 American LaFrance 75-foot aerial ladder. The men assigned to Engine 243's ladder truck made up its first crew. Ladder 168 has been awarded eight Unit Citations and six members have been awarded medals for their heroic actions. One member, Firefighter Charles A. Merz, earned the James Gordon Bennett Medal for rescuing several trapped firemen in the basement of a department store on April 17, 1939. He was awarded the Dr. Harry M. Archer Medal in 1942 for the same rescue.

*Battalion 42 in with Engine Company 243 and Ladder Company 168.

1st: Thomas Wollack, Lt. Victor Pace, Lt. Edmund Cashen, BC Stephen Ternland, Capt. Joseph Maganza, Lt. John Oddo, Thomas Cann 2nd: Patrick Parisi, Christopher Mangels, Paul Rini, John Rosati, James Burns, David Disanto 3rd: Frank Connelly, Carmine Ancona, John Scupelliti, Radames Torres

ENGINE CO. 247
1336 60th Street, Brooklyn

Brooklyn annexed the town of New Utrecht and several other towns on May 3, 1894, doubling the size of the City. Brooklyn placed Engine 47 and Ladder 19 in service on February 1, 1896, in new quarters at 1336 60th Street. This firehouse and Engine 243's house are identical. Additionally, it was one of the first houses to have a hot water tank for the men's comfort. On May 15, 1914, Ladder 19 was disbanded and the ladder truck became part of Engine 247's equipment. The ladder truck was removed from Engine 247 when Ladder 149 was placed in service at Engine 284's quarters. Engine 247 moved into the motor age on November 29, 1922, with an American LaFrance 700-gpm pumping engine and hose wagon. During 1929, the firehouse was updated and repaired, with removal of the lookout tower, replacement of the two small apparatus doors with one larger door and installation of new plumbing throughout. Two members have received medals for rescues and the company has garnered one Unit Citation.

ENGINE CO. 284
1157 79th Street, Brooklyn

Engine 284 was placed in service in a grand house on November 27, 1913. The three-story firehouse, at 1157 79th Street, is located in a neighborhood of single- and two-family homes. Since the firehouse is a rather large structure for the area, the company earned the nickname of "The Castle on the Hill." When this house was built, the area was mostly marshland and just beginning to develop. The two-bay house also was built for a ladder company that was put in service as Ladder 149 on May 15, 1914. Assigned to Engine 284 since April 20, 1991, is Satellite 3, part of the Maxi Water System, which replaced the Super Pumper in 1982. Engine 284 responds with a 1988 Mack Ward 79 2000-gpm pumper. Two members have been killed in the line of duty. One medal has been awarded to a member of Engine 284 for his heroic actions.

1st: James Dimeo, Lt. Robert Pugliese, Capt. Michael Steinman, Lt. John Giunta, Lt. James Katen 2nd: Glenn Ahlquist, Raymond Hauber, Anthony Borsellega, John Marchetta 3rd: Daniel Lettis, Joseph LaPolla, Vincent Coco, Edward Learning

LADDER CO. 149
1161 79th Street, Brooklyn

Ladder 149 went into service on May 15, 1914, in the quarters of Engine 284 at 1161 79th Street. They went in service with a used ladder truck, but on October 15, 1915, they received a new 1915 Mack City Service ladder truck. Ladder 149 replaced the horse-drawn ladders of Engines 241, 242 and 247. In the beginning, the area was mostly rural, but as it was being developed, large private homes were built, along with apartment buildings and commercial structures. Today, the area is made up of well-kept private homes and many stores and churches. On July 23, 1973, Ladder 149 received its first tower, a used 1973 model Mack. Three members have earned medals. The company has been awarded one Unit Citation. Two members have lost their lives in the performance of their duties. Ladder 149 rolls with a 1994 FWD/Saulsbury 75-foot tower-ladder.

1st: Steven Richards, Matt Larstanna, Lt. Stephen Rossiter, Paul Mulvey, Bill Ritter 2nd: Timothy Day, Fred Marsilla, John Gleave, John Galan, John Sini, Larry Ciarcia 3rd: Jake Pisano, Jesse Correale, Mike DePaola, Joe Cilento, Tim Tichenor, Dan Conklin, Jim Imbro

ENGINE CO. 330

2312 65th Street, Brooklyn

This Bensonhurst Engine Company was organized on April 28, 1965, at 2312 65th Street. This new company was put in service to cut down on response time in the East Bensonhurst area. A medal for valor was awarded to Firefighter John P. Fassari in 1987. Engine 330 has been awarded five Unit Citations as well. From 1975 to 1981, Engine 330 operated with Satellite 3—a hose wagon with 3000 feet of five-inch hose and a large stang gun—part of the Super Pumper system. In 1982, the Super Pumper was disbanded and Engine 330 received a 2000-gpm engine to operate with the Satellite. In 1991, the 2000-gpm engine and Satellite were relocated to Engine 284. Engine 330 has a response area of single and multiple dwellings, storefronts and two elevated subways. Engine 330 currently operates with a 1989 Mack 1000-gpm engine and is quartered with the "65th Street Bravest," Ladder 172.

1st: James Stoffers, Lt. Roderick Lewis, Capt. Christopher Scalone, Lt. Joseph Procopio, Lt. Dominic Genovese, Camillo Messina *2nd:* Stephen Lombardi, Mark Weber, Paul Collica, Joseph Dipierro, Frank Pepe, John Stringile *3rd:* Arturo Fioribello, John Diodato, Michael Passantino, Joseph Livolsi, Michael Bernstein, Thomas Ferranola, Michael Kennedy *4th:* Christopher Hyland, Norman Schlosser, Nicholas Barbieri

1st: Michael Behette, Lt. James Sammarco, Capt. John Stafford, Lt. John Reilly, Michael Pietracatella, Richard Ferro *2nd:* Russell Weissheier, Joseph Edrehi, Anthony Ciero, Lt. Dennis Munday, Michael Laurinaitis, Marc Bruni, Robert Fitting, Douglas Miller, Joseph Cioffi *3rd:* James Ventre, Gene Baginski, John Maguire, Christopher Bruno, Christopher Storch, James Sechiano, Mark Connelly, Michael Bacigalupo, Stephen McDade, Frank Denver, Michael Rehberg

LADDER CO. 172

2318 65th Street, Brooklyn

Ladder 172 went into service with Engine 330 on April 28, 1965. Located at 2318 65th Street, they filled a large void without ladder coverage, as did Engine 330. This house was in the works as early as 1940, but was delayed because of World War II. Ladder 172 went into service with a 1938 FWD 85-foot wood aerial and a 1947 Ward LaFrance tractor. They received their first tower-ladder in 1971 with a new Mack. Today, they have a 1999 Seagrave Saulsbury 95-foot tower-ladder. Their first-due area includes many apartment buildings, as well as private homes. They also have a large shopping and retail district. Three members have been awarded medals and the company has earned three Unit Citations. On October 22, 1965, Lieutenant Robert Niebling, of Battalion 41, lost his life while covering in Ladder 172.

ENGINE CO. 245

2929 West 8th Avenue, Brooklyn

Brooklyn placed Engine 45 in service on December 9, 1895, in the former quarters of Atlantic Engine 1 of the Coney Island Fire Department at 2919 West 8th Street. The City replaced the old volunteer house with a new brick house next door in 1904. Because of Coney Island's remoteness and a heavy fire load, a second Engine 245 was placed in service on December 22, 1904. The second section of Engine 245 was renamed Engine 326 on August 16, 1939, and disbanded on May 8, 1955. The 1904 house was replaced on July 23, 1971, on the same site. Initially, Engine 245 was not a busy company. However, a fire fought on May 26, 1899, burned nine blocks along the beach. Engine 245 served at many Borough Calls in this area. Two members of Engine 245 have been killed while protecting the people of Coney Island. Seven Unit Citations have been awarded to the Company and two members have earned medals.

1st: Kenneth Grof, Joseph Callahan, Lt. Donald Brown, Capt. Glenn Hawkins, Lt. Thomas O'Conner, Lt. Michael Capasso, Donald Halikias, Joseph DeGaetano *2nd:* Lt. Salvatore Brillante, Frank Giordano, John Laureno, Richard Danetti, Capt. Luke Lynch, Robert Wallen, John Scanlon, Alan Callahan, Steven Socci, Lt. Michael Massucci *3rd:* Brian Claro, Paul Cortes, Steven Francese, Sean Murphy, Michael Nasta, Sean Hanley, Louis Demontreux, Wayne Goehring

LADDER CO. 161

2929 West 8th Street, Brooklyn

Ladder 161 was placed in service in the quarters of Engine 245 at 2929 West 8th Street on November 5, 1927. Combination Engine 244's ladder truck was placed out of service and Ladder 161 was placed in service. Their first rig was a 1927 Seagrave 75-foot aerial. During the heyday of Coney Island, the beach resort was jam-packed with visitors to the beach and amusement parks. The wood buildings of the amusement parks were packed tightly together and a fire in one would spread to the adjoining buildings very quickly. Ladder 161 has responded to many of these conflagrations—Luna Park, the 23rd Street fire and the Bathhouses. On July 24, 1968, Ladder 161 moved into the former quarters of Engine 244, while the old house on East 8th Street was torn down and rebuilt. On August 16, 1971, Ladder 161 moved into new quarters at the former site of the old house. The company has been awarded 14 Unit Citations. Eight members have garnered medals.

1st: Michael Rizzi, Thomas Geiger, Lt. Donald Kelly, Capt. James Kelly, Lt. Richard McCluskey, Lt. John Petersen, Michael Feldman, Layne Plompen 2nd: Xavier Tufano, Emil Albano, Peter Archer, Patrick Gibbons, Walter Clark, Richard McClean, Anthony Nicosia, Anthony Petrarca, John Knutsen, Gary Sally, James Butler 3rd: John McMullen, Stephen Stroh, Richard DeSimone, John Iammatteo, William Pepitone, Anthony Buzzeo, Anthony Guida, John Emma, Albert Barry, Joseph Lennon

1st: Kevin Quinn, Lt. John Rementeria, Lt. Louis Terrusa, Capt. Michael Devoy, Lt. Michael Thompson, Lt. Frank Vultaggio, Lt. John Errico, Salvatore Antignano 2nd: Michael Renert, Andrew Ciarlo, Vincent D'Orio, Edward Fastaia, Steve Johnston, Michael Egan, James Caddell, Joseph Siano, Enrico Boletti 3rd: Edward Fitzpatrick, James Ervolino, John O'Keefe, Thomas McCandless, Edward Cowan, Gregory Castellano, Timothy Lockwood

ENGINE CO. 246

2732 East 11th Street, Brooklyn

Brooklyn Engine 46 and Ladder 17 were organized on December 9, 1895, in the former quarters of the Sheepshead Bay Fire Department at 2728 East 23rd Street. Ladder 17 was disbanded and placed under the control of the captain of Engine 46 on April 15, 1898. On December 20, 1904, a new, three-bay house was opened at 2731 East 23rd Street. Because of the large area covered by Engine 246 and the distances traveled, a second engine was added to Engine 246 on the same day the new house opened. At the turn of the century, Sheepshead Bay was a big resort area, similar to Coney Island, and the extra engine was needed. On August 16, 1939, the second section of Engine 246 was renamed Engine 327 and disbanded on July 16, 1960, when Engine 246 moved into new quarters at 2732 East 11th Street. One member died in the performance of his duty. Three medals have been awarded for bravery and one Unit Citation has been earned.

LADDER CO. 169

2732 East 11th Street, Brooklyn

Brooklyn Ladder 17 was placed in service with Engine 46 on December 8, 1895. Their first quarters were leased from the former volunteer department of Sheepshead Bay Fire Department. On April 15, 1898, Ladder 17 was made part of Engine 46 by the FDNY. Other than the area around Sheepshead Bay, the district was mostly marsh and swamps. In December of 1904, Combination Engine 246 was made into a double engine company and moved into new quarters at 2731 East 23rd Street. Combination Engine 246 had a very large response area, sometimes running in with Engines 255 and 257. Ladder 169 was organized on October 18, 1929, with a new American LaFrance 75-foot aerial. On July 16, 1960, Engine 246 and Ladder 169 moved into new quarters at 2732 East 11th Street. Ladder 169 has been awarded five Unit Citations and three members have been honored with medals for heroic acts. The current apparatus is a 1999 Seagrave 100-foot rearmount aerial.

1st: Robert Benvenuto, Richard Andersen, Lt. John Koch, Lt. Ralph Pepe, Capt. John Plant, Lt. Michael Hyland, Daniel Gerrity, William Ellis 2nd: Stephen Salzano, Thomas Deangelis, Juan Medina, Anthony Matteo, Christopher Banker, Gabriel Buonincontri, George Farinacci, John Kroczynski, Gary Lyons, Roy Nichols 3rd: William Graham, William Davison, Darren Jacobs, Robert Orlando, Richard Quinn, Donald Wallace, Michael Colgan, Robert Crimmins, Paul Francomano, Robert Colligan, Fred Rissland

ENGINE CO. 253
2429 86th Street, Brooklyn

Brooklyn Engine 53 and Ladder 24 were placed in service on February 1, 1896, in new quarters built for them at 2429 86th Street, in the growing Bensonhurst area of Brooklyn. On April 15, 1898, Ladder 24 was disbanded and became part of Engine 253's equipment. While the "el" was being built along 86th Street, Engine 253 moved to temporary quarters on the corner of Harway Street and 25th Avenue on September 7, 1915. This building was nothing more than a stable and Engine 253 remained there until December 31, 1918, before moving back to the old location. On August 18, 1920, Engine 253 received a 1919 American LaFrance 700-gpm pumper. Engine 253 lost its ladder truck on October 18, 1929, when Ladder 161 and Ladder 168 were placed in service. Engine 253 is using a 1997 Seagrave 1000-gpm pumper. The company has earned nine Unit Citations and one member has earned a medal. One member was killed in the line of duty.

1st: Lt. John Crowe, John Zarrella, Edward Gormley, Frank Donato, Capt. Edward Del Balso, Michael Carelli, John Falconite, James Gillespie, Michael Wood 2nd: Edward Hughes, Patrick Kearney, James Hyland, Charles Szoke, Howard Flugmacher, Frank Somma, Gerard Finegan, Mark Lotito, Lt. Timothy O'Leary

1st: Brian Ahr, Lt. Joseph Carlsen, Robert Dwyer, Vicent Piccolino, Edward Henry, Michael Bernstein, Ralph Tufano, Gerard Fitzgerald, Michael Olsen, Salvatore Lupia, Capt. Daniel O'Donnell 2nd: Patrick Keegan, Joseph Flack, Jaime Resker, Ryan Moriarty, Pasquale Tesi, John Mahoney, Robert Treiland, Lt. Leonard Sottile, Daniel Lind, Charles Barraco, Vincent LaMalfa, John Keenan, Matthew MacKittrick, Tellef Tellefsen, Steven Asaro, Thomas McDonald, Thomas Harty, James Ciano, Kevin Dooley, James Passadino, James Hurson, Michael Ostermann, Lt. Michael Carletti, Capt. Vincent Lyons, James Cahill, Joseph Walz, Thomas Marino, Joseph Kammer, Anthony Gaglia

ENGINE CO. 318
2510 Neptune Avenue, Brooklyn

Engine 318 was placed in service in new quarters at 2510 Neptune Avenue on November 1, 1929. A new 1929 American LaFrance 700-gpm pumper was assigned to the company on opening day. Located in the western end of Coney Island, it has responded to and fought some of the area's biggest fires. In 1932, 172 buildings were burned when children set fire to rubbish under the boardwalk. The Luna Park Amusement fire in 1944 destroyed most of the park. The area protected by Engine 318 features high-rise apartments, housing projects, single-family homes, the beach and the gated community of Seagate, with its mostly large private homes. Although not a fire-related duty, Engine 318 always is involved when a nor'easter is blowing. Seagate floods with high winds and waves, usually washing a house away. Engine 318 is assigned a 1998 Seagrave 1000-gpm pumper.

LADDER CO. 166
2510 Neptune Avenue, Brooklyn

Ladder 166 and Engine 318 were placed in service on the western half of Coney Island on November 1, 1929, where they have been ever since. Organized in new quarters at 2510 Neptune Avenue, Ladder 166 was assigned a new 1929 American LaFrance 75-foot aerial. Located outside the amusement areas, they protected mostly large apartment houses, housing projects and private dwellings. Several years after being placed in service, Ladder 166 fought one of its largest fires in 1932. Children set fire to rubbish under the Boardwalk and the wind blowing off the beach spread the fire over four city blocks, destroying 172 buildings. In 1944, they responded to a fire that wiped out half of the Luna Park amusement area. Ladder 166 has been awarded 11 Unit Citations and nine members have received medals for acts of bravery. One member was killed in the line of duty. Today, the company responds with a 1991 Seagrave 100-foot rear-mount aerial.

43rd Battalion

DIVISION 11

Robert Bonistalli, James Woods, Leon Morris, DC Charles Blaich, DC Philip Burns, DC David Corcoran, DC John Kelly, Lt. John Henricksen, Edward Cooper

BATTALION 28

BC William Conway, BC John Linkletter, Kevin Gillen

BATTALION 31

BC Gerard Canavan, BC Robert Cornwall, Michael Shea, BC Edward Collins, BC Brian O'Boyle

BATTALION 32

1st: BC John Podlucky, BC Robert Stock, BC James Jackson, BC James McGrath, BC Arthur Lakiotes, BC Charles Gussmann 2nd: John Scharfenberg, Robert Mulligan, Paul Brincat, Charles Migan, Joseph Williams

BATTALION 35

1st: BC George Eysser, BC John Dillon, BC Michael Burke, BC Joseph Bryant, BC Robert Turner 2nd: Chris Steidinger, Angelo Blanda, John Kolb, Samuel Giamo

BATTALION 48

1st: BC Richard Dailey, BC Frank Conguista, BC Peter Begley, BC Thomas Carrig 2nd: Richard Lang, Michael Bocchino, Michael Vindigni

BATTALION 57

Vladimir Kowal, BC Roderick O'Connor, BC Dennis Cross, BC Michael Canty, BC Richard DiPadova, BC Edward Cashman, Lois Mungay

28th Battalion

1st: Thomas Smyth, William Drewes, Lt. Lawrence Famigietti, Lt. Edward Coakley, Capt. Edward Baggott, Lt. Robert Mannina, James McGee 2nd: Andrew Szabo, Reginald Bonner, Lawrence Vitiello, Casey Colwell, Andrew Harris, James Giordano 3rd: Daniel Mugan, Andrew Mussler, Joseph Kadillak, Peter Walsh, Alfred Francis, Michael Arbuiso, Phillip Reilly, Joseph Monahan, Ronald Stortz

ENGINE CO. 206
1201 Grand Street, Brooklyn

Engine 206 started as Brooklyn Engine 6 on September 19, 1869, at 14 High Street, in the former volunteer quarters of Atlantic Hose 1. On August 1, 1892, the house was closed and Engine 6 was moved to new quarters at 189 Pearl Street. This new house was a block and a half away from Engine 207 at 245 Pearl Street. Times changed and Engine 206 was moved to the Brooklyn/Queens boarder at 1196 Metropolitan Avenue on January 1, 1915. When opened, the house also was lettered for Ladder 133, which was supposed to be placed in service on the same day, but never was. On December 6, 1976, Engine 206 moved into its fourth home, at 1201 Grand Street. Sharing quarters with Engine 206 is Foam Unit 206, which was placed in service on June 17, 1978. One member lost his life in the performance of his duty. The 1904 Brooklyn Citizens Medal was awarded to a member of Engine 206. The company has earned four Unit Citations.

ENGINE CO. 218
650 Hart Street, Brooklyn

Engine 218 has been located in two different houses. They were put in service on November 30, 1877, at 112 Seigel Street in the Williamsburg section. The next move was on December 1, 1887, to new quarters at 650 Hart Street in Bushwick. Ladder 8, now 108, was placed in service in Engine 18's old house. They received their first motorized pumper on July 19, 1917, a new American LaFrance 700-gpm pumper. Engine 218 has a mixed response area of commercial, residential and factory buildings. Engine 218 saw a lot of work when Bushwick was burning in the early 1970s. One of Engine 218's more unusual fire responses occurred during the mid-1970s: the Federal Government came to Bushwick for a burn test of wood-frame buildings. The Government set fire to two buildings which, in turn, set fire to several blocks, going for another multiple-alarm fire. Engine 218 has earned 19 Unit Citations and two members have received medals. Three members have died in the performance of their duty.

28th Battalion

1st: Thomas McCann, Timothy Murray, Capt. John McEneaney, Lt. Richard Steyert, Ronald Pinaud, Christopher Turner 2nd: John Wolfe, Paul Morongello, Steven Rios, Joseph Hatzelman, Richard LaFauci, Kenneth Stumpf, Robert Urgo, Joseph Daly 3rd: William Newport, Conway McMahon, Barry Kipp, Richard Hofmann, Richard Mercado, Ronald Blair, John Gibbons, William Day, Daniel Newman

1st: Lt. John Abbruzzese, Lt. Clifford Jackson 2nd: James Pfeiffer, Stephen Schmittgall, Richard Smith, Martin McNamara 3rd: John Wallace, William Luciani, Victor Bruno, Chris Balducci, Brian Dillon, Stephen Cristello, Robert Baran 4th: Gregory Quinn, Jeffrey Vought, Thomas Gander, Vincent Dour

ENGINE CO. 237
43 Morgan Avenue, Brooklyn

Brooklyn's Engine 37 was placed in service on July 15, 1895, in new quarters at 43 Morgan Avenue. Also placed in service on the same day was Engine 38 in Greenpoint. Both of these companies were added because of the growing number of commercial buildings in the area. Engine 237, located between East Williamsburg and Bushwick, has a unique response area. To the north of quarters are commercial occupancies, with varying kinds of industries, and to the south are mostly residential wood-frame houses. Engine 237's first motorized apparatus was a 1922 American LaFrance 700-gpm pumper, delivered on November 6, 1922. During the arson years of the late 1960s, Engine 237 was kept busy to the point that Squad 7 had to be relocated there on July 15, 1964. On July 8, 1966, Squad 7 was disbanded to reorganize Engine 232 in the Brownsville section of Brooklyn. One member has been killed in the line of duty. The company has been awarded 12 Unit Citations and one member has received a medal.

ENGINE CO. 238
205 Greenpoint Avenue, Brooklyn

Engine 38 was placed in service at 176 Norman Avenue on July 15, 1895. This area of Greenpoint contains many plants and factories. Gasoline storage tanks and gas works make this area very combustible. The wood-frame houses are built one next to each other and some homes have a second tenement in the rear of the first. The area is well kept and there was little fire activity during the arson years. On November 2, 1972, Engine 238 and Ladder 106 moved into new quarters at 205 Greenpoint Avenue. Engine 215 also was included in this move, but was disbanded on September 15, 1972. Eleven Unit Citations adorn the walls of the firehouse and three members of the company have been awarded medals. Six members of Engine 238 have been killed in the line of duty, including three who were overcome and died from jute fumes (hemp rope) in 1904 and two who were killed (with four other firemen from different companies) in a 1962 building collapse.

1st: Lt. Glen Wilkinson, Capt. Chris McKnight, Lt. Charles Wegener, Leonard Sisco 2nd: Robert Crinnion, Christian Daley, Michael Balfe, Chris Sakellarion, William Romaka, Stanley Trojanouski, Robert Florio, John McCurry 3rd: William Gaughan, Pete Grossmann, Dennis Wirbickas, Michael Morrow, Kevin Flaherty, Vincent Cartafalsa, Anthony Citera

1st: Raymond Mayr, Lt. Michael Kenney, Lt. Kevin Griffith, Capt. Kenneth Whelan, Lt. Gerald Duffy, Robert Rametta 2nd: Chris Chakwin, John Burke, Paul Nugent, Mario Polit, John Szczech, Kenneth Bohan, Domenic Coribello 3rd: Paul Ruckdeschel, James Galatro, Paul Tokarski, Robert Varese, Peter Quinn, Dermot Kearns

LADDER CO. 106
205 Greenpoint Avenue, Brooklyn

Ladder 6 was the last ladder company placed in service by Brooklyn on September 15, 1869. It was located in the former quarters of Excelsior Ladder 4 at 124 Greenpoint Avenue. Ladder 6 went in service with a ladder truck from the volunteer department. Motorization came to 106 on December 16, 1914, when they received a new American LaFrance 65-foot aerial. Ladder 106 has been in three different firehouses on the same site. The original house was built in 1867 and replaced in 1880 with a standard Brooklyn house. On January 1, 1910, Ladder 106 moved into its third house on this site. This house was closed and Ladder 106 moved into new quarters with Engine 238 on September 5, 1972. Ladder 106 has responded to some major fires—especially at the turn of the century—with the oil and gas works along the East River and Newtown Creek. Ladder 106 has earned 15 Unit Citations. Ten members have garnered medals. Four members have been killed in the line of duty.

ENGINE CO. 271

394 Himrod Street, Brooklyn

Engine 271 was placed in service on September 23, 1908, as Engine 171. The firehouse they share with Ladder 124 is located at 394 Himrod Street. This firehouse has a wall between the engine and truck. When built, this was the style, combining companies in one building, but each with separate quarters. Over the years, many houses were built like this, but this is the only one that has not breached the wall or combined housewatches. Engine 271 was right in the middle of the action during the 1970s. On July 18, 1977, Engine 271 was first-due to a fully involved, five-story vacant warehouse. They operated alone and protected exposures for several minutes before any other company arrived. The fire spread to exposures 2 and 3, destroying several frame homes, a church and the original fire building. For this work, Engine 271 earned a Unit Citation, one of 16 Citations accumulated in their history. One member has been killed in the performance of his duty.

1st: John Sassano, Tom Murphy, Lt. William Fitchett, Capt. Michael Wilkinson, Lt. Reinaldo Natal, Joseph Cavalcante, Timmy Noon 2nd: Paul Kanapes, Joseph Lavin, James Smagala, Chris Ferro, Dominick Carone, Dennis Valsamedis 3rd: Frank Scarpa, Frank Tortorella, George Walker, John Heegan, Gary Tracy

1st: Lt. Robert Hannon, Lt. John Fortunato, Lt. James McDermott, Patrick Schweiger 2nd: Robert Giuglianotti, Brian Reehil, Patrick Sheridan, Michael Killoran, Vincent Brindisi, Edward Checchia, Thomas Hughes, Patrick Giblin, Richard Hoffmann, Kevin Gillen, VanDorn Johnson, Brian Kelly, John Regler, Scott Riegel, Robert Roscoe, David Steinhauer, Craig Santandrea, Kevin McGinty, Brian Johnston Banner: John Finn, Thomas Kempf

LADDER CO. 124

394 Himrod Street, Brooklyn

Ladder 124 was the last truck company placed in service in Brooklyn with the old numbering system. Organized as Ladder 74 on September 23, 1908, it is located with Engine 271 at 394 Himrod Street. This firehouse has a wall down the center and is two separate houses. It is the only house that has not cut a hole through the walls. The first ladder truck assigned to 124 was a used 1900 LaFrance 85-foot aerial. A 1915 front-wheel-drive tractor replaced the horses that pulled the 1910 LaFrance 65-foot aerial. Ladder 124 has been a very busy company, especially during the 1970s. Just a few blocks from the Queens border, half of its response area includes wood-frame homes and brownstones. It has a large commercial area of factories and many retail stores. The company has been awarded 29 Unit Citations and 19 members have received medals for heroism. Three members have been killed in the performance of their duty.

ENGINE CO. 207

172 Tillary Street, Brooklyn

Engine 207 was placed in service on September 15, 1869, as Engine 7 of the Brooklyn Department. Its first home was in the former quarters of Protector Engine 6, a volunteer company that dates back to 1825. On May 1, 1946, Engine 207 moved into the former quarters of Rescue 2 and the old Headquarters Building, at 365 Jay Street, of the BFD. When it was opened as Headquarters for Brooklyn in 1892, it had no companies responding from the building. Engine 207 moved into new quarters at 172 Tillary Street on December 22, 1971. On October 6, 1983, the last alarm given by the old telegraph system was sent to Engine 207. The box sent out was Box 458, Brooklyn Borough Hall, Court and Joralemon Streets that, just like Engine 205, ended an era that went back to 1869 in Brooklyn and 1865 in Manhattan. Three members of Engine 207 have paid the Supreme Sacrifice with their lives. Four members have earned medals for bravery and two Unit Citations have been awarded to the company.

1st: Robert Ventriglia, Lt. Thomas Gogarty, Capt. Abraham Spector, Lt. Kevin Nerney, James Brennan 2nd: Kevin O'Neill, Edward Puccio, Thomas Corrigan, Edward O'Neil, Mathew Dwyer

LADDER CO. 110
172 Tillary Street, Brooklyn

Brooklyn organized Ladder 10 on August 1, 1891, with a new 1890 LaFrance Hayes 75-foot aerial. The new quarters—one of three identical houses—was located at 264 State Street in downtown Brooklyn. They moved in with Engine 207 at 365 Jay Street on June 26, 1949. A super house was built for Engine 207, Ladder 110, the Super Pumper and Super Tender at 172 Tillary Street. Ladder 110 was the last of the four companies to move in on June 12, 1972. In 1918, a 1918 American LaFrance 65-foot aerial was assigned to the company, replacing the horses. The first metal aerial, a 1948 Seagrave 85-footer was assigned to Ladder 110 on March 19, 1948. Today, they respond with a 1994 Seagrave 100-foot rear-mount aerial. The company has earned 13 Unit Citations and 11 members have received medals. Two members were killed in the line of duty. A third member, Firefighter Kevin C. Kane, was killed on September 13, 1991, and is remembered each year with the Kevin C. Kane Medal.

1st: Lt. Louis Napoli, Lt. Charles Daly, Capt. Emilio Longo, Lt. Robert Pav 2nd: Paul Mitchell, Thomas O'Brien, Robert Kelly, John Watt, Chris Gunn, James Lang, Scott Maraio, Bruce Delgiorno, Matt Mills, Mike McClelland, Victor Ruzicka 3rd: Ken Wade, Ed Martin, Mike Brown, Matt Ferris, Chris Jensen, Steve Klein, Carlos Font, David Rodriguez, Don Williams, Brian O'Donnell

ENGINE CO. 210
160 Carlton Avenue, Brooklyn

Engine 210 has been located at 160 Carlton Avenue since being placed in service on September 15, 1869. They were placed in the former quarters of Continental Engine 9. Like all of the volunteer houses that the paid department moved into, this one was rebuilt in 1912. On April 15, Engine 210 moved into leased quarters at 189 Vanderbilt Avenue and moved into their current house on October 7, 1913. Engine 210's response area includes a variety of buildings and occupancies, brownstones, housing projects, commercial buildings, factories and the Brooklyn Navy Yard. One of the worst fires to which Engine 210 responded was aboard the aircraft carrier Constellation in December 1960. This fire killed 50 and injured more than 300 construction workers while the carrier was being built. Several days before this, Engine 210 had responded to a plane crash that killed 134 people at Sterling Place and 7th Avenue. The company has been awarded six Unit Citations and two medals—the Fire College Medal in 1920 and the Third Alarm Association Medal in 1971.

1st: Paul Yodice, Lt. Tom Farrell, Lt. Hector Colon, Patrick Quinn 2nd: Andrew Burns, Thomas Cappiello, Bob Labas, James Knaver, Daniel Woods, Michael Brodbeck, Robert Cristadoro, Shaun Logan, Bill Smith 3rd: Thomas Mangus, Vincent Mastropasqua, James Corollo, Kevin Flood, Hermenio Rodriguez, Nicholas Sasso

ENGINE CO. 211
26 Hooper Street, Brooklyn

The paid department was extended to the Eastern District on September 15, 1869. Engine 11, now 211, first occupied the home of Victory Engine 13 at 173 Clymer Street. During 1888, Engine 211 moved to 166 Clymer Street and new quarters. This new building was torn down and rebuilt in 1909. On May 1, 1910, Engine 211 moved from 190 Clymer Street, temporary quarters, to new quarters on the same site as the old house. When Engine 251's house was closed and torn down, they moved in with Engine 211 on November 24, 1941. Engines 211 and 251 and Ladder 119 moved into a temporary building at 26 Hooper Street on May 24, 1944. Engine 251 was disbanded on November 1, 1946, but Engine 211 has remained at Hooper Street. Their first-due district is a mix of commercial buildings, tenements and the waterfront. Three members have earned medals, including a James Gordon Bennett Medal in 1935. Eight Unit Citations for teamwork have been awarded to Engine 211.

1st: William Corsello, Capt. Steven Zaderiko, Lt. Thomas Burns, Lt. John Shoemaker 2nd: Peter Laplace, Hon. Chief Norman Posnick, Anthony Primus, Michael Rossello, James Rosas, Wilfred Vasquez, Michael Walsh, David Lewis, Sr. 3rd: Matthew Beatty, Edward Kuhrt, Mario Lopez, Frank Lopesti, Ralph Caruso, Victor Cantelmo, Theodore Trombettas

LADDER CO. 119
26 Hooper Street, Brooklyn

Placed in service on June 8, 1901, Ladder 69 was quartered with Engine 251 at 47/48 Washington Avenue in the Brooklyn Navy Yard. It received a new LaFrance Hayes 85-foot aerial. On November 24, 1941, the firehouse was closed, torn down and a new Navy dry dock was built. Ladder 119 relocated to the quarters of Engine 210 at 160 Carlton Avenue. This location was unsuitable and temporary quarters—a large warehouse—were located at 26 Hooper Street, just outside the gate of the Navy Yard. On May 18, 1944, Engines 211, 251 and Ladder 119 moved in. The Super Pumper and Super Tender were placed in these temporary quarters in 1965 and moved out in 1972. The Department Photographer makes his nighttime quarters here also. In 1965, Ladder 119 received a 1962 Mack Margirus 146-foot aerial. On April 11, 1969, Ladder 119 received a new Mack 75-foot tower-ladder, the first one for Brooklyn. The company has earned 12 Unit Citations and six members have received medals.

1st: Thaddius Stanowicz, Lt. William Gaffney, Lt. William Bach, Patrick Sorger 2nd: Matthew Corrigan, Hon. Chief Norman Posnick, Richard Buckheit, Kevin Hannafin, Joseph Esposito, Lt. Peter Salatino, Patrick Hayden, Vito Berretta, Arthur Riccio, Edward Miller, Frank Corono 3rd: Paul Sarubbi, Mike Haberlack, Domenic Mushello, Steven Sharp, Frank Sweeney, Paul Maguire, Fred O'Neill, Daniel Hall

1st: Pete Culkin, Pete Chiodo, Lt. Robert Gleeson, Capt. William Carew, Lt. Matthew Nelson, William Clark, Brian McAleese 2nd: Dave DeRubbio, Anthony Sutera, Robert Unger, Matthew Jacoby, Thomas Casatelli 3rd: Mike Mason, David Arce, Tom Klonowski, Stan Smagala, Gerard Scarnato

ENGINE CO. 226
409 State Street, Brooklyn

Located in Downtown Brooklyn, Engine 226 was placed in service on January 9, 1889, in new quarters at 409 State Street where they have remained. Engine 226 filled the gap between Engines 205 and 204 in the downtown area. With the number of stores and other commercial establishments in the area, Engine 226 became one of Brooklyn's busiest companies for many years. In 1898, they were the third busiest Engine in Brooklyn with 200 runs. When first placed in service, Engine 226 received a spare steamer before receiving a new 1890 Amoskeag second-size steamer. Engine 226's first motorized pumper was a 1919 American LaFrance with a 700-gpm pump, which they received on May 26, 1919. Two members of Engine 226 have been killed in the performance of their duty. Four members have earned medals for bravery and four Unit Citations have been awarded to the Company. One of the Unit Citations was for operations at the World Trade Center bombing in 1993.

1st: Lt. Leo Fragapano, Capt. Terrance Sweeney, Lt. Thomas Calkin, Lt. Clarence McClean, Lt. Cosmo Romeo 2nd: Adolpho Otano, Anthony Gerrera, Mike Kuper, Anthony Catapano, David Coleman, Vincent Anderson, Anthony Reinecke, Michael Mahony, Kevin Thurlow, Robert Spadaro 3rd: Robert Norris, Albert Nocella, Robert O'Neill, Robert Clarke, Paul Brincat, Maurice Scarinci, Mark Loftus, Kevin Zaneski

ENGINE CO. 202
31 Richards Street, Brooklyn

The Brooklyn Fire Department originally organized Engine 2 on September 15, 1869. Engine 2's dock area was a picturesque assortment of three- and four-masted ships. The Red Hook section is home to many factories and warehouses and today, several large housing projects. Engine 202 always has been a busy company. Engine 202's first location was in the former quarters of Hope Hose Company 9 at Van Brunt and Hamilton Streets. This small, cramped house was not suited to the Department's needs and larger and more comfortable accommodations were built for this company. The new house was opened on March 1, 1872, at 199 Van Brunt Street with Ladder 101. This was Brooklyn's first house built for the paid department. This building served Red Hook until 1960. Both Engine 202 and Ladder 101 moved to 31 Richards Street on March 10. The members of Engine 202 have earned two Unit Citations and one member has received a medal. During its history, Engine 202 has had five members killed in the line of duty.

LADDER CO. 101

31 Richards Street, Brooklyn

Ladder 101 was placed in service on September 15, 1869, as Ladder 1 of the Brooklyn Fire Department. They were located in the former quarters of Degraw Ladder 4 on 19th Street, just west of 4th Avenue. The first rig assigned to Ladder 1 was an unknown type ladder truck from the volunteers. Located in what was southern Brooklyn, most of their runs were to the north, along the waterfront. Their house was unsuitable for a fire company and a new location was selected. A new building for both Engine 2 and Ladder 1 opened on March 1, 1872. Motorization came to Ladder 101 on July 17, 1917, with a used 1914 American LaFrance 65-foot aerial. New quarters again were built for Ladder 101 and Engine 202 at 31 Richards Street and they moved in on March 10, 1960. Ladder 101 has received six Unit Citations. Three members have earned medals for bravery. Two members have died in the line of duty.

1st: Lt. Thomas Pigott, Lt. Joseph Gullickson, Capt. Thomas Giordano, Lt. Michael Del Grosso 2nd: John Scharfenberg, Edward Davis, Robert Mulligan, Thomas Kennedy, Gerard Hall, Gary Box, Joseph Farinacci, Joseph Williams, Charles Marshall, Brian Cannizzaro 3rd: Matthew Nevins, Arthur Fitzpatrick, Anthony Corsaro, Thomas Gannon, Raymond Giovanniello, Ronald Kingsley, Michael O'Gorman, Salvatore Calabro

1st: Lt. Lawrence Sloan, Lt. Christopher Green, Capt. Daniel O'Gara, Lt. Paul DiGeorgio 2nd: Gregory Garaizar, Richard Puricelli, Thomas Westhoff, Sean Danis, Gary Ziegler, Michael Curly, Michael McKenna, Timothy Kenny, Charles Molluzzo, Steven Murphy 3rd: Richard Eggstein, Jovica Stojanovic, Gary Mancini, Edward Rodriguez, Mark Lavardera, Steven Holihan, Steven Piccerill, Salvatore Pugliese 4th: Patrick West, Michael Baumeister, Shawn Roudi, Mark Poppe, Thomas Killan

ENGINE CO. 204

299 Degraw Street, Brooklyn

Engine 204 has been in the same location—299 Degraw Street—for its entire history. Engine 204 started out as Engine 4 of the Brooklyn Fire Department on September 15, 1869. They took over the former quarters of Montauk Engine 22 of the volunteer department. In 1893, the old volunteer house was torn down for the currant house, which opened during 1894. Most of Engine 204's first-due area is residential, with a large shopping area along Court and Smith Streets. During World War II, Engine 204 was disbanded to organize Squad 24, a manpower unit, from December 3, 1943, to May 10, 1945. Two days after the War in Europe ended, Engine 204 was back in service, protecting the Carroll Gardens section of Brooklyn. On November 12, 1892, two members of Engine 204 were killed at the Harbeck Stores fire. Engine 204 has earned nine Unit Citations and two members have received medals for their actions at fires. Engine 204 also earned the New York Firefighters Burn Center Foundation Medal.

ENGINE CO. 205

74 Middagh Street, Brooklyn

In Downtown Brooklyn, Engine 205 dates back to September 15, 1869. Engine 5, of the B.F.D., was located in the former quarters of volunteer Pacific Engine 14. On December 20, 1922, Engine 205 responded to Box 458, Brooklyn Borough Hall, Court and Joralemon Streets, with the last horse-drawn steamer run. After making the "Last Run," Engine 205 received a new American LaFrance 700-gpm pumper. New quarters were built for Engine 205 and Ladder 118 at 74 Middagh Street and opened on October 22, 1929. The deadliest fire for Engine 205 occurred on December 5, 1876, when 300 people were killed in the Brooklyn Theater fire. Other fires of note include the Furman Street fire of 1935, which burned out of control for 18 hours and injured 1068 firefighters, the Margaret Hotel fire in 1980, which turned Orange Street and Columbia Heights into a winter ice palace and the St. George Hotel fire of 1995, which went to 18 alarms. Engine 205 has received two Unit Citations and two members have received medals for bravery.

1st: Lt. Thomas Hayes, Lt. Robert Wallace, Capt. David Fenton, Lt. John Bongiorno, Capt. Nick Delre 2nd: Daniel Lopez, John Urso, Richard Murray, John Stonick, Frank Visco, John Leavy, Joe Sciurca 3rd: Thomas Baccarosa, George Clancy, Neil Schoer, Brian Forsyth, Christopher Murray, John Sorrentino, Andrew McCord

LADDER CO. 118
76 Middagh Street, Brooklyn

Placed in service as Ladder 68 on June 8, 1901, it was the first company placed in service after the merger of the BFD and FDNY in 1898. Ladder 68 first was quartered in the old Brooklyn Headquarters building at 365 Jay Street in downtown Brooklyn. It was relocated to Engine 205's quarters at 76 Middagh Street on October 22, 1929, where they have remained. Their first apparatus was a used 1889 LaFrance Hayes 75-foot aerial. On November 27, 1913, they received a new American LaFrance 75-foot aerial. Ladder 118 also shared its quarters with Water Tower 6, Divisions 6 and 10 and Searchlight 2. When Ladder 118 moved out of Jay Street, Rescue 2 moved in on the same day. One of the larger fires to which Ladder 118 responded was the Hotel St. George in 1995. The blaze went to 18 alarms and extended to several exposures. Three members have earned medals. Three Unit Citations have been awarded to the company. Four members have been killed in the line of duty.

1st: Robert O'Rourke, Vernon Cherry, Lt. Martin Egan, Capt. John Martorana, Lt. Pasquale Abatangelo, Darryl Patterson, Eddie Greene, Gerard Belletiere 2nd: Joseph Agnello, James Mangracina, Timothy Julian, Robert Forte, Michael Gallino, Michael Luzopone, James Gibbons, Anthony Gonzalez, Rick Fowler, Jeff Oakland 3rd: Kevin Clifford, Peter Vega, James McAlevey, Ray Thomas, Kevin Byrnes, Scott Davidson, Donald Rosas, Paul Gotlieb, Leon Smith, Michael Merced

ENGINE CO. 224
274 Hicks Street, Brooklyn

Engine 24 was placed in service at 153 Furman Street in leased quarters on January 18, 1886. The leased building, a first for Brooklyn's Fire Department, was four stories high with Engine 24 using the first two floors and paying rent of $500 a year. This company covered an important waterfront area, which had seen numerous dock and ship fires. Their first rig was the 1874 self-propelled steamer that Engine 4 had used. It proved unsatisfactory and was replaced by horses. Their first run came only a few short hours after being placed in service; 347 to 355 Furman Street. The three-story cooperage building kept Engine 24 busy for more than 20 hours before they returned to their new quarters. At the turn of the century, most of the leased buildings were replaced with new quarters and Engine 224 moved to 274 Hicks Street in a beautiful and ornate, single-bay, three-story building on April 30, 1904. Engine 224 has earned three Unit Citations and four medals have been awarded to its members.

1st: Michael Hazel, John Simoncini, Lt. John Kelly, Capt. Jerry Quinn, Lt. George Desimone, Richard Saulle, Thomas Smith 2nd: Stuart Bailey, George Heck, Jorge Pacheco, Sean Newman, Michael Roberts, Michael Gatto, Fredrick Domini, Irwin Edelstein, Joseph Avignone, Kevin Bradbury 3rd: Anthony Palminteri, Christopher Pillal, Anthony Ventrano, Richard Miranda

1st: Steven Vicino, Lt. Kevin Lunny, Lt. Thomas St. Pierre, Capt. Michael O'Brien, Lt. Jorge Palacio, Richard J. Marucheau 2nd: Thomas Darnaud, William Murray, Edward Quinn, Steven Troche, Edward Kuohn, Nicholas Turner 3rd: Craig Moore, Philip McKenna, James Fortmeyer, Joseph Brautigam, Troy Owens, Kenneth Sheich, Michael Golding

ENGINE CO. 279
252 Lorraine Street, Brooklyn

Located at 252 Lorraine Street, Engine 279 was placed in service on March 20, 1913, as part of the Brooklyn expansion. Engine 279 is located in the Red Hook section of Brooklyn, an area of factories, waterfront, housing projects and residential housing. This two-bay, three-story firehouse has a wall down the center, making it two firehouses in one. Sharing the house is Ladder 131, which was placed in service later in the same year. Engine 279 went into service with a 1912 American LaFrance second-size steamer with a Christie front-wheel-drive tractor and a new Mack Boyd combination chemical and hose wagon. Engine 279 was assigned a new 1939 Ahrens Fox 1000-gpm pumper, which they kept until 1958. They are nicknamed the "Happy Hookers" because of their solid relationship with the citizens of Red Hook. Today, Engine 279 responds with a 1993 Seagrave 1000-gpm pumper. One member of Engine 279 has earned a medal for bravery and the Company has received three Unit Citations.

LADDER CO. 131

254 Lorraine Street, Brooklyn

Ladder 131 was one of the first ladder companies in Brooklyn to be placed in service with a motorized apparatus. On November 27, 1913, Ladder 131 went into service at 254 Lorraine Street in the southern end of Red Hook. Engine 279 had been placed in service earlier in March. The firehouse was built as one building, but a wall separated the engine and truck from each other. Ladder 131's response area has it all—private homes, housing projects, heavy commercial and industrial buildings, a major highway and the docks along the waterfront. For years, this area was served by Ladder 101 and Ladder 131, a big asset for the citizens of Red Hook. The first apparatus assigned to Ladder 131 was a 1913 American LaFrance 65-foot aerial. Today, they respond with a 1989 Mack 95-foot tower-ladder. Ladder 131 has been awarded eight Unit Citations and seven members have received medals for rescues. Four members have lost their lives in the line of duty.

1st: Jake Sexton, Lt. Terrance Nicosia, Capt. Martin Ford, Lt. Gary Wood, Lt. Thomas Coleman, James Grogan
2nd: Scott Trivolis, Gerald Cox, Mike Jezycki, Joe Thompson, Greg Gutkes, Gerald Sweeney, Mike DeStafano
3rd: Roger Kilfoil, Charles Migan, Harry Gillen, Kevin Dillon, Chris Kielczewski, Chris Gaffney, Paul D'emic, Andrew Serra

ENGINE CO. 212

136 Wythe Avenue, Brooklyn

Engine 212 was placed in service on September 15, 1869, in the former quarters of Engine 5, known as the Northern Liberties, at 136 Wythe Avenue. Engine 212 has been in two different houses, both on the same site. On June 1, 1908, Engine 212 moved into a stable, north of 9th Street on Wythe Avenue. The steamer and horses were left outside while the men lived in the stables until December 1, 1908. This mostly commercial area along the waterfront has seen some of Brooklyn's most disastrous fires. Engine 212 was closed on November 22, 1975, due to budget cuts. The local citizens were so upset with the closing of their firehouse that they took it over before it was closed. After the City felt the pressure of the protest group for a year and half, they reopened the house with Utility 1 on March 19, 1977. Engine 212 replaced Utility 1 on June 17, 1978. Engine 212 has earned two Unit Citations. Two members have been killed protecting the citizens of Brooklyn.

1st: Arthur Tassiello, Michael Guglielmo, Lt. John Clifford, Lt. Gary Rivano, Bernard Duignan, Benjamin Ortiz, Thomas Olszewski *2nd:* Eugene Reilly, Thomas Shulz, Richard Wylie, Timothy Tolan, Nicholas Falotico, John Sexton, Edward Snyder, John Tiska, John Winter

1st: Daniel Suhr, Lt. Thomas Hosford, Capt. Thaddeus Jankowski, Lt. Edward Schollmeier, Kenneth Collins *2nd:* James Tierney, John Schatzle, Charles Gildersleeve, Robert Hillary *3rd:* John Orlando, Timothy McGuinness, Donald Ferguson, Mike McCaffrey, Anthony Sanseviro

ENGINE CO. 216

187 Union Avenue, Brooklyn

Brooklyn Engine 16 was placed in service on September 15, 1872, in the former quarters of Eagle Engine 6 at Stagg Street and Union Avenue. Engine 16 was one of two engines placed in service on the same day; Engine 15 in Greenpoint was the other. This temporary house lasted until 1893, when new quarters were built for the company at 11 Scholes Street. Engine 16 remained on Scholes Street until new quarters were built for them and Ladder 108. Engine 216 moved into 187 Union Avenue on October 13, 1971. The first member of the Brooklyn Fire Department to be killed in the line of duty was Captain William Baldwin of Engine 16. He was buried by a falling wall on January 14, 1880, and died six days later. Engine 216's response area has a variety of hazards and buildings—commercial, industrial, residential wood-frames and brownstones. Engine 216 is an active company and has earned 16 Unit Citations. Four medals have been awarded to members for their bravery.

1st: Glen Tracy, Lt. James Hanly, Capt. Terrance Thornton, Lt. Brian Malone, Robert Bonistalli 2nd: Bruce Foss, John Driscoll, Andrew Isolano, Allen Nevendorf, Dan Hyland, Bob Natalicchio, Dan Conniff, Gerard Brickman 3rd: Thomas Cotter, Ray McCarthy, William Hasseck, Dan Bowman, Rich Cadotte

LADDER CO. 108

187 Union Avenue, Brooklyn

Ladder 8 was placed in service on November 30, 1887, in the former quarters of Engine 18 at 112 Seigel Street. Located in the Williamsburg section of the borough, Ladder 8 was placed between Ladder 4 and Ladder 2. Williamsburg is an older section of Brooklyn that was annexed in 1855 and heavily developed with tenements, retail, commercial and heavy industrial buildings. Originally, the area was served by Ladder 5. The first apparatus assigned to Ladder 8 was a new 1886 LaFrance Hayes 75-foot aerial. Today, they share quarters with Engine 216 and Battalion 35 at 187 Union Avenue, which opened on August 9, 1971. Firefighter Gregory J. Smith received the James Gordon Bennett Medal for rescuing a mother and child from a fire in 1994. Besides Smith, the company had another James Gordon Bennett Medal winner in 1974, plus 35 other medal winners. Ladder 108 has earned 30 Unit Citations. Two members have lost their lives in the line of duty.

1st: Lt. Joseph Murphy, Capt. Bruce Lindahl, Lt. Robert Nola 2nd: Donald Filete, Gregory Gallagher, Timothy Walsh, Michael Herold, Vito Oliva, Joseph Badger, Thomas Petti, Thomas Dalgish, James Keeney 3rd: Paul Warhola, Eric Dellaquila, Robert Johnson, William Rooney, David Kelnhofer, Benjamin Suarez, Christopher Egan

ENGINE CO. 221

163 South 2nd Street, Brooklyn

Brooklyn placed Engines 221 and 222 in service on the same day, January 16, 1885. Engine 221 was located at 163 South 2nd Street in the Williamsburg section of Brooklyn. This section is very old and Engine 221 has seen some disastrous fires, including the Diamond Candy Factory fire on November 6, 1915, which killed 12 workers. Four days before this fire, 13 people were killed in a double rear-tenement fire. With this kind of work, Engine 221 has earned 19 Unit Citations and three members have earned medals. On December 15, 1913, Engine 221 and Chemical Engine 1 exchanged quarters. Engine 221 went to 712 Driggs Street. Chemical Engine 1 was disbanded on January 1, 1915, and Ladder 104 moved in on the same day. Ladder 104 moved to 166 Clymer Street on December 22, 1931, and the old quarters were torn down and replaced with a new, two-story firehouse. Engine 221 moved in with Ladder 104 on October 29, 1932. Two members have died in the line of duty.

LADDER CO. 104

163 South 2nd Street, Brooklyn

Brooklyn Ladder 4 was organized in the former quarters of Zephyr Hose 4 at 114 South 3rd Street. Starting on September 15, 1869, Ladder 4's first rig also came from the volunteer department. The quarters were torn down and rebuilt during 1888. This location only lasted until December 15, 1913, and then Ladder 104 moved into the former quarters of Engine 221 at 163 South 2nd Street. Sharing these quarters with Ladder 104 was Chemical Engine 1. A 1914/15 Christie front-wheel-drive tractor was placed under the 1907 Seagrave 75-foot aerial. Again, Ladder 104 was relocated into the quarters of Engine 211 at 166 Clymer Street on December 22, 1931. On October 29, 1932, Ladder 104 and Engine 221 moved into new quarters on the same site, 163 South 2nd Street. Ladder 104 has garnered 25 Unit Citations. Six members have received medals for their heroic actions. Three members have lost their lives in the line of duty.

1st: Joseph Cicha, Lt. Kevin Kalb, Capt. Edward Flynn, John Rizzo 2nd: Walter Rogers, Frederick Mallet, Louis Gorgano, Umberto Gallo, James Bert, Francis Cleary, Timothy Murphy, John Leimeister 3rd: Christopher DelGiorno, Joseph Quinn, Patrick Williams, Michael Smith, Richard McDade, Peter Maslinski, John DeResto

35th Battalion

35th Battalion

35th Battalion

1st: Ed Hronec, Lt. Steven Opitz, Lt. Jerry Horton, Lt. Artie Barnett, Capt. Bob Sutherland, Thomas Gentile 2nd: David Treco, Pat Martin, Tim Devine, Rob Olsen, James Sommers, Enzo Sozzi, William Wilson, Mark Broccolo, John Maurer, Kerry Deto, Mike Scheibe, Kenneth Ruddick

ENGINE CO. 229
75 Richardson Street, Brooklyn

The 29th engine company placed in service by the Brooklyn Fire Department on November 1, 1890, was located at 246 Frost Street. Engine 229's response area is a mix of heavy industrial, light commercial and residential buildings. On July 12, 1915, Engine 229 and Division 11 moved into new quarters at 75 Richardson Street. Division 11 has occupied these quarters for three different periods before moving to Engine 207's quarters in 1990. This building was lettered for Water Tower 7, which never went into service. Instead, Ladder 146 was added to quarters on January 1, 1916. Engine 229 received a new, second-size American steamer with a Van Blerck tractor on April 17, 1913. The first motorized hose wagon received was a 1914 Mack Boyd regulation-size wagon. Today, Engine 229 responds with a 1997 Seagrave 1000-gpm pumper. Engine 229 has earned 11 Unit Citations. Three medal winners can be counted among its ranks. Three members have been killed protecting the citizens of New York City.

LADDER CO. 146
75 Richardson Street, Brooklyn

Ladder 146 was organized in the quarters of Engine 229 at 75 Richardson Street on January 1, 1916. The building was constructed for Engine 229 and Water Tower 7 in 1915. The water tower never was placed in service and Ladder 146 was added. Located between Williamsburg and Greenpoint, Ladder 146's first-due area includes large factories, commercial and retail buildings and three-story, wood-frame tenements. One of the worst fires to which Ladder 146 responded was the Standard Oil Company conflagration of 1919. The fire went to two Borough Calls over the fifth alarm and destroyed a thousand barrels of flammable liquids and 25 tanks of naphtha and gasoline. The fire spread to several large industrial buildings. Their first rig was a used 1913 American LaFrance 75-foot aerial. On January 25, 1973, they received a new Mack 75-foot tower-ladder. Today, they operate with a 1987 Mack 75-foot tower-ladder. The company has received nine Unit Citations and seven members have garnered medals for acts of bravery.

1st: Frank Moody, James Korzeniewski, Lt. Angelo Figueroa, Capt. Patrick Savage, Lt. John Caltagirone, Hon. Chief Anthony Lanza, Thomas Steffens, Joseph McGrory, Michael Giammanco, Daniel McGrath 2nd: Alfred Doyle, William Sergio, William Lambert, Kevin Farrell, Richard Capito, Joseph Lagone, John Leahy, Steven Holihan, Anthony Malfi

ENGINE CO. 220
532 11th Street, Brooklyn

Engine 220 was placed in service on November 1, 1882, in a single-bay house at 532 11th Street. Most of their first-due area is residential with some commercial and industrial buildings along the Avenues. The growing area of Park Slope started around 1870 with new brownstones being constructed. The area was built up by the turn of the century. Placed on top of the hill, Engine 20—as it was known in Brooklyn—filled in a big hole among Engines 202, 204 and 201, the closest companies. At the time, the horses had a hard time pulling the heavy steamers up the hills. A new house was built for Engine 220—next door at 530 11th Street—and it opened on December 31, 1907. Ladder 122 moved into their old quarters on the same day. One member of the company was killed at a fire in 1889. Three members have earned medals for bravery and four Unit Citations have been awarded to the company.

1st: Edward Plunkett, Lt. Mark Barra, Lt. Edward McDonough, Capt. Richard O'Grady, Lt. Wayne Trivelli, Anthony Pantone 2nd: Keithroy Maynard, Vincent Maniscalco, Brian McCann, Dominick Polignone, Dean Coutsouros, William Monteverde, Richard Martin, Joseph Rocha 3rd: Dion Kelly, James Murphy, John McLean, Kenneth Micco, Brian Sheehan, Kevin Farrell, George Marsh

LADDER CO. 122
532 11th Avenue, Brooklyn

Ladder 122 was organized as Ladder 72. Ladder 72 was placed in service in the former quarters of Engine 120 at 532 11th Avenue. Built in 1882, this is the oldest house in continuous use in Brooklyn. Engine 120 moved next door into a new building on December 31, 1907. Ladder 72 went in service with a 1905 Fire Engine Company 50-foot straight-frame combination ladder and chemical truck. Ladder 122 received its first aerial in 1910 with a new American LaFrance 65-foot ladder truck. It was motorized in 1917 with a front-wheel-drive tractor. Today, they respond with a 1995 Seagrave 100-foot rear-mount aerial. During 1996 to 1997, Ladder 122 relocated to the quarters of Engine 239 while both houses on 11th Avenue were remodeled. When they moved back on November 7, 1997, Ladder 122's quarters were new, inside and out. Eight members have received medals. Eight Unit Citations have been earned. Three members have been killed in the line of duty, two while serving in the military during World War II.

1st: James Sweeney, Lt. James Munday, Capt. Michael Feminella, Lt. John Ducey, Lt. Gregory McLetchie, Robert Jackson 2nd: Owen Carlock, Vincent DeMarinis, Steve Scotto, Michael Martorana, Barry Buss, Kevin Burns, Matthew Hanley, Kevin McCabe, Robert Unger 3rd: Edward Gonzalez, Dennis Quinn, Dave Koyles, James Finnegan, Christopher Kane, Arthur Oschmann, Frank McLoughlin, Kevin Walker, Dennis Brantley, Brian Sullivan, John Leanza, William Miranda

1st: Peter Brown, Stephen Elis, Lt. Patrick Scollan, Capt. Robert Moccia, Lt. Anthony Mancuso, Lawrence Burns, Neil Malone 2nd: Ronald Sessa, James Bledsoe, Michael Radicella, William McMahon, Glen Griffin, Josef Pruden, Kevin Martin 3rd: Thomas Ryan, William Wheeler, Jeffery Conti, Stephen Love, Ronald DeRosa, Daniel Yaccarino, Matthew Mulham

ENGINE CO. 239
395 4th Avenue, Brooklyn

Brooklyn's Engine 39 was placed in service just south of the downtown area. The firehouse, located at 395 4th Avenue, has been home for Engine 239 since being placed in service on November 30, 1895. When built, Engine 239's firehouse was the only building on the block. The three-story firehouse has the BFD interwoven in limestone on the front of the building. Engine 239 fills the gap between Engines 226 and 204 to the north and Engine 228 to the south. Sandwiched between the Gowanus Canal and Park Slope, Engine 239 has a diverse response area of commercial and industrial buildings and residential homes. The 1895 Amoskeag third-size steamer had a 1915 tractor placed under it, replacing the horses on August 25,1915. The James Gordon Bennett medal was awarded to a member in 1921, the first firefighter from Brooklyn to receive this honor. Four other members of the company have received medals. Eight Unit Citations have been earned. Three members have been killed in the line of duty.

ENGINE CO. 240
1307 Prospect Avenue, Brooklyn

On January 11, 1888, Windsor Terrace Hose 3 was placed in service at 1288 Prospect Avenue and it became part of the Flatbush Fire Department. The City of Brooklyn annexed the town of Flatbush on April 24, 1894. Engine 40 and Ladder 21 were organized on January 20, 1896, in new quarters at 1307 Prospect Avenue. After New York City took over the Brooklyn Fire Department, Engine 40 and Ladder 21 were combined into Combination Engine 40. On May 15, 1914, the ladder truck was taken away from Engine 240 when Ladder 147 went into service at Engine 281. Today, Engine 240 shares its house with Battalion 48. Engine 240's firehouse, with its unique Romanesque style, is the only house of this design. Originally, the building had two apparatus doors in front. These were removed in 1925 at a cost of $13,210. The building cost only $15,000 to build in 1895. Five members have lost their lives in the performance of their duty. Four Unit Citations have been bestowed on Engine 240.

1st: Edward Witkowski, Kelvin Alcala, Lt. Anthony Auciello, Capt. Matthew Sabatello, Lt. David Winston, Lt. Leonard Merola, Paul Bardo, Dedie Plasencia 2nd: Richard Lang, Mike Schiraldi, John Winkler, Tom Mahoney, Mike Duzant, Philip Benigno, Pat Sullivan 3rd: Darren Jacobs, Charles Puza, Mike Pasquarello, Frank Sweeney, Mike Murray, Martin Farrell, John Mooney

48th Battalion

1st: Douglas Riechel, Lt. Stephen Auciello, Lt. William Heintz, John Pecora 2nd: Robert Schmidt, James Cassidy, Thomas Matteo, Thomas Connelly, Peter Conelli 3rd: Joseph Scollan, John Mahon, Peter Easop, Gilbert Montalvo, Henry Jablonsky

ENGINE CO. 282

4210 12th Avenue, Brooklyn

The last engine to be placed in service on March 20, 1913, Engine 282 is located in the Boro Park section of Brooklyn. Engine 282 and 281 filled a large void in fire coverage among Engines 239, 240, 247 and 250. This house, which has the center wall, also was built for a ladder company, which was placed in service on April 15, 1914. A 1912 American LaFrance second-size steamer with a Christie front-wheel-drive tractor and a 1912 Mack Boyd combination chemical and hose wagon were the company's first apparatus. Today, Engine 282 responds with a 1998 Seagrave 1000-gpm pumper that they received on October 29, 1998. Engine 282 has a unique response area of commercial buildings, factories and single-family homes, as well as apartment houses. Engine 282 has earned six Unit Citations and one member received a medal for his heroic actions at a fire. Two members were killed in the line of duty.

LADDER CO. 148

4210 12th Avenue, Brooklyn

Ladder 148 was placed in service at 4210 12th Avenue on May 15, 1914. Sharing the quarters with Engine 282, which went into service on March 20, 1913, these two companies protect the Borough Park section of Brooklyn. A 1914 American LaFrance 65-foot aerial was assigned to Ladder 148. Like Ladder 147, Ladder 148 also replaced three older horse-drawn ladder trucks in Combination Engine Companies 240, 247 and 250. Ladder 148's response area is mostly apartment buildings, with several streets of commercial buildings and retail stores. Four members have earned medals for their heroic actions. Seven Unit Citations have been awarded to Ladder 148. Three members have been killed in the line of duty. Currently, Ladder 148 is assigned a 1995 Seagrave 100-foot rear-mount aerial.

1st: Chris Romeo, Lt. Phil Petti, Lt. Donald Murphy, Capt. Robert Baumann, Lt. Michael Gala, George Bachmann 2nd: Chris Wagner, James Urkonis, Gordon Reebe, Michael Kendall, Gerard Chipura, Stephen Molino, Kevin McConville 3rd: David Zdanok, Michael Vindigni, William Doody, Brian Gorman, Peter DiSalvo, Alfonse Calato

ENGINE CO. 209

850 Bedford Street, Brooklyn

Brooklyn Engine 9, now Engine 209, was placed in service in the former quarters of Phoenix Engine 12 at 159 Taaffe Place on September 15, 1869. During 1887, the old house was torn down and replaced by a two-story firehouse with all the modern conveniences of the day for the comfort of the men and horses. On March 9, 1966, Engine 209 vacated its old quarters and moved in with Ladder 102 at 850 Bedford Street. Located in the northern part of Bed-Stuy, Engine 209 always has been in the center of fire activity. During the "War Years" of 1969 to the mid-1970s, Engine 209 experienced two or three fires each tour. Engine 209 is known for its reliable response in Bed-Stuy, Bushwick and elsewhere. This company still serves this area with pride and efficiency. The horses are gone, but the dedication of the members remains. Over the years, Engine 209 has earned nine Unit Citations. One member of Engine 209 was killed in the line of duty.

1st: Daniel Kane, Lt. Christopher Bowles, Lt. William Hayes, Capt. John Papadimitrios, Capt. John Postel, Lt. Joseph Buda, David Duigan 2nd: Todd Heaney, Joseph Adinolfi, Thomas Carrera, Michael Young, James Murphy, Allen Murphy, Frank Dileo, Kevin McGarry 3rd: Patrick Hastings, Elroy Braswell, Leif Kreuscher, James Martin, Thomas Hansard, Christopher McKeon, John Cunniff, Brian Donovan, Michael Minogue, Eugenio Gonzalez

LADDER CO. 102

850 Bedford Avenue, Brooklyn

Ladder 102 was organized in the former quarters of Empire Ladder 3 at 898 Bedford Avenue. Brooklyn Ladder 2—as it was known then—received a ladder truck from the volunteer department and went in service on September 15, 1869. New quarters were built for them at 894 Bedford Avenue and they moved into them in February 1892. It had all the modern amenities to outfit a firehouse, for both the men and horses. They received a 1912 Webb 75-foot aerial, replacing the horses. From September 1, 1946, to March 10, 1950, Engine 230 was quartered here. On March 9, 1966, Ladder 102 moved again to new quarters with Engine 209 at 850 Bedford Avenue. Located in the Bedford-Stuyvesant section of Brooklyn, they have been a very active fire company. Thirty-five Unit Citations have been awarded to the company. Twenty-three members have been presented with medals for bravery, including the James Gordon Bennett Medal given to Firefighter Steven C. DeRosa in 1972. Three members have died in the line of duty.

1st: Richard Radziewicz, Lt. Robert Oehler, Capt. James Graham, Lt. Lawrence Quinn, Lt. Bruce Silas, Lt. Joseph Lasher, Richard Croce 2nd: Joseph Rogers, Joseph Mondello, Edward Dowd, Daniel Insardi, Dennis Pace, Robert Magnusen, James Gorman, Kenneth Sinkevitch, Lanaird Granger 3rd: Andrew Hassell, William Orfanos, Robert Laible, Raymond Pollard, James McCutcheon, Christopher Gregory, William Byrnes, Robert Endall, Thomas Mooney, Steve King

1st: Lt. Patrick Albertelli, Capt. Eugene Vellia, Lt. Thomas McGoff, Capt. Ciro Migliore 2nd: Michael Gallo, John O'Reagan, Frank Ardizzone, Brian Gibbons, John Senese, Robert Watts, Sean Cummins, Mark Bartoletti, Brian Clarke, David Feddern, Jack Hayden, Richard Brady, John Byrne, John Cottrell, Gerard Dewan, James Hart, Neil Leavy

ENGINE CO. 217

940 Dekalb Avenue, Brooklyn

Placed in service on July 1, 1876, Brooklyn Engine 17 was placed in a new house at 940 Dekalb Avenue. Not much is known about the house, but it was probably a wood-frame building. Engine 217 received the first motorized steamer in Brooklyn on October 4, 1912. The first-size 1907 Nott steamer had a 1912 Webb Couple gear tractor replacing the horses. The first-due area of Engine 217 includes mostly wood-frame and brownstone houses. As the area grew, so did 217's responses, to the point that a second Engine 217 was added from August 10, 1968, until November 25, 1972. During the "war years" of 1968 to 1975, both sections of Engine 217 were kept very busy with four or five building fires per tour, plus many rubbish and car fires. Engine 217 has earned 12 Unit Citations; the second section earned one. Four members were awarded medals for bravery, including the James Gordon Bennett Medal in 1968. One member was killed in the line of duty.

ENGINE CO. 219

494 Dean Street, Brooklyn

Engine 219 was placed in service on December 24, 1880, in new quarters built for them at 735 Dean Street. This area, known as Prospect Heights, was built and completed from 1870 to 1880. There were mostly homes for the working class and many factories in the area. The company's first-due district included the area bounded by Park Avenue, Kingston Avenue, the City Line (with the village of New Lots) and Carrol and Nevins Streets, a total of 112 boxes. Today, Engine 219's response area—which is smaller—consists of factories, loft buildings, railroad yards and residential units. The first motorized pumper for 219 was placed in service on August 1, 1917, with a 700-gpm American LaFrance pumper. On June 2, 1977, they moved into new quarters with Ladder 105 at 494 Dean Street. Four members of Engine 219 have received medals and the company has earned 10 Unit Citations. Three members have been killed in the performance of their duty, protecting the citizens of New York City.

1st: Richard Loeber, Lt. Joseph Carey, Capt. Donald Howard, Lt. Steven Balkunas 2nd: Regina Wilson, Joseph Castelli, Natalio Conanan, John Chipura, Peter DiSalvo, Keith McElwain, Marc Anderson 3rd: Scott Quinlan, Hollis Flanagan, Thomas Carroll, Kevin Maloney, Stephen Peteley

LADDER CO. 105

494 Dean Street, Brooklyn

Ladder 105 was placed in service on September 15, 1869, in the former quarters of United States Engine 4, located at Manhattan Avenue and Ten Eyck Street. For unknown reasons, Brooklyn Ladder 5 was disbanded during 1873. It was reorganized in new quarters at 648 Pacific Street on June 15, 1885. Its district first included the area bounded by Dekalb Avenue, Nostrand Avenue, Bond Street to 5th Street and an area that now is covered by Ladder Companies 132, 122 and 123. Ladder 105's first motorized truck was a 1910 Seagrave with a 1915 Christie front-wheel-drive tractor. A new firehouse was built for Engine 219 and Ladder 105 at 494 Dean Street and it opened on June 2, 1977. On December 19, 1969, Ladder 105 received the second tower-ladder assigned to Brooklyn when they received a new, 75-foot Mack tower-ladder. Ladder 105 has 26 medal winners among its ranks and 13 Unit Citations. Six members of the company have lost their lives in the performance of their duty.

1st: James Nola, Lt. Vincent Brunton, Capt. Edward Moriarty, Edward Cooper 2nd: Steven Corcoran, Thomas Wohltjen, Frank Palombo, Albert Petrocelli, John Lynott, Joseph McAllister, Henry Miller, Patrick Mitchell, Robert Castaldo 3rd: Michael Brady, Shamus Connelly, Charles Saladis, Keith McTarsney, Arthur Herlihy, James Dillon, James Kearney, Richard Doody, William Sarro, Timothy Grogan, Thomas Kelly

1st: Michael Mullarkey, Daniel Connolly, Lt. Joseph Chiafari, Lt. George Grossman, Robert Connolly, Frank Bonomo 2nd: Aidan Kelly, Dean Psathas, John Guarino, Jeffrey Stark, Scott Smith 3rd: Philip Polemeni, Edward White, Michael Carlo, Chris Perry, Stephen Mendolia, James Rybicki, Steven Lubrino

ENGINE CO. 230

701 Park Avenue, Brooklyn

Engine 230 was placed in service on July 2, 1891, in new quarters at 59 Ellery Street. When placed in service, their first-due district was mainly residential with some manufacturing in small factories. Today, its response area is more diversified with homes, factories and stores. The Ellery Street house was one of the most handsome in the Brooklyn Department. On September 1, 1946, the house was closed and Engine 230 moved in with Ladder 102 at 894 Bedford Avenue. New quarters were built at 701 Park Avenue and Engine 230 moved in on March 10, 1950. For many years, this house held the reputation of being the last single-bay house built by the Fire Department. During the 1960s and 1970s, Engine 230 became very busy with arson fires. Squad 3 relocated here on July 8, 1966, and was disbanded on May 1, 1976. Two members were killed when a wall fell on them on August 21, 1923. Eighteen Unit Citations have been awarded to the company. Two members have earned medals.

ENGINE CO. 235

206 Monroe Street, Brooklyn

Engine 35 was added to the growing section of Bedford-Stuyvesant on July 1, 1895. The firehouse, located at 206 Monroe Street, is a sister house to Engine 36, which opened on the same day. Engine 235's response area includes brownstone homes, with stores along Fulton Street and Atlantic Avenue. With the growing population, the single-family brownstones were converted into apartments with substandard work, causing many fires that drove out the working class. The area deteriorated quickly and Engine 235 was kept very busy during the 1960s and 1970s. Squad 3, a manpower unit, was organized on November 16, 1955, in this house because of the growing workload. They moved to Engine 230's quarters on July 8, 1966. Engine 235 was the first company certified in CFR-D responses and on the first day, responded to 25 EMS runs, along with a couple of all-hands fires. Two members have been awarded medals and the company has earned 25 Unit Citations. Engine 235 and Squad 3 lost one member each in the line of duty.

1st: BC Dennis Cross, Lt. Eugene Marmann, Capt. John Bevacqua, Lt. John Cullen, BC Michael Canty 2nd: Kevin MacBride, Kevin Mahoney, Louis Testani, John Deprizio, Rodney Riddick, Brian Muldoon, Richard Colabella, Lois Mungay, Michael Ramos, Ryan Moriarty 3rd: Philip Scarfi, Anthony DeRubbio, James Cashin, Walter Merecka, Steven Vincent, Lee Fehling, Simon Ressner, Kevin Doody 4th: Lawrence Veling, Valdimir Kowal, Apolinar LaGrandier, Chris McKlusky

DIVISION 13

1st: DC Daniel Butler, DC Joseph Curry, DC Alexander Parzych, DC John Bambury 2nd: Lawrence Rottkamp, Walter Schroeder

BATTALION 50

1st: Richard Brown, Warren Bushing, Chris Guglielmo 2nd: BC Walter Murphy, BC Vincent Moore, BC James Manahan, BC John Bley

BATTALION 51

1st: BC Richard McGuire, BC Michael Quinn, BC Thomas Narbutt, BC Howard Carlson, BC Kenneth Grabowski 2nd: Mark Presti, Ralph Scerbo, John Mazzullo, Ralph Nicholes

BATTALION 54

Thomas Abramski, Michael Bonura, BC Ed Power, BC James Campbell, BC Edward Weber, BC Peter Campbell, BC Patrick Ruddick, Tony Petro, John Duncan

BATTALION 47

1st: BC Robert Burns, BC Gerald Esposito, BC Bruce DiPietro 2nd: Thomas McVeigh, Mark Tricone

ENGINE CO. 275

111-36 Merrick Boulevard, Queens

This company was organized July 5, 1907, as Hose Co. 7 in the former volunteer quarters of Fosdick Hose Company 4 at 89-19 168th Place. Their first apparatus was a 1903 George B. Marx third-size hose wagon. On October 15, 1909, they received an 1894 Clapp & Jones third-size steam engine. Hose Co. 7 was reorganized as Engine Co. 175 and on January 1, 1913, Engine 175 again was reorganized as Engine Co. 275. On September 5, 1925, they relocated to 89-56 162nd Street with Engine Companies 298 and 299, Ladder 127 and the 50th Battalion. They moved into their current quarters on March 18, 1960. One member has died in the line of duty. One member has received a medal. Engine 275 has garnered seven Unit Citations. One of the busiest engine companies in Queens, they have a response area of single and multiple dwellings, taxpayers and housing projects. They respond on a 1989 Mack 1000-gpm pumper. Their "Merrick Boulevard Magic" quarters are shared with newly organized Ladder 133.

1st: BC Walter Murphy, Lt. Henry Hinton, Capt. Thomas Auer, Lt. Daniel DiMartino, Capt. John Gullota, Thomas Lyons 2nd: Kevin Hannan, Steven Johnston, Edmund Catano, Fred Heffel, Richard Flynn, Michael Broschart 3rd: Robert Winterfeldt, Tyrone Clark, Peter Schmitt, Michael Hanna, Charles Cottone, Paul Greco, Anthony Lembo, Christopher McGurk

LADDER CO. 133

111-36 Merrick Boulevard, Queens

This company was organized on November 1, 1998, at 111-36 Merrick Boulevard. Mayor Giuliani, Commissioner Von Essen and Queens Borough President Claire Shulman were at the opening of Ladder 133 in the South Jamaica, St. Albans, area of Queens. This was the first new fire company to be organized since August 1987. This new company has been a welcome addition to Ladder 165, 155, 127 and 126. In service for only 13 days, Lieutenant Gregory L. Picconi rescued a woman from a burning apartment house. He received a medal for his actions. Ladder 133 has the same busy response area as Engine 275. Ladder 133 operates with a 1994 Seagrave 100-foot rear-mount ladder truck. They are quartered at "Merrick Boulevard Magic" with Engine 275.

1st: Lawrence Brown, Donald Shields, Capt. William Youngson, Lt. Gregory Picconi, Lt. Steven Berube, Alan Beach, Thomas Butler 2nd: Christopher Burack, Robert Roughley, Glenn Healy, Hugh Gigfords, Victor Rosario, Daniel Nelson, Daniel White 3rd: Michael Checco, Thomas Richardson, William Schaefer, Michael Carlin, Craig McCarthy, John Nolan, Timothy Karp

1st: Lou LaFemina, Joe Tesoriero, Nef Albergo, Paul Moyik, Chris Guglielmo, Jim Mare, Richie Berkhout 2nd: Capt. Bruce Groth, Pat Rooney, Jim McMorrow, Hugh Diamond, Mike Cullen, Chris Lindberg, Rich Brown, Phil Milkovits, Joe Middlebrook, Lt. Bob Speck, Lt. Jim Ahern 3rd: Mike Klimchak, Bob Steinert, Tom Mituzas, Tom Staubister, Greg Miele, John Castles, Dave McDonough, Sal Pastore, Dave Sandvik, Bob Lang

ENGINE CO. 298

153-11 Hillside Avenue, Queens

They were organized on July 5, 1907, as Hose Co. 5 in the former volunteer quarters of Continental H&L 2 at 90-22 Grace Court. Their first apparatus was a 1903 George B. Marx third-size hose wagon. On August 1, 1918, Hose 5 received a 1917 Robinson 500-gpm engine and was reorganized as Engine Co. 298. On September 5, 1925, Engine 298 was relocated to new quarters with Engines 275 and 299, Ladder 127 and Battalion 50—the "First Big House"— at 89-56 162nd Street. On April 28, 1965, Engine 298 again was relocated to new quarters at 153-11 Hillside Avenue. Two members have made the Supreme Sacrifice. One member has received a medal. Engine 298 has garnered eight Unit Citations. On January 13, 1967, at 101st Avenue and Creskill Place, Engine 298's 1960 Ward LaFrance engine was destroyed in a 13-alarm gas fire. The "Hillside Hurricanes" operate with a 1992 Seagrave 1000-gpm pumper. They are quartered with Ladder 127 and Battalion 50.

1st: Lt. Dan Martinetion, Ray Cooney, Bill Frage, Mark Mushitello, Lt. Dave Bengyak 2nd: Tom McCarthy, Charlie Frame, Mike Gazzillo, Joe Miccio, Mike Borchick, John Rizzo 3rd: Ray Caluori, Wayne Ludewig, Ken Poulin, Kevin Forgarty, Brad Hores, Pat Kerley, Jim McFarland

LADDER CO. 127
153-11 Hillside Avenue, Queens

This Jamaica ladder company was organized as Ladder 77 on July 5, 1907, at 89-48 162nd Street in the former volunteer quarters of Atlantic H & L 1. Their first apparatus was a 1903 Seagrave city service 40-foot ladder truck. On January 1, 1913, they became Ladder 127. On September 5, 1925, Ladder 127 was relocated to new quarters in the first "Big House," at 89-56 162nd Street with Engines 275, 298 and 299 and Battalion 50. On April 28, 1965, Ladder 127 relocated to 153-11 Hillside Avenue with Engine 298 and Battalion 50. In 1995, Lieutenant John Clancy made the Supreme Sacrifice. Medals have been awarded to three members. Ladder 127 has garnered 10 Unit Citations. On January 13, 1967, at 101st Avenue and Creskill Place, Ladder 127's 1961 American LaFrance ladder truck was destroyed in a 13-alarm gas fire. Today, the "Hillside Hurricanes" operate with a 1995 FWD 75-foot tower-ladder. They are quartered with Engine 298 and Battalion 50.

1st: Lt. Robert Grieser, Lt. Paul Wachter, Capt. Kevin Duffy, Lt. John Saville 2nd: Timothy Burke, Jason Schmidt, Harold Herzog, Robert Adock, David Robrecht, Michael Whalen, John Brannen, William Johnson, Josef Pruden, Joseph Triolo, Kevin Darcy, William Conlon

ENGINE CO. 303
104-12 Princeton Street, Queens

They were organized in South Jamaica on July 7, 1907, as Hose 3 in the former volunteer quarters of Resolute Hose 5 at 146-39 105th Avenue. Hose 3 went into service with an 1894 P.J. Barrett first-size hose wagon, pulled by two horses. On July 15, 1922, Hose 3 received a 1922 American LaFrance 700-gpm engine and was reorganized as Engine Co. 303. On February 19, 1931, Engine 303 was relocated to new quarters at 104-12 Princeton Street. Two members have made the Supreme Sacrifice—Lieutenant Albert E. Donovan in 1924 and Firefighter Robert C. Pettit in 1944 in WW II. Engine 303 has garnered nine Unit Citations. Engine 303 has a response area of older single and multiple wood-frame dwellings, subways, Long Island Rail Road yards, junkyards and multiple apartments with storefronts. They are one of the first-due engines on Box 269 to Kennedy Airport. Engine 303 responds on a 1993 Seagrave 1000-gpm pumper. The "Princeton Street Tigers" are quartered with Ladder 126.

LADDER CO. 126
104-12 Princeton Street, Queens

Ladder 126 began as Ladder 76 on July 5, 1907, at 97-22 Cresskill Place, in South Jamaica, in the former volunteer quarters of Jamaica H & L 1. The first apparatus of Ladder 76 was a 1905 American LaFrance chemical combination ladder truck, pulled by two horses. On January 1, 1913, Ladder 76 was reorganized as Ladder 126. On February 19, 1931, the company was relocated to new quarters at 104-12 Princeton Street with Engine Co. 303. Firefighter Dennis McQueenie died in the line of duty in 1960. Ten medals have been awarded to members of Ladder 126—Steven J. Sheil, Richard Trampas (two), Steven J. Gladding, Thomas G. McAree, Kevin J. McCullagh, Dennis Sollin, John A. Signorile, Gerard L. Walsh and Thomas Reilly. Ladder 126 has garnered 17 Unit Citations. Today, they respond with a 1991 Seagrave 100-foot rear-mount ladder truck. They are quartered with the "Princeton Street Tigers," Engine 303.

1st: Lt. Michael Hart, Lt. Christian Corbin, Capt. Erick Weekes, Lt. Joseph Smithwick, Lt. Thomas Reilly 2nd: John Gremes, Michael D'Amico, Joseph Conner, Thomas Young, Thomas Irving, Robert Gabrielli, Robert Cook, James Flynn, Eugene DiTaronto, Raymond Werts, Frank Ferrara, Keith Williams, Robert Wind, Larry Byrnes, Timothy Killarney, John Maxwell, Gary Fortgang, Timothy Olson, James Stewart, William Denis, Robert Knapp, Steven DiBlasi, Dennis Sollin

ENGINE CO. 305

111-02 Queens Boulevard, Queens

Engine 305 entered service on November 15, 1924, at 111-02 Queens Boulevard in a new firehouse styled like an English Tudor to conform to the Forest Hills area. Engine 305's first apparatus was a 1924 American LaFrance 700-gpm engine. For his heroic actions, Lieutenant Thomas Gerrie received a medal in 1995. Engine 305 has a large response area. Their territory includes multiple dwellings, non-fireproof small and large apartments, Queen Annes, subways, apartments with storefronts and all kinds of store complexes. Engine 305 currently operates with a 1997 Seagram 1000-gpm pumper. They are quartered with Ladder 151 in "Deem DA Hills."

1st: Lt. Paul Duplatre, Lt. Thomas Gerrie, Capt. Joaquim DaSilva, Lt. Richard Skellington 2nd: Joseph Pomilla, Albert Ciraolo, John Winter, John Depierro, Robert Auciello, Ronald President, Robert Leonick, Douglas Edle, Richard Murry 3rd: James Bednar, Richard Truta, Sean Hayes, Terrance Sherod, Winzola Taylor, Christopher Pue, David Nelson

LADDER CO. 151

111-02 Queens Boulevard, Queens

Ladder 151 was organized on November 15, 1924, at 111-02 Queens Boulevard in Forest Hills. They have an English Tudor-style firehouse that conforms to the Forest Hills area. The first apparatus of Ladder 151 was a 1921 White Pirsch 50-foot city service ladder truck. Medals of valor were awarded to Lieutenant Walter J. Werner in 1991 and Lieutenant Nocenzo J. Cusemano in 1997. Ladder 151 has garnered two Unit Citations. The response area of Ladder 151 is the same as Engine 305. Today, Ladder 151 operates with a 1991 Seagrave 100-foot tiller ladder truck. They share quarters in the "Pride of the Hills" with Engine 305.

1st: Capt. Walter Werner, Lt. Edward Deery, Capt. Matthew Corrigan, Lt. Richard Gleave 2nd: John Holfester, Frederick Altano, Anthony Tavoulareas, James Tracy, Peter Nelson, James Carney, Joe Pilat 3rd: Joe Wisz, William Korinek, Paul Kenny, Anthony Vanacore, Arthur Leecock, John Redican, Anthony Migliore

1st: Dennis Kramer, Lt. Albert Molinaro, Capt. Peter Passaretti, Lt. Michael Cannava, John Bohn 2nd: Johnny Antoniadis, Timothy O'Connell, Andrew Hedges, John LaPadula, David Fontana, John Butcher, Peter Grandazza 3rd: Kevin Gilligan, Richard Downey, Lewis Nicolosi, Timothy Harrigan

LADDER CO. 125

159-06 Union Turnpike, Queens

This company was organized as Ladder 75 on May 5, 1907, at 91-45 121st Street in Richmond Hill in the former volunteer quarters of Richmond Hill Engine 1 and Richmond Hill Ladder 1. On January 1, 1913, they were reorganized as Ladder 125. On June 30, 1913, new quarters were constructed on the same site for Ladder 125 and Engine Co. 270 was relocated here on the same day. Ladder 125 relocated on July 20, 1953, to 159-06 Union Turnpike with Engine 315. In 1975, Firefighter John Flannigan died in the line of duty. Three members have been awarded medals—Captain Robert C. Williams in 1982, Firefighter John J. Flannigan in 1975 and Firefighter Kenneth Baumeist in 1975. Ladder 125 has received four Unit Citations. Their first apparatus as Ladder 75 was an 1899 Gleason & Bailey ladder truck, pulled by two horses. Today, they respond on a 1989 Seagrave 100-foot rear-mount ladder. They share their quarters at "Clown College" with Engine 315.

1st: George Beyer, Lt. Eric Reape, Lt. Kenneth Burbulak, Lucien Segot 2nd: Patrick Lavin, Donald Miller, Harry McCabe, Richard Bunger, Lawrence Cooke, Kevin Malone, Christopher Andres 3rd: Stephen Sanfilippo, Keith Devenish, Daniel Mayott, Thomas DaParma

ENGINE CO. 315

159-06 Union Turnpike, Queens

This company was organized on October 18, 1929, in a Mayor Jimmy Walker firehouse at 159-06 Union Turnpike in Kew Gardens and Jamaica Estates. The first apparatus of Engine 315 was a 1929 American LaFrance 700-gpm engine. Two members from Engine 315 have made the Supreme Sacrifice—Captain Daniel Murphy in 1940 and Firefighter Walter J. Bozenko in 1971. Four members have received medals for heroism—Firefighter Oscar Winegar in 1950, Firefighter Thomas E. Doyle in 1950, Firefighter James A. Mills in 1982 and Lieutenant Brian T. O'Connor in 1995. Engine 315 has garnered four Unit Citations. Engine 315 has a response territory with all kinds of buildings, single and multiple dwellings, apartments, high-rise apartments, a hospital across the street from their quarters and Queens College. They are first-due at St. John's University. Today, they operate with a 1998 Seagrave 1000-gpm engine. They are quartered at "Clown College" with Ladder 125.

1st: Fredrick Schmitt, Lt. Richard Abbott, Lt. Bruce Willman, Capt. Donald Spiegel, Steve Olberding, Lt. Michael Scully 2nd: Richard Sgro, Phillip D'Agostino, Mark Wallace, Raymond York, Charles Zachman 3rd: Dominic DeVito, Kevin Woods, Robert Brennan, Wayne Hulse, Joseph Fagan, Richard Scola, Thomas VanRossem

ENGINE CO. 285

103-17 98th Street, Queens

Organized in Ozone Park on January 1, 1915, at 103-17 98th Street, Engine 285 was one of the companies put into service with motorized apparatus. The first apparatus was a 1912 American LaFrance second-size steam engine with a Christie front-drive tractor and a 1914 Mack Boyd hose wagon. On January 1, 1925, Engine 286 received a 1924 American LaFrance 700-gpm engine to retire the steam engine. Two members made the Supreme Sacrifice—Lieutenant James Griffin in 1923 and Firefighter Thomas J. Earl in 1976. Medals have been awarded to Lieutenant Albert J. Lee in 1975 and Firefighter James A. Mills in 1987. The company has received two Unit Citations. Engine 285's response area features wood-frame dwellings—both single and multiple attached—and an elevated subway. They are one of the first-due units into Aqueduct Racetrack. Today, Engine 285 operates with a 1989 Mack 1000-gpm pumper. They are quartered with Ladder 142.

LADDER CO. 142

103-17 98th Street, Queens

This company was organized on January 1, 1915, at 103-17 98th Street in Ozone Park. Their first apparatus was a 1903 Seagrave straight frame 40-foot ladder truck. In 1916, they received a 1916 Mack city service 50-foot ladder truck to replace the tractor-drawn Seagrave. Three members have made the Supreme Sacrifice—Firefighter Michael E. Hanley in 1923, Firefighter John F. Dunne in 1923 and Firefighter Robert T. Smullen in 1966. Medals for acts of heroism have been awarded to Firefighter William B. Jacobs in 1922, Firefighter John F. Henglein in 1994 and Firefighter Lawrence Chernow in 1994. Ladder 142 has garnered five Unit Citations. Ladder 142 operates in the same response area as Engine 285. Today, Ladder 142 responds on a 1998 Seagrave 75-foot tower-ladder. They share quarters with Engine 285.

1st: James Russo, Francis Brennan, Lt. James Magas, Capt. James Mercir, Lt. Robert Castell, Lt. Salvatore Marchese, Philip Guarnieri, Lawrence Chernow 2nd: Kevin Delano, Joseph Parella, Philip Ruggierio, Frank Costa, Thomas Hyland, Victor Milukas, Edward Rissland, Robert Bynes 3rd: Michael McCarthy, Frank Ingoglia, Donald Gander, John Berna, William Harris, John Henglein, Joseph Ferrugia, Glen Stordeur

ENGINE CO. 286
66-44 Myrtle Avenue, Queens

This company was organized in Glendale on September 1, 1913, in the former volunteer quarters of Ivanhoe H&L 10 at 74-01 Cypress Hill Street. They went into service with a 1912 American LaFrance second-size steam engine with a Christie front-drive tractor and a 1912 Mack Boyd combination chemical hose wagon. On December 23, 1913, Engine 286 was relocated to new quarters at 66-44 Myrtle Avenue. Captain Raymond Koehler died in the line of duty in 1975. Engine 286 has a response area of two- and three-story brownstones, single and multiple frame dwellings and two- to three-story attached apartments with storefronts. Engine 286 was used so often for relocations that they acquired the name, "The Glendale Gypsies." Engine 286 responds with a 1993 Seagrave 1000-gpm pumper. They are quartered with Ladder 135.

1st: Joseph Lachase, Louis Rios, Lt. Marion Anderson, Lt. Richard Selig, Jerry Ross, Robert Duffy 2nd: Edward Dillon, Michael Russo, Frank Mitchell, Quentin Spencer, Patrick Flynn, Damian Duggan 3rd: Richard Kuerner, Daniel Haase, Timothy Coffey, Domenic Zito

LADDER CO. 135
66-44 Myrtle Avenue, Queens

This company was organized on September 1, 1913, at 71-55 Metropolitan Avenue in Middle Village in the former volunteer quarters of Fearless H&L 7. Their first apparatus was an 1897 Gleason & Bailey 40-foot city service ladder truck. On May 14, 1914, Ladder 135 was relocated to new quarters at 66-44 Myrtle Avenue in Glendale with Engine 286. In 1943, Firefighter George Smith made the Supreme Sacrifice. Ladder 135 has been awarded two Unit Citations. Ladder 135 has the same response area as Engine 286. Just like Engine 286, Ladder 135 so often is used for relocations that they, too, acquired the name, the "Glendale Gypsies." They operate today with a 1988 Mack 75-foot tower-ladder. They share their quarters with Engine 286.

1st: Sal Ventarola, Bill Hennessy, Capt. Steve Kinneary, Lt. Mark Guerra, Steve Harrigan, Dave Viola 2nd: Ken Woisin, Bill Knudsen, Gerry Baccari, Tom Bubelnik, John Coombs, Ralph Paprocki, Len Damelio, Tom Sweetman 3rd: Van Johnson, Bill Bell, Bill Aaron, Greg Chevalley, Eric Schroeder, Harold Brown, Mike Mazzo, Jose Morales

1st: Remo Belloli, John Palamaro, Capt. Robert Majeski, Andrew O'Connell, Kieran Colleary 2nd: Lt. Paul Rynston, Lt. John Byrne, Martin Sullivan, Bruce Isser, Jeffery Attridge, Richard Riccardi, Gregory Magi, Edward Peters 3rd: Christopher Staten, Paul Stein, Michael Iannazzo, Steven Huron, Jim Coakley, Matt Farrell, Steven Ross, Matthew Schmiemann, Glen Franke

ENGINE CO. 293
89-40 87th Street, Queens

This company was organized on July 5, 1907, as Hose Company 2 in the former volunteer quarters of Clarenceville H&L Co. 2 at 91-70 111th Street. It entered service with a four-wheel third-size hose wagon. On January 1, 1915, Hose 2 was relocated to new quarters at 89-40 87th Street. On the same day, Hose 2 was reorganized as Engine Co. 293. They operated with a 1912 American LaFrance second-size steam engine with a Van Blerek tractor and a 1913 Mack Boyd combination chemical hose wagon. Three members from Engine 293 have made the Supreme Sacrifice—Firefighter Ignatius F. Neusch in 1916, Firefighter Joseph Scanlon in 1936 and Firefighter Robert W. Johnson in 1943 during WW II. Engine 293 has been awarded four Unit Citations. Engine 293 has a response area of multiple attached wood-frame dwellings, single wood-frame dwellings, multiple apartments with storefronts and an elevated subway. The "Woodhaven Wild Cats" currently operate with a 1989 Mack 1000-gpm pumper.

ENGINE CO. 294

101-02 Jamaica Avenue, Queens

Engine 294 was organized on January 1, 1915, at 101-02 Jamaica Avenue in Richmond Hill. They entered service fully motorized with a 1912 American LaFrance second-size steam engine with a 1914 Mack Boyd hose wagon. On November 22, 1975, Engine 294 was disbanded and reorganized on July 1, 1981. Ten years later on March 3, 1991, Engine 294 again was disbanded. On February 28, 1994, they were reorganized again. Two members have died in the line of duty—Firefighter Arnold N. Hafner in 1955 and Firefighter Robert J. Denney in 1960. For his heroic actions, Firefighter Mark Janesky was given a medal in 1922. Engine 294 has received two Unit Citations. Their response area includes single and multiple wood-frame dwellings, Queen Ann residences, apartments with storefronts and an overhead subway. Engine 294 responds with a 1994 Seagrave 1000-gpm pumper. "El's Angels" are quartered with Ladder 143.

1st: John McCoy, Frederick Robinson, Lt. Joseph DiMartino, Capt. Thomas Howell, Lt. Arthur Spina, Robert Gless 2nd: John Piazza, Brian Gill, Anthony Pullo, Thomas Carmody, Richard Napolitano, Timothy Westhall, Gerald Liotta, Sherman Smalls 3rd: Joseph LeDeoux, Eugene Philcox, Benedict Rebecca, Joseph Tumulty, John Paolella, James Rodgers, Harold Yodice, Kevin Dunn

1st: Bobby Reich, Tom Lucas, Charlie Hayes, Capt. Paul Dombrowsky, Ed Galiani, Jim Werner, Mark Koetzner 2nd: Chris Coughlin, Bobby McGuire, Billy Tripp, John Donovan, Jim McCabe, Ray Moran, Eddy Valk, Jerry Nappo, Charlie Laclair, Tom Manzo, Ed Tully, Joe Mattiello, Fred Kirk, Billy Nolan, Mike Tedaldi, Rob Giardina

LADDER CO. 143

101-02 Jamaica Avenue, Queens

Ladder 143 was organized on January 1, 1915, at 101-02 Jamaica Avenue in Richmond Hill. When Ladder 143 entered into service, they operated with a 1905 American LaFrance straight frame combination chemical 50-foot ladder truck. Three members from Ladder 143 died in the line of duty—Firefighter Stanley Skinner in 1976, Lieutenant Joseph M. Beetle 1976 and Lieutenant Peter Canelli in 1987. Medals for valor have been awarded to Firefighter Arthur F. Shaw in 1922, Firefighter Alfred J. Bold in 1974, Lieutenant Walter C. Mischke in 1974 and Firefighter Kenneth Fitzpatrick in 1993. Ladder 143 has received five Unit Citations. The response area of Ladder 143 is the same as Engines 294 and 293 and Squad 270. Ladder 143 operates today with a 1991 Seagrave 100-foot tiller ladder truck. They are quartered with the "Els Angels," Engine 294.

ENGINE CO. 308

107-02 Lefferts Boulevard, Queens

This company was organized on November 30, 1926, at 107-02 Lefferts Boulevard in Richmond Hill South. Their first apparatus was a 1917 American LaFrance 700-gpm engine. Firefighter John C. Huggins was killed in the line of duty. Firefighter Randal H. Rodrigues was presented with a medal in 1993 for his heroic actions. Engine 308 received six Unit Citations from 1987 to 1998. Because of over-crowded, single-room occupancies and old wood-frame dwellings, Engine 308 worked in one of the highest fire fatality areas of the 1990s. Engine 308 operated at some major incidents, including the Jamaica Gas fire in 1967, the Long Island Rail Road crash in the 1950s and the Eastern Airline crash in 1975. Engine 308 has a 1980 American LaFrance engine converted by the Shops to hold 3000 feet of five-inch hose for use at KENNEDY AIRPORT. They operate with a 1997 Seagrave 1000-gpm pumper. They share their quarters with the JFK hose wagon and Battalion 51.

1st: Nicholas Donofrio, Randy Rodrigues, James Ferretti, Lt. Robert Urso, Lt. Cliff Payan, Capt. Robert Bell, Lt. Joe Mills, James Hall, Wayne Slater 2nd: Steve George, Pete D'Ancona, Jere Dineen, Phil Lanasa, Kevin Wilkinson, Joe Glick, John Ostrick, Kevin Crosby, Tom McAllister, Tom Lynch, Steve Kelly, Paul Sokol 3rd: Steve Lawrence, Craig Moore, Rob Wilson, Bob Meany, Chris Simmons, Al Merk, Steve Cox, Bob O'Hara, Tom Gathmann, Anthony Bonfiglio

1st: Michael Mulqueen, Michael Szewczuk, Lt. Kevin Callaghan, Lt. Richard Bleoth, Kevin Casey, Joseph Terry 2nd: Michael Keaser, Daniel Seller, Michael Coyle, Terry Horn, Joseph Mitchell, Donald Hoffman 3rd: Kevin Collins, George Barr, Kenneth Lorigan

ENGINE CO. 331
158-57 Cross Bay Boulevard, Queens

This company was organized on September 5, 1938, at Main Street for the World's Fair in Flushing Meadow Park. Their apparatus was a 1938 Ahrens Fox 1000-gpm engine. The second section was a 1938 Ahrens Fox 500-gpm engine. Engine 331 was disbanded when the World's Fair closed on March 31, 1941. On December 2, 1966, Engine 331 was reorganized in a new firehouse in the Howard Beach section in Queens at 158-57 Cross Bay Boulevard. Their new apparatus was a 1946 Ward LaFrance 750-gpm engine. Engine 331 is the only firehouse with a dock and waterway in the rear yard. The small fireboat, *Blaze*, operated here from May 16, 1968, until December 11, 1970. The *Hackett* operated until December 16, 1974. They have received one Unit Citation. Their response area includes residential homes and commercial stores and businesses. Engine 331 responds with a 1993 Seagrave 1000-gpm pumper. They are quartered "On Golden Pond" with Ladder 173. From May to October, the small fireboat, *Marine 3*, operates from Engine 331's quarters.

LADDER CO. 173
158-57 Cross Bay Boulevard, Queens

This company was organized on December 1, 1966, in a new firehouse at 158-57 Cross Bay Boulevard in Howard Beach. This new ladder company was put into service to reduce the response time in the areas of Howard Beach, South Ozone Park, West Hamilton Beach and into the Broad Channel area. Their first apparatus was a 1955 FWD 75-foot wooden ladder tiller truck. Ladder 173 has had one member make the Supreme Sacrifice—Lieutenant Robert J. Cahill in 1982. Ladder 173 has shared their quarters with the small fireboats, *Blaze* and the *Hackett* from 1968 to 1974. Ladder 173 operates in the same response area as Engine 331 and also is assisted by the West Hamilton Beach Volunteer Fire Department. Ladder 173 operates with a 1989 Seagrave 100-foot tiller ladder truck. They share their quarters, "On Golden Pond," with Engine 331 and—from May to October—the small rescue fireboat, *Marine Operations 3*.

1st: Lt. Michael Harty, Capt. Michael Kadel, Lt. Joseph Masterson 2nd: Kenneth Borgs, Daniel Kemmet, Angel Vasquez, Robert Green, Robert Massella 3rd: Peter Statis, Steve McCaffery, William Englund, Bruce Baxter

1st: Tim Hoyt, Joe Tursi, Jack Huttle, Steve Vella, Gary Lamb, Capt. Mike Degennaro, Capt. Bill Olson, Lt. Joe Bachety, Paul Armato, Ed Cusack, Tim Carney, George Finnerty, Jerry Fiore, John Degirolamo, E.J. Maloney, Adrian Keenan, Todd Smith 2nd: Jack Fullam, John Loeber, Kirk Leslie, Patty Wall, Joe Minicozzi, Joe Boyle, Mike Wolyneic, Mike Brown, Tom Reid 3rd: John Regan, Paul Monfre, John Morrissey, Ken Healy, Bob Middendorf, Bob Martens, Lee Streithorst, Sean Sammon, Al Ferguson

ENGINE CO. 301

91-02 197th Street, Queens

This Hollis company was organized on January 15, 1921, at 91-02 197th Street in the former volunteer quarters of Hollis H&L 1. They entered service with a 1917 American LaFrance 700-gpm engine. On May 5, 1933, Engine 301 was quartered in a new firehouse erected at the same location. Firefighter George L. Byrne died in the line of duty in 1931. For his heroic actions, Firefighter Walter C. Lehman received a medal in 1952. Engine 301 has been awarded three Unit Citations. Engine 301 has a response area of single and multiple wood-frame dwellings, apartments, taxpayers and two- and three-story apartments with storefronts. Today, Engine 301 operates with a 1998 Seagrave 1000-gpm pumper. The "Hollis Hogs" are quartered with Ladder Co. 150.

LADDER CO. 150

91-02 197th Street, Queens

Ladder 150 was organized on January 15, 1921, at 91-02 197th Street in Hollis in the former volunteer quarters of Hollis H&L 1. Their first apparatus was a 1915 Mack 50-foot city service ladder truck. New quarters were erected on the same site for Ladder 150 on January 1, 1933. Two members of Ladder 150 have been awarded medals for valor—Firefighter James R. McEnroe in 1985 and Captain Michael J. Uzzi in 1987. The company has received one Unit Citation. Ladder 150 has the same response area as Engine 301. Ladder 150 responds on a 1995 Seagrave 100-foot rear-mount ladder truck. They are quartered with the "Hollis Hogs," Engine 301.

1st: Lt. Rich O'Leary, Hector Faberlle, Jeff Ercolino, BC Pete Hart, Capt. Tom Farino, Kevin Monahan 2nd: Jim Jacobs, Lt. Frank Leto, Brian DePalmo, Chris Nelson, Frank Stark, Larry Troy, Greg Diliello 3rd: Capt. Jim Dalton, Jim Murray, Lt. Joe Ferguson, Dan Dorrian, Frank Lobue, Greg McLoughlin

ENGINE CO. 302

143-15 Rockaway Boulevard, Queens

This South Ozone Park Company was organized on July 5, 1907, as Hose Co. 4 in former volunteer quarters of Distler Hose 3 at 92-11 150th Street in Jamaica. The first apparatus of Hose Co. 4 was a 1903 George B. Marx third-size hose wagon. On November 9, 1912, Hose 4 was relocated to new quarters at 137-24 Rockaway Boulevard in South Ozone Park. On October 21, 1921, Hose 5 received a 1921 American LaFrance 700-gpm engine and was reorganized as Engine Co. 302. On January 31, 1931, Engine 302 again was relocated to new quarters at 143-15 Rockaway Boulevard. Firefighter Bernard Tully died in the line of duty in 1957. Engine 302 has received four Unit Citations. Engine 302's response area includes older single and multiple wood-frame dwellings, apartments and apartments with storefronts. They are the first-due engine into Kennedy Airport. They operate a 1993 Seagrave 1000-gpm engine. They are quartered in the "Vipers Nest" with Ladder 155.

LADDER CO. 155
143-15 Rockaway Boulevard, Queens

Ladder 155 was organized on November 30, 1926, at 107-12 Lefferts Boulevard in the South Richmond Hill area of Queens in the quarters of Engine 308. Their apparatus was a 1921 White Pirsch 50-foot city service ladder truck. On March 1, 1947, Ladder 155 was relocated to 143-15 Rockaway Boulevard in South Ozone Park. Lieutenant Victor Prokop made the Supreme Sacrifice in 1970. Medals have been awarded to Firefighter Gerade V. Albro in 1965, Firefighter Raymond Nelson in 1937, Firefighter Martin Schmidt in 1976, Firefighter Robert R. Maynes in 1989 and 1987, Firefighter Herman C. Bringe in 1988 and Firefighter Bruce Baxter in 1982. The company has received seven Unit Citations. Ladder 155 operates in the same response area as Engine 302. They respond with a 1995 FWD 75-foot tower-ladder. They share their quarters in the "Vipers Nest" with Engine 302.

1st: Lt. Allen Williams, Bruce DiPietro, Ed Gaynor, Lt. John Stack, Oscar Thompson, Frank Papalia, Steven Kuefner 2nd: Bruce Gerrie, Don Wunderlich, Dan Donohue, John McCormack, Joe DiPinto, Dave Gettens, Larry Vitiello, Andy Badamo 3rd: Lt. Dan Karp, Joe Abramski, Jim Connolly, Lt. Casey Politi, Mike Schramn, Scott Thomson, Randy Feifel, Lou Grappone 4th: Tim Scully, Jim Radin, Phil Davey, Tom Ryan, Ron Pannicia, Capt. Boudreau

1st: Robert Murphy, Lt. Michael Abele, Capt. Nicholas Schiralli, Lt. John Brennan, Alan Locascio 2nd: Joseph Calvacca, Arthur Schwab, Robert Constant, Albert Saponieri, Douglas Dematteo, Fred Ostrick, Charles Jones 3rd: Christopher Cirino, Kenneth McCormick, Frank Romano, Joseph Barrow, Bryan Edgar, Thomas Meny, Timothy Culley

ENGINE CO. 311
145-50 Springfield Boulevard, Queens

This engine company was organized on October 16, 1927, at 145-50 Springfield Boulevard in Springfield Gardens, to replace the volunteer companies, Springfield Chemical Engine 1 and Springfield Hose 1. Engine 311 entered service with a 1917 American LaFrance 700-gpm engine. Lieutenant Joseph P. Connelly made the Supreme Sacrifice in 1972. Engine 311 has garnered two Unit Citations. Their response territory includes single and double wood-frame dwellings, garden apartments, two large schools, the Belt Parkway and a large brush area. Additionally, Engine 311 is one of the first-due units into Kennedy Airport. Today, they respond with a 1993 Seagrave 1000-gpm pumper. The "Swamp Dogs" are quartered with Ladder 158.

LADDER CO. 158
145-50 Springfield Boulevard, Queens

Ladder 158 was organized on September 16, 1927, at 145-50 Springfield Boulevard in Springfield Gardens to replace the volunteer company Rosedale Ladder 1. The apparatus used by Ladder 158 was a 1916 Mack 50-foot city service ladder truck. On July 13, 1974, Ladder 158 was reorganized with Engine 311 into a combination unit, Combination Co. 151, and reorganized back to Ladder 158 on November 12, 1977. A medal of valor was awarded to Firefighter Frank J. Walsh in 1949. Ladder 158 has received one Unit Citation. Ladder 158 was one of the last companies to operate with a wooden aerial ladder, as late as 1971. They operate in the same response area as Engine 311. Ladder 158 responds with a 1994 FWD 75-foot tower-ladder. They are quartered with the "Swamp Dogs," Engine 311.

1st: Thomas Spagnola, Michael VanRoten, Lt. John Esposito, Capt. Leroy O'Neill, Lt. Hank Bringe, Edmund Costigan 2nd: Thomas Heschl, Chris Meyer, Ray Moss, Michael Gregory, William Duncan, Jack Cappadora, James Miller 3rd: Juan Pacheco, Chris Kalata, Edward Walsh, Joseph Andryuk, Dennis McSweeney, Craig Pitz, Donald Meyer, Anthony Monaco

ENGINE CO. 314
142-04 Brookville Boulevard, Queens

This Rosedale company was organized on September 27, 1929, at 142-04 Brookville Boulevard. When Engine 314 entered into service, it replaced the volunteer company, Rosedale Chemical Engine 1. The first apparatus of Engine 314 was a 1929 American LaFrance 700-gpm engine. Firefighter William J. Farrell died in the line of duty in 1966. They have a response area of mostly single and multiple wood-frame dwellings, two large schools, two- and three-story apartments with storefronts and a large brush area adjacent to Kennedy Airport. Engine 314 relocates to Far Rockaway on all 10-75s in the Rockaway area. Occasionally, Engine 314 has operated in Nassau County, providing mutual aid to the volunteer Valley Stream Fire Department. Today, they operate with a 1993 Seagrave 1000-gpm engine and are quartered by themselves "On the Edge" of Runway 22 Left at JFK.

1st: Lt. Charles Marsh, Lt. Michael Dulko, Capt. Kevin Munnelly, Lt. John Schilling 2nd: John Perretti, Richard Oliveri, John Acritani, Charles Incarnato, Michael Stuart, Sean Griffin 3rd: Timothy McConnell, Chris Eckhoff, William White, Scott Hummel, Donald Maher

ENGINE CO. 317
117-11 196th Street, Queens

Engine 317 originated on October 18, 1929, at 117-11 196th Street in St. Albans. When Engine 317 entered service, it operated with a 1929 American LaFrance 700-gpm engine. From 1983 to 1995, Engine 317 has garnered four Unit Citations. Engine 317 is one of the busiest engine companies in Queens with a very large response area to protect. Their territory still has many old pull boxes. Their first-due area is made up of primarily residential single and multiple wood-frame dwellings, taxpayers and small apartments with storefronts. Today, Engine 317 responds with a 1997 Seagrave 1000-gpm pumper. The "St. Albans Sleepless Knights" are quartered with Ladder 165 and Battalion 54.

1st: BC Peter Campbell, Lt. Robert Collis, Lt. Robert Smillie, Lt. Paul Deo, Capt. Patrick Hawkins 2nd: William Carlson, Dave Amon, Matthew Kelleher, Robert Tucker, Steven McEvoy, Ronald Bonomo, Thomas Immello, John Hartmann, Louis Dimino, Mathew Zitz, Frank Santonastaso 3rd: Vincent Schieda, John Amzler, Frederic Bienz, John Urbanski, James Ritchie, Robert Korfman, Daniel Filosa, Mark Montgomery, Anthony Liantonio

LADDER CO. 165
117-11 196th Street, Queens

Ladder 165 was organized on October 18, 1929, at 117-11 196th Street in St. Albans. This ladder company was put in service to replace the disbanded volunteer company, St. Albans Ladder Co. 1. Their first piece of apparatus was a 1929 American LaFrance 75-foot tiller truck. One member from Ladder 165 has made the Supreme Sacrifice—Lieutenant Robert E. Rummel in 1949. A medal for valor was awarded to Firefighter Clarence Waldron in 1953. Two Unit Citations have been garnered by Ladder 165. They have the same response area as Engine 317, with a great number of old pull boxes. The company averages approximately 4000 runs a year. Ladder 165 operates with a 1989 Seagrave 110-foot rear-mount ladder truck. They are quartered with the "St. Albans Sleepless Knights," Engine 317.

1st: James Yuskevich, Paul Pfeifer, BC Peter Campbell, Lt. Philip DeLuca, Capt. Patrick Hawkins, Lt. James Pepio, Lt. John Brown, Donald Chrisville 2nd: Robert Engel, James Johnsen, Joseph Lucchese, Mark Barrett, Michael Yannucci, Vincent Hefferen, Michael O'Donnell, Laurence Mooney, Albert Schmidt, Anthony Marden, Thomas Valentine, James Setter 3rd: Michael Bonura, Howard Kleinschmidt, Brian Janelli, Michael Koncz, William Robinson, James Doherty, Michael Stack, Joseph Joy, Wayne Calder, Patrick Astegher, Frank Durr

ENGINE CO. 264

16-15 Central Avenue, Queens

This company was organized as combination Engine Co. 164 in the former volunteer quarters of Protection Engine 1, Oceanic Hose 1 and Protection H&L 1 at 16-15 Central Avenue in Far Rockaway on September 1, 1905. On January 1, 1913, Combination Engine 164 was reorganized as Combination Engine 264. On May 24, 1913, Combination Engine 264 moved into new quarters at the same location and was reorganized as Engine 264. That same day, the ladder section was reorganized as Ladder Co. 134. Two members have been awarded medals. Engine 264 has received two Unit Citations. Engine 264 had a busy day on June 15, 1922: the home of Broadway star Lillian Russell burned on Reids Lane, Far Rockaway, and two members were killed in a chimney collapse. In the afternoon, 141 homes were destroyed in the Arverne conflagration. They operate a 1998 Seagrave 1000-gpm pumper. This is the only firehouse in the FDNY with two engines and a ladder in a three-bay building. They are quartered with Engine 328 and Ladder 134.

1st: Lt. Patrick Featherson, Capt. William Schelling, Lt. Kevin Kelly 2nd: Christopher Pagano, Glenn McAuley, Richard Porcelli, Tim Rowe 3rd: James Rae, Robert Ricciardi, Gregory Ruggiero, Arthur Poore, Kenneth Nichtern

LADDER CO. 134

16-19 Central Avenue, Queens

This company was organized on May 24, 1913, in Far Rockaway at 16-19 Central Avenue in the newly constructed quarters of Engine 264. Their first apparatus was a 1905 American LaFrance straight frame combination chemical 50-foot ladder truck acquired from combination Engine 264's ladder section. Three members have died in the line of duty. Four members have received medals—Firefighter Thomas J. Brady in 1933, Captain Timothy F. Costello in 1933, Lieutenant Kevin J. Coyle in 1993 and Firefighter Kenneth Rogers in 1994. The company has garnered three Unit Citations. On the morning of June 15, 1922, the home of Broadway star Lillian Russell burned to the ground. Ladder 134 Firefighter Emmet F. Donnelly and an off-duty member from Engine 26, Firefighter Adrian Curran, were killed in the line of duty. That afternoon, Ladder 134 worked at the Arverne conflagration that destroyed 141 houses. Ladder 134 operates with a 1992 Seagrave 100-foot rear-mount ladder truck. They are quartered at the "Big House" with Engine 264 and Engine 328.

1st: Rich Porcelli, Lt. Gerry McParland, Lt. Phil Duncan, Timmy Rowe 2nd: Ben Laube, Robert Riccardi, Mike Krol, Frank Vanderlofske, Jimmy Rae, Mike Savino 3rd: Greg Ruggierio, Jeff James, Chris Pagano, Anthony Mauro, Arthur Poore

1st: Lt. Patrick Kilgallen, Capt. John Seibert, Lt. James O'Brien 2nd: Timothy Rowe, Arthur Poore, William McAuley, William Hopkins, Wally Torres, James Rae, Frank Gatto 3rd: Richard Porcelli, Gregory Ruggiero, Chris Paggano, Anthony Mauro, Kenneth Nichtern

ENGINE CO. 328

16-15 Central Avenue, Queens

This company had its beginnings on August 16, 1939, at 16-15 Central Avenue in Far Rockaway. Engine 328 was the second section of Engine 264, which was put into service after the Arverne conflagration in 1922. Its first apparatus as Engine 328 was a 1931 American LaFrance 700-gpm engine. Engine 328 has been awarded two unit citations for exemplary work—one in 1992 and the other in 1994. This company has a response area of mostly residential structures, single and multiple dwellings, Queen Annes, apartments, housing projects, beach high-rise apartments and an energy power plant in Far Rockaway. Today, they respond with a 1998 Seagrave 1000-gpm engine. They share quarters at the "Big House" with Engine 264 and Ladder 134.

1st: Michael Weinschreider, Paul Dieringer, Salvatore Thompson, Lt. Lee Fisher, Capt. Brian White, Lt. Robert Pfeiffer, Michael Gambino, Lawrence Intrabartola 2nd: Richard Nash, Christopher Farrell, Kenneth Dolney, Guy LaCognata, Anthony DiMonda, Michael Schreiner, James Botta

ENGINE CO. 265
58-03 Rockaway Beach Boulevard, Queens

This company was organized as Engine Co. 165 in the former volunteer quarters of Arverne Engine and Hose Co. 2 at 63-21 Rockaway Beach Boulevard on September 1, 1905. Engine 165's apparatus was an 1897 Clapp & Jones third-size steam engine assisted by an 1896 Gleason & Bailey third-size hose wagon. On January 1, 1913, Engine 165 was reorganized as Engine 265. They faced a conflagration in Arverne that destroyed a five-block area from Rockaway Beach Boulevard to the ocean. They could not restart the Christie front drive on their Clapp & Jones steamer and it, too, was destroyed in the fire. On September 27, 1929, Engine 265 relocated to their new and current quarters. One member has been awarded a medal. The company has one Unit Citation. Engine 265's response area features single and multiple dwellings, housing projects, high-rises, the Cross Bay Bridge and the Key Span Energy Power Plant. After the Arverne conflagration, they received a 1923 American LaFrance 700-gpm engine. Today, they respond on a 1992 Seagrave 1000-gpm engine.

LADDER CO. 121
58-03 Rockaway Beach Boulevard, Queens

This Arverne company was organized on September 1, 1905, as Ladder 71 at 88-03 Rockaway Beach Boulevard in the former volunteer quarters of Oceanus Hose Co. 2. On January 1, 1913, Ladder 71 was reorganized as Ladder 121. They relocated to new quarters at 92-20 Rockaway Beach Boulevard on December 21, 1922, with Engines 266 and 267 and Battalion 47. On March 1, 1954, Ladder 121 was relocated to 58-03 Rockaway Beach Boulevard with Engine 265. Four members have died in the line of duty. Medals have been awarded to Firefighter Ambrose Morgan in 1929, Firefighter Richard J. Gillen in 1967, Firefighter John J. Frain in 1967 and Firefighter James B. Williams in 1991. Ladder 121 has garnered seven Unit Citations. Ladder 121's first apparatus was a 1903 Seagrave city service truck with a 40-foot ladder. Today, they respond with a 1991 Mack 95-foot tower-ladder. They share their quarters with Engine 265.

1st: Peter Murphy, Kevin Shannon, Kevin Brown, Lt. Kelly McDonald, Capt. John Rokee, Thomas Hall, Robert Gates, Michael Tripptree, John Komorowski 2nd: Vincent Vaccaro, Frank Haskell, Thomas Begley, Michael Peterson, Glenn Heidenfelder, Brian Gallagher, Matthew Cody, Joseph Carey, Richard McDonough 3rd: James Byrne, Michael Sandhaas, Dennis Boyle, Michael Murray, William Gallagher, Rodger Buck, John Olsen, Richard Hill, Michael Baumeister

ENGINE CO. 266
92-22 Rockaway Beach Boulevard, Queens

This company was organized as Engine 166 in the former volunteer quarters of Atlantic Hose Co. 1 at 211 Beach 86th Street on September 1, 1905. Its first apparatus was an 1893 LaFrance fourth-size steam engine with a 1903 George B. Marx third-size hose wagon. On January 1, 1913, Engine 166 was reorganized as Engine 266. On June 15, 1922, Engine 266 operated at the Arverne conflagration with the rest of the Rockaway companies. On December 21, 1922, they were relocated to new quarters at 92-22 Rockaway Beach Boulevard with Engine 267, Ladder 121 and Battalion 47. One member has died in the line of duty. They have garnered four Unit Citations. Engine 266 has a response area of one- and two-family dwellings, housing projects, high-rise apartments and an elevated subway. They are the first-due engine over the Cross Bay Bridge into Broad Channel. Engine 266 acquired a new brush fire unit on October 17, 1997. They operate a 1997 Seagrave 1000-gpm engine. They share quarters with Brush Unit 7 and the 47th Battalion.

1st: Lt. Daniel O'Brien, William Hartman, Capt. Keith Fairchild, Capt. Timothy Tubridy, Lt. William Magale 2nd: William Smith, Leroy McGinnis, Glen Ott, Michael Hynes, Charles Wendland, Frank Esposito, Michael Chojnacki 3rd: Timothy Gallagher, Stephen Conklin, Robert Tilearcio, Gary Olsen, Charles Weinsheimer, John Jordan

ENGINE CO. 268

259 Beach 116th Street, Queens

This Rockaway Park company was organized in the former volunteer quarters of Atlantic Engine Co. 1 as Engine Company 168 at 111-02 Rockaway Beach Boulevard on November 28, 1905. They went into service with an 1886 Clapp & Jones third-size steam engine and an 1896 P.J. Barrett second-size hose wagon. On January 1, 1913, Engine 168 was reorganized as Engine 268. They relocated to their new and current quarters with newly organized Ladder 137 on November 27, 1913. In 1913, they received a motorized Mack Boyd combination chemical hose wagon. Three years later, a Van Blerek tractor was installed on the American LaFrance steam engine, which retired all the horses. Engine 268 has been awarded two Unit Citations. Their response area includes single and multiple dwellings, apartments, taxpayers and overhead subways. They are second-due engine to Rockaway Point and Broad Channel. In 1922, Engine 268 also operated at the Arverne conflagration. They respond with a 1993 Seagrave 1000-gpm pumper and share quarters at the "Beach House" with Ladder 137.

1st: Tom Wilson, John Considine, Kevin Swift, Al McSaveny 2nd: Bob Koeth, Lt. Dan Fucella, Glenn Bubbenheimer, Lt. Ray Creede, Tom Reilly

LADDER CO. 137

259 Beach 116th Street, Queens

This Rockaway Park ladder company was organized on November 27, 1913, at 259 Beach 116th Street in the new quarters built for Engine 268. When they entered service, their apparatus was a 1913 American LaFrance 65-foot ladder truck. One member from Ladder 137 has made the Supreme Sacrifice—Firefighter Bertram Butler in 1941. Three members have been awarded medals for their acts of heroism—Firefighter Joseph A. Courtney in 1950, Firefighter Conrad J. Rohe, Jr., in 1965 and Firefighter Eugene Gentile in 1999. Ladder 137 has received six Unit Citations. Ladder 137 has the same response area as Engine 268. Ladder 137 operated on June 15, 1922, at the Arverne conflagration that destroyed 141 homes. Today, Ladder 137 responds on a 1999 Seagrave 100-foot rear-mount ladder truck. They are quartered at "The Beach House" with Engine 268.

1st: Brendan Kearns, Tom Costa, Kevin Judge, Jim Murphy, Brennan Savage 2nd: Peter Blum, Bob Knoop, Bill Kalletta, Rich Ferrin, Capt. Pete Murray, Terrance O'Donnell

ENGINE CO. 329

402 Beach 169th Street, Queens

This company was organized on December 2, 1961, at 402 Beach 169th Street in the Neoponsit section of the Rockaways. Their first apparatus was a 1954 Ward LaFrance 750-gpm engine. Lieutenant Eugene B. Murtagh received a medal for heroism in 1993. Engine 329 has received one Unit Citation. From January 27, 1963, until December 11, 1970, Engine 329 had a small fireboat, the Flame, which was launched from the nearby Coast Guard station. Engine 329 has a response area of single and multiple dwellings in Neponsit and one- and two-story dwellings in Roxbury and Rockaway Point. They are the first-due engine to Floyd Bennett Field (Gateway Park). Engine 329 is assisted by three volunteer fire departments—Roxbury, Point Breeze and the Breezy Point Fire Departments. The "Beach Boys" operate with a 1993 Seagrave 1000-gpm pumper and a four-wheel drive GMC manifold hose wagon, equipped with a deck pipe, hose and firefighting equipment, to operate in the sand on the beach at houses not accessible by a road.

1st: John O'Brien, Lt. Mark Pinsent, Capt. Donald Mischke, Lt. Thomas Healy, Lt. Mike Ferrarese 2nd: Steven Snapper, Michael Woods, Virginia Spinelli, Jack Paglino, Robert Stark, Robert Portano, Elizabeth Featherston 3rd: John Tubridy, Daniel Archbold

DIVISION 14

*1st: DC Seamus McNeela, DC Thomas Dunne, DC Michael Butler, DC Michael Giovinazzo **2nd:** Capt. Michael Stefano, John Frohlich, Theodore Monte, Kim Paolino, Gene Van Vort, Thomas Greco, Lt. Martin Cass*

BATTALION 45

BATTALION 46

BC Michael Rowley, BC Joseph Molfeto, BC Joseph Dwyer, BC Daniel Conlisk, BC James Gerrish, Kenneth McDermott

*1st: BC Vinny Mavaro, BC John Acerno, BC John Kleehaas **2nd:** Jeff Meister, Rich Cleary*

BATTALION 49

*1st: BC George Lonergan, BC William Seelig, BC William McGovern **2nd:** Van Don Williams, Jerry DeMeo, Miguel Berrios, James Roy*

BATTALION 52

Mitch Tropin, BC Robert Stampfel, BC John Gleeson, Dave Brandman

BATTALION 53

1st: BC Walter Worontzoff, BC Richard Rewkowski, BC Michael O' Keefe, BC Gerard Koziak
2nd: Robert Feinsilver, Vincent Bulzomi

ENGINE CO. 258
10-14 47th Avenue, Queens

Engine 258 was organized as Engine 1 of the Long Island City Fire Department at 12-17 Jackson Avenue with Ladder 1 on February 1, 1891. On January 28, 1898, Queens County became part of the City of New York and Engine 1 became Engine 58. They were reorganized as Engine 158 on October 1, 1899. On September 3, 1904, Engine 158 was relocated with Ladder 65 to 10-14 47th Avenue and on January 1, 1913, Engine 158 was reorganized again to Engine 258. Two members have made the Supreme Sacrifice. Two members have received medals. Engine 258 has been awarded four Unit Citations. Engine 258's response area includes multiple dwellings, factories, apartments, overhead roadways and bridges, waterfronts, subways, the Long Island Rail Road, Sunnyside Yards and the Midtown Tunnel. They are second-due engine into Greenpoint, Brooklyn. Engine 258 has a 1993 Seagrave high-pressure pumper. Engine 258 has been the home of the fictional Engine 57 and Ladder 100 for the NBC television series, *Third Watch*. Engine 258 is quartered with Ladder 115.

1st: Steve Denaro, Lt. Pete Stein, Capt. Frank Shanagan, Lt. Bob Doherty, Tim Heidrich 2nd: Charlie Dankenbrink, Dan McGuinn, Greg Salone, Frank Larkin, Scott Freeze, Mike Essig, Mick Rafferty, Wayne Dutton, Dan Corrigan 3rd: Dave Santiago, Frank Montaruli, Jim O'Hara, Jim Schade, Mike Treiland, Frank Carney, Tom Johnston, Phil Ercolano, Bill Schenone

LADDER CO. 115
10-40 47th Avenue, Queens

This company was organized on January 1, 1891, as Ladder 1 of the Long Island City Fire Department at 12-16 47th Road. On January 28, 1898, Queens became part of the City of New York and Ladder 1 was reorganized as Ladder 15 of the FDNY. On October 1, 1899, Ladder 15 was reorganized as Ladder 65. They were relocated to new quarters on October 3, 1904, at 10-40 47th Avenue with Engine 158. On January 1, 1913, Ladder 65 became Ladder 115. Firefighter Francis X. Egan and Lieutenant John W. Smith were killed in the line of duty. Medal recipients include Firefighter Gregory Pirozzi in 1962, Firefighter Sasha W. Burak in 1947 and Firefighter Thomas J. Lucas in 1913. Ladder 115 received four Unit Citations. Ladder 115 responds with a 1994 FWD 75-foot tower-ladder. They share quarters with Engine 258. The fictional Engine 57 and Ladder 100 are portrayed here in the NBC television series, *Third Watch*.

1st: Richard Huttie, Lt. Thomas Albert, Capt. Gerard McMahon, Lt. Roy Richburg, Lt. Steven Guise, Samuel Maldonado 2nd: Paul Lang, Patrick Carew, Gary McGuggart, Lawrence Klingener, Charles Roberts, Stephen Hoch, Ray Ward, Steve Golden, Howard Tewes 3rd: John Maniaci, Leo Russ, Rich Paolone, Scott Prinz, Robert Kuhnle, John Balkunas, William Sesselman, Derek Kelly

45th Battalion

45th Battalion

1st: Daniel Dillon, Adam Torres, Paul Santoro, Capt. Richard Hogan, Lt. James Berghorn, David Cane, James O'Boyle, Richard Boscarino 2nd: Mike McDonald, Mike Conklin, Charles Guttman, Carl Reich, Sam Bello

ENGINE CO. 259
33-51 Greenpoint Avenue, Queens

Organized March 1, 1894, as Engine Co. 2 of the Long Island City Fire Department at 71 Gale Street in the Hunters Point section of Queens, their first apparatus was an 1886 Clapp & Jones, fourth-size steam engine with an 1892 Gleason & Bailey hose wagon. On January 28, 1898, Queens became part of the City of New York and Engine Co. 2 was reorganized as Engine Co. 59. On October 1, 1899, Engine 59 was reorganized as Engine Co. 159. On February 7, 1910, Engine 159 was relocated to new quarters at 33-51 Greenpoint Avenue and on January 1, 1913, was reorganized as Engine Co. 259. One member made the Supreme Sacrifice. Engine 259 has been awarded three Unit Citations. Engine Co. 259 has a response area including dwellings, waterfront, factories, waterways, the Queens Midtown Tunnel, overhead roadways and bridges. They are second-due engine into Greenpoint, Brooklyn, and first-due at Fleet Maintenance. They operate a 1993 Seagrave 1000-gpm pumper. They are quartered with Ladder Co. 128 and Battalion 45.

LADDER CO. 128
33-49 Greenpoint Avenue, Queens

This Hunters Point ladder company was organized on February 7, 1910, as Ladder 78 at 33-49 Greenpoint Avenue. Their first piece of apparatus was a 1910 Seagrave AMSA 75-foot ladder truck, pulled by horses. On January 1, 1913, Ladder 78 was reorganized as Ladder 128. Three members from Ladder 128 have made the Supreme Sacrifice—Firefighter Caesar J. Macari in 1939, Firefighter Edwin C. Remhild in 1964 and Firefighter James W. Kojac in 1956. Ladder 128 has received one Unit Citation. In 1921, Ladder 128 received a 1921 White Pirsch city service ladder truck to retire the horses. Today, Ladder 128 operates with a 1989 Seagrave 100-foot rear-mount ladder truck. They are quartered at "Tombstone Territory" with Engine 259 and the 45th Battalion.

ENGINE CO. 260
11-15 37th Street, Queens

Engine 6 was organized at 685 Vernon Boulevard in the former quarters of Ladder 3 on May 15, 1895. Their first apparatus was an 1894 American fourth-size steam engine with a four-wheel hose tender. On January 28, 1898, Engine 6 was reorganized as Engine 60. In 1899, Engine 60 was relocated to new quarters at 36-33 Vernon Boulevard. On October 1, 1899, Engine 60 was reorganized as Engine 160 and on January 1, 1913, was reorganized as Engine 260. On March 31, 1939, Engine 260 was relocated to their current quarters. One member made the Supreme Sacrifice. Engine 260 has been awarded three Unit Citations. Water Tower 5 and Searchlight 1 operated here until they were disbanded. On September 5, 1972, a foam unit was relocated to Engine 260 and on May 10, 1988, was reorganized as Foam Unit 81 and on December 29, 1998, Foam 260. The apparatus is a 1978 Mack pumper converted for a foam operation. Engine 260 operates a 1988 Mack 1000-gpm pumper.

1st: David Lynott, Lt. Frank Donodeo, Capt. Joseph Saccente, Capt. Glen Judson, Lt. Michael Burke, Lt. Jim Daly, Clifford Hawkins 2nd: David Carpio, Michael Gallo, Keith Tanico, Tim Delaney, Glen Taylor, Louis Celestino, Michael Agosta, Dean Beltrami, Joseph Cataldi, Christopher Long, Salvatore Chillemi 3rd: Frank Nash, Jay Frango, John O'Malley, Christopher Lenny, Thomas Greco, Eddie Rodriguez, John Nietzschmann, Richard Pyryt

LADDER CO. 116

37-20 29th Street, Queens

This company was organized on January 1, 1894, at 443 Buckley Street, as Ladder 2 of the Long Island City Fire Department. The first apparatus was an 1889 Gleason & Bailey 60-foot ladder truck. On January 28, 1898, Ladder 2 became Ladder 16 of the FDNY. On October 1, 1899, Ladder 16 was reorganized as Ladder 66. Ladder 66 was relocated to new quarters on 38-11 Northern Boulevard on October 3, 1904. On January 1, 1913, Ladder 66 was reorganized as Ladder 116. On March 1, 1947, they relocated to 37-20 29th Street with Engine Co. 261. Two members from Ladder 116 have made the Supreme Sacrifice. Ladder 116 has received six Unit Citations. On November 29, 1921, they received a 1921 Mack 65-foot ladder truck to retire the horses. Today, they respond with a 1989 Seagrave 100-foot rear-mount. They are quartered with Engine 261.

1st: Lt. Bryan O'Neill, Lt. James O'Donnell, Capt. Ralph Gismondi *2nd:* John Westfield, Dave Schleyer, Dennis McGoldrick, John Drew, John Griffin, Kevin Tonkin, Kenneth Holler, Daniel Kelly, Warren Degan *3rd:* Brian Lavan, Robert Demott, William Russell, Joseph Vosilla, Carl Italiano, John Dallao, Richard Larocca, Thomas Rizzi, James Rooney, Robert Clarke, Richard Motta

1st: Lt. Thomas Westman, Joseph Anzalone, Lt. Patrick Vissichelli, Lt. Thomas McKenna *2nd:* Nicholas Demasi, Jeffery Bednar, Michael Kilcommons, Michael Musich, Peter Miele, Jimmy Georgilis, Steven Cycan *3rd:* Andrew Braun, Thomas Regan, Juan Flores, Christopher Dimaria, Daniel Kipnes, Joseph Parrino, Christopher Marino, Richard Scott, Christopher Yudt

ENGINE CO. 261

37-20 29th Street, Queens

Organized as Engine Co. 3 on June 12, 1984, located at 38-08 28th Street. On January 28, 1898, Engine 3 was reorganized as Engine 61. On October 1, 1899, Engine 61 was reorganized as Engine 161 and on January 1, 1913, was reorganized as Engine 261. On October 22, 1931, Engine 261 relocated to new quarters at 37-20 29th Street in what was called a Mayor Jimmy Walker firehouse. Three members have died in the line of duty. Their unique response area includes residential dwellings, factories and one of the busiest transportation hubs—four subway lines converging into Queens Plaza and the Long Island Rail Road, Amtrak and the Conrail all converging into the Sunnyside Yards. Engine 3 was organized with an American fourth-size steam engine and four-wheel hose tender. Engine 261 operates a 1989 Mack 1000-gpm pumper. Engine 262 is quartered with Ladder 116.

ENGINE CO. 291

56-07 Metropolitan Avenue, Queens

Engine 291's history began on October 1, 1915, at 56-097 Metropolitan Avenue in Ridgewood. When put into service, their apparatus was a 1912 American LaFrance second-size steam engine with a 1914 Mack hose wagon. Engine 291 replaced the volunteer company, Metropolitan Engine 12, located at 57-10 Metropolitan Avenue. Two members from Engine 291 have made the Supreme Sacrifice: Lieutenant John Mayer in 1929 and Lieutenant Joseph Sparacino, Jr., in 1976. Engine 291 has a response area of brownstones, single and multiple wood-frame houses, taxpayers, multiple store complexes and apartment houses. A good part of their runs are made into Brooklyn and they often are called the "Ridgewood Border Patrol." Today, Engine 291 responds on a 1993 Seagrave 1000-gpm pumper. They are quartered with Ladder 140.

1st: Lorraine Cziko, Capt. Walsh, Capt. Cicola, John Hackett *2nd:* John Donovan, John Panzone, John Manzione, Steve Intrabartola, Ray Anderson *3rd:* Dennis Lee, Rich Kugler, Bill Magnus, John Whalen, Jim Stang, Mike Messineo, Jim Ross

45th Battalion

LADDER CO. 140
56-07 Metropolitan Avenue, Queens

This company was organized on October 1, 1915, at 56-07 Metropolitan Avenue in the Ridgewood section of Queens. Ladder 140 entered service with a 1903 Seagrave straight frame 40-foot ladder truck. Approximately two months later, a 1915 motorized Mack city service 50-foot ladder truck replaced it. Ladder 140 has been awarded one Unit Citation. Ladder 140 covers the same response area as Engine 291 and frequently operates in Brooklyn. Today, they respond on a 1991 Seagrave 100-foot rear-mount ladder truck. The "Ridgewood Raiders" are quartered with Engine 291.

1st: Eddie Lawler, Lt. Edmund Lucia, Capt. Donald Csorny, Lt. John Roiy, Rich Casta 2nd: Mark Lopez, Al Barroca, Peter Lazarcheck, John Joy, Brian Barrett, Brian Mitchell, Tom Anderson, Evan King, Chris McQueen 3rd: James Scaglione, Robert Quinn, Fred Ford, Steve Wojsnis, Chris Goehring, Thomas Kaminski, Anthony Conte, Bill Roesch

ENGINE CO. 287
86-53 Grand Avenue, Queens

They were organized in Elmhurst on September 1, 1913, in the former volunteer quarters of Wandownock Engine Company 1 at 86-18 Broadway. Engine 287 had a second section until August 1, 1918, when it was disbanded. Engine 287 went into service with a 1912 American LaFrance second-size steam engine and 1912 Mack Boyd combination chemical hose wagon. On October 1, 1914, Engine 287 was relocated to new quarters at 86-53 Grand Avenue with Ladder 136. Engine 287 has been awarded five Unit Citations. Engine 287 has a varied response area of many small and large apartments, retail stores, subways and single and multiple dwellings. Today, Engine 287 operates with a 1992 Seagrave 1000-gpm pumper. The Elmhurst Eagles share quarters with Ladder 136 and the 46th Battalion.

1st: Greg Lemko, Alfred O'Dea, Brian Griffin, Lt. Eric Sands, William Vesely, James Holmes 2nd: Edward Higgins, Michael Savino, Keith Lippert, Steve Carlino 3rd: John Venticinque, Dudley Cox, John Kearns, William Murphy, Rodger Rudezwick

1st: George Schaaf, Michael Risso, Lt. George Hosle, Capt. James McNally, Lt. Richard Gonzalez, Scott Cowan 2nd: William Pence, Richard Cleary, Robert Ferrara, Paul Archer, Thomas Foy 3rd: Michael Gunning, William Pedersen, Scott Annicelli, John Weber, Duery Smith

LADDER CO. 136
86-53 Grand Avenue, Queens

This Elmhurst company was organized on September 1, 1913, at 91-12 43rd Avenue in the former volunteer quarters of Elmhurst Ladder 1. Ladder 136 entered service with a 1905 American LaFrance straight frame 50-foot combination chemical ladder truck. On October 1, 1914, Ladder 136 relocated to new quarters at 86-53 Grand Avenue, their current location. Three members from Ladder 136 have made the Supreme Sacrifice—Firefighter Peter Farley in 1943, Firefighter Joseph P. Dugan in 1954 and Captain Wayne E. Smith in 1994. Medals for heroism have been awarded to Firefighter James J. Flood in 1944, Lieutenant John W. Collins in 1986, Firefighter Anthony Sannella in 1992 and Firefighter James T. Finnell in 1998. Ladder 136 has garnered 12 Unit Citations. They have the same response area as Engine 287. They respond on a 1994 Seagrave 100-foot rear-mount ladder truck. Ladder 136, the "Elmhurst Eagles," are quartered with Engine 287 and Battalion 46.

ENGINE CO. 289

97-28 43rd Avenue, Queens

This Corona company was organized on September 1, 1913, in the former volunteer quarters of Pioneer Ladder 6 and Pioneer Hose Co. 6 at 41-19 102nd Street. Their first apparatus was a 1912 American LaFrance second-size steam engine with a 1912 Mack Boyd combination chemical hose wagon. On December 1, 1914, Engine 289 was relocated to their new and current quarters on 97-28 43rd Avenue. Two members have been killed in the line of duty—Firefighter Patrick O'Connor in 1917 and Firefighter Jacob G. Gulde in 1928. A medal for heroic actions was awarded to Raymond Dee in 1964. Engine 289 has accumulated 12 Unit Citations. One of the busiest companies in Queens, Engine 289 has a large response area of multiple dwellings, apartment houses, taxpayers and other store complexes. Today, Engine 289 operates a 1994 Seagrave 1000-gpm pumper. They share quarters with Ladder 138. The firehouse of the "Corona Tigers" recently was given landmark status.

1st: Joseph Minogue, David McAndrews, Lt. Peter Melly, Lt. Edward Byrne, Capt. Peter Mulhall, Lt. Richard Bruno, Christopher Revere, Dennis Siry 2nd: John O'Brien, Gerald Farina, Michael Grogan, Michael King, John Gallager, Dennis Stefanak, Keith Calabrese, Michael Schmid, William Lynch, Michael Dunphy 3rd: Stephen Poppe, Randolph Supuk, James Weldon, Eric Figueroa, Greg Hirschfield, Kenneth Speecht, Glenden Bell, Steven Troche, John DeBenedittis

LADDER CO. 138

97-28 43rd Avenue, Queens

This company was organized on October 25, 1929, in the Corona section of Queens at 97-28 43rd Road. When Ladder 138 entered service, their first piece of apparatus was a 1929 American LaFrance 75-foot tiller truck. Medals have been awarded to Captain Patrick M. Larkin in 1940, Lieutenant Sidney S. Stenson in 1953, Firefighter William F. Poventud in 1979, Firefighter Neil G. Yank in 1989, Firefighter Daniel G. Delargy in 1994 and Firefighter Raymond A. Fassberger in 1999. Ladder 138 has garnered 13 Unit Citations. Ladder 138 operates in the same response area as Engine 289. They respond on a 1997 Seagrave 75-foot tower-ladder. They share quarters with Engine 289. The quarters of the "Corona Tigers" recently have been given landmark status.

1st: Peter Gunther, Ken Gunther, Mike Prior, Lt. Mike Moran, Capt. John Maloney, Lt. Mike McLoughlin, Kevin Smith, Don Wilson 2nd: Joe Tarantini, Paul Fanara, Jim Weisenburger, John Gennosa, John Wojcik, John Malley, Vic Rosa, Jim Fearon, Pete McGrath, Bob Stanton 3rd: Dennis Donovan, Rich Jones, Ted Monte, Joe Fernicola, Joe Lauria, Tom Marino, Phil Piarulli, Bob Wright, Dean Marino, Ray Fassberger

1st: William Pollack, Lt. Robert O'Keefe, Lt. Alan Maurer, Capt. Rocco Citeno, Lt. Louis Guzzo, Scott Ringle 2nd: William Waring, Christopher Gaidis, Richard Welliver, Richard Miranda, Dean Spadaro, Joe Lavan 3rd: Kenneth Strohl, Damon Alston, Kenneth Michitsch, Alan Blazkiewicz, Sean McPherson, Anthony Chaimowitz

ENGINE CO. 292

64-18 Queens Boulevard, Queens

Engine 292 was organized on September 1, 1913, as the second section of Engine 287 in the former volunteer quarters of Gooderson Engine 2 at 67-32 Queens Boulevard. When Engine 287 (2) was put into service, its apparatus was a 1912 Mack Boyd combination chemical hose wagon. This apparatus was used for seven years until they received a 1920 American LaFrance 700-gpm engine. On December 1, 1914, Engine 287 (2) was relocated to new quarters at 64-18 Queens Boulevard. On August 1, 1918, Engine 287 (2) was reorganized as Engine Company 292. Three members have died in the line of duty—Firefighter Howard V. Colbert in 1944 in WW II, Firefighter Vincent A. Schmitt in 1944 in WW II and Firefighter William McEvoy in 1956. Firefighter John Marshall received a medal in 1956. The company has garnered five Unit Citations. Engine 292 responds on a 1994 Seagrave 1000-gpm pumper. The "Winfield Cougars" share their quarters with Rescue 4.

ENGINE CO. 319
78-11 67th Road, Queens

This Middle Village engine company was organized on November 18, 1930, at 78-11 67th Road. Engine 319 entered service with a 1921 American LaFrance 700-gpm engine and two months later received a new, 1930 Mack 700-gpm engine. The 1930 Mack lasted until 1951 when Engine 319 received a 1951 Ward LaFrance 750-gpm engine. Firefighter Daniel Sullivan made the Supreme Sacrifice in 1954. Three members have been awarded medals for their acts of heroism—Firefighter Frank Knoph in 1941, Firefighter William V. Groening in 1946 and Lieutenant Edward G. Rankin in 1947. Engine Company 319 has received three Unit Citations. They have a response area of single and multiple attached wood-frame dwellings, taxpayers and small apartments with storefronts. From July 1, 1984, until it was disbanded on November 29, 1989, Battalion 59 was quartered with Engine 319. Today, Engine 319 responds with a 1993 Seagrave 1000-gpm pumper. "The Lone Wolf" is quartered by itself.

1st: Stanley Bohenek, Michael Staten, Lt. Dennis O'Connor, Capt. Charles Feyh, Lt. Joseph Baccari, Lt. Bradley Walls, John Sahtila, Michael Of **2nd:** *Mark Morello, Jesus Mercado, Joseph Slattery, Thomas Vanwallendael, Vincent Mattone, John Reynolds, James Manganaro, James Seney, Joseph Schettino, Joseph Woska, James Daley, Nicholas Carpenter, Charles Kotov* **3rd:** *James Gregoretti, Michael Pontone, Robert Westerberg*

ENGINE CO. 324
108-01 Horace Harding Boulevard, Queens

This company was organized on March 18, 1940, at 108-01 Horace Harding Boulevard in Flushing Meadows. They entered service in a new firehouse before Engines 331, 332 and 333 were disbanded after the 1939 World's Fair closed. Their first apparatus were a 1939 Ahrens Fox 1000-gpm engine, the first and only fire apparatus built entirely by FDNY Shops personnel, and a 1938 Ahrens Fox 500-gpm engine, which was acquired from Engine 332. Engine 324 has had two members make the Supreme Sacrifice—Firefighter Samuel A. Schiller in 1954 and Firefighter Denis J. Corrodan in 1952. Engine 324 has been awarded six Unit Citations. Their response area includes single and multiple dwellings, two major highways, shopping complexes, small apartments and high-rise apartment complexes. Engine 324 is also Satellite 4 of the Maxi Water System and can operate anywhere in the borough. The "Queens Burros" of Engine 324 respond with a 1987 Mack 2000-gpm pumper and a 1993 Mack hose wagon with a large stang gun and 3000 feet of five-inch hose. They share their quarters with Division 14.

1st: Matthew Linitz, Lt. Thomas O'Brien, Lt. Joseph Colleluori, Lt. Dennis Madden, Capt. Dennis Kenahan, Daniel Drolet **2nd:** *Chris Paglia, Richard Draves, Gerard Lee, Vincent Fondacaro, Brian Moloney, William Keegan, John Cipriano, Thomas Dandola* **3rd:** *James Pescatore, Edward McDonagh, Joseph Napoli, Gary Smaldon, James Takes, Salvatore Bologna, Mark Bacenet, Michael Gunning, Gary Kresse*

ENGINE CO. 262
30-89 21st Street, Queens

This company originally was organized as Engine 4 on March 20, 1891, in a firehouse on 12 Main Street for the volunteer companies, Tiger Hose Co. 8, Columbia Hose 9 and Astoria H&L 1. Their first apparatus was a horse-drawn hose wagon, followed by an 1894 LaFrance fourth-size steam engine and Gleason & Bailey second-size hose wagon. On January 25, 1898, Engine 4 was reorganized as Engine 62. On October 1, 1899, Engine 62 was reorganized as Engine 162 and on January 1, 1913, was reorganized as Engine 262. On May 10, 1972, Engine 262 was relocated to their current quarters. One member has made the Supreme Sacrifice. Two members have received medals. Engine 262 has been awarded nine Unit Citations. Engine 262's response area includes dwellings, housing projects, Roosevelt Island, factories, the Triborough Bridge and a large Con Edison power plant. In 1915, Engine 262 operated an experimental engine built by Westinghouse in 1910. Today, they respond on a 1993 Seagrave 1000-gpm pumper.

1st: Lt. Mark Foris, Lt. Eric Michelsen, Claude Kebbe, John McKenna, Robert Daly, Paul Rut, Francis Brancato, Dennis Langrock, Daniel Gorwitz, James Heerey, Capt. Frank Conners **2nd:** *William Freese, Rich Coyle, James Long, Dean Neligan, Dennis Quinci, Robert Rindfleisch, James Martin* **3rd:** *Brian Caglione, Robert Wieber, Robert Brown, Cliff Lesmeister*

*1st: Lt. Bill Stubbs, Capt. Mike Barry, Lt. Kevin Kefer **2nd:** Joe Abbamonte, Jeff Brown, Gorden Thomas, Joe Knapik, Alan Arias, Bob Antonelli **3rd:** Richie Appenzeller, Jim Maguire, Gene St. John, Gerard Cox, Lainard Granger, Phil Russo*

ENGINE CO. 263
40-08 Astoria Boulevard, Queens

This company began as Engine 5 with Ladder 4 at 40-08 Astoria Boulevard on December 8, 1894. Its first apparatus was an 1894 LaFrance fourth-size steam engine and a Gleason & Bailey second-size hose wagon. On January 28, 1898, Engine 5 became Engine 63. On October 1, 1899, Engine 63 was reorganized as Engine 163. Engine 163 moved into new quarters at 40-08 Astoria Boulevard on May 1, 1909. On January 1, 1913, Engine 163 was reorganized as Engine 263. One member has died in the line of duty. Two members have been awarded medals. Engine 263 received five Unit Citations. Their very busy response area includes all kinds of structures, highways, the Triborough Bridge and a large Con Edison power plant in Ravenswood. They are one of the first-due engines at LaGuardia Airport. The first motorized apparatus of Engine 263 was a 1920 American LaFrance 700-gpm engine. Today, the "Road Runners" respond with a 1993 Seagrave 1000-gpm pumper. They are quartered with Ladder 117.

LADDER CO. 117
40-08 Astoria Boulevard, Queens

They were organized on December 8, 1894, as Ladder 4 of the Long Island City Fire Department at 40-08 Astoria Boulevard with Engine 5. On January 28, 1898, Ladder 4 was reorganized as Ladder 17. On October 1, 1899, Ladder 17 was reorganized as Ladder 67. Quarters were built for Ladder 67 on May 1, 1909, further back from its original site, but at the same address. On January 1, 1913, they became Ladder 117. For heroic actions, Firefighter Eberhard Von Uchtrap received a medal in 1955. Ladder 117 has garnered 10 Unit Citations. Their response area spans the Fire Academy and Rikers Island, "Between a rock and a hard place." Ladder 117 went into service with an 1894 LaFrance Hayes 55-foot ladder truck. Today, they operate with a 1991 95-foot Mack tower-ladder. They are quartered with Engine 263.

1st: Thomas McDougall, Patrick Baker, Capt. Dennis Ruckdeschel, Lt. James Hay, Ricardo Soria, Kevin Mathis 2nd: Matthew Swan, Peter Konopka, Michael Morrisey, Frank McCartin, Richard Smithwick, John Bonadio 3rd: Brian Kearney, Neil Volz, Robert Poncel, Thomas Ingram, Craig Baldwin

1st: David Forland, Kevin Kelly, Jorge Faberlle, Lt. Robert Ginley, Charles Bruno, Ralph Seiter 2nd: Matthew Dwyer, Bayard Carmiencke, John Tew, Eugene Reaccuglia, Richard DePrima, Gary Santosus, Raymond Arcos

ENGINE CO. 307
81-17 Northern Boulevard, Queens

This company was organized on February 2, 1925, at 81-17 Northern Boulevard in Jackson Heights. Upon entering service, their first piece of apparatus was a 1924 American LaFrance 700-gpm engine. While responding to an alarm in 1935, Firefighter Raymond M. Sands made the Supreme Sacrifice. Two members from Engine 307 have been awarded medals—Lieutenant Stephen Passion in 1972 and Lieutenant Louis Monteleone in 1990. Engine 307 has garnered seven Unit Citations from 1980 to 1998. Engine 307 has a response area that features single wood-frame dwellings, multiple wood-frame attached dwellings, small and large apartments and apartment complexes with storefronts. They are also one of the first-due engines into Shea Stadium and LaGuardia Airport. The "Jackson Heights Knights" operate with a 1988 Mack 1000-gpm pumper. They share their quarters with Ladder 154.

LADDER CO, 154
81-17 Northern Boulevard, Queens

This ladder company was organized on February 1, 1925, at 81-17 Northern Boulevard in the Jackson Heights area of Queens. Their first apparatus was a 1925 American LaFrance 75-foot tiller truck. Medals of valor have been awarded to Lieutenant Howard Kennedy (2) in 1980, Firefighter Michael R. DiGiorgio in 1986, Lieutenant Carl S. DiLallo in 1994 and Firefighter Charles Wiemann in 1994. Ladder 154 has been awarded an impressive 12 Unit Citations. Ladder 154 operates in the same response area as Engine 307. They respond on a 1999 Seagrave 100-foot rear-mount ladder truck. The "Jackson Heights Knights" share their quarters with Engine 307.

1st: Scott Duryea, Dean Stephen, William Quinn, John Fratangelo, Lt. Carl DiLallo, Lt. Daniel Buckheit, Virgil Sanchez, Glenn Berube 2nd: Ron Kirchner, Michael Fitall, Mike McCrory, Michael Gagliano, Richard Schmidt, George Carl, Scott Pflume

1st: Robert Goetz, Patrick Varian, Capt. William McLaughlin, Lt. Charles Harris, Steven Vano 2nd: Edward Ganassa, Glenn Fitchett, James Roy, John Sottile, James Pustelniak, Kevin Pidgeon 3rd: David Higgins, Robert Hilke, Miguel Berrios, James Morris, Italo Colasante

ENGINE CO. 312
22-63 35th Street, Queens

This company was organized on November 1, 1928, at 22-63 35th Street in Astoria. Engine 312's first apparatus was a 1928 American LaFrance 700-gpm engine. Lieutenant George G. Goger made the Supreme Sacrifice in 1963. Three Engine 312 members have been awarded medals for heroism—Captain Denis W. Lane in 1948, Lieutenant George R. Goger in 1953 and Firefighter Ronald S. Sessa in 1964. Engine 312 has been awarded three Unit Citations. Engine 312 has a response area that includes all kinds of single and multiple wood-frame dwellings, the Triborough Bridge, a large Con Edison power plant in Ravenswood, apartments with storefronts, an elevated subway and Rikers Island. They are one of the first-due units into LaGuardia Airport. They respond on a 1993 Seagrave 1000-gpm pumper. The "Hell's Gate Firefighters" share their quarters with Battalion 49.

ENGINE CO. 316
27-12 Kearney Street, Queens

This company was organized on November 25, 1929, at 27-12 Kearney Street in East Elmhurst. Their first piece of apparatus was a 1929 American LaFrance 700-gpm engine. For his act of heroism, Firefighter James A. Mills received a medal in 1982. Engine 316 has been awarded 12 Unit Citations. Engine 316 has a varied response area with all kinds of single and multiple wood-frame dwellings, storefronts and large airport hotels. Their first-alarm assignment includes Shea Stadium and Flushing Bay Marina. They respond first-due at LaGuardia Airport. Today, Engine 316 operates with a 1993 Seagrave 1000-gpm pumper.

1st: Paul Quinnonez, Peter Cosgrave, Lt. Robert Mungiguerra, Capt. William Cetto, Lt. John Lombardi, Lt. Frank Manetta, Gary Giannone 2nd: John Murphy, Michael Keller, Leroy Jonas, Carmelo Mercado, Peter Naldrett, Glenn Sieber, Vincent Marino 3rd: John Helmke, Peter Sollenne, Donald Hohmann, Ralph Portoghese, Joseph Riccardi, Mark Wrobleski, Nichlos Wowk, Joseph Turner

ENGINE CO. 325
41-24 51st Street, Queens

Engine 325 was organized on September 8, 1941, at 41-24 51st Street in the Woodside section of Queens. They entered into service with a 1941 Mack 1000-gpm engine. Three members from Engine 325 have made the Supreme Sacrifice—Firefighter James F. Marino, Firefighter Richard Andrews and Captain William F. Russell. All three perished in a building collapse in 1962. Three other firefighters were injured fatally at the same location. Engine 325 has a response area of two- and three-story attached multiple dwellings, large apartment buildings, taxpayers, a complex of underground and elevated subways, the Long Island Rail Road and the Sunnyside Rail Yards. "The Woodside Warriors" of Engine 325 operate with a 1988 Mack 1000-gpm pumper. They are quartered with Ladder 163.

1st: Lt. Nichlos D. Alessandro, Capt. Thomas White, Lt. John Margherita 2nd: Keith Ruby, Thomas D'Alto, Bernard Cornell, James Lavin, Marek Jaworski, Robert Meyer, Robert Ammann, Stephen Dominick, Eric Huber, Matthew McDougall, Thomas Moore 3rd: William Sieter, Michael Potter, Steven Greco, Scott Cassese

LADDER CO. 163
41-14 51st Street, Queens

Ladder 163 was organized on November 1, 1928, at 22-31 35th Street in Astoria in the quarters of Engine 312. Their first apparatus was a 1913 American LaFrance 65-foot tiller ladder with a 1926 FWD tractor. On April 1, 1952, Ladder 163 was relocated to 41-24 51st Street in Woodside with Engine 325. Members of Ladder163 who have made the Supreme Sacrifice are Lieutenant James O'Donnell in 1932 and Firefighter Charles Will in 1939. Medals have been awarded to Firefighter James S. Norton in 1948, Firefighter Edward J. Stegmaie in 1947, Firefighter Christof Burns in 1964, Firefighter Harry Martin in 1987, Firefighter Thomas M. Harrington in 1996, Lieutenant John S. Colbert in 1988 and Firefighter Owen P. James in 1988. Ladder 163 has received two Unit Citations. Ladder 163 operates in the same response area as Engine 325. In 1985, Ladder 163 operated with a 100-foot American LaFrance tower-ladder. Now, they respond with a 1989 Mack 95-foot tower-ladder. The "Woodside Warriors" are quartered with Engine 325.

1st: Lt. John Messina, Lt. Charles Zuba, Capt. Kevin Benes, Lt. Mark Boyd 2nd: Kevin McKenna, Harry Ohnigian, Larry Krepela, John VanWallendael, Nicholas Dolce, Jon Mastrodomenico, Thomas Harrington, James Quinn, James Pue, Robert O'Neill, Joseph Depperman, Robert Mas, Brian Cleary, Cono Manzione, Gerard Brannigan, Scott Grubert 3rd: Anthony Leonick, Timothy Johnston, Scott Larsen, Richard Miccio, Chris Messana, Thomas Gambino, Kenneth Warns, Kevin Sconzo, Duncan Cooke

ENGINE CO. 273

40-18 Union Street, Queens

This Flushing company was organized on December 1, 1908, as Engine Co. 173 in the former volunteer quarters of Mutual Engine 1 at 40-16 Union Street. Engine Co. 173's first apparatus was an 1897 fire extinguisher company chemical engine and hose, pulled by two horses. On January 1, 1913, Engine 173 was reorganized as Engine 273. New quarters were erected on the same site and on February 3, 1932, they moved in with Ladder 129, with whom they still share quarters in the "Mouse House." Engine 273 has been awarded five Unit Citations. Their response area includes single and multiple dwellings, apartment complexes, expressways, taxpayers and multiple store complexes. They are one of the first-due engines into Shea and Arthur Ashe Stadiums in Flushing Meadow Park. Engine 273 responds on a 1988 Mack 1000-gpm pumper.

1st: Richard Gramolini, Jeffery Baer, Lt. Robert Mulzac, Lt. John Lorenz, Christopher Fusaro, Laurence Parker 2nd: Ronald Schankin, Jeffery Teta, Thomas Woods, Steven Gawrych, Jason Choi 3rd: Lawrence Migliore, Robert Kiernan, Brian Whiston, James Walther

1st: Edward Murphy, Thomas Mott, Lt. Richard McCarthy, Capt. Salvatore Cusumano, Lt. Peter Antine, Lt. James Smithwick, Shawn Murphy, Kevin LaClair 2nd: Pasquale Caggiano, Louis Minutoli, Michael D'Antuono, Thomas Doherty, Raymond Lamboin, Thomas Colvin, John Walis, Michael Lavin 3rd: William Sander, Richard Margino, James Interdonati, Craig Dunn, Wayne Mera, Joseph Cundari, Thomas Coughlin, James Carroll

LADDER CO. 129

40-18 Union Street, Queens

This company was organized on December 1, 1908, as Ladder 79 at 133-76 40th Road in Flushing in the former volunteer quarters of Rescue Ladder 1. Their first apparatus was a 1903 Seagrave straight frame 40-foot ladder truck, pulled by two horses. On January 1, 1913, they became Ladder 129. On November 3, 1928, Ladder 129 relocated to new quarters with Engine 272 at 135-16 38th Avenue. On February 3, 1931, they moved to their current location with Engine 273. Two members have died in the line of duty—Firefighter Ernest Mattes in 1935 and Firefighter Richard Schultz in 1959. For their heroic actions, nine members have been awarded medals. Ladder 129 has garnered six Unit Citations. Ladder 129 responds on a 1994 Seagrave 100-foot rear-mount ladder truck. They are quartered at the "Mouse House" with Engine 273.

ENGINE CO. 274

41-20 Murry Street, Queens

Organized December 1, 1908, as Engine Co. 174 in the former volunteer quarters of Murry Hill Hose Co. 4 at 150-18 41st Avenue, their first apparatus was an 1896 Charles T. Holloway combination chemical engine and hose wagon. On January 1, 1913, Engine 174 was reorganized as Engine Co. 274. To make room for the Long Island Rail Road in 1914, Engine 274's quarters were picked up and moved to a new location at 41-20 Murry Street. On July 19, 1940, a new firehouse was erected on the same site. The company's one medal was garnered by Lieutenant Francis R. Shanagan in 1995. Engine 274 has been awarded nine Unit Citations. Engine 274 has a response area in Flushing that includes every kind of dwelling, apartment complexes and store complexes. They operate a 1993 Seagrave 1000-gpm pumper and share their quarters, "The Orient Express," with Battalion 52.

1st: Kevin Biscardi, Jorge Albert, Scott Bentley, Frank Digristina, Eamonn McLoughlin 2nd: Mark Hamilton, BC Gleeson, Capt. Johnson, Tom Porti, James Gunther, David Brandman, Peter Giammarino 3rd: Lt. Thomas LeDeoux, Michael Gunther, Charles Horak, Michael Farsang, Paul Rogers

1st: Victor Sailor, Michael Spyntiuk, John Zangara, Carl Nicolosi, Christopher Traahey, Peter Scally, Steven Baretta, William Bonilla, Sean Hickey, Peter Freshour, James Checco, Christopher Fallon 2nd: Walter Voight, Steve Newman, Robert Digiovanni, Darren Cook, Ray Grace, Timothy Coan, Brian Heffernan, Scott Schaffer, Robert Montgomery, Derron Peck, Jim Myers, Michael Claffey, Domenick Pastore, Fred Cortese, Brian Lane, Jim Brown 3rd: Peter Tripp, Fred Bishoff, John Peteroy, Kevin Sheehy, Brian Trummer

ENGINE CO. 295
12-49 149th Street, Queens

Engine 295 began operations in Whitestone at 14-09 149th Street on October 1, 1915. They were put into service to replace the volunteer companies Whitestone Engine 1, Columbia Hose 1 and Indian Hose 2. Their first apparatus was a 1914 Ahrens Fox 700-gpm engine. In 1938, Engine 295 was relocated to the old volunteer quarters of Whitestone Ladder 1 at 150-43 14th Avenue. Their firehouse was moved 1 blocks north to 12-49 149th Street to make way for the new Cross Island Parkway. On November 10, 1939, they relocated back into their old quarters. Three members have received medals. Engine 295 has been awarded one Unit Citation. Their response area includes single and multiple dwellings, small apartments and highways. They are first-due over the Whitestone Bridge and first-due engine at the future Fire Academy at Fort Totten. Engine 295 responds with a 1993 Seagrave 1000-gpm pumper and shares its quarters with Ladder 144.

LADDER CO. 144
12-49 149th Street, Queens

This ladder company was organized on October 1, 1915, at 14-09 149th Street in Whitestone. Their first apparatus was a motorized 1915 Mack city service 50-foot ladder truck. On November 15, 1938, Ladder 144 was relocated to the old volunteer quarters of Whitestone Ladder 1 at 150-43 14th Avenue. Their quarters were moved north 1½ blocks to 12-49 149th Street to make way for the new Cross Island Parkway. On November 10, 1939, they moved back into their quarters. Ladder 144 has had two members make the Supreme Sacrifice—Firefighter Frederick Ziegler and Firefighter William D. Austin, both as a result of an exploding gas can at a boat fire in 1947. For his heroic actions, Firefighter James T. Kelleher received a medal in 1941. Ladder 144 has garnered three Unit Citations. Ladder 144 responds on a 1994 FWD Baker Saulsbury 75-foot tower-ladder. They are quartered with Engine 295.

ENGINE CO. 297
119-11 14th Road, Queens

This College Point company was organized on December 1, 1908, as Hose Co. 9 in the former volunteer quarters of Enterprise Hose Company 2 at 14-11 114th Street. Its first apparatus was an 1898 Sebastian second-size hose wagon pulled by two horses. On August 1, 1918, Hose 9 received a 1917 motorized Robinson 500-gpm engine and Hose Co. 9 was reorganized as Engine Co. 297. On February 21, 1931, they relocated to new quarters at 119-11 14th Road. Two members have made the Supreme Sacrifice—Firefighter Gerald T. Ganley in 1978 and Firefighter Tony Shands in 1984. For their heroic actions, two members have been awarded medals—Firefighter Guy V. Avezzano in 1979 and Lieutenant James E. Reinheime in 1987. Engine 297 received one Unit Citation. Engine 297's response area includes single and multiple frame dwellings, apartments with storefronts and small and large factories. The "Pride of the Point" operates with a 1989 Mack 1000-gpm pumper. They are quartered with Ladder 130.

1st: Michael Amberg, Lt. George O'Doherty, Lt. James Pappas, Lt. Richard Bauser, Alvin Kevelier 2nd: Tom Carney, James Fleming, Carl Fassberger, David Santise 3rd: Steven Letscher, Phil Senra, Joe Green

1st: Paul Shannon, Capt. Tim Sullivan, Lt. Keith Hulse, Ron Anderson 2nd: Nat Johnson, George Faller, John McCarthy, Adam Taylor 3rd: Chris Costi, Joe Karney

LADDER CO. 130
119-11 14th Road, Queens

This company was organized on December 1, 1908, as Ladder Co. 80 at 18-18 125th Street in College Point in the former volunteer quarters of Eagle Ladder 1. Their first apparatus was an 1898 Hoepfner and Wuest roller frame 40-foot ladder truck, pulled by two horses. On January 1, 1913, Ladder 80 was reorganized as Ladder 130. On February 21, 1931, Ladder 130 relocated to new quarters at 119-11 14th Road. Lieutenant William Munda made the Supreme Sacrifice in 1952. Ladder 130 has been awarded one Unit Citation. Ladder 130 has the same response area as Engine 297. In 1921, Ladder 130 received a 1921 White Pirsch city service 50-foot ladder truck to retire the horses. Today, they operate with a 1994 Seagrave 100-foot rear-mount ladder truck. They are quartered in "Sleepy Hollow" with the "Pride of the Point," Engine 297.

ENGINE CO. 299
61-20 Utopia Parkway, Queens

They were organized on July 5, 1907, as Hose 6 in the former volunteer quarters of Woodhull Hose 1, at 90-26 161st Street in Jamaica. Their first piece of apparatus was a 1906 George B. Marx third-size hose wagon. On October 1, 1920, Hose 6 received a 1920 American LaFrance 700-gpm engine and was reorganized as Engine Co. 299. On September 5, 1925, Engine 299 was relocated to new quarters at 89-59 162nd Street with Engines 275 and 298, Ladder 127 and Battalion 50. On July 16, 1960, Engine 299 was relocated to new quarters at 61-20 Utopia Parkway in Fresh Meadows. Firefighter John W. Eiserman made the Supreme Sacrifice in 1945. Engine 299 has been awarded two Unit Citations. The response area of Engine 299 is primarily residential single and multiple dwellings, small apartments, storefronts and the Long Island Expressway. Engine 299 responds with a 1993 Seagrave 1000-gpm pumper. The "Utopia Express" shares their quarters with Ladder 152.

1st: Amnon Szanto, Michael Keely, Lt. Thomas Finnerty, Capt. John Marinaro, James Watson, John Driscoll 2nd: Frank DeCesare, Christopher England, Thomas Vanasco, Anton Endriss, Daniel Gilmore, Bruce Clark

1st: Jeffery Salvatore, Richard Boeri, Lt. Joseph Donlevy, Richard Garcia, Kevin Michaels, Herbert Parmentor 2nd: Charles Silvia, Charles McGroary, Michael Brennan, William Brown, Patrick McGiveney, Joseph Cooney, Robert Senetore

LADDER CO. 152
61-20 Utopia Parkway, Queens

Ladder 152 was organized on November 15, 1924, at 40-18 214th Place in Bayside at the quarters of Engine 306 to replace the volunteer company, Bayside Ladder 1. Their first apparatus was a 1918 Van Blerek 50-foot city service ladder truck. On July 16, 1960, Ladder 152 relocated to a new firehouse at 61-20 Utopia Parkway. Three members from Ladder 152 have made the Supreme Sacrifice – Firefighter John J. Whelan in 1930, Firefighter Paul C. Wrigley in 1958 and Firefighter Donald P. Aversa in 1977. A medal of valor was awarded to John J. Whelan in 1926. Ladder 152 has received one Unit Citation. They have the same response area as Engine 299. They respond with a 1989 Mack 75-foot tower-ladder. Ladder 152 is quartered at the "Utopia Express" with Engine 299.

ENGINE CO. 251

254-20 Union Turnpike, Queens

This company was organized as Engine 51 of the Brooklyn Fire Department on December 15, 1897, in what is now the Brooklyn Navy Yard. On January 28, 1898, it was reorganized as Engine 51. On October 1, 1899, it was reorganized as Engine 151 and on January 1, 1913, reorganized as Engine 251. From December 1, 1907, to May 1, 1915, Engine 251 had a second section. On November 24, 1941, Engine 251 was relocated to 173 Clymer Street with Engine 211 and on May 24, 1944, both companies moved to 26 Hooper Street. Engine 251 was disbanded on November 1, 1946. Six members have died in the line of duty. In 1927, Engine 251 was awarded the Fire College Citation. Engine 251 has received three Unit Citations. On October 1, 1952, Engine 251 was reorganized into new quarters at 254-20 Union Turnpike in Floral Park, Queens. Engine 251's response area includes single-family dwellings, taxpayers, garden apartments, two high-rises and Long Island Jewish Hospital. Today, they operate a 1993 Seagrave pumper.

1st: Joseph Cleary, Louis Morales, Lt. Orest Daszo, Capt. Sheldon Barocas, Lt. Nocenzo Cusumano, Lt. Robert Wiecezak, Joseph Joyce, George Friedell 2nd: Michael Miller, Francis Ulmer, Robert Kelly, Wayne Roser, Robert Dellatto, Terrance Hirten, Daniel Kerr 3rd: James Coyne, Thomas McMahon

ENGINE CO. 304

218-44 97th Avenue, Queens

This Queens Village company began its history on November 16, 1923, at 217-16 Hempstead Avenue. Their first piece of apparatus was a 1917 American LaFrance 700-gpm motorized engine. On January 14, 1928, Engine 304 was relocated to new quarters at 218-44 97th Avenue. Engine 304 has had one member make the Supreme Sacrifice—Firefighter Edward Winewski in 1975. The company has received three Unit Citations. Their response area consists of older single and multiple wood-frame dwellings, small apartments and apartment complexes with storefronts. Occasionally, Engine 304 has provided mutual aid with the Nassau County fire departments. Engine 304, "The Border Patrol," operates with a 1998 Seagrave 1000-gpm pumper. They share their quarters with Ladder 162.

1st: Edward Seymour, Frank DeAngelo, Lt. Joseph Petrucci, Capt. Michael Gorman, Lt. Ruben Vega, Miguel Moreno 2nd: Jane Toohig, Michael Maher, Michael Graham, Joseph Leoncavallo, Jeffrey Stroehlein, John Rogan, Todd Townsend, Richard Cheek, James Pannullo 3rd: Bruce Lyall, Brian Wendland, Robert Knapp, Paul Rodriguez, Paul Rosati, Lewis DeChiaro, Michael Steck, Kurt Endelmann, Joseph Malatestinic

LADDER CO. 162

218-44 97th Avenue, Queens

This Queens Village ladder company was organized on January 1, 1928, at 218-44 97th Avenue. The first apparatus of Ladder 162 was a 1921 Mack 50-foot city service ladder truck. Two members from Ladder 162 have made the Supreme Sacrifice—Firefighter John F. Whelan in 1969 and Lieutenant Joseph P. Faughnan in 1987. Firefighter Joseph R. Peterson has been awarded two medals for valor, one in 1973 and the other in 1987. Ladder 162 has garnered two Unit Citations. Ladder 162 operates in the same response area as Engine 304. They respond with a 1999 Seagrave 75-foot tower-ladder. They are quartered at the "Border Patrol" with Engine 304.

1st: Robert Halliday, Fredrick Aronsen, Lt. Mark Kugler, Capt. Barry Meade, Lt. James Kelly, Lt. Joseph Regan, Rudolf Kohlroser, Mark Renganeschi 2nd: James Ippolito, Robert O'Neill, Michael Kollman, Peter Gale, James Fenn, Joseph Dimino, Jason Daly, Michael Alberico, Brian Tobin, Stephen Tumulty, Frank Trezza, Donald Whiston 3rd: Joseph Shelton, Vincent Aleixo, James Teemsma, James Fitzpatrick, Francis Doherty, John Patterson, Michael DiBenedetto, Robert Cleary, Robert Christensen, Patrick DiMichele

1st: Frank Gaccione, Joseph Beltrani, Lt. Anthony Variale, Capt. Thomas Thompson, Lt. Daniel Rella, Lt. Thomas Wojcik, Anthony Kennedy 2nd: Michael Pagliuca, Adam Vilagos, Michael Schaefer, David Fitton, Dennis McGrath, Carlo Casoria, John Lograsso 3rd: John Hartel, Charles Fisher, James Pfeiffer, James Poppe, Scott Santmyers, Joseph Digilio, Raymond Leidner

ENGINE CO. 306
40-18 214th Place, Queens

This Bayside engine company entered service on November 15, 1924, at 40-18 214th Place to replace the volunteer company, Bayside Engine 1. Their first apparatus was a 1924 American LaFrance 700-gpm engine. Two members of Engine 306 have made the Supreme Sacrifice – Firefighter Antonio J. Assente in 1951 and Firefighter Charles R. Nagle in 1926. In 1926, Charles R. Nagle received a medal for his heroic actions. Engine 306 has received three Unit Citations. Their response area is widespread and consists primarily of residential dwellings of newer construction, small apartments and storefronts. Engine 306 is one of the first-due engines into the future Fire Academy located at Fort Totten. The "Bayside Bulls" currently respond with a 1993 Seagrave 1000-gpm pumper.

ENGINE CO. 313
44-01 244th Street, Queens

Engine 313 was organized on November 30, 1929, at 44-01 244th Street in Douglaston. When Engine 313 went into service, it replaced the last volunteer company attached to the FDNY, Douglaston Hose Co. 1. Their first apparatus was a 1929 American LaFrance 700-gpm engine. Two Engine 313 members have made the Supreme Sacrifice—Captain Orestes Hantjiles in 1959 and Captain Thomas F. Munroe in 1968. Engine 313 has been awarded two Unit Citations. Engine 313's response area includes residential homes of newer construction, single wood-frame dwellings, Queen Annes and large and small apartments with storefronts. Occasionally, Engine 313 has provided mutual aid to Nassau County volunteer fire departments. Today, they operate with a 1993 Seagrave 1000-gpm engine. They are quartered with Ladder 164 at the "End of the Rainbow."

1st: Richard Pandolf, William Brideson, Lt. Steven Hintze, Capt. Edward Ireland, Lt. Larry Griffin, Joseph Touhy, Frank Lasalle 2nd: William Mitchell, Michael Loscalzo, Jack Nash, Timothy Dowd, Terence McMahon, Michael Moskowitz, Gary Slattery 3rd: Edward Manly, John Spencer, Timothy McCormack, Edward Kester, Gregory Keane, David Sinclair, Fredrick Devito

LADDER CO. 164
44-01 244th Street, Queens

This company was organized on November 30, 1929, at 44-01 244th Street in Douglaston. This ladder company replaced the last volunteer ladder company—Active Ladder Company 1. They were the last volunteer ladder company attached to the FDNY and were quartered in Little Neck at 250th Street and Northern Boulevard. Their first apparatus was a 1926 Pierce Arrow 50-foot city service ladder truck. Ladder 164 has been awarded one Unit Citation. Ladder 164 covers the same response area as Engine 313. They, too, have provided mutual aid to some of the Nassau County volunteer fire departments. Today, Ladder 164 operates with a 1991 Mack 95-foot tower-ladder. They are quartered at the "End of the Rainbow" with Engine 313.

1st: Lt. Neil Conway, Lt. Michael Holian, Capt. William Canner, Capt. Ronald Meehan, Lt. Michael Sialiano, John Grappone 2nd: James Thornton, Frank DiLorenzo, Marshal Glenz, Edward Murray, Terance Quinn, Alan Akers, Larry Colby 3rd: John Tyrrell, John Law, Michael Mahon, Brian Gavin, Kevin Stahl, Robert Reilly, Christopher Menna 4th: Andrew Burkard, Steven Healy, James Leonard, Kevin McEnery

ENGINE CO. 320

36-18 Francis Lewis Boulevard, Queens

This company was organized on February 11, 1931, at 36-18 Francis Lewis Boulevard in the Auburndale-Bayside area of Queens. When Engine 320 tapped into service, its first apparatus was a 1930 Mack 700-gpm engine. From 1956 until 1986, Engine 320 has been awarded three Unit Citations. They have a response area of mostly residential structures, single wood-frame dwellings, garden apartments, multiple two- and three-story duplexes, taxpayers, store complexes and small and large apartments. Today, Engine 320 operates with a 1997 Seagrave 1000-gpm pumper. The Francis Lewis Boulevard "Patriots" share their quarters with Ladder 167.

1st: Lt. Kenneth Galanek, Capt. Robert Wells, Lt. James Casey 2nd: Richard Steinmuller, Thomas Scally, Keith Palumbo, Gary Fezza, Donald Honey, Peter Sciurca, James Pisani, Michael McCarthy 3rd: Peter Connolly, James Hein, Robert Scalia, Paul Porcello, Paul Wilt, Joseph Ronde, James Cosgrove, John Schnaufer

LADDER CO. 167

36-18 Francis Lewis Boulevard, Queens

This ladder company was put into service on February 11, 1931, at 36-18 Francis Lewis Boulevard in the Auburndale-Bayside section of Queens. Their first piece of apparatus was a 1921 Mack 65-foot ladder truck. Captain Thomas Herlihy died in the line of duty in 1955. Medals for valor have been awarded to Firefighter Julius P. Boertlein in 1947 and Firefighter James G. Powderly in 1988. Ladder 167 has garnered four Unit Citations. Ladder 167 has the same response area—mostly residential structures—as Engine 320. Today, Ladder 167 responds with a 1995 Seagrave 100-foot rear-mount ladder truck. The Francis Lewis Boulevard "Patriots" are quartered with Engine 320.

1st: Gregor McConnell, Lt. Edwin Camilleri, Capt. Rocco Fertoli, Capt. McNamara, Lt. John Nykiel, Kenneth Hutchinson 2nd: Richard Peterson, Thomas Minelli, Michael McKnight, Richard Duden, Joseph Sorrentino, Martin Liptak, Joseph Proscia, Thomas Johnson, Lawrence Vowinkel, Derek Kuhland, Mark Lavardera 3rd: Gregory Jerome, Mark Aglietti, Thomas Profeta, Daniel McGovern, Vincent Prisco, Theodore Bouchard, Stephen Schmittgall, Thomas Marx, Daniel McCarvil

1st: Brian O'Leary, Lt. Robert Aponte, Lt. Andrew Borgese, Capt. John Gallagher, Lt. Gerard Uzzi, Walter Feit 2nd: John Signorelli, Orsilio Oquendo, John Patten, Donald Spurrell, Eugene Hanlon, Eric Brown 3rd: Kevin Walker, Kevin Farrelly, Karl Vankassten, James Beltrami, Stephen Bumb

ENGINE CO. 326

64-04 Springfield Boulevard, Queens

Engine 326 was organized on August 16, 1939, in Coney Island, Brooklyn, in the quarters of Engine Co. 245 at 2929 West 8th Street. Its first apparatus was a 1926 American LaFrance 700-gpm engine. On October 1, 1952, Engine 326 was disbanded to reorganize Engine 251 in Floral Park, Queens. On August 20, 1984, Engine Co. 326 was reorganized at 64-04 Springfield Boulevard in the Creedmore section of Queens. The apparatus for the reorganized company was a 1980 American LaFrance 1000-gpm engine. They have a response area of mostly new construction, single and multiple dwellings, garden apartments, high-rise apartments and the Long Island Expressway. Engine 326 operates today with a 1998 Seagrave 1000-gpm engine. They are quartered at the "Springfield Express" with Ladder 160 and Battalion 53.

LADDER CO. 160

64-02 Springfield Boulevard, Queens

This is a relatively new ladder company that was organized on July 1, 1984, in the Creedmore section of Queens at 64-02 Springfield Boulevard. One member has made the Supreme Sacrifice—Arthur Tuck in 1993. Ladder 160 has greatly reduced the response time of Ladder 164, 162 and 152. They cover a large residential area and are one of the first-due ladder trucks to the Long Island Jewish Hospital complex. Ladder 160 went into service with a 1972 Mack 75-foot tower-ladder. Today, they respond with a 1994 FWD 75-foot tower-ladder. Ladder 160 is quartered at the "Springfield Express" with Engine 326 and Battalion 53.

1st: Charles Piotrowski, Lt. Thomas Reilly, Lt. Brendan Keys, Capt. Bill Herlihy, Lt. Richard Killian, Lt. Joseph Gruosso, Lawrence Bell 2nd: Christopher Massaria, John Senica, Ted Dulka, Michael Monaghan, Robert Sgro, Gary Sims, David Fischbein, Robert Kelly, Peter Santelli 3rd: Edward Cunn, Eugene Fallon, Keith Green, Sebastian Raspanti, Edward Reilly, Daniel Von Braunsberg, Thomas Roew, Jeffery Brauchler

DIVISION 15

1st: DC Arthur Messbauer, DC Terrence Roche, DC James Murtagh, DC Charles Blaich, DC Dennis Petrocelli 2nd: Joseph Breen, Lt. Thomas Hughes, Lolita Gray, Lee Morris, Mark Horak, Michael O'Hara

BATTALION 33

Winston Lawrence, BC Frank Milio, Joseph Napoli

BATTALION 37

BC Eugene L. Jesinkey, Wayne Wichern, Denis Weidner, BC Robert E. Gleason

BATTALION 38

1st: BC Eugene McGowan, BC Michael Marrone, BC Edward Kilduff, BC Joseph Grzelak 2nd: Daniel Marzano, John Rafferty

BATTALION 39

Walter McKee, BC Edward White, BC Michael Falotico, BC Ronald Quartuccio, Michael Mongelli

BATTALION 41

*1st: BC Thomas McEnroe, BC Edward O'Connor **2nd:** Larry Murphy, William Rohe, BC Paul Ferro, BC Robert Maynes, BC Edward Ellison, BC Steve Ternlund, Scott Stromer*

BATTALION 44

*1st: BC Kevin Scanlon, BC John Ievolo, BC Robert Brown, BC William Gillespie **2nd:** Charles Van Rossem, Michael Reutter, William Rossiter, Thomas McKeon*

BATTALION 58

Dan Forland, BC Ralph Leoce, BC Gil Frank, BC Frank Montagna, BC Frank Sikorski, Joe Costello, Ed McNoble

33rd Battalion

*1st: Lt. William D'Emic, Capt. Joseph Russo, BC John Fox **2nd:** James Ryan, John Arias, Thomas Kennedy, Robert Cuollo, Brian Gibbons, Edward McGrath*

ENGINE CO. 254

901 Avenue U, Brooklyn

Engine 54 was placed in service in the former quarters of the Gravesend Neck Volunteer Fire Department on December 9, 1895. The firehouse located at 56 Gravesend Neck Road was part of the town hall of the former town. Engine 54 went in service with a 50-gallon chemical engine and hose wagon, which they kept until 1899. The town hall, built in the late 1700s, was in deplorable condition and a replacement firehouse was planned in the 1908 budget. For unknown reasons, it was scrapped and Engine 254 moved to temporary quarters, the stables of a riding club, at 2310 Ocean Parkway on August 1, 1911. This one-year lease lasted until December 23, 1924, when new quarters were built for them at 901 Avenue U. On March 1, 1925, Ladder 153 was placed in service with Engine 254. Engine 254 was first-due at the Waldbaum's fire on August 2, 1978, where six firefighters were killed in a roof collapse. Six Unit Citations have been awarded to Engine 254.

1st: Lt. James Coyne, Lt. Richard Palmer, Capt. James Carpenter, Lt. Thomas Faherty 2nd: Ronald Parker, James Gallicchio, Larry Spalter, Christopher Reiser, Michael Tadduni 3rd: James DelBianco, Joseph Adinolfi, Brian McManus, Timothy Duffy

LADDER CO. 153
901 Avenue U, Brooklyn

Ladder 153 was placed in service with a used 1906 American LaFrance 75-foot aerial with a 1913 Christie front-wheel-drive tractor. Ladder 153 was established in the quarters of Engine 254 at 901 Avenue U on March 1, 1925, where they have been located ever since. In 1983, Ladder 153 received its first tower-ladder, a used 1973 model Mack. Today, they respond with a 1991 Mack 95-foot tower-ladder. The first-due district for Ladder 153 is a mixed bag of residential, commercial and retail buildings. Ladder 153 has received three Unit Citations and three members have earned medals for heroic actions. Three members have been killed in the line of duty. Two of these members, Firefighters James P. McManus and George S. Rice, were killed—along with four other firefighters—while operating on the roof when it collapsed into the blazing Waldbaum's Supermarket on August 2, 1978.

ENGINE CO. 276
1635 East 14th Street, Brooklyn

Engine 276 has the distinction of being the last company to be placed in service using the old numbering system. Organized as Combination Engine 176 on February 11, 1911, it was re-numbered to Engine 276 on January 1, 1913. The new firehouse built for the company is located at 1635 East 14th Street. As a combination company, they had three pieces of apparatus, a steamer, hose wagon and ladder truck. Engine 276's first motorized pumper was a 1923 American LaFrance with a 700-gpm pump, which they received on October 1, 1923. Ladder 156 was organized on February 1, 1927, replacing the ladder truck assigned to Engine 276. One of the worst fires to which Engine 276 responded was the Waldbaum's Supermarket fire on August 2, 1978, when the roof collapsed. Three Unit Citations have been awarded to Engine 276 and one member has earned a medal for bravery. Two members have been killed in the line of duty.

1st: Robert Yuli, Lt. William Howley, Capt. Salvatore Palmeri, Lt. Michael Burns, Lt. Francis Woods, Philip Scafuri 2nd: Michael Henry, Dermott Clowe, Joseph Valenti, Douglas Price, Richard Mannetta, Eugene McEnroe, Scott Gaffney, John Miskanic 3rd: Edward Snyder, Robert Angelone, Robert Ryan, William Cromas, Steven Orr, Robert Sputh

LADDER CO. 156
1635 East 14th Street, Brooklyn

On February 11, 1911, Combination Engine 276 was placed in service with an engine, hose cart and ladder truck. The ladder truck did not have its own identity and responded as either part of Engine 276 or Ladder 276, if it was responding by itself. On February 1, 1927, the ladder truck received its own identification and became Ladder 156. They went into service with a 1921 Mack City Service ladder truck with a 50-foot Bangor ladder. Today, Ladder 156 is running with a 1999 Seagrave 100-foot aerial. Ladder 156's first-due area includes large private homes, apartment buildings and many retail stores along Kings Highway. Four members have earned medals for brave acts, while the company has been awarded eight Unit Citations. Four members have been killed in the line of duty. One was killed while detailed to Engine 40 in Manhattan. Two others, Firefighters Charles S. Bouton and William O'Connor, were killed in the Waldbaum's Supermarket roof collapse on August 2, 1978.

1st: James Mulligan, Capt. George Cassidy, Thomas Haeger, Gerard Davan 2nd: Michael Brody, William Simpson, Patrick Battle, George Storz, Stephen Schwarzrock, Adam Polanish 3rd: Neil Cronin, Patrick Klein, John Sullivan, William Murphy, James McBrien

1st: Michael Wilson, David Lamar, John Veracka, Charles Franzo, William Chesney, John Jackson, Michael Haddican, Justin Van Wert, James Willsen, Lt. John Ricketts *2nd:* Arturo Grant, Capt. William Mundy, Richard Peredo, Carl Fargione, Philip Cappadora, Joseph Gavitt, Randell Boucher, Edward Farrell, Capt. Rochelle Jones, Lt. Richard Flood, Capt. Brian Lanci, Thomas Farrell *3rd:* Michael Spyntiuk, Daniel Poore, Barry Albrecht, John Hanning, Michael Basmagy, Gregory Visco, Raymond Bennett, Brian Collins, Lt. William Stark, Kenneth Haskell, Scott Bellman *4th:* James McHugh, James Yearsley, Michael O'Brien, Andrew Sochinski, Thomas Stackpole, John Lynch

ENGINE CO. 309

1851 East 48th Street, Brooklyn

Engine 309 was placed in service on September 27, 1927, in a new house built for them at 1851 East 48th Street in the Flatlands section of Brooklyn. This part of the city was mostly farmlands and was not developed until the early 1920s. Engines 255 and 257 first served this area. Engine 309's first apparatus was a used 1919 American LaFrance 700-gpm pumper from Engine 21. Ladder 159 was added to the quarters on January 1, 1947. Their response area is a mix of residential and commercial buildings. Engine 309 is active with the community and has earned the name, "The Friendly Firehouse." Company members even painted a big yellow smiley face on the apparatus door. Today, the company operates with a 1993 Seagrave 1000-gpm pumper. The company has earned one Unit Citation. Two members have been killed in the line of duty.

LADDER CO. 159

1851 East 48th Street, Brooklyn

Ladder 159 was added to the growing area of Flatlands, Marine Basin and Marine Park on January 1, 1947, in the quarters of Engine 309 at 1851 East 48th Street. Their first rig was a used 1934 Walters 75-foot aerial. Ladder 159's area includes many single-family homes, apartment buildings, retail stores, a mall and the Gateway National Recreation Area—a wildlife management area. During brush season, the companies in this area are kept quite busy, fighting large brush fires in the marsh areas. Ladder 159 is the second-due truck to the Rockaways in Queens, over the Marine Parkway Bridge, a distance of more than four miles. The company has been awarded five Unit Citations. Eight members have earned medals for their heroic actions. Four of these medals were bestowed for work performed at a building collapse at 3851 Flatlands Avenue on August 6, 1997.

ENGINE CO. 321

2165 Gerritsen Avenue, Brooklyn

This Marine Park engine company was organized on October 4, 1930, at 2165 Gerritsen Avenue. The first apparatus of Engine 321 was a 1922 American LaFrance 700-gpm engine. Two months later, they received a new 1930 Mack 700-gpm engine. Two members from Engine 321 have made the Supreme Sacrifice. Several medals for valor have been awarded to members and the company has received six Unit Citations. The response area of Engine 321 is mainly residential, with single and multiple dwellings, small apartment houses, storefronts and a large brush area. The Gerritsen Beach Volunteer Fire Department provides an assist. On October 1, 1986, Engine 321 received a 1978 Mack engine, converted by fleet maintenance to operate as a foam unit. On October 17, 1997, a 1997 International/Saulsbury 500-gpm brush fire unit was assigned to them. Today, Engine 321 operates with a 1989 Mack 1000-gpm engine and still responds with BFU 6 and Foam Unit 321.

1st: John Carrera, Capt. Richard Donnelly, Lt. Neil Wilson, Bruce Jacoby, John Ross *2nd:* John Deresto, Anthony Smaldone, Michael Sturgis, Andrew Mastrota, Anthony Borruso, Lt. Robert Scott, Joseph Napoli, Matthew Adee, Robert Breivogel, Stephen Schneider *3rd:* Gerard Sini, Lawrence Murphy, Steven Closs, Andrew Rasavongeuk, Robert Boldi, John Dorn

ENGINE CO. 214

495 Hancock Street, Brooklyn

Engine 14 was the first engine expansion company that Brooklyn placed in service after the paid department went in service in 1869. Organized on July 4, 1872, Engine 14 was placed into new quarters built for them at 231 Herkimer Street. At the time, this was considered out in the country and Engine 14 was a slow company. After World War II, many single company houses were closed and the company moved in with a neighboring unit. Engine 214 moved in with Ladder 111 at 399 Halsey Street on February 9, 1948. Ladder 111's house was very cramped with Engine 214 in it and on June 26, 1957, both companies moved into new quarters at 495 Hancock Street. The area expanded and Engine 214 has become one of the busier companies in the City, earning 24 Unit Citations. Two members received medals for their heroic actions. Their first-due area includes mostly brownstones with commercial buildings and older warehouses along Atlantic Avenue and Fulton Street. One member was killed in the line of duty.

1st: Jimmy Noon, Lt. Roscoe Brown, Lt. Tony Fernandez, Capt. Sorrentino, Lt. Mike Bell, Ed Steffens, Chris Norris, Gene Johnston *2nd:* Greg Lamanna, Jose Montalvo, Ken Watson, Frank Barvo, Carl Bedigian, Ken Ditata, Malcolm Moore, Mike Curran, Tim McMahon, Roy Nichols, Tim Kuveikis

1st: Richard McCabe, Robert Austin, Lt. Kenny Connelly, Lt. Louis Pistani, Richard Spatafora, James Ellson, Joseph Higgins *2nd:* Thomas Cleary, Gerard Slevin, Thomas Hannan, Chris Eysser, Fred Saporito, Ray Strong, Scott Sivert, William Carlson, Martin Fullam

LADDER CO. 111

495 Hancock Street, Brooklyn

Placed in service on April 26, 1892, Ladder 11 was located in new quarters at 399 Halsey Street. This area features mostly single-family homes, apartments and some retail buildings. They went in service with the standard Brooklyn ladder truck, a LaFrance Hayes 75-foot aerial, an 1891 model. The first motorized apparatus assigned to the company was a 1918 Seagrave 75-foot aerial on April 23, 1918. They received their first tower-ladder on June 9, 1973, a 1973 Mack 75-foot tower. Today, they respond with a 1994 Saulsbury 75-foot tower. Engine 214 moved in with Ladder 111 on February 9, 1948, and moved into the current house on June 26, 1957. Three members have earned the James Gordon Bennett Medal with two of them also receiving the Dr. Harry M. Archer Medal, including senior member Kenneth Connelly. Thirty-eight other members have garnered medals. Thirty Unit Citations adorn the walls of the firehouse. One member was killed in the line of duty.

ENGINE CO. 222 & RECUPERATION & CARE UNIT 2

32 Ralph Avenue, Brooklyn

Placed in service with Engine 221 on the same day—January 16, 1885—Engine 222 was located in a residential area. The firehouse, located at 836 Quincy Street, was in the eastern section of Bedford-Stuyvesant. When placed in service, Engine 222 was alone, except for Engine 217 to the north. Close to Bushwick, Engine 222 protected the southern section that had a large commercial area with many breweries. Engine 222 has seen many fires during the late 1960s and 1970s and has 21 Unit Citations for their hard work. Five members have been awarded medals for their heroic actions. Engine 222 moved to new quarters at 32 Ralph Avenue on April 13, 1973. Also sharing quarters with Engine 222 are the 37th Battalion and the Recuperation and Care Unit 2, known as RAC 2. Earlier, the RAC Unit was known by many different names, including Rehab, Mobile Medical Unit 2 and Ambulance 2. Mobile Medical Unit 2 moved in with Engine 222 on June 13, 1990.

1st: Daniel Quinn, Lt. Thomas Melia, Lt. Eugene Pandolfi, Capt. Kevin Malone, Lt. Gary Esposito, Timothy Aas *2nd:* Charles Hendry, William Zimmerman, Anthony Kennedy, Vincent Cammarasana, Thomas Schecker, John Clacher, Christopher Meehan, Michael Weglarz *3rd:* Thomas Minelli, Craig Kobes, Michael Johnson, Kenneth Kennedy, Stephen O'Sullivan, Michael Healy, Kevin McGowan, Stephen Harvazinski

37th Battalion

1st: Lt. Greg Wellbrock, Lt. Austin Csorny, Capt. Michael Legge, Lt. Sal Curiale 2nd: Steve Stock, Mike Schuh, Robert Malone, Joe Smith, Benny Ortiz, Richard Duffy, Tom Imbornoni 3rd: Steve Murphy, Dennis Keane, Joe McConnell, Dan Zucchini, Vincent Lonegro, Steve Scott, Doug Guercia

ENGINE CO. 277

582 Knickerbocker Avenue, Brooklyn

Placed in service on March 20, 1913, Engine 277 was located in a new building at 582 Knickerbocker Avenue in the middle of Bushwick. They were the first of six engine companies placed in service that day in Brooklyn. The single-bay, three-story firehouse is known as a Johnson House, named after Commissioner Joseph Johnson, who approved the design of the building. These houses were the first houses to be built without stables for the horses. Engine 277 went in service with a new American LaFrance second-size steam fire engine. During the 1940s and 1950s, Engine 277 operated one of the 1938 World's Fair Ahrens Foxes. Located in Bushwick, Engine 277 has been very busy and earned its nickname, "Wood City Workers." A good portion of their response area includes wood-frame dwellings. Engine 277 has earned 15 Unit Citations. Two members have been awarded medals for their heroic actions. Two members have died in the line of duty.

LADDER CO. 112

582 Knickerbocker Avenue, Brooklyn

Brooklyn Ladder 12 was placed in service on November 20, 1893, in new quarters built for them at 1171 Madison Street. This company was organized to fill the gap in Bushwick between Ladder 8 to the north and Ladder 7 to the south. They went in service with an 1892 LaFrance Hayes 75-foot aerial. In 1918, they received a 1918 American LaFrance 65-foot motorized ladder truck. On September 19, 1973, Ladder 112 moved in with Engine 277 at 582 Knickerbocker Avenue and has been there ever since. This is the only house with the engine and ladder in tandem on the apparatus floor, as opposed to side by side. Working in an active fire area, 19 members have earned medals for heroism. Two of the medal winners earned their medals in the same building—486 Central Avenue—four years apart. The company has been awarded 30 Unit Citations. Two members have lost their lives in the performance of duty.

1st: BC Mark Ferran, Lt. Thomas Kuefner, Capt. Ronald Carritue, Capt. Michael Borst 2nd: Mike Harty, Anthony Messina, Robert Trascoy, Stephen Brooks, Ronald Broome, Thomas Prin, Daniel Gimpel, Richard Duffy, Francis McCarthy, James Fehling 3rd: Daniel Taylor, Eugene Cummings, Daniel Gillis, Vincent Sobal, Brian Kelly, Mark Loftus, Eugene Hickey, Bernard Floody, John Gayron

1st: Roy Ferlisi, Lt. Serge Burack, Lt. James Lemonda, Lt. Daniel Delargy, Sean Goodridge 2nd: Michael Butt, John Spillane, John Turkus, Joseph Morro, Stephen Cross, Frank Rosciano, Kingsley Taylor, Chris McSorley, Glenn Sheridan

ENGINE CO. 234

1352 St. Johns Place, Brooklyn

Brooklyn placed Engine 34 in service on October 2, 1893, at 1472 Bergen Street in the Crown Heights section. Engine 234's house was the last of the two-story, flat-roof houses built by the Brooklyn Fire Department. All the houses built after this were different in layout and looks. Engine 234 received one of the last horse-drawn steamers purchased in 1910, a 1910 Nott third-size steamer. Over the years, Engine 234 has seen a lot of fire with the bulk of their work coming in the 1960s, 1970s and early 1980s. During the 1970s, Engine 234 was featured in an ad for Mack Trucks when they received the 1000th Mack apparatus delivered to New York City. On March 22, 1979, Engine 234 moved into new quarters with Ladder 123 at 1352 St. Johns Place. Three members have made the Supreme Sacrifice. In 1927, one member earned the James Gordon Bennett Medal for a rescue. Two other members have earned medals for bravery and the company has been awarded 18 Unit Citations.

LADDER CO. 123

1352 St. Johns Place, Brooklyn

Placed in service in its own quarters on November 7, 1907, Ladder 73 was located at 423 Ralph Avenue. They went in service with a used 1899 LaFrance Hayes 85-foot aerial. The horses were replaced in 1915 with a 1915 Christie front-wheel-drive tractor on its 1910 Seagrave 65-foot aerial. Engine 227 moved into these quarters on June 26, 1949, as part of a consolidation plan of combining single companies. Ladder 123 moved to new quarters at 1352 St. Johns Place on June 7, 1977, leaving Engine 227 behind. Joining Ladder 123 was Engine 234 on March 22, 1979. Ladder 123's response area is mixed with apartment buildings, some brownstones and many shops and stores. The area has seen its share of fires through the years, making Ladder 123 an active company. Twenty-four Unit Citations have been awarded and 28 members have garnered medals for heroic actions. Two members have died in the line of duty. Ladder 123 responds with a 1999 Seagrave 100-foot rear-mount aerial.

1st: Marvin Robinson, Lt. Thomas Zuhlke, Lt. Raymond Clancy, Capt. Philip Gaetani 2nd: Robert Wiedmann, William Mangus, Robert Morris, Richard LaPiedra, Richard Davan, John Taylor 3rd: Thomas Buttaro, Thomas Davide, Michael Zechewytz, Joseph Calvanese

ENGINE CO. 249

493 Rogers Avenue, Brooklyn

Brooklyn put Engine 49 and Ladder 23 in service on January 23, 1896, in new quarters at 493 Rogers Avenue. Both companies replaced the volunteer department in the town of Flatbush. Engine 49 was placed in service with just a hose wagon and no steam fire engine until 1896. The two-bay, two-story firehouse had been in continuous use for more than 100 years before it was rebuilt on the inside and a third floor added. This is the only firehouse in Brooklyn that has Brooklyn Fire Department spelled out above the apparatus door. Although the area remained residential, the number of fires increased, due to the drugs and turf wars fought in the area. Engine 249 is now one of the busier companies in Brooklyn. They respond with a 1998 Seagrave 1000-gpm pumper. Engine 249 has received eight Unit Citations and two members have earned medals. One of the original members of Engine 249 lost his life in the performance of his duty in 1908.

1st: Frank Munafo, Capt. Peter Gannon, Lt. Jim Goelz, Lt. Dan LaRocco, Nick Malter 2nd: Denis Twomey, Ronald Vitale, Bill Sweeney, Charles Tozzo, Tom Fleming, Bobby Hart, Joe Scaramuzzino, David Rosenzwieg 3rd: John Gemmel, Howard Waltzer, John Gagliano, Joseph Cavagnaro

1st: Lt. Raymond Brown, Lt. Thomas Kreuzer, Capt. James Savastano, Capt. Peter Frontera 2nd: Joseph Garafola, Robert Bohack, Anthony Arcello, Kevin Redden, Kevin Dempsey, Bill Hansen, John Hand, Brian Healey, Michael Manza, Thomas Manley

LADDER CO. 113

493 Rogers Avenue, Brooklyn

Brooklyn Ladder 23 was placed in service with Engine 49 on January 20, 1896, at 493 Rogers Avenue. When the BFD and FDNY merged in 1898, the ladder companies in Brooklyn and Queens were re-numbered. Brooklyn Ladders 13 through 25 were combined with the engine companies with which they were housed, except Ladders 23 and 18, which became Ladder 13 and 14. Their first apparatus was an 1886 LaFrance Hayes 75-foot aerial. On July 26, 1921, Ladder 113 received its first motorized ladder truck, a new American LaFrance 75-foot aerial. For many years, Ladder 113 had a very large response area, now covered by Ladders 132, 120, 123, 174 and 147. This area was not developed for many years. Most of the area now includes private homes, some apartment buildings and retail stores. In recent years, Ladder 113 became one of the busier companies in Brooklyn. Ten members have been honored with medals and the company has earned 17 Unit Citations.

1st: Joe Ferrantelli, Joe D'Amico, Lt. Mike Brunton, Lt. Richard Lafata, Capt. Matthew Ryan, Lt. John Newman, Lt. Terry McKay, Mike Desiante, Phil Cortes 2nd: Mike Chiarulli, Patrick Murtagh, Mark Nicola, Mark Holstrom, Kevin Gallagher, Bruce Edwards, Ray McPolin, Ralph Mandia, Tom Mingione 3rd: Chris Atwell, Bob Ryan, Anthony Zopich, Kevin Charlie, Steve Campanella, Randy Foss, Tim O'Toole, Glen Zwosta, John Zwilinske, Gerard Triglia

ENGINE CO. 280
489 St. Johns Place, Brooklyn

One of six engine companies placed in service on March 20, 1913, Engine 280 has called 489 St. Johns Place home since being organized. Engine 280 was a "fill in" company. Placed among Engine 219, 235, 269 and 249, it filled a large hole in fire coverage. On the western side of Bedford-Stuyvesant, Engine 280 has seen a lot of fire since being placed in service. Engine 280's first-due response area includes mostly large apartment buildings and brownstones. With a wall down the center, it is also home for Ladder 132. The first unit assigned to Engine 280 was a 1912 American LaFrance second-size steamer with a Christie front-wheel tractor and a new Mack Boyd combination chemical and hose wagon. Because of the amount of work they have done, Engine 280 has earned 17 Unit Citations. One member has been awarded a medal for his heroic actions at a fire. One member has made the Supreme Sacrifice, killed in the line of duty.

1st: Ken Svenningsen, Lt. John Graziano, Capt. Mike Rogers, Lt. Mike Coccurullo, Lt. Tom Bierne, Gerard Triglia, Greg Farinacci 2nd: Joe Donatelli, Ken DeFranco, Brian Faherty, Jack Collins, Joe Fiorino, John Vigiano, Horacio Maldonado 3rd: Keith Loughlin, John Colella, Darrel Adone, Bob Karcher, Mike Mulligan, Tony Zaccaro, Steve Schreck

LADDER CO. 132
489 St. Johns Place, Brooklyn

Placed in service on November 27, 1913, Ladder 132 is located at 489 St. Johns Place. Engine 280 was placed in service earlier in the year. Like Ladder 131, Ladder 132 went into service with a motorized 1913 American LaFrance 65-foot aerial. Located in Prospect Heights, Ladder 132 is located among Ladders 105, 111, 123 and 113. Their response area has many large apartment buildings, brownstone homes, commercial and industrial buildings. Always in the thick of the action, Ladder 132 is a very busy company. During the arson years of the 1970s, they responded to three or four vacant building fires per tour. Because of this work, Ladder 132 has been awarded 21 Unit Citations over the years. Twenty-two members have earned medals for their heroic work. One Firefighter, Gerard J. Triglia, earned the James Gordon Bennett Medal, as well as the Dr. Harry M. Archer Medal, for a rescue in 1995. One member was killed in the line of duty. Ladder 132's rig is a 1994 Seagrave 100-foot rear-mount aerial.

ENGINE CO. 225
799 Lincoln Avenue, Brooklyn

With the town of New Lots annexed by the City of Brooklyn on August 4, 1886, Engine 25 and Ladder 7 replaced the volunteer department. Engine 25's first house was at 420 Liberty Avenue. The company went in service with only a hose wagon and protected almost eight square miles. Most of the district was residential at first, but as it grew, manufacturing played an important part in the development of the area. On June 10, 1890, the company moved into a modern firehouse at 657 Liberty Avenue. Initially, Engine 225 was a slow company, but by 1968, they were so busy that a second Engine 225 was placed in service on October 1. On November 29, 1969, Engine 225 (2) was renamed as a Tactical Control Unit. TCU 531 was disbanded on February 19, 1972. On February 21, 1970, Engine 225 and Ladder 107 moved to new quarters at 799 Lincoln Avenue. Engine 225 received four Unit Citations and members earned three medals for bravery.

1st: Frank Zampaglione, Lt. Robert Madden, Lt. Steve Casquarelli, Capt. James O'Donnell, Lt. Stephen Trogele, Fred Stavans, Michael Brecciano 2nd: Salvatore DiBlasi, Robert Lee, Richard Galeazzi, David Lang, Andre Majors, Kevin Burke, Michael Basile 3rd: Kevin Sherod, John DiRienzo, Richard Mattone, John Farrell, John Cassidy, Brian Trontz, Kevin Daly, Michael Gagliano

1st: Lt. Joseph Thomas, Stephen Russack, Lt. Kenneth Fink, Capt. James Corcoran, Lt. Hugh O'Donnell, Lt. John Snow, Herman Williams 2nd: Gregory Kerr, Stephen Sullivan, Joseph Stavola, Michael Alvarez, Matthew Yellico, Timothy Sonnenberg, Richard Lorenzen, Joseph Ward, Clinton Evans, John McNamara, Paul Rhodes, Andrew Smith, Bruce Stanley 3rd: Daniel Brennan, Martin Tripptree, Frank Campisi, Richard Kenney, John Curley, Ronald Curaba, Robert Kittelberger, James Duggan, John Brown

LADDER CO. 107

799 Lincoln Avenue, Brooklyn

When Brooklyn annexed the village of New Lots on August 4, 1886, they placed Ladder 7 and Engine 25 in service in different houses. Ladder 7's first quarters were at 104 Jamaica Avenue in the former quarters of Union Ladder 1 of the New Lots Fire Department. They went in service with a new 1886 LaFrance/Hayes 75-foot aerial ladder truck. On December 23, 1890, Ladder 7 moved into new quarters at 79 New Jersey Avenue. The horses were removed from quarters during 1915-16 when their 1910 Seagrave 65-foot aerial was outfitted with a new front-wheel-drive tractor. Located in East New York, Ladder 107 was a very active company during the 1960s and 1970s when many vacant buildings were burning. On February 21, 1970, Ladder 107 and Engine 225 moved some distance away to new quarters at 799 Lincoln Avenue. Ladder 107's old quarters were occupied by Ladder 175, a new company organized to replace 107. Ten Unit Citations have been awarded to 107. Seven members have earned medals.

ENGINE CO. 236

998 Liberty Avenue, Brooklyn

Placed in service on the same day as Engine 235—July 1, 1895—Engine 236 was placed in the farm area of Brooklyn. Located at 998 Liberty Avenue, it was only a few blocks from the Queens County border. After the merger of the FDNY with BFD in 1898, Engine 236 responded into Queens to assist the volunteer departments that serviced the area. The area has remained residential since it was laid out in the mid-1880s. East New York was hit hard during the mid-1960s and the area was devastated by arson, keeping Engine 236 very busy. Although the area is rejuvenating, Engine 236 is still a very busy company. Sixteen Unit Citations have been awarded to the company and there are three medal winners among the ranks. One member was killed in the line of duty. A second member was promoted to Lieutenant, assigned to Battalion 45 and killed in his first fire as an officer when the floor gave way.

1st: Stephen Cassidy, John Lennon, Kenneth Gianelli, Lt. Vincent Louis, Capt. Kevin McCabe, Lt. Michael Dilena, Lt. William Boltja, Kevin Sheehan, Peter Strahl, James Saverese 2nd: Peter Carino, Joseph Cestari, Brian Harvey, Joseph Bachert, Steven Razickas, Patrick McGreen, Edward Ireland, James Kinneary, Glen Bullock, James Helfrich, Neil McCarthy 3rd: Robert Spinelli, Michael Pritchett, Julius Ellison, Richard Resto, Keith Gross, Bernard Keegan, Scott Frazer, Lt. Brian McDade, Joseph McGovern, John Crawford

1st: Stephen Alexander, Lt. Richard Duemig, Lt. Michael Carbone, Lt. Michael Donovan, Stephen O'Keefe 2nd: Louis Caserta, John Collins, Joseph Beissel, Lawrence O'Donnell, James Gersbeck, Albert Kessner, Martin Scialpi 3rd: James Mullen, Kevin Curran, James Schwicke, James McGetrick, James Draude, Michael Dzwlewicz

ENGINE CO. 290

480 Sheffield Avenue, Brooklyn

Brownsville first was settled in 1865 with the construction of several hundred homes. On October 1, 1915, a new firehouse opened at 480 Sheffield Avenue for an engine and ladder company. Originally, the building was lettered for Engine 296 and Ladder 145, but when opened, only Engine 290 was placed in service. At the last minute, Engine 290 replaced Engine 296. Engine 290 was placed in service with a new 1915 Ahrens Fox, 700-gpm pumper. The East New York area started suffering from urban blight during the 1950s and 1960s. The middle class moved out and poorer people moved into the area. Buildings started to deteriorate and the fire load skyrocketed. Engine 290 was responding to many more fires, as were other companies throughout the city. As fires decreased in other parts of the city, Engine 290's area has remained busy. Over the years, they have earned 17 Unit Citations and two members garnered medals for heroic work. One member was shot and killed on a payroll delivery in 1938.

LADDER CO. 103

480 Sheffield Avenue, Brooklyn

Ladder 103 has been in two areas of Brooklyn since being placed in service on September 15, 1869, as Ladder 3 of the Brooklyn Fire Department. First located in Downtown Brooklyn, they occupied the former volunteer quarters of Clinton Ladder 2 at 236 Gold Street. This building was replaced on April 29, 1875, with the erection of new quarters at 183 Concord Street. On September 21, 1932, Ladder 103 was moved to the East New York section of Brooklyn. This area was growing and an additional ladder company was needed. During the "arson years," Ladder 103 responded to 30 runs or more a day and most of these were fires. Ladder 193 was placed in service with Ladder 103 from September 1, 1966, until August 10, 1968. It was re-numbered to Ladder 103, the second section. They lasted until December 16, 1974. Seventeen Unit Citations have been garnered and 17 members have received medals for heroism, including a James Gordon Bennett medal. Two members have lost their lives in the line of duty.

1st: Lt. Kevin Schamberger, Capt. John Mooney, Lt. Timothy Stackpole, Lt. James Connelly, Lt. Ralph Celentani
2nd: Peter Touhy, John Hands, Daniel Libretti, Joseph Cavanaugh, Neil Brandes, Michael Brady, John Colon
3rd: Robert Mosier, Joseph Trezza, George Glenday, Michael Pinsent, Richard Scally, Kevin Mundinger, John Mulcahy

1st: Robert Farrell, Lt. Daniel Walsh, Lt. Anthony Urti, Capt. Robert Albanese, BC Edward O'Connor, Lt. Thomas Rivicci, Lt. Raymond Reilly, Thomas Morgan 2nd: George Curran, Richard Mills, James Moran, James Coakley, Kevin Mullee, Larry Prather, Larry Murphy 3rd: William Horohoe, Christopher Ciardiello, Anthony Marasco, Mark Connolly, John Mraz, David Drake, Michael Hart

ENGINE CO. 248

2900 Snyder Avenue, Brooklyn

The City of Brooklyn annexed the town of Flatbush on April 24, 1894. The Flatbush Fire Department had been in existence since 1821. On January 20, 1896, Brooklyn replaced the volunteer department with several paid companies. Engine 48, Ladder 22 and District Chief 11 were placed in service in new quarters built for them at 2261 Church Avenue. Ladder 22 was disbanded on April 15, 1898, and the ladder truck became part of Engine 48. When Ladder 147 and 148 were placed in service on May 15, 1914, the horse-drawn ladder truck of Engine 248 was disbanded. On October 20, 1921, Engine 248 received a new American LaFrance 700-gpm motorized pumping engine. During the 1960s and 1970s, they saw heavy fire duty in the heart of Flatbush. On October 18, 1972, Engine 248 and Battalion 41 moved to new quarters—a combination fire station and police precinct—at 2900 Snyder Avenue. In 1997, they ranked number one in occupied structural workers. They have received 12 Unit Citations and two members have earned medals.

ENGINE CO. 250

126 Foster Avenue, Brooklyn

Brooklyn's Engine 50 and Ladder 20 were placed in service in the former quarters of Woodbine Hose 4 and Farmers Ladder 2 on January 20, 1896. The two-bay, two-story, wood-frame firehouse at 147 Lawrence Avenue, between Ocean Parkway and Seton Place, was built for Woodbine Hose 4 in 1886 and opened on February 1, 1887. Farmers Ladder 2 was added to the firehouse on September 1, 1888. This house was owned by the Flatbush Fire Department and rented to Brooklyn. Ladder 20 was disbanded on April 15, 1898, and assigned to Engine 50. On May 15, 1914, the ladder truck was removed from service when Ladders 147 and 148 were put into service. On November 23, 1929, Engine 250 moved to its current quarters at 126 Foster Avenue. Today, Engine 250 operates a 1998 Seagrave 1000-gpm pumper. Five Unit Citations have been awarded to the company and one medal winner is counted among its ranks. Two members have made the Supreme Sacrifice in the performance of their duty.

1st: Robert Fulco, Lt. Gerard McDevitt, Capt. Robert DiTrani, Lt. Charles Entrieri, Lt. Jan Midbo, Roman Ducalo
2nd: Michael Mandala, Chris Franz, John Maloney, John Reilly, Fred Bernard, Eileen Gregan, Robert Brant, John Castronova, Kevin Martin 3rd: Harold Jackson, Joseph Monteperto, Kevin Monahan, Frank Baldassare, Kevin McNamara, John Coobs, John Byrnes

1st: Robert Hess, Peter Scipilliti, Patrick Campbell, Lt. James Yakimovich, Capt. Michael Meagher, BC John Pritchard, Lt. Richard Smith, Lt. James Morgan, Kevin Kelly 2nd: Steven Weltner, Sean Taylor, Joseph Rea, John Sarubbi, George Polito, Roy Cottignola 3rd: George Johnson, Antonio Martino, Charles Restaino, Randy Ballentine, Steven Stora, Michael Nigro

ENGINE CO. 255
1367 Rogers Avenue, Brooklyn

On December 15, 1897, just 16 days before consolidation of New York City and Brooklyn, Engine 55 and Ladder 25 were organized. The three-bay house, located at 1367 Rogers Avenue, has been home for Engine 255 since it was placed in service. During those 16 days of 1897, Engine 255 responded on only two runs and were released once they got on the scene. Ladder 25 lost its identity on April 15, 1898, and the truck was kept and assigned to Engine 55. On February 1, 1927, Ladder 157 was organized with Engine 255. During 1925, two of the three apparatus doors were removed and replaced with one larger door, changing the looks of the house. On September 3, 1915, the 1898 LaFrance fourth-size steamer had a two-wheel tractor added, replacing the horses. Two members have earned medals in the performance of their duty. One of these is Captain John Pritchard, who earned his second James Gordon Bennett Medal while assigned to 255. Seven Unit Citations have been awarded to the company.

LADDER CO. 157
1369 Rogers Avenue, Brooklyn

Ladder 157 originally was placed in service as Brooklyn Ladder 25 on December 15, 1897, in new quarters with Engine 55 at 1369 Rogers Avenue. They were part of the Brooklyn Fire Department for only 16 days before being merged with the FDNY. On April 15, 1898, Ladder 25 was disbanded and consolidated with Engine 55, making it a combination company. On February 1, 1927, Ladder 157 was placed in service with a 1913 American LaFrance 65-foot aerial, replacing a city service ladder truck. Located in an area featuring mostly private homes and apartment buildings, Ladder 157 is a very active fire company. Currently, they respond to calls in a 1994 FWD Saulsbury 75-foot tower-ladder. There have been 16 medal winners and eight Unit Citations have been awarded to the company. One member, Firefighter Thomas F. Shortell, was killed while serving his country as a Marine on Iwo Jima during World War II.

1st: Michael Cunningham, Michael King, Lt. Gerard Clinton, Capt. Charles Magrath, Lt. Anthony Tricarico, William Ruhnau, Daniel Dempsey, Thomas Mazaras, Peter Furio 2nd: Dennis Barnes, Lt. Terrance McKay, Dennis Washington, Lt. Thomas Gardner, Lt. Stephen Harrell, Edward Mullen, George Shea, Justin Horigan 3rd: Matthew Martin, Donald Rudden, Mark D'Avino, Ronald Darcy, Frank Cummins, Frederick Forgione, Christopher Viviano

ENGINE CO. 281
1210 Cortelyou Road, Brooklyn

Engine 281 was placed in service on March 20, 1913, in new quarters built for them and a ladder company at 1210 Cortelyou Road. Built during the 1912 expansion program, this house is exactly like the houses of Engine 279 and Engine 280. Because of the angle of the street to the building, backing into quarters can be tricky. If not done right, a chauffeur could back through the side wall. Engine 281 went in service with a second-size steamer built by American LaFrance. It was powered by a Christie front-wheel-drive tractor. The wagon was a 1912 Mack Boyd combination chemical and hose wagon. Engine 281 now responds with a 1993 Seagrave 1000-gpm pumper. Ladder 147 was added to the house on May 15, 1914. One member has been killed in the line of duty. Two medals for bravery have been awarded to members and three Unit Citations have been garnered.

1st: Roger Scott, Lt. Patrick Ward, Capt. George Murphy, Lt. Arthur Darby, Lt. Henry Clifford, Robert Polacik 2nd: James Lunny, Joseph LaCorte, Lesly Alvarez, Frank Presia, William Gleeson, Thomas King 3rd: Brian Foster, Kevin Cummings, Thomas Petrizzo, Edward Hughes, Daniel Reddy, Joseph Richter

LADDER CO. 147

1210 Cortelyou Road, Brooklyn

Ladder 147 was placed in service on May 15, 1914, in the quarters of Engine 281 at 1210 Cortelyou Road. When placed in service, Ladder 147 replaced the horse-drawn ladder trucks in Combination Engine Companies 240, 248 and 250. Their first piece of apparatus was a 1913 American LaFrance 65-foot aerial. The first-due area for Ladder 147 is made up of large apartment houses, large "Queen Anne" single-family homes and industrial buildings. The company has been awarded five Unit Citations and 17 members have been awarded medals for their heroic actions. Two members, Firefighters Thomas H. Gavitt and John W. Hagemann, received medals for rescuing a mother and a child from a burning bedroom of a private house. Two members have been killed in the line of duty. Their current apparatus is a 1994 Seagrave 100-foot tiller aerial.

1st: Frank Witkowski, Lt. Dave Deering, Capt. Michael McGrath, Lt. Gerry O'Donnell, Lt. Mike Irwin, Chris King 2nd: Steve Collins, Mark Morello, Kenny Klipp, Pete Brady, Buddy Pantaleo, Dennis Quealy 3rd: Billy Johnson, Mike Finnegan, Jimmy Kelly, Tom Gavitt, Frank Vultaggio, Bob Fraumeni, Bob Ryan 4th: Tony Srour, Joe McGeary, John Hagemann, Chris Deszcz

1st: Lt. Neil Ferro, Lt. Mike Dorkings, Tom Laudicina, BC Frank Ryan, Lt. James Raymond 2nd: Paul Medordi, Michael Hubert, Eric Szillus, Anthony Careleo, Shaun O'Sullivan, Joseph Driscoll, John Clifford, Jeffery Monsen, James Ackerman, Barnard Randell, Brian Ricker, William Gilmartin, Daniel Kaiser, Robert Dolney, Paul Ioveno, Harry Mills, Ian Perdikou, John Pearson, James Ryan, Joseph Lennon, Joseph Matthews

ENGINE CO. 227

423 Ralph Avenue, Brooklyn

Engine 227 was placed in service on January 11, 1889, two days after Engine 226 was organized. Located at 979 Herkimer Street for its first 60 years, Engine 227 moved in with Ladder 123 at 423 Ralph Avenue. Engine 227 received one of the last horse-drawn steamers bought in 1910—a third-size Nott. This move was part of the program of combining older, single-bay firehouses with other companies in the area, thus saving money for the City. Ladder 123 moved into new quarters at 1352 St. Johns Place with Engine 234 on June 7, 1977. Engine 227's area includes mixed occupancies of residential and housing projects and commercial and industrial buildings. During the glory years of the 1970s, Engine 227 witnessed heavy fire duty. On November 5, 1973, Engine 227 earned two different Unit Citations for operating at 1483 Lincoln Place and 719 Kingsboro 7th Walk. All told, Engine 227 has earned 21 Unit Citations and six members have earned medals. Two members have died in the line of duty.

ENGINE CO. 231

107 Watkins Street, Brooklyn

Engine 231 was organized on March 12, 1892, in a wooden house built for them at 1772 Pitkin Avenue. On March 3, 1905, Engine 231 moved into new quarters at 107/109 Watkins Street. Originally, Engine 231 had a very large response area. They responded with Engine 225 to Canarsie and with Engine 246 in the Marine Park section. The area was not built up and the runs were few. Closer to home, Engine 231 has been a very busy company with a great deal of fire duty over the years. They were in the top 10 busiest companies for many years. Due to their heavy workload, Engine 232, a former fireboat, was reorganized and placed in service as a land company on July 8, 1966. Engine 232 responded from Watkins Street until September 24, 1971, when they moved to their own quarters. Three members have lost their lives protecting the citizens of Brownsville. Medals for bravery have been awarded to six members. The company has earned nine Unit Citations.

1st: William Braxton, Lt. Raymond Heuser, Lt. Robert Alford, Capt. Robert Higgins, Capt. Joseph Coniglio, Lt. Peter Ioveno, Lt. Timothy Riordan, Michael Polifrone 2nd: Charles Staten, William McLaughlin, George Kelly, Brian Storz, Daniel Hunt, John Fee, James Blow, Michael Laffan, James O'Brien, John Speck 3rd: Daniel Donleavy, Patrick Dilena, Robert Mooney, Daniel Wetzel, Thomas Quinn, Michael Callan, John Hillery, Michael Kalish, Alfonso Guarascio

LADDER CO. 120

109 Watkins Street, Brooklyn

Ladder 120 was organized as Ladder 70 on April 8, 1905. They have been located in only one location, 109 Watkins Street, with Engine 231 and the 44th Battalion. Their first rig was a new 1905 Seagrave 75-foot aerial ladder. A 1916 Christie front-wheel-drive tractor was placed under it, replacing the horses in 1916. The Brownsville section part of East New York and Ladder 120 have seen a tremendous amount of fire over the years. They have been one of the top 10 truck companies in runs and workers for the past 50 or more years. A good night tour would be 25 or more runs with four or five all-hands fires. Twenty-eight members have earned medals with one, Firefighter Victor Rossi, receiving the James Gordon Bennett Medal in 1950 and the Dr. Harry M. Archer Medal in 1953. Ladder 120 has 14 Unit Citations for outstanding work. One member was killed in the performance of his duty. Today, they respond with a 1996 FWD Saulsbury 75-foot tower-ladder.

1st: Daniel Brandenberger, Lt. Michael Hart, Lt. Joseph Cunningham, Capt. Harold Werner, Lt. Ernie Gentile, Lt. Robert McBride, Frank Nolan, Kevin Canham 2nd: Michael Guardino, Thomas McKeon, Larry Schneckenburger, Timothy Byrne, Dominick Michelli, Thomas Butler, Michael Shepherd, Brian Cross, Charles Van Rossem, Robert Forde, John Vicenti, Thomas Cascio, John Quealy 3rd: Kevin Condon, David Dietz, Michael Kelly, Brian Davan, Kevin Heaney, William Gallagher, John Narbutt, Emmitt Daly, Michael Cummings, John Dooley, Sean Nealon

1st: Alan Schwall, Lt. Dennis Murphy, Capt. Daniel Willis, Lt. James McMahon, Lt. Michael Edwards, Kevin Tracy 2nd: Donald Hodgkinson, Stephen Kearns, Richard Pearsall, Charles Buser, Paul Pfundstein, Robert Miller, William Dalton, Jeffrey Scherer 3rd: Joseph Sesack, Joseph Heptig, Ronald Kraemer, Michael D'Alessandro, Christopher Kelleher, John Ginley, Gary Celentani

ENGINE CO. 233

25 Rockaway Avenue, Brooklyn

Engine 33 of the Brooklyn Fire Department was organized on October 2, 1893, in new quarters at 243 Hull Street. With the extension of several railroads through the area, it became known as Broadway Junction. Engine 33 was located just to the north of this junction. Engine 233's area includes stores and residential properties on either side of the elevated tracks. In 1907, Engine 233 moved to temporary quarters at 1894 Broadway while the firehouse was rebuilt and a third floor added. From August 10, 1966, to November 24, 1972, a second section of Engine 233 was added because of the increased workload in the area. When the second section of Engine 233 was disbanded, they organized Ladder 176. On June 22, 1987, Engine 233 moved into new quarters at 25 Rockaway Avenue. This house is unique because the second floor is rotated 45 degrees to the first floor. Engine 233 has earned 18 Unit Citations. Five members have been awarded medals for bravery. Four members have died in the line of duty.

LADDER CO. 176

266 Rockaway Avenue, Brooklyn

Tactical Control Unit 732, a ladder company that operated during the evening hours, was relocated to new quarters at 266 Rockaway Avenue with Engine 232 on September 24, 1971. The experimental program, which was started in 1969, was unsuccessful and all six units were disbanded in 1972. The fire load was beginning to escalate and the need for an additional ladder company was great. Ladder 176 was placed in service with Engine 232 on November 24, 1972, with a 1969 American LaFrance 100-foot rear-mount aerial. Today, they respond with a 1991 Seagrave 100-foot rear-mount aerial, only their fourth rig. On June 29, 1987, Ladder 176 and Engine 233 moved into new quarters at 25 Rockaway Avenue. Ladder 176 has been active since being placed in service and has been awarded 20 Unit Citations. Twelve members have earned medals for their heroic actions. Fireman James A. Battillo received the James Gordon Bennett Medal for rescuing two children from a fire at 345 Saratoga Avenue on March 3, 1977. On June 5, 1998, Captain Scott LaPiedra, covering in Ladder 176, was injured in a floor collapse. He was pitched into the fire and died from his injuries on July 4, 1998.

1st: Henry Seegar, Lt. George Guinan, Capt. Jim Marketti, Lt. George Wallace, Lt. Daniel Murphy, Mike Pagano 2nd: Tim Watkins, Tom Daly, Matt Corless, John Schulken, David Donatelli, Tim Lee, Lenny Eberlien, Paul Bader, Chris Carri 3rd: Joe Duggan, Joe Fischer, Jim Reilly, Jim Mills, Eamon Charles, Mike Viglietta, Brian McCarrick

ENGINE CO. 332
165 Bradford Street, Brooklyn

This company was organized on September 5, 1938, at South Gate and Horace Harding Boulevard, Queens, in a temporary firehouse for the 1939 World's Fair. Their apparatus consisted of two 1938 Ahrens Fox 500-gpm engines. After the World's Fair, Engine 332 was disbanded on April 30, 1941. On February 21, 1970, Engine 332 was reorganized in East New York in the vacated quarters of Engine 225 at 657 Liberty Avenue. On July 15, 1985, they were relocated to new quarters at 165 Bradford Street. Two members from Engine 332 have made the Supreme Sacrifice – Robert R. Dolney and James W. Blackmore. Two members have received medals for heroism. Engine 332 has been awarded 11 Unit Citations. Engine 332 has a busy response area featuring all kinds of dwellings, apartment houses and factories. Today, they average about 3300 runs a year. They operate with a 1998 Seagrave 1000-gpm engine. Engine 332 is quartered with "The East New York Trucking Company," Ladder 175.

1st: Lt. Michael Lopez, Capt. Francis Johnston, Lt. Gary Wegener *2nd:* Gerard Von Essen, Paul Conboy, Gary Deleraba, Eugene D'Auria, Brian Baiker, Michael Golini, Thomas Guarnieri *3rd:* Stephen Koenig, Daniel Higgins, Walter Zoeller, Thomas Renda, Timothy Smith, Timothy Donlon, Kenneth Grzelaczyk

LADDER CO. 175
165 Bradford Street, Brooklyn

Ladder 175 was organized in the former quarters of Ladder 107, at 79 New Jersey Avenue, on February 21, 1970. Ladder 107 had moved to new quarters with Engine 225 on the same day. Ladder 175 and Engine 332 moved to new quarters on July 15, 1985, at 165 Bradford Street. Ladder 175's first apparatus was a 1963 Seagrave 100-foot tiller aerial. Ladder 175's first-due area includes wood-frame dwellings, commercial properties and factories. Since being placed in service, Ladder 175 has been a very active fire company. Ten members have been awarded medals for heroism and the company has received 15 Unit Citations. On March 28, 1971, Captain John T. Dunne was killed while searching the top floor of a wood-frame dwelling. Today, Ladder 175 responds with a 1994 Seagrave 100-foot tiller aerial.

1st: Peter Scarlatos, James Lowe, Joseph Marotta, Capt. Gerard Dombrowsky, Lt. John Buckheit, Anthony Nuccio, Joseph Sardo, Dean Psathas *2nd:* Edward Fulford, John Regan, Jerome Morrissey, Daniel Donoghue

ENGINE CO. 257

1361 Rockaway Parkway, Brooklyn

The last company Brooklyn put in service was Engine 57 on December 15, 1897. Located in the town of Canarsie, it was housed in the former town morgue at 1517 Rockaway Parkway. Engine 57 replaced the entire Flatlands Volunteer Department of one engine, truck and hose company. Canarsie consisted of several streets and mostly marshland and when first placed in service, Engine 57 was not a very busy company. In fact, in 1899, Engine 57 responded to only nine runs for the entire year. Also assigned to the company was a chemical engine and hose wagon. The old morgue was in very bad shape with the second floor sagging into the stables. There were only two small rooms on the second floor for the 11 men assigned to the company. New quarters were built and opened on February 1, 1908, at 1361 Rockaway Parkway. Four Unit Citations have been awarded to the company and one member has earned a medal for a rescue. Three members have been killed in the line of duty.

1st: Jack Paglino, Philip Ceparano, Lt. Charles Young, Capt. Michael O'Kelly, Lt. Gary Chamberlain, John Adinolfi, James Faria 2nd: Michael Bianco, Joe Delligatti, Alphonse Trapanese, Thomas Mastrodomenico, Charles Murphy, Ray Devine, Cary Walsh, Corey Hannah, Steve Letscher, Steven Leggio, Gerard Casey 3rd: Kevin Roth, Kevin Lynch, Andre Fletcher, Sal Butera, John Brunkard, Michael Ryan, Robert Bollman, Michael Ryan, Kevin Murphy

LADDER CO. 170

1361 Rockaway Parkway, Brooklyn

Ladder 170 went into service on October 18, 1929, in the quarters of Engine 257 at 1361 Rockaway Parkway. They replaced the ladder truck that had been assigned to Engine 257 since 1899. Their first apparatus was a 1921 White Pirsch 50-foot City Service ladder truck that was assigned to Engine 257. Located in Canarsie, their first-due area includes a little of everything—private homes, housing projects, heavy commercial and industrial buildings, subways, marshland and Jamaica Bay. Activity in this area has been increasing steadily in the past 10 years. During 1972 and 1973, Ladder 170 responded with a 1972 Seagrave 100-foot rear-mount aerial. It was replaced by a new 1974 Mack 75-foot tower-ladder. Today, they respond with a 1994 FWD Saulsbury 75-foot tower-ladder. Ladder 170 has been awarded three Unit Citations and two members have earned medals. Three members—Lieutenant Joseph P. Cavalieri and Firefighters Christopher Bopp and James F. Bohan—were killed on December 18, 1998, at 17 Vandalia Avenue.

1st: Lt. Thomas Ray, Lt. William Croak, Lt. William Grant, Capt. Timothy Joyce 2nd: David Giardina, Gerard Curran, Steven Mormino, Michael Keane, Michael Sullivan, Joseph Abruzzino, Sean Johnson, Edward Slow, James Savarese, Anthony Modica, Paul Peterson, Andrew Walters, John Moschella, Hector Tyler, Anthony Lombardo, Matthew James, Robert Ostrander, John Farina, John Hinchey, John Poly, Richard Amthor 3rd: Salvatore Belmonte, Francis Nastro, Anthony Cairo, Timothy Wodicka, Alexander Brown, John Halleran, Lawrence Kieley, Edward Purpora, Kevin Pfundstein, Peter Milisci

1st: Ella McNair, Thomas Goodheart, Lt. Robert Sarno, Capt. Rocco Rinaldi, Lt. Craig Silvino, John Hughes 2nd: Scott Colquhoun, Wayne Pyatt, Mike O'Neill, Vincent O'Grady, Robert Johnston, Mike O'Malley, Chris Childs, Gerard McGibbon, James Lang 3rd: Steve Supek, James Heegan, Christopher Joyce, Thomas Boyd, Edward DiSanza, John Flynn, James LoFaso

ENGINE CO. 283

885 Howard Avenue, Brooklyn

Engine 283 was placed in service on November 27, 1913, in a single-bay firehouse. Located at 214 Bristol Street, it was in the heart of Brownsville. Once the large apartment buildings were built, the population exploded. With this large influx of people, the number of fires also increased. A second section of Engine 283 was placed in service from December 25, 1931, to November 1, 1946. The fires increased and so did the workload for Engine 283. During the arson years, Engine 283 responded to fires and observed columns of smoke from other fires in the neighborhood. Squad 4 moved here from Engine 231's quarters on January 1, 1956, and lasted until May 1, 1976. On November 19, 1973, Engine 283 and Squad 4 moved to new quarters at 885 Howard Avenue. Engine 283 has earned 12 Unit Citations and six members have been awarded medals for their actions. One member of the company was killed in the performance of his duty.

1st: Lennart Stromstedt, Joseph Pigott, Walter Blum, Garry Knott, Richard Jackson, James Steen, Dominic Cassase **2nd:** *Thomas O'Day, Lt. Richard Tarello, Lt. Karl Kramer, Lt. Michael McShea, Capt. Patrick Clifford, Capt. Roger Beehler, Lt. Thomas Riley, Lt. James Graham, Lt. Brian Foley, William Howley* **3rd:** *Richard Tanner, Joel Rutsky, Steven Galucci, Daniel McSwiggan, Anthony Saccavino, John Schnaars, William Gromley, William Hastings, Daniel Reid, Thomas Woods, Michael Duffy, Thomas Daly, Gerard O'Donnell, Richard Alles, Patrick Sullivan* **4th:** *Charles O'Neill, Glenn Clapp, Christopher Spencer, Daniel Sullivan, Irving Rosenthal, Steven Homan, Edward McNoble, Kevin Judson, John Kelly, John Gregorio, Timothy Jacob, Kieran Kilduff, Robert Doyle, Gil Frank, Thomas Ryan* **5th:** *Thomas Mooney, Rich Savarese, Luke Schreiner, Thomas McNoble, James Shea, Charles Brady, Robert Greiser, Brian Smith, Donald Howard, Edward Mehnert, Michael Reilly, Thomas Lambui, Joseph Bachert, Mauricio Suarez, Edward Watt, John Brunner, Gerard Kennedy, Daniel Pyle, Thomas Coleman, Harold Werner, Gregory Bruno, Robert Stegmeier, Michael Burns, Richard Brower, Robert Savarese, Michael Kilduff, Jay Patton, Brian Gorman, James Geraghty*

ENGINE CO. 310

5105 Snyder Avenue, Brooklyn

Placed in service on September 27, 1927, Engine 310 is located at 5105 Snyder Avenue. Like Engine 309, it was another "fill in" company. The area was developed in the 1920s and first served by Engines 248, 249, 283 and 255, which made for long response distances. Engine 310's first truck was a used 1917 American LaFrance 700-gpm pumper from Engine 81. On February 11, 1957, Engine 310 received a used 1951 Ward LaFrance 750-gpm Quad from Engine 96. This unit was given to Engine 310 because of the remoteness of aerial ladder companies in the area. Another unique rig for Engine 310 was the 1970 Mack 1000-gpm pumper with a 54-foot Squrt boom. It was assigned to the company on May 14, 1971. Today, the company responds with a 1998 Seagrave 1000-gpm pumper. The company has earned one Unit Citation. One member was killed in the performance of his duty.

LADDER CO. 174

5105 Snyder Avenue, Brooklyn

Ladder 174 was placed in service in the quarters of Engine 310 on April 22, 1966. Ladder 174 replaced the 1951 Ward LaFrance Quad that Engine 310 was using. The area needed an additional ladder company and the workload demanded it. This was the beginning of the "arson years" and Ladder 174 has seen a lot of work since being established. First placed in service with a used 1938 FWD wood aerial being pulled by a 1947 Ward LaFrance tractor, they now respond with a 1994 Seagrave 100-foot rear-mount aerial. The area protected by Ladder 174 is mostly large apartment buildings. Additionally, they are first-due at Kings County Hospital and Kingsboro Psychiatric Center, a complex that is a block wide and 17 blocks long. Ladder 174 has earned six Unit Citations. Three members have been awarded medals for their heroic acts.

ENGINE CO. 323

6405 Avenue N, Brooklyn

The company was organized on November 5, 1932, in the Flatlands/Mill Basin area of Brooklyn at 6405 Avenue N. When Engine 323 entered service, it operated with a 1925 American LaFrance 700-gpm engine. One member from Engine 323 has made the Supreme Sacrifice—Lieutenant Thomas P. Sheridan in 1971. A medal for valor was awarded to Firefighter Paul J. Stroessner in 1995. Engine 323 has been awarded three Unit Citations, too. Engine 323 has a response area of mostly residential, single and multiple dwellings, small apartments, storefronts, a large brush area and the Mill Basin oil storage facility. On May 10, 1962, Engine 323 was the first-due engine at the largest oil storage fire in the history of New York City. The fire quickly went to eight alarms. With the help of three fireboats and after three hours of operations, it was declared under control. Today, Engine 323 responds with a 1989 Mack 1000-gpm engine.

1st: Victor Carlucci, Lt. Paul Como, Capt. Gennaro Bonfiglio, Lt. Thomas Silecchia, Lt. Donnell Jordan, Kevin App **2nd:** *Anthony Desimone, Michael Fazio, Richard Appenzeller, Larrie Placide, Salvatore Poma, Paul Stroessner* **3rd:** *Leonard Friedlander, William Fitzpatrick, Raymond Longo, Robert Mylan, Richard Jones, Kieran Mills, Bernard Donaghy*

SAFETY OPERATIONS BATTALION

*1st: BC James Jackson, BC Hugh A. Hagan, BC James P. Duggan, BC Jon Malkin **2nd:***
Robert Crawford, Lt. Dennis Eberhart, BC Michael Telesca, Michael Bosco, Daniel Prince

SPECIAL OPERATIONS COMMAND

SOC 1st: Thomas Murray, Lt. James McQuade, BC William Siegel, BC Raymond Downey, Capt. Peter O' Donohue, Lt. Frank Piarulli, Ralph Williams 2nd:
Wayne Ludwig, Robert Foley, Kenneth Sullivan, Michael Musich, Mark Bowden, Thomas Ciangiola, Edward Monahan, William St. George, Dennis Maher

MARINE DIVISION

*1st: Hector Andrade, Kathleen Dugan, Kirk Zoller **2nd:** Tom Andrews, DC William Guido, Bill Zoller*

Marine Division

Pt. Dan Zecchini, Pt. Gene Gorman, Wp. Bruce Peat, John Cassidy, Pt. John Tonner, ME Dennis Thomson, Capt. Tom Tracy, Rich Vanstry, ME Bill O'Brien, Lt. Harry Wanamaker, Wp. Bob Peterson, ME Jim Briordy, Bob Spadaro, ME Joe Stark, Tom Harnisher

MARINE CO. 1
Foot of Bloomfield Street, North River

This company was organized February 1, 1891, as Engine Company 57 at Castle Garden. In 1895, Engine 57 was relocated to new quarters at Battery Park. On October 6, 1941, they relocated to new quarters at Pier A, North River. On June 1, 1959, Engine 57 was disbanded and reorganized as Marine Company 1. On October 9, 1992, Marine Company 1 was relocated at the foot of Bloomfield Street, North River, in the old quarters of Marine Co. 2. From 1966 to 1995, Marine 1 was awarded three Unit Citations. Famous fires to which Marine Co. 1 responded include the 35th Street pier explosion in Brooklyn on December 3, 1956, and the aircraft carrier Constellation in the Brooklyn Navy Yard, where 50 civilian workers were killed on December 19, 1960. Fireboats used by Marine 1 include *The New Yorker*, *John Purroy Mitchel*, *John J. Harvey*, *The Fire Fighter* and the *John D. McKean*, named after the marine engineer fatally injured on the *George B. McClellan* and is currently in operation.

MARINE CO. 6
Building 292, Brooklyn Navy Yard

Marine 6 was organized on June 4, 1898, as Engine Co. 66, at the foot of Grand Street, East River. On October 16, 1941, new quarters were erected at the same location. On May 1, 1955, Engine 66 was disbanded. It was reorganized as Marine Co. 6. One member from Marine 6 has made the Supreme Sacrifice – Firefighter James J. Farrell was killed in action in World War II. Marine Company 6 has been awarded six Unit Citations. Major fires to which Marine Co. 6 has responded include the 35th Street pier explosion, the aircraft carrier *Constellation* fire and the *Esso Brussels*/*Sea Witch* ship collision underneath the Verrazano Bridge on June 2, 1973. On December 9, 1992, Marine 6 was relocated to Building 292 at the Brooklyn Navy Yard. Fireboats used by Marine 6 include the *William Strong*, *George B. McClellan*, *Cornelius W. Lawrence* and the *Harry M. Archer*. Today, Marine 6 operates with the *Kevin Kane* and shares their quarters with the Marine Division.

*1st: ME George Nikosey, Pt. Neil Yellen, Thomas Woska, ME Paul Fornuto, Robert Dixon, Kenneth Courtney, ME John Buhler, Pt. Martin Accardi, Capt. Phillip Garaizar, Edward Weyhrauch, Thomas Touhey, James Larkin, James Romeika, Pt. Daniel Garvey **2nd:** Lt. Thomas Guldner, Pt. Scott Hanson, Fred Roberts*

Marine Division

1st: Wp. Roy Campbell, Bill Ruhl, ME Ray Gierer, Ed Mauro, Pt. Ted Lukawski, ME Don Pantina 2nd: Jim Donovan, ME Tim Maloney, Wp. Sam Melisi, ME Rich Souto, Capt. Willie Marszalkiewicz, Bill Hannan, Bob Spadaro, Paul Coulbourne, Pt. Joe Gagliardi

MARINE CO. 9
355 Front Street,
Navy Home Port, Staten Island

Marine Co. 9 was organized on April 14, 1883, as Engine Company 51 at Pier 42 in the East River. Engine 51 was relocated to three other locations in Manhattan before relocating to Staten Island in 1908. Engine 51 has been disbanded and reorganized on three different occasions, most recently in 1949. On June 1, 1959, Engine 51 was disbanded and reorganized as Marine Co. 9. On September 17, 1953, Marine Engineer John D. McKean, detailed from Engine 85, made the Supreme Sacrifice when a steam explosion occurred on the fireboat *George B. McClellan*. Marine 9 has been awarded five Unit Citations and one member garnered a medal. On June 2, 1973, *Sea Witch* and *Esso Brussels* collided and burned under the Verrazano Bridge. Marine 9 rescued 35 crewmen and received the "Gallant Ship Award" from the Department of Commerce. On September 8, 1997, Marine 9 relocated to 355 Front Street, Navy Home Port. On June 30, 1989, *The Fire Fighter* was designated a National Landmark by the National Park Service.

RESCUE CO. 1
530 West 43rd Street, Manhattan

Rescue 1, the first Rescue Company in the United States, was organized on January 18, 1915. After a period of intensive training, the unit went into service on March 8, 1915, in the quarters of Engine Company 33, at 42 Great Jones Street in lower Manhattan. The company also has been quartered with Engine Company 30 at 278 Spring Street, now the Fire Museum, the former quarters of Engine Company 20 at 243 Lafayette Street, Engine Company 65 at 33 West 43rd Street and with Engine Company 34 and Ladder Company 21 at 440 West 38th Street. Members of Rescue 1 have received a total of 53 unit citations and 61 individual medals of valor, including James Gordon Bennett medals in 1919, 1933, 1948 and 1998. The original apparatus was a rebuilt 1914 Cadillac touring car. The current rig is a 1996 HME/Saulsbury heavy rescue.

1st: Paul Hashagen, Lt. Mike Pena, Lt. Dennis Mojica, Capt. Terry Hatton, Lt. John Kiernan, Joe Angelini 2nd: Mike Montesi, Gerry Nevins, Kevin Kroth, David Weiss, Lloyd Infanzon, Dan Duddy, Frank Fee, Pat O'Keefe 3rd: Brian Foy, Ed Myslinski, Steve Mockler, Dave Marmann, George Healy, Thor Johannessen, John Flatley

RESCUE CO. 2
1472 Bergen Street, Brooklyn

Rescue 2 was placed in service on March 1, 1925. Attempts at extinguishing a fire aboard a submarine in the Brooklyn Navy Yard was delayed until Rescue 1 could respond with their smoke masks. This delay spread the fire and prompted the establishment of Rescue 2. Their first quarters were with Engine 210 at 160 Carlton Avenue from 1925 until October 22, 1929. They then moved to 365 Jay Street until May 1, 1946, and then back to Engine 210's quarters. On July 26, 1985, Rescue 2 moved into the former quarters of Salvage 1 at 1472 Bergen Street. This house was built in 1893 for Engine 234. Rescue 2's first apparatus was a 1925 Mack rescue truck. Today, they respond with a 1996 HME Saulsbury heavy rescue. Because of the nature of their work, their members are well represented on the Roll of Merit. They have 81 medal winners, including four who have received the James Gordon Bennett Medal. The company has garnered 52 Unit Citations. Three members have paid the Supreme Sacrifice.

1st: Robert Galione, Capt. Joseph Downey, Capt. Philip Ruvolo, Lt. Peter Lund, Salvatore Civitillo 2nd: Kevin O'Rourke, James Sandas, Ray Smith, Cliff Pase 3rd: Mark Gregory, Michael Quinn, John Driscoll, Joseph Jardin 4th: William Eisengrein, Lincoln Quappe, Peter Romeo, James Kiesling

RESCUE CO. 3

451-453 East 176th Street, Bronx

Rescue 3 was organized in the quarters of Ladder 17 on June 1, 1931. They have moved five times since, finally settling in their current home, the former quarters of Engine 46 and Ladder 27, on July 1, 1992. The Collapse Rescue Unit, manned by Rescue 3, also is quartered here, as is RAC (Recuperation and Care) 3. Members of this company have received 54 unit citations and 42 individual medals for valor, including James Gordon Bennett Medals in 1932, 1944 and 1990, the most recent of which was awarded to Firefighter (now Lieutenant) Gerard Murtha. In 1944, their former captain received the Stephenson Medal for having the most efficient and best-disciplined company in the department. They have had three line-of-duty deaths, including Firefighter Alfred Ronaldson, who was killed on March 5, 1991, at a 3-3 at 126 East Fordham Road. Their apparatus includes a 1996 HME/Saulsbury rescue van and the 1995 Ford/SuperVac collapse truck.

1st: John W. Femina, Gerard Schrang, Lt. John W. Olson, Capt. Ralph Tiso, Lt. Kevin Williams, Robert Knabbe, Michael Davis 2nd: Richard Tana Gretta, Thomas Clair, Nicholas Giordano, Michael Conboy, Thomas Conroy, John Conroy, Robert Athanas, Greg Einsfeld 3rd: Garret Lindgren, Raymond Phillips, Clifford Stabner, David Drury, Michael Morrissey, Stan Sussina, Douglas Hantusch, Christopher Ryan, Donald Reagan

---

1st: Tony Meier, Lt. Larry Gray, Terry Farrell, Mark Bowden, Capt. Brian Hickey, Bill Mahoney 2nd: Ed Monohan, Mike Loftus, Lt. Kevin Dowdell, Butch Foley, Tony Tarrabocchia, Paul Mendoza, Bill Ryan, Ed Curley, Harry Ford, Mike Travers, Ed Morrison, Lt. Chuck Downey, Liam Flaherty, Dave Raynor, Tom McAree, Jim Trainor, Brian Fahey, Mike Roy, Mike Fitzgerald, Mike Milner, Chris Young

RESCUE CO. 4

64-18 Queens Boulevard, Queens

Rescue 4 was organized on June 1, 1931, at 64-18 Queens Boulevard in the Winfield section of Queens in the quarters of Engine 292. Their first apparatus was a 1925 AC (10) Bull Dog Mack. Members killed in the line of duty include Lieutenant Thomas B. Dore in 1955, Lieutenant Thomas A. Williams in 1992 and Firefighter Peter F. McLoughlin in 1995. From 1951 to 1995, 21 medals of valor have been bestowed on members of Rescue 4. The company has garnered 41 Unit Citations. On February 1, 1982, Rescue 4 received a 1975 GMC mechanics truck that was modified by members of the Hazardous Material Team to carry specialized equipment. On October 15, 1984, the unit was disbanded to organize a new company, Haz-Mat Co. 1 in the quarters of Engine 288 (Squad 288). Rescue 4 responds to all 10-75s in Queens, but can operate anywhere in the city. They respond with a 1995 HME/Saulsbury rescue van. The members of "Popeye" are quartered with the "Winfield Cougars," Engine 292.

RESCUE CO. 5

1850 Clove Road, Staten Island

Rescue 5 was established on May 16, 1948, in the quarters of Ladder 78 at 14 Brighton Avenue. Ladder 78 had an extra chauffeur assigned to the Rescue. If Rescue 5 was needed and Ladder 78 was out of quarters, the extra chauffeur would take Rescue 5 to Ladder 78, pick up the men and proceed to the call. They were disbanded on June 1, 1962. Their first rig was a used 1941 Ward LaFrance hose wagon. Reorganized on August 20, 1984, Rescue 5 has been located in the quarters of Engine 160 at 1850 Clove Road. On September 27, 1996, a second piece of apparatus was added—a Hazardous Material Technician Unit, which makes the Rescue a back-up Haz-Mat Unit. The company has earned 14 Unit Citations, with four members earning medals for heroic acts. Today, they respond with a 1996 HME/Saulsbury heavy rescue. One member of Ladder 78, while assigned to Rescue 5, was killed while operating at a store fire on November 16, 1959.

1st: Peter Brunaes, Brian Stoffers, Lt. Richard Tarkenton, Capt. John Ferry, Lt. Nat DiPrisco, Lt. Louis Raimondi, Lt. Harvey Harrell, Carl Bini, Larry Nelson 2nd: Arthur Barry, Christopher Dowd, Rod Zarelli, Thomas Droppa, Charles Frizziola, Michael Fiore, John Drury, David King, Kevin Reilly, Lawrence Sullivan, Joseph Sykes, William Spade, Danny Beyer, Donald Dillon, Gerard Koenig, Robert Brown, Anthony Cavalieri 3rd: William Hodgens, Robert Milmore, Joseph Mascali, Allan Tarasiewicz, Scott Fox, Michael Lombardi, John Farrell, Thomas Ihnken, John Bergin, Raymond Tremer

SQUAD CO. 1

786 Union Street, Brooklyn

Squad 1 was placed in service at Engine 59 on April 16, 1955. The company was moved to Ladder 58's quarters in the Bronx in 1972 and to Engine 45 in 1975. On May 1, 1976, Squad 1 was disbanded. On November 22, 1975, Engine 269 was disbanded and the firehouse at 786 Union Street was left vacant. The people of Park Slope were so outraged by the closing of Engine 269, which was organized on October 5, 1908, that the City reopened the house on December 1, 1977, with Squad 1. The Squads were manpower units that responded to all fires in the borough. Today, besides responding to fires, Squad 1 is trained to mitigate hazardous materials incidents. On February 4, 1993, the Technical Response Unit 1 was added and cross-manned by Squad 1. When in Manhattan, three members earned medals and while in the Bronx, two members earned medals. Today, Squad 1 can boast of five medal winners, including a James Gordon Bennett winner in 1993. Eighteen Unit Citations have been awarded.

1st: Robert Mannarino, Lt. Edward D'Atri, Lt. Michael Esposito, Capt. Donald Hayde, Capt. Louis Modafferi, Lt. Dennis Farrell, Joseph O'Donnell 2nd: Gregory Fagen, Robert West, Thomas Butler, Tim Rogers, Michael Russo, Stephen Siller, Phil Solimeo, Ken Michitsch, Stephen Beyar 3rd: David Fontana, John Hindle, Fred Lawrence, Hugh Lynch, George Ebert, Tony Edwards, Mike Stackpole, William Spiess, Durrell Pearsall

1st: John Flynn, Lt. William McGinn, Lt. Brian Smith, Capt. Gerald Tracy, Fire Comm. Thomas Von Essen, Lt. Peter Campanelli, Harry Davis, Peter Runfola, Lawrence Virgilio 2nd: Lawrence Cohen, Philip Vincenzo, Richard Scalfani, John Esposito, Kevin Scanlon, Christopher Calamia, Gary Moore, Thomas Oswald, Stephen Mickiewicz, Manuel Mojica 3rd: Andrew Fredericks, Patrick Kelly, Daniel Castellano, Charles Powers, Daniel Murray, Timothy Haskell, Nicholas Guglielmo

SQUAD CO. 18

132 West 10th Street, Manhattan

Squad 18 was organized as Engine 18 in the former quarters of volunteer Guardian Engine 29, on September 14, 1865. They moved into their current house, at the same location, on May 21, 1892. They operated as a double engine company from March 1, 1884, until July 8, 1891, again from May 21, 1892, until May 1, 1918, and yet again from March 25, 1926, until July 1, 1939. They became a Squad company on July 1, 1998. While still an engine company, they had five unit citations and nine individual medals for valor. Firefighter William Mitchell received the James Gordon Bennett Medal in 1926. In 1927, he was awarded the Dr. Harry M. Archer Medal for the same action. They have had seven line-of-duty deaths, five of which occurred at the tragic 23rd Street fire on October 17, 1966, when Lieutenant Joseph Priore and Firefighters James Galanaugh, Daniel Rey, Joseph Kelly and Bernard Tepper were killed in the collapse. Their apparatus includes a 1998 Seagrave 1000-gpm pumper and a 1998 GMC/Union City step-van.

SQUAD CO. 41

330 East 150th Street, Bronx

Squad 41 was organized as Engine 41, one of the earliest Bronx companies, in a former volunteer house of Jackson Engine 4 at 2801 Third Avenue, on January 1, 1874. They moved to their current quarters on April 4, 1904. Due to budget problems, they were disbanded on May 3, 1989, but reinstated on July 1, 1990. They officially were designated as a Squad company on July 1, 1998. A second section, using the apparatus and manpower of the disbanded Manhattan Engine 72, was in service from 1957 until 1958, and again from 1968 until 1974, when Engine 41-2 was disbanded to reorganize Squad 5 in these quarters. Squad 5 was disbanded in 1976. While still an engine company, they have had 20 unit citations and 10 members were awarded medals for valor. They have a specially constructed 1998 Seagrave 1000-gpm rescue-pumper and a 1997 Chevrolet/Union City step-van.

1st: Bruce VanNosdall, Lt. Charles Schmid, Lt. Denis Mironchik, Capt. Russell Vomero, Lt. Christopher King, Lt. Richard Portello, Lawrence Sullivan 2nd: Richard Ting, Kevin Quinn, Thomas Foley, John Citarella, Scott Maxwell, John Hassett, Michael Kilker 3rd: John Schof, Kevin Murphy, Joseph Beltrani, Kevin McArdle, Luis Torres, Steven Gillespie, Scott Schrimpe

SQUAD CO. 61
1518 Williamsbridge Road, Bronx

Squad 61, originally Engine 61, was organized on February 1, 1896, at temporary quarters in the Club Stables of the Morris Park Race Track and later moved to 1518 Williamsbridge Road. On July 20, 1896, they were re-designated as a combination engine company. They were designated as a regular engine on September 7, 1904, and moved to their new and current quarters on December 4, 1929, where the 20th Battalion also is located. They became a Squad company on July 1, 1998. While operating as an engine company, they were awarded three unit citations and endured three line-of-duty deaths. Their apparatus includes a 1998 Seagrave 1000-gpm pumper, as well as a 1998 GMC/Union City step-van.

1st: Jeremy Cassel, Joe DiBernardo, Lt. Sean Genovese, Capt. Mike Banker, Lt. Mike Fitzgerald, Lt. Tom McKiernan, Pat Tuohy, Mitch Amerbach 2nd: Lou Rufrano, Tom Mayerhauser, Tony Zeolla, Chris Mandeville, Andy Gaughan, Charlie Dodenhoff, Pete Kearney, Thomas Cegielski, Thomas Day, Jason Faso, John Grasso, Joe Light, Kevin Yoos, Robert Hauryluck, Al Luchetti

SQUAD CO. 252
617 Central Avenue, Brooklyn

Engine 252 was established on April 1, 1897, in the southern end of Bushwick, a fast-growing area of the city. Engine 252's firehouse was a model of what firehouses in the future would be like. It was the first house to have a garden on the second-floor roof with shade awnings over the stables. It turned out to be the only one built. The very ornate facade of this firehouse is the only one like it in the city. On July 1, 1998, Engine 252's mission was changed to a Squad Company. Squad 252 received many hours of training in the mitigation of hazardous materials, as well as other specialized training. They respond as an engine company in their first- and second-due areas. At other times, they respond as a Squad or a back-up haz-mat unit. This action-packed company has received 18 Unit Citations, including two on the same day, December 29, 1979. One member lost his life while responding to a fire in 1920.

1st: Hank Fried, Wimpy, Kevin Prior, Larry Tompkins, Mush, Woody McHale, Rich Meyers, Pete Langone, Ken Kazokas, John Feehan, Joe Harris 2nd: Jeff Converse, Jack Donnelly, Arel Coleman, Jim McGuiness, Jim O'Conner, John DeFilippo, Lt. Jim Schumeyer, Capt. Steve Rasweiler, Lt. Ed Metcalf, Rob McDermott, Bob Chuisano, Rich Sweeney, Tom Kuveikis, Greg Pastos

SQUAD CO. 270
91-45 121st Street, Queens

This company was organized on September 5, 1907, as Engine 170 at 86-40 122nd Street in the former volunteer quarters of Colombia Hose Co. 1 and Colombia H&L Co. 1. Their first apparatus were an 1883 Clapp and Jones fourth-size steam engine and a 1906 George B. Marx third-size hose wagon. On January 1, 1913, Engine 170 was reorganized as Engine 270 and relocated to new quarters on June 30, 1913, at 91-45 121st Street with Ladder 125. Lieutenant Herman G. Berny died in the line of duty in 1972. Four members have been awarded medals for their acts of heroism. They have received 10 Unit Citations. On July 1, 1998, Engine 270 became Squad 270. Squad 270 covers 24 other engine companies at all 10-75 alarms. Squad 270 operates with a 1996 Seagrave 1000-gpm pumper and a 1998 GMC/Union City/Haz-mat Tender. Squad 270 has a second truck that carries tools and haz-mat equipment. They share their quarters with Division 13.

1st: Gregory Haynes, Lt. Christher Rigoli, Capt. Thomas Richardson, Lt. James Earl, Lt. Douglas Sloan, Raymond Seeley 2nd: Michael Smithwick, Thomas Bohn, Vincent Pickford, Robert Reinhardt, Kenneth Barry, Bruce Smith, James Giovanniello, Frank Leeb, John Fordham, David Dangerfield 3rd: Joseph Vaccaro, Donald Schneider, Celia Thompson, Fred Herrmann, Anthony Tedeschi, Adam Bell, Michael Sullivan, John Hogan, Edward Ginley, Vincent Tavella, Frank Paliotta, Stephen Witter

SQUAD CO. 288

56-29 68th Street, Queens

This Maspeth company was organized as Engine 288 on September 1, 1913, in the former volunteer quarters of Maspeth Engine Co. 4 at 61-55 Maspeth Avenue. Their first piece of apparatus was a 1912 American LaFrance second-size steam engine with a 1912 Mack Boyd combination chemical hose wagon. On October 1, 1914, Engine 288 was relocated to new quarters at 56-29 68th Street. Engine 288 Firefighter William S. Wadling made the Supreme Sacrifice in 1946. Engine 288 has one Unit Citation. On July 1, 1998, Engine 288 was reorganized as Squad 288. Squad 288 covers 30 other engine companies at all 10-75 alarms. Squad 288 responds with a 1989 Mack 1000-gpm pumper. They also operate with a second apparatus, a Chevy/Union Haz-mat Tender, equipped with special tools and haz-mat equipment. The "Maspeth Mutts" share their quarters with the Haz-Mat Co. 1.

1st: Hank Molle, Lt. Anthony Bellisari, Capt. Denis Murphy, Lt. Vincent Ungaro, Lt. Timothy Kelly, Paul Baldwin 2nd: Kevin Kubler, Louis Rufrano, Ronnie Gies, Gerald Murphy, Paul Patsos, James D'Avolio, William Hill, Timothy Murphy, Matthew Neary, 3rd: Timothy Geraghty, Timothy Welty, Christopher Carangi, Anthony Tito, Joseph Fable, Jonathan Ielpi, Brian Sweeney, Peter Brennan, John Walters

TACTICAL SUPPORT UNIT 1

750 Main Street, Roosevelt Island, Manhattan

Tactical Support Unit 1 was organized on Roosevelt Island on August 24, 1990. It replaced Searchlight 1, a 1959 Mack searchlight truck. The first searchlight dates back to 1900, when Searchlight Engine 1 was placed in service with a LaFrance fourth-size steamer that carried a 5KW generator to power two removable, 9000-candle power lights. It was disbanded in 1916. Searchlight 1 was placed in service on September 19, 1922, in the quarters of Engine 7. When disbanded in 1990, it was located in the quarters of Engine 260 and responded to 56 runs the year before. Tac-1 was designed to replace the light truck and given additional duties, including responses to water rescues and building collapses. Tac-1's first apparatus was a 1989 Ford/Saulsbury unit that carried an inflated boat and crane, in addition to the lights. It also carried many different kinds of tools for haz-mat incidents, collapse equipment and water rescue equipment. Tac-1's current apparatus is a 1998 International with a Saulsbury body.

Ralph Williams, Nicholas Giordano, David Riechel, Paul Jaeger

Robert Milmore, Robert Brown, Scott Fox, William Spade

TACTICAL SUPPORT UNIT 2

1850 Clove Road, Staten Island

Tactical Support Unit 2 was placed in service on August 24, 1990, in the quarters of Engine 160 and Rescue 5. They were assigned a 1989 Ford/Saulsbury unit that is identical to Tac-1. These one-man units respond on all second alarms throughout the City, plus major emergencies, building collapses, confined space rescues, high-rise fires, water emergencies and any haz-mat incident. They also can be special-called by the Incident Commander if needed. Tac-2 covers all of Staten Island, Brooklyn south of Atlantic Avenue and the 13th Division in Queens. The rest of the City is covered by Tac-1. Tac-2's current apparatus is a 1998 International with a Saulsbury body.

Anthony Confessore, Jeffrey Borkowski, Lt. Stanley Rybak, Anthony Mussorfiti, BC Jack Fanning, Capt. Robert Ingram, John Olewnicki

HAZARDOUS - MATERIALS OPERATIONS

Haz-Mat

1st: Neil Yank, Lt. John Crisci, Lt. Ed Connelly, Capt. Vin Doherty, Lt. Steve Bacci, Jack Hack 2nd: Frank Derop, Kevin Smith, Cliff Hollywood, Bob Hunter, Dennis Scauso, Dom Tralli, John Gagliano, Tony Mussorfiti, Dennis Carey, Phil McArdle 3rd: Tom Gardner, George Hough, Ed Tomaszewski, Rick Gimbl, Richard Smith, Tim Regan, Bob Crowe, John Larocchia

HAZARDOUS - MATERIALS CO. 1
56-29 68th Street, Queens

The predecessor of Haz-Mat Company 1 was the former Hazardous Materials Response Team, organized as a part of Rescue 4, on February 1, 1982. The actual Haz-Mat company was organized officially in their current quarters on October 15, 1984, but did not become operational until December 3, 1984. The interim period from mid-October until December was used for training the newly assigned personnel of this highly specialized unit. With normal manning of an officer and seven firefighters on duty on each tour, this is the largest single company in the FDNY. They respond only on special calls, with an ever-growing number of dangerous incidents each year. They share quarters with Squad Company 288. Haz-Mat 1 responds with two pieces of apparatus–a 1989 Mack/Saulsbury and a smaller 1996 International/Saulsbury, both specially built for their needs. Haz-Mat 1 has had one medal winner–Firefighter Kevin J. Smith was awarded the LaGuardia Medal on September 20, 1989.

MASK SERVICE UNIT

Mask Service

1st: James Russell, Lt. Edward Alston, Eric Kosak 2nd: Joe Polizzi, Lt. Charles Coletti, Nick Dolce, Roy Alford, Lt. Peter Martino, Steve Sbordone, Ana Andrade, John Juranich, Walter Dunlop, DC Eugene Garvin, Lt. Brian Pritchard, Ronald Sparnroft, Rick DeRosso

BOARD OF TRUSTEES

1st: Michael Currid, Dr. Kerry Kelly, Christine Lee, Magda DeConinck, Marta Soja, Thaddius McTigue 2nd: John Corr, Arthur Parrinello, David Clinton, Augostino Cangemi, Seth Cohen, Edward Lee 3rd: Kevin Gallagher, John Buhler, Thomas LaMacchia, Michael Carter, Louis Sforza, Jerome Huntzinger

UNIFORMED FIREFIGHTERS ASSOCIATION

1st: William Mirro, Kevin Gallagher, Thomas LaMacchia 2nd: Rudy Sanfilippo, Edward Burke, Matthew James, Jerome Huntzinger, Thomas Manley, Thomas Daparma, Robert Staub

SECURITY BENEFIT FUND & UFA OFFICE STAFF

1st: Joey Matuszwski, Debbie Lynch, Fern Iodice, Theresa Carapella, Marie Walsh, Phyllis Coniglio 2nd: Arthur Turner, Tom Butler, Paul Polizzi, Sheila Pettit, Tama Reilly, Jude Gaddis, Maria Zingone, Denise Keeley, Carmen Llado, Jennifer James, Amy Sullivan, Joe Crawley, Will Lincifort

UNIFORMED FIRE OFFICERS ASSOCIATION

*1st: DC Arthur J. Parrinello, Capt. Peter L. Gorman, BC Richard Goldstein, Lt. John F. Corr **2nd:** Lt. Steve Carbone, BC James T. Ciulla, Capt. John J. McDonnell, Lt. John E. Ginty, Capt. Michael C. Currid*

UNIFORMED FIRE OFFICERS ASSOCIATION STAFF

*1st: Kevin Sullivan, Tom O'Connor, Dennis Cummins **2nd:** Janet Toohill, Danette Crocker, Ellen Tuohey, Audrey Jones, Susan Kokol*

FIRE MUSEUM STAFF

*1st: Tom Walters, Mike Krempaski, Tim Shea **2nd:** John Kennedy, Geoff Giglierano, Ray Eger, Lt. Angel Carrero, John Jermyn **3rd:** Jane Toohig, Joe Frascati*

399

Tom Behan, Lt. Joe Buell, DC Phil Burns, Ted Carstensen, Gerard Coughlin, Lt. Jack Clarke, Lt. Chris Corbin, Bill Crowley, Tom Cunneen, Bill Duffy, Jr., Lt. Bill Duffy, Sr., Hugh Duffy, Tom Dooley, Jack Dugan, Charles Fitzpatrick, Tom Foy, Gene Fraher, Lt. John Cox, Lt. Ed Geraghty, Lt. Tom Gerondel, Jim Ginty, Kevin Grace, Brian Grogan, BC Hugh Hagan, Kevin Hayes, Capt. Bill Hopkins, Brian Kearney, BC Jack Kelly, Bob King, Jim Leach, Frank McCutchen, Lt. Jim McEnaney, Dan McEnroe, Tom McEnroe, Lt. Tom McEnroe, Sr., Tom McGonigal, Jack McLaughlin, Lt. Ed McLoughlin, Lt. Mike McShea, John McSweeney, Tom McTigue, Sr., Tom McTigue, Jr., Lt. Gerard Murtha, Dennis O'Connell, Durrell Pearsall, Joe Quinn, John O'Hagan, Jimmy O'Neill, Lt. Jim Schumeyer, Al Schwartz, Ken Sullivan, Chris Walsh, Lt. Al Warta, Capt. Bob Wright, Chris Waugh, Bill Woods, Bill Murphy, Lt. Pete Sheridan

F.D.N.Y. EMERALD SOCIETY BAGPIPE BAND

Organized January of 1962, the bagpipers made their first appearance at an Emerald Society dance held at City Center, New York City, in November 1962. The following March 17th, they made their first trek up Fifth Avenue as part of our annual St. Patricks's Day Parade and were received warmly by the huge throng of Gaels. The pipe band tartan was acquired from Grainger and Campbell Ltd. of Glasgow, Scotland. One can easily see the significance of the colors. The bright red tunic represents the New York City Fire Department. The green stands for our Emerald Society. The light blue represents the rank of firefighter, with the white taking in the officers rank of the Department. Although the tartan is relatively new, one can be assured that the organization, which it represents, is rich in a colorful history and tradition, dedicated to the protection of life and property in this great city. For the sake of posterity, the tartan has been duly recorded and registered with the Scottish Tartans Society in Stirling, Scotland. The group is also a member of the United States Pipe Band Association. They have played for too many audiences to mention them all. They've been everywhere! They've played for Ed Sullivan, Jerry Lewis and his Muscular Dystrophy Telethon, visiting foreign dignitaries, official Fire Department functions, such as Medal Day and Memorial Services, and at the personal request of His Honor, the Mayor. They've played in hundreds of parades and at Shea Stadium, Madison Square Garden, the NYC Marathon, the Waldorf Astoria and, of course, the Emerald Isle. They were the first band to march up lower Broadway in the ticker-tape parade that welcomed home the hostages from Iran. During the summer months, they play in competition against other pipe bands at the New York Feis, various Scottish games and other events up and down the East Coast. Needless to say, they have garnered their share of trophies and awards. Their ultimate goal is to compete in the Emerald Isle and Canada. They are a credit to the New York City Fire Department and the Emerald Society. Visit their Web site at www.FDNYpipesanddrums.com

This index represents only those names contained in the history section of this publication. The personnel section was not indexed.